SEVENTH EDITION

Patterns for College Writing

A RHETORICAL READER AND GUIDE

SEVENTH EDITION

Patterns for College Writing

A RHETORICAL READER AND GUIDE

LAURIE G. KIRSZNER

UNIVERSITY OF THE SCIENCES
IN PHILADELPHIA

STEPHEN R. MANDELL

DREXEL UNIVERSITY

BEDFORD/ST. MARTIN'S

Boston ◆ New York

Sponsoring editor: Donna Erickson
Development editor: Talvi Laev
Editorial assistants: Griff Hansbury, Jason Noe
Manager, publishing services: Emily Berleth
Associate editor, publishing services: Meryl Gross
Project management: York Production Services
Production supervisor: Scott Lavelle
Text design: Anna George
Cover design: Evelyn Horovicz
Cover art: © 1997 Succession H. Matisse, Paris / Artist's Rights Society (ARS)
New York. Private Collection.

Library of Congress Catalog Card Number: 97-65181

Copyright © 1998 by St. Martin's Press, Inc.

All rights reserved. No part of this book may be reproduced, stored in a retrieval system, or transmitted by any form or by any means, electronic, mechanical, photocopying, recording, or otherwise, except as may be expressly permitted by the applicable copyright statutes or in writing by the Publisher.

Manufactured in the United States of America.

3   2   1   0   9
f   e

For information, write:
Bedford/St. Martin's
75 Arlington Street
Boston, MA 02116
(617-426-7440)

ISBN: 0-312-19044-1
       0-312-25581-0 (hardcover)

Acknowledgments

Acknowledgments and copyrights are continued at the back of the book on pages 676–678, which constitute an extension of the copyright page.

Maya Angelou, "Finishing School." Excerpt from *I Know Why the Caged Bird Sings* by Maya Angelou. Copyright © 1969 by Maya Angelou. Reprinted by permission of Random House, Inc.

Bruno Bettelheim, "The Holocaust." From *Surviving and Other Essays* by Bruno Bettelheim. Copyright © 1979 by Bruno Bettelheim and Trude Bettelheim as Trustees. Reprinted by permission of Alfred A. Knopf, Inc.

Judy Brady, "I Want a Wife." First appeared in *Motherlode.* Published in the premier issue of *Ms.* Copyright © 1970 by Judy Syfers. Reprinted by permission of the author.

Peter Brimelow, "What, Then, Is to be Done?" From *Alien Nation* by Peter Brimelow. Copyright © 1995 by Peter Brimelow. Reprinted by permission of Random House, Inc.

Larry Brown, Excerpt from *On Fire.* Copyright © 1994 by Larry Brown. Reprinted by permission of Algonquin Books of Chapel Hill, a division of Workman Publishing.

José Antonio Burciaga, "Tortillas." Originally titled "I Remember Masa" by José Antonio Burciaga. From *Weedee Peepo* by José Antonio Burciaga. Published by Pan American University Press, Edinburgh, TX (1988). Reprinted by permission.

It is a violation of the law to reproduce these selections by any means whatsoever without the written permission of the copyright holder.

For Peter Phelps (1936–1990), with thanks

CONTENTS

2 NARRATION   *61*

"Being only a daughter for my father meant my destiny would lead me to become someone's wife. That's what he believed."

"It went without saying that all girls could iron and wash, but the fine touches around the home, like setting a table with real silver, baking roasts and cooking vegetables without meat, had to be learned elsewhere. . . . During my tenth year, a white woman's kitchen became my finishing school."

"From her wheelchair she canned pickles, baked bread, ironed clothes, wrote dozens of letters weekly to her friends and her 'half dozen or more kids,' and made three patchwork housecoats and one quilt."

"For more than half an hour 38 respectable, law-abiding citizens in Queens watched a killer stalk and stab a woman in three separate attacks. . . . Not one person telephoned the police during the assault; one witness called after the woman was dead."

3 DESCRIPTION   107

"My Principle is the key to an understanding of all hierarchical systems,
and therefore to an understanding of the whole structure of civilization."

"We recently participated in an environmental festival at the Mall of
America. . . . Having spoken with literally thousands of parents, children, and teachers, we were appalled at the public's wealth of environmental misunderstanding."

"Why is it that when the sun or the moon or the stars are out, they
are visible, but when the lights are out, they are invisible, and that
when I wind up my watch, I start it, but when I wind up this essay, I
shall end it?"

"It was in the echo of that terrified woman's footfalls that I first began to
know the unwieldy inheritance I'd come into—the ability to alter public
space in ugly ways."

"Do we possess the character and courage to address a problem which so
many nations, poorer than our own, have found it natural to correct?"

"Some boys are very tough. They're afraid of nothing. They are
the ones who climb a wall and take a bow at the top. . . . They also

jiggle and hop on the platform between the locked doors of the subway cars."

    "My first view in the mirror blotted out the hurting. I'd seen some pretty conks, but when it's the first time, on your *own* head, the transformation, after the lifetime of kinks, is staggering."

    "In the feeding and safeguarding of their progeny insects and spiders exhibit some interesting analogies to reasoning and some crass examples of blind instinct."

    "While it may suit Leno's image to portray the 'Tonight' show monologue as something that's banged out over late night pizza with a few cronies, in fact each joke requires the concerted effort of a crack team of six highly disciplined comedy professionals."

    "You learn that you are only human flesh, not Superman, and that you can burn like a candle."

    "For those who have the stomach for it, let us part the formaldehyde curtain."

    "There was a great deal of fussing to be done before Mr. Summers declared the lottery open. There were the lists to make up—of heads of families, heads of households in each family, members of each household in each family."

"He never learned a trade, he just sells gas,
Checks oil, and changes flats. Once in a while,
As a gag, he dribbles an inner tube,
But most of us remember anyway.
His hands are fine and nervous on the lug wrench,
It makes no difference to the lug wrench, though."

"What I wish for all my students is some release from the clammy grip of the future. I wish them a chance to savor each segment of their education as an experience in itself and not as a grim preparation for the next step. I wish them the right to experiment, to trip and fall, to learn that defeat is as instructive as victory and is not the end of the world."

"So I was baffled when the women at college accused me and my sex of having cornered the world's pleasures. I think something like my bafflement has been felt by other boys (and by girls as well) who grew up in dirt-poor farm country, in mining country, in black ghettos, in Hispanic barrios, in the shadows of factories, in Third World nations—any place where the fate of men is as grim and bleak as the fate of women."

"I spend a great deal of my time thinking about the power of language—the way it can evoke an emotion, a visual image, a complex idea, or a simple truth. Language is the tool of my trade. And I use them all—all the Englishes I grew up with."

"What these incidents show is that sexism is not something existing independently in American English or in the particular dictionary that I happened to read. Rather, it exists in people's minds."

9 DEFINITION   *443*

THEMATIC GUIDE TO THE CONTENTS

FAMILY RELATIONSHIPS

LANGUAGE

EDUCATION

BUSINESS AND WORK

SPORTS

RACE AND CULTURE

GENDER

NATURE AND THE ENVIRONMENT

THE MEDIA

HISTORY AND POLITICS

ETHICS

PREFACE

Patterns for College Writing was first published in 1980 and since then has been adopted at more than four hundred colleges and universities across the country. We have been gratified at the praise the first six editions of *Patterns* have received, and we continue to be both humbled and awed by the many instructors (including some who have used it through all of its editions) who find *Patterns* to be the most accessible and most pedagogically sound rhetoric-reader they have ever used. In preparing the seventh edition, we have worked hard to sharpen and refine the features that have kept longtime users returning and new users turning to *Patterns* for the first time.

What Students and Instructors Like about *Patterns for College Writing*

An Introduction to Critical Reading

The text begins with "Introduction: Reading to Write," which gives students an overview of critical reading and illustrates its application to the selections and apparatus in the book.

A Comprehensive Treatment of the Writing Process

Chapter 1, "The Writing Process," functions as a mini-rhetoric, offering extensive advice on planning, writing, and revising, including brainstorming, clustering, journal writing, and editing.

Detailed Coverage of the Patterns of Development

Chapters 2 through 10 explain and illustrate the patterns of development that students use in their college writing assignments: narration, description, exemplification, process, cause and effect, comparison and contrast, classification and division, definition, and argumentation. Each chapter begins with a comprehensive introduction that first presents a definition and a para-

graph-length example of the pattern to be discussed; then explains the particular writing strategies and applications associated with it; and finally, analyzes one or more annotated student papers to show how the pattern can be
used in particular college writing situations. The pattern's use is then further
illustrated in essays—diverse in subject, style, and cultural perspective—by
professional writers and in a short story or poem.

Extensive Apparatus

Each essay is followed by four types of questions designed to help students measure their comprehension of the essay's content, their understanding of the writer's purpose and audience, their recognition of the stylistic
and structural techniques used to shape the essay, and their sensitivity to the
nuances of word choice and figurative language. Each essay is also accompanied by a prompt for a "Journal Entry," "Writing Workshop" topics (suggestions for full-length writing assignments), and the popular "Thematic
Connections" feature, which suggests other works in the text that are the-
matically related to that particular essay. In addition, a new "Combining the
Patterns" feature highlights the ways in which patterns are blended in the
essay. The stories and poems in the text are accompanied by "Thinking
about Literature" questions, "Journal Entry" suggestions, and "Thematic
Connections." Each chapter ends with a list of "Writing Assignments" and a
"Collaborative Writing Activity."

What's New in This Edition

New Readings

In the seventh edition more than 30 percent of the readings are new.
We have retained the selections that our colleagues and their students
found most useful and added a number of fresh and timely selections—
for example, Lawrence Otis Graham's "The 'Black Table' Is Still There,"
Robert M. Lilienfeld and William L. Rathje's "Six Enviro-Myths,"
Christopher B. Daly's "How the Lawyers Stole Winter," Melanie
Scheller's "On the Meaning of Plumbing and Poverty," and Edward
Mendelson's "The Word and the Web."

An Expanded Chapter on the Writing Process

Chapter 1 includes new material on the writing process, including expanded discussions of thesis and support, developing body paragraphs,
and outlining. It has also been strengthened and updated with boxed
editing tips and computer strategies.

A New Debate and a New Casebook
in the Argumentation Chapter

In Chapter 10, three sets of paired essays take opposing positions on controversial issues: multicultural education, date rape, and (new to this edition) immigration. The chapter is enhanced by a casebook of four essays, designed to show students that there can be more than two sides to an issue. The new casebook in this edition focuses on violence in the media—in particular, on whether the media should be held responsible for violent behavior that it may have caused. Students can use this convenient collection of essays to develop their own ideas about this topic or as a resource for a research project.

An Expanded Chapter on Combining the Patterns

Chapter 11, "Combining the Patterns," illustrates how various patterns of development can work together in an essay. The chapter includes three professional essays: Lars Eighner's "On Dumpster Diving," Jonathan Swift's "A Modest Proposal," and Alice Walker's "In Search of Our Mothers' Gardens." Each essay is accompanied by the same kinds of questions and other features that follow the book's other essays, as well as a student essay. Both the student essay and the first professional essay are annotated to illustrate the use of multiple rhetorical patterns within a single essay.

A New Appendix on Documentation, with 1998 MLA Guidelines for Citing Internet Sources

Also new to this edition is the appendix, "Using and Documenting Sources," which covers summary, paraphrase, integrating quotations, and avoiding plagiarism. Relying on the *MLA Handbook for Writers of Research Papers,* the appendix gives students a concise guide to the principles of documentation, including the Modern Language Association's newly published (1998) guidelines for citing and documenting Internet sources. It also includes a sample student essay that cites sources drawn from the casebook on media violence.

A Complete Supplements Package

Instructors who adopt *Patterns* now have access to a wide array of support materials, including the following:

- Comprehensive *Resources for Instructors* that give instructors guidance in approaching the assignments and provide answers to the questions following each reading
- An interactive Web site featuring additional writing activities and argument casebooks as well as links to other relevant Web sites: ⟨http://www.smpcollege.com/patterns⟩
- Transparency masters, which include peer editing worksheets and sample student essays

Acknowledgments

As always, friends, colleagues, students, and family all helped this project along. Of particular value were the responses to questionnaires sent to users of the sixth edition, and we thank each of the instructors who responded so frankly and helpfully: Kirk Adams, Tarrant County Junior College; F. K. Bartsch, Wharton County Junior College; David Bower, Northern Michigan University; Georgene Clark, Delta State University; Michael Cross, Tulsa Community College; Kitty Chen Dean, Nassau Community College; Priscilla Finely, Elmira College; Ray Foster, Scottsdale Community College; Joan Fry, Glendale Community College and Pasadena City College; Muriel Fuqua, Daytona Beach Community College; Loris Galford, McNeese State University; Ellen Gardiner, University of Mississippi; Gabrielle Gautreaux, University of New Orleans; Cynthia Greenwood, Wharton County Junior College; Ida Hagman, College of DuPage; Iris Rose Hart, Santa Fe Community College; Charles Hill, Gadsden State Community College; Joseph S. Horobetz, Northern Virginia Community College–Annandale; Arden Jensen, Gulf Coast Community College; Catherine L. Kasper, University of Denver; Sally Ann Kress, Hudson County Community College; Sue Lane McCulley, Wharton County Junior College; Nancy A. McMichael, Allentown College; Michael Moghtader, University of New Mexico; Barbara Murray, Daytona Beach Community College; Lisa Ostrom, Brooklyn College; Brendan Pieters, Santa Fe Community College; W. Allen Powell, Dallas Baptist University; Raychel Haugrud Reiff, University of Wisconsin–Superior; Michael Schroeder, Savannah State College; Anne Sheffield, University of Connecticut; Anne Slater, Frederick Community College; Ann Spicer, Wayne Community College; J. K. Van Dover, Lincoln University; Jane Wilcox, Christian Brothers University; and Trudy Zimmerman, Hutchinson Community College.

We are also grateful to the following colleagues, who provided useful commentary on various drafts of this new edition: T. Meleia Barnhill, Gadsden State Community College; Karen S. Becker, Richland Community College; Carin Bigrigg, University of New Mexico; John R. Boly, Marquette University; Tamara Ponzo Brattoli, Joliet Junior College; Sally Bright, Tulsa Community College; Barbara Broer, San Joaquin Delta College; Michel A. de Benedictis, Miami-Dade Community College; Kate Dobbins, Laney College; Scott Fisher, Rock Valley College; Joan Gagnon, Honolulu Community College; Loris D. Galford, McNeese State University; Keysha Ingram Gamor, Montgomery College; Gabrielle Gautreaux, University of New Orleans; Iris Rose Hart, Santa Fe Community College; Mary Piering Hiltbrand, University of Southern Colorado; Arden Jensen, Gulf Coast Community College; Kimberlie A. Johnson, Seminole Community College; Shannon Kiser, Shawnee State University; Teresa Kynell, Northern Michigan University; Mary Cole Larson, Tulsa Community College; Janice L. Lucas, Gulf Coast Community College; Virginia L. Macdonald, Loyola University; Wanda Martin, University of New Mexico; Deborah A. McDavis, Santa Fe Community College; Eleanor K. Montero, Daytona Beach Community College; Troy D. Nordman, Butler County Community College; Judy Ann

Pearce, Montgomery College; Brendan Pieters, Santa Fe Community College; Catherine Schwertman, Nassau Community College; Rosemary H. Shellander, Harper Community College; Ellen Shull, Palo Alto College; Anne Slater, Frederick Community College; Susan A. VanSchuyver, Oklahoma City Community College; Elisa Warford, Northern Virginia Community College; and Kathy Wyss, San Jose State University.

Special thanks go to Mark Gallaher, a true professional and a valued friend, for revising the headnotes and the *Resources for Instructors* for this edition.

Through seven editions of *Patterns of College Writing,* we have enjoyed a wonderful relationship with St. Martin's Press. We have always found the editorial and production staff to be efficient, cooperative, and generous with their time and advice. During our work on this edition, we benefited from the thoughtful comments and careful attention to detail of Talvi Laev, Development Editor, and from the helpful advice of Donna Erickson, English Editor. We are especially grateful to Judy Voss for her superb copyediting. We are also grateful to Emily Berleth, Manager of Publishing Services at St. Martin's, and to Dolores Wolfe of York Production Services for their work overseeing the book's production.

We are fortunate to have enjoyed our own twenty-two-year collaboration; we know how rare a successful partnership like ours is. We also know how lucky we are to have our families—Mark, Adam, and Rebecca Kirszner and Demi, David, and Sarah Mandell—to help keep us in touch with the things that really matter.

Laurie G. Kirszner
Stephen R. Mandell

SEVENTH EDITION

Patterns for College Writing

A RHETORICAL READER AND GUIDE

INTRODUCTION: READING TO WRITE

On a purely practical level, you will read the selections in this text to answer study questions and prepare for class discussions. However, you will also read to evaluate the ideas of others, to form judgments, and to develop original points of view. By introducing you to new ideas and new ways of thinking about familiar concepts, reading prepares you to respond critically to the ideas of others and to develop ideas of your own. When you understand what you read, you are able to form opinions, exchange ideas with others in conversation, ask and answer questions, and develop ideas that can be further explored in writing. For all of these reasons, reading is a vital part of your education.

READING CRITICALLY

Reading is a two-way street. Readers are presented with a writer's ideas, but they also bring their own responses and interpretations to what they read. After all, readers have different national, ethnic, cultural, and geographic backgrounds and different kinds of knowledge and experiences. Consequently, they may react differently to a particular essay or story. For example, urban readers may miss the point of an essay about the enriching powers of the wilderness, but they may nevertheless be able to spot bias in the essay or to challenge its assumptions. Readers from an economically and ethnically homogeneous suburban neighborhood may have difficulty understanding a story about class conflict, but these readers may also be more objective than readers who are struggling with such conflict on a personal level.

These differences in reactions do not mean that every interpretation is acceptable, that an essay or story or poem may mean whatever a reader wants it to mean. Readers must make sure they are not distorting the writer's words, overlooking (or ignoring) significant details, or seeing things in an essay or story that do not exist. It is not important for all readers to agree on a particular interpretation of a work. It is important, however, for each reader to develop an interpretation that can be supported by the work itself.

The study questions that accompany the essays in this text encourage you to question writers' ideas. Although some of the questions—particularly those listed under *Comprehension*—require fairly straightforward factual responses, other questions—particularly those designated *Journal Entry*—invite more complex responses, reflecting your individual reaction to the selections. (Note that different kinds of questions follow the literary works in this text.)

READING ACTIVELY

When you read an essay in this text, or any work that you expect to discuss in class (and perhaps to write about), you should read it carefully—and you should read it more than once.

Before You Read

Before you read, look over the essay to get an overview of its content. If the selection has a headnote, begin by reading it. Next, skim the work to get a general sense of the writer's ideas. As you read, note the title and any internal headings as well as the use of boldface type, italics, and other design elements. When approaching an essay, pay special attention to the introductory and concluding paragraphs, where a writer is likely to make (or reiterate) key points.

As You Read

As you read, ask yourself questions like the following:

- What is the writer's general subject?
- What is the writer's main point?
- Does the writer seem to have a particular purpose in mind?
- What kind of audience is the writer addressing?
- Are the writer's ideas consistent with your own?
- Do you have any knowledge that could challenge the writer's ideas?
- Is any information missing?
- Are any sequential or logical links missing?
- Can you identify themes or ideas that also appear in other works you have read?
- Can you identify parallels with your own experience?

HIGHLIGHTING AND ANNOTATING

As you read and reread, be sure to record your reactions in writing. These notations will help you to understand the writer's ideas and your own thinking about these ideas. Every reader develops a different system of recording such responses, but many readers use a combination of *highlighting* and *annotating.*

When you **highlight,** you mark the text with symbols. You might, for example, underline important ideas, box key terms, number a series of related points, circle an unfamiliar word (or place a question mark beside it), draw vertical lines in the margin beside a particularly interesting passage, draw arrows to connect related points, or place asterisks next to discussions of the work's central issues or themes.

When you **annotate,** you carry on a conversation with the text in marginal notes. You might, among other things, ask questions, suggest possible parallels with other reading selections or with your own experiences, argue with the writer's points, comment on the writer's style, or define unfamiliar terms and concepts.

The paragraph that follows, excerpted from Maya Angelou's "Finishing School" (page 75), illustrates the method of highlighting and annotating described above.

Date written?	(Recently) a white woman from Texas, who would quickly describe herself as a (liberal,) asked me about my hometown. When I told her that in Stamps my grandmother had owned the only Negro general merchandise store since the turn of the century, she exclaimed, "Why, you were a (debutante.") Ridiculous and even ludicrous. But Negro girls in small Southern towns, whether poverty-stricken or just munching along on a few of life's necessities, were given as extensive and irrelevant preparations for adulthood as rich white girls shown in magazines. Admittedly the training was not the same. While white girls learned to waltz and sit gracefully with a tea cup balanced on their knees, we were lagging behind, learning the (mid-Victorian values) with very little money to indulge them....

Serious or sarcastic?

What are these values?

Why does she mention this?

Also true of boys? In North as well as South? True today?

Remember that this process of highlighting and annotating is not an end in itself but rather a step toward understanding what you have read. Annotations suggest questions; in your search for answers, you may ask your instructor for clarification, or you may raise particularly puzzling or provocative points during class discussion or in small study groups. After your questions have been answered, you will be able to discuss and write about what you have read with greater confidence, accuracy, and authority.

READING THE SELECTIONS IN THIS BOOK

The selection that follows, " 'What's in a Name?' " by Henry Louis Gates Jr., is typical of the essays in this text. It is preceded by a headnote that provides information about the author's life and career. As you read the essay and the headnote, you should highlight and annotate them carefully.

HENRY LOUIS GATES JR.

Henry Louis Gates Jr. was born in 1950 in Keyser, West Virginia. He graduated from Yale University in 1973 and earned his doctorate from Cambridge University in 1979. He has taught at Yale, Cornell, and Duke universities and since 1991 has been the W. E. B. Du Bois Professor of the Humanities and chair of the Afro-American Studies Department at Harvard University. Gates has edited many collections of the works of African-American writers and numerous books of literary criticism. He is the author of *Figures in Black: Words, Signs, and the Racial Self* (1987); *The Signifying Monkey: A Theory of Afro-American Literary Criticism* (1988), which won an American Book Award in 1989; *Loose Canons: Notes on the Culture Wars* (1992); *Colored People: A Memoir* (1994); and, with Cornel West, *The Future of Race* (1996). Gates advocates broadening the representation of non-European cultures in the basic university curriculum and works to establish a strong community of African-American students and scholars. In this selection, originally published in the journal *Dissent* in 1989, Gates recalls an incident from his childhood that helped him understand the significance of race in his society.

"What's in a Name?"

The question of color takes up much space in these pages, but the question of color, especially in this country, operates to hide the graver questions of the self.
> —JAMES BALDWIN, *1961*

. . . blood, darky, Tar Baby, Kaffir, shine . . . moor, black-amoor, Jim Crow, spook . . . quadroon, meriney, red bone, high yellow . . . Mammy, porch monkey, home, homeboy, George . . . spearchucker, schwarze, Leroy, Smokey . . . mouli, buck. Ethiopian, brother, sistah. . . .
> —TREY ELLIS, *1989*

I had forgotten the incident completely, until I read Trey Ellis's essay, "Remember My Name," in a recent issue of the *Village Voice* (June 13, 1989). But there, in the middle of an extended italicized list of the bynames of "the race" ("the race" or "our people" being the terms my parents used in polite or reverential discourse, "jigaboo" or "nigger" more commonly used in anger, jest, or pure disgust) it was: "George." Now the events of that very brief exchange return to mind so vividly that I wonder why I had forgotten it.

My father and I were walking home at dusk from his second job. He "moonlighted" as a janitor in the evenings for the telephone company. Every day but Saturday, he would come home at 3:30 from his regular job at the paper mill, wash up, eat supper, then at 4:30 head downtown to his second job. He used to make jokes frequently about a union official who moonlighted. I never got the joke, but he and his friends thought it was hilarious. All I knew was that my family always ate well, that my brother and I had new clothes to wear, and that all of the white people in Piedmont, West Virginia, treated my parents with an odd mixture of resentment and respect that even we understood at the time had something directly to do with a small but certain measure of financial security.

He had left a little early that evening because I was with him and I   3 had to be in bed early. I could not have been more than five or six, and we had stopped off at the Cut-Rate Drug Store (where no black person in town but my father could sit down to eat, and eat off real plates with real silverware) so that I could buy some caramel ice cream, two scoops in a wafer cone, please, which I was busy licking when Mr. Wilson walked by.

Mr. Wilson was a very quiet man, whose stony, brooding, silent man-   4 ner seemed designed to scare off any overtures of friendship, even from white people. He was Irish, as was one-third of our village (another third being Italian), the more affluent among whom sent their children to "Catholic School" across the bridge in Maryland. He had white straight hair, like my Uncle Joe, whom he uncannily resembled, and he carried a black worn metal lunch pail, the kind that Riley* carried on the television show. My father always spoke to him, and for reasons that we never did understand, he always spoke to my father.

"Hello, Mr. Wilson," I heard my father say.   5

"Hello, George."   6

I stopped licking my ice cream cone, and asked my Dad in a loud   7 voice why Mr. Wilson had called him "George."

"Doesn't he know your name, Daddy? Why don't you tell him your   8 name? Your name isn't George."

For a moment I tried to think of who Mr. Wilson was mixing Pop up   9 with. But we didn't have any Georges among the colored people in Piedmont; nor were there colored Georges living in the neighboring towns and working at the mill.

"Tell him your name, Daddy."   10

"He knows my name, boy," my father said after a long pause. "He   11 calls all colored people George."

A long silence ensued. It was "one of those things," as my Mom   12 would put it. Even then, that early, I knew when I was in the presence of "one of those things," one of those things that provided a glimpse, through a rent curtain, at another world that we could not affect but that affected us. There would be a painful moment of silence, and you would wait for it to give way to a discussion of a black superstar such as Sugar Ray or Jackie Robinson.

"Nobody hits better in a clutch than Jackie Robinson."   13

"That's right. Nobody."   14

I never again looked Mr. Wilson in the eye.   15

---

*EDS. NOTE—The lead character in a 1950s sitcom titled *The Life of Riley.*

RESPONDING TO READING SELECTIONS

Once you have read a selection carefully and recorded your initial reactions to it, you should be able to respond to specific questions about it.
The study questions that follow each essay in Chapters 2 through 11 of
this text will guide you through the rest of the reading process and help
you think critically about what you are reading. These questions begin by
focusing on comprehension and then ask you to consider the writer's
purpose and the choices he or she has made. Some questions then ask
you to make connections between the selection and your own opinions or
personal experiences. Five types of study questions follow each essay:

Comprehension questions help you to measure your understanding of
what the writer is saying.

Purpose and Audience questions ask you to consider why, and for whom,
each selection was written and to examine the implications of the
writer's choices in view of a particular purpose or intended audience.

Style and Structure questions encourage you to examine the decisions the
writer has made about elements like arrangement of ideas, paragraph-
ing, sentence structure, diction, and imagery.

Vocabulary Projects ask you to define certain words, to consider the connotations of others, and to examine the writer's reasons for selecting particular words or word patterns.

Journal Entry questions ask you to respond informally to what you read
and to speculate freely about related ideas—perhaps exploring ethical issues raised by the selection or offering your opinions about the writer's
statements. Briefer, less polished, and less structured than full-length essays, journal entries not only allow you to respond critically to a reading
selection but may also suggest ideas for more formal kinds of writing.

Following these sets of questions are three additional features:

Writing Workshop assignments ask you to write essays structured according to the pattern of development explained and illustrated in the chapter.

Combining the Patterns questions focus on the other patterns of development—besides the essay's dominant pattern—that the writer uses. These
questions ask why a writer uses particular patterns—narration, description, exemplification, process, cause and effect, comparison and contrast,
classification and division, definition—what each pattern contributes to
the essay, and what other choices the writer had.

Thematic Connections identify other readings in the book that deal with
the same theme or a similar one. Reading these related works will enhance your understanding and appreciation of the original work. (The
Thematic Connections identify two or more works related to each reading selection; you should look for others as well.)

The final selection in each chapter, a story or poem, is followed by *Thinking
about Literature* questions, a *Journal Entry,* and *Thematic Connections.* Finally,

at the end of each chapter, *Writing Assignments* offer additional practice in writing essays structured according to a particular pattern of development, and a *Collaborative Activity* suggests an idea for a group project.

Following are some examples of study questions and possible responses as well as a Writing Workshop assignment and Thematic Connections for " 'What's in a Name?' " (pages 5–6). The numbers in parentheses after quotations refer to the paragraphs in which the quotations appear.

• • •

COMPREHENSION

1. *In paragraph 1 Gates wonders why he forgot about the exchange between his father and Mr. Wilson. Why do you think he forgot about it?* Gates may have forgotten about the incident simply because it was something that happened a long time ago, or because such incidents were commonplace when he was a child. Alternatively, he may *not* have forgotten the exchange between his father and Mr. Wilson but rather pushed it out of his mind because he found it so painful. (After all, he says he was never again able to look Mr. Wilson in the eye.)

2. *How was the social status of Gates's family different from that of other black families in Piedmont, West Virginia? How does Gates account for this difference?* Gates's family was different from other African-American families in town in that they were treated with "an odd mixture of resentment and respect" (2) by whites. Although other blacks were not permitted to eat at the drugstore, Mr. Gates was. Gates attributes this social status to his family's "small but certain measure of financial security" (2). Even so, when Mr. Wilson insulted Mr. Gates, the privileged status of the Gates family was revealed to be false.

3. *What does Gates mean when he says, "It was 'one of those things,' as my Mom would put it" (12)?* Gates's comment indicates that the family learned to see such mistreatment as routine. In context, the word *things* in paragraph 12 refers to the kind of incident that gave Gates and his family a glimpse of the way the white world operates.

4. *Why did Gates's family turn to discussions of "black superstars" after a "painful moment of silence" (12) such as the one he describes?* Although Gates does not explain the family's behavior, we can infer that they spoke of African-American heroes like prizefighter Sugar Ray Robinson and baseball player Jackie Robinson to make themselves feel better. Such discussions were a way of balancing the negative images of African-Americans created by incidents such as the one Gates describes and of bolstering the low self-esteem the family felt as a result. These heroes seemed to have won the respect denied to the Gates family; to mention them was to participate vicariously in their glory.

5. *Why do you think Gates "never again looked Mr. Wilson in the eye" (15)?* Gates may have felt that Mr. Wilson was somehow the enemy, not to be trusted, because he had insulted Gates's father. Or he may have been

ashamed to look him in the eye because he believed his father should have insisted on being addressed properly.

PURPOSE AND AUDIENCE

1. *Why do you think Gates introduces his narrative with the two quotations he selects? How do you suppose he expects his audience to react to them? How do you react?* Gates begins with two quotations, both by African-American writers, written nearly thirty years apart. Baldwin's words seem to suggest that, in the United States, "the question of color" is a barrier to understanding "the graver questions of the self." That is, the labels *black* and *white* may mask more fundamental characteristics or issues. Ellis's list of names (many pejorative) for African-Americans illustrates the fact that epithets can dehumanize people—they can, in effect, rob a person of his or her "self." This issue of the discrepancy between a name and what lies behind it is central to Gates's essay. In one sense, then, Gates begins with these two quotations because they are relevant to the issues he will discuss. More specifically, he is using the two quotations—particularly Ellis's string of unpleasant names—to arouse interest in his topic and provide an intellectual and emotional context for his story. He may also be intending to make his white readers uncomfortable and his black readers angry. How you react depends on your attitudes about race (and perhaps about language).

2. *What is the point of Gates's narrative? That is, why does he recount the incident?* It is difficult to isolate any one specific point this narrative makes. Certainly Gates wishes to make readers aware of the awkward, and potentially dangerous, position of his father (and, by extension, of other African-Americans) in a small southern town in the 1950s. He also shows us how names help to shape people's perceptions and actions: as long as Mr. Wilson can call all black men "George," he can continue to see them as insignificant and treat them as inferiors. The title of the piece does, however, suggest that the way names shape perceptions is the writer's main point.

3. *The title of this selection, which Gates places in quotation marks, is an allusion to act 2, scene 2 of Shakespeare's* Romeo and Juliet, *where Juliet says, "What's in a name? That which we call a rose / By any other name would smell as sweet." Why do you think Gates chose this title? Does he expect his audience to recognize the quotation?* Although Gates could not have been certain that all members of his audience would recognize the allusion to *Romeo and Juliet,* he could have been reasonably sure that if they did, the reference would enhance their understanding of the selection. In Shakespeare's play the two lovers are kept apart essentially because of their names: she is a Capulet and he is a Montague, and the two families are involved in a bitter feud. In the speech from which Gates takes the title quotation, Juliet questions the logic of such a situation. In her view, what a person is called should not determine how he or she is regarded—and this, of course, is one of Gates's points as well. Even if readers are not able to recognize the allusion, however, the title still foreshadows the selection's focus on names.

STYLE AND STRUCTURE

1. *Does paragraph 1 add something vital to the narrative, or would Gates's story make sense without the introduction? Could another kind of introduction work as well?* Gates's first paragraph supplies the context in which the incident is to be read—that is, it makes clear that Mr. Wilson's calling Mr. Gates "George" was not an isolated incident but rather part of a pattern of behavior that allowed those in positions of power to mistreat those they considered inferior. For this reason, it is an effective introduction. Although the narrative would make sense without paragraph 1, the story's full impact would probably not be as great. Still, Gates could have begun differently. For example, he could have started with the incident itself (paragraph 2) and interjected his comments about the significance of names later in the piece. He could also have begun with the exchange of dialogue in paragraphs 5 through 11 and then introduced the current paragraph 1 to supply the incident's context.

2. *What does the use of dialogue contribute to the narrative? Would the selection have a different impact without dialogue? Explain.* Gates was five or six years old when the incident occurred and the dialogue helps to establish the child's innocence as well as his father's quiet acceptance of the situation. In short, the dialogue is a valuable addition to the piece because it creates two characters, one innocent and one resigned to injustice, both of whom stand in contrast to the voice of the adult narrator: wise, worldly, but also angry and perhaps ashamed, the voice of a man who has benefited from the sacrifices of men like Gates's father.

3. *Why do you think Gates supplies the specific details he chooses in paragraphs 2 and 3? In paragraph 4? Is all this information necessary?* The details Gates provides in paragraphs 2 and 3 help to establish the status of the Gates family in Piedmont; because readers have this information, the fact that the family was ultimately disregarded and discounted by whites emerges as deeply ironic. The information in paragraph 4 also contributes to this **irony.** Here we learn that Mr. Wilson was not liked by many whites, that he looked like Gates's Uncle Joe, and that he carried a lunch box—in other words, that he had no special status in the town apart from that conferred by race.

VOCABULARY PROJECTS

1. *Define each of the following words as it is used in this selection.*

   by-names (1)—nicknames
   measure (2)—extent or degree
   uncannily (4)—strangely
   rent (12)—torn
   ensued (12)—followed

2. *Consider the connotations of the words* colored *and* black, *both of which are used by Gates to refer to African-Americans. What different associations does each word have? Why does Gates use both—for example,* colored *in paragraph 9 and* black

in paragraph 12? What is your response to the father's use of the term boy *in paragraph 11?* In the 1950s, when the incident Gates describes took place, the term *colored* was still widely used, along with *Negro,* to designate Americans of African descent. In the 1960s the terms *Afro-American* and *black* replaced the earlier names, with *black* emerging as the preferred term and remaining dominant through the 1980s. Today, although *black* is still preferred by many, others prefer *African-American.* (According to a recent survey conducted by the Joint Center for Political and Economic Studies, 72 percent of black Americans preferred the term *black,* with 15 percent favoring *African-American,* 3 percent preferring *Afro-American,* and 2 percent choosing *Negro.*) Because the term *colored* is the oldest designation, it may seem old-fashioned and even racist today; *black,* which connoted a certain degree of militancy in the 1960s, is probably now considered a neutral term by most people. Gates uses both words because he is speaking from two time periods. In paragraph 9, recreating the thoughts and words of a child in a 1950s southern town, he uses the term *colored;* in paragraph 12 the adult Gates, commenting in 1989 on the incident, uses *black.* The substitution of *African-American* for the older terms might give the narrative a more contemporary flavor, but it might also seem awkward or forced—and, in paragraph 9, inappropriately formal. As far as the term *boy* is concerned, different readers are apt to have different responses. Although the father's use of the term can be seen as affectionate, it can also be seen as derisive in this context since it echoes the bigot's use of *boy* for all black males, regardless of age or accomplishments.

JOURNAL ENTRY

Do you think Gates's parents should have used experiences like the one in "'What's in a Name?'" to educate him about the family's social status in the community? Why do you think they chose instead to dismiss such incidents as "one of those things" (12)? Your responses to these questions should reflect your own opinions and judgments, based on your background and experiences as well as on your interpretation of the reading selection.

WRITING WORKSHOP

Write about a time when you, like Gates's father, could have spoken out in protest but chose not to. Would you make the same decision today? By the time you approach the Writing Workshop questions, you will have read an essay, highlighted and annotated it, responded to study questions about it, discussed it in class, and perhaps considered its relationship to other essays in the text. Often your next step will be to write an essay in response to one of the Writing Workshop questions. (Chapter 1 follows Laura Bobnak, a first-year composition student, through the process of writing such an essay.)

COMBINING THE PATTERNS

Although **narration** *is the pattern of development that dominates "'What's in a Name?'" and gives it its structure, Gates also uses* **exemplification,** *presenting an extended exam-*

ple to support his thesis. What is this example? What does it illustrate? Would several brief examples have been more convincing? The extended example is the story of the encounter between Gates's father and Mr. Wilson, which compellingly illustrates the kind of behavior African-Americans were often forced to adopt in the 1950s. Because Gates's introduction focuses on "the incident" (1), one extended example is enough (although he alludes to other incidents in paragraph 12).

THEMATIC CONNECTIONS

- "Finishing School" (page 75)
- "Sexism in English: A 1990s Update" (page 401)

As you read and think about the selections in this text, you should begin to see thematic links among them. Such parallels can add to your interest and understanding as well as give you ideas for group discussion and writing. For example, Maya Angelou's "Finishing School," another autobiographical essay by an African-American writer, has many similarities with Gates's. Both essays describe the uneasy position of a black child expected to adhere to the white world's unfair code of behavior, and both deal squarely with the importance of being called by one's name. In fact, paragraph 26 of "Finishing School" offers some helpful insights into the problem Gates examines. A less obvious but equally valid thematic link exists between "'What's in a Name?'" and Alleen Pace Nilsen's "Sexism in English: A 1990s Update," which also considers the dangers of using language to separate and demean a group of people.

In the process of thinking about Gates's narrative, discussing it in class, or preparing to write an essay on a related topic (such as those listed under Writing Workshop), you might find it useful to consider (or reconsider) Angelou's and Nilsen's essays.

1

THE WRITING PROCESS

Every reading selection in this book is the result of a struggle between a writer and his or her material. If a writer's struggle is successful, the finished work is welded together without a seam, and readers have no sense of the frustration the writer experienced while hunting for the right word or rearranging ideas. Writing is no easy business, and even a professional writer can have a very difficult time. Still, although no simple formula for good writing exists, some approaches are easier and more productive than others.

At this point you may be asking yourself, "So what? What has this got to do with me? I'm not a professional writer." True enough, but during the next few years you will be doing a good deal of writing. Throughout your college career, you will need to write midterms, final exams, lab reports, short essays, and research papers. In your professional life, you may have to write progress reports, proposals, business correspondence, memos, and résumés. As diverse as these assignments may seem, they have something in common: they can be made easier if you are familiar with the **writing process**—the procedure experienced writers follow to produce a finished piece of writing.

In general, the writing process has three stages:

- Invention
- Arrangement
- Drafting and revision

During *invention,* also called *prewriting,* you decide what you will write about and gather information to support or explain what you want to say. During *arrangement,* you decide how you are going to organize your ideas. Finally, during *drafting and revision,* you write your essay, progressing through several drafts as you reconsider ideas and refine your style and structure. When you have finished revising, you move on to *editing,* correcting grammar, punctuation, and mechanics.

Although we discuss the writing process as a series of neatly defined steps, this model does not reflect the way people actually write. For one thing, ideas do not always flow easily, and the central point you set out to develop does not always wind up in the essay you ultimately write. Writing often progresses in fits and starts, with ideas occurring sporadically or not at all. In fact, much good writing occurs when a writer gets stuck or confused but continues to work until ideas take shape on the page or on the screen.

Furthermore, because the writing process is so erratic, its three stages overlap. Most writers engage in invention, arrangement, and drafting and revision simultaneously—finding ideas, considering possible methods of organization, and looking for the right words all at the same time. In fact, writing is an idiosyncratic process: no two writers approach the writing process in exactly the same way. Some people outline; others do not. Some take elaborate notes during the prewriting stage; others keep track of everything in their heads.

The writing process that we discuss throughout this book illustrates the many choices writers may make at various stages of composition. But regardless of writers' different approaches, one thing is certain: the more you write, the better acquainted you will become with your personal writing process and with ways to modify it to suit various writing tasks. This chapter will help you define your needs as a writer and understand your options as you approach writing assignments both in and out of college.

STAGE ONE: INVENTION

Invention, or **prewriting,** is an important part of the writing process. At this stage you discover what interests you about your subject and what ideas you will develop in your essay. When you are given a writing assignment, you may be tempted to plunge into a first draft immediately. Before writing, however, you should take the time to consider the assignment, explore your subject, and decide what you wish to say about it.

Understanding the Assignment

Almost everything you write in college will begin as an *assignment*. Some assignments will be direct and easy to understand:

Write about an experience that changed your life.

Discuss the procedure you used to synthesize ammonia.

But others will be difficult and complex:

According to Wayne Booth, point of view is central to understanding modern fiction. In a short essay, discuss how Henry James uses point of view in *The Turn of the Screw*.

Before beginning to write, you need to understand what you are being asked to do. If the assignment is a written question, read it carefully several times and underline its key ideas. If the assignment is read aloud by your instructor, be sure to copy it accurately. (A missed word can make quite a difference.) If you are confused about anything, ask your instructor for clarification. Remember that no matter how well written an essay is, it will miss the mark if it does not address the assignment.

Setting Limits

Once you understand the assignment, you should consider its *length, purpose, audience,* and *occasion* and your own *knowledge* of the subject. Each of these factors helps you determine what you will say about your subject and thus simplifies your writing task.

LENGTH. Often your instructor will specify an approximate length for a paper, or your writing situation will determine how much you can write. Your word or page limit has a direct bearing on your paper's focus. For example, you would need a narrower topic for a two-page essay than for a ten-page paper. Similarly, you could not discuss a question as thoroughly during an hour-long exam as you might in a paper prepared over several days.

If your instructor sets no page limit, consider how the nature of the assignment suggests its length. A *summary* of a chapter or an article, for instance, should be much shorter than the original, whereas as *analysis* of a poem will often be longer than the poem itself. If you are uncertain about the appropriate length for your paper, consult your instructor.

PURPOSE. Your **purpose** also limits what you say and how you say it. For example, if you were to write to a prospective employer, you would not emphasize the same aspects of college life that you would stress in a letter to a friend. In the first case, you would want to persuade the reader to hire you, so you might include your grade-point average or a list of the relevant courses you took. In the second case, you would want to inform and perhaps entertain. To accomplish these aims, you might share anecdotes about dorm life or describe one of your favorite instructors. In each case, your purpose would help you determine what information you should include to evoke a particular response in a specific audience.

In general, you can classify your purposes for writing according to your relationship to the audience. Thus, one purpose might be to express personal feelings or impressions to your readers. *Expressive* writing includes diaries, personal letters, journals, and often narrative and descriptive essays as well. Another purpose might be to inform readers about something. *Informative* writing includes essay exams, lab reports, book reports, expository essays, and some research papers. Or your purpose might be to persuade readers to think or act in a certain way. *Persuasive* writing includes editorials, argumentative essays, and many other essays and research papers.

In addition to these general purposes, you might have a more specific purpose—to analyze, entertain, hypothesize, assess, summarize, question, report, recommend, suggest, evaluate, describe, recount, request, instruct, and so on. For example, suppose you wrote a report on the incidence of AIDS in your community. Your general purpose might be to *inform* readers of the situation, but you might also want to *assess* the progression of the disease and *instruct* readers how to avoid contracting the virus that causes it.

AUDIENCE.   To be effective, your essay should be written with a particular **audience** in mind. An audience can be an *individual*—your instructor, for example—or it can be a *group,* like your classmates or coworkers. Your essay could address a *specialized* audience, such as a group of medical doctors or economists, or a *general* or *universal* audience whose members have little in common, such as the readers of a newspaper or newsmagazine.

In college, your audience is usually your instructor, and your purpose in most cases is to demonstrate your mastery of the subject matter, your reasoning ability, and your competence as a writer. Other audiences may include classmates, professional colleagues, or members of your community. Considering the age and gender of your audience, its political and religious values, its social and educational level, and its interest in your subject may help you define it. Certainly the approach you took in your report about the spread of AIDS in your community would depend on your intended audience. For example, a report written for students at a local middle school would be very different from one addressing a civic group or the city council—or the parents of those students.

Often, you may find that your audience is just too diverse to be categorized. In such cases, many writers imagine a universal audience and make points that they think will appeal to a variety of readers. Sometimes writers try to imagine one typical individual in the audience—perhaps a person they know—so that they can write to someone specific. At other times, writers identify a common denominator, a role that characterizes the entire audience. For instance, when a report on the dangers of smoking asserts "Now is the time for health-conscious individuals to demand that cigarettes be removed from the market," it automatically casts its audience in the role of health-conscious individuals.

After you define your audience, you have to determine how much or how little its members know about your subject. This helps you decide how much background information your readers will need in order to understand the discussion. Are they highly informed? If so, you will make your points directly. Are they relatively uninformed? If this is the

---

☑ **CHECKLIST FOR SETTING LIMITS**

LENGTH

- Has your instructor specified a length?
- Does your writing situation suggest a length?

PURPOSE

- Is your general purpose to express personal feelings? To inform? To persuade?
- In addition to your general purpose, do you have any more specific purposes?
- Does your assignment provide any guidelines about purpose?

AUDIENCE

- Is your audience a group or an individual?
- Are you going to address a specialized or a general audience?
- Should you take into consideration the audience's age, gender, education, biases, or political or social values?
- Should you cast your audience in a particular role?
- How much can you assume your audience knows about your subject?
- How much interest does your audience have in the subject?

OCCASION

- Are you writing an in-class exercise or an at-home assignment?
- Are you addressing a situation outside the academic setting?
- What special approaches does your occasion require?

KNOWLEDGE

- What do you know about your subject?
- What do you need to find out?
- What are your opinions about your subject?

---

case, you will have to include definitions of key terms, background information, and summaries of basic research. Keep in mind that experts in one field will still need background information in areas with which they are unfamiliar. If, for example, you were writing an essay analyzing the characters in Joseph Conrad's *Heart of Darkness,* you could assume that the literature instructor who assigned the novel would not need a plot summary. However, if you wrote an essay for your history instructor that used *Heart of Darkness* to illustrate the evils of European colonialism in nineteenth-century Africa, you would probably need to include a short plot summary. (Even though your history instructor would know a lot about colonialism in Africa, she might not be familiar with the details of Conrad's work.)

OCCASION.   In general terms, the occasion for academic writing can be either an in-class writing exercise or an at-home assignment. In addition, different subject areas create different occasions for writing. A response suitable for a psychology or history class might not be acceptable for an English class, just as a satisfactory answer on a quiz might be insufficient on a midterm.

Although college writing situations may seem artificial, they provide valuable practice for writing you do outside of college. Like these assignments, each writing task you do outside of college requires a special approach that suits the occasion. A memo to your coworkers, for instance, will be less formal and more limited in scope than a report to your company's president. An e-mail communication to your fellow beer-can collectors about an upcoming meeting might be strictly informational, whereas a letter to your senator about preserving a local historical landmark would be persuasive as well as informational.

KNOWLEDGE.   Obviously, what you know (and do not know) about a subject limits what you can say about it. Before writing about any subject, ask yourself the following questions:

- What do I know about the subject?
- What do I need to find out?
- What do I think about the subject?

Different writing situations require different kinds of knowledge. A personal essay may draw on your own experiences and observations; a term paper will require you to gain new knowledge through research. Sometimes you will be able to increase your knowledge about a topic easily because you already have a strong background in the general subject. At other times, when a general subject is unfamiliar to you, you will need to select a topic particularly carefully so that you do not get out of your depth. In many cases, the amount of time you are given to do the assignment and its page limit will guide you as you consider what you know and what you need to learn before you can write knowledgeably.

EXERCISES

1. Decide whether or not each of the following topics is appropriate for the stated limits, and then write a few sentences to explain why each topic is or is not acceptable.
   a. A *two-to-three page paper:* A history of animal testing in the cosmetics industry
   b. A *two-hour final exam:* The effectiveness of bilingual education programs
   c. A *one-hour in-class essay:* An interpretation of Andy Warhol's painting of Campbell's soup cans

    d. A *letter to your college newspaper:* A discussion of your school's policy on alcoholic beverages

2. Make a list of the different audiences to whom you speak or write in your daily life. (Consider all the different people you see regularly, such as family members, your roommate, your instructor, your boss, your friends, and so on.)

    a. Do you speak or write to each person in the same way and about the same things? If not, how do your approaches to these people differ?

    b. List some subjects that would interest some of these people but not others. How do you account for these differences?

    c. Choose one of the following subjects and describe how you would speak or write to each audience about it.

- a local political issue
- your favorite comic strip
- curfews
- academic cheating

Moving from Subject to Topic

Many writing assignments begin as broad areas of interest or concern. These general *subjects* always need to be narrowed to specific *topics* that can be reasonably discussed within the limits of the assignment. For example, a subject like DNA recombinant research is interesting, but it is too vast to write about for any college assignment except in a general way. You need to limit such a subject to a topic that can be covered within the time and space available.

Subject	*Topic*
DNA recombinant research	One outcome of DNA recombinant research
Herman Melville's *Billy Budd*	Billy Budd as a Christ figure
Constitutional law	One result of the Miranda ruling
Personal computers	The uses of personal computers in elementary education

As these examples illustrate, a topic does more than narrow a general subject. A topic also defines the manner in which you will treat a subject.

To narrow your subject, you need to discover the topics that the subject suggests. Probing systematically for a workable topic is a crucial stage of the writing process. If you skip this stage and wait for a topic to come to you, not only will you waste time but you may also fail to realize the potential of your subject. Instead, you can narrow your subject by using *questions for probing* and *freewriting.*

    QUESTIONS FOR PROBING.   You probe your subject by asking a series of questions about it. These questions are useful because they reflect ways in which your mind operates: finding similarities and differences, for instance, or dividing a whole into its parts. By going through the following list of questions, you can explore your subject systematically. Of course, not all questions will work for every subject. Still, any question may elicit many different answers, and each answer is a possible topic for your essay.

When applied to a particular subject, some of these questions can yield many workable topics—some you might never have considered had you not asked the questions. For example, by applying this approach

---

☑ QUESTIONS FOR PROBING

What happened?

When did it happen?

Where did it happen?

Who did it?

What does it look like?

What are its characteristics?

What impressions does it make?

What are some typical cases or examples of it?

How did it happen?

What makes it work?

How is it made?

Why did it happen?

What caused it?

What does it cause?

What are its effects?

How is it like other things?

How is it different from other things?

What are its parts or types?

How can its parts or types be separated or grouped?

Do its parts or types fit into a logical order?

Into what categories can its parts or types be arranged?

On what basis can it be categorized?

How can it be defined?

How does it resemble other members of its class?

How does it differ from other members of its class?

What are its limits?

💻 **COMPUTER STRATEGY**

If you are writing on a computer, you can store the questions for probing in a special file that you can open every time you have a new subject to probe. Make sure you also keep a record of your answers. If the topic you have chosen is too difficult or too narrow, you can return to the questions-for-probing file and select another topic.

---

to the general subject "the Brooklyn Bridge," you can generate more ideas and topics than you need:

What happened? A short history of the Brooklyn Bridge

What does it look like? A description of the Brooklyn Bridge

How is it made? The construction of the Brooklyn Bridge

What are its effects? The impact of the Brooklyn Bridge on American writers

How does it differ from other members of its class? Innovations in the design of the Brooklyn Bridge

At this point in the writing process, you mainly want to discover possible topics, and the more ideas you have, the wider your choice. So write down all the topics you think of. You can even repeat the process of probing several times to limit topics further. Once you have a list of topics, eliminate those that are not suitable—those that do not interest you or that are too complex or too simple to fit your assignment. When you have discarded these less promising ideas, you should still have several left. You can then select the topic that best suits your paper's length, purpose, audience, and occasion as well as your interests and your knowledge of the subject.

• • •

EXERCISES

1. Indicate whether the following are general subjects or topics that are narrow enough for a short essay.
   a. An argument against cigarette ads that are aimed at teenagers
   b. A comparison of the salaries of professional basketball and football players
   c. Children's television
   d. Two creation stories in the Book of Genesis
   e. Canadian and U.S. immigration law
   f. The Haber process for the fixation of atmospheric nitrogen
   g. The advantages of affirmative action programs
   h. The advantages of term over whole life insurance

    i. Managed health care
    j. An analysis of a political cartoon in your local newspaper
    k. Gender roles

2. Choose two of the following subjects, and generate three or four topics from each by using as many of the questions for probing as you can. (Assume that the essay you are preparing on each topic is due in one week for your composition class and that it should be about 750 words long.)
    a. Movie violence
    b. The Internet
    c. Popular music
    d. Vegetarianism
    e. Substance abuse
    f. Scientific experimentation on animals
    g. Styles of clothing
    h. Date rape
    i. Motorcycles
    j. Talk radio
    k. Diets
    l. Adolescence
    m. Grading
    n. The homeless
    o. Sex education

FREEWRITING.   You can use **freewriting** at any stage of the writing process—for example, to generate supporting information or to find a thesis. Freewriting is also a particularly useful way to narrow a general subject or assignment. When you freewrite, you write for a fixed period, perhaps five or ten minutes, without stopping and without paying attention to spelling, grammar, or punctuation. Your goal is to get your ideas down on paper so you can react to them. If you find you have nothing to say, write down anything until ideas begin to emerge—and in time they will. The secret is to *keep writing*. Try to focus on your subject, but don't worry if your ideas seem to wander off in other directions. The object of freewriting is to let your ideas flow. Often your best ideas will come to you from the unexpected connections you make as you write.

After completing your freewriting, read what you have written and look for ideas that you can write about. Some writers underline ideas they think they might explore in their essays. These ideas could become topics, or they could become subjects for other freewriting exercises. You might, for example, want to freewrite again, using a new idea as your focus. This process of writing more and more narrowly focused freewriting exercises—called **looping**—can yield a great deal of useful information and help you decide on a workable topic.

💻 COMPUTER STRATEGY

If you do your freewriting on a computer, you may find that staring at your own words causes you to go blank or lose your spontaneity. One possible solution is to turn down the brightness until the screen becomes dark and then freewrite. This technique allows you to block out distracting elements and concentrate on your ideas. Once you finish freewriting, turn up the brightness and see what you have. If you have come up with an interesting idea, you can move it onto a new page and use it as the subject of a new freewriting exercise.

▶ A STUDENT WRITER: FREEWRITING

After reading Henry Louis Gates Jr.'s " 'What's in a Name?' " (page 5), Laura Bobnak, a student in a composition class, chose to write an essay in response to this Writing Workshop question:

> Write about a time when you, like Gates's father, could have spoken out in protest but chose not to. Would you make the same decision today?

In an attempt to narrow this assignment to a workable topic, Laura freewrote the following:

> Write for ten minutes . . . ten minutes . . . at 9 o'clock in the morning—Just what I want to do in the morning—If you can't think of something to say, just write about anything. Right! Time to get this over with—An experience—should have talked—I can think of plenty of times I should have kept quiet! I should have brought coffee to class. I wonder what the people next to me are writing about. That reminds me. Next to me. Jeff Servin in chemistry. The time I saw him cheating. I was mad but I didn't do anything. I studied so hard and all he did was cheat. I was so mad. Nobody else seemed to care either. What's the difference between now and then? It's only a year and a half. . . . Honor code? Maturity? A lot of people cheated in high school. I bet I could write about this—Before and after, etc. My attitude then and now.

After some initial floundering, Laura discovered an idea that could be the basis for her essay. Although Laura's discussion of the incident still had to be developed, her freewriting had helped her discover a possible topic for her essay.

•   •   •

EXERCISES

1. Assume you have been asked to write a short in-class essay for your composition class. Do a ten-minute freewriting exercise on one of the following subjects:
   a. Exercise

    b. Movies
    c. Sports
    d. Raising children
    e. Books
    f. Jobs

2. Read what you have just written, underline the most interesting ideas, and choose one idea as a topic you might be able to write about in a short essay. Freewrite about this topic for another ten minutes to narrow it further and to generate ideas for your essay. Underline the ideas that seem most useful.

Finding Something to Say

Brainstorming and *journal writing* are useful tools for generating ideas, and both strategies can be helpful at this stage of the writing process and whenever you need to find something to say.

BRAINSTORMING. **Brainstorming** is one method of invention that can help you discover ideas about your topic. You can brainstorm in a group, exchanging ideas with several students in your composition class and writing down the useful ideas that come up. Or you can brainstorm on your own, quickly writing down every fact, idea, or association you can think of that relates to your topic. Your notes might include words, phrases, statements, questions, or even drawings or diagrams. Jot them down in whatever order you think of them, allowing your thoughts to wander freely. Some of the items may be inspired by your class notes; others may be ideas you got from reading or from talking with friends. Still other items may be ideas you have begun to wonder about, points you thought of while moving from subject to topic, or thoughts that occurred to you as you brainstormed.

▶ A STUDENT WRITER: BRAINSTORMING

After freewriting, Laura Bobnak decided to write about a time when she saw someone cheating and did not speak out. In order to narrow her topic further and find something to say, she made the brainstorming notes on page 25.

Laura obviously had plenty of ideas. After reading her brainstorming notes several times, she decided to concentrate on the differences between her attitude in high school and her current attitude. She knew that

---

🖳 **COMPUTER STRATEGY**

If you're a good typist, brainstorming on a computer can save you time and effort. Most word-processing programs make it easy to create bulleted or numbered lists. A computer also enables you to experiment with different ways of arranging and grouping items from your brainstorming notes.

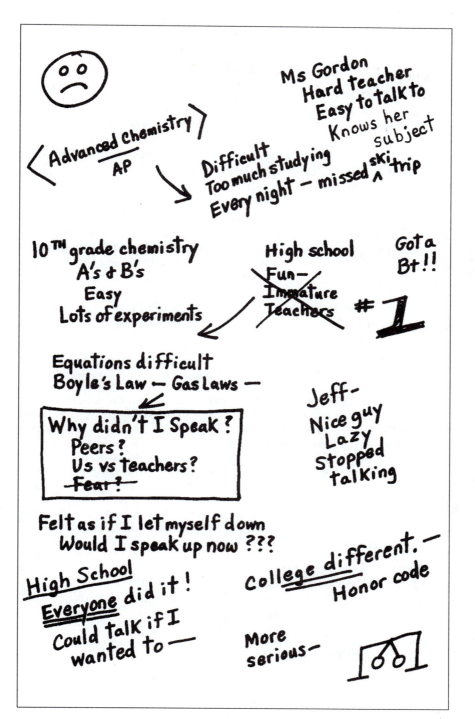

Brainstorming Notes

she could write a lot about this idea and relate it to the assignment, and she felt confident that her topic would be interesting both to her instructor and to the other students in the class.

JOURNAL WRITING.   **Journal writing** can be a useful source of ideas at any stage of the writing process. Many writers routinely keep a journal, jotting down experiences or exploring ideas they may want to use when they write. They write journal entries even when they have no particular writing project in mind. Often these journal entries are the kernels from which longer pieces of writing develop. Your instructor may ask you to keep a writing journal, or you may decide to do so on your own. In either case, you will find that your journal entries are likely to be more narrowly focused than freewriting or brainstorming, perhaps examining a small part of a reading selection or even one particular statement. Sometimes you will write in your journal in response to specific questions, like the Journal Entry assignments that appear throughout this book. Assignments such as these can help you start thinking about a reading selection you may later discuss in class or write about.

▶   A STUDENT WRITER: JOURNAL WRITING

The journal entry Laura Bobnak wrote after deciding on a topic for her paper appears below. In this entry she explores one idea from her brainstorming notes—her thoughts about her college's honor code.

> At orientation the dean of students talked about the college's honor code. She talked about how we were a community of scholars who were here for a common purpose—to take part in an intellectual dialogue. According to her, the purpose of the honor code is to make sure this dialogue continues uninterrupted. This idea sounded dumb at first, but now it makes more sense. If I saw someone cheating, I'd tell the instructor. First, though, I'd ask the *student* to go to the instructor. I don't see this as "telling" or "squealing." We're all here to get an education, and we should be able to assume everyone is being honest and fair. Besides, why should I go to all the trouble of studying while someone else does nothing and gets the same grade?

Although this journal entry is much narrower than the topic Laura eventually wrote about, it focuses on an issue relevant to her paper. Even though Laura included only a small part of this entry in her paper, it did help her clarify her ideas about her topic.

⌨   **COMPUTER STRATEGY**

Keeping your writing journal in a computer file has some obvious advantages, particularly if you type quickly and easily. Not only can you maintain a neat record of your ideas, but you can also easily move entries from your journal into an essay without recopying them.

Grouping Ideas

Once you have generated some material for your essay, you will want to group ideas that belong together. Doing so enables you to discover the connections that exist among various ideas.

CLUSTERING.   **Clustering** is a way of visually arranging your ideas so that you can tell at a glance where ideas belong and whether or not you need to generate more information. Although you can use clustering at an earlier stage of the writing process, it is especially useful for identifying major points and seeing how ideas fit together. (Clustering can also help you narrow your paper's topic to suit its length. If you find that your cluster diagram is too detailed, you can write about just one branch of the cluster.)

Begin clustering by writing your topic in the middle of a sheet of paper. After circling it, surround it with the words and phrases that identify the major points you intend to discuss. (You can get ideas from your brainstorming notes, from your journal, or from your freewriting.) Circle these words and phrases and connect them to the topic in the center. Next, construct other clusters of ideas relating to each major point and draw lines connecting them to the appropriate point. By dividing and subdividing your points, you get more specific as you move outward from the center of the page. In the process, you identify the facts, details, examples, and opinions that illustrate and expand your main points.

▶   A STUDENT WRITER: CLUSTERING

Because Laura Bobnak was not particularly visually oriented, she chose not to use this method of grouping her ideas. If she had, however, her cluster diagram might have looked like the one below.

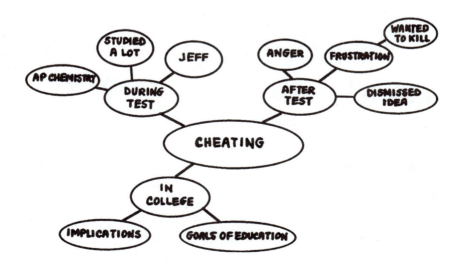

💻 **COMPUTER STRATEGY**

If you use a computer, you can easily arrange the notes generated from your prewriting activities into an informal outline. You can make an informal outline by typing words or phrases from your prewriting notes and rearranging them until the order makes sense. Later, you can use the categories from this informal outline to help you construct a more formal outline.

MAKING AN INFORMAL OUTLINE.   As an alternative or follow-up to clustering, you can organize your notes from brainstorming or other invention techniques into an *informal outline*. Quite often an informal outline is just a list of your major points, perhaps presented in some tentative order. Sometimes, however, an informal outline will include supporting details or suggest a pattern of development. Informal outlines do not specify all the major divisions and subdivisions of your paper or indicate the relative importance of your ideas the way formal outlines do (see page 36); they simply suggest the shape of your emerging essay.

▶ **A STUDENT WRITER: MAKING AN INFORMAL OUTLINE**

The following outline shows how Laura Bobnak grouped her ideas.

During test
    Found test hard
    Saw Jeff cheating

After test
    Got angry
    Wanted to tell
    Dismissed idea

In college
    Implications of cheating
    Goals of education

•   •   •

EXERCISE

Suppose your English composition instructor has given you the following list of subjects and told you to select one for a short essay, due in two days. Prepare one of these subjects using the invention strategies discussed above. First, apply the questions for probing. Next, do five minutes of freewriting on each of the three topics that seem most appealing. Then, pick the most promising topic and brainstorm about it. Finally, select the ideas you would use if you were actually writing the paper, and either cluster the ideas or group them into an informal outline.

    a. Grandparents
    b. Censoring the Internet

c. Gay rights
d. The drinking age
e. Equal pay for equal work
f. Divorce
g. Financial aid to college students
h. The environment
i. Campus security
j. Sex education in high schools

Understanding Thesis and Support

A **thesis** is the main idea of your essay, its central point. The concept of *thesis and support*—stating your thesis and developing ideas that explain and expand it—is central to your college writing. The academic essays you write will consist of several paragraphs: an *introduction* that presents your thesis statement, several *body paragraphs* that develop and support your thesis, and a *conclusion* that reinforces your thesis and provides closure. Your thesis holds this structure together; it is the center around which the rest of your essay develops.

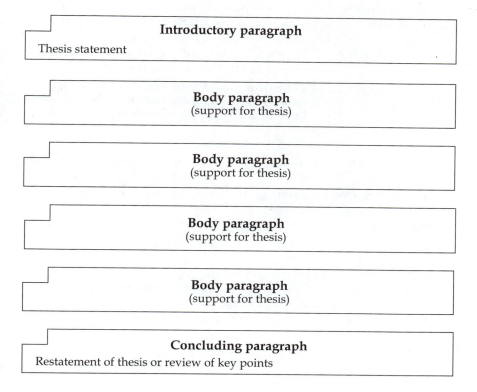

Introductory paragraph

Thesis statement

Body paragraph
(support for thesis)

Body paragraph
(support for thesis)

Body paragraph
(support for thesis)

Body paragraph
(support for thesis)

Concluding paragraph
Restatement of thesis or review of key points

Formulating a Thesis

DEFINING THE THESIS STATEMENT.   A thesis statement is always more than a title, an announcement of your intent, or a statement of fact. Although a descriptive title orients your readers, it is seldom detailed enough to reveal your essay's purpose or direction. An announcement of your intent can reveal more, but it is stylistically distracting. Finally, a statement of fact—such as a historical fact or a statistic—is typically a dead end and therefore cannot be developed into an essay. A statement like "Alaska became a state in 1959" or "Tuberculosis is highly contagious" or "The population of Greece is about ten million" provides your essay with no direction. However, a judgment or opinion in response to a fact *can* be an effective thesis—for instance, "The continuing threat of tuberculosis, particularly in the inner cities, suggests it is necessary to administer more frequent diagnostic tests among high-risk populations."

To gain an appreciation of the differences among titles, announcements, statements of fact, and thesis statements, compare the statements in each of the following groups:

Title:	The Fifty-Five-Mile-per-Hour Speed Limit: Pro and Con
Announcement:	I will examine the pros and cons of doing away with the fifty-five-mile-per-hour speed limit on major highways.
Statement of fact:	Nearly all states have now increased the speed limit from fifty-five to sixty-five miles per hour.
Thesis statement:	The federal government should withhold highway funds from all states that have increased the speed limit from fifty-five to sixty-five miles per hour.
Title:	Orwell's "A Hanging"
Announcement:	This paper will discuss George Orwell's attitude toward the death penalty in his essay "A Hanging."
Statement of fact:	In his essay, Orwell describes a hanging that he witnessed in Burma.
Thesis statement:	In "A Hanging," George Orwell shows that capital punishment is not only unpleasant but immoral.
Title:	Speaking Out
Announcement:	This essay will discuss a time when I could have spoken out but did not.
Statement of fact:	Once I saw someone cheating and did not speak out.
Thesis statement:	As I look back on the situation, I wonder why I kept silent and what would have happened had I acted.

DECIDING ON A THESIS.   No fixed rules determine when you formulate your thesis; the decision depends on such variables as the scope and difficulty of your assignment, your knowledge of the subject, and your method of writing. Sometimes, when you know a lot about a subject, you may be able to come up with a thesis before doing any invention activities like freewriting or brainstorming. At other times, you may have to wait until you review all your material and combine it into a single statement that indicates your position on the topic. Occasionally, your assignment may specify a thesis by telling you to take a particular position on a topic. Whatever the case, you should have a tentative thesis before you begin to write your first draft.

As you write, you will continue to discover new ideas, and you will probably move in directions that you did not anticipate. Still, because a tentative thesis gives you guidance and purpose, it is essential at the initial stages of writing. As you draft your essay, review the points you make in light of how they relate to your thesis, and revise the thesis statement or your support as necessary.

STATING YOUR THESIS.   Usually you will want to include a one-sentence statement of your thesis in your essay. An effective thesis statement has three characteristics.

1. *An effective thesis statement clearly expresses your essay's main idea.* It does more than just present your topic; it indicates what you will say about your topic, and it signals how you will approach your material. The following thesis statement, from the essay "Grant and Lee: A Study in Contrasts" by Bruce Catton (page 330), clearly communicates the writer's main idea:

> They [Grant and Lee] were two strong men, these oddly different generals, and they represented the strengths of two conflicting currents that, through them, had come into final collision.

This statement indicates that the essay will compare and contrast Grant and Lee; more specifically, it reveals that Catton will present the two Civil War generals as symbols of two historical currents that were also in opposition. If the statement had been less fully developed—for example, had Catton said "Grant and Lee were quite different from each other"—it would have communicated just the essay's title, without signaling the essay's purpose—or real subject—to his readers.

2. *An effective thesis statement reflects your essay's purpose.* Whether your purpose is to evaluate or analyze or simply to describe or recount, your thesis statement communicates that purpose to your readers. In general terms, your purpose may be to express personal feelings, to present information in a straightforward manner, or to persuade. Accordingly, your thesis can be *expressive,* conveying a mood or impression; it can be *informative,* perhaps listing the major points you will discuss or presenting an

objective overview of the essay; or it can be *persuasive,* taking a strong stand or outlining the position you will argue.

Each of the following thesis statements expresses a different purpose:

> The city's homeless families live in heartbreaking surroundings. (purpose—to express feelings)
>
> The plight of the homeless has become so serious that it is a major priority for many city governments. (purpose—to inform)
>
> The only responsible reaction to the crisis at hand is to renovate abandoned city housing to provide suitable shelter for homeless families. (purpose—to persuade)

3. *An effective thesis statement is clearly worded.* To communicate your essay's main idea, an effective thesis statement—often a single sentence— should be clearly and specifically worded. It should also speak for itself. It is not necessary to write, "My thesis is that . . ." or "The thesis of this paper is . . . ." The thesis statement should give an accurate indication of what follows and not mislead readers about the essay's direction, emphasis, content, or point of view. Vague language, confusing abstractions, irrelevant details, and complex terminology have no place in a thesis statement. Keep in mind, too, that your thesis statement should not make promises that your essay is not going to keep. For example, if you are going to discuss just the effects of a new immigration law, your thesis statement should not emphasize the sequence of events that led to the law's passage.

Your thesis statement cannot, or course, include every point you will discuss in your paper. Still, it should be specific enough to indicate the direction and scope of your essay. The statement "The new immigration law has failed to stem the tide of illegal immigrants" does not give your essay much focus. Which immigration law will you be examining? Which illegal immigrants? The following sentence, however, *is* an effective thesis statement. It clearly indicates what you are going to discuss, and it establishes a specific direction and purpose for the essay.

> Because it fails to take into account the economic causes of illegal immigration, the 1996 immigration law does not solve the problem of illegal immigration from Mexico into the United States.

IMPLYING A THESIS.   Although every essay should have a clear sense of purpose, not every kind of writing requires an explicitly stated thesis. Sometimes a thesis may only be *implied.* Like an explicitly stated thesis, an implied thesis conveys an essay's purpose, but it does not do so directly. Instead, the purpose is suggested by the selection and arrangement of the essay's points. Many professional writers prefer this option because an implied thesis is subtler than a stated thesis. An implied thesis is especially advantageous in narratives, descriptions, and some arguments, where an explicit thesis would seem heavy-handed or arbitrary. In most college writing, however, you should state your thesis explicitly to avoid any risk of being misunderstood or of allowing the organization of your essay to go astray.

► A STUDENT WRITER: FORMULATING A THESIS

After experimenting with different ways of arranging her ideas for her essay, Laura Bobnak was eventually able to sum them up in a tentative thesis statement: "As I look back on the situation, I wonder why I kept silent and what would have happened had I acted."

•   •   •

EXERCISES

1. Assess the strengths and weaknesses of the following as thesis statements, asking yourself which statements would most effectively establish the direction of an essay, and why.
   a. Myths and society.
   b. Myths serve an important function in society.
   c. Contrary to popular assumptions, myths are more than fairy tales; they express the underlying attitudes a society has toward important issues.
   d. Today, almost two marriages in four will end in divorce.
   e. Skiing, a popular sport for millions, is a major cause of winter injuries.
   f. If certain reforms are not instituted immediately, our company will be bankrupt within two years.
   g. Early childhood is an important period.
   h. By using the proper techniques, parents can significantly improve the learning capabilities of their preschool children.
   i. Fiction can be used to criticize society.
   j. Fiction, in the hands of an able writer, can be a powerful tool for social reform.

2. Rewrite the following factual statements to make them effective thesis statements. Make sure that each thesis statement is a clearly and specifically worded sentence.
   a. A number of hospitals have refused to admit patients without health insurance because they fear that such patients do not have the resources to pay their bills.
   b. Several recent Supreme Court decisions say that art containing a sexual theme is not necessarily pornographic.
   c. Many women earn less money than men do, in part because they drop out of the workforce during their child-rearing years.
   d. People who watch more than five hours of television a day tend to think the world is more violent than do people who watch less than two hours of television daily.
   e. In recent years the rate of suicide among teenagers—especially middle- and upper-middle-class teenagers—has risen dramatically.

3. Read the following sentences from *Broca's Brain* by Carl Sagan. Then, formulate a one-sentence thesis statement that draws together the points Sagan makes about robots.

- "Robots, especially robots in space, have received derogatory notices in the press."
- "Each human being is a superbly constructed, astonishingly compact, self-ambulatory computer—capable on occasion of independent decision making and real control of his or her environment."
- "If we do send human beings to exotic environments, we must also send along food, air, water, waste recycling, amenities for entertainment, and companions."
- "By comparison, machines require no elaborate life-support systems, no entertainment, and no companionship, and we do not feel any strong ethical prohibitions against sending machines on one-way, or suicide, missions."
- "Even exceptionally simple computers—those that can be wired by a bright ten-year-old—can be wired to play perfect tic-tac-toe."
- "With this . . . set of examples of the state of development of machine intelligence, I think it is clear that a major effort over the next decade could produce much more sophisticated examples."
- "We appear to be on the verge of developing a wide variety of intelligent machines capable of performing tasks too dangerous, too expensive, too onerous, or too boring for human beings."
- "The main obstacle seems to be a very human problem, the quiet feeling that there is something threatening or 'inhuman' about machines."
- "But in many respects our survival as a species depends on our transcending such primitive chauvinisms."
- "There is nothing inhuman about an intelligent machine; it is indeed an expression of all those superb intellectual capabilities that only human beings . . . now possess."

4. For three of the following general subjects and topics, go through as many steps as you need to formulate effective thesis statements.
   a. The importance of your family
   b. The World Wide Web
   c. Credit card debt
   d. Finding a summer job
   e. One thing you would change about your life
   f. Recycling
   g. Academic standards for college athletes
   h. The image of women in television commercials
   i. The sub-minimum wage for unskilled and teenage workers
   j. Plagiarism

STAGE TWO: ARRANGEMENT

Each of the tasks discussed so far represents a series of choices you have to make about your topic and your material. Now, before actually beginning to write, you have another choice to make: how to arrange your material into an essay. This extremely important choice helps to determine how clear and convincing your essay will be and how your audience will react to it.

Recognizing a Pattern

Sometimes deciding how to arrange your ideas will be easy because your assignment specifies a particular pattern of development. This may often be the case in a composition class, where the instructor may assign, say, a descriptive or a narrative essay. Also, certain assignments or examination questions suggest how your material should be structured. Probably no one except an English composition instructor will say to you "Write a narrative," but you will have assignments that begin "Give an account" or "Tell about." Likewise, few teachers will explicitly assign a process essay, but they *will* ask you to explain how something works. Similarly, an examination question might ask you to trace the circumstances leading up to an event. If you are perceptive, you will realize that this question calls for either a narrative or a cause-and-effect answer. The important thing is to recognize the clues such assignments give, or those you find in your topic or thesis statement, and to structure your essay accordingly.

One clue to the emerging structure of your essay may be found in the questions that proved most helpful when you probed your subject. For example, if questions like "What happened?" and "When did it happen?" suggested the most useful material, you might consider structuring your paper as a narrative. The chart below links various questions to the patterns of development they suggest. Notice that the terms in the right-hand column—narration, description, and so on—identify some useful patterns of development that can help order your ideas. Chapters 2 through 9 explain and illustrate each of these patterns.

☑ QUESTIONS FOR PROBING: RECOGNIZING A PATTERN

What happened? When did it happen? Where did it happen? Who did it?	Narration
What does it look like? What are its characteristics? What impression does it make?	Description
What are some typical cases or examples of it?	Exemplification

(cont'd)

(cont'd)

How did it happen? What makes it work? How is it made?	Process
Why did it happen? What caused it? What does it cause? What are its effects?	Cause and effect
How is it like other things? How is it different from other things?	Comparison and contrast

What are its parts or types?
How can its parts or types be
   separated or grouped?
Do its parts or types fit into a logical
   order?
Into what categories can its
   parts or types be arranged?
On what basis can it be categorized?
	Classification and division

What is it?
How does it resemble other
   members of its class?
How does it differ from other
   members of its class?
What are its limits?
	Definition

Constructing a Formal Outline

At this point you may want to construct a *formal outline* for your essay. Whereas informal outlines are preliminary lists that simply remind the writer which points to make in which order, formal outlines are detailed, multilevel constructions. The complexity of your assignment will determine how complete an outline you need. For short papers, informal outlines like the ones included in Chapters 2–10 are usually sufficient. For a longer, more complex essay, however, you may need to prepare a formal outline.

To construct an outline, review your thesis statement and all the ideas you compiled during prewriting. As you examine this material, you will see that some ideas seem more important than others. A good way to begin your formal outline is to copy down the main headings from your informal outline. Then, arrange ideas from your brainstorming notes or cluster diagram as subheadings under the appropriate headings. As you work on your outline, make sure that each idea supports your thesis. Ideas that don't seem to fit should be reworded or discarded entirely. In addition, make certain that your outline follows the proper format. As you revise your essay, continue to refer to your outline to make sure thesis and support are logically related. The following list of guidelines will help you prepare a formal outline (an example appears on page 37).

☑ **GUIDELINES FOR FORMAL OUTLINING**

- Write your thesis statement at the top of the page.
- Group main headings under roman numerals (I, II, III, IV, and so forth), and place them flush with the left-hand margin.
- Indent each subheading under the first word of the heading above it. Use capital letters before major points and numbers before subtopics.
- Capitalize the first letter of the first word of each heading.
- Make your outline as simple as possible, avoiding overly complex divisions of ideas. (Try not to go beyond third-level headings—1, 2, 3, and so on).
- Your outline should be either a *topic outline,* with headings expressed as short phrases or single words ("Advantages and disadvantages") *or* a *sentence outline,* with headings expressed as complete sentences ("The advantages of advanced placement chemistry outweigh the disadvantages"). *Never use both phrases and complete sentences in the same outline.*
- Express all headings at the same level in parallel terms. (If roman numeral I is a noun, II, III, and IV should also be nouns.)
- Make sure each heading contains at least two subdivisions. You cannot have a *1* without a *2,* or an *a* without an *b.*
- Make sure your headings don't overlap.

▶ A STUDENT WRITER: CONSTRUCTING A FORMAL OUTLINE

The outline Laura Bobnak constructed follows the guidelines discussed above. Notice that her outline focuses on the body of her paper and does not include the introduction or conclusion—these are usually developed after the body has been drafted. (Compare this formal outline with the informal outline on page 28 in which Laura simply grouped her brainstorming notes under three general headings.)

SPEAKING OUT

Thesis statement: As I look back on the situation, I wonder why I kept silent and what would have happened had I acted.

    I. The incident
       A. Taking test
       B. Witnessing cheating
       C. Reacting
          1. Anger
          2. Dismissal

   II. Reasons for keeping silent
       A. Other students' attitudes
       B. My fears

⌨ COMPUTER STRATEGY

If you use a computer to construct a formal outline, you can easily arrange and rearrange your headings until your outline is logical and complete. If you saved your prewriting notes in computer files, you can refer to them while working on your outline and perhaps add or modify headings to reflect what you find.

   III. Current opinion of cheating
       A. Effects of cheating on education
           1. Undercuts the process
           2. Is unfair to teachers
       B. Effects of cheating on students

This outline enabled Laura to order her points so that they supported her thesis. As she went on to draft her essay, the outline reminded her to arrange and support her points to highlight the contrast between her present and former attitudes toward cheating.

Understanding the Parts of the Essay

No matter what pattern of development you use, an essay should have a beginning, a middle, and an end—that is, an *introduction*, a *body*, and a *conclusion*.

THE INTRODUCTION. The **introduction** of your essay, usually one paragraph and rarely more than two, introduces your subject, engages your readers' interest, and often states your thesis. In so short a space, however, there is no room for an in-depth discussion of your topic.

You can introduce an essay and engage your readers' interest in a number of ways.

1. You can give some *background information* and then move directly to your thesis statement. This approach works well when you know that the audience is already interested in your topic and that you can therefore come directly to the point. This strategy is especially useful for exams, where there is no need (or time) for subtlety.

> With inflation slowing down, many companies have understandably lowered prices, and the oil industry should be no exception. Consequently, homeowners have begun wondering whether the relatively high price of home heating oil is justified given the economic climate. It makes sense, therefore, for us to start examining the pricing policies of the major American oil companies.   (economics essay)

2. You can introduce an essay with a *definition* of a relevant term or concept. (Keep in mind, however, that the "According to *Webster's Dictionary* . . ." formula is overused and trite.) This technique is especially useful for research papers or examinations, where the meaning of a specific term is crucial.

> Democracy is a form of government in which the ultimate authority is given to and exercised by the people. This may be so in theory, but some recent local elections have raised concerns about the future of democracy. Extensive voting-machine irregularities and ghost voting have seriously jeopardized people's faith in the democratic process.
>
> (political science exam)

3. You can begin your essay with an *anecdote* or *story* that leads readers to your thesis.

> Upon meeting the famous author James Joyce, a young student stammered, "May I kiss the hand that wrote *Ulysses?*" "No!" said Joyce. "It did a lot of other things, too." As this exchange shows, Joyce was a person who valued humor. His sense of humor is also present in his final work, *Finnegans Wake,* in which he uses humor to comment on the human condition.
>
> (English literature paper)

4. You can begin with a *question*.

> What was it like to live through the Holocaust? Elie Wiesel, in *One Generation After,* answers this question by presenting a series of accounts about ordinary people who found themselves imprisoned in Nazi death camps. As he does so, he challenges some of the assumptions we hold in our smug, materialistic society.   (sociology book report)

5. You can also begin with a *quotation.* If it is well chosen, it can encourage your audience to read further.

> "The rich are different," said F. Scott Fitzgerald more than fifty years ago. Apparently, they still are. As any examination of the tax laws shows, the wealthy receive many more benefits than the middle class or the poor do.   (business law paper)

No matter which strategy you select, your introduction should be consistent in tone and approach with the rest of your essay. If it is not, it can misrepresent your intentions and even destroy your credibility. (For this reason, it is a good idea to write your introduction after you have finished the rest of your rough draft.) A technical report, for instance, should have an introduction that reflects the formality and objectivity required by the occasion. The introduction to an autobiographical essay or a personal letter, however, may have a more informal, subjective tone.

THE BODY PARAGRAPHS.   The middle section, or body, of your essay develops your thesis. The **body paragraphs** present the details that convince your audience that your thesis is reasonable. To do so, each body paragraph should be *unified, coherent,* and *well developed.* It should also follow a particular pattern of development and should clearly support your thesis.

• *Each body paragraph should be unified.* A paragraph has **unity** when every sentence relates directly to the main idea of the paragraph.

Sometimes the main idea of a paragraph is stated in a **topic sentence.** Like a thesis statement, a topic sentence acts as a guidepost, making it easy for readers to follow your discussion. Although the placement of a topic sentence depends on your purpose and subject, beginning writers often make it the first sentence of a paragraph.

Sometimes the main idea of a paragraph is *implied* by the sentences in the paragraph. Professional writers frequently use this technique because they believe that in some situations—especially narratives and descriptions—a topic sentence can seem forced or awkward. Many beginning writers, however, find it helpful to use topic sentences. Topic sentences not only emphasize the ideas you are discussing in each paragraph, but they also keep you on track by reflecting the major divisions of your outline.

Whatever strategy you use, remember that each sentence in a paragraph should be consistent with your purpose and should develop the paragraph's main idea. If the sentences in a paragraph do not do these things, the paragraph will lack unity.

In the following excerpt from a student essay, notice how the topic sentence unifies the paragraph by summarizing its main idea:

> Built on the Acropolis overlooking the city of Athens in the fifth century B.C., the Parthenon illustrates the limitations of Greek architecture. As a temple of the gods, it was supposed to represent heavenly or divine perfection. However, although at first glance its structure seems to be perfect, on closer examination it becomes clear that it is a static, two-dimensional object. As long as you stand in the center of any of its four sides to look at it, its form appears to be perfect. The strong Doric columns seem to be equally spaced, one next to another, along all four of its sides. But if you take a step to the right or left, the Parthenon's symmetry is destroyed.

The explicit topic sentence, located at the beginning of the paragraph, enables readers to grasp the writer's point immediately. The examples that follow all relate to that point. The whole paragraph is therefore focused and unified.

• *Each body paragraph should be coherent.* A paragraph is coherent if its sentences are smoothly and logically connected to one another. **Coherence** can be achieved through three techniques. First, you can repeat key words to carry concepts from one sentence to another and to echo important terms. Second, you can use pronouns to refer to key nouns in previous sentences. Finally, you can use **transitions,** words or expressions that show chronological sequence, cause and effect, and so on (see the list of transitions on page 41). These strategies for connecting sentences—which you can also use to connect paragraphs within an essay—spell out for your readers the exact relationships among your ideas.

The following paragraph, from George Orwell's "Shooting an Elephant" (page 91), uses repeated key words, pronouns, and transitions to achieve coherence:

☑ TRANSITIONS

SEQUENCE OR ADDITION

again	first, . . . second, . . .	moreover
also	third	next
and	furthermore	one . . . another
besides	in addition	still
finally	last	too

TIME

afterward	finally	simultaneously
as soon as	immediately	since
at first	in the meantime	soon
at the same time	later	subsequently
before	meanwhile	then
earlier	next	until
eventually	now	

COMPARISON

also	in the same way
likewise	similarly
in comparison	

CONTRAST

although	in contrast	on the one hand . . .
but	instead	on the other hand . . .
conversely	nevertheless	still
despite	nonetheless	whereas
even though	on the contrary	yet
however		

EXAMPLES

for example	specifically
for instance	that is
in fact	thus
namely	

CONCLUSIONS OR SUMMARIES

as a result	in summary
in conclusion	therefore
in short	thus

CAUSES OR EFFECTS

as a result	so
because	then
consequently	therefore
since	

I got up. The Burmans were already racing past me across the mud. It was obvious that the elephant would never rise again, but he was not dead. He was breathing very rhythmically with long rattling gasps, his great mound of a side painfully rising and falling. His mouth was wide open—I could see far down into the caverns of pale pink throat. I waited a long time for him to die, but his breathing did not weaken. Finally I fired my two remaining shots into the spot where I thought his heart must be. The thick blood welled out of him like red velvet, but still he did not die. His body did not even jerk when the shots hit him, the tortured breathing continued without a pause. He was dying, very slowly and in great agony, but in some world remote from me where not even a bullet could damage him further. I felt that I had got to put an end to that dreadful noise. It seemed dreadful to see the great beast lying there, powerless to move and yet powerless to die, and not even be able to finish him. I sent back for my small rifle and poured shot after shot into his heart and down his throat. They seemed to make no impression. The tortured gasps continued as steadily as the ticking of a clock.

In this paragraph Orwell keeps his narrative coherent by using transitional expressions (*already, finally, when the shots hit him*) to signal the passing of time. He uses pronouns (*he, his*) in nearly every sentence to refer back to the elephant, the topic of his paragraph. Finally, he repeats key words like *shot* and *die* (and its variants *dead* and *dying*) to link the whole paragraph's sentences together. The result is a coherent, cohesive whole.

• *Each body paragraph should be well developed.* A paragraph is well developed if it contains the examples, facts, and explanations readers need to understand its main idea. If a paragraph is not adequately developed, readers will feel they have been given only a partial picture of your subject. Just how much information you need depends on your audience, your purpose, and the claims you make in your topic sentence.

If you decide you need more information in a paragraph, you can look back at your brainstorming notes. If this doesn't help, you can freewrite or brainstorm again, talk with friends and instructors, read more about your topic, or (with your instructor's permission) even do some research. Your assignment and your topic will determine the kind and amount of information you need.

The following student paragraph develops two examples to support the topic sentence:

Just look at how males have been taught that extravagance is a positive characteristic. Scrooge, the main character of Dickens's *A Christmas Carol,* is portrayed as an evil man until he is rehabilitated—meaning that he gives up his miserly ways and freely distributes gifts and money on Christmas day. This behavior, of course, is rewarded when people change their opinions about him and decide that perhaps he isn't such a bad person after all. Diamond Jim Brady is another interesting example. This individual was a financier who was known for his extravagant taste in women and food. On any given night, he would consume enough food to feed at least ten of the numerous poor who roamed the streets of late-nineteenth-century New York. Yet, despite his selfishness and infantile self-gratification, Diamond Jim Brady's name has become synonymous with the good life.

• *Each body paragraph should follow a particular pattern of development.* In addition to making sure that your body paragraphs are unified, coherent, and well developed, you need to organize each paragraph according to a specific pattern of development. (Chapters 2 through 9 each begin with a paragraph-length example of the pattern discussed in the chapter.)

• *Each body paragraph should clearly support the thesis statement.* No matter how many body paragraphs your essay has—three, four, five, or even more—each paragraph should introduce and develop an idea that supports the essay's thesis. Each paragraph's topic sentence should express one of these supporting points. The following diagram illustrates this thesis-and-support structure.

THE CONCLUSION.   Since readers remember best what they read last, your **conclusion** is extremely important. Always end your essay in a way that reinforces your thesis and your purpose.

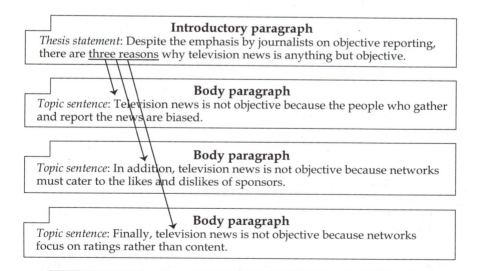

Introductory paragraph
Thesis statement: Despite the emphasis by journalists on objective reporting, there are <u>three reasons</u> why television news is anything but objective.

Body paragraph
Topic sentence: Television news is not objective because the people who gather and report the news are biased.

Body paragraph
Topic sentence: In addition, television news is not objective because networks must cater to the likes and dislikes of sponsors.

Body paragraph
Topic sentence: Finally, television news is not objective because networks focus on ratings rather than content.

Concluding paragraph
Restatement of thesis: Even though television journalists give much lip service to objective reporting, the truth is that this ideal has been impossible to achieve.

Like your introduction, your conclusion should be brief. In a short essay, it is rarely longer than a paragraph. Regardless of its length, however, your conclusion should be consistent with the content of your essay. It should not introduce supporting material that you have not discussed earlier. Frequently, a conclusion will restate the thesis, summarizing your essay's main idea in different words, or review your key points. Like thesis statements, effective conclusions need no announcement, and you should avoid beginning your conclusion with the artificial phrase *In conclusion.*

Conclusions can be as challenging to construct as introductions. Here are several ways to conclude an essay:

1. You can conclude your essay by *reviewing your key points* or *restating your thesis.*

> Rotation of crops provided several benefits. It enriched soil by giving it a rest; it enabled farmers to vary their production; and it ended the cycle of "boom or bust" that had characterized the prewar South's economy when cotton was the primary crop. Of course, this innovation did not solve all the economic problems of the postwar South, but it did lay the groundwork for the healthy economy this region enjoys today.
>
> (history exam)

2. You can end a discussion of a problem with a *recommendation of a course of action.*

> While there is still time, American engineering has to reassess its priorities. We no longer have the luxury of exotic and wasteful experiments in design for purely aesthetic reasons. Instead, we need technology grounded in common sense and economic feasibility. That the proposed space station seems to have few practical applications illustrates how far we have strayed from old-fashioned common sense and ingenuity.
>
> (engineering ethics report)

3. You can conclude with a *prediction.* Be careful, however, that your prediction follows logically from the points you have made in the essay. Your conclusion is no place to make new points or change direction.

> It is too late to save parts of the great swamps in northern Florida, but it is not too late to preserve the Everglades in the southern part of the state. With intelligent planning and an end to the dam building program by the Army Corps of Engineers, we will be able to halt the destruction of what Native Americans called the "Timeless Swamp."
>
> (environmental science essay)

4. You can also end with a *quotation.* If selected carefully, it can add weight to an already strong essay.

> In *Walden,* Henry David Thoreau says, "The mass of men lead lives of quiet desperation." This sentiment is reinforced by a drive through the

Hill District of our city. Perhaps the work of the men and women who run the clinic on Jefferson Street cannot totally change this situation, but it can give us hope to know that some people, at least, are working for the betterment of us all.

(public health essay)

STAGE THREE: DRAFTING AND REVISION

After you decide on a tentative thesis and an arrangement for your ideas, you can begin to draft and revise your essay. Keep in mind that even as you carry out these activities, you may have to generate more material or revise your thesis statement or outline.

Writing Your First Draft

The purpose of your first draft is to get your ideas down on paper so you can react to them. Experienced writers know that the first draft is nothing more than a work in progress; it exists to be revised. With this in mind, you should be prepared to cross out and extensively rearrange material. In addition, don't be surprised if you think of new ideas as you write. If a new idea comes to you, follow it to its conclusion. Some of the best writing results from unexpected turns or accidents. The following suggestions will help you with your first draft.

☑ **GUIDELINES FOR DRAFTING**

- *Begin with the body paragraphs.* Because your essay will probably be revised extensively, don't take time at this stage to write an introduction or conclusion. Instead, let your thesis statement guide you as you draft the body paragraphs of your essay.
- *Get your ideas down quickly.* Don't worry about correctness or word choice, and try not to interrupt the flow of your writing with concerns about style.
- *Take regular breaks as you write.* Don't continue writing until you are so exhausted you can't think straight. To avoid this problem, many writers divide their writing into stages, perhaps completing several body paragraphs and then taking a short break. This strategy reduces fatigue and in the long run is more efficient than trying to write without stopping.
- *Write with revision in mind.* If you type, triple-space so you will have room to make changes. (Use this technique even if you are writing on a computer because you will most likely be revising on hard copy.)
- *Leave yourself time to revise.* Remember, your first draft is called a *rough draft* for a good reason. All writing profits from revision, so try to allow enough time to write two or more drafts.

💻 COMPUTER STRATEGY

Drafting on a computer has several advantages. First, writing on a computer enables you to generate a clean, easy-to-read first draft of your essay. In addition, the computer makes it easy for you to move ideas from one part of your essay to another and to reformat text. Finally, the computer allows you to add new ideas instantly as you write.

Revising Your Essay

Remember that revision is not something you do after your paper is finished. It is a continuing process during which you consider the logic and clarity of your ideas as well as their effective and correct expression. Thus, revision is not simply a matter of proofreading or editing, of crossing out one word and substituting another or correcting errors in spelling and punctuation; revision means reexamining and rethinking what you have written. In fact, you may even find yourself adding and deleting extensively, reordering whole sentences or paragraphs as you reconsider what you want to communicate to your audience. Revision can take a lot of time, so don't be discouraged if you have to go through three or four drafts of your essay before you think it is ready to hand in. The following pointers can help you when you revise your essay.

How you revise—what specific strategies you decide to use—depends on your own preference, your instructor's directions, and the

☑ GUIDELINES FOR REVISION

- *Give yourself a cooling-off period.* After you have written your first draft, put it aside for several hours, or even a day or two if you can. This cooling-off period lets you distance yourself from your essay so that you can read it more objectively when you return to it. When you read it again, you will see things you missed the first time.

- *Try to work from a typed draft.* Because a typed or printed draft is neat and easy to read, you will be able to see connections and gaps more easily than you would if you were working with a handwritten copy. In addition, type enables you to distance yourself from your draft and evaluate it objectively.

- *Read your draft aloud.* Before you revise, read your draft aloud to spot choppy sentences, missing words, or phrases that do not sound right.

- *Take advantage of opportunities to get feedback.* Instructors often give students a number of opportunities to obtain information that will help them revise. For example, an instructor might organize peer critique sessions, hand out a revision checklist, refer students to a writing center, or offer suggestions during a one-on-one conference. Make use of as many of these sources of information as you can; each offers you a different way of gaining information about what you have written.

- *Try not to get overwhelmed.* It is easy to become overwhelmed by all the feedback you get about your draft. To avoid this, approach revision as a systematic process. Don't just automatically make all the changes that people suggest; consider the impact and the validity of each change. Also ask yourself whether comments suggest larger issues that are not being addressed. For example, does a comment about choppy sentences in a paragraph simply suggest a need for you to add transitions, or does it signal a need to rethink your ideas?

- *Don't let your ego get in the way.* All of us like praise, and receiving negative criticism of our writing is not a pleasant experience. Experienced writers know, however, that they must get feedback if they are going to improve their work. Learn to see criticism—whether by an instructor or by your peers—as a necessary (if painful) part of the revision process, a way of improving the effectiveness of your ideas.

- *Revise in stages.* Deal with the large elements (essay and paragraph structure) before moving on to the smaller elements (sentence structure and word choice).

time available. Like the rest of the writing process, revision varies from student to student and from assignment to assignment.

REVISING WITH A CHECKLIST.   If you have time, you can start your revision by using the following checklist, which can be adapted to your own writing process.

☑ **CHECKLIST FOR REVISION**

- **Thesis statement.** Is it clear and specific? Does it indicate the direction your essay is taking? Is it consistent with the body of your essay? If you departed from your essay's original direction while you were writing, you may need to revise your thesis statement so that it accurately sums up the ideas and information now contained in the body. Or you may need to delete from the body any material that is unrelated to the thesis statement—or revise it so it *is* relevant.

- **Body.** Are the body paragraphs unified? Coherent? Well developed? If not, you might have to add more facts or examples or smoother transitions. Does each body paragraph follow a particular pattern of development? Do the points you make in these paragraphs support your thesis?

- **Introduction and conclusion.** Are they appropriate for your material, your audience, and your purpose? Are they interesting? Do they reinforce your thesis?

- **Sentences.** Are they effective? Interesting? Varied in length and structure? Should any sentences be deleted, combined, or moved?

(cont'd)

(cont'd)

- **Words.** Should you make any substitutions?
- **Title.** Because it creates readers' first impression of your essay, your title should spark their interest. Usually, single-word titles ("Love") and cute ones ("The Cheery Cheerleader") do little to draw readers into your essay. To be effective, a title should reflect your purpose and your tone.

The essays in this book illustrate the various kinds of titles you can use.

Essay's focus: "Grant and Lee: A Study in Contrasts"

Question: "Who Killed Benny Paret?"

Unusual angle: "How the Lawyers Stole Winter"

Controversy: "Six Enviro-Myths"

Provocative Wording: "Frankenstein Must Be Destroyed: Chasing the Monster of TV Violence"

Quotation: "Memo to John Grisham: What's Next—'A Movie Made Me Do It'?"

REVISING WITH AN OUTLINE.   If you do not have time to consult a detailed checklist, you can check your essay's structure by making a *review outline*. Either an informal outline or a formal one can show you whether you have omitted any important points. An outline can also show you whether your essay follows the pattern of development you have chosen. Finally, an outline can clarify the relationship between your thesis statement and your body paragraphs.

REVISING WITH A PEER CRITIQUE.   Another revision strategy you might find helpful is seeking a *peer critique*—in other words, asking a friend to read your essay and comment on it. Sometimes a peer critique can be quite formal. An instructor may require students to exchange papers and evaluate their classmates' work according to certain standards, perhaps by completing a *peer editing worksheet* (see page 51). Often, however, a peer critique is informal. Even if a friend is unfamiliar with your topic, he or she can still tell you honestly whether you are getting your point across—and maybe even advise you about how to communicate more effectively. (Remember, though, that your critic should be only your reader, not your ghostwriter.)

The use of peer critiques mirrors the way people in the real world actually write. In the business world, reports are circulated in order to get feedback. Scientists and academics routinely collaborate when they write. And, as you may have realized, even this book is the result of collaboration.

Your classmates can be quite helpful during the early drafts of your essay, providing suggestions that can guide you through the revision process. In addition, they can respond to questions you may have about your essay—for example, whether your introduction works, or whether one of your supporting

☑ **GUIDELINES FOR PEER CRITIQUES**

- *Be positive.* Remember that your purpose is to help other students improve their essays.

- *Be tactful.* Be sure to emphasize the good points about the essay; mention one or two things the writer has done particularly well.

- *Be specific.* Offer concrete suggestions about what the writer could do better. Vague words like *good* or *bad* provide little guidance.

- *Be attentive.* If you are doing a critique orally, make sure you interact with the writer as you read. Ask questions, listen to responses, and explain your comments.

- *Be thorough.* Don't focus on the mechanics of the paper. Although spelling and punctuation matter, you shouldn't expect these elements to be perfect in a first draft. At this stage, the clarity of the thesis statement, the effectiveness of the support, and the organization of the writer's ideas are much more important.

- *Be helpful.* When possible, write down your comments—either on a form your instructor provides or in the margins of the paper.

points needs more explanation or additional examples. When friends ask *you* to critique their work, the guidelines on this page should help you.

▶ **A STUDENT WRITER: REVISING A FIRST DRAFT**

Here is the first draft of Laura Bobnak's essay.

When I was in high school, I had an experience like the one   1
Henry Louis Gates talks about in his essay. It was then that
I saw a close friend of mine cheat in chemistry class. As I
look back on the situation, I wonder why I kept silent and
what would have happened had I acted.

💻 **COMPUTER STRATEGY**

If you revise on a computer, you can add, delete, and move information quickly and effortlessly. Still, it is usually not a good idea to begin revising directly on the computer screen. Since most screens show only a portion of a page, the connections between ideas are hard to see and to keep track of. Even with the split-screen option that some word-processing programs offer, you cannot view several sections of a draft at once or easily compare one draft to another. For these reasons, it is a good idea to revise on a hard copy of your essay. Once you have made your handwritten corrections, you can enter them into the computer. Be sure to keep all the drafts of your essay in case you decide that an idea you deleted from one draft might be useful in another. (If you do revise on the screen, move all unwanted material to the end of your document until you are absolutely sure you don't want to use it.)

The incident I am going to describe took place during   2
the final examination for my advanced placement chemistry
class. I had studied hard for it, but even so, I found the
test difficult. As I struggled to balance a particularly
difficult equation, I noticed that my friend Jeff Servin,
who was sitting across from me, was acting strangely. I
noticed that he was copying material from a paper. After
watching him for a while, I dismissed the incident and got
back to my test.

After the test was over, I began to think about what I   3
had seen. The more I thought about it the angrier I got. It
seemed unfair that I had struggled for weeks to memorize
formulas and equations while all Jeff had done was to copy
them onto a cheat sheet. For a moment I considered going to
the teacher, but I quickly dismissed this idea. After all,
cheating was something everybody did. Besides, I was afraid
if I told on Jeff, my friends would stop talking to me.

Now that I am in college I see the situation differ-   4
ently. I find it hard to believe that I could ever have been
so calm about cheating. Cheating is certainly something that
students should not take for granted. It undercuts the education process and is unfair to teachers and to the majority
of students who spend their time studying.

If I could go back to high school and relive the expe-   5
rience, I now know that I would have gone to the teacher.
Naturally Jeff would have been angry at me, but at least I
would have known I had the courage to do the right thing.

Points for Special Attention

After writing this rough draft, Laura put it aside for a few hours and
then reread it. Later, Laura's instructor divided the class into small
groups and had them read and write critiques of each other's papers. As a
result of her own reading and three written critiques (one of which is
reproduced on page 51), Laura was able to focus on a number of areas
that needed revision.

THE INTRODUCTION.   Laura knew that she would eventually have to
present more detail in her introduction. (Because she was writing a first
draft, she had spent little time on this section.) At this stage, though, she
was more concerned with her thesis statement, and the students in her peer
editing group said that they didn't think it addressed the second half of the
assignment—to explain whether or not she would act differently today.

☑ **SAMPLE PEER EDITING WORKSHEET**

What is the essay's thesis? Is it clearly worded? Does it provide a focus for the rest of the essay? Is it appropriate for the assignment?

Thesis statement: "As I look back on the situation, I wonder why I kept silent and what would have happened had I acted." I don't really think the thesis talks about the second part of the assignment—would she have done the same thing today?

How clearly are the body paragraphs related to the essay's thesis? Which topic sentences could be more focused?

The topic sentences seem OK—each one seems to tell what the paragraph is about.

How do the body paragraphs develop the essay's main idea? Where could the writer have used more detail?

Each of the body paragraphs tells a part of the narrative, but as I said before, the paragraph that deals with the second part of the assignment is missing. You could add more detail—I really can't picture everything you're talking about.

Can you follow the writer's ideas? Does the essay need transitions?

I have no problem following your ideas. Maybe you could have added some more transitions, but I think the essay moves nicely.

Which points are especially clear? What questions do you have that are not answered in the essay?

I think the things you didn't like about Jeff's cheating were good. I'm not sure what AP chemistry is like, though. Do people cheat because it's hard?

If this were your essay, what would you change before you handed it in?

I'd change the thesis so it reflects the assignment. I'd add more detail and explain more about AP chemistry. Also, what were the other students doing while the cheating was going on?

Overall, do you think the paper is effective? Explain.

Good paper; cheating is an important issue, and I think your story really puts it in focus.

Keeping their comments in mind, Laura rewrote her introduction. First, she created a context for her discussion by more specifically linking her story to Gates's essay. Next, she decided to postpone mentioning her subject—cheating—until later in the paper, hoping that this strategy would stimulate the curiosity of her readers and make them want to read further. Finally, she revised her thesis statement to reflect the specific wording of the assignment.

THE BODY PARAGRAPHS. The students in her peer editing group also said that Laura needed to expand her body paragraphs. Although she had expected that most of her readers would be familiar with courses like advanced placement chemistry, she discovered this was not the case. One student suggested she explain how challenging it was. In addition, some students in her group thought she should expand the paragraph in which she described her reaction to the cheating. They wondered what the other students in the class had thought about the incident. Did they know? Did they care? Laura's classmates were curious, and they thought other readers would be, too.

Before revising the body paragraphs, Laura did some brainstorming to come up with additional ideas. She decided to describe the difficulty of advanced placement chemistry and the pressure that the students in the class had felt. She also decided to summarize discussions she had had with several of her classmates after the test. In addition, she wanted to explain in more detail her present views on cheating; she felt that the paragraph in which she presented these ideas did not contrast clearly enough with the paragraphs that dealt with her high school experiences.

To make sure that her sentences led smoothly into one another, Laura added transitions and rewrote entire sentences when necessary, signaling the progression of her thoughts by adding words and phrases like *therefore, for this reason, for example,* and *as a result.* In addition, she tried to repeat key words so that important concepts would be reinforced.

THE CONCLUSION.   Laura's biggest concern as she revised was to make sure her readers would see the connection between her essay and the assignment. To make this connection clear, she decided to mention in her conclusion a specific effect the incident had on her: its impact on her friendship with Jeff. She also decided to link her reactions to those of Henry Louis Gates Jr.: like him, she had been upset by the actions of someone she knew. By employing this strategy, she was able to bring her essay full circle and develop an idea she had alluded to in her introduction. Thus, rewriting her conclusion helped Laura to reinforce her thesis statement and provide closure to her essay.

▶   A STUDENT WRITER: REVISING A SECOND DRAFT

The following draft incorporates Laura's revisions as well as some preliminary editing of punctuation and grammar.

Speaking Out

In his essay "'What's in a Name?'" Henry Louis Gates   1
Jr. recalls an incident from his past in which his father
did not speak up. Perhaps he kept silent because he was
afraid or because he knew that nothing he said or did would
change the situation in Piedmont, West Virginia. Although I
have never encountered the kind of prejudice Gates describes, I did have an experience in high school where,
like Gates's father, I could have spoken up but did not. As
I now look back on the situation, I know I would not make
the same decision today.

The incident I am going to describe took place during   2
the final examination in my advanced placement chemistry
class. The course was very demanding and required hours of
studying every night. Every day after school, I would meet
with other students to outline chapters and answer homework questions. Sometimes we would even work on weekends.
We would often ask ourselves whether we had gotten in over
our heads. As the semester dragged on, it became clear to
me, as well as to the other students in the class, that
passing the course was not something we could take for
granted. Test after test came back with grades that were
well below the "As" and "Bs" I was used to getting in the
regular chemistry course I took in tenth grade. By the
time we were ready to take the final exam, most of us were
worried that we would fail the course--despite the
teacher's assurances that she would mark on a curve.

The final examination for advanced placement chemistry   3
was given on a Friday morning from nine to twelve o'clock.
As I struggled to balance a particularly complex equation,
I noticed that the person sitting across from me was acting
strangely. At first I thought I was imagining things, but
as I stared I saw Jeff Servin, my friend and study partner,
fumbling with his test booklet. About a minute passed before I realized that he was copying material from a paper
he had taped inside the cuff of his shirt. After a short
time, I dismissed the incident and finished my test.

Surprisingly, when I mentioned the incident to others in   4
the class, they all knew what Jeff had done. The more I
thought about Jeff's actions, the angrier I got. It seemed
unfair that I had struggled for weeks to memorize formulas
and equations while all Jeff had done was to copy them onto a
cheat sheet. For a moment I considered going to the teacher,
but I quickly dismissed this idea. Cheating was nothing new
to me or to others in my school. Many of my classmates
cheated at one time or another. Most of us saw school as a
war between us and the teachers, and cheating was just another weapon in our arsenal. The worst crime I could commit
would be to turn Jeff in. As far as I was concerned, I had no
choice. I fell in line with the values of my high school
classmates and dismissed the incident as "no big deal."

```
        I find it hard to believe that I could ever have been      5
so complacent about cheating. The issues that were simple in
high school now seem complex. I now ask questions that never
would have occurred to me in high school. Interestingly,
Jeff and I are no longer very close. Whenever I see him I
have the same reaction Henry Louis Gates Jr. had when he met
Mr. Wilson after he had insulted his father--I have a hard
time looking him in the eye.
```

Points for Special Attention

Laura could see that her second draft was stronger than her first. But after reading and analyzing it, she discovered a number of ways to improve her draft further.

THE TITLE.   Laura's original title was only a working title, and now she wanted one that would create interest and draw readers into her essay. She knew, however, that a humorous, cute, or catchy title would undermine the seriousness of her essay. After rejecting a number of possibilities, she decided on "The Price of Silence." Not only was this title thought provoking, but it was also descriptive; it prepared readers for what was to follow in the essay.

THE INTRODUCTION.   Although Laura was basically satisfied with her introduction, she identified one problem. She had assumed that everyone reading her essay would be familiar with Gates's essay. By adding material that summarized the problems Gates's father had faced, she could accommodate readers who didn't know or remember Gates's comments.

THE BODY PARAGRAPHS.   After reading her first body paragraph, Laura thought she could sharpen its focus. She decided to delete the first sentence of the paragraph because it seemed too conversational. She also deleted several other sentences that she thought gave too much detail about how difficult advanced placement chemistry was—even though she had added this material at the suggestion of a classmate. After all, cheating, not advanced placement chemistry, was the subject of her paper. If she included this kind of detail, she ran the risk of distracting readers with an irrelevant discussion.

In her second body paragraph, Laura noticed that her first and second sentences did not seem to be linked together, and she realized that a short discussion of her own reaction to the test would connect these two ideas. She also decided to add transitional words and phrases to the last part of the paragraph to clarify the sequence of events she described.

Phrases like *at first, about a minute passed,* and *after a short time* would help readers follow her discussion.

Laura thought that the third body paragraph was her best, but even so, she felt that she needed to add some material. After reading the paragraph several times, she decided to expand her discussion of the students' reactions to cheating. More information—perhaps some dialogue—would help her make the point that cheating was condoned by the students in her class.

THE CONCLUSION.   Laura realized her conclusion began by mentioning her present attitude toward cheating and then suddenly shifted to the effect cheating had on her relationship with Jeff. To remedy this situation, she decided to take her discussion about her current view of cheating out of her conclusion and put it in a separate paragraph. By doing this, she would be able to focus her conclusion on the effect cheating had on both Jeff and her. This strategy would enable Laura to present her views about cheating in more detail and also help her to end her essay forcefully.

▶ A STUDENT WRITER: PREPARING A FINAL DRAFT

Based on her analysis, Laura revised and edited her draft and handed in this final version of her essay.

The Price of Silence

Introduction (provides background)	In his essay "'What's in a Name?'" Henry 1 Louis Gates Jr. recalls an incident from his past in which his father encountered prejudice and did not speak up. Perhaps he kept silent because he was afraid or because he knew that nothing he said or did would change the racial situation in Piedmont, West Virginia. Although I have never encountered the kind of prejudice Gates describes, I did have an experience in high school where, like Gates's father, I could have spoken out but did not. As I think back on
Thesis statement	the situation, I realize that I have outgrown the immaturity and lack of confidence that made me keep silent.
Narrative begins	In my senior year in high school I, along 2 with fifteen other students, took advanced placement chemistry. The course was very de- manding and required hours of studying every

night. As the semester dragged on, it became clear to me, as well as to the other students in the class, that passing the course was not something we could take for granted. Test after test came back with grades that were well below the "As" and "Bs" I was used to getting in the regular chemistry course I had taken in tenth grade. By the time we were ready to take the final exam, most of us were worried that we would fail the course--despite the teacher's assurances that she would mark on a curve.

Key incident occurs

The final examination for advanced place-ment chemistry was given on a Friday morning between nine o'clock and noon. I had studied all that week, but even so, I found the test difficult. I knew the material, but I had a hard time answering the long questions that were asked. As I struggled to balance a partic-ularly complex equation, I noticed that the person sitting across from me was acting strangely. At first I thought I was imagining things, but as I stared I saw Jeff Servin, my friend and study partner, fumbling with his test booklet. About a minute passed before I realized that he was copying material from a paper he had taped to the inside of his shirt cuff. After a short time, I stopped watching him and finished my test.

3

Narrative continues: reactions to the incident

It was not until after the test that I began thinking about what I had seen. Surprisingly, when I mentioned the incident to others in the class, they all knew what Jeff had done. Some even thought that Jeff's actions were justified. "After all," one student said, "the test was hard." But the more I thought about Jeff's actions, the angrier I got. It seemed unfair that I had struggled for weeks to memorize formulas and equations while all Jeff had done was copy them onto a cheat sheet. For a moment I considered going to the teacher, but

4

I quickly dismissed this idea. Cheating was
nothing new to me or to others in my school.
Many of my classmates cheated at one time or
another. Most of us saw school as a war between
us and the teachers, and cheating was just another weapon in our arsenal. The worst crime I
could commit would be to turn Jeff in. As far
as I was concerned, I had no choice. I fell in
line with the values of my high school classmates and dismissed the incident as "no big
deal."

Narrative ends

**Analysis of
key incident**

Now that I am in college, however, I see   5
the situation differently. I find it hard to
believe that I could ever have been so complacent about cheating. The issues that were simple in high school now seem complex--especially
in light of the honor code that I follow in
college. I now ask questions that never would
have occurred to me in high school. What, for
example, are the implications of cheating? What
would happen to the educational system
if cheating became the norm? What are my obligations to all those who are involved in education? Aren't teachers and students interested
in achieving a common goal? The answers to
these questions give me a sense of the far-
reaching effects of my failure to act. If confronted with the same situation today, I know I
would speak out regardless of the consequences.

**Reinforcement
of thesis**

Jeff Servin is now a first-year student at   6
the state university and, like me, was given
credit for chemistry. I feel certain that not
only did I fail myself by not turning him in
but I also failed him. I gave in to peer pressure instead of doing what I knew to be the
right thing. The worst that would have happened
to Jeff had I spoken up is that he would have
had to repeat chemistry in summer school. By
doing so, he would have proven to himself that
he could, like the rest of us in the class,

Conclusion (aftermath of incident)

pass on his own. In the long run, this knowledge would serve him better than the knowledge that he could cheat whenever he faced a difficult situation.

Interestingly, Jeff and I are no longer very close. Whenever I see him I have the same reaction Henry Louis Gates Jr. had when he met Mr. Wilson after he had insulted his father--I have a hard time looking him in the eye.

7

With each draft of her essay, Laura sharpened the focus of her discussion. In the process, she clarified her thoughts about her subject and reached some new and interesting conclusions. Although much of Laura's paper is a narrative, it also contains a contrast between her current ideas about cheating and the ideas she had in high school. Perhaps Laura could have explained the reasons behind her current ideas about cheating more fully. Even so, her paper gives a straightforward account of the incident and analyzes its significance without lapsing into clichés or simplistic moralizing. Especially effective is Laura's conclusion, in which she examines the effects of cheating. By placing this material at the end of her discussion, she makes sure that her readers will not lose sight of the implications of her experience.

A Note on Editing

When you finish revising your essay, it is tempting to hand it in to your instructor and breathe a sigh of relief. This is one temptation you should resist. You still have to edit your paper to correct many of the small problems that remain even after you revise.

When you edit, you put the finishing touches on your essay. You correct misspellings, check punctuation, search for grammatical errors, look at your paper's format, and consider any other surface features that might weaken its message or undermine your credibility. Editing is your last chance to make sure your paper says what you want it to say.

Of course, you could spend literally hours checking your essay for every possible error, but this approach would be time-consuming and impractical. As you edit, keep in mind that certain errors occur more frequently than others. By concentrating on these errors, and by keeping a record of the specific errors that you make most often, you will be able to edit your essays quickly and efficiently.

💻 COMPUTER STRATEGY

Just as you do when you revise, you should edit on a hard copy of your essay. Seeing your work on the printed page makes it easy for you to spot surface-level errors in spelling, grammar, and punctuation. Before you print, however, you can use the *find* or *search* command to locate words or phrases that you know are troublesome. For instance, if you want to make sure you have not used the word *man* in a sexist way, you can use the *find* command to check all instances of the word's use in your paper. Finally, you can run a spell check to find words that are misspelled. Keep in mind, however, that a spell checker will not help you with many proper nouns, nor will it highlight words that are spelled correctly but used incorrectly—*there* for *their,* for example. Even if you run a spell check, you must still proofread carefully.

The following checklist includes many of the most common errors. Consult a handbook of grammar and usage for detailed discussions of these errors.

☑ CHECKLIST FOR EDITING

- **Subject-verb agreement.** Do all your verbs agree in number with their subjects? Remember that singular subjects take singular verbs and plural subjects take plural verbs.

- **Clear pronoun reference.** Do pronouns that refer back to specific nouns do so clearly? Be especially careful of unclear references involving *this.* To avoid this problem, always follow *this* with a word that clarifies the reference—*this problem, this event,* and so on.

- **Punctuation.** Are any commas misplaced, missing, or unnecessary? Remember to use commas before coordinating conjunctions (such as *and* or *but*) that join independent clauses in compound sentences.

- **Misspelled words and typos.** Proofread for spelling even if you have run a computer spell check. Also, be on the lookout for mistakes in capitalization as well as for improper spacing and omitted letters.

- **Commonly confused words.** Be alert for words that are often confused with each other. Remember, for example, that *it's* is a contraction meaning *it is,* and *its* is the possessive form of *it.*

- **Sentence fragments.** Does each group of words punctuated as a sentence have a subject and a verb? Does it make sense on its own, without being attached to another sentence?

- **Comma splices.** Is a comma used alone to connect two independent clauses? If so, correct this problem by adding the appropriate coordinating conjunction (*and* or *but,* for example), changing the comma to a semicolon, or making the clauses separate sentences.

(cont'd)

(cont'd)

- **Inconsistencies.** Are you consistent in expressing yourself throughout your paper? For example, do not shift from the present to the past tense unless your meaning requires you to do so.
- **Manuscript format.** Have you followed your instructor's guidelines? In addition, make sure that your essay is neat and clearly printed.

Each of the reading selections in the chapters that follow is organized around one dominant pattern of development. It is not at all unusual, however, to find more than one pattern used in a single work (see Chapter 11, Combining the Patterns, page 603). In any event, these patterns are not to be followed blindly; they should be adapted to your subject, your audience, and your writing occasion.

2

NARRATION

WHAT IS NARRATION?

Narration tells a story by presenting events in an orderly, logical sequence. In the following paragraph from her memoir *I Know Why the Caged Bird Sings*, Maya Angelou recalls her high school graduation:

Narrative presents events in orderly sequence

Topic sentence

The school band struck up a march and all classes filed in as had been rehearsed. We stood in front of our seats, as assigned, and on a signal from the choir director, we sat. No sooner had this been accomplished than the band started to play the national anthem. We rose again and sang the song, after which we recited the pledge of allegiance. We remained standing for a brief minute before the choir director and the principal signaled to us, rather desperately I thought, to take our seats. The command was so unusual that our carefully rehearsed and smooth-running machine was thrown off. For a full minute we fumbled for our chairs and bumped into each other awkwardly. Habits change or solidify under pressure, so in our state of nervous tension we had been ready to follow our usual assembly pattern: the American national anthem, then the pledge of allegiance, then the song every Black person I knew called the Negro National Anthem. All done in the same key, with the same passion, and most often standing on the same foot.

Narration can be the dominant pattern in many kinds of writing and speech. Histories, biographies, and autobiographies follow a narrative form, as do personal letters, diaries, and journals. Narration is the dominant pattern in many works of fiction and poetry, and it is an essential part of casual conversation. Narration also underlies folk and fairy tales and radio and television news reports. In short, any time you tell what happened, you are using narration.

Although a narrative's purpose may be simply to recount events or create a particular mood or impression, in college writing a narrative essay is more likely to present a sequence of events for the purpose of supporting a thesis. For instance, in a narrative about your first date, your purpose may be to show your readers that dating is a bizarre and often unpleasant ritual. Accordingly, you do not simply tell the story of your date. Rather, you select and arrange details to show your readers *why* dating is bizarre and unpleasant. As in any other kind of essay, you may state your thesis explicitly ("My experiences with dating have convinced me that this ritual should be abandoned entirely"), or you may imply your thesis through the selection and arrangement of events.

Narration can provide the structure for an entire essay, but narrative passages may also appear in essays that are not primarily narrative. In an *argumentative essay* supporting stricter gun-control legislation, for example, you might devote one or two paragraphs to the story of a child accidentally killed by a handgun. In this chapter, however, we focus on narration as the dominant pattern of a piece of writing. During your college career, many of your assignments will call for such writing. In an English composition class, for instance, you may be asked to write about an experience that was important to your development as an adult; on a European history exam, you may need to relate the events that led to Napoleon's defeat at the Battle of Waterloo; in a technical writing class, you may be asked to write a letter of complaint summarizing in detail a company's negligent actions. In each of these situations (as well as in many additional assignments), the piece of writing has a structure that is primarily narrative, and the narrative supports a particular thesis.

The skills you develop in narrative writing will also help you in other kinds of writing. A *process essay,* such as an explanation of a laboratory experiment, is like a narrative because it outlines a series of steps in chronological order; a *cause-and-effect essay,* such as your answer to an exam question that asks you to analyze the events that led to the Great Depression, also resembles a narrative in that it traces a sequence of events. A process essay, however, explains how to do something, and a cause-and-effect essay explains how items or events are related. Still, writing process and cause-and-effect essays will be easier after you master narration. (Process essays and cause-and-effect essays are dealt with in Chapters 5 and 6, respectively.)

Including Enough Detail

Narratives, like other types of writing, need rich, specific details if they are to be convincing. Each detail should help to create a picture for the reader; even exact times, dates, and geographical locations can be helpful. Look, for example, at the following paragraph from the essay "My Mother Never Worked," which appears later in this chapter.

In the winter she sewed night after night, endlessly, begging cast-off clothing from relatives, ripping apart coats, dresses, blouses, and trousers to remake them to fit her four daughters and son. Every morning and every evening she milked cows, fed pigs and calves, cared for chickens, picked eggs, cooked meals, washed dishes, scrubbed floors, and tended and loved her children. In the spring she planted a garden once more, dragging pails of water to nourish and sustain the vegetables for the family. In 1936 she lost a baby in her sixth month.

In the paragraph above, the list of details gives the narrative authenticity and makes it convincing. The central figure in the narrative is a busy, productive woman, and readers know this because they are presented with an exhaustive catalog of her activities.

Varying Sentence Structure

When narratives present a long series of events, all the sentences can begin to sound alike: "She sewed dresses. . . . She milked cows. . . . She fed pigs. . . . She fed calves. . . . She cared for chickens." Such a predictable string of sentences may become monotonous for your readers. You can eliminate this monotony by varying your sentence structure—for instance, by using a variety of sentence openings or by combining simple sentences: "In the winter she sewed night after night, endlessly. . . . Every morning and every evening she milked cows, fed pigs and calves, cared for chickens. . . . "

Maintaining Clear Narrative Order

Many narratives present events in the exact order in which they occurred, moving from first event to last. Whether or not you follow a strict **chronological order** depends on the purpose of your narrative. If you are writing a straightforward account of a historical event or summarizing a record of poor management practices, you will probably want to move from beginning to end. In a personal experience essay or a fictional narrative, however, you may engage your readers' interest by beginning with an event from the middle of your story, or even from the end, and then presenting the events that led up to it. You may also begin in the present and then use one or more *flashbacks* (shifts into the past) to tell your story.

USING ACCURATE VERB TENSES.   Verb tense is extremely important in writing that recounts events in a fixed order because tenses indicate temporal (time) relationships—*earlier, simultaneous, later.* When you write a narrative, you must be careful to keep verb tenses consistent and accurate so your readers can follow the sequence of events. Naturally, you must shift tenses to reflect an actual time shift in your narrative. For instance, convention requires that you use present tense when discussing works of literature ("When Hamlet's mother *marries* his uncle. . ."), but a flashback to an earlier point in the story calls for a shift from present to past tense ("Before their marriage, Hamlet *was*. . ."). Nevertheless, you should avoid unwarranted shifts in verb tense; they will make your narrative confusing.

USING TRANSITIONS.   Transitions—connecting words or phrases— help link events in time, enabling narratives to flow smoothly. Without them, narratives would lack coherence, and readers would be unsure of the correct sequence of events. Transitions can indicate the order in which events occur, and they also signal shifts in time. In narrative writing, the transitions commonly used for these purposes include *first, second, next, then, later, at the same time, meanwhile, immediately, soon, before, earlier, after, afterward, now,* and *finally.* In addition to these transitions, specific time markers—such as *three years later, in 1927, after two hours,* and *on January 3*—indicate how much time has passed between events. A more complete list of transitions appears on page 41.

STRUCTURING A NARRATIVE ESSAY

Like other essays, narratives have an introduction, a body, and a conclusion. If your essay's thesis is explicitly stated, it will, in most cases, appear in the *introduction*. The *body* of your essay will recount the events that make up your narrative, following a clear and orderly plan. Finally, the *conclusion* will give your readers the sense that your story is complete, perhaps by restating your thesis or summarizing key points or events.

Suppose you are assigned a short history paper about the Battle of Waterloo. You plan to support the thesis that if Napoleon had kept more troops in reserve, he might have defeated the British troops under Wellington. Based on this thesis, you decide that the best way to organize your paper is to present the five major phases of the battle in chronological order. An informal outline of your essay might look like this:

Introduction:	Thesis statement—Had Napoleon kept more troops in reserve, he might have broken Wellington's line with another infantry attack and thus won the battle of Waterloo.
Phase 1 of the battle:	Napoleon attacked the Château of Hougoumont.
Phase 2 of the battle:	The French infantry attacked the British lines.
Phase 3 of the battle:	The French cavalry staged a series of charges against the British lines that had not been attacked before. Napoleon committed his reserves.
Phase 4 of the battle:	The French captured La Haye Sainte, their first success of the day but an advantage that Napoleon, having committed troops elsewhere, could not maintain without reserves.

Phase 5 of the battle: The French infantry was decisively defeated by the combined thrust of the British infantry and the remaining British cavalry.

Conclusion: Restatement of thesis or review of key points or events.

By discussing the five phases of the battle in chronological order, you clearly support your thesis. As you expand your informal outline into a historical narrative, exact details, dates, times, and geographical locations are extremely important, for without them, your statements are open to question. In addition, to keep your readers aware of the order in which the events of the battle took place, you must select appropriate transitional words and phrases and pay careful attention to verb tenses.

▶ **A STUDENT WRITER: NARRATION**

The following essay is typical of the informal narrative writing many students are asked to do in English composition classes. It was written by Tiffany Forte in response to the assignment "Write an essay about a goal or dream you had when you were a child."

My Field of Dreams

Introduction   When I was young, I was told that when I   1 grew up I could be anything I wanted to be, and I always took for granted that this was true. I knew exactly what I was going to be, and I would spend hours dreaming about how wonderful my life would be when I grew up. One day, though, when I did grow up, I realized

Thesis statement   that things had not turned out the way I had always expected they would.

Narrative begins   When I was little, I never played with   2 baby dolls or Barbies. I wasn't like other little girls; I was a tomboy. I was the only girl in the neighborhood where I lived, so I always played with boys. We would play army or football or (my favorite) baseball.

     Almost every summer afternoon, all the   3 boys in my neighborhood and I would meet by the big oak tree to get a baseball game going. Surprisingly, I was always one of the first to be picked for a team. I was very fast, and (for my size) I could hit the ball far. I loved baseball more than anything, and I wouldn't miss a game for the world.

My dad played baseball too, and every   4
Friday night I would go to the field with my mother to watch him play. It was just like the big leagues, with lots of people, a snack bar, and lights that shone so high and bright you could see them a mile away. I loved to go to my dad's games. When all the other kids would wander off and play, I would sit and cheer on my dad and his team. My attention was focused on the field, and my heart would jump with every pitch.

Even more exciting than my dad's games   5
were the major league games. The Phillies were my favorite team, and I always looked forward to watching them on television. My dad would make popcorn, and we would sit and watch in anticipation of a Phillies victory. We would go wild, yelling and screaming at all the big plays. When the Phillies would win, I would be so excited I couldn't sleep; when they would lose, I would go to bed angry just like my dad.

Key experience introduced (¶s 6–7)

It was when my dad took me to my first   6
major league baseball game that I decided I wanted to be a major league baseball player. The excitement began when we pulled into the parking lot of Veterans Stadium. There were thousands of cars. As we walked from the car to the stadium, my dad told me to hold on to his hand and not to let go no matter what. When we gave the man our tickets and entered the stadium, I understood why. There were mobs of people everywhere. They were walking around the stadium and standing in long lines for hot dogs, beer, and souvenirs. It was the most wonderful thing I had ever seen. When we got to our seats, I looked down at the tiny base-

ball diamond below and felt as if I were on top of the world.

The cheering of the crowd, the singing, and the chants were almost more than I could stand. I was bursting with enthusiasm. Then, in the bottom of the eighth inning, with the score tied and two outs, Mike Schmidt came up to bat and hit the game-winning home run. The crowd went crazy. Everyone in the whole stadium was standing, and I found myself yelling and screaming along with everyone else. When Mike Schmidt came out of the dugout to receive his standing ovation, I felt a lump in my throat and butterflies in my stomach. He was everyone's hero that night, and I could only imagine the pride he must have felt. I slept the whole way home and dreamed of what it would be like to be the hero of the game.   7

Narrative continues

The next day, when I met with the boys at the oak tree, I told them that when I grew up, I was going to be a major league baseball player. They all laughed at me and said I could never be a baseball player because I was a girl. I told them that they were all wrong, and that I would show them.   8

Analysis of childhood experiences

In the years to follow I played girls' softball in a competitive fast-pitch league, and I was very good. I always wanted to play baseball with the boys, but there were no mixed leagues. After a few years, I realized that the boys from the oak tree were right: I was never going to be a major league baseball player. I realized that what I had been told when I was younger wasn't the whole truth. What no one had bothered to tell me was that I could be anything I wanted to be--as long as it was something that was appropriate for a girl to do.   9

Conclusion

In time, I would get over the loss of my dream. I found new dreams, acceptable for a   10

young woman, and I moved on to other things.
Still, every time I watch a baseball game and
someone hits a home run, I get those same butterflies in my stomach and think, for just a
minute, about what might have been.

Points for Special Attention

INTRODUCTION.   Tiffany's introduction is very straightforward, yet it arouses reader interest by setting up a contrast between what she expected and what actually happened. Her optimistic expectation—that she could be anything she wanted to be—is contradicted by her thesis statement, encouraging readers to read on to discover how things turned out, and why.

THESIS STATEMENT.   Tiffany's assignment was to write about a goal or dream she had when she was a child, but her instructor made it clear that the essay should have an explicitly stated thesis that made a point about the goal or dream. Tiffany knew she wanted to write about her passion for baseball, but she also knew that just listing a series of events would not fulfill the assignment. Her thesis statement—"One day, though, when I did grow up, I realized that things had not turned out the way I had always expected they would"—puts her memories in context, suggesting that she will use them to support a general conclusion about the gap between dreams and reality.

STRUCTURE.   The body of Tiffany's essay traces the chronology of her involvement with baseball: playing with the neighborhood boys, watching her father's games, watching baseball on television, and, finally, seeing her first major league game. Each body paragraph introduces a different aspect of her experience with baseball, culminating in the vividly described Phillies game. The balance of the essay (paragraphs 8–10) summarizes the aftermath of that game, gives a brief overview of Tiffany's later years in baseball, and presents her conclusion.

DETAIL.   Personal narratives like Tiffany's need a lot of detail because the writers want readers to see and hear and feel what they did. To present an accurate picture, Tiffany includes all the significant sights and sounds she can remember: the big oak tree, the lights on the field, the popcorn, the excited cheers, the food and souvenir stands, the crowds, and so on. She also names Mike Schmidt ("everyone's hero"), his team, and the stadium in which she saw him play. Despite all these details, though, she omits a few important ones—in particular, how old she was at each stage of her essay.

VERB TENSE.   Maintaining clear chronological order is very important in narrative writing, where unwarranted shifts in verb tenses can confuse readers. Knowing this, Tiffany avoids unnecessary tense shifts. In her conclusion, she shifts from past to present tense, but this shift is both necessary and clear. Elsewhere she uses *would* to identify events that recurred regularly. For example, in paragraph 5 she says, "My dad *would* make popcorn" rather than "My dad *made* popcorn," which would suggest that he did so only once.

TRANSITIONS.   Tiffany's skillful use of transitional words and expressions links her sentences and moves her readers smoothly through her essay. In addition to transitional words like *when* and *then*, she uses specific time markers—"When I was little," "Almost every summer afternoon," "every Friday night," "As we walked," "The next day," "In the years to follow," and "After a few years"—to advance the narrative and carry her readers along.

Focus on Revision

In their responses to an earlier draft of Tiffany's essay, several students in her peer editing group recommended that she revise one particularly monotonous paragraph. (As one student pointed out, all its sentences began with the subject, making the paragraph seem choppy and its ideas disconnected.)

> My dad played baseball too. I went to the field with my mother every Friday night to watch him play. It was just like the big leagues. There were lots of people and a snack bar. The lights shone so high and bright you could see them a mile away. I loved to go to my dad's games. All the other kids would wander off and play. I could sit and cheer on my dad and his team. My attention was focused on the field. My heart would jump with every pitch.

In the revised version of the paragraph (now paragraph 4 of her essay), Tiffany varies sentence length and opening strategies:

> My dad played baseball too, and every Friday night I would go to the field with my mother to watch him play. It was just like the big leagues, with lots of people, a snack bar, and lights that shone so high and bright you could see them a mile away. I loved to go to my dad's games. When all the other kids would wander off and play, I would sit and cheer on my dad and his team. My attention was focused on the field, and my heart would jump with every pitch.

After reading Tiffany's revised draft, another student suggested that she might still polish her essay a bit. For instance, she could add some dialogue, quoting the boys' taunts and her own reply in paragraph 8. She could also edit to eliminate **clichés** (overused expressions), substituting fresher, more original language for phrases like "I felt a lump in my throat and butterflies in my stomach" and "I felt as if I were on top of the world." In another draft of her essay, Tiffany followed up on these suggestions.

The selections that follow illustrate some of the many possibilities open to writers of narratives.

SANDRA CISNEROS

Sandra Cisneros was born in Chicago in 1954 to a Mexican father and a Chicana mother who took the family back to Mexico City regularly. Cisneros attended the University of Iowa's Writer's Workshop and has taught at California State University in Chico. She is the author of *The House on Mango Street* (1983), a collection of interlocking short stories that is sometimes classified as a novel; two collections of poetry, *My Wicked Wicked Ways* (1987) and *Loose Women* (1994); a collection of stories entitled *Woman Hollering Creek* (1991); and a children's book, *Hairs-Pelitos* (1994). She was awarded a MacArthur fellowship in 1995. Cisneros writes about a Latino culture that she believes is very different from the world of many of her readers. In the autobiographical "Only Daughter," which was published in *Glamour* in 1990, she describes the isolation and alienation she experienced as the only daughter in a family of six sons.

Only Daughter

Once, several years ago, when I was just starting out my writing career, I was asked to write my own contributor's note for an anthology I was part of. I wrote: "I am the only daughter in a family of six sons. *That* explains everything."

Well, I've thought about that ever since, and yes, it explains a lot to me, but for the reader's sake I should have written: "I am the only daughter in a *Mexican* family of six sons." Or even: "I am the only daughter of a Mexican father and a Mexican-American mother." Or: "I am the only daughter of a working-class family of nine." All of these had everything to do with who I am today.

I was/am the only daughter and *only* a daughter. Being an only daughter in a family of six sons forced me by circumstance to spend a lot of time by myself because my brothers felt it beneath them to play with a *girl* in public. But that aloneness, that loneliness, was good for a would-be writer—it allowed me time to think and think, to imagine, to read and prepare myself.

Being only a daughter for my father meant my destiny would lead me to become someone's wife. That's what he believed. But when I was in the fifth grade and shared my plans for college with him, I was sure he understood. I remember my father saying, "*Que bueno, ni'ja,* that's good." That meant a lot to me, especially since my brothers thought the idea hilarious. What I didn't realize was that my father thought college was good for girls—good for finding a husband. After four years in college and two more in graduate school, and still no husband, my father shakes his head even now and says I wasted all that education.

In retrospect, I'm lucky my father believed daughters were meant for husbands. It meant it didn't matter if I majored in something silly like English. After all, I'd find a nice professional eventually, right? This allowed me the liberty to putter about embroidering my little poems and stories without my father interrupting with so much as a "What's that you're writing?"

But the truth is, I wanted him to interrupt. I wanted my father to understand what it was I was scribbling, to introduce me as "My only daughter, the writer." Not as "This is only my daughter. She teaches." *Es maestra*—teacher. Not even *profesora*.   6

In a sense, everything I have ever written has been for him, to win his approval even though I know my father can't read English words, even though my father's only reading includes the brown-ink *Esto* sports magazines from Mexico City and the bloody *¡Alarma!* magazines that feature yet another sighting of *La Virgen de Guadalupe* on a tortilla or a wife's revenge on her philandering husband by bashing his skull in with a *molcajete* (a kitchen mortar made of volcanic rock). Or the *fotonovelas,* the little picture paperbacks with tragedy and trauma erupting from the characters' mouths in bubbles.   7

My father represents, then, the public majority. A public who is uninterested in reading, and yet one whom I am writing about and for, and privately trying to woo.   8

When we were growing up in Chicago, we moved a lot because of my father. He suffered bouts of nostalgia. Then we'd have to let go of our flat, store the furniture with mother's relatives, load the station wagon with baggage and bologna sandwiches, and head south. To Mexico City.   9

We came back, of course. To yet another Chicago flat, another Chicago neighborhood, another Catholic school. Each time, my father would seek out the parish priest in order to get a tuition break, and complain or boast: "I have seven sons."   10

He meant *siete hijos,* seven children, but he translated it as "sons." "I have seven sons." To anyone who would listen. The Sears Roebuck employee who sold us the washing machine. The short-order cook where my father ate his ham-and-eggs breakfasts. "I have seven sons." As if he deserved a medal from the state.   11

My papa. He didn't mean anything by that mistranslation, I'm sure. But somehow I could feel myself being erased. I'd tug my father's sleeve and whisper: "Not seven sons. Six! and *one daughter.*"   12

When my oldest brother graduated from medical school, he fulfilled my father's dream that we study hard and use this—our heads, instead of this—our hands. Even now my father's hands are thick and yellow, stubbed by a history of hammer and nails and twine and coils and springs. "Use this," my father said, tapping his head, "and not this," showing us those hands. He always looked tired when he said it.   13

Wasn't college an investment? And hadn't I spent all those years in college? And if I didn't marry, what was it all for? Why would anyone go to college and then choose to be poor? Especially someone who had always been poor.   14

Last year, after ten years of writing professionally, the financial rewards started to trickle in. My second National Endowment for the Arts   15

Fellowship. A guest professorship at the University of California, Berkeley. My book, which sold to a major New York publishing house.

At Christmas, I flew home to Chicago. The house was throbbing, same as always; hot *tamales* and sweet *tamales* hissing in my mother's pressure cooker, and everybody—my mother, six brothers, wives, babies, aunts, cousins—talking too loud and at the same time, like in a Fellini film, because that's just how we are.   16

I went upstairs to my father's room. One of my stories had just been translated into Spanish and published in an anthology of Chicano writing, and I wanted to show it to him. Ever since he recovered from a stroke two years ago, my father likes to spend his leisure hours horizontally. And that's how I found him, watching a Pedro Infante* movie on Galavisión** and eating rice pudding.   17

There was a glass filmed with milk on the bedside table. There were several vials of pills and balled Kleenex. And on the floor, one black sock and a plastic urinal that I didn't want to look at but looked at anyway. Pedro Infante was about to burst into song, and my father was laughing.   18

I'm not sure if it was because my story was translated into Spanish, or because it was published in Mexico, or perhaps because the story dealt with Tepeyac, the *colonia* my father was raised in and the house he grew up in, but at any rate, my father punched the mute button on his remote control and read my story.   19

I sat on the bed next to my father and waited. He read it very slowly. As if he were reading each line over and over. He laughed at all the right places and read lines he liked out loud. He pointed and asked questions: "Is this So-and-so?" "Yes," I said. He kept reading.   20

When he was finally finished, after what seemed like hours, my father looked up and asked: "Where can we get more copies of this for the relatives?"   21

Of all the wonderful things that happened to me last year, that was the most wonderful.   22

•   •   •

COMPREHENSION

1. What does Cisneros mean when she says being an only daughter in a family of six sons "explains everything" (1)?

2. What distinction does Cisneros make in paragraphs 2 and 3 between being "the only daughter" and being "only a daughter"?

3. What advantages does Cisneros see in being the only daughter? In being only a daughter?

---

*Eds. note—Mexican actor.
**Eds. note— A Spanish-language cable channel.

4. Why does her father think she has wasted her education? What is her re-action to his opinion?

5. Why was her father's reaction to her story the most wonderful thing that happened to Cisneros that year?

PURPOSE AND AUDIENCE

1. Although Cisneros uses many Spanish words in her essay, in most cases she defines or explains these words. What does this decision tell you about her purpose and audience?

2. What is Cisneros's thesis? What incidents and details support her point?

3. Do you think Cisneros intends to convey a sympathetic or an unsympathetic impression of her father? Explain.

STYLE AND STRUCTURE

1. "Only Daughter" is not a single continuous narrative but a series of brief related episodes. Where does Cisneros interrupt the narrative to comment on or analyze events? What does this strategy accomplish?

2. Are the episodes presented in chronological order? Explain.

3. What transitional expressions does Cisneros use to introduce new episodes?

4. Cisneros quotes her father several times. What do we learn about him from his words?

5. Why does Cisneros devote so much space to describing her father in paragraphs 16–18? How does this portrait compare to the one she presents in paragraphs 9–11?

VOCABULARY PROJECTS

1. Define each of the following words as it is used in this selection.

   embroidering (5)   stubbed (13)

2. What is the difference in connotation between *sons* and *children*? Between *teacher* and *professor*? Do you think these distinctions are as significant as Cisneros seems to think they are? Explain.

JOURNAL ENTRY

In what sense do the number and gender(s) of your siblings "explain everything" about who you are today?

WRITING WORKSHOP

1. Write a narrative essay consisting of a series of related episodes that show how you gradually gained the approval and respect of one of your parents, another relative, or a friend.

2. In "Only Daughter," Cisneros traces the development of her identity as an adult, a female, and a writer. Write a narrative essay in which you trace the development of your own personal or professional identity.

3. Are male and female children treated differently in your family? Have your parents had different expectations for their sons and daughters? Write a narrative essay recounting one or more incidents that illustrate these differences (or the lack of differences). If you and your siblings are all of the same gender, or if you are an only child, write about another family you know well.

COMBINING THE PATTERNS

Cisneros structures her essay as a narrative in which she is the main character and her brothers barely appear. To give her readers a clearer understanding of how her father's attitude toward her differs from his attitude toward her brothers, Cisneros could have added one or more paragraphs of **comparison and contrast,** focusing on the different ways she and her brothers are treated. What specific points of contrast would readers find most useful? Where might such paragraphs be added?

THEMATIC CONNECTIONS

- "My Field of Dreams" (page 65)
- "Words Left Unspoken" (page 121)
- "Suicide Note" (page 305)
- "The Men We Carry in Our Minds" (page 387)

MAYA ANGELOU

Maya Angelou was born Marguerita Johnson in 1928 in St. Louis and grew up in Stamps, Arkansas. Angelou has had a diverse career. She served as northern coordinator for the Southern Christian Leadership Conference, the civil rights group organized by Martin Luther King Jr., and worked as a journalist in Egypt and Ghana. Trained as a dancer, she has appeared in theatrical productions and a television drama and has also written for film and television. Angelou is the author of several autobiographical works, including *I Know Why the Caged Bird Sings* (1970) and *Wouldn't Take Nothing for My Journey Now* (1993). Her early volumes of poetry are published together in *The Complete Collected Poems* (1994). *On the Pulse of Morning* (1993), a long poem she composed and read for the 1992 inauguration of President Bill Clinton, was a best-seller, and her recording of it won a Grammy. She currently teaches at Wake Forest University. In "Finishing School," a chapter from *I Know Why the Caged Bird Sings,* Angelou explores a theme she returns to often: her inability to understand the ways of the whites in her hometown and their inability to understand her.

Finishing School

Recently a white woman from Texas, who would quickly describe herself as a liberal, asked me about my hometown. When I told her that in Stamps my grandmother had owned the only Negro general merchandise store since the turn of the century, she exclaimed, "Why, you were a debutante." Ridiculous and even ludicrous. But Negro girls in small Southern towns, whether poverty-stricken or just munching along on a few of life's necessities, were given as extensive and irrelevant preparations for adulthood as rich white girls shown in magazines. Admittedly the training was not the same. While white girls learned to waltz and sit gracefully with a tea cup balanced on their knees, we were lagging behind, learning the mid-Victorian values with very little money to indulge them. . . . 1

We were required to embroider and I had trunkfuls of colorful dishtowels, pillowcases, runners, and handkerchiefs to my credit. I mastered the art of crocheting and tatting, and there was a lifetime's supply of dainty doilies that would never be used in sacheted dresser drawers. It went without saying that all girls could iron and wash, but the finer touches around the home, like setting a table with real silver, baking roasts, and cooking vegetables without meat, had to be learned elsewhere. Usually at the source of those habits. During my tenth year, a white woman's kitchen became my finishing school. 2

Mrs. Viola Cullinan was a plump woman who lived in a three-bedroom house somewhere behind the post office. She was singularly unattractive until she smiled, and then the lines around her eyes and mouth which made her look perpetually dirty disappeared, and her face looked 3 like the mask of an impish elf. She usually rested her smile until late afternoon when her woman friends dropped in and Miss Glory, the cook, served them cold drinks on the closed-in porch.

The exactness of her house was inhuman. This glass went here and only here. That cup had its place and it was an act of impudent rebellion to place it anywhere else. At twelve o'clock the table was set. At 12:15 Mrs. Cullinan sat down to dinner (whether her husband had arrived or not). At 12:16 Miss Glory brought out the food.   4

It took me a week to learn the difference between a salad plate, a bread plate, and a dessert plate.   5

Mrs. Cullinan kept up the tradition of her wealthy parents. She was from Virginia. Miss Glory, who was a descendant of slaves that had worked for the Cullinans, told me her history. She had married beneath her (according to Miss Glory). Her husband's family hadn't had their money very long and what they had "didn't 'mount to much."   6

As ugly as she was, I thought privately, she was lucky to get a husband above or beneath her station. But Miss Glory wouldn't let me say a thing against her mistress. She was very patient with me, however, over the housework. She explained the dishware, silverware, and servants' bells. The large round bowl in which soup was served wasn't a soup bowl, it was a tureen. There were goblets, sherbet glasses, ice-cream glasses, wine glasses, green glass coffee cups with matching saucers, and water glasses. I had a glass to drink from, and it sat with Miss Glory's on a separate shelf from the others. Soup spoons, gravy boat, butter knives, salad forks, and carving platter were additions to my vocabulary and in fact almost represented a new language. I was fascinated with the novelty, with the fluttering Mrs. Cullinan and her Alice-in-Wonderland house.   7

Her husband remains, in my memory, undefined. I lumped him with all the other white men that I had ever seen and tried not to see.   8

On our way home one evening, Miss Glory told me that Mrs. Cullinan couldn't have children. She said that she was too delicate-boned. It was hard to imagine bones at all under those layers of fat. Miss Glory went on to say that the doctor had taken out all her lady organs. I reasoned that a pig's organs included the lungs, heart, and liver, so if Mrs. Cullinan was walking around without those essentials, it explained why she drank alcohol out of unmarked bottles. She was keeping herself embalmed.   9

When I spoke to Bailey* about it, he agreed that I was right, but he also informed me that Mr. Cullinan had two daughters by a colored lady and that I knew them very well. He added that the girls were the spitting image of their father. I was unable to remember what he looked like, although I had just left him a few hours before, but I thought of the Coleman girls. They were very light-skinned and certainly didn't look very much like their mother (no one ever mentioned Mr. Coleman).   10

*EDS. NOTE—Angelou's brother.

My pity for Mrs. Cullinan preceded me the next morning like the 11
Cheshire cat's smile. Those girls, who could have been her daughters,
were beautiful. They didn't have to straighten their hair. Even when they
were caught in the rain, their braids still hung down straight like tamed
snakes. Their mouths were pouty little cupid's bows. Mrs. Cullinan
didn't know what she missed. Or maybe she did. Poor Mrs. Cullinan.

For weeks after, I arrived early, left late and tried very hard to make 12
up for her barrenness. If she had her own children, she wouldn't have
had to ask me to run a thousand errands from her back door to the back
doors of her friends. Poor old Mrs. Cullinan.

Then one evening Miss Glory told me to serve the ladies on the 13
porch. After I set the tray down and turned toward the kitchen, one of the
women asked, "What's your name, girl?" It was the speckled-faced one.
Mrs. Cullinan said, "She doesn't talk much. Her name's Margaret."

"Is she dumb?" 14

"No. As I understand it, she can talk when she wants to but she's usu- 15
ally quiet as a little mouse. Aren't you, Margaret?"

I smile at her. Poor thing. No organs and couldn't even pronounce my 16
name correctly.

"She's a sweet little thing, though." 17

"Well, that may be, but the name's too long. I'd never bother myself. 18
I'd call her Mary if I was you."

I fumed into the kitchen. That horrible woman would never have the 19
chance to call me Mary because if I was starving I'd never work for her. . . .

That evening I decided to write a poem on being white, fat, old, and 20
without children. It was going to be a tragic ballad. I would have to watch
her carefully to capture the essence of her loneliness and pain.

The very next day, she called me by the wrong name. Miss Glory and 21
I were washing up the lunch dishes when Mrs. Cullinan came to the
doorway. "Mary?"

Miss Glory asked, "Who?" 22

Mrs. Cullinan, sagging a little, knew and I knew. "I want Mary to go 23
down to Mrs. Randall's and take her some soup. She's not been feeling
well for a few days."

Miss Glory's face was a wonder to see. "You mean Margaret, ma'am. 24
Her name's Margaret."

"That's too long. She's Mary from now on. Heat that soup from last night 25
and put it in the china tureen and, Mary, I want you to carry it carefully."

Every person I knew had a hellish horror of being "called out of his 26
name." It was a dangerous practice to call a Negro anything that could be
loosely construed as insulting because of the centuries of their having
been called niggers, jigs, dinges, blackbirds, crows, boots, and spooks.

Miss Glory had a fleeting second of feeling sorry for me. Then as she 27
handed me the hot tureen she said, "Don't mind, don't pay that no mind.
Sticks and stones may break your bones, but words. . . . You know, I been
working for her for twenty years."

She held the back door open for me. "Twenty years. I wasn't much   28
older than you. My name used to be Hallelujah. That's what Ma named
me, but my mistress give me 'Glory,' and it stuck. I likes it better too."

I was in the little path that ran behind the houses when Miss Glory   29
shouted, "It's shorter too."

For a few seconds it was a tossup over whether I would laugh (imag-   30
ine being named Hallelujah) or cry (imagine letting some white woman
rename you for her convenience). My anger saved me from either out-
burst. I had to quit the job, but the problem was going to be how to do it.
Momma wouldn't allow me to quit for just any reason.

"She's a peach. That woman is a real peach." Mrs. Randall's maid   31
was talking as she took the soup from me, and I wondered what her name
used to be and what she answered to now.

For a week I looked into Mrs. Cullinan's face as she called me Mary.   32
She ignored my coming late and leaving early. Miss Glory was a little annoyed because I had begun to leave egg yolk on the dishes and wasn't
putting much heart in polishing the silver. I hoped that she would complain to our boss, but she didn't.

Then Bailey solved my dilemma. He had me describe the contents of   33
the cupboard and the particular plates she liked best. Her favorite piece
was a casserole shaped like fish and the green glass coffee cups. I kept his
instructions in mind, so on the next day when Miss Glory was hanging out
clothes and I had again been told to serve the old biddies on the porch, I
dropped the empty serving tray. When I heard Mrs. Cullinan scream
"Mary!" I picked up the casserole and two of the green glass cups in readiness. As she rounded the kitchen door I let them fall on the tiled floor.

I could never absolutely describe to Bailey what happened next, be-   34
cause each time I got to the part where she fell on the floor and screwed up
her ugly face to cry, we burst out laughing. She actually wobbled around
on the floor and picked up shards of the cups and cried, "Oh, Momma.
Oh, dear Gawd. It's Mamma's china from Virginia. Oh Momma, I'm sorry."

Miss Glory came running in from the yard and the women from the   35
porch crowded around. Miss Glory was almost as broken up as her mistress. "You mean to say she broke our Virginia dishes? What we gone do?"

Mrs. Cullinan cried louder. "That clumsy nigger. Clumsy little black   36
nigger."

Old speckled-face leaned down and asked, "Who did it, Viola? Was it   37
Mary? Who did it?"

Everything was happening so fast I can't remember whether her ac-   38
tion preceded her words, but I know that Mrs. Cullinan said, "Her name's
Margaret, goddamn it, her name's Margaret." And she threw a wedge of
broken plate at me. It could have been the hysteria which put her aim off,
but the flying crockery caught Miss Glory right over her ear and she
started screaming.

I left the front door wide open so all the neighbors could hear.   39

Mrs. Cullinan was right about one thing. My name wasn't Mary.   40

• • •

COMPREHENSION

1. What was Angelou required to do in the white woman's kitchen? Why were these tasks so important to Mrs. Cullinan?

2. Why did Angelou feel sorry for Mrs. Cullinan at first? When did her attitude change? Why?

3. Why did Mrs. Cullinan's friend recommend that Angelou be called "Mary" (18)? Why did this upset Angelou so deeply?

4. When Angelou decided she wanted to quit, she realized she could not quit "for just any reason" (30). How did Bailey help her resolve her dilemma?

5. What did Angelou actually learn through her experience?

PURPOSE AND AUDIENCE

1. Is Angelou writing for southerners, blacks, whites, or a general audience? Identify specific details that support your answer.

2. Angelou begins her narrative by summarizing a discussion between herself and a white woman. What is her purpose in doing this?

3. What is Angelou's thesis?

STYLE AND STRUCTURE

1. What exactly is a *finishing school*? What image does it usually call to mind? How is the use of this phrase **ironic** in view of its meaning in this selection?

2. How does Angelou signal the passage of time in this narrative? Identify some transitional phrases that show the passage of time.

3. How does the use of dialogue highlight the contrast between the black and the white characters? In what way does this contrast strengthen the narrative?

4. What details does Angelou use to describe Mrs. Cullinan and her home to the reader? How does this detailed description help advance the narrative?

VOCABULARY PROJECTS

1. Define each of the following words as it is used in this selection.

tatting (2)	pouty (11)	dilemma (33)
sacheted (2)	barrenness (12)	shards (34)
impudent (4)	ballad (20)	
embalmed (9)	construed (26)	

2. According to your dictionary, what is the difference between *ridiculous* and *ludicrous* (1)? Between *soup bowl* and *tureen* (7)? Why do you think Angelou draws a distinction between the two words in each pair?

3. Try substituting an equivalent word for each of the following, paying careful attention to the context of each in the narrative.

perpetually (3)   station (7)   biddies (33)
exactness (4)   peach (31)

Does Angelou's original choice seem more effective in all cases? Explain.

JOURNAL ENTRY

Have you ever received any training or education that you considered at the time to be "extensive and irrelevant preparation for adulthood" (1)? Do you now see any value in the experience?

WRITING WORKSHOP

1. Think about a time in your life when an adult in a position of authority treated you unjustly. How did you react? Write a narrative essay in which you recount the situation and your responses to it.

2. Have you ever had an experience in which you were the victim of name calling—or in which you found yourself doing the name calling? Summarize the incident, including dialogue and description that will help your readers understand your motivations and reactions. Include a thesis statement that presents your attitude toward the incident.

3. Write a narrative essay that includes a brief summary of an incident from a work of fiction—specifically, an incident that serves as a character's initiation into adulthood. In your essay, focus on how the experience helps the character grow up.

COMBINING THE PATTERNS

Angelou's essay is a narrative, but it is rich with descriptive details. Identify specific passages of the essay that are structured as **descriptions** of people and places. Is the description primarily visual, or does it incorporate other senses (sound, smell, taste, and touch) as well? Do you think any person, setting, or object should be described in greater detail? Explain.

THEMATIC CONNECTIONS

- "Midnight" (page 165)
- "The 'Black Table' Is Still There" (page 284)
- "Revelation" (page 424)

▶▶▶▶▶▶▶▶▶▶▶▶▶▶▶▶▶▶

DONNA SMITH-YACKEL

Although this essay, which was first published in *Women: A Journal of Liberation* in 1975, draws on personal experience, it makes a pointed statement about what society thinks of "women's work." According to federal law, a woman who is a homemaker is entitled to Social Security benefits only through the earnings of her husband. Therefore, a homemaker who becomes disabled receives no disability benefits, and her husband and children are allowed no survivors' benefits if she should die. Although this law has been challenged in the courts, a woman who does not work for wages outside the home is still not entitled to Social Security benefits in her own right. Without explicitly stating her thesis, Donna Smith-Yackel comments on this situation in her narrative.

My Mother Never Worked

"Social Security Office." (The voice answering the telephone sounds very self-assured.)   1

"I'm calling about... my mother just died... I was told to call you and see about a... death-benefit check, I think they call it...."   2

"I see. Was your mother on Social Security? How old was she?"   3

"Yes... she was seventy-eight...."   4

"Do you know her number?"   5

"No... I, ah... don't you have a record?"   6

"Certainly. I'll look it up. Her name?"   7

"Smith. Martha Smith. Or maybe she used Martha Ruth Smith?... Sometimes she used her maiden name... Martha Jerabek Smith?"   8

"If you'd care to hold on, I'll check our records—it'll be a few minutes."   9

"Yes...."   10

Her love letters—to and from Daddy—were in an old box, tied with ribbons and stiff, rigid-with-age leather thongs: 1918 through 1920; hers written on stationery from the general store she had worked in full-time and managed, single-handed, after her graduation from high school in 1913; and his, at first, on YMCA or Soldiers and Sailors Club stationery dispensed to the fighting men of World War I. He wooed her thoroughly and persistently by mail, and though she reciprocated all his feelings for her, she dreaded marriage....   11

"It's so hard for me to decide when to have my wedding day—that's all. I've thought about these last two days. I have told you dozens of times that I won't be afraid of married life, but when it comes down to setting the date and then picturing myself a married woman with half a dozen or more kids to look after, it just makes me sick.... I am weeping right now—I hope that some day I can look back and say how foolish I was to dread it all."   12

They married in February, 1921, and began farming. Their first baby, 13
a daughter, was born in January, 1922, when my mother was 26 years old.
The second baby, a son, was born in March, 1923. They were renting
farms; my father, besides working his own fields, also was a hired man
for two other farmers. They had no capital initially, and had to gain it
slowly, working from dawn until midnight every day. My town-bred
mother learned to set hens and raise chickens, feed pigs, milk cows, plant
and harvest a garden, and can every fruit and vegetable she could
scrounge. She carried water nearly a quarter of a mile from the well to fill
her wash boilers in order to do her laundry on a scrub board. She learned
to shuck grain, feed threshers, shock and husk corn, feed corn pickers. In
September, 1925, the third baby came, and in June, 1927, the fourth
child—both daughters. In 1930, my parents had enough money to buy
their own farm, and that March they moved all their livestock and be-
longings themselves, 55 miles over rutted, muddy roads.

In the summer of 1930 my mother and her two eldest children re- 14
claimed a 40-acre field from Canadian thistles, by chopping them all out
with a hoe. In the other fields, when the oats and flax began to head out,
the green and blue of the crops were hidden by the bright yellow of wild
mustard. My mother walked the fields day after day, pulling each mustard plant. She raised a new flock of baby chicks—500—and she spaded
up, planted, hoed, and harvested a half-acre garden.

During the next spring their hogs caught cholera and died. No cash 15
that fall.

And in the next year the drought hit. My mother and father trudged 16
from the well to the chickens, the well to the calf pasture, the well to the
barn, and from the well to the garden. The sun came out hot and bright,
endlessly, day after day. The crops shriveled and died. They harvested
half the corn, and ground the other half, stalks and all, and fed it to the
cattle as fodder. With the price at four cents a bushel for the harvested
crop, they couldn't afford to haul it into town. They burned it in the fur-
nace for fuel that winter.

In 1934, in February, when the dust was still so thick in the 17
Minnesota air that my parents couldn't always see from the house to the
barn, their fifth child—a fourth daughter—was born. My father hunted
rabbits daily, and my mother stewed them, fried them, canned them,
and wished out loud that she could taste hamburger once more. In the
fall the shotgun brought prairie chickens, ducks, pheasant, and grouse.
My mother plucked each bird, carefully reserving the breast feathers for
pillows.

In the winter she sewed night after night, endlessly, begging cast-off 18
clothing from relatives, ripping apart coats, dresses, blouses, and trousers
to remake them to fit her four daughters and son. Every morning and
every evening she milked cows, fed pigs, and calves, cared for chickens,
picked eggs, cooked meals, washed dishes, scrubbed floors, and tended
and loved her children. In the spring she planted a garden once more,

dragging pails of water to nourish and sustain the vegetables for the family. In 1936 she lost a baby in her sixth month.

In 1937 her fifth daughter was born. She was 42 years old. In 1939 a   19
second son, and in 1941 her eighth child—and third son.

But the war had come, and prosperity of a sort. The herd of cattle had   20
grown to 30 head; she still milked morning and evening. Her garden was
more than a half acre—the rains had come, and by now the Rural
Electricity Administration and indoor plumbing. Still she sewed—dresses
and jackets for the children, housedresses and aprons for herself, weekly
patching of jeans, overalls, and denim shirts. She still made pillows, using
feathers she had plucked, and quilts every year—intricate patterns as
well as patchwork, stitched as well as tied—all necessary bedding for her
family. Every scrap of cloth too small to be used in quilts was carefully
saved and painstakingly sewed together in strips to make rugs. She still
went out in the fields to help with the haying whenever there was a threat
of rain.

In 1959 my mother's last child graduated from high school. A year   21
later the cows were sold. She still raised chickens and ducks, plucked
feathers, made pillows, baked her own bread, and every year made a new
quilt—now for a married child or for a grandchild. And her garden, that
huge, undying symbol of sustenance, was as large and cared for as in all
the years before. The canning, and now freezing, continued.

In 1969, on a June afternoon, mother and father started out for town   22
so that she could buy sugar to make rhubarb jam for a daughter who
lived in Texas. The car crashed into a ditch. She was paralyzed from the
waist down.

In 1970 her husband, my father, died. My mother struggled to regain   23
some competence and dignity and order in her life. At the rehabilitation
institute, where they gave her physical therapy and trained her to live
usefully in a wheelchair, the therapist told me: "She did fifteen pushups
today—fifteen! She's almost seventy-five years old! I've never known a
woman so strong!"

From her wheelchair she canned pickles, baked bread, ironed clothes,   24
wrote dozens of letters weekly to her friends and her "half dozen or more
kids," and made three patchwork housecoats and one quilt. She made
balls and balls of carpet rags—enough for five rugs. And kept all her love
letters.

"I think I've found your mother's records—Martha Ruth Smith; mar-   25
ried to Ben F. Smith?"

"Yes, that's right."   26

"Well, I see that she was getting a widow's pension. . . ."   27

"Yes, that's right."   28

"Well, your mother isn't entitled to our $255 death benefit."   29

"Not entitled! But why?"   30

The voice on the telephone explains patiently: 31

"Well, you see—your mother never worked."   32

• • •

COMPREHENSION

1. What kind of work did Martha Smith do while her children were growing up? List some of the chores she performed.

2. Why isn't Martha Smith eligible for a death benefit?

3. How does the government define *work*?

PURPOSE AND AUDIENCE

1. What is the essay's thesis? Why do you suppose it is never explicitly stated?

2. This essay appeared in *Ms.* magazine and other publications whose audiences are sympathetic to feminist goals. Could it just as easily have appeared in a magazine whose audience was not? Explain.

3. Smith-Yackel mentions relatively little about her father in this essay. How can you account for this?

STYLE AND STRUCTURE

1. Is the title effective? If so, why? If not, what title can you suggest?

2. Smith-Yackel could have outlined her mother's life without framing it with the telephone conversation. Why do you think she includes this frame?

3. What strategies does Smith-Yackel use to indicate the passing of time in her narrative?

4. This narrative piles details one on top of another almost like a list. Why does the writer list so many details?

5. In paragraphs 20 and 21, what is accomplished by the repetition of the word *still*?

VOCABULARY PROJECTS

1. Define each of the following words as it is used in this selection.

scrounge (13)	rutted (13)	intricate (20)
shuck (13)	reclaimed (14)	sustenance (21)
shock (13)	flax (14)	
husk (13)	fodder (16)	

2. Try substituting equivalent words for those italicized in this sentence:

He *wooed* her *thoroughly* and *persistently* by mail, and though she *reciprocated* all his feeling for her, she *dreaded* marriage. . . (11).

How do your substitutions change the sentence's meaning?

3. Throughout her narrative, Smith-Yackel uses concrete, specific verbs. Review her choice of verbs, particularly in paragraphs 13–24, and comment on how such verbs serve the essay's purpose.

JOURNAL ENTRY

Do you believe homemakers should be entitled to Social Security death benefits? Explain your reasoning.

WRITING WORKSHOP

1. If you can, interview one of your parents or grandparents (or another person you know who might remind you of Donna Smith-Yackel's mother) about his or her work, and write a chronological narrative based on what you learn. Include a thesis statement that your narrative can support.

2. Write Martha Smith's obituary as it might have appeared in her hometown newspaper. If you are not familiar with the form of an obituary, read a few in your local paper.

3. Write a narrative account of the worst job you ever had. Include a thesis statement that expresses your negative feelings.

COMBINING THE PATTERNS

Because of the repetitive nature of the farm chores Smith-Yackel describes in her narrative, some passages come very close to explaining a **process**, a series of repeated steps that always occur in a predictable order. Identify several such passages. If Smith-Yackel's essay were written entirely as a process explanation, what material would have to be left out? How would these omissions change the essay?

THEMATIC CONNECTIONS

- "Midnight" (page 165)
- "On Fire" (page 283)
- "I Want a Wife" (page 461)
- "The Company Man" (page 465)

MARTIN GANSBERG

Martin Gansberg (1920–1995), a native of Brooklyn, New York, was a reporter and editor for the *New York Times* for forty-three years. A graduate of St. John's University, he also taught at Fairleigh Dickinson University and wrote for numerous magazines. The following article, written for the *Times* two weeks after the murder it recounts, earned Gansberg an award for excellence from the Newspaper Reporters Association of New York. The murder of Kitty Genovese, which shocked the entire country and has been the subject of countless articles and editorials, as well as a television movie, is still cited as an example of public indifference, and Gansberg's article is frequently reprinted. Its thesis, though not explicitly stated, retains its power.

Thirty-Eight Who Saw Murder Didn't Call the Police

For more than half an hour 38 respectable, law-abiding citizens in Queens watched a killer stalk and stab a woman in three separate attacks in Kew Gardens.

Twice their chatter and the sudden glow of their bedroom lights interrupted him and frightened him off. Each time he returned, sought her out, and stabbed her again. Not one person telephoned the police during the assault; one witness called after the woman was dead.

That was two weeks ago today.

Still shocked is Assistant Chief Inspector Frederick M. Lussen, in charge of the borough's detectives and a veteran of 25 years of homicide investigations. He can give a matter-of-fact recitation on many murders. But the Kew Gardens slaying baffles him—not because it is a murder, but because the "good people" failed to call the police.

"As we have reconstructed the crime," he said, "the assailant had three chances to kill this woman during a 35-minute period. He returned twice to complete the job. If we had been called when he first attacked, the woman might not be dead now."

This is what the police say happened beginning at 3:20 A.M. in the staid, middle-class, tree-lined Austin Street area:

Twenty-eight-year-old Catherine Genovese, who was called Kitty by almost everyone in the neighborhood, was returning home from her job as manager of a bar in Hollis. She parked her red Fiat in a lot adjacent to the Kew Gardens Long Island Rail Road Station, facing Mowbray Place. Like many residents of the neighborhood, she had parked there day after day since her arrival from Connecticut a year ago, although the railroad frowns on the practice.

She turned off the lights of her car, locked the door, and started to walk the 100 feet to the entrance of her apartment at 82–70 Austin Street, which is in a Tudor building, with stores in the first floor and apartments on the second.

The entrance to the apartment is in the rear of the building because the front is rented to retail stores. At night the quiet neighborhood is shrouded in the slumbering darkness that marks most residential areas.   9

Miss Genovese noticed a man at the far end of the lot, near a seven-story apartment house at 82–40 Austin Street. She halted. Then, nervously, she headed up Austin Street toward Lefferts Boulevard, where there is a call box to the 102nd Police Precinct in nearby Richmond Hill.   10

She got as far as a street light in front of a bookstore before the man grabbed her. She screamed. Lights went on in the 10-story apartment house at 82–67 Austin Street, which faces the bookstore. Windows slid open and voices punctuated the early-morning stillness.   11

Miss Genovese screamed: "Oh, my God, he stabbed me! Please help me! Please help me!"   12

From one of the upper windows in the apartment house, a man called down: "Let that girl alone!"   13

The assailant looked up at him, shrugged, and walked down Austin Street toward a white sedan parked a short distance away. Miss Genovese struggled to her feet.   14

Lights went out. The killer returned to Miss Genovese, now trying to make her way around the side of the building by the parking lot to get to her apartment. The assailant stabbed her again.   15

"I'm dying!" she shrieked. "I'm dying!"   16

Windows were opened again, and lights went on in many apartments. The assailant got into his car and drove away. Miss Genovese staggered to her feet. A city bus, 0–10, the Lefferts Boulevard line to Kennedy International Airport, passed. It was 3:35 A.M.   17

The assailant returned. By then, Miss Genovese had crawled to the back of the building, where the freshly painted brown doors to the apartment house held out hope for safety. The killer tried the first door; she wasn't there. At the second door, 82–62 Austin Street, he saw her slumped on the floor at the foot of the stairs. He stabbed her a third time—fatally.   18

It was 3:50 by the time the police received their first call, from a man who was a neighbor of Miss Genovese. In two minutes they were at the scene. The neighbor, a 70-year-old woman, and another woman were the only persons on the street. Nobody else came forward.   19

The man explained that he had called the police after much deliberation. He had phoned a friend in Nassau County for advice and then he had crossed the roof of the building to the apartment of the elderly woman to get her to make the call.   20

"I didn't want to get involved," he sheepishly told police.   21

Six days later, the police arrested Winston Moseley, a 29-year-old business machine operator, and charged him with homicide. Moseley   22 had no previous record. He is married, has two children and owns a home at 133–19 Sutter Avenue, South Ozone Park, Queens. On Wednesday, a court committed him to Kings County Hospital for psychiatric observation.

When questioned by the police, Moseley also said that he had slain   23
Mrs. Annie May Johnson, 24, of 146–12 133d Avenue, Jamaica, on Feb. 29 and Barbara Kralik, 15, of 174–17 140th Avenue, Springfield Gardens, last July. In the Kralik case, the police are holding Alvin L. Mitchell, who is said to have confessed to that slaying.

The police stressed how simple it would have been to have gotten in   24
touch with them. "A phone call," said one of the detectives, "would have done it." The police may be reached by dialing "0" for operator or SPring 7–3100.

Today witnesses from the neighborhood, which is made up of one-   25
family homes in the $35,000 to $60,000 range with the exception of the two apartment houses near the railroad station, find it difficult to explain why they didn't call the police.

A housewife, knowingly if quite casually, said, "We thought it was a   26
lovers' quarrel." A husband and wife both said, "Frankly, we were afraid." They seemed aware of the fact that events might have been different. A distraught woman, wiping her hands in her apron, said, "I didn't want my husband to get involved."

One couple, now willing to talk about that night, said they heard the   27
first screams. The husband looked thoughtfully at the bookstore where the killer first grabbed Miss Genovese.

"We went to the window to see what was happening," he said, "but   28
the light from our bedroom made it difficult to see the street." The wife, still apprehensive, added: "I put out the light and we were able to see better."

Asked why they hadn't called the police, she shrugged and replied: 29
"I don't know."

A man peeked out from a slight opening in the doorway to his apart-   30
ment and rattled off an account of the killer's second attack. Why hadn't he called the police at the time? "I was tired," he said without emotion. "I went back to bed."

It was 4:25 A.M. when the ambulance arrived to take the body of Miss   31
Genovese. It drove off. "Then," a solemn police detective said, "the people came out."

• • •

COMPREHENSION

1. How much time elapsed between the first stabbing of Kitty Genovese and the time when the people finally came out?

2. What excuses did the neighbors make for not coming to Kitty Genovese's aid?

PURPOSE AND AUDIENCE

1. This article appeared in 1964. What effect was it intended to have on its audience? Do you think it has the same impact today, or has its impact changed or diminished?

2. What is the article's main point? Why does Gansberg imply his thesis rather than stating it explicitly?

3. What is Gansberg's purpose in describing the Austin Street area as "staid, middle-class, tree-lined" (6)?

4. Why do you suppose Gansberg provides the police department's phone number in his article?

STYLE AND STRUCTURE

1. Gansberg is very precise in this article, especially in his references to time, addresses, and ages. Why?

2. The objective newspaper style is dominant in this article, but the writer's anger shows through. Point to words and phrases that reveal his attitude toward his material.

3. Because this article was originally set in the narrow columns of a newspaper, there are many short paragraphs. Would it be more effective if some of these brief paragraphs were combined? If so, why? If not, why not? Give examples to support your answer.

4. Review the dialogue. Does it strengthen Gansberg's presentation? Would the article be more compelling without dialogue? Explain.

5. This article does not have a formal conclusion; nevertheless, the last paragraph sums up the writer's attitude. How?

VOCABULARY PROJECTS

1. Define each of the following words as it is used in this section.

   stalk (1)   adjacent (7)   distraught (26)
   baffles (4)   punctuated (11)   apprehensive (28)
   staid (6)   sheepishly (21)

2. The word *assailant* appears frequently in this article. Why is it used so often? What impact is this repetition likely to have on readers? What other words could have been used?

JOURNAL ENTRY

In a similar situation, would you have called the police? Would you have gone outside to help? What do you think might have influenced your decision?

WRITING WORKSHOP

1. In your own words, write a ten-sentence summary of the article. Try to reflect Gansberg's order and emphasis as well as his ideas.

2. Rewrite the article as if it were a diary entry of one of the thirty-eight people who watched the murder. Summarize what you saw, and explain why you decided not to call for help. (You may invent details that Gansberg does not include.)

3. If you have ever been involved in or witnessed a situation in which someone was in trouble, write a narrative essay about the incident. If people failed to help the person in trouble, explain why you think no one acted. If people did act, tell how. Be sure to account for your own actions.

COMBINING THE PATTERNS

Because the purpose of this newspaper article is to inform, it has no extended descriptions of the victim, the witnesses, or the crime scene. It also does not explain why those who watched did not act. Where might passages of **description** or **cause and effect** be added? How might such additions change the essay's impact on readers? Do you think they would strengthen the essay?

THEMATIC CONNECTIONS

- "Samuel" (page 202)
- "Who Killed Benny Paret?" (page 270)
- "It's Just Too Late" (page 294)

GEORGE ORWELL

George Orwell (1903–1950) was born Eric Blair in Bengal, India, where his father was a British civil servant. Instead of going to a university, Orwell joined the Imperial Police in Burma (now renamed Myanmar by its military dictatorship), where he remained for five years. His sense of guilt about British colonialism and his role as its defender led Orwell to leave Burma to live and write in Paris and London. Wishing to learn about the life of the poor first-hand, Orwell struggled to survive on his income from menial jobs. He wrote about his experiences in his first book, *Down and Out in Paris and London* (1933). His other books include *The Road to Wigan Pier* (1937), about the lives of unemployed coal miners and factory workers in the north of England; *Homage to Catalonia* (1938), about his experiences fighting in the Spanish Civil War in 1936 and 1937; and *Animal Farm* (1945) and *1984* (1949), novels portraying the dangers of totalitarianism. Orwell also wrote many essays and articles for the left-wing British journal *Tribune* and other periodicals; his nonfiction writings are published in four volumes entitled *Collected Essays, Journalism and Letters* (1968). "Shooting an Elephant," set in Burma, relates an incident that clarified for Orwell the nature of British colonial rule.

Shooting an Elephant

In Moulmein, in Lower Burma, I was hated by large numbers of people—the only time in my life that I have been important enough for this to happen to me. I was sub-divisional police officer of the town, and in an aimless, petty kind of way anti-European feeling was very bitter. No one had the guts to raise a riot, but if a European woman went through the bazaars alone somebody would probably spit betel juice over her dress. As a police officer I was an obvious target and was baited whenever it seemed safe to do so. When a nimble Burman tripped me up on the football field and the referee (another Burman) looked the other way, the crowd yelled with hideous laughter. This happened more than once. In the end the sneering yellow faces of young men that met me everywhere, the insults hooted after me when I was at a safe distance, got badly on my nerves. The young Buddhist priests were the worst of all. There were several thousands of them in the town and none of them seemed to have anything to do except stand on street corners and jeer at Europeans.

All this was perplexing and upsetting. For at that time I had already made up my mind that imperialism was an evil thing and the sooner I chucked up my job and got out of it the better. Theoretically—and secretly, of course—I was all for the Burmese and all against their oppressors, the British. As for the job I was doing, I hated it more bitterly than I can perhaps make clear. In a job like that you see the dirty work of Empire at close quarters. The wretched prisoners huddling in the stinking cages of the lockups, the grey, cowed faces of the long-term convicts, the scarred buttocks of the men who had been flogged with bamboos—all these oppressed me with an intolerable sense of guilt. But I could get nothing into perspective. I was young and ill-educated and I had had to think out my problems in the utter silence that is imposed on every Englishman in the East. I did not even know that the British Empire is dying, still less did I know that it is a great deal better than the younger empires that are going to supplant it.* All I knew was that I was stuck between my hatred of the empire I served and my rage against the evil-spirited little beasts who tried to make my job impossible. With one part of my mind I thought of the British Raj** as an unbreakable tyranny, as something clamped down, in *saecula saeculorum*,*** upon the will of prostrate peoples; with another part I thought that the greatest joy in the world would be to drive a bayonet into a Buddhist priest's guts. Feelings like these are the normal by-products of imperialism; ask any Anglo-Indian official, if you can catch him off duty.

One day something happened which in a roundabout way was enlightening. It was a tiny incident in itself, but it gave me a better glimpse than I had had before of the real nature of imperialism—the real motives for which despotic governments act. Early one morning the sub-inspector at a police station the other end of the town rang me up on the phone and said that an elephant was ravaging the bazaar. Would I please come and do something about it? I did not know what I could do, but I wanted to see what was happening and I got on to a pony and started out. I took my rifle, an old .44 Winchester and much too small to kill an elephant, but I thought the noise might be useful *in terrorem.*† Various Burmans stopped me on the way and told me about the elephant's doings. It was not, of course, a wild elephant, but a tame one which had gone "must."‡ It had been chained up, as tame elephants always are when their attack of "must" is due, but on the previous night it had broken its chain and escaped. Its mahout,¶ the only person who could manage it when it was in that state, had set out in pursuit, but had taken the wrong direction and was now twelve hours' journey away, and in the morning the elephant had suddenly reappeared in the town. The Burmese population had no weapons and were quite helpless against it. It had already destroyed somebody's bamboo hut, killed a cow, and raided some fruit-stalls and devoured the stock; also it had met the municipal rubbish van and, when the driver jumped out and took to his heels, had turned the van over and inflicted violences upon it. 3

The Burmese sub-inspector and some Indian constables were waiting for me in the quarter where the elephant had been seen. It was a very poor 4

---

    *EDS. NOTE—Orwell was writing in 1936, when Hitler and Stalin were in power and World War II was only three years away.
    **EDS. NOTE—*Raj:* sovereignty.
    ***EDS. NOTE—From time immemorial.
    †EDS. NOTE—*In terrorem:* in terrorizing him.
    ‡EDS. NOTE—That is, gone into an uncontrollable frenzy.
    ¶EDS. NOTE—A keeper and driver of an elephant.

quarter, a labyrinth of squalid bamboo huts, thatched with palm-leaf, winding all over a steep hillside. I remember that it was a cloudy, stuffy morning at the beginning of the rains. We began questioning people as to where the elephant had gone, and, as usual, failed to get any definite information. That is invariably the case in the East; a story always sounds clear enough at a distance, but the nearer you get to the scene of events the vaguer it becomes. Some of the people said that the elephant had gone in one direction, some said that he had gone in another, some professed not even to have heard of an elephant. I had almost made up my mind that the whole story was a pack of lies, when we heard yells a little distance away. There was a loud, scandalized cry of "Go away, child! Go away this instant!" and an old woman with a switch in her hand came round the corner of a hut, violently shooing away a crowd of naked children. Some more women followed, clicking their tongues and exclaiming; evidently there was something that the children ought not to have seen. I rounded the hut and saw a man's dead body sprawling in the mud. He was an Indian, a black Dravidian coolie,* almost naked, and he could not have been dead many minutes. The people said that the elephant had come suddenly upon him round the corner of the hut, caught him with its trunk, put its foot on his back, and ground him into the earth. This was the rainy season and the ground was soft, and his face had scored a trench a foot deep and a couple of yards long. He was lying on his belly with arms crucified and head sharply twisted to one side. His face was coated with mud, the eyes wide open, the teeth bared and grinning with an expression of unendurable agony. (Never tell me, by the way, that the dead look peaceful. Most of the corpses I have seen looked devilish.) The friction of the great beast's foot had stripped the skin from his back as neatly as one skins a rabbit. As soon as I saw the dead man I sent an orderly to a friend's house nearby to borrow an elephant rifle. I had already sent back the pony, not wanting it to go mad with fright and throw me if it smelled the elephant.

The orderly came back in a few minutes with a rifle and five cartridges, and meanwhile some Burmans had arrived and told us that the elephant was in the paddy** fields below, only a few hundred yards away. As I started forward practically the whole population of the quarter flocked out of the houses and followed me. They had seen the rifle and were all shouting excitedly that I was going to shoot the elephant. They had not shown much interest in the elephant when he was merely ravaging their homes, but it was different now that he was going to be shot. It was a bit of fun to them, as it would be to an English crowd; besides they wanted the meat. It made me vaguely uneasy. I had no intention of shooting the elephant—I had merely sent for the rifle to defend myself if necessary—and it is always unnerving to have a crowd following you. I marched down the hill, looking and feeling a fool, with the rifle over my

5

---

*EDS. NOTE—An unskilled laborer.
**EDS. NOTE—Wet land in which rice grows.

shoulder and an ever-growing army of people jostling at my heels. At the bottom, when you got away from the huts, there was a metalled road and beyond that a miry waste of paddy fields a thousand yards across, not yet ploughed but soggy from the first rains and dotted with coarse grass. The elephant was standing eight yards from the road, his left side towards us. He took not the slightest notice of the crowd's approach. He was tearing up bunches of grass, beating them against his knees to clean them and stuffing them into his mouth.

I had halted on the road. As soon as I saw the elephant I knew with   6 perfect certainty that I ought not to shoot him. It is a serious matter to shoot a working elephant—it is comparable to destroying a huge and costly piece of machinery—and obviously one ought not to do it if it can possibly be avoided. And at that distance, peacefully eating, the elephant looked no more dangerous than a cow. I thought then and I think now that his attack of "must" was already passing off; in which case he would merely wander harmlessly about until the mahout came back and caught him. Moreover, I did not in the least want to shoot him. I decided that I would watch him for a little while to make sure that he did not turn savage again, and then go home.

But at that moment I glanced round at the crowd that had followed   7 me. It was an immense crowd, two thousand at the least and growing every minute. It blocked the road for a long distance on either side. I looked at the sea of yellow faces above the garish clothes—faces all happy and excited over this bit of fun, all certain that the elephant was going to be shot. They were watching me as they would watch a conjurer about to perform a trick. They did not like me, but with the magical rifle in my hands I was momentarily worth watching. And suddenly I realized that I should have to shoot the elephant after all. The people expected it of me and I had got to do it; I could feel their two thousand wills pressing me forward, irresistibly. And it was at this moment, as I stood there with the rifle in my hands, that I first grasped the hollowness, the futility of the white man's dominion in the East. Here was I, the white man with his gun, standing in front of the unarmed native crowd—seemingly the leading actor of the piece; but in reality I was only an absurd puppet pushed to and fro by the will of those yellow faces behind. I perceived in this moment that when the white man turns tyrant it is his own freedom that he destroys. He becomes a sort of hollow, posing dummy, the conventionalized figure of a sahib.* For it is the condition of his rule that he shall spend his life in trying to impress the "natives," and so in every crisis he has got to do what the "natives" expect of him. He wears a mask, and his face grows to fit it. I had got to shoot the elephant. I had committed myself to doing it when I sent for the rifle. A sahib has got to act like a sahib; he has got to appear resolute, to know his own mind and do definite

*EDS. NOTE—Term used among Hindus and Muslims in Colonial India when speaking of an official.

things. To come all that way, rifle in hand, with two thousand people marching at my heels, and then to trail feebly away, having done nothing—no, that was impossible. The crowd would laugh at me. And my whole life, every white man's life in the East, was one long struggle not to be laughed at.

But I did not want to shoot the elephant. I watched him beating his   8
bunch of grass against his knees, with the preoccupied grandmotherly air that elephants have. It seemed to me that it would be murder to shoot him. At that age I was not squeamish about killing animals, but I had never shot an elephant and never wanted to. (Somehow it always seems worse to kill a *large* animal.) Besides, there was the beast's owner to be considered. Alive, the elephant was worth at least a hundred pounds; dead, he would only be worth the value of his tusks, five pounds, possibly. But I had got to act quickly. I turned to some experienced-looking Burmans who had been there when we arrived, and asked them how the elephant had been behaving. They all said the same thing: he took no notice of you if you left him alone, but he might charge if you went too close to him.

It was perfectly clear to me what I ought to do. I ought to walk up to   9
within, say, twenty-five yards of the elephant and test his behavior. If he charged I could shoot, if he took no notice of me it would be safe to leave him until the mahout came back. But also I knew that I was going to do no such thing. I was a poor shot with a rifle and the ground was soft mud into which one would sink at every step. If the elephant charged and I missed him, I should have about as much chance as a toad under a steamroller. But even then I was not thinking particularly of my own skin, only of the watchful yellow faces behind. For at that moment, with the crowd watching me, I was not afraid in the ordinary sense, as I would have been if I had been alone. A white man mustn't be frightened in front of "natives"; and so, in general, he isn't frightened. The sole thought in my mind was that if anything went wrong those two thousand Burmans would see me pursued, caught, trampled on, and reduced to a grinning corpse like that Indian up the hill. And if that happened it was quite probable that some of them would laugh. That would never do. There was only one alternative. I shoved the cartridges into the magazine and lay down on the road to get a better aim.

The crowd grew very still, and a deep, low, happy sigh, as of people   10
who see the theatre curtain go up at last, breathed from innumerable throats. They were going to have their bit of fun after all. The rifle was a beautiful German thing with cross-hair sights. I did not then know that in shooting an elephant one would shoot to cut an imaginary bar running from ear-hole to ear-hole. I ought, therefore, as the elephant was sideways on, to have aimed straight at his ear-hole; actually I aimed several inches in front of this, thinking the brain would be further forward.

When I pulled the trigger I did not hear the bang or feel the kick—one   11
never does when a shot goes home—but I heard the devilish roar of glee

that went up from the crowd. In that instant, in too short a time, one would have thought, even for the bullet to get there, a mysterious, terrible change had come over the elephant. He neither stirred nor fell, but every line on his body had altered. He looked suddenly stricken, shrunken, immensely old, as though the frightful impact of the bullet had paralyzed him without knocking him down. At last, after what seemed a long time—it might have been five seconds, I dare say—he sagged flabbily to his knees. His mouth slobbered. An enormous senility seemed to have settled upon him. One could have imagined him thousands of years old. I fired again into the same spot. At the second shot he did not collapse but climbed with desperate slowness to his feet and stood weakly upright, with legs sagging and head drooping. I fired a third time. That was the shot that did for him. You could see the agony of it jolt his whole body and knock the last remnant of strength from his legs. But in falling he seemed for a moment to rise, for as his hind legs collapsed beneath him he seemed to tower upwards like a huge rock toppling, his trunk reaching skywards like a tree. He trumpeted, for the first and only time. And then down he came, his belly towards me, with a crash that seemed to shake the ground even where I lay.

I got up. The Burmans were already racing past me across the mud. 12
It was obvious that the elephant would never rise again, but he was not dead. He was breathing very rhythmically with long rattling gasps, his great mound of a side painfully rising and falling. His mouth was wide open—I could see far down into the caverns of pale pink throat. I waited a long time for him to die, but his breathing did not weaken. Finally, I fired my two remaining shots into the spot where I thought his heart must be. The thick blood welled out of him like red velvet, but still he did not die. His body did not even jerk when the shots hit him, the tortured breathing continued without a pause. He was dying, very slowly and in great agony, but in some world remote from me where not even a bullet could damage him further. I felt that I had got to put an end to that dreadful noise. It seemed dreadful to see the great beast lying there, powerless to move and yet powerless to die, and not even to be able to finish him. I sent back for my small rifle and poured shot after shot into his heart and down his throat. They seemed to make no impression. The tortured gasps continued as steadily as the ticking of a clock.

In the end I could not stand it any longer and went away. I heard later 13
that it took him half an hour to die. Burmans were bringing dahs* and baskets even before I left, and I was told they had stripped his body almost to the bones by the afternoon.

Afterwards, of course, there were endless discussions about the 14
shooting of the elephant. The owner was furious, but he was only an Indian and could do nothing. Besides, legally I had done the right thing, for a mad elephant has to be killed, like a mad dog, if its owner fails to

*EDS. NOTE—Heavy knives.

control it. Among the Europeans opinion was divided. The older men said I was right, the younger men said it was a damn shame to shoot an elephant for killing a coolie, because an elephant was worth more than any damn Coringhee coolie. And afterwards I was very glad that the coolie had been killed; it put me legally in the right and it gave me a sufficient pretext for shooting the elephant. I often wondered whether any of the others grasped that I had done it solely to avoid looking a fool.

• • •

COMPREHENSION

1. Why was Orwell "hated by large numbers of people" (1) in Burma? Why did he have mixed feelings toward the Burmese people?

2. Why did the local officials want something done about the elephant? Why did the crowd want Orwell to shoot the elephant?

3. Why did Orwell finally decide to kill the elephant? What made him hesitate at first?

4. Why does Orwell say at the end that he was glad the coolie had been killed?

PURPOSE AND AUDIENCE

1. One of Orwell's purposes in telling his story is to show how it gave him a glimpse of "the real nature of imperialism" (3). What does he mean? How does the story illustrate this purpose?

2. Do you think Orwell wrote this essay to inform or to persuade his audience? How did Orwell expect his audience to react to his ideas? How can you tell?

3. What is the essay's thesis?

STYLE AND STRUCTURE

1. What does Orwell's first paragraph accomplish? Where does the introduction end and the narrative itself begin?

2. The essay includes almost no dialogue. Why do you think Orwell's voice as narrator is the only one readers hear? Is the absence of dialogue a strength or a weakness? Explain.

3. Why do you think Orwell devotes so much attention to the elephant's misery (11–12)?

4. Orwell's essay includes a number of editorial comments, which appear within parentheses or dashes. How would you characterize these comments? Why are they set off from the text?

5. Consider the following passages: "Some of the people said that the elephant had gone in one direction, some said that he had gone in another . . ." (4); "Among the Europeans opinion was divided. The older men said I was

right, the younger men said it was a damn shame to shoot an elephant . . ."
(14). How do these comments reinforce the theme expressed in paragraph 2
("All I knew was that I was stuck between my hatred of the empire I served
and my rage against the evil-spirited little beasts . . .")? What other examples
reinforce this theme?

VOCABULARY PROJECTS

1. Define each of the following words as it is used in this selection.

baited (1)	despotic (3)	conjurer (7)
perplexing (2)	labyrinth (4)	dominion (7)
oppressors (2)	squalid (4)	magazine (9)
lockups (2)	professed (4)	cross-hair (10)
flogged (2)	ravaging (5)	remnant (11)
supplant (2)	miry (5)	trumpeted (11)
prostrate (2)	garish (7)	pretext (14)

2. Because Orwell is British, he frequently uses words or expressions that
an American writer would not be likely to use. Substitute a contemporary American word or phrase for each of the following, making sure it is
appropriate in Orwell's context.

raise a riot (1)	rubbish van (3)	a bit of fun (5)
rang me up (3)	inflicted violences (3)	I dare say (11)

What other expressions might need to be "translated" for a contemporary American audience?

JOURNAL ENTRY

Do you think Orwell is a coward? Do you think he is a racist? Explain your
feelings.

WRITING WORKSHOP

1. Orwell says that even though he hated British imperialism and sympa-
   thized with the Burmese people, he found himself a puppet of the system. Write a narrative essay about a time when you had to do something
   that went against your beliefs or convictions.

2. Orwell's experience taught him something not only about himself but
   also about something beyond himself—the way British imperialism
   worked. Write a narrative essay that reveals how an incident in your life
   taught you something about some larger social or political force as well
   as about yourself.

3. Write an objective, factual newspaper article recounting the events
   Orwell describes.

COMBINING THE PATTERNS

Implicit in this narrative essay is an extended **comparison and contrast** that highlights the differences between Orwell and the Burmese people. Review the essay, and list the most obvious differences Orwell perceives between himself and them. Do you think his perceptions are accurate? If all of the differences were set forth in a single paragraph, how might such a paragraph change your perception of Orwell's dilemma? Of his character?

THEMATIC CONNECTIONS

- "Thirty-Eight Who Saw Murder Didn't Call the Police" (page 86)
- "Just Walk On By" (page 186)
- "The Untouchable" (page 448)

SAKI (H. H. MUNRO)

Hector Hugh Munro, who took the pen name Saki, was born in 1870 in Akyab, Burma (now known as Myanmar), the son of an officer in the British military police. Following his mother's death when Munro was not yet two years old, he was sent to England to be raised by his aunts. In 1893 Munro himself joined the military police in Burma, but he was forced to leave after a year because of ill health. He then worked in London as a writer for the *Westminster Gazette,* the *Bystander,* the *Daily Express,* and the *Morning Post,* for which he was a foreign correspondent for six years in the Balkans, Russia, and Paris. Munro enlisted in the army at the beginning of World War I and was killed in November 1916 by a German sniper during a British attack on Beaumont-Hamel in France. Although he also wrote political sketches and plays, he is best known for his humorous, often cynical fiction, including the novel *The Unbearable Bassington* (1912) and the short stories collected in *The Westminster Alice* (1902), *Reginald in Russia* (1910), and *Beasts and Super-Beasts* (1914). In "The Open Window," from *Beasts and Super-Beasts,* Munro tells the story of a man's disturbing visit to the home of an excessively imaginative young girl.

The Open Window

"My aunt will be down presently, Mr. Nuttel," said a very self-possessed young lady of fifteen; "in the meantime you must try and put up with me." 1

Framton Nuttel endeavored to say the correct something which should duly flatter the niece of the moment without unduly discounting the aunt that was to come. Privately he doubted more than ever whether these formal visits on a succession of total strangers would do much towards helping the nerve cure which he was supposed to be undergoing. 2

"I know how it will be," his sister had said when he was preparing to migrate to this rural retreat; "you will bury yourself down there and not speak to a living soul, and your nerves will be worse than ever from moping. I shall just give you letters of introduction to all the people I know there. Some of them, as far as I can remember, were quite nice." 3

Framton wondered whether Mrs. Sappleton, the lady to whom he was presenting one of the letters of introduction, came into the nice division. 4

"Do you know many of the people round here?" asked the niece, when she judged that they had had sufficient silent communion. 5

"Hardly a soul," said Framton. "My sister was staying here, at the rectory, you know, some four years ago, and she gave me letters of introduction to some of the people here." 6

He made the last statement in a tone of distinct regret. 7

"Then you know practically nothing about my aunt?" pursued the self-possessed young lady. 8

"Only her name and address," admitted the caller. He was wondering whether Mrs. Sappleton was in the married or widowed state. An undefinable something about the room seemed to suggest masculine habitation.   9

"Her great tragedy happened just three years ago," said the child; "that would be since your sister's time."   10

"Her tragedy?" asked Framton; somehow in this restful country spot tragedies seemed out of place.   11

"You may wonder why we keep that window wide open on an October afternoon," said the niece, indicating a large French window that opened on to a lawn.   12

"It is quite warm for the time of the year," said Framton; "but has that window got anything to do with the tragedy?"   13

"Out through that window, three years ago to a day, her husband and her two young brothers went off for their day's shooting. They never came back. In crossing the moor to their favorite snipe-shooting ground they were all three engulfed in a treacherous piece of bog. It had been that dreadful wet summer, you know, and places that were safe in other years gave way suddenly without warning. Their bodies were never recovered. That was the dreadful part of it." Here the child's voice lost its self-possessed note and became falteringly human. "Poor aunt always thinks that they will come back, some day, they and the little brown spaniel that was lost with them, and walk in at that window just as they used to do. That is why the window is kept open every evening till it is quite dusk. Poor dear aunt, she has often told me how they went out, her husband with his white waterproof coat over his arm, and Ronnie, her youngest brother, singing, 'Bertie, why do you bound?' as he always did to tease her, because she said it got on her nerves. Do you know, sometimes on still, quiet evenings like this, I almost get a creepy feeling that they will all walk in through that window—"   14

She broke off with a little shudder. It was a relief to Framton when the aunt bustled into the room with a whirl of apologies for being late in making her appearance.   15

"I hope Vera has been amusing you?" she said.   16

"She has been very interesting," said Framton.   17

"I hope you don't mind the open window," said Mrs. Sappleton briskly; "my husband and brothers will be home directly from shooting, and they always come in this way. They've been out for snipe in the marshes today, so they'll make a fine mess over my poor carpets. So like you men-folk, isn't it?"   18

She rattled on cheerfully about the shooting and the scarcity of birds, and the prospects for duck in the winter. To Framton it was all purely horrible. He made a desperate but only partially successful effort to turn the talk on to a less ghastly topic; he was conscious that his hostess was giving him only a fragment of her attention, and her eyes were constantly straying past him to the open window and the lawn beyond. It was cer-   19 tainly an unfortunate coincidence that he should have paid his visit on this tragic anniversary.

"The doctors agree in ordering me complete rest, an absence of men- 20 tal excitement, and avoidance of anything in the nature of violent physical exercise," announced Framton, who labored under the tolerably wide-spread delusion that total strangers and chance acquaintances are hungry for the least detail of one's ailments and infirmities, their cause and cure. "On the matter of diet they are not so much in agreement," he continued.

"No?" said Mrs. Sappleton, in a voice which only replaced a yawn at 21 the last moment. Then she suddenly brightened into alert attention—but not to what Framton was saying.

"Here they are at last!" she cried. "Just in time for tea, and don't they 22 look as if they were muddy up to the eyes!"

Framton shivered slightly and turned towards the niece with a look 23 intended to convey sympathetic comprehension. The child was staring out through the open window with dazed horror in her eyes. In a chill shock of nameless fear Framton swung round in his seat and looked in the same direction.

In the deepening twilight three figures were walking across the lawn 24 towards the window; they all carried guns under their arms, and one of them was additionally burdened with a white coat hung over his shoulders. A tired brown spaniel kept close at their heels. Noiselessly they neared the house, and then a hoarse young voice chanted out of the dusk: "I said, Bertie, why do you bound?"

Framton grabbed wildly at his stick and hat; the hall-door, the gravel- 25 drive, and the front gate were dimly noted stages in his headlong retreat. A cyclist coming along the road had to run into the hedge to avoid imminent collision.

"Here we are, my dear," said the bearer of the white mackintosh, 26 coming in through the window; "fairly muddy, but most of it's dry. Who was that who bolted out as we came up?"

"A most extraordinary man, a Mr. Nuttel," said Mrs. Sappleton; 27 "could only talk about his illness, and dashed off without a word of good-bye or apology when you arrived. One would think he had seen a ghost."

"I expect it was the spaniel," said the niece calmly; "he told me he 28 had a horror of dogs. He was once hunted into a cemetery somewhere on the banks of the Ganges by a pack of pariah dogs, and had to spend the night in a newly dug grave with the creatures snarling and grinning and foaming just above him. Enough to make any one lose their nerve."

Romance at short notice was her specialty. 29

• • •

THINKING ABOUT LITERATURE

1. Why is it essential that the story Vera tells Mr. Nuttel be extremely detailed?

2. How does the dialogue included in "The Open Window" characterize Mrs. Sappleton, Nr. Nuttel, and Vera? Give specific examples to support your answer.

3. Why is each of these details important to "The Open Window"?
   a. Mr. Nuttel is recovering from a nervous breakdown.
   b. Mr. Nuttel knows almost nothing about Mrs. Sappleton.
   c. Vera is "a very self-possessed young lady" (1).
   d. The window is open.

   How would the story be different without each of these details?

JOURNAL ENTRY

Explain the meaning of the story's last line (29). In what sense does it serve as a thesis statement for the story? How would the story be different if this "thesis statement" appeared earlier?

THEMATIC CONNECTIONS

- "The Spider and the Wasp" (page 223)
- "The Ways We Lie" (page 414)

WRITING ASSIGNMENTS FOR NARRATION

1. Trace the path you expect to follow to establish yourself in your chosen profession, considering possible obstacles you may face and how you expect to deal with them. Include a thesis statement that conveys the importance of your goals. If you like, you may consult some essays elsewhere in this book that focus on work—for example, "The Peter Principle" (page 169), "On Fire" (page 235), or "The Men We Carry in Our Minds" (page 387).

2. Write a personal narrative in which you look back from some point in the far future on your own life as you hope it will be seen by others. Use third person if you like, and write your own obituary; or use first person, assessing your life in the form of a letter to your great-grandchildren.

3. Write a news article recounting in objective terms the events described in "My Mother Never Worked" or "Shooting an Elephant." Include a descriptive headline.

4. Write a historical narrative tracing the roots of your family or your hometown or community. Be sure to include the kinds of specific details—including dialogue and descriptions of people and places—used by Cisneros and Angelou.

5. Write an account of one of these "firsts": your first date; your first serious argument with your parents; your first experience with physical violence or danger; your first extended stay away from home; your first encounter with someone whose culture was very different from your own; your first experience with the serious illness or death of a close friend or relative. Make sure your essay includes a thesis statement that your narrative can support.

6. Both George Orwell and Martin Gansberg deal with the consequences of failing to act. Write an essay or story in which you recount what would have happened if Orwell had *not* shot the elephant or if one of the eyewitnesses *had* called the police right away.

7. Maya Angelou's "finishing school" was Mrs. Cullinan's kitchen. What institution served as your finishing school? What did you learn there, and how did this knowledge serve you later?

8. Write a short narrative summarizing a class, a short story, a television show, a conversation, a fable or fairy tale, or a narrative poem. Include as many details as you can.

9. Write a narrative about a time when you were an outsider, isolated because of social, intellectual, or ethnic differences between you and others. Did you resolve the problems your isolation created? Explain. If you like, you may refer to the Angelou or Orwell essays in this chapter or to "Just Walk On By" (page 186) or "Aria: A Memoir of a Bilingual Childhood" (page 357).

10. Imagine a meeting between any two characters in this chapter's reading selections. Using dialogue as well as narrative, write an account of this meeting.

COLLABORATIVE ACTIVITY FOR NARRATION

Working with a group of students of about your own age, write a history of your television-viewing habits. Start by working individually to list all your most-watched television shows in chronological order, beginning as far back as you can remember. Then compile a single list that reflects a consensus of the group's preferences, perhaps choosing one or two representative programs for each stage of your life (preschool, elementary school, and so on). Have a different student write a paragraph on each stage, describing the chosen programs in as much detail as possible. Finally, combine the individual paragraphs to create a narrative essay that traces the group's changing tastes in television shows. The essay's thesis statement should express what your group's television preferences reveal about your generation's development.

3

DESCRIPTION

WHAT IS DESCRIPTION?

You use **description** whenever you want to tell readers about the physical characteristics of a person, place, or thing. Description relies on the five senses—sight, hearing, taste, touch, and smell. In the following paragraph from "Knoxville: Summer 1915," James Agee uses sight, sound, and touch to recreate a scene for his audience:

Topic sentence	It is not of games children play in the evening that I want to speak now, it is of a contemporaneous atmosphere that has little to do with them; that of fathers and
Description using sight	families, each in his space of lawn, his shirt fishlike pale in the unnatural light and his face nearly anonymous, hosing their lawns. The hoses were attached to spigots that stood out of the brick foundations of the houses. The nozzles were variously set but usually so there was a
Description using touch	long sweet stream of spray, the nozzle wet in the hand, the water trickling the right forearm and the peeled-back cuff, and the water whishing out a long loose and low-
Description using sound	curved cone, and so gentle a sound. First an insane noise of violence in the nozzle, then the still irregular sound of adjustment, then the smoothing into steadiness and a pitch as accurately tuned to the size and style of stream as any violin. So many qualities of sound out of one hose: so many choral differences out of those several hoses that were in earshot. Out of any one hose, the almost dead silence of the release, and the short still arch of the separate big drops, silent as a held breath, and the only noise the flattering noise on leaves and the slapped grass at the fall of each big drop. That, and the intense hiss with the intense stream; that, and the same intensity not growing less but growing more quiet and delicate with the turn of the nozzle, up to that extreme tender whisper when the water was just a wide bell of film.

Before we make judgments about the world, before we compare or contrast or classify our experiences, we describe. Scientists describe their observations whenever they conduct experiments, and you use description whenever you write a paper. In a comparison-and-contrast essay, for example, you may describe the appearance of two cars to show that one is better designed than the other. In an argumentative essay, you may describe a fish kill in a local river to show that industrial waste dumping is a problem. Through description, you communicate your view of the world to your readers. If your readers come to understand or share your view, they are more likely to accept your observations, your judgments, and your conclusions. Therefore, in almost every essay you write, knowing how to write effective description is important.

A narrative essay presents a series of events; it tells a story. As was mentioned in Chapter 2, a good narrative may depend heavily on descriptive details. A narrative, however, always presents events in time, in some sort of chronological order, whereas a description presents things in spatial order.

A descriptive essay tells what something looks like or what it feels like, sounds like, smells like, or tastes like. Description often goes beyond personal sense impressions: novelists can create imaginary landscapes, historians can paint word pictures of historical figures, and scientists can describe physical phenomena they have never seen. When you write description, you use language to create a vivid impression for your readers.

Writers of descriptive essays often use an implied thesis when they describe a person, place, or thing. This technique allows them to convey an essay's **dominant impression**—the mood or quality that is emphasized in the piece of writing—subtly through the selection and arrangement of details. When they use description to support a particular point, however, many writers prefer to use an explicitly stated thesis. This strategy eliminates ambiguity by letting readers see immediately what point the writer is making—for example, "The sculptures that adorn Philadelphia's City Hall are a catalog of nineteenth-century artistic styles." Whether you state or imply your thesis, the details of your descriptive essay must work together to create a single dominant impression. In many cases your thesis may be just a statement of the dominant impression; sometimes, however, your thesis may go further and make a point about that dominant impression.

Objective and Subjective Descriptions

Descriptions can be *objective* or *subjective*. In an **objective description,** you focus on the object itself rather than on your personal reactions to it. Your purpose is to present a precise, literal picture of your subject. Many writing situations require exact descriptions of apparatus or conditions, and in these cases your goal is to construct an accurate and straightforward picture for your audience. A biologist describing what he sees through a microscope and a historian describing a Civil War battlefield would both write objectively. The biologist would not, for instance, say how exciting his observations were, nor would the historian say how disappointed she was at the outcome of the battle. Many newspaper reporters also try to achieve this impersonal objectivity, and so do writers of technical reports, scientific papers, and certain types of business correspondence. Still, objectivity is an ideal that writers strive for but never achieve. In fact, even by selecting some details and leaving out others, writers are making subjective decisions.

In the following descriptive passage, Thomas Marc Parrott aims for objectivity by giving his readers all the factual information they need to visualize Shakespeare's theater:

> When James Burbage built the Theatre in 1576 he naturally designed it along the lines of inn-yards in which he had been accustomed to play. The building had two entrances—one in front for the audience; one in the rear for actors, musicians, and the personnel of the theatre. Inside the building a rectangular platform projected far out into what was called "the yard"—we know the stage of the Fortune ran halfway across the "yard," some twenty-seven and a half feet.

Note that Parrott is not interested in responding to or evaluating the theater he describes. Instead, he chooses words that convey sizes, shapes, and distances, such as *two* and *rectangular*. Only one word in the paragraph—*naturally*—suggests an opinion.

In contrast to objective description, **subjective description** conveys your personal response to your subject and tries to get your readers to share it. Your subjective response is not necessarily expressed directly, through a straightforward statement of your opinion or perspective. Often it is revealed indirectly, through your choice of words and phrasing. If an English composition assignment asks you to describe a place that has special meaning to you, you could give a subjective reaction to your topic by selecting and emphasizing details that show your feelings about the place. For example, you could write a subjective description of your room by focusing on particular objects—your desk, your window, and your bookshelves—and explaining the meanings these things have for you. Thus, your desk could be a "warm brown rectangle of wood whose surface contains the scratched impressions of a thousand school assignments."

A subjective or impressionistic description should convey not just a literal record of sights and sounds but also their significance. For example, if you objectively described a fire, you might include its temperature, duration, and scope. In addition, you might describe, as accurately as possible, the fire's color, movement, and intensity. If you subjectively described the fire, however, you would include more than these factual observations. Through your choice of words, you would try to recreate for your audience a sense of how the fire made you feel: your reactions to the crackling noise, to the dense smoke, to the sudden destruction.

In the following passage, notice how Mark Twain subjectively describes a sunset on the Mississippi River:

> I still kept in mind a certain wonderful sunset which I witnessed when steamboating was new to me. A broad expanse of the river was turned to blood; in the middle distance the red hue brightened into gold, through which a solitary log came floating, black and conspicuous; in one place a long, slanting mark lay sparkling upon the water; in another the surface was broken by boiling, tumbling rings, that were as many-tinted as an opal.

In this passage, Twain conveys his strong emotional reaction to the sunset by using vivid, powerful images such as the river "turned to blood," the "solitary log . . . black and conspicuous," and the "boiling, tumbling rings." He also chooses words that convey great value, such as *gold* and *opal*.

Neither objective nor subjective description exists independently. Objective descriptions usually contain some subjective elements, and subjective descriptions need some objective elements to convey a sense of reality. The skillful writer adjusts the balance between objectivity and subjectivity to suit the topic, thesis, audience, purpose, and occasion of an essay.

Objective and Subjective Language

As the passages by Parrott and Twain illustrate, both objective and subjective descriptions depend on specific and concrete words to appeal to readers' senses. But these two types of description use different kinds of language. On the one hand, objective descriptions rely on precise, factual language that presents a writer's observations without conveying his or her attitude toward the subject. They use unambiguous words and phrases. Subjective descriptions, on the other hand, generally use richer or more suggestive language. They are more likely to rely on the **connotations** of words, their emotional associations, than on their **denotations,** or more direct meanings. They may deliberately provoke the reader's imagination with striking phrases or vivid comparisons. For example, a subjective description might compare the actions of a person at a party to those of a pet Siamese cat posturing and posing, thus evoking a lively image in the reader's mind.

Although both kinds of description may use comparisons, subjective descriptions tend to rely more on elaborate or imaginative comparisons than objective descriptions do. When you write subjective descriptions, you can compare two similar things, using the familiar parakeet to describe the unfamiliar cockatoo. Or you can find similarities between things that are dissimilar, such as a peacock and a person, and provide a fresh view of both. Such special comparisons fall under the heading of **figures of speech.** Three of the most common figures of speech are simile, metaphor, and personification.

A **simile** uses *like* or *as* to compare two dissimilar things. These comparisons occur frequently in everyday speech—for example, when someone claims to be "happy as a clam," "free as a bird," or "hungry as a bear." As a rule, however, you should avoid overused expressions like these in your writing. Effective writers constantly strive to use original similes. In his short story "A & P," for instance, John Updike uses a striking simile when he likens people going through the checkout aisle of a supermarket to balls dropping down a slot in a pinball machine.

A **metaphor** compares two dissimilar things without using *like* or *as.* Instead of saying that something is like something else, a metaphor says it *is* something else. Twain uses a metaphor when he says "A broad expanse of river was turned to blood."

Personification speaks of concepts or objects as if they were endowed with life or human characteristics. If you say that the wind whispered or that an engine died, you are using personification.

In addition to these figures of speech, writers of subjective descriptions also use allusions to enrich their writing. An **allusion** is a reference to a person, place, event, or quotation that the writer assumes readers will recognize. In "Letter from Birmingham Jail" (page 513), for example, Martin Luther King Jr. enhances his argument by alluding to biblical passages and proverbs with which he expects his audience of clergy to be familiar.

Your purpose and audience determine whether you should use predominantly objective or subjective description. An assignment that specifically asks for reactions calls for a subjective description. Legal, medical, technical, business, and scientific writing assignments, however, frequently require objective descriptions because their primary purpose is to give the audience factual information. (Even in these areas, of course, figures of speech may be used. Scientists often use such language to describe an unfamiliar object or concept to an audience. In their pioneering article on the structure of DNA, for example, James Watson and Francis Crick use a simile when they describe a molecule of DNA as looking like two spiral staircases winding around each other.)

Selection of Detail

Sometimes inexperienced writers pack their descriptions with empty words like *nice, great, terrific,* or *awful,* substituting their own reactions to an object for the qualities of the object itself. To produce an effective description, however, you must do more than just *say* something is wonderful—you must use details that evoke this response in your readers, as

Twain does with the sunset. (Twain does in fact use the word *wonderful* at the beginning of his description, but he then goes on to supply many concrete details that make the scene he describes vivid and specific.)

All good descriptive writing, whether objective or subjective, relies on specific details. Your aim is not simply to *tell* readers what something looks like but to *show* them. Every person, place, or thing has its special characteristics, and you should use your powers of observation to detect them. Then you need to select the concrete words that will convey your dominant impression, that will enable your readers to imagine what you describe. Don't be satisfied with "He looked angry" when you can say "His face flushed, and one corner of his mouth twitched as he tried to control his anger." What is the difference? In the first case, you simply identify the man's emotional state. In the second, you provide enough detail so that readers can tell not only that he was angry but also how he revealed the intensity of his anger.

Of course, you could have provided even more detail by describing the man's beard, or his wrinkles, or any number of other features. Keep in mind, however, that not all details are equally useful or desirable. You should take care to include only those that contribute to the dominant impression you wish to create. Thus, in describing a man's face to show how angry he was, you would probably not include the shape of his nose or the color of his hair. (After all, a person's hair color does not change when he or she gets angry.) In fact, the number of particulars you use is less important than their quality and appropriateness. You should select and use only those details relevant to your purpose.

Factors like the level, background, and knowledge of your audience also influence the kinds of details you include. For example, a description of a DNA molecule written for first-year college students would contain more basic details than a description written for junior biology majors. In addition, the more advanced description would contain details—the sequence of amino acid groups, for instance—that might be inappropriate for first-year students.

STRUCTURING A DESCRIPTIVE ESSAY

When you write a descriptive essay, you usually begin by writing down details in no particular order. You then arrange these details in a way that supports your thesis and communicates your dominant impression. As you consider how to arrange your details, you have a number of options. For example, you can move from a specific description of an object to a general description of other things around it. Or you can reverse this order, beginning with the general and proceeding to the specific. You can progress from the least important feature to the most important one. You can also move from the smallest to the largest item or from the least unusual to the most unusual detail. You can present the details of your description in a straightforward spatial order, moving from left to right or right to left, from top to bottom or bottom to top. Another option you have is to combine approaches, using different organizing schemes in different parts of the essay. The particular strategy you choose depends on the dominant impression you want to convey, your thesis, and your purpose and audience.

As you write, be sure to supply the transitional words and phrases that readers will need to follow your discussion. Throughout your description, and especially in the topic sentences of your body paragraphs, include words or phrases that indicate the spatial arrangement of details—for example, *at the top, in the middle,* and *at the bottom.*

Suppose your English composition instructor has asked you to write a short essay describing a person, place, or thing. After thinking about the assignment for a day or two, you decide to write an objective description of the Air and Space Museum in Washington, D.C., because you have visited it recently and many details are fresh in your mind. The museum is large and has many different exhibits, so you know you will not be able to describe them all. Therefore, you decide to concentrate on one, the heavier-than-air flight exhibit, and you choose as your topic the particular display that you remember most vividly: Charles Lindbergh's airplane, *The Spirit of St. Louis.* You begin by brainstorming to recall all the details you can. When you read over your notes, you realize that the organizing scheme of your essay could reflect your actual experience in the museum. You decide to present the details of the airplane in the order in which your eye took them in, from front to rear. The dominant impression you wish to create is how small and fragile *The Spirit of St. Louis* appears, and your thesis statement communicates this impression. An informal outline for your essay might look like this:

Introduction:	Thesis statement—It is startling that a plane as small as *The Spirit of St. Louis* could fly across the Atlantic.
Front of plane:	Single engine, tiny cockpit
Middle of plane:	Short wing span, extra gas tanks
Rear of plane:	Limited cargo space filled with more gas tanks
Conclusion:	Restatement of thesis or review of key points or details

▶ **STUDENT WRITERS: DESCRIPTION**

Each of the following student essays illustrates the principles of effective description. The first one, an objective description of the light microscope, by Joseph Tessari, was written for a scientific writing class. His assignment was to write a detailed, factual description of an instrument, mechanism, or piece of equipment used in his major field of study. The second essay, a subjective description of a place in Burma, was written by Mary Lim for her composition class. Her assignment was to write an essay about a place that has had a profound effect on her.

The Light Microscope

Introduction

The simple light microscope is a basic   1
tool for biologists. The function of the microscope is to view objects or biological
specimens that would otherwise be invisible to
the naked eye. Light microscopes come in a variety of shapes and sizes, with different degrees of magnification and complexity. Most
microscopes, however, are made of metal or
plastic (primarily metal) and stand approxi-

**Thesis
statement**

mately ten to thirteen inches tall. A description of the microscope's design illustrates
its function.

**Description of
stand**

A simple light microscope consists of sev-   2
eral integrated parts (see diagram). The
largest piece is the stand. The base of the
stand, which is wishbone-shaped, rests on the
tabletop. A vertical section approximately nine
inches tall extends out of the base and is
shaped like a question mark.

**Description
of optic tube**

At the end of the vertical piece of the   3
stand is the black metal optic tube, a vertical
cylinder approximately three to four inches
long. One entire side of this tube is attached
to the stand, so that the tube sits in front of
the stand when the microscope is viewed from
the front.

**Description of
eyepiece**

Directly on top of this tube is a cylin-   4
drical eyepiece. The eyepiece, slightly smaller
in diameter than the optic tube, is approximately two inches long. The top of the eyepiece
is fitted with a clear glass lens called the
fixed lens.

**Description of
coarse and fine
adjustment knobs**

On the stand, adjacent to the point where   5
it meets the optic tube, are two circular
coarse adjustment knobs--one on each side of the
microscope. When rotated, these knobs raise and
lower the optic tube, focusing the image being
viewed. Two fine adjustment knobs at the bottom

of the stand permit finer adjustments in focus.
These knobs are especially useful at high mag-
nifications, where smaller adjustments are
needed.

**Description of
objective
lenses**

Attached to the bottom of the optic tube   6
is a rotating disk that contains two small
silver objective lenses spaced one hundred
eighty degrees apart. These lenses have different magnification powers. When an objective lens is locked into place, the eyepiece,
optic tube, and objective lens fall in a vertical line.

**Description of
viewing stage**

Directly below the objective lens, at-   7
tached to the bend in the question mark of the
vertical stand, is the viewing stage, a square
horizontal plate with a small circular hole in
the center. This circular hole is approximately the same diameter as the objective lens
and falls along the same vertical line. On either side of the hole are metal clips that
hold a glass slide or a specimen plate in
place.

**Description of
mirror**

A few inches below the viewing stage is a   8
small circular mirror that can pivot around a
horizontal axis. It is attached to the stand by
a Y-shaped clamp. When the mirror is adjusted,
light is reflected up through the hole in the
viewing stage and into the objective lens,
optic tube, and eyepiece.

Conclusion

The simple light microscope has been an   9
extremely useful biological tool for many
years. It has helped scientists learn more
about human anatomy and physiology as well as a
number of diseases. With modern technology, new
and more complex instruments, such as the elec-
tron microscope, have been developed. Still,
the light microscope remains an important tool
for both students and serious
researchers.

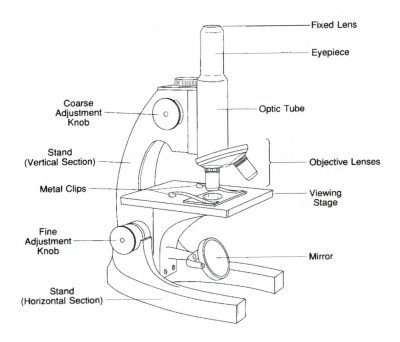

Fixed Lens

Eyepiece

Optic Tube

Coarse
Adjustment
Knob

Stand
(Vertical Section)

Objective Lenses

Metal Clips

Viewing
Stage

Fine
Adjustment
Knob

Mirror

Stand
(Horizontal Section)

Points for Special Attention

OBJECTIVE DESCRIPTION. Joseph Tessari, a toxicology major, wrote this paper as an exercise for a class in scientific writing. Because he is writing an objective description, he does not make subjective comments or point out the microscope's strengths and weaknesses; instead, he describes its physical features. Joseph's thesis statement emphasizes his purpose and conveys his straightforward intention to his readers.

OBJECTIVE LANGUAGE. Because his essay is written for a class in scientific writing, Joseph keeps his description technical. His factual, concrete language concentrates on the size, shape, and composition of each part of the microscope and on the physical relationship of each part to other parts and to the whole. Although he does not use subjective language, he does use several figures of speech to help his readers visualize what he is describing (the "wishbone-shaped base," for example).

STRUCTURE. Joseph chooses to describe the microscope piece by piece. He starts at the bottom of the microscope with its largest part—the stand. He next directs the reader's attention upward from the optic tube to the eyepiece and then downward past the coarse adjustment knobs to the bottom of the optic tube (where the objective lens is located) and down to the viewing stage and the mirror. In his introduction, Joseph comments on the microscope's purpose and general appearance; in his conclusion, he summarizes the microscope's historical significance and briefly considers its future.

SELECTION OF DETAIL.   Joseph's instructor defined his audience as a group of nonscientists. Joseph was told he could assume that his readers would know generally what a microscope looked like, but that he would have to describe the individual components in some detail.

DIAGRAM.   Joseph knew that describing the relationship among the parts of the microscope would not be easy. In fact, his initial attempts to do so produced sentences like "When viewed from the side, the objective lens makes a forty-five degree angle with the front of the optic tube and is higher in front of the microscope than in the back." In order to avoid complicated and tedious passages of description such as this, Joseph included a diagram. Not only does the diagram present the parts of the microscope in relationship to one another, but it also depicts certain parts—like the objective lenses—that are difficult to visualize. Notice that the diagram is clearly labeled.

Focus on Revision

The peer critics of Joseph's paper identified two areas that they thought needed work. One student said that some of Joseph's sentences were wordy. Another suggested that he delete some of the details he had included because his diagram made them unnecessary. As a result of these criticisms, Joseph decided to edit for wordiness and to eliminate phrases such as "Y-shaped clamp" and "a small circular mirror." Since readers can see these structures on the diagram, he doesn't need to describe them in precise detail.

Unlike "The Light Microscope," Mary Lim's essay uses subjective description so that readers can share, as well as understand, her experience.

The Valley of Windmills

Introduction   In my native country of Burma, strange   1
happenings and exotic scenery are not unusual.
For Burma is a mysterious land that in some
areas seems to have been ignored by time.
Mountains stand jutting their rocky peaks into
the clouds as they have for thousands of
years. Jungles are so dense with exotic vege-
tation that human beings or large animals cannot even enter. But one of the most fascinat-

Description (identifying the scene)

ing areas in Burma is the Valley of Windmills, nestled between the tall mountains near the fertile and beautiful city of Taungaleik. In this valley there is beautiful and breathtaking scenery, but there are also old, massive, and gloomy structures that can disturb a person deeply.

Description (moving toward the valley)

The road to Taungaleik twists out of the coastal flatlands into those heaps of slag, shale, and limestone that are the Tennesserim Mountains in the southern part of Burma. The air grows rarer and cooler, and stones become grayer, the highway a little more precarious at its edges, until, ahead, standing in ghostly sentinel across the lip of a pass, is a line of squat forms.

Description (immediate view)

They straddle the road and stand at intervals up hillsides on either side. Are they boulders? Are they fortifications? Are they broken wooden crosses on graves in an abandoned cemetery?

These dark figures are windmills standing in the misty atmosphere. They are immensely old and distinctly evil, some merely turrets, some with remnants of arms hanging derelict from their snouts, and most of them covered with dark green moss. Their decayed but still

Description (more distant view)

massive forms seem to turn and sneer at visitors. Down the pass on the other side is a circular green plateau that lies like an arena below, where there are still more windmills. Massed in the plain behind them, as far as the eye can see, in every field, above every hut, stand ten thousand iron windmills, silent and sailless. They seem to await only a call from a watchman to clank, whirr, flap, and groan into action. Visitors suddenly feel cold. Perhaps it is a sense of loneliness, the cool air, the desolation, or the weird-

2

3

```
ness of the arcane windmills--but something
chills them.
```
```
        As you stand at the lip of the valley,      4
contrasts rush as if to overwhelm you.
```

Conclusion

Description (windmills contrasted with city)

```
Beyond, glittering on the mountainside like a
solitary jewel, is Taungaleik in the territo-
ry once occupied by the Portuguese. Below, on
rolling hillsides, are the dark windmills,
still enveloped in morning mist. These
ancient windmills can remind you of the
impermanence of life and the mystery that
```

Thesis statement

```
still surrounds these hills. In a strange
way, the scene in the valley can disturb you,
but it also can give you an insight into the
contrasts that seem to define our lives here
in my country.
```

Points for Special Attention

SUBJECTIVE DESCRIPTION.   One of the first things her classmates noticed when they read Mary's essay was her use of vivid details. The road to Taungaleik is described in specific terms: it twists "out of the coastal flatlands" into the mountains, which are "heaps of slag, shale, and limestone." The iron windmills are decayed and stand "silent and sailless" on a green plateau that "lies like an arena." Through her use of detail, Mary creates her dominant impression of the Valley of Windmills as dark, mysterious, and disquieting. The point of her essay—the thesis—is stated in the last paragraph: the Valley of Windmills embodies the contrasts that characterize life in Burma.

SUBJECTIVE LANGUAGE.   By describing the windmills, Mary conveys the sense of foreboding she felt. When she first introduces them, she questions whether these "squat forms" are "boulders," "fortifications," or "broken wooden crosses," each of which has a menacing connotation. After telling readers what they are, she uses personification, describing the windmills as dark, evil, sneering figures with "arms hanging derelict." She sees them as ghostly sentinels awaiting "a call from a watchman" to spring into action. Through this figure of speech, Mary skillfully recreates the unearthly quality of the scene.

STRUCTURE.   Mary's purpose in writing this paper was to give her readers the sensation of actually being in the Valley of Windmills. She uses an organizing scheme that takes readers along the road to

Taungaleik, up into the Tennesserim Mountains, and finally to the pass where the windmills wait. From her perspective on the lip of the valley, she describes the details closest to her and then those farther away, as if following the movement of her eyes. She ends by bringing her readers back to the lip of the valley, contrasting Taungaleik "glittering on the mountainside" with the windmills "enveloped in morning mist." Through her description, she builds up to her thesis about the nature of life in her country. She withholds the explicit statement of her main point until her last paragraph, when readers have been fully prepared for it.

Focus on Revision

One of Mary's peer critics thought that the essay's thesis about life in Burma needed additional support. The student pointed out that although Mary's description is quite powerful, it does not really convey the contrasts she alludes to in her conclusion. Mary decided that adding another paragraph in which she discussed something about her life, perhaps her reasons for visiting the windmills, could help supply this missing information. She could, for example, tell her reader that right after her return from the valley, she found out that a friend had been accidentally shot by border guards, and that it was this event that caused her to characterize the windmills as she did. Such information would explain the somber mood of the passage and underscore the ideas presented in the conclusion.

The following selections illustrate various ways in which description can shape an essay. As you read them, pay particular attention to the differences between objective and subjective description.

LEAH HAGER COHEN

Although she is not deaf, Leah Hager Cohen (1967–   ) lived for much of her childhood at the Lexington School for the Deaf in Queens, New York, where her mother was a teacher and her father was an administrator. (Both her paternal grandparents were deaf.) Her strong identification with the deaf students at the school led her to see deafness as "not a pathology but a cultural identity." A graduate of the Columbia University School of Journalism, Cohen has been a writing instructor at Emerson College in Boston and an interpreter for deaf students in mainstream classes. In 1994 she published a book about deaf culture; its title, *Train Go Sorry,* is a translation of the American Sign Language symbols meaning "to miss the boat" or "to be left behind." Her latest book is *Glass, Paper, Beans: Revelations on the Nature and Value of Ordinary Things* (1997). In the following selection from *Train Go Sorry,* Cohen remembers her grandfather, Sam Cohen, whose parents had to hide their son's deafness from immigration officials when they passed through Ellis Island in the early 1900s. Once a student at the Lexington School, her grandfather provides Cohen with another connection to the deaf community.

Words Left Unspoken

My earliest memories of Sam Cohen are of his chin, which I remember as fiercely hard and pointy. Not pointy, my mother says, jutting; Grandpa had a strong, jutting chin. But against my very young face it felt like a chunk of honed granite swathed in stiff white bristles. Whenever we visited, he would lift us grandchildren up, most frequently by the elbows, and nuzzle our cheeks vigorously. This abrasive ritual greeting was our primary means of communication. In all my life, I never heard him speak a word I could understand.

Sometimes he used his voice to get our attention. It made a shapeless, gusty sound, like a pair of bellows sending up sparks and soot in a blacksmith shop. And he made sounds when he was eating, sounds that, originating from other quarters, would have drawn chiding or expulsion from the table. He smacked his lips and sucked his teeth; his chewing was moist and percussive; he released deep, hushed moans from the back of his throat, like a dreaming dog. And he burped out loud. Sometimes it was all Reba, Andy, and I could do not to catch one another's eyes and fall into giggles.

Our grandfather played games with us, the more physical the better. He loved that hand game: he would extend his, palms up, and we would hover ours, palms down, above his, and lower them, lower, lower, until they were just nesting, and *slap!* he'd have sandwiched one of our hands, trapping it between his. When we reversed, I could never even graze his, so fast would he snatch them away, like a big white fish.

121

He played three-card monte* with us, arranging the cards neatly be-   4
tween his long fingers, showing us once the jack of diamonds smirking,
red and gold, underneath. And then, with motions as swift and implausi-
ble as a Saturday morning cartoon chase, his hands darted and faked and
blurred and the cards lay still, face down and impassive. When we
guessed the jack's position correctly, it was only luck. When we guessed
wrong, he would laugh—a fond, gravelly sound—and pick up the cards
and begin again.

He mimicked the way I ate. He compressed his mouth into dainty   5
proportions as he nibbled air and carefully licked his lips and chewed
tiny, precise bites, his teeth clicking, his eyelashes batting as he gazed
shyly from under them. He could walk exactly like Charlie Chaplin and
make nickels disappear, just vanish, from both his fists and up his sleeves;
we never found them, no matter how we crawled over him, searching. All
of this without any words.

He and my grandmother lived in the Bronx, in the same apartment   6
my father and Uncle Max had grown up in. It was on Knox Place, near
Mosholu Parkway, a three-room apartment below street level. The
kitchen was a tight squeeze of a place, especially with my grandmother
bending over the oven, blocking the passage as she checked baked apples
or stuffed cabbage, my grandfather sitting with splayed knees at the
dinette. It was easy to get each other's attention in there; a stamped foot
sent vibrations clearly over the short distance, and an outstretched arm
had a good chance of connecting with the other party.

The living room was ampler and dimmer, with abundant floor and   7
table lamps to accommodate signed conversation. Little windows set up
high revealed the legs of passerby. And down below, burrowed in black
leather chairs in front of the television, we children learned to love physical comedy. Long before the days of closed captioning, we listened to our
grandfather laugh out loud at the snowy black-and-white antics of
Abbott and Costello, Laurel and Hardy, the Three Stooges.

During the time that I knew him, I saw his hairline shrink back and   8
his eyes grow remote behind pairs of progressively thicker glasses. His
athlete's bones shed some of their grace and nimbleness; they began curving in on themselves as he stood, arms folded across his sunken chest.
Even his long, thin smile seemed to recede deeper between his nose and
his prominent chin. But his hands remained lithe, vital. As he teased and
argued and chatted and joked, they were the instruments of his mind, the
conduits of his thoughts.

As far as anyone knows, Samuel Kolominsky was born deaf (according   9
to Lexington** records, his parents "failed to take note until child was about
one and a half years old"). His birthplace was Russia, somewhere near Kiev.
Lexington records say he was born in 1908; my grandmother says it was

---

*EDS. NOTE—A sleight-of-hand card game often played on urban streets, in which
the dealer gets onlookers to place bets that they can pick the jack of diamonds.
**EDS. NOTE—The Lexington School for the Deaf.

1907. He was a child when his family fled the czarist pogroms. Lexington records have him immigrating in 1913, at age five; my grandmother says he came to this country when he was three. Officials at Ellis Island altered the family name, writing down Cohen, but they did not detect his deafness, so Sam sailed on across the last ribbon of water to America.

His name-sign at home: *Daddy*. His name-sign with friends: the 10
thumb and index finger, perched just above the temple, rub against each other like grasshopper legs. One old friend attributes this to Sam's hair, which was blond and thick and wavy. Another says it derived from his habit of twisting a lock between his fingers.

Lexington records have him living variously at Clara, Moore, Siegel, 11
Tehema, and Thirty-eighth streets in Brooklyn and on Avenue C in Manhattan. I knew him on Knox Place, and much later on Thieriot Avenue, in the Bronx. Wherever he lived, he loved to walk, the neighborhoods revolving silently like pictures in a Kinetoscope,* unfurling themselves in full color around him.

Shortly before he died, when I was thirteen, we found ourselves walk- 12
ing home from a coffee shop together on a warm night. My family had spent the day visiting my grandparents at their apartment. My grandmother and the rest of the family were walking half a block ahead; I hung back and made myself take my grandfather's hand. We didn't look at each other. His hand was warm and dry. His gait was uneven then, a long slow beat on the right, catch-up on the left. I measured my steps to his. It was dark except for the hazy pink cones of light cast by streetlamps. I found his rhythm, and breathed in it. That was the longest conversation we ever had.

He died before I was really able to converse in sign. I have never seen 13
his handwriting. I once saw his teeth, in a glass, on the bathroom windowsill. Now everything seems like a clue.

• • •

COMPREHENSION

1. Why was Cohen's grandfather unable to speak? How did Cohen communicate with him?

2. What kind of relationship did Cohen have with her grandfather? Warm? Distant?

3. What is the significance of the essay's title? What does Cohen mean when she says, "That was the longest conversation we ever had" (12)?

4. In paragraph 13 Cohen says that now, after her grandfather's death, "everything seems like a clue." What does she mean?

5. What do you think the "words left unspoken" are? Is the speaker of these words Cohen, her grandfather, or both? Explain.

---

*EDS. NOTE—A device for viewing a sequence of moving pictures as it rotates over a light source, creating the illusion of motion.

PURPOSE AND AUDIENCE

1. Does "Words Left Unspoken" have an explicitly stated thesis? Why or why not?

2. What dominant impression is Cohen trying to create in this essay? How successful is she?

3. How much do you think Cohen expects her readers to know about deaf culture? How can you tell?

STYLE AND STRUCTURE

1. Why do you think Cohen begins with a description of her grandfather's chin?

2. What is the organizing principle of this essay? Would another organizing principle be more effective? Explain.

3. Are you able to picture Cohen's grandfather after reading her description? Do you think she expects you to?

4. Does Cohen develop her description fully enough? At what points could she have provided more detail?

5. What figures of speech does Cohen use in this essay? Where might additional figures of speech be helpful?

VOCABULARY PROJECTS

1. Define each of the following words as they are used in this selection.

   honed (1)   abundant (7)
   expulsion (2)   prominent (8)
   percussive (2)   lithe (8)
   smirking (4)   conduits (8)
   splayed (6)   gait (12)

2. Supply a synonym for each of the words listed above. In what way is each synonym different from the original word?

JOURNAL ENTRY

In what ways does Cohen's grandfather fit the traditional stereotype of a grandfather? In what ways does he not fit this stereotype?

WRITING WORKSHOP

1. Write a description of a person. Concentrate on one specific feature or quality that you associate with this person as Cohen does in her essay.

2. Choose three or four members of your family, and write a one-paragraph description of each. Combine these descriptions into a "family album" essay that has an introduction, a thesis statement, and a conclusion.

3. Write an essay in which you describe your earliest memories of a family member or close family friend. Before you write, decide on the dominant impression you want to convey.

COMBINING THE PATTERNS

Cohen uses **narration** to develop paragraph 9. Why does she include this narrative paragraph? Does it add to or detract from the dominant impression she is trying to convey? Explain.

THEMATIC CONNECTIONS

- "Only Daughter" (page 70)
- "The Way to Rainy Mountain" (page 136)
- "Mother Tongue" (page 393)

MARK TWAIN

Samuel L. Clemens (1835–1910), or Mark Twain, the pen name by which he is known, was born in Florida, Missouri, and raised in the river town of Hannibal, Missouri. He left school at the age of twelve and traveled extensively throughout the West, working as a riverboat pilot, a printer, and a newspaper reporter. When the Civil War broke out, Twain joined a volunteer company in the Confederate army but left after one week to become a prospector. After the war, he began a career as a humorist and writer, achieving great success as a lecturer. Among his most popular works are the novels *The Adventures of Tom Sawyer* (1876) and *The Adventures of Huckleberry Finn* (1885) and three autobiographical works: *Innocents Abroad* (1869), about his travels to Europe and the Holy Land; *Roughing It* (1872), about his life as a traveler and prospector in the Nevada territory and California; and *Life on the Mississippi* (1883), about his experiences as a riverboat pilot.

Reading the River

The face of the water, in time, became a wonderful book—a book that was a dead language to the uneducated passenger but which told its mind to me without reserve, delivering its most cherished secrets as clearly as if it uttered them with a voice. And it was not a book to be read once and thrown aside, for it had a new story to tell every day. Throughout the long twelve hundred miles there was never a page that was void of interest, never one that you could leave unread without loss, never one that you would want to skip, thinking you could find higher enjoyment in some other thing. There never was so wonderful a book written by man, never one whose interest was so absorbing, so unflagging, so sparklingly renewed with every reperusal. The passenger who could not read it was charmed with a peculiar sort of faint dimple on its surface (on the rare occasions when he did not overlook it altogether) but to the pilot that was an *italicized* passage; indeed it was more than that, it was a legend of the largest capitals with a string of shouting exclamation-points at the end of it, for it meant that a wreck or a rock was buried there that could tear the life out of the strongest vessel that ever floated. It is the faintest and simplest expression the water ever makes, and the most hideous to a pilot's eye. In truth, the passenger who could not read this book saw nothing but all manner of pretty pictures in it, painted by the sun and shaded by the clouds, whereas to the trained eye these were not pictures at all, but the grimmest and most dead-earnest of reading matter.

Now when I mastered the language of this water, and had come to know every trifling feature that bordered the great river as familiarly as I knew the letters of the alphabet, I had made a valuable acquisition. But I had lost something, too. I had lost something which could never be restored to me while I lived. All the grace, the beauty, the poetry, had gone out of the majestic river! I still kept in mind a certain wonderful sunset which I witnessed when steamboating was new to me. A broad expanse of the river was turned to blood; in the middle distance the red hue brightened into gold, through which a solitary log came floating, black and conspicuous; in one place a long, slanting mark lay sparkling upon the water; in another the surface was broken by boiling, tumbling rings, that were as many-tinted as an opal; where the ruddy flush was faintest, was a smooth spot that was covered with graceful circles and radiating lines, ever so delicately traced; the shore on our left was densely wooded, and the somber shadow that fell from this forest was broken in one place by a long, ruffled trail that shone like silver; and high above the forest wall a clean-stemmed dead tree waved a single leafy bough that glowed like a flame in the unobstructed splendor that was flowing from the sun. There were graceful curves, reflected images, woody heights, soft distances; and over the whole scene, far and near, the dissolving lights drifted steadily, enriching it every passing moment with new marvels of coloring.

I stood like one bewitched. I drank it in, in a speechless rapture. The world was new to me, and I had never seen anything like this at home. But as I have said, a day came when I began to cease from noting the glories and the charms which the moon and the sun and the twilight wrought upon the river's face; another day came when I ceased altogether to note them. Then, if that sunset scene had been repeated, I should have looked upon it without rapture, and should have commented upon it, inwardly, after this fashion: "This sun means that we are going to have wind tomorrow; that floating log means that the river is rising, small thanks to it; that slanting mark on the water refers to a bluff reef which is going to kill somebody's steamboat one of these nights, if it keeps on stretching out like that; those tumbling 'boils' show a dissolving bar and a changing channel there; the lines and circles in the slick water over yonder are a warning that that troublesome place is shoaling up dangerously; that silver streak in the shadow of the forest is the 'break' from a new snag, and he has located himself in the very best place he could have found to fish for steamboats; that tall dead tree, with a single living branch, is not going to last long, and then how is a body ever going to get through this blind place at night without the friendly old landmark?"

No, the romance and beauty were all gone from the river. All the value any feature of it had for me now was the amount of usefulness it could furnish toward compassing the safe piloting of a steamboat. Since those days, I have pitied doctors from my heart. What does the lovely flush in a beauty's cheek mean to a doctor but a "break" that ripples above some deadly disease? Are not all her visible charms sown thick with what are to him the signs and symbols of hidden decay? Does he ever see her beauty at all, or doesn't he simply view her professionally and comment upon her unwholesome condition all to himself? And doesn't he sometimes wonder whether he has gained most or lost most by learning his trade?

• • •

COMPREHENSION

1. How is the Mississippi River like a book?

2. When a passenger sees a dimple in the water's surface, what does a steamboat pilot see?

3. What did Twain gain as he became a skilled pilot? What did he lose?

4. Why does Twain say, in his conclusion, that he feels sorry for doctors? What do doctors and riverboat pilots have in common?

PURPOSE AND AUDIENCE

1. State Twain's thesis in your own words.

2. Is Twain writing primarily for an audience of pilots or of passengers? Explain your conclusion.

3. What is Twain's attitude toward passengers? Toward pilots?

STYLE AND STRUCTURE

1. In the first lines of the selection, Twain compares the Mississippi River to a book. Trace this metaphor and the variations of it (other references to language, punctuation, or reading) throughout the selection. Are the comparisons between the river and the book effective? Explain.

2. How does Twain arrange the details in his description? What other organizational scheme could he have used? What are the advantages and disadvantages of this other scheme?

3. Why does Twain include the description of the sunset in paragraph 2? Would this description have the same effect if it were briefer? Why or why not?

4. Where does Twain restate his thesis? Do you think this restatement is necessary? Why or why not?

5. Why does Twain end his essay with observations about doctors? Why do you suppose he feels the need to include these comments?

VOCABULARY PROJECTS

1. Define each of the following words as it is used in this selection.

unflagging (1)	conspicuous (2)	somber (2)
reperusal (1)	opal (2)	rapture (3)
italicized (1)	ruddy (2)	wrought (3)
trifling (2)	radiating (2)	

2. Make a list of the adjectives Twain uses to describe the river. What dominant impression do you think Twain seeks to convey with these adjectives? Is he successful? Explain.

3. What other adjectives could you substitute for the ones Twain uses? What are the advantages and disadvantages of your choices?

JOURNAL ENTRY

Do you agree with Twain's point that acquiring knowledge necessarily results in a loss of appreciation for beauty? What examples from your own experience illustrate the opposite point—that is, that knowledge increases the appreciation of beauty?

WRITING WORKSHOP

1. Write a subjective description of a scene you remember from your childhood. In your thesis statement and in your conclusion, explain how your adult impressions of the scene differ from those of your childhood.

2. Write an essay in which you show how increased knowledge of a subject actually increased your enthusiasm for it.

3. Think of a situation in which you were once a "passenger" but are now a "pilot." Write an essay in which you describe how becoming a pilot changed your perceptions of events. You may want to consult "How the Lawyers Stole Winter" (page 345) to get ideas for your essay.

COMBINING THE PATTERNS

In addition to containing a great deal of description, this essay also **compares and contrasts** two ways of reading the river. What points about each view of the river does Twain compare? What other points might he have included?

THEMATIC CONNECTIONS

- "Shooting an Elephant" (page 91)
- "Once More to the Lake" (page 142)
- "How the Lawyers Stole Winter" (page 345)

ANNIE DILLARD

Born in Pittsburgh, Pennsylvania, in 1945, Annie Dillard attended Hollins College in Virginia's rural Roanoke Valley. There she kept a journal in which she recorded her observations of nature and wildlife; these journal entries served as the basis for her first, highly acclaimed essay collection, *Pilgrim at Tinker Creek* (1974), which won the Pulitzer Prize for nonfiction. A second essay collection, *Teaching a Stone to Talk* (1982), was preceded by the brief, intensely contemplative *Holy the Firm* (1977), a meditation on the universe and the mysteries of the human spirit. Later works include a memoir, *An American Childhood* (1987); an examination of the creative act of writing, *A Writer's Life* (1989); a historical novel, *The Living* (1992), set in the Pacific Northwest around Puget Sound, where Dillard now lives; and a collection of poems, *Mornings Like This: Found Poems* (1996). "In the Jungle" (from *Teaching a Stone to Talk*) is an essay about her visit to a remote village in the Ecuadorian rain forest. This essay is typical of Dillard's work: closely observed, lyrically descriptive, and imbued with the sense of wonder Dillard finds in seemingly insignificant things.

In the Jungle

Like any out-of-the-way place, the Napo River in the Ecuadorian jungle seems real enough when you are there, even central. Out of the way of *what?* I was sitting on a stump at the edge of a bankside palm-thatch village, in the middle of the night, on the headwaters of the Amazon. Out of the way of human life, tenderness, or the glance of heaven? 1

A nightjar in deep-leaved shadow called three long notes, and hushed. The men with me talked softly in clumps: three North Americans, four Ecuadorians who were showing us the jungle. We were holding cool drinks and idly watching a hand-sized tarantula seize moths that came to the lone bulb on the generator shed beside us. 2

It was February, the middle of summer. Green fireflies spattered lights across the air and illumined for seconds, now here, now there, the pale trunks of enormous, solitary trees. Beneath us the brown Napo River was rising, in all silence; it coiled up the sandy bank and tangled its foam in vines that trailed from the forest and roots that looped the shore. 3

Each breath of night smelled sweet, more moistened and sweet than any kitchen, or garden, or cradle. Each star in Orion seemed to tremble and stir with my breath. All at once, in the thatch house across the clearing behind us, one of the village's Jesuit priests began playing an alto recorder, playing a wordless song, lyric, in a minor key, that twined over the village clearing, that caught in the big trees' canopies, muted our talk on the bankside, and wandered over the river, dissolving downstream. 4

This will do, I thought. This will do, for a weekend, or a season, or a home. 5

Later that night I loosed my hair from its braids and combed it   6
smooth—not for myself, but so the village girls could play with it in the
morning.

We had disembarked at the village that afternoon, and I had slumped   7
on some shaded steps, wishing I knew some Spanish or some Quechua*
so I could speak with the ring of little girls who were alternately staring at
me and smiling at their toes. I spoke anyway, and fooled with my hair,
which they were obviously dying to get their hands on, and laughed, and
soon they were all braiding my hair, all five of them, all fifty fingers, all
my hair, even my bangs. And then they took it apart and did it again,
laughing, and teaching me Spanish nouns, and meeting my eyes and each
other's with open delight, while their small brothers in blue jeans climbed
down from the trees and began kicking a volleyball around with one of
the North American men.

Now, as I combed my hair in the little tent, another of the men, a free-   8
lance writer from Manhattan, was talking quietly. He was telling us the
tale of his life, describing his work in Hollywood, his apartment in
Manhattan, his house in Paris. . . . "It makes me wonder," he said, "what
I'm doing in a tent under a tree in the village of Pompeya, on the Napo
River, in the jungle of Ecuador." After a pause he added, "It makes me
wonder why I'm going *back*."

The point of going somewhere like the Napo River in Ecuador is not   9
to see the most spectacular anything. It is simply to see what is there. We
are here on the planet only once, and might as well get a feel for the place.
We might as well get a feel for the fringes and hollows in which life is
lived, for the Amazon basin, which covers half a continent, and for the life
that—there, like anywhere else—is always and necessarily lived in detail:
on the tributaries, in the riverside villages, sucking this particular white-
fleshed guava in this particular pattern of shade.

What is there is interesting. The Napo River itself is wide (I mean   10
wider than the Mississippi at Davenport) and brown, opaque, and
smeared with floating foam and logs and branches from the jungle.
White egrets hunch on shoreline deadfalls and parrots in flocks dart in
and out of the light. Under the water in the river, unseen, are anacon-
das**—which are reputed to take a few village toddlers every year—
and water boas, stingrays, crocodiles, manatees, and sweet-meated fish.

Low water bares gray strips of sandbar on which the natives build   11
tiny palm-thatch shelters, arched, the size of pup tents, for overnight fishing trips. You see these extraordinarily clean people (who bathe twice a
day in the river, and whose straight black hair is always freshly washed)
paddling down the river in dugout canoes, hugging the banks.

---

*EDS. NOTE—Language spoken by native peoples of South America.
**EDS. NOTE—Large constricting snake of the boa family.

Some of the Indians of this region, earlier in the century, used to sleep   12
naked in hammocks. The nights are cold. Gordon MacCreach, an
American explorer in these Amazon tributaries, reported that he was startled to hear the Indians get up at three in the morning. He was always
more startled, night after night, to hear them walk down to the river
slowly, half asleep, and bathe in the water. Only later did he learn what
they were doing: they were getting warm. The cold woke them; they
warmed their skins in the river, which was always ninety degrees; then
they returned to their hammocks and slept through the rest of the night.

The riverbanks are low, and from the river you see an unbroken wall   13
of dark forest in every direction, from the Andes to the Atlantic. You get a
taste for looking at trees: trees hung with the swinging nests of yellow
troupials,* trees from which ant nests the size of grain sacks hang like
black goiters, trees from which seven-colored tanagers flutter, coral trees,
teak, balsa and breadfruit, enormous emergent silk-cotton trees, and the
pale-barked *samona* palms.

When you are inside the jungle, away from the river, the trees vault out   14
of sight. It is hard to remember to look up the long trunks and see the fans,
strips, fronds, and sprays of glossy leaves. Inside the jungle you are more
likely to notice the snarl of climbers and creepers round the trees' boles,**
the flowering bromeliads and epiphytes in every bough's crook, and the
fantastic silk-cotton tree trunks thirty or forty feet across, trunks buttressed
in flanges of wood whose curves can make the three high walls of a room—
a shady, loamy-aired room where you would gladly live, or die. Butterflies,
iridescent blue, striped, or clear-winged, thread the jungle paths at eye
level. And at your feet is a swath of ants bearing triangular bits of green
leaf. The ants with their leaves look like a wide fleet of sailing dinghies—
but they don't quit. In either direction they wobble over the jungle floor as
far as the eye can see. I followed them off the path as far as I dared, and
never saw an end to ants or to those luffing chips of green they bore.

Unseen in the jungle, but present, are tapirs, jaguars, many species of   15
snake and lizard, ocelots, armadillos, marmosets, howler monkeys, toucans
and macaws and a hundred other birds, deer, bats, peccaries, capybaras,
agoutis, and sloths. Also present in this jungle, but variously distant, are
Texaco derricks and pipelines, and some of the wildest Indians in the world,
blowgun-using Indians, who killed missionaries in 1956 and ate them.

Long lakes shine in the jungle. We traveled one of these in dugout ca-   16
noes, canoes with two inches of freeboard, canoes paddled with machete-
hewn oars chopped from buttresses of silk-cotton trees, or poled in the
shallows with peeled cane or bamboo. Our part-Indian guide had cleared
the path to the lake the day before; when we walked the path we saw
where he had impaled the lopped head of a boa, open-mouthed, on a
pointed stick by the canoes, for decoration.

---

*EDS. NOTE—A species of large bird.
**EDS. NOTE—Trunks.

This lake was wonderful. Herons, egrets, and ibises plodded the saw-   17
grass shores, kingfishers and cuckoos clattered from sunlight to shade,
great turkeylike birds fussed in dead branches, and hawks lolled overhead. There was all the time in the world. A turtle slid into the water. The
boy in the bow of my canoe slapped stones at birds with a simple sling, a
rubber thong and leather pad. He aimed brilliantly at moving targets, always, and always missed; the birds were out of range. He stuffed his
sling back in his shirt. I looked around.

The lake and river waters are as opaque as rain-forest leaves; they   18
are veils, blinds, painted screens. You see things only by their effects. I
saw the shoreline water roil and the sawgrass heave above a thrashing
paichi, an enormous black fish of these waters; one had been caught the
previous week weighing 430 pounds. Piranha fish live in the lakes, and
electric eels. I dangled my fingers in the water, figuring it would be
worth it.

We would eat chicken that night in the village, and rice, yucca,   19
onions, beets, and heaps of fruit. The sun would ring down, pulling darkness after it like a curtain. Twilight is short, and the unseen birds of twilight wistful, uncanny, catching the heart. The two nuns in their dazzling
white habits—the beautiful-boned young nun and the warm-faced old—
would glide to the open cane-and-thatch schoolroom in darkness, and
start the children singing. The children would sing in piping Spanish,
high-pitched and pure; they would sing "Nearer My God to Thee" in
Quechua, very fast. (To reciprocate, we sang for them "Old MacDonald
Had a Farm"; I thought they might recognize the animal sounds. Of
course they thought we were out of our minds.) As the children became
excited by their own singing, they left their log benches and swarmed
around the nuns, hopping, smiling at us, everyone smiling, the nuns'
faces bursting in their cowls, and the clear-voiced children still singing,
and the palm-leafed roofing stirred.

The Napo River: it is not out of the way. It is *in* the way, catching sun-   20
light the way a cup catches poured water; it is a bowl of sweet air, a basin
of greenness, and of grace, and, it would seem, of peace.

•　•　•

COMPREHENSION

1. How does Dillard define an "out-of-the-way place" (1)? Does she consider the Napo River an out-of-the-way place? Explain.

2. Why does Dillard loosen her hair? How does her doing so help her communicate with the village girls?

3. What does Dillard find interesting about the Napo River? Why is she there?

4. How at home in the jungle are the Europeans and Americans? What do
   they find in the jungle that they cannot find at home?

5. Does Dillard see the jungle as a place "of peace" (20) or a place of danger? Explain.

PURPOSE AND AUDIENCE

1. What is Dillard's purpose in writing this essay? To instruct? To entertain? To persuade? Or does she have some other purpose?

2. What dominant impression does Dillard try to convey? Is she successful? Why or why not?

3. Does this essay have an explicit thesis? In your own words, summarize this thesis.

4. Is Dillard's essay an objective or a subjective description? What are the advantages and disadvantages of her choice?

STYLE AND STRUCTURE

1. This essay is divided into three distinct sections. What does each section discuss, and how do the sections fit together?

2. Paragraphs 14 through 18 develop a detailed description of the jungle. What does Dillard accomplish by including such a description?

3. Dillard concludes her essay with a description of schoolchildren singing. Why does she do this? What point is she trying to make?

VOCABULARY PROJECTS

1. Define each of the following words as it is used in this selection.

thatch (1)	vault (14)
solitary (3)	fronds (14)
alto (4)	iridescent (14)
muted (4)	luffing (14)
basin (9)	derricks (15)
tributaries (9)	hewn (16)
opaque (10)	impaled (16)
reputed (10)	lolled (17)
goiters (13)	wistful (19)
emergent (13)	uncanny (19)

2. Throughout this essay, Dillard uses colorful and specific adjectives to describe the Napo River. Underline ten of these adjectives and try to substitute other ones that convey the same impression. What conclusion can you draw about Dillard's use of descriptive adjectives?

JOURNAL ENTRY

What do you think Dillard learns by visiting the Napo River? What does the man described in paragraph 8 learn?

WRITING WORKSHOP

1. Write an essay in which you describe an out-of-the-way place. Be sure to describe the qualities that make the place out of the way.

2. Elsewhere, Dillard calls herself a "stalker" of nature who delights in the wonders and terrors it inspires. Taking the point of view of such a stalker, write a descriptive essay that conveys the mysteries and delights of a place you have visited.

3. Write a descriptive essay about a place that you go to when you want to escape from your everyday life. What is this place like? What attracts you to it? In what ways does visiting this place help you return to your normal routine?

COMBINING THE PATTERNS

What pattern structures paragraph 19? What does this particular pattern contribute to the essay?

THEMATIC CONNECTIONS

- "Shooting an Elephant" (page 91)
- "The Spider and the Wasp" (page 223)
- "The Park" (page 604)

N. SCOTT MOMADAY

N. Scott Momaday was born in 1934 in Lawton, Oklahoma, of Kiowa ancestry. He graduated from the University of New Mexico in 1958 and received a doctorate from Stanford University in 1963. He has taught English at the University of California campuses at Santa Barbara and Berkeley as well as at Stanford, and he currently teaches at the University of Arizona. In 1969 Momaday won a Pulitzer Prize for his first novel, *House Made of Dawn* (1968). His second book, The *Way to Rainy Mountain* (1969), is a collection of Kiowa legends and folk tales. *The Names: A Memoir* (1976) describes a personal quest for a Native American identity. Momaday's poetry collections include *Angle of Geese and Other Poems* (1974) and *The Gourd Dancer* (1976). His most recent books are *In the Presence of the Sun: Stories and Poems, 1961–1991* (1992); *Circle of Water: A Native American Christmas Story* (1994); and *The Man Made of Words: Essays, Stories, Passages* (1997). In addition to writing poetry and prose, Momaday is an accomplished artist. The following essay is excerpted from the introduction to *The Way to Rainy Mountain,* in which Momaday traces the migration of the Kiowas to Oklahoma.

The Way to Rainy Mountain

A single knoll rises out of the plain in Oklahoma, north and west of the [1] Wichita Range. For my people, the Kiowas, it is an old landmark, and they gave it the name Rainy Mountain. The hardest weather in the world is there. Winter brings blizzards, hot tornadic winds arise in the spring, and in summer the prairie is an anvil's edge. The grass turns brittle and brown, and it cracks beneath your feet. There are green belts along the rivers and creeks, linear groves of hickory and pecan, willow and witch hazel. At a distance in July or August the steaming foliage seems almost to writhe in fire. Great green-and-yellow grasshoppers are everywhere in the tall grass, popping up like corn to sting the flesh, and tortoises crawl about on the red earth, going nowhere in the plenty of time. Loneliness is an aspect of the land. All things in the plain are isolate; there is no confusion of objects in the eye, but *one* hill or *one* tree or *one* man. To look upon that landscape in the early morning, with the sun at your back, is to lose the sense of proportion. Your imagination comes to life, and this, you think, is where Creation was begun.

I returned to Rainy Mountain in July. My grandmother had died in [2] the spring, and I wanted to be at her grave. She had lived to be very old and at last infirm. Her only living daughter was with her when she died, and I was told that in death her face was that of a child.

I like to think of her as a child. When she was born, the Kiowas were [3] living that last great moment of their history. For more than a hundred years they had controlled the open range from the Smoky Hill River to the

Red, from the headwaters of the Canadian to the fork of the Arkansas and Cimarron. In alliance with the Comanches, they had ruled the whole of the southern Plains. War was their sacred business, and they were among the finest horsemen the world has ever known. But warfare for the Kiowas was preeminently a matter of disposition rather than of survival, and they never understood the grim, unrelenting advance of the U.S. Cavalry. When at last, divided and ill-provisioned, they were driven onto the Staked Plains in the cold rains of autumn, they fell into panic. In Palo Duro Canyon they abandoned their crucial stores to pillage and had nothing then but their lives. In order to save themselves, they surrendered to the soldiers at Fort Sill and were imprisoned in the old stone corral that now stands as a military museum. My grandmother was spared the humiliation of those high gray walls by eight or ten years, but she must have known from birth the affliction of defeat, the dark brooding of old warriors.

Her name was Aho, and she belonged to the last culture to evolve in   4
North America. Her forebears came down from the high country in western Montana nearly three centuries ago. They were a mountain people, a mysterious tribe of hunters whose language has never been positively classified in any major group. In the late seventeenth century they began a long migration to the south and east. It was a long journey toward the dawn, and it led to a golden age. Along the way the Kiowas were befriended by the Crows, who gave them the culture and religion of the Plains. They acquired horses, and their ancient nomadic spirit was suddenly free of the ground. They acquired Tai-me, the sacred Sun Dance doll, from that moment the object and symbol of their worship, and so shared in the divinity of the sun. Not least, they acquired the sense of destiny, therefore courage and pride. When they entered upon the southern Plains, they had been transformed. No longer were they slaves to the simple necessity of survival; they were a lordly and dangerous society of fighters and thieves, hunters and priests of the sun. According to their origin myth, they entered the world through a hollow log. From one point of view, their migration was the fruit of an old prophecy, for indeed they emerged from a sunless world.

Although my grandmother lived out her long life in the shadow of   5
Rainy Mountain, the immense landscape of the continental interior lay like memory in her blood. She could tell of the Crows, whom she had never seen, and of the Black Hills, where she had never been. I wanted to see in reality what she had seen more perfectly in the mind's eye, and traveled fifteen hundred miles to begin my pilgrimage.

Yellowstone, it seemed to me, was the top of the world, a region of   6
deep lakes and dark timber, canyons and waterfalls. But, beautiful as it is, one might have the sense of confinement there. The skyline in all directions is close at hand, the high wall of the woods and deep cleavages of shade. There is a perfect freedom in the mountains, but it belongs to the eagle and the elk, the badger and the bear. The Kiowas reckoned their stature by the distance they could see, and they were bent and blind in the wilderness.

Descending eastward, the highland meadows are a stairway to the   7
plain. In July the inland slope of the Rockies is luxuriant with flax and
buckwheat, stonecrop and larkspur. The earth unfolds and the limit of
the land recedes. Clusters of trees and animals grazing far in the distance
cause the vision to reach away and wonder to build upon the mind. The
sun follows a longer course in the day, and the sky is immense beyond
all comparison. The great billowing clouds that sail upon it are shadows
that move upon the grain like water, dividing light. Farther down, in the
land of the Crows and Blackfeet, the plain is yellow. Sweet clover takes
hold of the hills and bends upon itself to cover and seal the soil. There
the Kiowas paused on their way; they had come to the place where they
must change their lives. The sun is at home in the plains. Precisely there
does it have the certain character of a god. When the Kiowas came to the
land of the Crows, they could see the dark lees of the hills at dawn across
the Bighorn River, the profusion of light on the grain shelves, the oldest
deity ranging after the solstices. Not yet would they veer southward to
the caldron of the land that lay below; they must wean their blood from
the northern winter and hold the mountains a while longer in their view.
They bore Tai-me in procession to the east.

A dark mist lay over the Black Hills, and the land was like iron. At the   8
top of a ridge I caught sight of Devil's Tower upthrust against the gray
sky as if in the birth of time the core of the earth had broken through its
crust and the motion of the world was begun. There are things in nature
that engender an awful quiet in the heart of man; Devil's Tower is one of
them. Two centuries ago, because they could not do otherwise, the
Kiowas made a legend at the base of the rock. My grandmother said:

> "Eight children were there at play, seven sisters and their brother.
> Suddenly the boy was struck dumb; he trembled and began to run upon
> his hands and feet. His fingers became claws, and his body was covered
> with fur. Directly there was a bear where the boy had been. The sisters
> were terrified; they ran, and the bear after them. They came to the stump
> of a great tree, and the tree spoke to them. It bade them climb upon it,
> and as they did so, it began to rise into the air. The bear came to kill them,
> but they were just beyond its reach. It reared against the tree and scored
> the bark all around with its claws. The seven sisters were borne into the
> sky, and they became the stars of the Big Dipper."

From that moment, and so long as the legend lives, the Kiowas have
kinsmen in the night sky. Whatever they were in the mountains, they
could be no more. However tenuous their well-being, however much
they had suffered and would suffer again, they had found a way out of
the wilderness.

My grandmother had a reverence for the sun, a holy regard that now   9
is all but gone out of mankind. There was a wariness in her, and an ancient awe. She was a Christian in her later years, but she had come a long
way about, and she never forgot her birthright. As a child she had been to

the Sun Dances; she had taken part in those annual rites, and by them she had learned the restoration of her people in the presence of Tai-me. She was about seven when the last Kiowa Sun Dance was held in 1887 on the Washita River above Rainy Mountain Creek. The buffalo were gone. In order to consummate the ancient sacrifice—to impale the head of a buffalo bull upon the medicine tree—a delegation of old men journeyed into Texas, there to beg and barter for an animal from the Goodnight herd. She was ten when the Kiowas came together for the last time as a living Sun Dance culture. They could find no buffalo; they had to hang an old hide from the sacred tree. Before the dance could begin, a company of soldiers rode out from Fort Sill under orders to disperse the tribe. Forbidden without cause the essential act of their faith, having seen the wild herds slaughtered and left to rot upon the ground, the Kiowas backed away forever from the medicine tree. That was July 20, 1890, at the great bend of the Washita. My grandmother was there. Without bitterness, and for as long as she lived, she bore a vision of deicide.

Now that I can have her only in memory, I see my grandmother in the several postures that were peculiar to her: standing at the wood stove on a winter morning and turning meat in a great iron skillet; sitting at the south window, bent above her beadwork, and afterwards, when her vision had failed, looking down for a long time into the fold of her hands; going out upon a cane, very slowly as she did when the weight of age came upon her; praying. I remember her most often at prayer. She made long, rambling prayers out of suffering and hope, having seen many things. I was never sure that I had the right to hear, so exclusive were they of all mere custom and company. The last time I saw her she prayed standing by the side of her bed at night, naked to the waist, the light of a kerosene lamp moving upon her dark skin. Her long, black hair, always drawn and braided in the day, lay upon her shoulders and against her breasts like a shawl. I do not speak Kiowa, and I never understood her prayers, but there was something inherently sad in the sound, some merest hesitation upon the syllables of sorrow. She began in a high and descending pitch, exhausting her breath to silence; then again and again—and always the same intensity of effort, of something that is, and is not, like urgency in the human voice. Transported so in the dancing light among the shadows of her room, she seemed beyond the reach of time. But that was illusion; I think I knew that I should not see her again.

• • •

COMPREHENSION

1. What is the significance of the essay's title?

2. What does Momaday mean when he says that his grandmother was born when the Kiowas were living the "last great moment of their history" (3)?

3. How did meeting the Crows change the Kiowas (4)?

4. What effect did the soldiers have on the religion of the Kiowas?

5. What significance does Momaday's grandmother have for him?

PURPOSE AND AUDIENCE

1. Is Momaday writing only to express emotions, or does he have other purposes as well? Explain.

2. What assumptions does Momaday make about his audience? What elements of the essay lead you to your conclusion?

3. Why do you think Momaday includes the legend of Devil's Tower in his essay?

STYLE AND STRUCTURE

1. Why do you think Momaday begins his essay with a description of Rainy Mountain?

2. What determines the order in which Momaday arranges details in his description of his grandmother?

3. Why do you think Momaday ends his essay with a description of his grandmother praying?

4. Momaday includes many passages that describe landscapes. What do these descriptions add to readers' understanding of Momaday's grandmother?

VOCABULARY PROJECTS

1. Define each of the following words as it is used in this selection.

infirm (2)	billowing (7)	consummate (9)
preeminently (3)	profusion (7)	impale (9)
nomadic (4)	engender (8)	deicide (9)
luxuriant (7)	tenuous (8)	inherently (10)

2. Find three examples of figurative language in the essay. How do these examples help Momaday convey his impressions to his readers?

JOURNAL ENTRY

Which people in your family connect you to your ethnic or cultural heritage? How do they do so?

WRITING WORKSHOP

1. Write an essay describing a grandparent or any other older person who has had a great influence on you. Make sure that you include background information as well as a detailed physical description.

2. Describe a place that has played an important part in your life. Include a narrative passage that conveys the significance of the place to your readers.

3. Describe a ritual—such as a wedding or a confirmation—that you have witnessed or participated in.

COMBINING THE PATTERNS

Momaday weaves passages of **narration** throughout this descriptive essay. Bracket the narrative passages that Momaday uses in this essay, and explain how each one helps him describe his grandmother.

THEMATIC CONNECTIONS

- "Only Daughter" (page 70)
- "My Mother Never Worked" (page 81)
- "Aria: A Memoir of a Bilingual Childhood" (page 357)

E. B. WHITE

Elwyn Brooks White (1899–1985) was born in Mount Vernon, New York, and graduated from Cornell University in 1921. He joined the newly founded *New Yorker* in 1925 and was associated with the magazine until his death. In 1937 White moved to a farm in North Brooklin, Maine, and began a monthly column for *Harper's Magazine* entitled "One Man's Meat," which revealed a more serious side to his writing than had been evident in the earlier *New Yorker* pieces. His numerous writings are collected in several volumes, including *Every Day Is Saturday* (1934), *Quo Vadimus?* (1939), *One Man's Meat* (1944), *The Second Tree from the Corner* (1954), *The Points of My Compass* (1962), *Letters* (1976), *Essays of E. B. White* (1977), and *Poems and Sketches of E. B. White* (1981). His published books also include the children's classics *Stuart Little* (1945) and *Charlotte's Web* (1952). In 1959, White revised a grammar handbook by William Strunk, a professor of English at Cornell, that he had used as a student; this handbook, *The Elements of Style*, remains a national best-seller. "Once More to the Lake" (1941), reprinted from *One Man's Meat*, is a classic essay of personal reminiscence. Using precise detail and vivid language, White recreates the lakeside camp he visited with his son.

Once More to the Lake

One summer, along about 1904, my father rented a camp on a lake in Maine and took us all there for the month of August. We all got ringworm from some kittens and had to rub Pond's Extract on our arms and legs night and morning, and my father rolled over in a canoe with all his clothes on; but outside of that the vacation was a success and from then on none of us ever thought there was any place in the world like that lake in Maine. We returned summer after summer—always on August 1st for one month. I have since become a salt-water man, but sometimes in summer there are days when the restlessness of the tides and the fearful cold of the sea water and the incessant wind which blows across the afternoon and into the evening make me wish for the placidity of a lake in the woods. A few weeks ago this feeling got so strong I bought myself a couple of bass hooks and a spinner and returned to the lake where we used to go, for a week's fishing and to revisit old haunts.

I took along my son, who had never had any fresh water up his nose and who had seen lily pads only from train windows. On the journey over to the lake I began to wonder what it would be like. I wondered how time would have marred this unique, this holy spot—the coves and streams, the hills that the sun set behind, the camps and the paths behind the camps. I was sure that the tarred road would have found it out and I wondered in what other ways it would be desolated. It is strange how much you can remember about places like that once you allow your mind to return into the grooves which lead back. You remember one thing, and that suddenly reminds you of another thing. I guess I remembered clearest of all the early mornings, when the lake was cool and motionless, re-membered how the bedroom smelled of the lumber it was made of and the wet woods whose scent entered through the screen. The partitions in the camp were thin and did not extend clear to the top of the rooms, and as I was always the first up I would dress softly so as not to wake the oth-ers, and sneak out into the sweet outdoors and start out in the canoe, keeping close along the shore in the long shadows of the pines. I remem-bered being very careful never to rub my paddle against the gunwale for fear of disturbing the stillness of the cathedral.

The lake had never been what you would call a wild lake. There were 3 cottages sprinkled around the shores, and it was in farming country al-though the shores of the lake were quite heavily wooded. Some of the cot-tages were owned by nearby farmers, and you would live at the shore and eat your meals at the farmhouse. That's what our family did. But al-though it wasn't wild, it was a fairly large and undisturbed lake and there were places in it which, to a child at least, seemed infinitely remote and primeval.

I was right about the tar: it led to within half a mile of the shore. But 4 when I got back there, with my boy, and we settled into a camp near a farmhouse and into the kind of summertime I had known, I could tell that it was going to be pretty much the same as it had been before—I knew it, lying in bed the first morning, smelling the bedroom, and hearing the boy sneak quietly out and go off along the shore in a boat. I began to sustain the illusion that he was I, and therefore, by simple transposition, that I was my father. This sensation persisted, kept cropping up all the time we were there. It was not an entirely new feeling, but in this setting it grew much stronger. I seemed to be living a dual existence. I would be in the middle of some simple act, I would be picking up a bait box or laying down a table fork, or I would be saying something, and suddenly it would be not I but my father who was saying the words or making the gesture. It gave me a creepy sensation.

We went fishing the first morning. I felt the same damp moss cover- 5 ing the worms in the bait can, and saw the dragonfly alight on the tip of my rod as it hovered a few inches from the surface of the water. It was the arrival of this fly that convinced me beyond any doubt that everything was as it always had been, that the years were a mirage and there had been no years. The small waves were the same, chucking the rowboat under the chin as we fished at anchor, and the boat was the same boat, the same color green and the ribs broken in the same places, and under the floor-boards the same freshwater leavings and débris—the dead hel-gramite,* the wisps of moss, the rusty discarded fishhook, the dried blood from yesterday's catch. We stared silently at the tips of our rods, at the dragonflies that came and went. I lowered the tip of mine into the water, tentatively, pensively dislodging the fly, which darted two feet away,

*EDS. NOTE—An insect larva often used as bait.

poised, darted two feet back, and came to rest again a little farther up the rod. There had been no years between the ducking of this dragonfly and the other one—the one that was part of memory. I looked at the boy, who was silently watching his fly, and it was my hands that held his rod, my eyes watching. I felt dizzy and didn't know which rod I was at the end of.

We caught two bass, hauling them in briskly as though they were   6
mackerel, pulling them over the side of the boat in a businesslike manner without any landing net, and stunning them with a blow on the back of the head. When we got back for a swim before lunch, the lake was exactly where we had left it, the same number of inches from the dock, and there was only the merest suggestion of a breeze. This seemed an utterly enchanted sea, this lake you could leave to its own devices for a few hours and come back to, and find that it had not stirred, this constant and trustworthy body of water. In the shallows, the dark, water-soaked sticks and twigs, smooth and old, were undulating in clusters on the bottom against the clean ribbed sand, and the track of the mussel was plain. A school of minnows swam by, each minnow with its small individual shadow, doubling the attendance, so clear and sharp in the sunlight. Some of the other campers were in swimming, along the shore, one of them with a cake of soap, and the water felt thin and clear and unsubstantial. Over the years there had been this person with the cake of soap, this cultist, and here he was. There had been no years.

Up to the farmhouse to dinner through the teeming, dusty field, the   7
road under our sneakers was only a two-track road. The middle track was missing, the one with the marks of the hooves and the splotches of dried, flaky manure. There had always been three tracks to choose from in choosing which track to walk in; now the choice was narrowed down to two. For a moment I missed terribly the middle alternative. But the way led past the tennis court, and something about the way it lay there in the sun reassured me; the tape had loosened along the backline, the alleys were green with plantains and other weeds, and the net (installed in June and removed in September) sagged in the dry noon, and the whole place steamed with midday heat and hunger and emptiness. There was a choice of pie for dessert, and one was blueberry and one was apple, and the waitresses were the same country girls, there having been no passage of time, only the illusion of it as in a dropped curtain—the waitresses were still fifteen; their hair had been washed, that was the only difference—they had been to the movies and seen the pretty girls with the clean hair.

Summertime, oh summertime, pattern of life indelible, the fade-proof   8
lake, the woods unshatterable, the pasture with the sweetfern and the juniper forever and ever, summer without end; this was the background, and the life along the shore was the design, the cottages with their innocent and tranquil design, their tiny docks with the flagpole and the American flag floating against the white clouds in the blue sky, the little paths over the roots of the trees leading from camp to camp and the paths

leading back to the outhouses and the can of lime for sprinkling, and at the souvenir counters at the store the miniature birch-bark canoes and the post cards that showed things looking a little better than they looked. This was the American family at play, escaping the city heat, wondering whether the newcomers in the camp at the head of the cove were "common" or "nice," wondering whether it was true that the people who drove up for Sunday dinner at the farmhouse were turned away because there wasn't enough chicken.

It seemed to me, as I kept remembering all this, that those times and   9 those summers had been infinitely precious and worth saving. There had been jollity and peace and goodness. The arriving (at the beginning of August) had been so big a business in itself, at the railway station the farm wagon drawn up, the first smell of the pineladen air, the first glimpse of the smiling farmer, and the great importance of the trunks and your father's enormous authority in such matters, and the feel of the wagon under you for the long ten-mile haul, and at the top of the last long hill catching the first view of the lake after eleven months of not seeing this cherished body of water. The shouts and cries of the other campers when they saw you, and the trunks to be unpacked, to give up their rich burden. (Arriving was less exciting nowadays, when you sneaked up in your car and parked it under a tree near the camp and took out the bags and in five minutes it was all over, no fuss, no loud wonderful fuss about trunks.)

Peace and goodness and jollity. The only thing that was wrong now,   10 really, was the sound of the place, an unfamiliar nervous sound of the outboard motors. This was the note that jarred, the one thing that would sometimes break the illusion and set the years moving. In those other summertimes all motors were inboard; and when they were at a little distance, the noise they made was a sedative, an ingredient of summer sleep. They were one-cylinder and two-cylinder engines, and some were make-and-break and some were jump-spark, but they all made a sleepy sound across the lake. The one-lungers throbbed and fluttered, and the twin-cylinder ones purred and purred, and that was a quiet sound too. But now the campers all had outboards. In the daytime, in the hot mornings, these motors made a petulant, irritable sound; at night, in the still evening when the afterglow lit the water, they whined about one's ears like mosquitoes. My boy loved our rented outboard, and his great desire was to achieve singlehanded mastery over it, and authority, and he soon learned the trick of choking it a little (but not too much), and the adjustment of the needle valve. Watching him I would remember the things you could do with the old one-cylinder engine with the heavy flywheel, how you could have it eating out of your hand if you got really close to it spiritually. Motor boats in those days didn't have clutches, and you would make a landing by shutting off the motor at the proper time and coasting in with a dead rudder. But there was a way of reversing them, if you learned the trick, by cutting the switch and putting it on again exactly on the final dying revolution of the flywheel, so that it would kick back against compression and begin reversing. Approaching a dock in a strong following breeze, it was difficult to slow up sufficiently by the ordinary coasting method, and if a boy felt he had complete mastery over his motor, he was tempted to keep it running beyond its time and then reverse it a few feet from the dock. It took a cool nerve, because if you threw the switch a twentieth of a second too soon you could catch the flywheel when it still had speed enough to go up past center, and the boat would leap ahead, charging bull-fashion at the dock.

We had a good week at the camp. The bass were biting well and the sun shone endlessly, day after day. We would be tired at night and lie down in the accumulated heat of the little bedrooms after the long hot day and the breeze would stir almost imperceptibly outside and the smell of the swamp drift in through the rusty screens. Sleep would come easily and in the morning the red squirrel would be on the roof, tapping out his gay routine. I kept remembering everything, lying in bed in the mornings—the small steamboat that had a long rounded stern like the lip of a Ubangi,* how quietly she ran on the moonlight sails, when the older boys played their mandolins and the girls sang and we ate doughnuts dipped in sugar, and how sweet the music was on the water in the shining night, and what it had felt like to think about girls then. After breakfast we would go up to the store and the things were in the same place—the minnows in a bottle, the plugs and spinners disarranged and pawed over by the youngsters from the boys' camp, the fig newtons and the Beeman's gum. Outside, the road was tarred and cars stood in front of the store. Inside, all was just as it had always been, except there was more Coca-Cola and not so much Moxie** and root beer and birch beer and sarsaparilla.*** We would walk out with a bottle of pop apiece and sometimes the pop would backfire up our noses and hurt. We explored the streams, quietly, where the turtles slid off the sunny logs and dug their way into the soft bottom; and we lay on the town wharf and fed worms to the tame bass. Everywhere we went I had trouble making out which was I, the one walking at my side, the one walking in my pants.   11

One afternoon while we were there at that lake a thunderstorm came up. It was like the revival of an old melodrama that I had seen long ago with childish awe. The second-act climax of the drama of the electrical disturbance over a lake in America had not changed in any important respect. This was the big scene, still the big scene. The whole thing was so familiar, the first feeling of oppression and heat and a general air around camp of not wanting to go very far away. In midafternoon (it was all the same) a curious darkening of the sky, and a lull in everything that had made life tick; and then the way the boats suddenly swung the other way   12

---

*EDS. NOTE—An African tribe whose members wear mouth ornaments that stretch their lips into a saucerlike shape.

**EDS. NOTE—A soft drink that at one time was very popular.

***EDS. NOTE—A sweetened carbonated beverage flavored with birch oil and sassafras.

at their moorings with the coming of a breeze out of the new quarter, and the premonitory rumble. Then the kettle drum, then the snare, then the bass drum and cymbals, then crackling light against the dark, and the gods grinning and licking their chops in the hills. Afterward the calm, the rain steadily rustling in the calm lake, the return of light and hope and spirits, and the campers running out in joy and relief to go swimming in the rain, their bright cries perpetuating the deathless joke about how they were getting simply drenched, and the children screaming with delight at the new sensation of bathing in the rain, and the joke about getting drenched linking the generations in a strong indestructible chain. And the comedian who waded in carrying an umbrella.

When the others went swimming my son said he was going in too. He   13
pulled his dripping trunks from the line where they had hung all through the shower, and wrung them out. Languidly, and with no thought of going in, I watched him, his hard little body, skinny and bare, saw him wince slightly as he pulled up around his vitals the small, soggy, icy garment. As he buckled the swollen belt suddenly my groin felt the chill of death.

•   •   •

COMPREHENSION

1. In what ways are the writer and his son alike? In what ways are they different? What does White mean when he says, "I seemed to be living a dual existence" (4)?

2. In paragraph 5 White says there seemed to be "no years" between past and present; elsewhere, he senses that things are different. How do you account for these conflicting feelings?

3. Why does White feel disconcerted when he discovers that the road to the farmhouse has two tracks, not three? What do you make of his comment that "now the choice was narrowed down to two" (7)?

4. In what way does sound "break the illusion and set the years moving" (10)?

5. To what is White referring in the last sentence?

PURPOSE AND AUDIENCE

1. What is the thesis of this essay? Is it stated or implied?

2. Do you think White expects the ending of his essay to be a surprise to his audience? Explain.

3. To what age group do you think this essay would appeal most? Why?

STYLE AND STRUCTURE

1. At what points in the essay does White describe the changes that have taken place on the lake? Does White emphasize these changes or play them down? Explain.

2. What ideas and images does White repeat throughout his essay? What is the purpose of this repetition?

3. White goes to great lengths to describe how things look, feel, smell, taste, and sound. How does this help him achieve his purpose in this essay?

4. In what way does White's conclusion refer to the first paragraph of the essay?

VOCABULARY PROJECTS

1. Define each of the following words as it is used in this selection.

placidity (1)	pensively (5)	melodrama (12)
gunwale (2)	jollity (9)	premonitory (12)
primeval (3)	petulant (10)	perpetuating (12)
transposition (4)	imperceptibly (11)	languidly (13)

2. Underline ten words in the essay that refer to one of the five senses. Make a list of synonyms you could use for these words. How close do your substitutions come to capturing White's meaning?

JOURNAL ENTRY

Do you identify more with the father or the son in this essay? Explain why you feel the way you do.

WRITING WORKSHOP

1. Write a description of a scene you remember from your childhood. In your essay, discuss how your current view of the scene differs from the view you had when you were a child.

2. Assume you are a travel agent. Write a descriptive brochure designed to bring tourists to the lake. Be specific, and stress the benefits White mentions in his essay.

3. Write an essay in which you describe yourself from the perspective of one of your parents. Make sure your description conveys both the qualities your parent likes and the qualities he or she would want to change.

COMBINING THE PATTERNS

White opens his essay with a short narrative about his trip to the lake in 1904. How does this use of **narration** provide a context for the entire essay?

THEMATIC CONNECTIONS

- "Only Daughter" (page 70)
- "It's Just Too Late" (page 294)
- "How the Lawyers Stole Winter" (page 345)
- "The Men We Carry in Our Minds" (page 387)

KATHERINE ANNE PORTER

Katherine Anne Porter (1890–1980) was born in Indian Creek, Texas, where she was raised by her paternal grandmother after her mother's death in 1892 and educated in convent schools. Porter worked on newspapers in Texas, Denver, and Chicago before and during World War I and lived for extended periods in Mexico and Europe; later, she did some screenwriting for MGM. She also lectured widely, gave public readings of her work, and succeeded William Faulkner as writer in residence at the University of Virginia in 1958. Her short story collections are *Flowering Judas and Other Stories* (1930); *Pale Horse, Pale Rider* (1939); and *The Leaning Tower and Other Stories* (1944); Porter also published a selection of her reviews, essays, and translations in *The Days Before* (1952), and she wrote one novel, *Ship of Fools* (1962). Her *Collected Stories* were published in 1965. In "The Grave," published in *The Leaning Tower,* Porter describes a childish afternoon of rabbit hunting that brings death close enough to be seen and understood.

The Grave

The grandfather, dead more than thirty years, had been twice dis- 1
turbed in his long repose by the constancy and possessiveness of his widow. She removed his bones first to Louisiana and then to Texas as if she had set out to find her own burial place, knowing well she would never return to the places she had left. In Texas she set up a small cemetery in a corner of her first farm, and as the family connection grew, the oddments of relations came over from Kentucky to settle, it contained at last about twenty graves. After the grandmother's death, part of her land was to be sold for the benefit of certain of her children, and the cemetery happened to lie in the part set aside for sale. It was necessary to take up the bodies and bury them again in the family plot in the big new public cemetery, where the grandmother had been buried. At last her husband was to lie beside her for eternity, as she had planned.

The family cemetery had been a pleasant small neglected garden of 2
tangled rose bushes and ragged cedar trees and cypress, the simple flat stones rising out of uncropped sweet-smelling wild grass. The graves were lying open and empty one burning day when Miranda and her brother Paul, who often went together to hunt rabbits and doves, propped their twenty-two Winchester rifles carefully against the rail fence, climbed over and explored among the graves. She was nine years old and he was twelve.

They peered into the pits all shaped alike with such purposeful accu- 3
racy, and looking at each other with pleased adventurous eyes, they said in solemn tones: "These were graves!" trying by words to shape a special, suitable emotion in their minds, but they felt nothing except an agreeable thrill of wonder: they were seeing a new sight, doing something they had not done before. In them both there was also a small disappointment at the entire commonplaceness of the actual spectacle. Even if it had once con-

tained a coffin for years upon years, when the coffin was gone a grave was just a hole in the ground. Miranda leaped into the pit that had held her grandfather's bones. Scratching around aimlessly and pleasurably as any young animal, she scooped up a lump of earth and weighed it in her palm. It had a pleasantly sweet, corrupt smell, being mixed with cedar needles and small leaves, and as the crumbs fell apart, she saw a silver dove no larger than a hazel nut, with spread wings and a neat fan-shaped tail. The breast had a deep round hollow in it. Turning it up to the fierce sunlight, she saw that the inside of the hollow was cut in little whorls. She scrambled out, over the pile of loose earth that had fallen back into one end of the grave, calling to Paul that she found something, he must guess what. . . . His head appeared smiling over the rim of another grave. He waved a closed hand at her. "I've got something too!" They ran to compare treasures, making a game of it, so many guesses each, all wrong, and a final showdown with opened palms. Paul had found a thin wide gold ring carved with intricate flowers and leaves. Miranda was smitten at sight of the ring and wished to have it. Paul seemed more impressed by the dove. They made a trade, with some little bickering. After he had the dove in his hand, Paul said, "Don't you know what this is? This is a screw head for a *coffin!* . . . I'll bet nobody else in the world has one like this!"

Miranda glanced at it without covetousness. She had the gold ring on   4
her thumb; it fitted perfectly. "Maybe we ought to go now," she said, "maybe one of the niggers'll see us and tell somebody." They knew the land had been sold, the cemetery was no longer theirs, and they felt like trespassers. They climbed back over the fence, slung their rifles loosely under their arms—they had been shooting at targets with various kinds of firearms since they were seven years old—and set out to look for the rabbits and doves or whatever small game might happen along. On these expeditions Miranda always followed at Paul's heels along the path, obeying instructions about handling her gun when going through fences; learning how to stand it up properly so it would not slip and fire unexpectedly; how to wait her time for a shot and not just bang away in the air without looking, spoiling shots for Paul, who really could hit things if given a chance. Now and then, in her excitement at seeing birds whizz up suddenly before her face, or a rabbit leap across her very toes, she lost her head, and almost without sighting she flung her rifle up and pulled the trigger. She hardly ever hit any sort of mark. She had no proper sense of hunting at all. Her brother would be often completely disgusted with her. "You don't care whether you get your bird or not," he said. "That's no way to hunt." Miranda could not understand his indignation. She had seen him smash his hat and yell with fury when he had missed his aim. "What I like about shooting," said Miranda, with exasperating inconsequence, "is pulling the trigger and hearing the noise."

"Then, by golly," said Paul, "whyn't you go back to the range and   5
shoot at bulls-eyes?"

"I'd just as soon," said Miranda, "only like this, we walk around   6
more."

"Well, you just stay behind and stop spoiling my shots," said Paul,   7
who, when he made a kill, wanted to be certain he had made it. Miranda,
who alone brought down a bird once in twenty rounds, always claimed
as her own any game they got when they fired at the same moment. It
was tiresome and unfair and her brother was sick of it.

"Now, the first dove we see, or the first rabbit, is mine," he told her.   8
"And the next will be yours. Remember that and don't get smarty."

"What about snakes?" asked Miranda idly. "Can I have the first   9
snake?"

Waving her thumb gently and watching her gold ring glitter,   10
Miranda lost interest in shooting. She was wearing her summer roughing
outfit: dark blue overalls, a light blue shirt, a hired-man's straw hat, and
thick brown sandals. Her brother had the same outfit except his was a
sober hickory-nut color. Ordinarily Miranda preferred her overalls to any
other dress, though it was making rather a scandal in the countryside, for
the year was 1903, and in the back country the law of female decorum
had teeth in it. Her father had been criticized for letting his girls dress like
boys and go careering around astride barebacked horses. Big sister Maria,
the really independent and fearless one, in spite of her rather affected
ways, rode at a dead run with only a rope knotted around her horse's
nose. It was said the motherless family was running down, with the
Grandmother no longer there to hold it together. It was known that she
had discriminated against her son Harry in her will, and that he was in
straits about money. Some of his old neighbors reflected with vicious satisfaction that now he would probably not be so stiff-necked, nor have any
more high-stepping horses either. Miranda knew this, though she could
not say how. She had met along the road old women of the kind who
smoked corn-cob pipes, who had treated her grandmother with most sincere respect. They slanted their gummy old eyes side-ways at the grand-
daughter and said, "Ain't you ashamed of yoself, Missy? It's aginst the
Scriptures to dress like that. Whut yo Pappy thinkin about?" Miranda,
with her powerful social sense, which was like a fine set of antennae radiating from every pore of her skin, would feel shamed because she knew
well it was rude and ill-bred to shock anybody, even bad-tempered old
crones, though she had faith in her father's judgment and was perfectly
comfortable in the clothes. Her father had said, "They're just what you
need, and they'll save your dresses for school. . . ." This sounded quite
simple and natural to her. She had been brought up in rigorous economy.
Wastefulness was vulgar. It was also a sin. These were truths; she had
heard them repeated many times and never once disputed.

Now the ring, shining with the serene purity of fine gold on her   11
rather grubby thumb, turned her feelings against her overalls and sock-
less feet, toes sticking through the thick brown leather straps. She wanted
to go back to the farmhouse, take a good cold bath, dust herself with
plenty of Maria's violet talcum powder—provided Maria was not present
to object, of course—put on the thinnest, most becoming dress she
owned, with a big sash, and sit in a wicker chair under the trees. . . . These

things were not all she wanted, of course; she had vague stirrings of desire for luxury and a grand way of living which could not take precise form in her imagination but were founded on family legend of past wealth and leisure. These immediate comforts were what she could have, and she wanted them at once. She lagged rather far behind Paul, and once she thought of just turning back without a word and going home. She stopped, thinking that Paul would never do that to her, and so she would have to tell him. When a rabbit leaped, she let Paul have it without dispute. He killed it with one shot.

When she came up with him, he was already kneeling, examining the   12
wound, the rabbit trailing from his hands. "Right through the head," he said complacently, as if he had aimed for it. He took out his sharp, competent bowie knife and started to skin the body. He did it very cleanly and quickly. Uncle Jimbilly knew how to prepare the skins so that Miranda always had fur coats for her dolls, for though she never cared much for her dolls she liked seeing them in fur coats. The children knelt facing each other over the dead animal. Miranda watched admiringly while her brother stripped the skin away as if he were taking off a glove. The flayed flesh emerged dark scarlet, sleek, firm; Miranda with thumb and finger felt the long fine muscles with the silvery flat strips binding them to the joints. Brother lifted the oddly bloated belly. "Look," he said, in a low amazed voice. "It was going to have young ones."

Very carefully he slit the thin flesh from the center ribs to the flanks, and   13
a scarlet bag appeared. He slit again and pulled the bag open, and there lay a bundle of tiny rabbits, each wrapped in a thin scarlet veil. The brother pulled these off and there they were, dark gray, their wet down lying in minute even ripples, like a baby's head just washed, their unbelievably small delicate ears folded close, their little blind faces almost featureless.

Miranda said, "Oh, I want to *see*," under her breath. She looked and   14
looked—excited but not frightened, for she was accustomed to the sight of animals killed in hunting—filled with pity and astonishment and a kind of shocked delight in the wonderful little creatures for their own sakes, they were so pretty. She touched one of them ever so carefully. "Ah, there's blood running over them," she said and began to tremble without knowing why. Yet she wanted most deeply to see and to know. Having seen, she felt at once as if she had known all along. The very memory of her former ignorance faded, she had always known just this. No one had ever told her anything outright, she had been rather unobservant of the animal life around her because she was so accustomed to animals. They seemed simply disorderly and unaccountably rude in their habits, but altogether natural and not very interesting. Her brother had spoken as if he had known about everything all along. He may have seen all this before. He had never said a word to her, but she knew now a part at least of what he knew. She understood a little of the secret, formless intuitions in her own mind and body, which had been clearing up, taking form, so gradually and so steadily she had not realized that she was learning what she had to know.

Paul said cautiously, as if he were talking about something forbidden: "They were just about ready to be born." His voice dropped on the last word. "I know," said Miranda, "like kittens. I know, like babies." She was quietly and terribly agitated, standing again with her rifle under her arm, looking down at the bloody heap. "I don't want the skin," she said, "I won't have it." Paul buried the young rabbits again in their mother's body, wrapped the skin around her, carried her to a clump of sage bushes, and hid her away. He came out again at once and said to Miranda, with an eager friendliness, a confidential tone quite unusual in him, as if he were taking her into an important secret on equal terms: "Listen now. Now you listen to me, and don't ever forget. Don't you ever tell a living soul that you saw this. Don't tell a soul. Don't tell Dad because I'll get into trouble. He'll say I'm leading you into things you ought not to do. He's always saying that. So now don't you go and forget and blab out sometime the way you're always doing. . . . Now, that's a secret. Don't you tell."

Miranda never told, she did not even wish to tell anybody. She   15
thought about the whole worrisome affair with confused unhappiness for a few days. Then it sank quietly into her mind and was heaped over by accumulated thousands of impressions, for nearly twenty years. One day she was picking her path among the puddles and crushed refuse of a market street in a strange city of a strange country, when without warning, plain and clear in its true colors as if she looked through a frame upon a scene that had not stirred nor changed since the moment it happened, the episode of that far-off day leaped from its burial place before her mind's eye. She was so reasonlessly horrified she halted suddenly staring, the scene before her eyes dimmed by the vision back of them. An Indian vendor had held up before her a tray of dyed sugar sweets, in the shapes of all kinds of creatures: birds, baby chicks, baby rabbits, lambs, baby pigs. They were in gay colors and smelled of vanilla, maybe. . . . It was a very hot day and the smell in the market, with its piles of raw flesh and wilting flowers, was like the mingled sweetness and corruption she had smelled that other day in the empty cemetery at home: the day she had remembered always until now vaguely as the time she and her brother found treasure in the opened graves. Instantly upon this thought the dreadful vision faded, and she saw clearly her brother, whose childhood face she had forgotten, standing again in the blazing sunshine, again twelve years old, a pleased sober smile in his eyes, turning the silver dove over and over in his hands.

• • •

THINKING ABOUT LITERATURE

1. What is the significance of the dove? The ring? The rabbit?

2. What is so meaningful about the event described in the story that Miranda remembers it twenty years later?

3. In what way do specific, concrete details contribute to the effect of the story?

JOURNAL ENTRY

In "The Grave," Porter describes how a memory "leaped from its burial place" (15) years later. Write an entry about a childhood incident you remembered and understood only after having forgotten about it for some years.

THEMATIC CONNECTIONS

- "Shooting an Elephant" (page 91)
- "Once More to the Lake" (page 142)
- "Samuel" (page 202)

WRITING ASSIGNMENTS FOR DESCRIPTION

1. Choose a character from a work of fiction or film who you think is truly interesting. Write a descriptive essay that conveys what makes this character so special.

2. Describe a particularly memorable movie, concert, or sports event you have attended. Include both your own reactions and the reactions of other spectators.

3. Locate some photographs of your relatives. Describe three of these pictures, including details that provide insight into the lives of the people you discuss. Use your descriptive paragraphs to support a thesis about your family.

4. Visit a local art museum, and select a painting that interests you. Study it carefully, and write an essay-length description of it. Before you write, decide on the type of description you will write as well as an organizing scheme.

5. Select an object that you are familiar with, and write an objective description of it. Include a diagram.

6. Assume you are writing a letter to someone in another country who knows little about life in the United States. Describe to this person something that you consider to be typically American—a baseball stadium or a shopping mall, for example.

7. Visit your college library, and write an objective description of the reference section. Be specific, and select an organizing principle before you begin your essay. Your goal is to acquaint students with some of the reference materials they will use.

8. Describe your neighborhood to a visitor who knows nothing about it. Include as much specific detail as you can.

9. After reconsidering "In the Jungle," "The Way to Rainy Mountain," or "Samuel," write a description of a sight or scene that fascinated, surprised, or shocked you. Your description should explain why you were so deeply affected by what you saw.

10. Write an essay in which you describe an especially frightening horror film. What specific sights and sounds make this film so horrifying? Include a thesis statement that assesses the film's success as a horror film. (Be careful not to merely recount the plot of the film.)

COLLABORATIVE ACTIVITY FOR DESCRIPTION

Working in groups of three or four students, select a famous person—one you can reasonably expect your classmates to recognize. Then work as a group to write a physical description of that individual, including as much physical detail as possible. (Avoid any details that will be an instant giveaway.) Give your description a general title—*politician, movie* or *television star,* or *person in the news,* for example. Finally, have one person read the description aloud to the class, and see whether your classmates can guess the person's identity.

4

EXEMPLIFICATION

WHAT IS EXEMPLIFICATION?

Exemplification uses one or more particular cases, or **examples,** to make a general point specific or an abstract concept concrete. In the following paragraph from *Sexism and Language,* Alleen Pace Nilsen uses a number of well-chosen examples to support her statement that the armed forces use words that have positive masculine connotations to encourage recruitment:

Topic sentence

The armed forces, particularly the Marines, use the positive masculine connotation as part of their recruitment psychology. They promote the idea that to join the Marines (or the Army, Navy, or Air Force) guarantees that you will become a man. But this brings up a problem, because much of the work that is necessary to keep a large organization running is what is traditionally thought of as *woman's work.* Now, how can the Marines ask someone who has signed up for a *man-sized job* to do *woman's work?* Since they can't, they euphemize and give the jobs titles that are more prestigious or, at least, don't

Series of related examples

make people think of females. Waitresses are called *orderlies,* secretaries are called *clerk-typists,* nurses are called *medics,* assistants are called *adjutants,* and cleaning up an area is called *policing* the area. The same kind of word glorification is used in civilian life to bolster a man's ego when he is doing such tasks as cooking and sewing. For example, a *chef* has higher prestige than a *cook* and a *tailor* has higher prestige than a *seamstress.*

You have probably noticed, when watching television talk shows or listening to classroom discussions, that the most interesting and persuasive exchanges take place when those involved support their points with specific examples. Sweeping generalizations and vague statements are not nearly as effective as specific observations, anecdotes, details, and opinions. It is one thing to say, "The mayor is corrupt and should not be reelected," and another to illustrate your point by saying, "The mayor should not be reelected because he has fired two city workers who refused to contribute to his campaign fund, has put his family and friends on the city payroll, and has used public employees to make improvements to his home." The same principle applies to writing: many of the most effective essays use examples extensively. Exemplification is used in every kind of writing situation to explain and clarify, to add interest, and to persuade.

Using Examples to Explain and Clarify

On a midterm exam in a film course, you might write, "Even though horror movies seem modern, they really aren't." You may think your statement is perfectly clear, but if this is all you say about horror movies, you should not be surprised if your exam comes back with a question mark in the margin next to this sentence. After all, you have only made a general statement or claim about your subject. It is not specific, nor does it anticipate readers' questions about the ways in which horror movies are not modern. Furthermore, it includes no examples, which are your best means of ensuring clarity and avoiding ambiguity. To be certain your audience knows exactly what you mean, state your point precisely: "Despite the fact that horror movies seem modern, the two most memorable ones are adaptations of nineteenth-century Gothic novels." Then, you could illustrate your point by discussing these two films— *Frankenstein,* directed by James Whale, and *Dracula,* directed by Todd Browning—and linking them to the novels on which they are based. With the benefit of these specific examples, readers would know what you mean: that the literary roots of such movies are in the past, not that their cinematic techniques or production methods are dated. Moreover, readers would know which particular horror movies you are talking about.

Using Examples to Add Interest

Well-chosen examples add life to otherwise bland or straightforward statements. Laurence J. Peter and Raymond Hull use examples skillfully in their essay "The Peter Principle," which appears later in this chapter. Their claim that each employee in a system rises to a level of authority at which he or she is incompetent is not particularly intriguing. This statement becomes interesting, however, when it is supported by specific examples—the affable foreman who becomes the indecisive supervisor, the exacting mechanic who becomes the disorganized foreman, and the charismatic battlefield general who becomes the ineffective and self-destructive field marshal.

When you use exemplification, look for examples that are interesting as well as pertinent. Test the effectiveness of your examples by putting yourself in your readers' place. If you don't find your essay lively and absorbing, chances are your readers won't either. If this is the case, try to add more engaging, more spirited examples. After all, your goal is to communicate ideas to your readers, and imaginative examples can make the difference between an engrossing essay and one that is a chore to read.

Using Examples to Persuade

Although you may use examples simply to explain an idea or to entertain your readers, examples are also an effective way to demonstrate that what you are saying is reasonable and worth considering. A few well-chosen examples can eliminate pages of general, and often unconvincing, explanations. For instance, a statement that adequate health insurance is now too expensive for many Americans needs support. If you make such a statement on an exam, you need to back it up with appropriate examples—such as the fact that in one typical working-class neighborhood one out of every six primary wage earners is now jobless and that most of these unemployed workers can no longer afford health insurance. Similarly, a statement in a biology paper that DDT should continue to be banned is unconvincing without persuasive examples such as these to support it:

- Although DDT has been banned since December 31, 1972, traces are still being found in the eggs of various fish and waterfowl.
- Certain lakes and streams still cannot be used for sport and recreation because DDT levels are dangerously high, presumably because of farmland runoff.
- Because of its stability as a compound, DDT does not degrade quickly; therefore, existing residues will threaten the environment well into the twenty-first century.

Using Examples to Test Your Thesis

Examples can help you test your own ideas as well as the ideas of others. For instance, suppose you plan to write a paper for a composition class about students' writing skills. Your tentative thesis is that writing well is an inborn talent and that teachers can do little to help people write better. But is this really true? Has it been true in your own life? To test your point, you go back over your academic career and brainstorm about the various teachers who tried to help you improve your writing.

As you assemble your list, you remember Mrs. Colson, a teacher you had when you were a junior in high school. She was strict, required lots of writing, and seemed to accept nothing less than perfection. At the time neither you nor your classmates liked her; in fact, her nickname was Warden Colson. But looking back, you recall her one-on-one conferences, her organized lessons, and her pointed comments. You also remember her careful review of essay tests, and you realize that after being in her class, you felt much more comfortable taking such tests. After examining some papers that you saved, you are surprised to see how much your writing actually improved that year. These examples lead you to reevaluate your ideas and revise your tentative thesis. Now you conclude that even though some people seem to have a natural flair for writing, a good teacher can make a difference.

Providing Enough Examples

Unfortunately, no general rule exists to tell you how many examples you need to support your ideas. The number you use depends on your thesis. If, for instance, your thesis is that an educational institution, like a business, needs careful financial management, a detailed examination of your own college or university could work well. This single example might provide all the detail you need to make your point. In this case, you wouldn't need to include examples from a number of schools. In fact, too many examples could be tedious and cause your readers to lose interest.

If, however, your thesis is that conflict between sons and fathers is a major theme in the writing of Franz Kafka, several examples would be necessary. A single example would show only that the theme is present in *one* of Kafka's works. In this case, the more examples you include, the more effectively you prove your point. Of course, for some thesis statements, even several examples would not be enough. Examples alone, for instance, could not demonstrate convincingly that children from small families have more successful careers than children from large families. This thesis would have to be supported with a statistical study—that is, by collecting and interpreting numerical data representing a great many examples.

Selecting a sufficient *range* of examples is just as important as choosing an appropriate number. If you want to persuade readers that Colin Powell was an able general, you should choose examples from several stages of his career. Likewise, if you want to convince readers that outdoor advertising is ruining the scenic view from local highways, you should discuss an area larger than your immediate neighborhood. Your objective in each case is to select a cross section of examples appropriate for the boundaries of your topic.

Choosing Representative Examples

Just as professional pollsters take great pains to ensure that their samples reflect the makeup of the group they are polling, you should make sure that your examples fairly represent the group you are discussing. If you want to express support for a ban on smoking in all public buildings, you should not limit your examples to restaurants. To be convincing, you should include examples involving many public places, such as government office buildings, hospital lobbies, and sports stadiums. For the same reason, one person's experience is not enough to support a conclusion about many others unless you can establish that the experience is typical.

If you decide that you cannot cite enough representative examples to support your thesis, reexamine it. Rather than switching to a new topic, you may be able to narrow your thesis. After all, the only way your paper will be convincing is if your readers believe that your examples and your claim about your topic correspond—that is, that your thesis is supported by your examples and that your examples fairly represent the scope of your topic.

Of course, to be convincing you must not only choose examples effectively but also *use* them effectively. One way to reinforce the connection between your examples and your thesis is by using transitional words and phrases ("*Another* example of successful programs for the homeless . . . ") to introduce your examples. In addition, you should keep your thesis in mind as you write, taking care not to get so involved with one example that you digress from your main point. No matter how carefully developed, no matter how specific, lively, and appropriate, your examples accomplish nothing if they do not support your essay's main idea.

STRUCTURING AN EXEMPLIFICATION ESSAY

Exemplification essays usually begin with an *introduction* that includes the thesis statement, which is supported by examples in the body of the essay. Each *body paragraph* may develop a separate example, present a point illustrated by several brief examples, or explore one aspect of a single extended example that is developed throughout the essay. The *conclusion* reinforces the main idea of the essay, perhaps restating the thesis. At times, however, variations of this basic pattern are advisable and even necessary. For instance, beginning your paper with a striking example might stimulate your reader's interest and curiosity; ending with one might vividly reinforce your thesis.

Exemplification presents one special organizational problem. In an essay of this type, a large number of examples is not unusual. If these examples are not handled properly, your paper can become a thesis statement followed by a list or by ten or fifteen very brief, choppy paragraphs. One way to avoid this problem is to select only your best examples, developing them fully in separate paragraphs and discarding the others. Another way is to group related examples in paragraphs. Within each paragraph, examples can then be arranged in order of increasing importance or persuasiveness, to allow your audience's interest to build. The following informal outline for a paper evaluating the nursing care at a hospital illustrates one way to arrange examples. Notice how the writer groups his examples under three general headings: *patient rooms, emergency room,* and *clinics.*

Introduction:	Thesis statement—The quality of nursing care at Montgomery Hospital can serve as a model for nursing personnel at other medical facilities.

Patient Rooms
Example 1:	Responsiveness
Example 2:	Effective rapport
Example 3:	Good bedside care

Emergency Room
Example 4:	Adequate staffing
Example 5:	Nurses circulating among patients in the waiting room
Example 6:	Satisfactory working relationships between doctors and nursing staff

Clinics
Example 7:	Nurses preparing patients
Example 8:	Nurses assisting during treatment
Example 9:	Nurses instructing patients after treatment

Conclusion:	Restatement of thesis or review of key points or examples

▶ **STUDENT WRITERS: EXEMPLIFICATION**

Exemplification is frequently used in nonacademic writing situations, such as fiscal reports, memos, progress reports, and proposals. One of the most important situations in which you will use exemplification is in a letter applying for a job. Elizabeth Bensley's letter of application to a prospective employer follows this pattern of development. (Grace Ku's essay on page 165 illustrates a more conventional academic use of the exemplification pattern.)

295 Main Street
Mount Kisco, NY 10549
October 3, 1996

Mr. Steven Seltzer
Wall Street Journal
420 Lexington Avenue
New York, NY 10017

Dear Mr. Seltzer:

Opening

Please consider my application for the position of management trainee that you advertised in the October 1, 1996 edition of the Wall Street Journal. My advisor, Dr. David Sutton, an editorial consultant to the Journal, has inspired much of my enthusiasm about my field and about this opportunity to work in your

Thesis statement

business office. I am confident that my education and experience qualify me to fulfill the responsibilities of this job.

1

Series of brief examples

I am currently a senior in the College of Business at Drexel University and will graduate in June with a degree in management. I have completed courses in accounting, data processing, economics, management, and communications. In addition, I have taken a number of computer courses and have a working knowledge of systems programming. Throughout my college career, I have maintained a 3.3 average and have been secretary of the Management Society.

2

Major example

Drexel's five-year curriculum includes four work-study periods, during which students gain practical experience in the business world. During my most recent work-study period, I worked in the business office of the

3

Philadelphia Inquirer, where I was responsible
for accounts payable and worked closely with a
number of people in the accounting department.
During my six months in this position, I
gained a working knowledge of both IBM and
Macintosh computer systems and used them to
record charges, payments, and work schedules.
Eventually my supervisor, Ms. Nancy Viamonte,
put me in charge of training and supervising
two other work-study students. At the
Inquirer, I also developed a computer program
that verified charges and ensured the prompt
disposition and payment of accounts.

Closing   I believe that my education and work experi-   4
ence make me a good candidate for your posi-
tion. I have enclosed a résumé for your convenience and will be available for an interview
anytime after October 15. I look forward to
meeting with you to discuss my qualifications.

Sincerely,

Elizabeth Bensley

Elizabeth Bensley

Points for Special Attention

ORGANIZATION.   Exemplification is ideally suited for letters of application. The only way Elizabeth Bensley can support her claims about her qualifications for the management trainee job is to set forth her experience and knowledge. The body of her letter is divided into two categories: her educational record and her work-study experience. Each of the body paragraphs has a clear purpose and function. Paragraph 2 contains a series of brief examples pertaining to Elizabeth's educational record. Paragraph 3 contains a more fully developed example that deals with her work-study experience. These examples tell the prospective employer what qualifies Elizabeth for the job. In her body paragraphs, she arranges her points and her examples in order of increasing importance. Although her academic record is relevant, in this case it is not as important to a potential employer as her experience. Because her work-study experience relates directly to the position she wants, Elizabeth considers this her strongest point and wisely chooses to present it last.

Elizabeth ends her letter on a strong note. She not only asserts her willingness to be interviewed but also gives the date after which she will be available. Because people remember best what they read last, a strong conclusion is as essential here as it is in other writing situations.

PERSUASIVE EXAMPLES.   To support a thesis convincingly, examples should convey specific information, not just generalizations. Saying "I am a good student who works hard at her studies" means very little. It is better to say, as Elizabeth does, "Throughout my college career, I have maintained a 3.3 average." A letter of application should show a prospective employer how your strengths and background correspond to the employer's needs, and specific examples can help you accomplish this.

Focus on Revision

Elizabeth showed her letter to her work-study advisor, who thought it was effective but could be improved. She suggested that in addition to outlining her experience, Elizabeth could explain how her work at the *Philadelphia Inquirer* would make her an asset to the *Wall Street Journal.* She noted that Elizabeth could point out that her experience in the accounting department at the *Inquirer* would enable her to work either in the accounting department or in collections. Elizabeth could also explain why training and supervising two work-study students was important. Her advisor made the following recommendation as well: if Elizabeth's purpose is to show that she is able to assume responsibility, she should say so; if it is to illustrate that she has managerial ability, she should make this clear. Finally, Elizabeth's advisor suggested that she list the software programs with which she is familiar. This information would give the employer a clear idea of her extensive experience with computers.

The following essay by Grace Ku was written for a composition class, in response to the assignment "Write an essay about the worst job you (or someone you know) ever had."

Midnight

Introduction   It was eight o'clock, and like millions   1
of other Americans, I was staring at the television set wondering what kind of lesson Mr. Huxtable was going to teach his children next on The Bill Cosby Show. I was glued to the set like an average eleven-year-old couch potato while leisurely eating a can of cold Chef Boyardee spaghetti in my empty living room. As I watched the show, I gradually fell asleep on the floor fully clothed in a pair of blue

jeans and a T-shirt, wondering when my parents would come home. Around midnight I suddenly woke up to a rustling noise when my parents finally arrived from a long day at work. I

Thesis statement

could see in their tired faces the grief and the hardship of working at a dry cleaner.

Transitional paragraph provides background

My parents worked in modern times, but in conditions like those of nineteenth-century factory workers. Because they were immigrants with little formal education and spoke broken English, they could get only hard, physically demanding jobs. Therefore, they worked at a dry cleaner that was as big as a factory, a place where smaller cleaners sent their clothes to be cleaned.

2

Series of brief examples: physical demands

My parents had to meet certain quotas: each day they had to clean and press several hundred garments--shirts, pants, and other clothing. By themselves, every day, they did the work of four laborers. The muscles of my mother's shoulders and arms became as hard as iron from working with the press, a difficult job even for a man. In addition to pressing, my father washed the clothes in the machines, which is the reason a strong odor of oil was permanently embedded in his work clothes.

3

Example: long hours

Not only were my parents' jobs physically demanding, but they also required long hours. My parents went to work at five o'clock in the morning and came home anytime between nine o'clock at night and midnight. They worked over twelve hours daily at the dry cleaner, where the eight-hour work day and labor unions did not exist. Their only rest was two ten- to twenty-minute breaks--one for lunch and one for dinner. They did not stop even when they were burned by the hot press or by the steam

4

Example: frequent burns

rising from it. The scars on their arms made it obvious that they worked at a dry cleaner. Their burned skin would blister and later peel off, showing their raw flesh. In time they

Example: low pay

would heal, but other burns would soon follow.

Along with having to work overtime with-   5
out compensation and suffering injuries without treatment, my parents were paid below the
minimum wage. These two people (who did the
work of four) together received a paycheck
equivalent to that of a single worker. They
then used this money to feed and care for a
household of five people.

Conclusion

As my parents silently entered our home   6
around midnight, they did not have to complain
about their jobs. I could see their anguish in
the wrinkles on their foreheads and their
fatigue in the languid movements of their bod-

Restatement of thesis

ies. Their eyes looked toward me, saying, "We
hate our jobs, but we work so our children
will have better lives than we do."

Points for Special Attention

ORGANIZATION.   Grace Ku begins her introduction by describing herself as an eleven-year-old sitting on the floor watching television. At first, her behavior seems typical of many American children, but two things suggest problems: first, she is eating her cold dinner out of a can, and second, even though it is quite late, she is waiting for her parents to return from work. This opening prepares readers for her thesis that her parents' jobs produce only grief and hardship.

In the body of her essay, Grace presents the examples that support her thesis. In the second paragraph she sets the stage for the discussion to follow, explaining that her parents' working conditions were similar to those of nineteenth-century factory workers, and in paragraph 3 she presents a series of examples that illustrate how physically demanding her parents' job were. In the remaining body paragraphs, she gives three other examples to show how unpleasant the jobs were: how long her parents worked, how often they were injured, and how little they were paid. Grace concludes her essay by returning to the scene in her introduction, using a quotation that is intended to stay with her readers after they have finished the essay.

ENOUGH EXAMPLES.   Certainly no single example, no matter how graphic, could adequately support the thesis of this essay. To establish the pain and difficulty of her parents' jobs, Grace uses several well-chosen examples. Although more examples could add depth to the essay, the ones she uses are vivid and compelling enough to reinforce her thesis that her parents had to endure great hardship to make a living.

REPRESENTATIVE EXAMPLES.   Grace selects examples that illustrate the full range of her subject. She draws from the daily experience of her parents and does not include examples that are atypical. She also includes enough detail so that her readers, who she assumes do not know much about working in a dry cleaner, will understand her points. She does not, however, use so much detail that her readers will get bogged down and lose interest.

EFFECTIVE EXAMPLES.   All of Grace's examples support her thesis. While developing these examples, she never loses sight of her main idea; consequently, she does not get sidetracked in irrelevant digressions. She also avoids the temptation to preach to her readers about the injustice of her parents' situation. By allowing her examples to speak for themselves, Grace presents a powerful portrait of her parents and their hardships.

Focus on Revision

After reading this draft, a peer critic thought Grace could go into more detail about her parents' situation and could explain her examples in more depth—perhaps writing about the quotas her parents had to meet or the other physical dangers of their jobs. In addition, Grace thought she should expand the discussion in paragraph 5 about her parents' low wages, perhaps anticipating questions some of her readers might have about working conditions. For example, was it legal for her parents' employer to require them to work overtime without compensation or to pay them less than the minimum wage? If not, how was the employer able to get away with such practices? Grace also thought she should move the information about her parents' work-related injuries from paragraph 4 to paragraph 3, where she discusses the physical demands of their jobs. Finally, she decided to follow the advice of another student and include comments by her parents to make their experiences more immediate to readers.

The selections that appear in this chapter all depend on exemplification to explain and clarify, to add interest, or to persuade.

▶▶▶▶▶▶▶▶▶▶▶▶▶▶▶▶▶▶▶

LAURENCE J. PETER AND RAYMOND HULL

Laurence J. Peter (1919–1990) was an educator and academic, and Raymond Hull (1919–1985) was a writer and dramatist. Together they wrote *The Peter Principle: Why Things Always Go Wrong* (1969), a book that so pointedly analyzes American organizations and the way their social structures foster and reward ineptitude that the term *Peter Principle* has been absorbed into our language. This term refers to Peter's contention that in a hierarchy every employee tends to be promoted to a level at which he or she is incompetent to perform the duties of the position. Peter wrote two sequels, *Why Things Go Wrong: Or, the Peter Principle Revisited* (1984), containing anecdotes, historical footnotes, and autobiographical illustrations of the principle; and *The Peter Pyramid: Or, Will We Ever Get the Point?* (1986), using the image of the inverted pyramid to illustrate how most systems start small and grow until they are no longer stable. The following selection, the first chapter of *The Peter Principle*, presents the book's thesis along with several supporting examples.

The Peter Principle

When I was a boy I was taught that the men upstairs knew what they were doing. I was told, "Peter, the more you know, the further you go." So I stayed in school until I graduated from college and then went forth into the world clutching firmly these ideas and my new teaching certificate. During the first year of teaching I was upset to find that a number of teachers, school principals, supervisors, and superintendents appeared to be unaware of their professional responsibilities and incompetent in executing their duties. For example my principal's main concerns were that all window shades be at the same level, that classrooms should be quiet, and that no one step on or near the rose beds. The superintendent's main concerns were that no minority group, no matter how fanatical, should ever be offended and that all official forms be submitted on time. The children's education appeared farthest from the administrator's mind.

At first I thought this was a special weakness of the school system in which I taught so I applied for certification in another province. I filled out the special forms, enclosed the required documents, and complied willingly with all the red tape. Several weeks later, back came my application and all the documents!

No, there was nothing wrong with my credentials; the forms were correctly filled out; an official departmental stamp showed that they had been received in good order. But an accompanying letter said, "The new regulations require that such forms cannot be accepted by the Department of Education unless they have been registered at the Post Office to ensure safe delivery. Will you please remail the forms to the Department, making sure to register them this time?"

I began to suspect that the local school system did not have a monop-   4
oly on incompetence.

As I looked further afield, I saw that every organization contained a   5
number of persons who could not do their jobs.

A UNIVERSAL PHENOMENON

Occupational incompetence is everywhere. Have you noticed it?   6
Probably we have all noticed it.

We see indecisive politicians posing as resolute statesmen and the   7
"authoritative source" who blames his misinformation on "situational
imponderables." Limitless are the public servants who are indolent and
insolent, military commanders whose behavioral timidity belies their
dreadnought rhetoric, and governors whose innate servility prevents
their actually governing. In our sophistication, we virtually shrug aside
the immoral cleric, corrupt judge, incoherent attorney, author who cannot
write, and English teacher who cannot spell. At universities we see
proclamations authored by administrators whose own office communications are hopelessly muddled, and droning lectures from inaudible or incomprehensible instructors.

Seeing incompetence at all levels of every hierarchy—political,   8
legal, educational, and industrial—I hypothesized that the cause was
some inherent feature of the rules governing the placement of employees. Thus began my serious study of the ways in which employees
move upward through a hierarchy, and of what happens to them after
promotion.

For my scientific data hundreds of case histories were collected. Here   9
are three typical examples.

Municipal Government File, Case No. 17

J. S. Minion[1] was a maintenance foreman in the public works depart-   10
ment of Excelsior City. He was a favorite of the senior officials at City
Hall. They all praised his unfailing affability.

"I like Minion," said the superintendent of works. "He has good   11
judgment and is always pleasant and agreeable."

This behavior was appropriate for Minion's position: he was not sup-   12
posed to make policy, so he had no need to disagree with his superiors.

The superintendent of works retired and Minion succeeded him.   13
Minion continued to agree with everyone. He passed to his foreman
every suggestion that came from above. The resulting conflicts in policy,
and the continual changing of plans, soon demoralized the department.

---

[1]Some names have been changed, in order to protect the guilty.

Complaints poured in from the Mayor and other officials, from taxpayers and from the maintenance-workers' union.

Minion still says "Yes" to everyone, and carries messages briskly   14
back and forth between his superiors and his subordinates. Nominally a superintendent, he actually does the work of a messenger. The maintenance department regularly exceeds its budget, yet fails to fulfill its program of work. In short, Minion, a competent foreman, became an incompetent superintendent.

Service Industries File, Case No. 3

E. Tinker was exceptionally zealous and intelligent as an apprentice   15
at G. Reece Auto Repair Inc., and soon rose to journeyman mechanic. In this job he showed outstanding ability in diagnosing obscure faults, and endless patience in correcting them. He was promoted to foreman of the repair shop.

But here his love of things mechanical and his perfectionism be-   16
came liabilities. He will undertake any job that he thinks looks interesting, no matter how busy the shop may be. "We'll work it in somehow," he says.

He will not let a job go until he is fully satisfied with it.   17

He meddles constantly. He is seldom to be found at his desk. He is usu-   18
ally up to his elbows in a dismantled motor and while the man who should be doing the work stands watching, other workmen sit around waiting to be assigned new tasks. As a result the shop is always overcrowded with work, always in a muddle, and delivery times are often missed.

Tinker cannot understand that the average customer cares little about   19
perfection—he wants his car back on time! He cannot understand that most of his men are less interested in motors than in their pay checks. So Tinker cannot get on with his customers or with his subordinates. He was a competent mechanic, but is now an incompetent foreman.

Military File, Case No. 8

Consider the case of the late renowned General A. Goodwin. His   20
hearty, informal manner, his racy style of speech, his scorn for petty regulations, and his undoubted personal bravery made him the idol of his men. He led them to many well-deserved victories.

When Goodwin was promoted to field marshal he had to deal, not   21
with ordinary soldiers, but with politicians and allied generalissimos.

He would not conform to the necessary protocol. He could not turn   22
his tongue to the conventional courtesies and flatteries. He quarreled with all the dignitaries and took to lying for days at a time, drunk and sulking, in his trailer. The conduct of the war slipped out of his hands into those of his subordinates. He had been promoted to a position that he was incompetent to fill.

AN IMPORTANT CLUE

In time I saw that all such cases had a common feature. The employee   23
had been promoted from a position of competence to a position of incompetence. I saw that, sooner or later, this could happen to every employee
in every hierarchy.

Hypothetical Case File, Case No. 1

Suppose you own a pill-rolling factory, Perfect Pill Incorporated.   24
Your foreman pill roller dies of a perforated ulcer. You need a replacement. You naturally look among your rank-and-file pill rollers.

Miss Oval, Mrs. Cylinder, Mr. Ellipse, and Mr. Cube all show various   25
degrees of incompetence. They will naturally be ineligible for promotion.
You will choose—other things being equal—your most competent pill
roller, Mr. Sphere, and promote him to foreman.

Now suppose Mr. Sphere proves competent as foreman. Later, when   26
your general foreman, Legree, moves up to Works Manager, Sphere will
be eligible to take his place.

If, on the other hand, Sphere is an incompetent foreman, he will get   27
no more promotion. He has reached what I call his "level of incompetence." He will stay there till the end of his career.

Some employees, like Ellipse and Cube, reach a level of incompetence   28
in the lowest grade and are never promoted. Some, like Sphere (assuming
he is not a satisfactory foreman), reach it after one promotion.

E. Tinker, the automobile repair-shop foreman, reached his level of in-   29
competence on the third stage of the hierarchy. General Goodwin reached
his level of incompetence at the very top of the hierarchy.

So my analysis of hundreds of cases of occupational incompetence   30
led me on to formulate *The Peter Principle:*

In a Hierarchy Every Employee Tends to Rise to His Level of Incompetence

A NEW SCIENCE!

Having formulated the Principle, I discovered that I had inadver-   31
tently founded a new science, hierarchiology, the study of hierarchies.

The term "hierarchy" was originally used to describe the system of   32
church government by priests graded into ranks. The contemporary
meaning includes any organization whose members or employees are
arranged in order of rank, grade, or class.

Hierarchiology, although a relatively recent discipline, appears to   33
have great applicability to the fields of public and private administration.

THIS MEANS YOU!

My Principle is the key to an understanding of all hierarchical sys-   34
tems, and therefore to an understanding of the whole structure of civilization. A few eccentrics try to avoid getting involved with hierarchies, but
everyone in business, industry, trade-unionism, politics, government, the
armed forces, religion, and education is so involved. All of them are controlled by the Peter Principle.

Many of them, to be sure, may win a promotion or two, moving from   35
one level of competence to a higher level of competence. But competence
in that new position qualifies them for still another promotion. For each
individual, for *you*, for *me*, the final promotion is from a level of competence to a level of incompetence.[2]

So, given enough time—and assuming the existence of enough ranks   36
in the hierarchy—each employee rises to, and remains at, his level of incompetence. Peter's Corollary states:

> *In time, every post tends to be occupied by an employee who is incompetent to
> carry out its duties.*

WHO TURNS THE WHEELS?

You will rarely find, of course, a system in which *every* employee has   37
reached his level of incompetence. In most instances, something is being
done to further the ostensible purposes for which the hierarchy exists.

> *Work is accomplished by those employees who have not yet reached their level of
> incompetence.*

•   •   •

COMPREHENSION

1. What things disillusioned Peter during his first year of teaching? What
   did he find out about organizations?

2. What is the Peter Principle? What happens when employees reach their
   "level of incompetence"?

3. What do Peter and Hull mean by *hierarchiology* (31)? How did hierarchiology lead Peter to the Peter Principle?

4. If the Peter Principle operates in hierarchies such as corporations, who
   does the work?

---

[2]The phenomena of "percussive sublimation" (commonly referred to as "being
kicked upstairs") and of "the lateral arabesque" are not, as the casual observer might
think, exceptions to the Principle. They are only pseudo-promotions. . . .

PURPOSE AND AUDIENCE

1. Is this essay aimed at a general or an expert audience? What led you to your conclusion?

2. What is the essay's thesis? Why do you think Peter and Hull wait so long to state it?

3. How serious are Peter and Hull? What words or phrases indicate whether their purpose is to instruct or to entertain—or both?

STYLE AND STRUCTURE

1. Why do you think Peter and Hull begin the essay with an example? Why do they present a series of brief examples before introducing the typical case histories?

2. Why do Peter and Hull say they collected hundreds of case histories for data? How are the three case histories analyzed here typical?

3. Does the reliance on hypothetical examples strengthen or weaken the writers' case? Explain.

4. Do Peter and Hull use a sufficient range of examples? Explain.

VOCABULARY PROJECTS

1. Define each of the following words as it is used in this selection.

imponderables (7)	incomprehensible (7)	protocol (22)
indolent (7)	hypothesized (8)	subordinates (22)
insolent (7)	hierarchy (8)	eccentrics (34)
dreadnought (7)	minion (10)	ostensible (37)
inaudible (7)	dismantled (18)	

2. Do Peter and Hull use **figures of speech** in their discussion? Why do you think they do or do not?

JOURNAL ENTRY

What examples of the Peter Principle have you encountered in your life?

WRITING WORKSHOP

1. Do Peter and Hull overstate their case? Write a letter to them in the form of an exemplification essay pointing out the weaknesses of their position.

2. Study a school, business, or organization with which you are familiar. Write an exemplification essay showing how the Peter Principle applies (or does not apply).

3. Do you know someone who has progressed to the highest level of his or her incompetence? Supporting your thesis with a single extended example, write an exemplification essay showing how the Peter Principle applies.

COMBINING THE PATTERNS

Peter and Hull use a series of narrative examples. What are the advantages and disadvantages of using **narration** here? Would other kinds of examples—such as statistics—have been more effective? Explain.

THEMATIC CONNECTIONS

- "Shooting an Elephant" (page 91)
- "The Company Man" (page 465)
- "The Catbird Seat" (page 474)

ROBERT M. LILIENFELD AND WILLIAM L. RATHJE

Robert M. Lilienfeld (1953–), a writer and professional consultant, works with businesses and other organizations to make sure that their long-term plans include ways of sustaining the environment. An expert on the subject of reducing waste at the source, he lives in Ann Arbor and edits a newsletter, *The ULS Report* (ULS stands for Use Less Stuff). Lilienfeld holds a B.A. in behavioral psychology and an M.B.A. in marketing and organizational behavior, both from Northwestern University. William L. Rathje (1945–), who has a B.A. from the University of Arizona and a Ph.D. from Harvard, has taught anthropology at the University of Arizona since 1971. He is widely known as the director of the Garbage Project, which uses archaeological methods to analyze the household refuse disposed of in public landfills in order to determine how waste can be most effectively reduced. With Cullen Murphy, he wrote *Rubbish! The Archaeology of Garbage* (1992). In the following essay, which appeared in the *New York Times* in 1996, Lilienfeld and Rathje try to counter the "sound-bite-based, factoid-heavy" misperceptions that even well-intentioned people have about how to protect the environment.

Six Enviro-Myths

We recently participated in an environmental festival at the Mall of America in Bloomington, Minn., the largest indoor shopping center in the country. Having spoken with literally thousands of parents, children, and teachers, we were appalled at the public's wealth of environmental misunderstanding. 1

We were equally chagrined by the superficiality of what we heard, and have coined a new term for this type of sound-bite-based, factoid-heavy understanding: eco-glibberish. Here are half a dozen examples: 2

RECYCLING IS THE KEY

Myth: The most important thing we can do is to recycle. Actually, it's one of the least important things we can do, if our real objective is to conserve resources. Remember the phrase "reduce, reuse, and recycle"? Reduce comes first for a good reason: it's better to not create waste than to have to figure out what to do with it. And recycling, like any other form of manufacturing, uses energy and other resources while creating pollution and greenhouse gases. 3

Rather, we need to make products more durable, lighter, more energy efficient, and easier to repair rather than to replace. Finally, we need to reduce and reuse packaging. 4

GARBAGE WILL OVERWHELM US

Myth: There's a garbage crisis. The original garbage crisis occurred   5
when people first settled down to farm and could no longer leave their
campsites after their garbage grew too deep.

Since then, every society has had to figure out what to do with dis-   6
cards. That something was usually unhealthy, odiferous, and ugly—
throwing garbage in the streets, piling it up just outside of town,
incorporating it into structures, or simply setting it on fire.

Today we can design history's and the world's safest recycling facili-   7
ties, landfills, and incinerators. We even have a national glut of landfill capacity, thanks to the fact that we've been building large regional landfills
to replace older, smaller local dumps.

The problem is political. No one wants to spend money on just get-   8
ting rid of garbage or to have a garbage site in the backyard.

The obvious solution is to stop generating so much garbage in the   9
first place. Doing so requires both the knowledge and self-discipline to
conserve energy and to do more with less stuff.

INDUSTRY IS TO BLAME

Myth: It's all industry's fault. No, it's all people's fault. Certainly indus-   10
try has played a significant role in destroying habitats, generating pollution, and depleting resources. But we're the ones who signal businesses
that what they're doing is acceptable—every time we open our wallets.

And don't just blame industrial societies. In his recent book "Earth   11
Politics," Ernst Ulrich von Weizsäcker wrote that "perhaps 90 percent of the
extinction of species, soil erosion, forest and wilderness destruction, and also
desertification are taking place in developing countries." Thus, even non-
industrialized, subsistence economies are creating environmental havoc.

THE EARTH IS IN PERIL

Myth: We have to save the earth. Frankly, the earth doesn't need to be   12
saved.

Nature doesn't give a hoot if human beings are here or not. The   13
planet has survived cataclysmic and catastrophic changes for millions
upon millions of years. Over that time, it is widely believed, 99 percent of
all species have come and gone while the planet has remained.

Saving *the* environment is really about saving *our* environment—   14
making it safe for ourselves, our children, and the world as we know it. If
more people saw the issue as one of saving themselves, we would probably see increased motivation and commitment to actually doing so.

PACKAGING IS THE PROBLEM

Myth: Packaging accounts for a growing percentage of our solid waste. If you were to examine a dumpster of garbage from the 1950s and a dumpster of garbage from the 1980s, you would find more discarded packaging in the first one. Packaging has actually decreased as a proportion of all solid wastes—from more than half in the 1950s to just over one-third today.   15

One reason is that there was more of other kinds of wastes—old appliances, magazines, office paper—in the 1980s. But the main causes were two changes in the packaging industry.   16

First, the heavy metal cans and glass bottles of the 1950s gave way to far lighter and more crushable containers—about 22 percent lighter by the 1980s. At the same time, many metal and glass containers were replaced by paper boxes and plastic bottles and bins, which are even lighter and more crushable.   17

Second, the carrying capacity of packages—the quantity of product that can be delivered per ounce of packaging material—increased hugely.   18

Glass, for example, has a carrying capacity of 1.2, meaning that 1.2 fluid ounces of milk or juice are delivered for every ounce of glass in which they are contained. Plastic containers have a carrying capacity of about 30.   19

AMERICANS ARE WASTING MORE

Myth: Americans are overconsumers, since the per capita creation of solid waste continues to climb. Each person generates about 4.4 pounds of garbage a day—a number that has been growing steadily. The implication is that we partake in an unstoppable orgy of consumption. The truth is far more mundane.   20

In reality, increases in solid waste are based largely on the mathematics of households, not individuals. That's because regardless of the size of a household, fixed activities and purchases generate trash.   21

As new households form, they create additional garbage. Think about a couple going through a divorce. Once there was one home. Now there are two. Building that second house or condo used lots of resources and created lots of construction debris. Where once there was one set of furniture, one washing machine, and one refrigerator, now there are two. Each refrigerator contains milk cartons, meat wrappers, and packages of mixed vegetables. Each pantry contains cereal boxes and canned goods.   22

To make matters worse, households are growing at a fairly rapid rate, almost double the rate of population growth. That's because we're all living longer and away from our children, divorcing more frequently, and becoming far more accepting of single-parent households.   23

Census Bureau numbers tell this story: From 1972 to 1987, the population grew by 16 percent. The number of households grew by 35 percent. Municipal solid waste increased by 35 percent, too.   24

If Americans were really creating more trash by overindulging, we would be spending more on trash-generating items: nondurable goods like food and cosmetics. These all generate lots of garbage, since they are used and discarded quickly, along with their packaging. But household expenditures for nondurable goods, as measured by constant dollars, declined slightly from 1972 to 1987—by about one-half of 1 percent.   25

Does all of this mean we can sit back and relax? No. The earth's resources are finite. Habitats are being destroyed. Biodiversity is declining. And the consumption of resources is expanding.   26

But it does mean that we must be less willing to accept glib, ideological pronouncements of right and wrong, good and evil, cause and effect. Thus, to truly change the world for the better, we need more facts, not simply more faith.   27

• • •

COMPREHENSION

1. What prompted Lilienfeld and Rathje to write this essay?

2. Why do the writers think it is important to correct the mistaken ideas people have about the environment?

3. According to the writers, who is to blame for generating pollution and depleting resources?

4. What, according to the writers, is the primary danger of accepting the six myths they discuss?

PURPOSE AND AUDIENCE

1. What is the thesis of this essay? At what point is it stated?

2. What preconceptions do you think the writers expect their readers to have about the environment?

3. Do the writers seem to assume that readers will be sympathetic, neutral, or hostile to their ideas? On what do you base your conclusions?

4. What do you suppose Lilienfeld and Rathje hope to accomplish by writing their essay?

STYLE AND STRUCTURE

1. How effective is the essay's introduction? Does it create interest? What other strategy could the writers have used?

2. The body of this essay consists of six examples. What would the writers have gained or lost by using more examples? By developing each of the examples in more depth? By using one single extended example instead of six individual ones?

3. Do Lilienfeld and Rathje select the most effective examples? What other examples could they have used to make their point?

4. How effective is the essay's conclusion? Do you think the writers should have recommended a specific course of action to improve the environment? Why or why not?

VOCABULARY PROJECTS

1. Define each of the following words as it is used in this selection.

   literally (1)   odiferous (6)
   sound bite (2)   glut (7)
   factoid (2)   habitats (10)
   greenhouse gasses (3)   desertification (11)
   durable (4)   cataclysmic (13)

2. Lilienfeld and Rathje use recently coined words, such as *sound bite* and *factoid*, in their essay. Underline as many of these words as you can find. Could the writers have used other words to express the same ideas? What would be the advantages and disadvantages of using more traditional language?

JOURNAL ENTRY

Could Lilienfeld and Rathje be accused of suggesting that there is little individuals can or should do to save the environment? For example, by dismissing the usefulness of recycling, do they suggest that "we can sit back and relax" (26)?

WRITING WORKSHOP

1. Using a single extended example, write an essay about something you did to improve the environment.

2. Write a letter to Lilienfeld and Rathje in which you agree or disagree with their ideas. Include a thesis statement and support it with examples from your own experience.

3. Survey your house, apartment, or dormitory. List all the things you see that hurt the environment—for example, cans or newspapers that are not recycled. Then, write an essay in which you use your observations to support the following thesis statement: "In spite of all the publicity the environmental movement has gotten, individuals still do a lot to hurt the planet."

COMBINING THE PATTERNS

List the places where Lilienfeld and Rathje use a **cause-and-effect** pattern. Why do you think they use it so often?

THEMATIC CONNECTIONS

- "In the Jungle" (page 130)
- "The Spider and the Wasp" (page 223)
- "On Dumpster Diving" (page 609)

RICHARD LEDERER

Richard Lederer (1938–) was born in Philadelphia and attended Haverford College, Harvard, and the University of New Hampshire. From 1962 to 1989 he taught English at St. Paul's School, a private preparatory academy in Concord, New Hampshire. Lederer retired from teaching at the age of fifty-one so that he could, in his words, "extend my mission as a user-friendly English teacher," and he has succeeded, according to critic Paul Dickinson, in "transforming the use of English into an activity that rivals sex as a source of pleasure." His popular, lighthearted works on the wonders and oddities of the English language—and how it is fractured by politicians and bureaucrats, among others—include *Anguished English* (1987), *Crazy English* (1989), *The Miracle of Language* (1991), and *Adventures of a Verbivore* (1995). Author of more than a thousand articles on writing and language, Lederer writes a weekly syndicated newspaper column, "Looking at Language," in addition to contributing the monthly "Grammar Grappler" column to *Writer's Digest*. In the following essay, he offers a wide array of amusing examples to support the bold thesis stated in his title.

English Is a Crazy Language

English is the most widely spoken language in the history of our planet, used in some way by at least one out of every seven human beings around the globe. Half of the world's books are written in English, and the majority of international telephone calls are made in English. English is the language of over sixty percent of the world's radio programs, many of them beamed, ironically, by the Russians, who know that to win friends and influence nations, they're best off using English. More than seventy percent of international mail is written and addressed in English, and eighty percent of all computer text is stored in English. English has acquired the largest vocabulary of all the world's languages, perhaps as many as two million words, and has generated one of the noblest bodies of literature in the annals of the human race.

Nonetheless, it is now time to face the fact that English is a crazy language.

In the crazy English language, the blackbird hen is brown, blackboards can be blue or green, and blackberries are green and then red before they are ripe. Even if blackberries were really black and blueberries really blue, what are strawberries, cranberries, elderberries, huckleberries, raspberries, boysenberries, mulberries, and gooseberries supposed to look like?

To add to the insanity, there is no butter in buttermilk, no egg in eggplant, no grape in grapefruit, neither worms nor wood in wormwood, neither pine nor apple in pineapple, neither peas nor nuts in peanuts, and no ham in a hamburger. (In fact, if somebody invented a sandwich consisting of a ham patty in a bun, we would have a hard time finding a name for it.) To make matters worse, English muffins weren't invented in England, french fries in France, or danish pastries in Denmark. And we discover even more culinary madness in the revelations that sweetmeat is candy, while sweetbread, which isn't sweet, is made from meat.

In this unreliable English tongue, greyhounds aren't always grey (or   5
gray); panda bears and koala bears aren't bears (they're marsupials); a woodchuck is a groundhog, which is not a hog; a horned toad is a lizard; glowworms are fireflies, but fireflies are not flies (they're beetles); ladybugs and lightning bugs are also beetles (and to propagate, a significant proportion of ladybugs must be male); a guinea pig is neither a pig nor from Guinea (it's a South American rodent); and a titmouse is neither mammal nor mammaried.

Language is like the air we breathe. It's invisible, inescapable, indis-   6
pensable, and we take it for granted. But when we take the time, step back, and listen to the sounds that escape from the holes in people's faces and explore the paradoxes and vagaries of English, we find that hot dogs can be cold, darkrooms can be lit, homework can be done in school, nightmares can take place in broad daylight, while morning sickness and daydreaming can take place at night, tomboys are girls, midwives can be men, hours—especially happy hours and rush hours—can last longer than sixty minutes, quicksand works *very* slowly, boxing rings are square, silverware can be made of plastic and tablecloths of paper, most telephones are dialed by being punched (or pushed?), and most bathrooms don't have any baths in them. In fact, a dog can go to the bathroom under a tree—no bath, no room; it's still going to the bathroom. And doesn't it seem at least a little bizarre that we go to the bathroom in order to go to the bathroom?

Why is it that a woman can man a station but a man can't woman   7
one, that a man can father a movement but a woman can't mother one, and that a king rules a kingdom but a queen doesn't rule a queendom? How did all those Renaissance men reproduce when there don't seem to have been any Renaissance women?

A writer is someone who writes, and a stinger is something that   8
stings. But fingers don't fing, grocers don't groce, hammers don't ham, and humdingers don't humding. If the plural of *tooth* is *teeth,* shouldn't the plural of *booth* be *beeth*? One goose, two geese—so one moose, two meese? One index, two indices—one Kleenex, two Kleenices? If people ring a bell today and rang a bell yesterday, why don't we say that they flang a ball? If they wrote a letter, perhaps they also bote their tongue. If the teacher taught, why isn't it also true that the preacher praught? Why is it that the sun shone yesterday while I shined my shoes, that I treaded water and then trod on soil, and that I flew out to see a World Series game in which my favorite player flied out?

If we conceive a conception and receive at a reception, why don't   9
we grieve a greption and believe a beleption? If a horsehair mat is

made from the hair of horses and a camel's hair brush from the hair of camels, from what is a mohair coat made? If a vegetarian eats vegetables, what does a humanitarian eat? If a firefighter fights fire, what does a freedom fighter fight? If a weightlifter lifts weights, what does a shoplifter lift? If *pro* and *con* are opposites, is congress the opposite of progress?

Sometimes you have to believe that all English speakers should be committed to an asylum for the verbally insane. In what other language do people drive in a parkway and park in a driveway? In what other language do people recite at a play and play at a recital? In what other language do privates eat in the general mess and generals eat in the private mess? In what other language do men get hernias and women get hysterectomies? In what other language do people ship by truck and send cargo by ship? In what other language can your nose run and your feet smell? 10

How can a slim chance and a fat chance be the same, "what's going on?" and "what's coming off?" be the same, and a bad licking and a good licking be the same, while a wise man and a wise guy are opposites? How can sharp speech and blunt speech be the same and *quite a lot* and *quite a few* the same, while *overlook* and *oversee* are opposites? How can the weather be hot as hell one day and cold as hell the next? 11

If *button* and *unbutton* and *tie* and *untie* are opposites, why are *loosen* and *unloosen* and *ravel* and *unravel* the same? If *bad* is the opposite of *good*, *hard* the opposite of *soft*, and *up* the opposite of *down*, why are *badly* and *goodly*, *hardly* and *softly*, and *upright* and *downright* not opposing pairs? If harmless actions are the opposite of harmful actions, why are shameless and shameful behavior the same and pricey objects less expensive than priceless ones? If appropriate and inappropriate remarks and passable and impassable mountain trails are opposites, why are flammable and inflammable materials, heritable and inheritable property, and passive and impassive people the same and valuable objects less treasured than invaluable ones? If *uplift* is the same as *lift up*, why are *upset* and *set up* opposite in meaning? Why are *pertinent* and *impertinent, canny* and *uncanny,* and *famous* and *infamous* neither opposites nor the same? How can *raise* and *raze* and *reckless* and *wreckless* be opposites when each pair contains the same sound? 12

Why is it that when the sun or the moon or the stars are out, they are visible, but when the lights are out, they are invisible, and that when I wind up my watch, I start it, but when I wind up this essay, I shall end it? 13

English is a crazy language. 14

• • •

COMPREHENSION

1. According to Lederer, in what sense is English a crazy language?

2. Why is English such an important language?

3. What does Lederer mean when he says that language is "like the air we breathe" (6)? Why does he believe this?

4. According to Lederer, what are "the paradoxes and vagaries of English" (6)?

PURPOSE AND AUDIENCE

1. What is the thesis of this essay? Where is this thesis stated?

2. What is Lederer's purpose in writing this essay? To instruct? To entertain? To persuade? Do you think he is serious or playful? Explain.

3. At whom are Lederer's comments aimed? Students of the English language? Those who know little about the language? Both? Explain.

STYLE AND STRUCTURE

1. What information does Lederer provide in his introduction? Why do you think he provides this background material?

2. What point does Lederer make in each of his body paragraphs? How do the examples in these paragraphs help to support each point?

3. Do you think Lederer uses too many examples? Should he have used fewer examples and discussed them in more depth? Should he have devoted one paragraph to a single example? Explain your position.

4. Lederer uses a one-sentence paragraph to end his essay. How appropriate is this conclusion? Is it too brief? Why or why not?

VOCABULARY PROJECTS

1. Define each of the following words as it is used in this selection.

annals (1)	mammaried (5)	canny (12)
culinary (4)	passive (12)	uncanny (12)
sweetbread (4)	pertinent (12)	infamous (12)
marsupials (5)	impertinent (12)	reckless (12)

2. At several points in the essay, Lederer says that English is a crazy language. What connotations does the word *crazy* have? Can you think of another word with a more precise meaning that he could have used? What might he have gained or lost by substituting this word for *crazy*?

JOURNAL ENTRY

Assume that you are learning to speak English. What expressions give you the most trouble? Do you, like Lederer, believe that English is a crazy language?

WRITING WORKSHOP

1. Write an essay in which you use your own list of words to support the idea that English is a crazy language. Use numerous short examples to support your thesis.

2. Make a list of the words you use at work, at home, or with your friends that have special associations for you. (These may be **slang, jargon,** or technical terms.) Then write an essay in which you make the point that your different uses of English reflect the different roles you play.

3. Make a list of occupational terms that indicate gender. Then, list their neutral equivalents—for example, *mailman* and *letter carrier; policeman* and *police officer; waiter, waitress,* and *waitstaff.* Write an essay in which you discuss whether or not English is a sexist language. (You may want to read, or reread, "Sexism in English: A 1990s Update," page 401.)

COMBINING THE PATTERNS

This essay's primary pattern of development is **exemplification.** Does Lederer use any other patterns? How would a paragraph of **comparison and contrast,** comparing English to another language, help support Lederer's thesis? Do you think he should have included such a paragraph? Why or why not?

THEMATIC CONNECTIONS

- "The Human Cost of an Illiterate Society" (page 192)
- "Sexism in English: A 1990s Update" (page 401)
- "Our Forked Tongue" (page 453)

![decorative border]

BRENT STAPLES

Born in Chester, Pennsylvania, in 1951, Brent Staples received his bachelor's degree from Widener University in 1973 and his doctorate in psychology from the University of Chicago in 1982. After deciding on a career in journalism, he wrote for the *Chicago Sun-Times,* the *Chicago Reader, Chicago* magazine, and *Down Beat* magazine. Staples joined the *New York Times* in 1985, writing on culture and politics, and he became a member of its editorial board in 1990. He contributes articles to many other publications, including *Ms.* and *Harper's,* in which the following article was published in 1986. Staples has also written a memoir, *Parallel Time: Growing Up in Black and White* (1994), about his escape from the violence and poverty of his childhood. In "Just Walk On By," Staples recounts the many instances in which people have reacted to him as a potentially dangerous person solely because of the color of his skin.

Just Walk On By: A Black Man Ponders His Power to Alter Public Space

My first victim was a woman—white, well dressed, probably in her 1 early twenties. I came upon her late one evening on a deserted street in Hyde Park, a relatively affluent neighborhood in an otherwise mean, impoverished section of Chicago. As I swung onto the avenue behind her, there seemed to be a discreet, uninflammatory distance between us. Not so. She cast back a worried glance. To her, the youngish black man—a broad six feet two inches with a beard and billowing hair, both hands shoved into the pockets of a bulky military jacket—seemed menacingly close. After a few more quick glimpses, she picked up her pace and was soon running in earnest. Within seconds she disappeared into a cross street.

That was more than a decade ago. I was 22 years old, a graduate stu- 2 dent newly arrived at the University of Chicago. It was in the echo of that terrified woman's footfalls that I first began to know the unwieldy inheritance I'd come into—the ability to alter public space in ugly ways. It was clear that she thought herself the quarry of a mugger, rapist, or worse. Suffering a bout of insomnia, however, I was stalking sleep, not defenseless wayfarers. As a softy who is scarcely able to take a knife to a raw chicken—let alone hold it to a person's throat—I was surprised, embarrassed, and dismayed all at once. Her flight made me feel like an accomplice in tyranny. It also made it clear that I was indistinguishable from the muggers who occasionally seeped into the area from the surrounding ghetto. That first encounter, and those that followed, signified that a vast, unnerving gulf lay between nighttime pedestrians—particularly women—and me. And I soon gathered that being perceived as dangerous is a hazard in itself. I only needed to turn a corner into a dicey situation, or crowd some frightened, armed person in a foyer somewhere, or make an errant move after being pulled over by a policeman. Where fear and weapons meet—and they often do in urban America—there is always the possibility of death.

In that first year, my first away from my hometown, I was to become thoroughly familiar with the language of fear. At dark, shadowy intersections in Chicago, I could cross in front of a car stopped at a traffic light and elicit the *thunk, thunk, thunk, thunk* of the driver—black, white, male, or female—hammering down the door locks. On less traveled streets after dark, I grew accustomed to but never comfortable with people who crossed to the other side of the street rather than pass me. Then there were the standard unpleasantries with police, doormen, bouncers, cab drivers, and others whose business it is to screen out troublesome individuals *before* there is any nastiness.

I moved to New York nearly two years ago and I have remained an avid night walker. In central Manhattan, the near-constant crowd cover minimizes tense one-on-one street encounters. Elsewhere—visiting friends in SoHo, where sidewalks are narrow and tightly spaced buildings shut out the sky—things can get very taut indeed.

Black men have a firm place in New York mugging literature. Norman Podhoretz in his famed (or infamous) 1963 essay, "My Negro Problem—and Ours," recalls growing up in terror of black males; they "were tougher than we were, more ruthless," he writes—and as an adult on the Upper West Side of Manhattan, he continues, he cannot constrain his nervousness when he meets black men on certain streets. Similarly, a decade later, the essayist and novelist Edward Hoagland extols a New York where once "Negro bitterness bore down mainly on other Negroes." Where some see mere panhandlers, Hoagland sees "a mugger who is clearly screwing up his nerve to do more than just *ask* for money." But Hoagland has "the New Yorker's quick-hunch posture for broken-field maneuvering," and the bad guy swerves away.

I often witness that "hunch posture," from women after dark on the warrenlike streets of Brooklyn where I live. They seem to set their faces on neutral and, with their purse straps strung across their chests bandolier style, they forge ahead as though bracing themselves against being tackled. I understand, of course, that the danger they perceive is not a hallucination. Women are particularly vulnerable to street violence, and young black males are drastically overrepresented among the perpetrators of that violence. Yet these truths are no solace against the kind of alienation that comes of being ever the suspect, against being set apart, a fearsome entity with whom pedestrians avoid making eye contact.

It is not altogether clear to me how I reached the ripe old age of 22 without being conscious of the lethality nighttime pedestrians attributed to me. Perhaps it was because in Chester, Pennsylvania, the small, angry industrial town where I came of age in the 1960s, I was scarcely noticeable against a backdrop of gang warfare, street knifings, and murders. I grew up one of the good boys, had perhaps a half-dozen fist fights. In retrospect, my shyness of combat has clear sources.

Many things go into the making of a young thug. One of those things   8 is the consummation of the male romance with the power to intimidate. An infant discovers that random flailings send the baby bottle flying out of the crib and crashing to the floor. Delighted, the joyful babe repeats those motions again and again, seeking to duplicate the feat. Just so, I recall the points at which some of my boyhood friends were finally seduced by the perception of themselves as tough guys. When a mark cowered and surrendered his money without resistance, myth and reality merged—and paid off. It is, after all, only manly to embrace the power to frighten and intimidate. We, as men, are not supposed to give an inch of our lane on the highway; we are to seize the fighter's edge in work and in play and even in love; we are to be valiant in the face of hostile forces.

Unfortunately, poor and powerless young men seem to take all this   9 nonsense literally. As a boy, I saw countless tough guys locked away; I have since buried several, too. They were babies, really—a teenage cousin, a brother of 22, a childhood friend in his mid-twenties—all gone down in episodes of bravado played out in the streets. I came to doubt the virtues of intimidation early on. I chose, perhaps even unconsciously, to remain a shadow—timid, but a survivor.

The fearsomeness mistakenly attributed to me in public places often   10 has a perilous flavor. The most frightening of these confusions occurred in the late 1970s and early 1980s when I worked as a journalist in Chicago. One day, rushing into the office of a magazine I was writing for with a deadline story in hand, I was mistaken for a burglar. The office manager called security and, with an ad hoc posse, pursued me through the labyrinthine halls, nearly to my editor's door. I had no way of proving who I was. I could only move briskly toward the company of someone who knew me.

Another time I was on assignment for a local paper and killing time   11 before an interview. I entered a jewelry store on the city's affluent Near North Side. The proprietor excused herself and returned with an enormous red Doberman pinscher straining at the end of a leash. She stood, the dog extended toward me, silent to my questions, her eyes bulging nearly out of her head. I took a cursory look around, nodded, and bade her good night. Relatively speaking, however, I never fared as badly as another black male journalist. He went to nearby Waukegan, Illinois, a couple of summers ago to work on a story about a murderer who was born there. Mistaking the reporter for the killer, police hauled him from his car at gunpoint and but for his press credentials would probably have tried to book him. Such episodes are not uncommon. Black men trade tales like this all the time.

In "My Negro Problem—and Ours," Podhoretz writes that the hatred he feels for blacks makes itself known to him through a variety of avenues—one being his discomfort with that "special brand of paranoid touchiness" to which he says blacks are prone. No doubt he is speaking here of black men. In time, I learned to smother the rage I felt at so often being taken for a criminal. Not to do so would surely have led to madness—via that special "paranoid touchiness" that so annoyed Podhoretz at the time he wrote the essay.

I began to take precautions to make myself less threatening. I move about with care, particularly late in the evening. I give a wide berth to nervous people on subway platforms during the wee hours, particularly when I have exchanged business clothes for jeans. If I happen to be entering a building behind some people who appear skittish, I may walk by, letting them clear the lobby before I return, so as not to seem to be following them. I have been calm and extremely congenial on those rare occasions when I've been pulled over by the police.

And on late-evening constitutionals along streets less traveled by, I employ what has proved to be an excellent tension-reducing measure: I whistle melodies from Beethoven and Vivaldi and the more popular classical composers. Even steely New Yorkers hunching toward nighttime destinations seem to relax, and occasionally they even join in the tune. Virtually everybody seems to sense that a mugger wouldn't be warbling bright, sunny selections from Vivaldi's *Four Seasons*. It is my equivalent of the cowbell that hikers wear when they know they are in bear country.

• • •

COMPREHENSION

1. Why does Staples characterize the woman he encounters in paragraph 1 as a "victim"?

2. What does Staples mean when he says he has the power to "alter public space" (2)?

3. Why does Staples walk the streets at night?

4. What things does Staples say go "into the making of a young thug" (8)? According to Staples, why are young, poor, and powerless men especially likely to become thugs?

5. In what ways does Staples attempt to make himself less threatening?

PURPOSE AND AUDIENCE

1. What is Staples's thesis? Does he state it or imply it?

2. Does Staples use logic, emotion, or a combination of the two to appeal to his readers? How appropriate is his strategy?

3. What preconceptions does Staples assume his audience has? In what ways does he challenge these preconceptions?

4. What is Staples trying to accomplish with his first sentence? Do you think he succeeds? Why or why not?

STYLE AND STRUCTURE

1. Why does Staples mention Norman Podhoretz? Could he make the same points without referring to Podhoretz's essay?

2. Staples begins his essay with an anecdote. How effective is this strategy? Do you think another opening strategy would be more effective? Explain.

3. Does Staples present enough examples to support his thesis? Are they representative? Would other types of examples be more convincing? Explain.

4. In what order does Staples present his examples? Would another order be more effective? Explain.

VOCABULARY PROJECTS

1. Define each of the following words as it is used in this selection.

discreet (1)	quarry (2)	constrain (5)
uninflammatory (1)	insomnia (2)	bravado (9)
billowing (1)	wayfarers (2)	constitutionals (14)

2. In his essay, Staples uses the word *thug*. List as many synonyms as you can for this word. Do these words convey the same idea, or are there differences in connotation? Explain.

JOURNAL ENTRY

Have you ever been in a situation such as the ones Staples describes, where you perceived someone as threatening? How did you react? After reading Staples's essay, do you think you would react the same way now? Discuss.

WRITING WORKSHOP

1. Use your journal entry to help you write an essay in which you use an extended example to support this statement: "When walking alone at night, you can (or cannot) be too careful."

2. Relying on examples from your own experience, write an essay in which you discuss what part you think race plays in people's reactions to Staples. Do you think his perceptions are accurate?

3. How accurate is Staples's observation concerning the "male romance with the power to intimidate" (8)? What does he mean by this statement? What examples from your own experience illustrate that this "romance" is an element of male upbringing in our society?

COMBINING THE PATTERNS

In paragraph 8, Staples uses **cause and effect** to demonstrate what goes "into the making of a young thug." Would a **narrative** example have better illustrated how a youth becomes a thug?

THEMATIC CONNECTIONS

- "The 'Black Table' Is Still There" (page 284)
- "Brains versus Brawn" (page 317)
- "The Ways We Lie" (page 414)

JONATHAN KOZOL

Jonathan Kozol was born in Boston in 1936 and graduated from Harvard University in 1958. After studying as a Rhodes scholar at Oxford University, he began teaching in public schools in Boston and its suburbs. He has also taught at numerous colleges, including Yale University, Trinity College in Connecticut, and the University of Massachusetts at Amherst. Kozol has written for the *Los Angeles Times, USA Today,* the *New York Times Book Review,* and the *New Yorker.* His numerous books on education and literacy and their social impact include the critically acclaimed *Death at an Early Age* (1967) as well as *Illiterate America* (1985), *Rachel and Her Children: Homeless Families in America* (1988), *Savage Inequalities: Children in America's Schools* (1991), and *Amazing Grace: The Lives of Children and the Conscience of a Nation* (1995). He received the Lannon Literary Award in 1994. In *Illiterate America,* Kozol examines the human and financial costs of illiteracy in America, contending that more than thirty-five million people read below the level needed to function in this society, and that, in certain cities, almost 40 percent of the adult population is functionally illiterate. The following essay, taken from that book, uses examples to convey to readers what it means to be illiterate.

The Human Cost of an Illiterate Society

PRECAUTIONS. READ BEFORE USING.
Poison: Contains sodium hydroxide (caustic soda-lye).
Corrosive: Causes severe eye and skin damage, may cause blindness.
Harmful or fatal if swallowed.
If swallowed, give large quantities of milk or water.
Do not induce vomiting.
Important: Keep water out of can at all times to prevent contents from violently erupting. . . .
—*warning on a can of Drano*

Questions of literacy, in Socrates' belief, must at length be judged as matters of morality. Socrates could not have had in mind the moral compromise peculiar to a nation like our own. Some of our Founding Fathers did, however, have this question in their minds. One of the wisest of those Founding Fathers (one who may not have been most compassionate but surely was more prescient than some of his peers) recognized the special dangers that illiteracy would pose to basic equity in the political construction that he helped to shape.

"A people who mean to be their own governors," James Madison wrote, "must arm themselves with the power knowledge gives. A popular government without popular information or the means of acquiring it, is but a prologue to a farce or a tragedy, or perhaps both."

Tragedy looms larger than farce in the United States today. Illiterate   3
citizens seldom vote. Those who do are forced to cast a vote of questionable worth. They cannot make informed decisions based on serious print
information. Sometimes they can be alerted to their interests by aggressive voter education. More frequently, they vote for a face, a smile, or a
style, not for a mind or character or body of beliefs.

The number of illiterate adults exceeds by 16 million the entire vote   4
cast for the winner in the 1980 presidential contest. If even one third of all
illiterates could vote, and read enough and do sufficient math to vote in
their self-interest, Ronald Reagan would not likely have been chosen
president. There is, of course, no way to know for sure. We do know this:
Democracy is a mendacious term when used by those who are prepared
to countenance the forced exclusion of one third of our electorate. So long
as 60 million people are denied significant participation, the government
is neither of, nor for, nor by, the people. It is a government, at best, of
those two-thirds whose wealth, skin color, or parental privilege allows
them opportunity to profit from the provocation and instruction of the
written word.

The undermining of democracy in the United States is one "expense"   5
that sensitive Americans can easily deplore because it represents a contradiction that endangers citizens of all political positions. The human price
is not so obvious at first.

Since I first immersed myself within this work I have often had the   6
following dream: I find that I am in a railroad station or a large department store within a city that is utterly unknown to me and where I cannot
understand the printed words. None of the signs or symbols is familiar.
Everything looks strange: like mirror writing of some kind. Gradually I
understand that I am in the Soviet Union. All the letters on the walls
around me are Cyrillic. I look for my pocket dictionary but I find that it
has been mislaid. Where have I left it? Then I recall that I forgot to bring it
with me when I packed my bags in Boston. I struggle to remember the
name of my hotel. I try to ask somebody for directions. One person stops
and looks at me in a peculiar way. I lose the nerve to ask. At last I reach
into my wallet for an ID card. The card is missing. Have I lost it? Then I
remember that my card was confiscated for some reason, many years before. Around this point, I wake up in a panic.

This panic is not so different from the misery that millions of adult il-   7
literates experience each day within the course of their routine existence
in the U.S.A.

Illiterates cannot read the menu in a restaurant.   8

They cannot read the cost of items on the menu in the *window* of the   9
restaurant before they enter.

Illiterates cannot read the letters that their children bring home from   10
their teachers. They cannot study school department circulars that tell
them of the courses that their children must be taking if they hope to pass
the SAT exams. They cannot help with homework. They cannot write a

letter to the teacher. They are afraid to visit in the classroom. They do not want to humiliate their child or themselves.

Illiterates cannot read instructions on a bottle of prescription medi- 11
cine. They cannot find out when a medicine is past the year of safe consumption; nor can they read of allergenic risks, warnings to diabetics, or the potential sedative effect of certain kinds of nonprescription pills. They cannot observe preventive health care admonitions. They cannot read about "the seven warning signs of cancer" or the indications of blood-sugar fluctuations or the risks of eating certain foods that aggravate the likelihood of cardiac arrest.

Illiterates live, in more than literal ways, an uninsured existence. 12
They cannot understand the written details on a health insurance form. They cannot read the waivers that they sign preceding surgical procedures. Several women I have known in Boston have entered a slum hospital with the intention of obtaining a tubal ligation and have emerged a few days later after having been subjected to a hysterectomy. Unaware of their rights, incognizant of jargon, intimidated by the unfamiliar air of fear and atmosphere of ether that so many of us find oppressive in the confines even of the most attractive and expensive medical facilities, they have signed their names to documents they could not read and which nobody, in the hectic situation that prevails so often in those overcrowded hospitals that serve the urban poor, had even bothered to explain.

Childbirth might seem to be the last inalienable right of any female 13
citizen within a civilized society. Illiterate mothers, as we shall see, already have been cheated of the power to protect their progeny against the likelihood of demolition in deficient public schools and, as a result, against the verbal servitude within which they themselves exist. Surgical denial of the right to bear that child in the first place represents an ultimate denial, an unspeakable metaphor, a final darkness that denies even the twilight gleamings of our own humanity. What greater violation of our biological, our biblical, our spiritual humanity could possibly exist than that which takes place nightly, perhaps hourly these days, within such overburdened and benighted institutions as the Boston City Hospital? Illiteracy has many costs; few are so irreversible as this.

Even the roof above one's head, the gas or other fuel for heating that 14
protects the residents of northern city slums against the threat of illness in the winter months become uncertain guarantees. Illiterates cannot read the lease that they must sign to live in an apartment which, too often, they cannot afford. They cannot manage check accounts and therefore seldom pay for anything by mail. Hours and entire days of difficult travel (and the cost of bus or other public transit) must be added to the real cost of whatever they consume. Loss of interest on the check accounts they do not have, and could not manage if they did, must be regarded as another of the excess costs paid by the citizen who is excluded from the common instruments of commerce in a numerate society.

"I couldn't understand the bills," a woman in Washington, D.C., reports, "and then I couldn't write the checks to pay them. We signed things we didn't know what they were."   15

Illiterates cannot read the notices that they receive from welfare offices or from the IRS. They must depend on word-of-mouth instruction from the welfare worker—or from other persons whom they have good reason to mistrust. They do not know what rights they have, what deadlines and requirements they face, what options they might choose to exercise. They are half-citizens. Their rights exist in print but not in fact.   16

Illiterates cannot look up numbers in a telephone directory. Even if they can find the names of friends, few possess the sorting skills to make use of the yellow pages; categories are bewildering and trade names are beyond decoding capabilities for millions of nonreaders. Even the emergency numbers listed on the first page of the phone book—"Ambulance," "Police," and "Fire"—are too frequently beyond the recognition of nonreaders.   17

Many illiterates cannot read the admonition on a pack of cigarettes. Neither the Surgeon General's warning nor its reproduction on the package can alert them to the risks. Although most people learn by word of mouth that smoking is related to a number of grave physical disorders, they do not get the chance to read the detailed stories which can document this danger with the vividness that turns concern into determination to resist. They can see the handsome cowboy or the slim Virginia lady lighting up a filter cigarette; they cannot heed the words that tell them that this product is (not "may be") dangerous to their health. Sixty million men and women are condemned to be the unalerted, high-risk candidates for cancer.   18

Illiterates do not buy "no-name" products in the supermarkets. They must depend on photographs or the familiar logos that are printed on the packages of brand-name groceries. The poorest people, therefore, are denied the benefits of the least costly products.   19

Illiterates depend almost entirely upon label recognition. Many labels, however, are not easy to distinguish. Dozens of different kinds of Campbell's soup appear identical to the nonreader. The purchaser who cannot read and does not dare to ask for help, out of the fear of being stigmatized (a fear which is unfortunately realistic), frequently comes home with something which she never wanted and her family never tasted.   20

Illiterates cannot read instructions on a pack of frozen food. Packages sometimes provide an illustration to explain the cooking preparations; but illustrations are of little help to someone who must "boil water, drop the food—*within* its plastic wrapper—in the boiling water, wait for it to simmer, instantly remove."   21

Even when labels are seemingly clear, they may be easily mistaken. A woman in Detroit brought home a gallon of Crisco for her children's dinner. She thought that she had bought the chicken that was pictured on the   22 label. She had enough Crisco now to last a year—but no more money to go back and buy the food for dinner.

Recipes provided on the packages of certain staples sometimes tempt a semiliterate person to prepare a meal her children have not tasted. The longing to vary the uniform and often starchy content of low-budget meals provided to the family that relies on food stamps commonly leads to ruinous results. Scarce funds have been wasted and the food must be thrown out. The same applies to distribution of food-surplus produce in emergency conditions. Government inducements to poor people to "explore the ways" by which to make a tasty meal from tasteless noodles, surplus cheese, and powdered milk are useless to nonreaders. Intended as benevolent advice, such recommendations mock reality and foster deeper feelings of resentment and of inability to cope. (Those, on the other hand, who cautiously refrain from "innovative" recipes in preparation of their children's meals must suffer the opprobrium of "laziness," "lack of imagination. . . .")   23

Illiterates cannot travel freely. When they attempt to do so, they encounter risks that few of us can dream of. They cannot read traffic signs and, while they often learn to recognize and to decipher symbols, they cannot manage street names which they haven't seen before. The same is true for bus and subway stops. While ingenuity can sometimes help a man or woman to discern directions from familiar landmarks, buildings, cemeteries, churches, and the like, most illiterates are virtually immobilized. They seldom wander past the streets and neighborhoods they know. Geographical paralysis becomes a bitter metaphor for their entire existence. They are immobilized in almost every sense we can imagine. They can't move up. They can't move out. They cannot see beyond. Illiterates may take an oral test for drivers' permits in most sections of America. It is a questionable concession. Where will they go? How will they get there? How will they get home? Could it be that some of us might like it better if they stayed where they belong?   24

Travel is only one of many instances of circumscribed existence. Choice, in almost all of its facets, is diminished in the life of an illiterate adult. Even the printed TV schedule, which provides most people with the luxury of preselection, does not belong within the arsenal of options in illiterate existence. One consequence is that the viewer watches only what appears at moments when he happens to have time to turn the switch. Another consequence, a lot more common, is that the TV set remains in operation night and day. Whatever the program offered at the hour when he walks into the room will be the nutriment that he accepts and swallows. Thus, to passivity, is added frequency—indeed, almost uninterrupted continuity. Freedom to select is no more possible here than in the choice of home or surgery or food.   25

"You don't choose," said one illiterate woman. "You take your wishes from somebody else." Whether in perusal of a menu, selection of highways, purchase of groceries, or determination of affordable enjoyment,   26 illiterate Americans must trust somebody else: a friend, a relative, a stranger on the street, a grocery clerk, a TV copywriter.

"All of our mail we get, it's hard for her to read. Settin' down and writing a letter, she can't do it. Like if we get a bill . . . we take it over to my sister-in-law. . . . My sister-in-law reads it." 27

Billing agencies harass poor people for the payment of the bills for purchases that might have taken place six months before. Utility companies offer an agreement for a staggered payment schedule on a bill past due. "You have to trust them," one man said. Precisely for this reason, you end up by trusting no one and suspecting everyone of possible deceit. A submerged sense of distrust becomes the corollary to a constant need to trust. "They are cheating me. . . . I have been tricked. . . . I do not know. . . . " 28

Not knowing: This is a familiar theme. Not knowing the right word for the right thing at the right time is one form of subjugation. Not knowing the world that lies concealed behind those words is a more terrifying feeling. The longitude and latitude of one's existence are beyond all easy apprehension. Even the hard, cold stars within the firmament above one's head begin to mock the possibilities for self-location. Where am I? Where did I come from? Where will I go? 29

"I've lost a lot of jobs," one man explains. "Today, even if you're a janitor, there's still reading and writing. . . . They leave a note saying 'Go to room so-and-so. . . . ' You can't do it. You can't read it. You don't know." 30

"The hardest thing about it is that I've been places where I didn't know where I was. You don't know where you are. . . . You're lost." 31

"Like I said: I have two kids. What do I do if one of my kids starts choking? I go running to the phone. . . . I can't look up the hospital phone number. That's if we're at home. Out on the street, I can't read the sign. I get to a pay phone. 'Okay, tell us where you are. We'll send an ambulance.' I look at the street sign. Right there, I can't tell you what it says. I'd have to spell it out, letter for letter. By that time, one of my kids would be dead. . . . These are the kinds of fears you go with, every single day. . . . " 32

"Reading directions, I suffer with. I work with chemicals. . . . That's scary to begin with. . . ." 33

"You sit down. They throw the menu in front of you. Where do you go from there? Nine times out of ten you say, 'Go ahead. Pick out something for the both of us.' I've eaten some weird things, let me tell you!" 34

Menus. Chemicals. A child choking while his mother searches for a word she does not know to find assistance that will come too late. Another mother speaks about the inability to help her kids to read: "I can't read to them. Of course that's leaving them out of something they should have. Oh, it matters. You *believe* it matters! I ordered all these books. The kids belong to a book club. Donny wanted me to read a book to him. I told Donny: 'I can't read.' He said: 'Mommy, you sit down. I'll read it to you.' I tried it one day, reading from the pictures. Donny looked at me. He said, 'Mommy, that's not right.' He's only five. He knew I couldn't read. . . . " 35

A landlord tells a woman that her lease allows him to evict her if her   36
baby cries and causes inconvenience to her neighbors. The consequence
of challenging his words conveys a danger which appears, unlikely as it
seems, even more alarming than the danger of eviction. Once she admits
that she can't read, in the desire to maneuver for the time in which to call
a friend, she will have defined herself in terms of an explicit impotence
that she cannot endure. Capitulation in this case is preferable to self-hu-
miliation. Resisting the definition of oneself in terms of what one cannot
do, what others take for granted, represents a need so great that other imperatives (even one so urgent as the need to keep one's home in winter's
cold) evaporate and fall away in face of fear. Even the loss of home and
shelter, in this case, is not so terrifying as the loss of self.

"I come out of school. I was sixteen. They had their meetings. The di-   37
rectors meet. They said that I was wasting their school paper. I was wasting pencils. . . . "

Another illiterate, looking back, believes she was not worthy of her   38
teacher's time. She believes that it was wrong of her to take up space
within her school. She believes that it was right to leave in order that
somebody more deserving could receive her place.

Children choke. Their mother chokes another way: on more than   39
chicken bones.

People eat what others order, know what others tell them, struggle not   40
to see themselves as they believe the world perceives them. A man in
California speaks about his own loss of identity, of self-location, definition:

"I stood at the bottom of the ramp. My car had broke down on the   41
freeway. There was a phone. I asked for the police. They was nice. They
said to tell them where I was. I looked up at the signs. There was one that
I had seen before. I read it to them: ONE WAY STREET. They thought it was a
joke. I told them I couldn't read. There was other signs above the ramp.
They told me to try. I looked around for somebody to help. All the cars
was going by real fast. I couldn't make them understand that I was lost.
The cop was nice. He told me: 'Try once more.' I did my best. I couldn't
read. I only knew the sign above my head. The cop was trying to be nice.
He knew that I was trapped. 'I can't send out a car to you if you can't tell
me where you are.' I felt afraid. I nearly cried. I'm forty-eight years old. I
only said: 'I'm on a one-way street. . . .'"

The legal problems and the courtroom complications that confront il-   42
literate adults have been discussed above. The anguish that may underlie
such matters was brought home to me this year while I was working on
this book. I have spoken [in an earlier part of the book] of a sudden
phone call from one of my former students, now in prison for a criminal
offense. Stephen is not a boy today. He is twenty-eight years old. He
called to ask me to assist him in his trial, which comes up next fall. He
will be on trial for murder. He has just knifed and killed a man who first
enticed him to his home, then cheated him, and then insulted him—as
"an illiterate subhuman."

Stephen now faces twenty years to life. Stephen's mother was illiter-   43
ate. His grandparents were illiterate as well. What parental curse did not
destroy was killed off finally by the schools. Silent violence is repaid with
interest. It will cost us $25,000 yearly to maintain this broken soul in
prison. But what is the price that has been paid by Stephen's victim?
What is the price that will be paid by Stephen?

Perhaps we might slow down a moment here and look at the realities   44
described above. This is the nation that we live in. This is a society that
most of us did not create but which our President and other leaders have
been willing to sustain by virtue of malign neglect. Do we possess the
character and courage to address a problem which so many nations,
poorer than our own, have found it natural to correct?

The answers to these questions represent a reasonable test of our be-   45
lief in the democracy to which we have been asked in public school to
swear allegiance.

•   •   •

COMPREHENSION

1. Why is illiteracy a danger to a democratic society?

2. According to Kozol, why do our reactions to the problem of illiteracy in
   America test our belief in democracy?

3. What does Kozol mean when he says that an illiterate person leads a "circumscribed existence" (25)? How does being illiterate limit a person's
   choices?

4. What legal problems and courtroom complications confront illiterate
   adults?

5. According to Kozol, what is being done to solve the problem of illiteracy
   in the United States?

PURPOSE AND AUDIENCE

1. What is Kozol's thesis? Where does he state it?

2. Kozol aims his essay at a wide general audience. How does he address
   the needs of this audience? In what ways would his discussion differ if it
   were intended for an audience of reading specialists? Of politicians?

3. Is Kozol's purpose to inform, to persuade, to express emotions, or some
   combination of these three? Does he have additional, more specific purposes as well? Explain.

STYLE AND STRUCTURE

1. Why does Kozol introduce his essay with references to Socrates and
   James Madison? How does this strategy help him support his thesis?

2. In paragraph 6 Kozol recounts a dream that he often has. Why does he include this anecdote? How does it help him move from his introduction to the body of his essay?

3. Kozol uses many short examples to make his point. Do you think fewer examples developed in more depth would be more effective? Why or why not?

4. How effective is Kozol's use of statistics? Do the statistics complement or undercut his illustrations of the personal cost of illiteracy?

VOCABULARY PROJECTS

1. Define each of the following words as it is used in this selection.

prescient (1)	sedative (11)	opprobrium (23)
farce (2)	admonitions (11)	concession (24)
mendacious (4)	incognizant (12)	firmament (29)
countenance (4)	jargon (12)	capitulation (36)
Cyrillic (6)	numerate (14)	

2. Reread paragraphs 24 and 25 and determine which words or phrases convey Kozol's feelings toward his subject. Rewrite these two paragraphs, eliminating as much subjective language as you can. Do you think your changes make the paragraphs more appealing or less so to a general audience? To a group of sociologists? To a group of reading teachers?

JOURNAL ENTRY

Keep a journal for a day, noting the difficulty you would have carrying out each activity in your daily routine if you were illiterate.

WRITING WORKSHOP

1. Using your journal entry as a starting point, write an essay in which you describe the tasks you would have difficulty accomplishing if you could not read. Include an explicit thesis statement, and use examples to illustrate your points.

2. People have not always had to read to function in society. Six hundred years ago, in fact, most people could not read. Similarly, the majority of people today are not computer literate. Write an essay giving examples of the kinds of jobs a person cannot hold today if he or she cannot use a computer.

3. Using Kozol's essay as source material, write an essay in which your thesis is Madison's statement, "A people who mean to be their own governors must arm themselves with the power knowledge gives" (2). Be sure to document any information you borrow from Kozol.

COMBINING THE PATTERNS WITH EXEMPLIFICATION

Why does Kozol choose to end his essay with a **narrative** about Stephen, one of his former students, who is in jail awaiting trial for murder? How does this anecdote help Kozol set up his concluding remarks in paragraphs 44 and 45?

THEMATIC CONNECTIONS

- "Words Left Unspoken" (page 121)
- "Aria: A Memoir of a Bilingual Childhood" (page 357)
- "Mother Tongue" (page 393)

GRACE PALEY

Grace Paley (1922–) grew up in New York City. She attended Hunter College and taught at Columbia University, Syracuse University, City College of New York, and Sarah Lawrence College, from which she retired in 1988. Paley's short stories have appeared in the *New Yorker, Ms., Mother Jones,* and many other magazines, and they have been published in the collections *The Little Disturbances of Man* (1959); *Enormous Changes at the Last Minute* (1974), in which "Samuel" appeared; *Later the Same Day* (1985); and *The Collected Stories of Grace Paley* (1994), which was nominated for the National Book Award. Paley received the Rea Award for short stories in 1993. She has also published two collections of poems, *Leaning Forward* (1985) and *New and Collected Poems* (1992), and two books of stories and poems on peace, *365 Reasons Not to Have Another War* (1989) and *Long Walks and Intimate Talks* (1991). In "Samuel," Paley uses a simple story to touch on complex emotions and questions.

Samuel

Some boys are very tough. They're afraid of nothing. They are the ones who climb a wall and take a bow at the top. Not only are they brave on the roof, but they make a lot of noise in the darkest part of the cellar where even the super hates to go. They also jiggle and hop on the platform between the locked doors of the subway cars. 1

Four boys are jiggling on the swaying platform. Their names are Alfred, Calvin, Samuel, and Tom. The men and women in the cars on either side watch them. They don't like them to jiggle or jump but don't want to interfere. Of course some of the men in the cars were once brave boys like these. One of them had ridden the tail of a speeding truck from New York to Rockaway Beach without getting off, without his sore fingers losing hold. Nothing happened to him then or later. He had made a compact with other boys who preferred to watch: starting at Eighth Avenue and Fifteenth Street, he would get to some specified place, maybe Twenty-third and the river, by hopping the tops of the moving trucks. This was hard to do when one truck turned a corner in the wrong direction and the nearest truck was a couple of feet too high. He made three or four starts before succeeding. He had gotten this idea from a film at school called *The Romance of Logging.* He had finished high school, married a good friend, was in a responsible job, and going to night school. 2

These two men and others looked at the four boys jumping and jiggling on the platform and thought, It must be fun to ride that way, especially now the weather is nice and we're out of the tunnel and way high over the Bronx. Then they thought, These kids do seem to be acting sort of stupid. They *are* little. Then they thought of some of the brave things they had done when they were boys and jiggling didn't seem so risky. 3

The ladies in the car became very angry when they looked at the four   4
boys. Most of them brought their brows together and hoped the boys
could see their extreme disapproval. One of the ladies wanted to get up
and say, be careful you dumb kids, get off that platform or I'll call a cop.
But three of the boys were Negroes and the fourth was something else she
couldn't tell for sure. She was afraid they'd be fresh and laugh at her and
embarrass her. She wasn't afraid they'd hit her, but she was afraid of embarrassment. Another lady thought, their mothers never know where
they are. It wasn't true in this particular case. Their mothers all knew that
they had gone to see the missile exhibit on Fourteenth Street.

Out on the platform, whenever the train accelerated, the boys would   5
raise their hands and point them up to the sky to act like rockets going
off, then they rat-tat-tatted the shatterproof glass pane like machine guns,
although no machine guns had been exhibited.

For some reason known only to the motorman, the train began a sud-   6
den slowdown. The lady who was afraid of embarrassment saw the boys
jerk forward and backward and grab the swinging guard chains. She had
her own boy at home. She stood up with determination and went to the
door. She slid it open and said, "You boys will be hurt. You'll be killed.
I'm going to call the conductor if you don't just go into the next car and sit
down and be quiet."

Two of the boys said, "Yes'm," and acted as though they were about   7
to go. Two of them blinked their eyes a couple of times and pressed their
lips together. The trains resumed its speed. The door slid shut, parting the
lady and the boys. She leaned against the side door because she had to
get off at the next stop.

The boys opened their eyes wide at each other and laughed. The lady   8
blushed. The boys looked at her and laughed harder. They began to
pound each other's back. Samuel laughed the hardest and pounded
Alfred's back until Alfred coughed and the tears came. Alfred held tight
to the chain hook. Samuel pounded him even harder when he saw the
tears. He said, "Why you bawling? You a baby, huh?" and laughed. One
of the men whose boyhood had been more watchful than brave became
angry. He stood up straight and looked at the boys for a couple of seconds. Then he walked in a citizenly way to the end of the car, where he
pulled the emergency cord. Almost at once, with a terrible hiss, the pressure of air abandoned the brakes and the wheels were caught and held.

People standing in the most secure places fell forward, then back-   9
ward. Samuel had let go of his hold on the chain so he could pound Tom
as well as Alfred. All the passengers in the cars whipped back and forth,
but he pitched only forward and fell head first to be crushed and killed
between the cars.

The train had stopped hard, halfway into the station, and the conduc-   10
tor called at once for the trainmen who knew about this kind of death and
how to take the body from the wheels and brakes. There was silence except for passengers from the other cars who asked, What happened! What

happened! The ladies waited around wondering if he might be an only child. The men recalled other afternoons with very bad endings. The little boys stayed close to each other, leaning and touching shoulders and arms and legs.

When the policeman knocked at the door and told her about it, Samuel's mother began to scream. She screamed all day and moaned all night, though the doctors tried to quiet her with pills.   11

Oh, oh, she hopelessly cried. She did not know how she could ever find another boy like that one. However, she was a young woman and she became pregnant. Then for a few months she was hopeful. The child born to her was a boy. They brought him to be seen and nursed. She smiled. But immediately she saw that this baby wasn't Samuel. She and her husband together have had other children, but never again will a boy exactly like Samuel be known.   12

• • •

THINKING ABOUT LITERATURE

1. Paley supports the main point of the story with a single example. What is the example?

2. The story begins with the observation, "Some boys are very tough." Is Samuel really tough? What do you think Paley wants her readers to realize about Samuel?

3. What point do you think the story makes about bravery? Which of the characters do you consider brave? Why?

4. What effect does the incident have on the other characters? What do their reactions reveal about them?

JOURNAL ENTRY

Do you consider Samuel a hero? Is it true, as the narrator asserts, that "never again will a boy exactly like Samuel be known" (12)?

THEMATIC CONNECTIONS

- "Thirty-Eight Who Saw Murder Didn't Call the Police" (page 86)
- "It's Just Too Late" (page 294)
- "The Men We Carry in Our Minds" (page 387)

WRITING ASSIGNMENTS FOR EXEMPLIFICATION

1. Interview several businesspeople in your community. Begin by explaining the Peter Principle to them if they are unfamiliar with it. Then ask them to express their feelings about this concept, and take notes on their responses. Finally, write an essay about your findings that includes quotations from your notes.

2. Write a humorous essay about a ritual you experienced and the types of people who participated in it. Make a point about the ritual, and use the participants as examples to support your point.

3. Write an essay in which you establish that you are an optimistic or a pessimistic person. Use two or three extended examples to support your case.

4. If you could change three or four things at your school, what would they be? Use examples from your own experience to support your claims, and tie the three examples together with a single thesis statement.

5. Write an essay in which you discuss two or three of the greatest challenges facing the United States today. If you like, you may refer to essays in this chapter, such as "Just Walk On By" or "Six Enviro-Myths," or to essays elsewhere in this book, such as "Two Ways to Belong in America" (page 340) or "On Dumpster Diving" (page 609).

6. Using your family and friends as examples, write an essay in which you suggest some of the positive or negative characteristics of Americans.

7. Write an essay in which you present your formula for achieving success in college. You may, if you wish, talk about things like scheduling time, maintaining a high energy level, and learning how to relax. Use examples from your own experience to make your point. You may wish to refer to "College Pressures" (page 378).

8. Write an exemplification essay in which you discuss how cooperation has helped you achieve some important goal. Support your thesis with a single extended example.

9. Choose an event that you believe illustrates a less-than-admirable moment in your life. Write an essay explaining your feelings.

10. Write an essay in which you identify and discuss what you believe is the most pressing personal problem you have faced and overcome.

COLLABORATIVE ACTIVITY FOR EXEMPLIFICATION

The following passage appeared in a handbook given to parents of entering students at a midwestern university:

The freshman experience is like no other—at once challenging, exhilarating, and fun. Students face academic challenges as they are exposed to many new ideas. They also face personal challenges as they meet many new people from diverse backgrounds. It is a time to mature and grow. It is an opportunity to explore new subjects and familiar ones. There may be no more challenging and exciting time of personal growth than the first year of university study.

Working in groups of four, brainstorm to identify examples that support or refute the idea that there "may be no more challenging and exciting time of personal growth" than the first year of college. Then, choose one person from each group to tell the class what position the group took and explain the examples you collected. Finally, work together to write an essay that presents your group's position. Have one student write the first draft, two others revise this draft, and the last student edit and proofread the revised draft.

5

PROCESS

WHAT IS PROCESS?

A **process** essay explains how to do something or how something occurs. It presents a sequence of steps and shows how those steps lead to a particular result. In the following paragraph from *Language in Thought and Action,* the semanticist S. I. Hayakawa uses process to explain how an editor of a dictionary decides on a word's definition:

Process presents series of steps in chronological order
    To define a word, then, the dictionary-editor places before him the stack of cards illustrating that word; each of the cards represents an actual use of the word by a writer of some literacy or historical importance. He reads the cards carefully, discards some, rereads the rest, and divides up the stack according to what he thinks are the several senses of the word. Finally, he writes his definitions, following the hard-and-fast rule that each definition *must* be based on what the quotations in front of him reveal about the meaning of the word. The editor cannot be influenced by what *he* thinks a given word **Topic sentence** *ought* to mean. He must work according to the cards or not at all.

Process, like narrative, presents events in chronological order. Unlike a narrative, however, a process essay details a particular series of events that produces the same outcome whenever it is duplicated. Because these events form a sequence that has a fixed order, clarity is extremely important. Whether your readers are actually going to perform the process or are simply trying to understand how it occurs, your essay must make clear the exact order of the individual steps as well as their relationships to one another and to the process as a whole. You need to provide clear, logical transitions between the steps in a process, and you also need to present the steps in *strict* chronological order—that is, in the order in which they occur or are to be performed.

Instructions and Process Explanations

Depending on its purpose, a process essay can use either of two formats: *instructions* or *process explanation.*

The purpose of a set of **instructions** is to enable readers to perform the process. Instructions have many practical uses. A recipe, a handout about using your library's online databases, and the operating manual for your VCR are all sets of instructions. So are directions for locating an office building in Washington, DC, or driving from Houston to Pensacola. Instructions use the present tense and, like commands, the imperative mood, speaking directly to the readers who are to perform the tasks described: "*Disconnect* the system and *check* the electrical source."

The purpose of a **process explanation** is not to enable readers to perform a process but rather to help them understand how it is carried out. Such essays may examine anything from how silkworms spin their cocoons to how Michelangelo and Leonardo da Vinci painted their masterpieces on plaster walls and ceilings. A process explanation may employ the first person *(I, we)* or the third *(he, she, it, they)*, the past tense or the present. (Because its readers need to understand, not perform, the process, process explanation does not use the second person or the imperative mood.) The style of a process explanation varies, depending on whether a writer is explaining a process that takes place regularly or one that occurred in the past, and on whether the writer or someone else carries out the steps. The chart that follows suggests some of the options available to writers of process explanations.

	First person	*Third person*
Present tense	"After I place the chemicals in the tray, I turn out the lights in the darkroom." *(habitual process performed by the writer)*	"After photographers place the chemicals in the tray, they turn out the lights in the darkroom." *(habitual process performed by person other than the writer)*
Past tense	"After I placed the chemicals in the tray, I turned out the lights in the darkroom." *(process performed in the past by the writer)*	"After the photographer placed the chemicals in the tray, she turned out the lights in the darkroom." *(process performed in the past by someone other than the writer)*

Uses of Process Essays

College writing frequently calls for instructions or process explanations. In a biology term paper on some aspect of genetic engineering, you might devote a paragraph to an explanation of the process of amniocentesis; in an editorial about the negative side of fraternity life, you might decide to include a brief summary of the process of pledging. Or, you can organize an entire paper around a process pattern: in a literature essay, you might trace the steps through which a fictional character reaches some new insight; on a finance midterm, you might explain the procedure for approving a commercial loan.

You can use process writing to persuade or simply to present information. If its purpose is persuasive, a process paper may take a strong stand like "Applying for food stamps is a needlessly complex process that discourages many potential recipients" or "The process of slaughtering baby seals is inhumane and sadistic." Many process essays, however, communicate nothing more debatable than the procedure for blood typing. Even in such a case, though, a process should have a clear thesis statement that identifies the process and perhaps why it is performed: "Typing your own blood can familiarize you with some fundamental laboratory procedures."

STRUCTURING A PROCESS ESSAY

Like other essays, a process essay generally consists of three main sections. The *introduction* identifies the process and indicates why and under what circumstances it is performed. This section may include information about materials or preliminary preparations, or it may present an overview of the process, perhaps even listing its major stages. The paper's thesis is also usually stated in the introduction.

Each paragraph in the *body* of the essay typically treats one major stage of the procedure. Each stage may group several steps, depending on the nature and complexity of the process. These steps are presented in chronological order, interrupted only for essential definitions, explanations, or cautions. Every step must be included and must appear in its proper place. Throughout the body of a process essay, transitional words and phrases ensure that each step, each stage, and each paragraph leads logically to the next. Transitions like *first, second, meanwhile, after this, next, then, when you have finished,* and *finally* help to establish sequential and chronological relationships so that readers can follow the process.

A short process essay may not need a formal *conclusion*. If an essay does have a conclusion, however, it will often briefly review the procedure's major stages. Such an ending is especially useful if the paper has outlined a very long or particularly technical procedure that may seem complicated to general readers. The conclusion may also reinforce the thesis by summarizing the results of the process or explaining its significance.

As you plan a process essay's structure, remember that your goal is to depict the process accurately. This means that you should distinguish between what usually or always happens and what occasionally or rarely happens, between necessary steps and optional ones. You should also mentally test all the steps in sequence to be sure that the process really works as you say it does. Check carefully for omitted steps or incorrect information. If you are writing about a process you witnessed, try to test your written explanation by observing the process again.

As you write, remember to keep your readers' needs in mind. When necessary, explain the reasons for performing the steps, describe unfamiliar materials or equipment, define unfamiliar terms, and warn readers about possible snags that may occur during the process. (Sometimes you may even need to include illustrations.) Besides complete information, your readers need a clear and consistent discussion without ambiguities or surprises. For this reason, you should avoid unnecessary shifts in tense, person, voice, and mood. You should also include appropriate articles (*a*, *an*, and *the*) so that your discussion moves smoothly, like an essay—not abruptly, like a cookbook.

Suppose you are taking a midterm examination in a course in childhood and adolescent behavior. One essay question calls for a process explanation: "Trace the stages that children go through in acquiring language." After thinking about the question, you formulate the following thesis statement: "Although individual cases may differ, most children acquire language in a predictable series of stages." You then plan your essay and develop an informal outline, which might look like this.

Introduction:	Thesis statement—Although individual cases may differ, most children acquire language in a predictable series of stages.
First stage (two to twelve months):	Prelinguistic behavior, including "babbling" and appropriate responses to nonverbal cues.
Second stage (end of first year):	Single words as commands or requests; infant catalogs his or her environment.
Third stage (beginning of second year):	Expressive jargon (flow of sounds that imitates adult speech); real words along with jargon.
Fourth (and final) stage (middle of second year to beginning of third year):	Two-word phrases; longer strings; missing parts of speech.
Conclusion:	Restatement of thesis or review of major stages of process.

This essay, when completed, will show not only what the stages of the process are but also how they relate to one another. In addition, it will support the thesis that children learn language through a well-defined process.

▶ **STUDENT WRITERS: PROCESS**

The following student essays, Joseph Miksitz's set of instructions and Melany Hunt's explanation of how a process was conducted, were both written in response to the same assignment: "Write an essay in which you give instructions for a process that can change a person's appearance—or explain a process that changed your own appearance in some way."

Pumping Iron

Introduction

Students of high school and college age   1
are often dissatisfied with their appearance.
They see actors and models on television and
in magazines, and they want to be thinner,
stronger, or better looking. Sometimes this
quest for perfection gets young adults into
trouble, leading them to eating disorders or
drug use. A healthier way to improve your

Thesis statement

appearance is through a weight-training program, which can increase not only your
strength but also your self-esteem.

Overview of the
process; getting
started

If you want to avoid injury, you should   2
begin gradually. In the first week you might
lift weights only two days, concentrating on
thigh and calf muscles in the lower body and
on triceps, biceps, chest, back, and shoulders
in the upper body. For the next three or four
weeks, lift three days a week, adding more
exercises each week. By the fourth week, you
will probably start to feel stronger. At this
point, you can begin a four-day lifting program, which many experts believe is the most
productive and shows the best results.

Steps in process
of upper-body
workout

On Monday and Thursday, concentrate on   3
your upper body. Begin with the bench press (to
work chest muscles) and then move on to the
military press (for the shoulders). After that,
work your back muscles with the lats pull-down
exercise on the Universal machine or with some
heavy and light dead lifts. Finally, concentrate on your arms, doing bicep curls, tricep
extensions, and wrist curls (for the forearms).
To cool down, do a few sets of sit-ups.

Steps in process
of lower-body
workout

On Tuesday and Friday, focus on your   4
lower body with a leg workout. Start with the
weight-gaining bulk exercise, the leg press.
(Always begin your workout with your most
strenuous exercise, which is usually the exercise that works the largest muscles.) Next, do
some leg extensions to build the thigh muscles

in the front of your leg, and then move on to
leg curls to strengthen your hamstring muscle.
After that, do calf raises to work your calf
muscles. When you are finished, be sure to
stretch all the major muscles to prevent
tightness and injuries.

Warnings and   Of course, a balanced weight-training   5
reminders   program involves more than just lifting
weights. During your weight training, you
should eat four high-protein/high-carbohydrate
meals a day, limiting fat and eating four or
five servings of fruit and vegetables daily.
You should also monitor your progress carefully, paying attention to your body's aches and
pains and consulting a professional trainer
when necessary--especially if you think you
may have injured yourself.

Conclusion   Above all, don't let your weight-training   6
regimen take over your life. If you integrate
it into the rest of your life, balancing exercise with school, work, and social activities,
a weight-training program can make you look
and feel terrific.

Points for Special Attention

INTRODUCTION.   The first paragraph of Joseph Miksitz's essay includes a thesis statement that presents the advantages of embarking on a
weight-training program. Joseph begins with an overview of the image
problems faced by young adults and then narrows his focus to present
weight training as a possible solution to those problems.

STRUCTURE.   After his introduction, Joseph includes a paragraph
that presents guidelines for getting started. The third and fourth paragraphs enumerate the steps in each of the two processes he describes:
upper- and lower-body workouts. In his fifth paragraph, Joseph includes
reminders and cautions so that his readers will get the most out of their
exercise program while avoiding overexertion or injury. (The parenthetical sentence in paragraph 4 offers another helpful tip.) In his conclusion
Joseph advises readers to keep their exercise program in perspective and
(echoing his thesis statement) reminds them of its benefits.

PURPOSE AND STYLE.   Because Joseph's readers should be able to
perform the process themselves, he wrote it as a set of instructions.

Therefore, he uses the second person ("*you* will probably start to feel stronger") and present-tense verbs in the form of commands ("*Begin* with the bench press").

TRANSITIONS.   To make his essay clear and easy to follow, Joseph includes transitions that indicate the order in which each step is to be performed ("After that," "Next," "Finally") as well as specific time markers ("On Monday and Thursday," "On Tuesday and Friday") to distinguish the two related processes on which his essay focuses.

Focus on Revision

Joseph is careful to name various parts of the body and to identify different exercises as well as the general objective of each. He has, however, omitted many other key details, as several students noted in their peer critiques of his essay. For example, how much time should be spent on each exercise? What exactly is a bench press? A bicep curl? How are "light" and "heavy" defined? How many is "some" leg extensions or "a few sets" of sit-ups? How many repetitions of each exercise are necessary? What specific danger signs should alert readers to possible overexertion or injury? Is the routine Joseph describes appropriate for females as well as males? When revising his essay, Joseph needs to remember that most members of his audience are not familiar with the processes he describes and therefore will need much more detailed explanations.

In contrast to "Pumping Iron," Melany Hunt's essay is a process explanation.

Medium Ash Brown

Introduction	The beautiful chestnut-haired woman pictured on the box seemed to beckon to me. I reached for the box of Medium Ash Brown hair dye just as my friend Veronica grabbed the box labeled Sparkling Sherry. I can't remember our reasons for wanting to change our hair color, but they seemed to make sense at the time. Maybe we were just bored. I do remember that the idea of transforming our appearance came up unexpectedly. Impulsively, we decided to change our hair color--and, we hoped, our-	1
Thesis statement	selves--that very evening. Now I know that some impulses should definitely be resisted.	
Materials assembled	We decided to use my bathroom to dye our hair. Inside each box of hair color, we found two little bottles and a small tube wrapped in	2

a page of instructions. Attached to the instruction page itself were two very large, one-size-fits-all plastic gloves, which looked and felt like plastic sandwich bags. The directions recommended having some old towels around to soak up any spills or drips that might occur. Under the sink we found some old, frayed towels that I figured my mom had forgotten about, and we spread them around the

First stage of process: preparing the dye

bathtub. After we put our gloves on, we began the actual dyeing process. First we poured the first bottle into the second, which was half-full of some odd-smelling liquid. The smell was not much better after we combined the two bottles. The directions advised us to cut off a small section of hair to use as a sample. For some reason, we decided to skip this step.

Second stage of process: applying the dye

At this point, Veronica and I took turns leaning over the tub to wet our hair for the dye. The directions said to leave the dye on the hair for fifteen to twenty minutes, so we found a little timer and set it for fifteen minutes. Next, we applied the dye to our hair. Again, we took turns squeezing the bottle in order to cover all our hair. We then wrapped the old towels around our sour-smelling hair and went outside to get some fresh air.

3

Third stage of process: rinsing

After the fifteen minutes were up, we rinsed our hair. According to the directions, we were to add a little water and scrub as if we were shampooing our hair. The dye lathered up, and we rinsed our hair until the water ran clear. So far, so good.

4

Last stage of process: applying conditioner

The last part of the process involved applying the small tube of conditioner to our hair (because dyed hair becomes brittle and easily damaged). We used the conditioner as directed, and then we dried our hair so that

5

we could see the actual color. Even before I looked in the mirror, I heard Veronica's

Outcome of process

gasp.

"Nice try," I said, assuming she was just   6
trying to make me nervous, "But you're not
funny."

"Mel," she said, "look in the mirror."   7
Slowly, I turned around. My stomach turned
into a lead ball when I saw my reflection. My
hair was the putrid greenish-brown color of a
winter lawn, dying in patches yet still a nice
green in the shade.

The next day in school, I wore my hair   8
tied back under a baseball cap. I told only my
close friends what I had done. After they were
finished laughing, they offered their deepest,
most heartfelt condolences. They also offered
many suggestions--none very helpful--on what
to do to get my old hair color back.

Conclusion

It is now three months later, and I still   9
have no idea what prompted me to dye my hair.
My only consolation is that I resisted my
first impulse--to dye my hair a wild color,
like blue or fuchsia. Still, as I wait for my
hair to grow out, and as I assemble a larger
and larger collection of baseball caps, it is
small consolation indeed.

Points for Special Attention

STRUCTURE.   In her opening paragraph, Melany's thesis statement makes it very clear that the experience she describes is not one she would recommend to others. The temptation she describes in her introduction's first few sentences lures readers into her essay just as the picture on the box lured her. Her second paragraph lists the contents of the box of hair dye and explains how she and her friend assembled the other necessary materials. Then, she explains the first stage in the process, preparing the dye. Paragraphs 3–5 describe the other stages in the process in chronological order, and paragraphs 6–8 record Melany's and Veronica's reaction to their experiment. In paragraph 9 Melany sums up the impact of her experience and once again expresses her annoyance with herself for her impulsive act.

PURPOSE AND FORMAT.   Melany's purpose is *not* to enable others to duplicate the process she explains; on the contrary, she is trying to discourage readers from doing what she did. Consequently, she presents her process not as a set of instructions but as a process explanation, using first person and past tense to explain the actions of herself and her friend. She also largely eliminates cautions and reminders that her readers, who are not likely to undertake the process, will not need to know.

DETAIL.   Melany's essay was enthusiastically received by her peer critics largely because it includes vivid descriptive detail that gives readers a clear sense of the process and its outcome. Throughout, her emphasis is on the negative aspects of the process—the "odd-smelling liquid" and the "putrid greenish-brown color" of her hair, for instance—and this emphasis is consistent with her essay's purpose.

TRANSITIONS.   To move readers smoothly through the process, Melany includes clear transitions ("First," "At this point," "Next," "then") and clearly identifies the beginning of the process ("After we put our gloves on, we began the actual dyeing process") and the end ("The last part of the process").

Focus on Revision

Students who read Melany's essay thought that it was clearly written and structured and that its ironic, self-mocking tone was well suited to her audience and purpose. They felt, however, that some minor revisions would make her essay even more effective. Paragraph 2, for example, needs a bit of work. For one thing, this paragraph begins quite abruptly: paragraph 1 records the purchase of the hair dye, and paragraph 2 opens with the sentence "We decided to use my bathroom to dye our hair," leaving readers wondering how much time has passed between purchase and application. Since the thesis rests on the idea of the foolishness of an impulsive gesture, it is important for readers to understand that the girls presumably went immediately from the store to Melany's house. After thinking about this criticism, Melany decided to write a clearer opening for paragraph 2: "As soon as we paid for the dye, we returned to my house, where, eager to begin our transformation, we locked ourselves in my bathroom. Inside each box. . . ." She also decided to divide paragraph 2 into two paragraphs, one describing the materials and another beginning with "After we put our gloves on," which introduces the first step in the process.

Another possible revision Melany considered was to develop further the character of Veronica. Although both girls purchase and apply hair color, readers never learn what happens to Veronica. Melany knew she could easily add a brief paragraph after paragraph 7, describing Veronica's "Sparkling Sherry" hair in humorous terms.

The following selections illustrate how varied the purposes of process writing can be. Each essay, however, provides orderly and clear explanations so that readers can follow the process easily.

MALCOLM X

Malcolm X was born Malcolm Little in Omaha, Nebraska, in 1925 and was assassinated in New York City in 1965. The son of a Baptist minister, he converted to Islam while serving a prison term for burglary and became a
Muslim minister and an advocate of black separatism upon his release in
1952. Malcolm X was a vocal member of the Black Muslims (now known as
the Nation of Islam) and a disciple of their leader, Elijah Muhammad. In 1963,
however, he left the Black Muslim movement. Following a 1964 trip to
Mecca, he converted to orthodox Islam and founded the black nationalist
Organization for Afro-American Unity. Many believe his assassination was
motivated by the tension between the two movements after Malcolm X left
the Black Muslims. *The Autobiography of Malcolm X* (1964), from which the following excerpt is taken, relates his rise from poverty to national prominence
as a lecturer and religious leader. (The autobiography was dictated to Alex
Haley, who later wrote *Roots*.) "My First Conk" explains a process that was
part of Malcolm X's young manhood and also reflects his adult view of the
process.

My First Conk

Shorty soon decided that my hair was finally long enough to be   1
conked. He had promised to school me in how to beat the barber shops'
three- and four-dollar price by making up congolene, and then conking
ourselves.

I took the little list of ingredients he had printed out for me, and went   2
to a grocery store, where I got a can of Red Devil lye, two eggs, and two
medium-sized white potatoes. Then at a drugstore near the poolroom, I
asked for a large jar of vaseline, a large bar of soap, a large-toothed comb
and a fine-toothed comb, one of those rubber hoses with a metal spray-
head, a rubber apron, and a pair of gloves.

"Going to lay on that first conk?" the drugstore man asked me. I   3
proudly told him, grinning, "Right!"

Shorty paid six dollars a week for a room in his cousin's shabby apart-   4
ment. His cousin wasn't at home. "It's like the pad's mine, he spends so
much time with his woman," Shorty said. "Now, you watch me—"

He peeled the potatoes and thin-sliced them into a quart-sized Mason   5
fruit jar, then started stirring them with a wooden spoon as he gradually
poured in a little over half the can of lye. "Never use a metal spoon; the
lye will turn it black," he told me.

A jelly-like, starchy-looking glop resulted from the lye and potatoes,   6
and Shorty broke in the two eggs, stirring real fast—his own conk and
dark face bent down close. The congolene turned pale-yellowish. "Feel
the jar," Shorty said. I cupped my hand against the outside, and snatched

it away. "Damn right, it's hot, that's the lye," he said. "So you know it's going to burn when I comb it in—it burns bad. But the longer you can stand it, the straighter the hair."

He made me sit down, and he tied the string of the new rubber apron   7
tightly around my neck, and combed up my bush of hair. Then, from the big vaseline jar, he took a handful and massaged it hard all through my hair and into the scalp. He also thickly vaselined my neck, ears and forehead. "When I get to washing out your head, be sure to tell me anywhere you feel any little stinging," Shorty warned me, washing his hands, then pulling on the rubber gloves, and tying on his own rubber apron. "You always got to remember that any congolene left in burns a sore into your head."

The congolene just felt warm when Shorty started combing it in. But   8
then my head caught fire.

I gritted my teeth and tried to pull the sides of the kitchen table to-   9
gether. The comb felt as if it was raking my skin off.

My eyes watered, my nose was running. I couldn't stand it any   10
longer; I bolted to the washbasin. I was cursing Shorty with every name I could think of when he got the spray going and started soap lathering my head.

He lathered and spray-rinsed, lathered and spray-rinsed, maybe ten   11
or twelve times, each time gradually closing the hot-water faucet, until the rinse was cold, and that helped some.

"You feel any stinging spots?"   12

"No," I managed to say. My knees were trembling.   13

"Sit back down, then. I think we got it all out okay."   14

The flame came back as Shorty, with a thick towel, started drying my   15
head, rubbing hard. "*Easy, man, easy!*" I kept shouting.

"The first time's always worst. You get used to it better before long.   16
You took it real good, homeboy. You got a good conk."

When Shorty let me stand up and see in the mirror, my hair hung   17
down in limp, damp strings. My scalp still flamed, but not as badly; I could bear it. He draped the towel around my shoulders, over my rubber apron, and began again vaselining my hair.

I could feel him combing, straight back, first the big comb, then the   18
fine-tooth one.

Then, he was using a razor, very delicately, on the back of my neck.   19
Then, finally, shaping the sideburns.

My first view in the mirror blotted out the hurting. I'd seen some   20
pretty conks, but when it's the first time, on your *own* head, the transformation, after the lifetime of kinks, is staggering.

The mirror reflected Shorty behind me. We both were grinning and   21
sweating. And on top of my head was this thick, smooth sheen of shining red hair—real red—as straight as any white man's.

How ridiculous I was! Stupid enough to stand there simply lost in ad-   22
miration of my hair now looking "white," reflected in the mirror in

Shorty's room. I vowed that I'd never again be without a conk, and I never was for many years.

This was my first really big step toward self-degradation: when I en-   23 dured all of that pain, literally burning my flesh to have it look like a white man's hair. I had joined that multitude of Negro men and women in America who are brainwashed into believing that the black people are "inferior"—and white people "superior"—that they will even violate and mutilate their God-created bodies to try to look "pretty" by white standards.

Look around today, in every small town and big city, from two-bit   24 catfish and soda-pop joints into the "integrated" lobby of the Waldorf-Astoria, and you'll see conks on black men. And you'll see black women wearing these green and pink and purple and red and platinum-blonde wigs. They're all more ridiculous than a slapstick comedy. It makes you wonder if the Negro has completely lost his sense of identity, lost touch with himself.

You'll see the conk worn by many, many so-called "upper class"   25 Negroes, and, as much as I hate to say it about them, on all too many Negro entertainers. One of the reasons that I've especially admired some of them, like Lionel Hampton and Sidney Poitier, among others, is that they have kept their natural hair and fought to the top. I admire any Negro man who has never had himself conked, or who has had the sense to get rid of it—as I finally did.

I don't know which kind of self-defacing conk is the greater shame—   26 the one you'll see on the heads of the black so-called "middle class" and "upper class," who ought to know better, or the one you'll see on the heads of the poorest, most downtrodden, ignorant black men. I mean the legal-minimum-wage ghetto-dwelling kind of Negro, as I was when I got my first one. It's generally among these poor fools that you'll see a black kerchief over the man's head, like Aunt Jemima; he's trying to make his conk last longer, between trips to the barbershop. Only for special occasions is this kerchief-protected conk exposed—to show off how "sharp" and "hip" its owner is. The ironic thing is that I have never heard any woman, white or black, express any admiration for a conk. Of course, any white woman with a black man isn't thinking about his hair. But I don't see how on earth a black woman with any race pride could walk down the street with any black man wearing a conk—the emblem of his shame that he is black.

To my own shame, when I say all of this, I'm talking first of all about   27 myself—because you can't show me any Negro who ever conked more faithfully than I did. I'm speaking from personal experience when I say of any black man who conks today, or any white-wigged black woman, that if they gave the brains in their heads just half as much attention as they do their hair, they would be a thousand times better off.

• • •

COMPREHENSION

1. What exactly is a conk? Why did Malcolm X want to get his hair conked? What did the conk symbolize to him at the time he got it? What does it symbolize at the time he writes about it?

2. List the materials Shorty asked Malcolm X to buy. Is the purpose of each explained? If so, where?

3. Outline the major stages in the procedure Malcolm X describes. Are they presented in chronological order? Which, if any, of the major stages are out of place?

PURPOSE AND AUDIENCE

1. Why does Malcolm X write this selection as a process explanation instead of as a set of instructions?

2. This process explanation has an explicitly stated thesis that makes its purpose clear. What is this thesis?

3. *The Autobiography of Malcolm X* was published in 1964, when many African-Americans got their hair straightened regularly. Is the thesis of this selection still relevant today?

4. Why do you think Malcolm X includes so many references to the pain and discomfort he endures as part of the process?

5. What is the relationship between Malcolm X's personal experience and the universal statement he makes about conking in this selection?

STYLE AND STRUCTURE

1. Identify some of the transitional words Malcolm X uses to move from step to step.

2. Only about half of this selection is devoted to the process explanation. Where does the process begin? Where does it end?

3. In paragraphs 22–26, Malcolm X encloses several words in quotation marks, occasionally prefacing them with the phrase *so-called.* What is the effect of these quotation marks?

VOCABULARY PROJECTS

1. Define each of the following words as it is used in this selection.

vowed (22)	mutilate (23)	downtrodden (26)
self-degradation (23)	slapstick (24)	emblem (26)
multitude (23)	self-defacing (26)	

2. Because this is an informal essay, Malcolm X uses many **colloquialisms** and **slang** terms. Substitute a more formal word for each of the following.

beat (1)	glop (6)	"sharp" (26)
pad (4)	real (6)	"hip" (26)

Evaluate the possible impact of your substitutions. Do they improve the essay or weaken it?

JOURNAL ENTRY

Did you ever engage in behavior that you later came to view as unacceptable as your beliefs changed or your social consciousness developed? What made you change your attitude toward this behavior?

WRITING WORKSHOP

1. Write a process explanation of an unpleasant experience you or someone you know has often gone through in order to conform to others' standards of physical beauty (for instance, dieting or undertaking strenuous exercise). Include a thesis statement that conveys your disapproval of the process.

2. Rewrite Malcolm X's process explanation as he might have written it when he still considered conking a desirable process, worth all the trouble. Include all his steps, but change his thesis and choose words that make conking sound painless and worthwhile.

3. Rewrite this essay as a set of instructions that Shorty might have written for a friend who is about to help someone conk his hair. Begin by telling the friend what materials to purchase.

COMBINING THE PATTERNS

Although "My First Conk" is very detailed, it does not include an extended **definition** of a conk. Do you think a definition paragraph should be added? If so, where could it be inserted? What patterns could be used to develop such a definition?

THEMATIC CONNECTIONS

- "Finishing School" (page 75)
- "Medium Ash Brown" (page 213)
- "Aria: A Memoir of a Bilingual Childhood" (page 357)

ALEXANDER PETRUNKEVITCH

Alexander Petrunkevitch (1875–1964) was born in Pliski, Russia, and was educated at the University of Moscow and the University of Freiburg in Germany, where he received his doctorate in 1901. Petrunkevitch taught zoology at several universities in the United States, including Yale University from 1910 to 1944. He wrote a number of scholarly books, including *An Inquiry into the Natural Classification of Spiders* (1933) and *Principles of Classification* (1952). In addition to producing scientific works, Petrunkevitch also translated the poetry of Lord Byron into Russian and that of the Russian writer Alexander Pushkin into English, and he wrote an essay, "The Role of the Intellectuals in the Liberating Movement in Russia," that was published in 1918 in a collection entitled *The Russian Revolution*. "The Spider and the Wasp," first published in *Scientific American* in 1952, examines how a wasp is able to attack and kill a tarantula without any resistance from the spider until the last moment.

The Spider and the Wasp

In the feeding and safeguarding of their progeny insects and spiders   1
exhibit some interesting analogies to reasoning and some crass examples of blind instinct. The case I propose to describe here is that of the tarantula spiders and their archenemy, the digger wasps of the genus *Pepsis*. It is a classic example of what looks like intelligence pitted against instinct—a strange situation in which the victim, though fully able to defend itself, submits unwittingly to its destruction.

Most tarantulas live in the tropics, but several species occur in the   2
temperate zone and a few are common in the southern U.S. Some varieties are large and have powerful fangs with which they can inflict a deep wound. These formidable-looking spiders do not, however, attack man; you can hold one in your hand, if you are gentle, without being bitten. Their bite is dangerous only to insects and small mammals such as mice; for man it is no worse than a hornet's sting.

Tarantulas customarily live in deep cylindrical burrows, from which   3
they emerge at dusk and into which they retire at dawn. Mature males wander about after dark in search of females and occasionally stray into houses. After mating, the male dies in a few weeks, but a female lives much longer and can mate several years in succession. In a Paris museum is a tropical specimen which is said to have been living in captivity for 25 years.

A fertilized female tarantula lays from 200 to 400 eggs at a time; thus   4
it is possible for a single tarantula to produce several thousand young. She takes no care of them beyond weaving a cocoon of silk to enclose the

"The Spider and the Wasp" by Alexander Petrunkevitch. Copyright © 1952 by Scientific American, Inc. All rights reserved.

eggs. After they hatch, the young walk away, find convenient places in which to dig their burrows, and spend the rest of their lives in solitude. The eyesight of tarantulas is poor, being limited to a sensing of change in the intensity of light and to the perception of moving objects. They apparently have little or no sense of hearing, for a hungry tarantula will pay no attention to a loudly chirping cricket placed in its cage unless the insect happens to touch one of its legs.

But all spiders, and especially hairy ones, have an extremely delicate   5
sense of touch. Laboratory experiments prove that tarantulas can distinguish three types of touch: pressure against the body wall, stroking of the body hair, and riffling of certain very fine hairs on the legs called trichobothria. Pressure against the body, by the finger or the end of a pencil, causes the tarantula to move off slowly for a short distance. The touch excites no defensive response unless the approach is from above where the spider can see the motion, in which case it rises on its hind legs, lifts its front legs, opens its fangs, and holds this threatening posture as long as the object continues to move.

The entire body of a tarantula, especially its legs, is thickly clothed   6
with hair. Some of it is short and wooly, some long and stiff. Touching this body hair produces one of two distinct reactions. When the spider is hungry, it responds with an immediate and swift attack. At the touch of a cricket's antennae the tarantula seizes the insect so swiftly that a motion picture taken at the rate of 64 frames per second shows only the result and not the process of capture. But when the spider is not hungry, the stimulation of its hairs merely causes it to shake the touched limb. An insect can walk under its hairy belly unharmed.

The trichobothria, very fine hairs growing from disklike membranes   7
on the legs, are sensitive only to air movement. A light breeze makes them vibrate slowly, without disturbing the common hair. When one blows gently on the trichobothria, the tarantula reacts with a quick jerk of its four front legs. If the front and hind legs are stimulated at the same time, the spider makes a sudden jump. This reaction is quite independent of the state of its appetite.

These three tactile responses—to pressure on the body wall, to moving of the common hair, and to flexing of the trichobothria—are so different from one another that there is no possibility of confusing them. They serve the tarantula adequately for most of its needs and enable it to avoid most annoyances and dangers. But they fail the spider completely when it meets its deadly enemy, the digger wasp *Pepsis.*   8

These solitary wasps are beautiful and formidable creatures. Most   9
species are either a deep shiny blue all over, or deep blue with rusty wings. The largest have a wing span of about 4 inches. They live on nectar. When excited, they give off a pungent odor—a warning that they are ready to attack. The sting is much worse than that of a bee or common wasp, and the pain and swelling last longer. In the adult stage the wasp lives only a few months. The female produces but a few eggs, one at a

time at intervals of two or three days. For each egg the mother must provide one adult tarantula, alive but paralyzed. The mother wasp attaches the egg to the paralyzed spider's abdomen. Upon hatching from the egg, the larva is many hundreds of times smaller than its living but helpless victim. It eats no other food and drinks no water. By the time it has finished its single Gargantuan meal and become ready for wasphood, nothing remains of the tarantula but its indigestible chitinous skeleton.

The mother wasp goes tarantula-hunting when the egg in her ovary is almost ready to be laid. Flying low over the ground late on a sunny afternoon, the wasp looks for its victim or for the mouth of a tarantula burrow, a round hole edged by a bit of silk. The sex of the spider makes no difference, but the mother is highly discriminating as to species. Each species of *Pepsis* requires a certain species of tarantula, and the wasp will not attack the wrong species. In a cage with a tarantula which is not its normal prey, the wasp avoids the spider and is usually killed by it in the night.   10

Yet when a wasp finds the correct species, it is the other way about. To identify the species the wasp apparently must explore the spider with her antennae. The tarantula shows an amazing tolerance to this exploration. The wasp crawls under it and walks over it without evoking any hostile response. The molestation is so great and so persistent that the tarantula often rises on all eight legs, as if it were on stilts. It may stand this way for several minutes. Meanwhile the wasp, having satisfied itself that the victim is of the right species, moves off a few inches to dig the spider's grave. Working vigorously with legs and jaws, it excavates a hole 8 to 10 inches deep with a diameter slightly larger than the spider's girth. Now and again the wasp pops out of the hole to make sure that the spider is still there.   11

When the grave is finished, the wasp returns to the tarantula to complete her ghastly enterprise. First she feels it all over once more with her antennae. Then her behavior becomes more aggressive. She bends her abdomen, protruding her sting, and searches for the soft membrane at the point where the spider's legs join its body—the only spot where she can penetrate the horny skeleton. From time to time, as the exasperated spider slowly shifts ground, the wasp turns on her back and slides along with the aid of her wings, trying to get under the tarantula for a shot at the vital spot. During all this maneuvering, which can last for several minutes, the tarantula makes no move to save itself. Finally the wasp corners it against some obstruction and traps one of its legs in her powerful jaws. Now at last the harassed spider tries a desperate but vain defense. The two contestants roll over and over on the ground. It is a terrifying sight and the outcome is always the same. The wasp finally manages to thrust her sting into the soft spot and holds it there for a few seconds while she pumps in the poison. Almost immediately the tarantula falls paralyzed on its back. Its legs stop twitching; its heart stops beating. Yet it is not dead, as is shown by the fact that if taken from the wasp it can be restored to some sensitivity by being kept in a moist chamber for several months.   12

After paralyzing the tarantula, the wasp cleans herself by dragging her   13
body along the ground and rubbing her feet, sucks a drop of blood oozing
from the wound in the spider's abdomen, then grabs a leg of the flabby, helpless animal in her jaws and drags it down to the bottom of the grave. She
stays there for many minutes, sometimes for several hours, and what she
does all that time in the dark we do not know. Eventually she lays her egg
and attaches it to the side of the spider's abdomen with a sticky secretion.
Then she emerges, fills the grave with soil carried bit by bit in her jaws, and
finally tramples the ground all around to hide any trace of the grave from
prowlers. Then she flies away, leaving her descendant safely started in life.

In all this the behavior of the wasp evidently is qualitatively different   14
from that of the spider. The wasp acts like an intelligent animal. This is
not to say that instinct plays no part or that she reasons as man does. But
her actions are to the point; they are not automatic and can be modified to
fit the situation. We do not know for certain how she identifies the tarantula—probably it is by some olfactory or chemo-tactile sense—but she
does it purposefully and does not blindly tackle a wrong species.

On the other hand, the tarantula's behavior shows only confusion.   15
Evidently the wasp's pawing gives it no pleasure, for it tries to move
away. That the wasp is not simulating sexual stimulation is certain because male and female tarantulas react in the same way to its advances.
That the spider is not anesthetized by some odorless secretion is easily
shown by blowing slightly at the tarantula and making it jump suddenly.
What, then makes the tarantula behave as stupidly as it does?

No clear, simple answer is available. Possibly the stimulation by the   16
wasp's antennae is masked by a heavier pressure on the spider's body, so
that it reacts as when prodded by a pencil. But the explanation may be
much more complex. Initiative in attack is not in the nature of tarantulas;
most species fight only when cornered so that escape is impossible. Their
inherited patterns of behavior apparently prompt them to avoid problems rather than attack them. For example, spiders always weave their
webs in three dimensions, and when a spider finds that there is insufficient space to attach certain threads in the third dimension, it leaves the
place and seeks another, instead of finishing the web in a single plane.
This urge to escape seems to arise under all circumstances, in all phases of
life, and to take the place of reasoning. For a spider to change the pattern
of its web is as impossible as for an inexperienced man to build a bridge
across a chasm obstructing his way.

In a way the instinctive urge to escape is not only easier but often   17
more efficient than reasoning. The tarantula does exactly what is most efficient in all cases except in an encounter with a ruthless and determined
attacker dependent for the existence of her own species on killing as
many tarantulas as she can lay eggs. Perhaps in this case the spider follows its usual pattern of trying to escape, instead of seizing and killing
the wasp, because it is not aware of its danger. In any case, the survival of
the tarantula species as a whole is protected by the fact that the spider is
much more fertile than the wasp.

• • •

COMPREHENSION

1. List some of the tarantula's most striking physical features. List some of the wasp's most striking physical features.

2. Why *must* the wasp paralyze the tarantula?

3. What does Petrunkevitch see as the single most obvious contrast between the behavior of the wasp and that of the spider?

4. Why, according to Petrunkevitch, does the spider behave with such apparent stupidity in its encounter with the wasp?

5. Why is the fact that the tarantula is more fertile than the wasp so important?

PURPOSE AND AUDIENCE

1. Does "The Spider and the Wasp" include an explicitly stated thesis? If so, what is it? If not, why not?

2. *Scientific American,* in which "The Spider and the Wasp" first appeared, is a periodical aimed not at scientists but at a well-educated audience with an interest in science. What techniques does Petrunkevitch, a zoologist, use to attract and hold the interest of this audience?

3. What do you think is Petrunkevitch's purpose in spending so much more time describing the spider than the wasp? Does he accomplish this purpose? Explain.

STYLE AND STRUCTURE

1. Where does Petrunkevitch actually begin his discussion of the process by which a wasp kills a tarantula?

2. In the essay's opening paragraphs, Petrunkevitch describes first the spider and then the wasp. How does he indicate his movement from one subject to the other?

3. In the section of the essay devoted to the process explanation, what transitional words and phrases help readers follow the steps of the process?

4. What verb tense does Petrunkevitch use in his explanation of the process? Why do you think he selects this tense?

5. In paragraph 11 Petrunkevitch uses an **analogy** to help readers visualize the tarantula's reaction to the wasp. What is this analogy? Where else does Petrunkevitch use analogies to clarify his explanations?

6. Petrunkevitch makes frequent use of **parallelism** in his essay. One example of this technique is "They serve the tarantula adequately. . . . But they fail the spider completely" (8). Give some additional examples of parallel constructions. How does parallelism strengthen the essay?

VOCABULARY PROJECTS

1. Define each of the following words as it is used in this selection.

   progeny (1)   tactile (8)   olfactory (14)
   crass (1)   Gargantuan (9)
   unwittingly (1)   chitinous (9)

2. Although Petrunkevitch knows his audience is not composed of zoologists, his scientific topic requires that he use technical terms occasionally. Still, he is careful to accommodate his audience by defining such terms or by placing them in a context that suggests their meaning. Give examples of two or three such technical terms, and explain the concessions Petrunkevitch makes to his audience in each case.

3. At times Petrunkevitch uses distinctly unscientific language—for example, "the wasp pops out of the hole" (11); "her ghastly enterprise" (12). Give other examples of such language, and explain why you think Petrunkevitch uses it.

JOURNAL ENTRY

Choose one paragraph of "The Spider and the Wasp," and rewrite it so that it is appropriate for an elementary school science textbook. When you have finished your revision, make a list of the kinds of changes you have made, and explain why each was necessary. (Note: You will need to use a dictionary for this exercise.)

WRITING WORKSHOP

1. In paragraph 1 Petrunkevitch calls the spider-wasp confrontation "a classic example of what looks like intelligence pitted against instinct—a strange situation in which the victim, though fully able to defend itself, submits unwittingly to its destruction." Write a process essay in which you explain a similar "strange situation" from your own reading or experience—for example, deciding not to respond to a dangerous physical challenge or not to pursue an argument even though you believed you were right.

2. Retell the "story" of the encounter between the spider and the wasp as an animal fable like Aesop's "The Fox and the Grapes." Keep the process structure of the original essay, but try to portray the spider and the wasp as more fully developed characters. Include dialogue if you like, and be sure to include a moral at the end of your story.

3. Describe the process Petrunkevitch outlines from the point of view of either the spider or the wasp. Use first person and present tense.

COMBINING THE PATTERNS

Petrunkevitch supplies a very detailed **description** of the spider and the wasp before he launches into an explanation of the process. What function do these passages of description serve? Are they necessary? Why or why not?

THEMATIC CONNECTIONS

░░░░░░░░░░░░░░░░░░

GARRY TRUDEAU

Garry Trudeau was born in 1948 in New York City and attended Yale University and Yale's School of Art and Architecture, from which he received a master's degree in fine arts in 1970. He is the creator of the comic strip *Doonesbury,* which is syndicated nationwide. The strips have been collected in numerous books, most recently in *Doonesbury Nation* (1995) and *Virtual Doonesbury* (1996). Trudeau won a Pulitzer Prize for editorial cartooning in 1975 and was nominated for an Academy Award in 1977 for the animated film *A Doonesbury Special.* He is also an occasional contributor to the Op-Ed page of the *New York Times,* where "Anatomy of a Joke" appeared in 1993. In this piece, Trudeau outlines the detailed procedure by which a single joke for *The Tonight Show* is developed from the initial idea to the comic's delivery.

Anatomy of a Joke

In the wake of last week's press "availabilities" of funnymen Dave   1
Letterman, Jay Leno, Chevy Chase et al., there was much rim-shot cri-
tiquing, all of it missing the point.

The real jokes, the ones that count, occur not at press events but dur-   2
ing those extraordinary little pieces called monologues. Despite the popular conception of the monologue as edgy and unpredictable, it is actually
as formal and structured as anything found in traditional kabuki. The
stakes are too high for it to be otherwise. Even the ad-libs, rejoinders, and
recoveries are carefully scripted. While it may suit Leno's image to portray the "Tonight" show monologue as something that's banged out over
late-night pizza with a few cronies, in fact each joke requires the concerted effort of a crack team of six highly disciplined comedy professionals. To illustrate how it works, let's follow an actual topical joke, told the
night of Monday, July 26, as it makes its way through the pipeline.

The inspiration for a topical joke is literally torn from the headlines by   3
a professional comedy news "clipper." Comedy news reading is sometimes
contracted out to consultants, but the big-budget "Tonight" show has 12 of
its own in-house clippers who peruse some 300 newspapers every day.
Clippers know that the idea for the joke must be contained in the headline
or, at worst, the subhead. If the idea is in the body text, then the general
public has probably missed it and won't grasp the reference the joke is built
around. In this case, the clipper has spied an item about flood relief.

A20 FRIDAY, JULY 23, 1993

House Delays Final Flood Aid Vote
$3 Billion Package Stalls in Dispute Over Budget Limits

The Washington Post

230

The news clip is then passed on to a comedy "engineer," whose job is   4
to decide what shape the joke should take. After analyzing the headline,
the engineer decides how many parts the joke should have, the velocity of
its build, whether it contains any red herrings (rare on the "Tonight"
show), and the dynamics of the payoff and underlaughing. With
Monday's joke, the engineer chose a simple interrogatory setup, which
telegraphs to the often sleepy audience that the next line contains a payoff. The finished sequencing is then sent on to the "stylist."

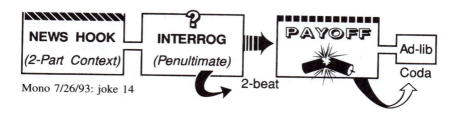

NEWS HOOK — INTERROG ▮▮▮➤ PAYOFF — Ad-lib

(2-Part Context) (Penultimate)   Coda

Mono 7/26/93: joke 14   2-beat

The comedy stylist is the writer who actually fashions the raw joke.   5
The stylist is the prima donna of the team, the best paid, the worst
dressed—and never in the office. The stylist, who is typically a per
diem session player, is faxed the original headline, the structural
scheme, and a gross time count, and from those elements creates the
rough draft for the joke. It's up to him to find the joke's "spring," that
tiny component of universal truth that acts as the joke's fulcrum. In this
case, the joke hinges on the public's resentment of Congress, a hoary
but proven truism. The stylist then faxes his finished rough to the "polish man."

```
1./It looks like the House of Representatives is hav-
ing trouble voting flood relief because they're wor-
ried about where to appropriate the money from./
2. /Here's my question./
3./ How come when the House votes itself a pay raise,
they never worry about that appropriation?
```

The polish man, usually a woman, is the joke's editor, charged with   6
burnishing the joke until it gleams. Obscure references, awkward phrasing, and puns are all removed, and any potentially offensive material is
run by an outside anti-defamation consultant. Unlike the stylist, who
usually works at his beach house, the polish man is always on the
premises, available in the event of emergency rewrites. For Monday's
joke, the polish man adds a "fall from the sky" coda that will allow Leno
some physical business. The decision to use it, however, ultimately rests
with the "timing coach."

> @ too long   ⸤Senate⸥
> It looks like the ~~House of Representatives~~ is
> ⸤passing,⸥ @ where? ⸤for the midwest⸥
> having troubl~~e voting~~ flood relief because ~~they're~~
> ⸤some Senators are⸥
> ₅worried about where ~~to appropriate~~ the money from.
> ⸤Now,⸥
> ₅Here's my question: How come when the ~~House~~ ⸤Senate⸥ votes
> ⸤big⸥
> itself a pay raise, they never ~~worry about~~ ⸤wonder where⸥ that
> money's coming from?
> ~~appropriation?~~   ad-libs: Ever notice that?
>
> It just seems to fall from the sky.

The timing coach is responsible for timing out the phrasing and pauses, and bringing the 21-joke routine in under its seven-minute limit. Running over is a major no-no. During the Carson era, a timing coach, who asked not to be identified, signed off on a monologue that ran 13.5 seconds long, a deficit that came out of Barbra Streisand's guest segment. The coach was summarily sacked. Such errors are rare today, however, as the monologues are now digitalized on disk. A timer can modulate the phrasing pattern to within 0.01 of a second, well beyond the performance sensitivity of any comic but Robin Williams.

(6.3 sec. to pause) IT LOOKS LIKE...FLOOD RELIEF...WORRIED... MONEY IS GOING TO COME FROM. (.95 sec. beat) NOW, HERE'S MY QUESTION; (.6 second beat; 3.45 sec. to ad-lib) HOW COME...BIG PAY RAISE...WHERE THAT MONEY'S COMING FROM? (ad-lib under laugh; see menu).

The final joke is then e-mailed to the "talent," in this case Jay Leno. Leno dry-runs the joke in his office, adding spin and body movement, and locks in his ad-libs, including recovery lines in case the joke bombs. (Carson had such good recovery material that he used to commission intentionally bad jokes, but Leno has not yet reached that pinnacle of impeccability.) Once Leno approves the joke, it is transferred to a hard disk and laser-printed on cue cards with a special font to make it look hand-lettered. Finally, at exactly 5:30 P.M., California taping time, Leno walks on stage and reads it to 15 million people.

• • •

COMPREHENSION

1. Identify each of the six people involved in writing a typical joke, and explain what each contributes to the process.

2. What is the inspiration for most of the jokes that are told in late-night talk-show monologues? Why do you suppose this is so?

PURPOSE AND AUDIENCE

1. Trudeau, the creator of the *Doonesbury* comic strip, is known primarily as a cartoonist, yet this essay originally appeared as a column in the *New York Times*. What, if anything, do these details and Trudeau's comments in paragraphs 1 and 2 suggest about his purpose for explaining how a joke is created?

2. Does Trudeau assume his audience is familiar with late-night comedy programs? How can you tell?

3. Where does Trudeau state his essay's thesis? Restate it in your own words. Do you think such a restatement of the thesis should appear in the essay's conclusion? Explain.

STYLE AND STRUCTURE

1. Identify each stage in the process Trudeau describes.

2. What transitional expressions does Trudeau use to move his readers through each stage of the process? How does he connect one stage to the next? Would additional transitions improve the clarity? Explain.

3. Do you think Trudeau is being serious when he refers to the joke writers as a "crack team of six highly disciplined comedy professionals" (2)? Explain your reasoning.

4. What elements typically included in a process explanation are absent here? Why?

5. Do you think the illustrations are necessary? Do they add to or detract from the essay's effectiveness? Explain.

VOCABULARY PROJECTS

1. Define each of the following words as it is used in this selection.

anatomy (title)	fulcrum (5)	summarily (7)
kabuki (2)	hoary (5)	spin (8)
rejoinders (2)	truism (5)	pinnacle (8)
velocity (4)	burnishing (6)	impeccability (8)
red herrings (4)	coda (6)	
per diem (5)	business (6)	

2. Trudent's essay includes many examples of **colloquialisms**, such as paragraph 2's *cronies* and *banged out*. Choose one paragraph and identify additional examples of colloquialisms. What other features help to make this essay's style informal?

3. The essay also includes a good deal of **jargon**, such as paragraph 4's *underlaughing* and *sequencing*. Do you think Trudeau should define these terms? Why?

JOURNAL ENTRY

Does Trudeau's essay change the way you view your favorite late-night television talk-show host or stand-up comedian? If so, how?

WRITING WORKSHOP

1. Write an essay (serious or humorous) in which you explain your process of writing and revision. Include a thesis statement that assesses the effectiveness of your writing process.

2. Write a set of instructions in which your goal is to convince a younger student of the importance of revision. Be sure to include an illustration like the one that follows paragraph 6 in Trudeau's essay.

3. Record the process of writing your own topical joke. Begin with an idea "literally torn from the headlines," and include a thesis that comments on how difficult the process is.

COMBINING THE PATTERNS

Although Trudeau's essay is structured as a process, he uses **exemplification** throughout his discussion. Why are examples so important to this essay?

THEMATIC CONNECTIONS

- "The Open Window" (page 100)
- "Television: The Plug-In Drug" (page 274)
- "The Catbird Seat" (page 474)

LARRY BROWN

Larry Brown (1951–) was born into a farming family in Oxford, Mississippi. After serving as a marine during the Vietnam War, he attended the University of Mississippi and held a variety of odd jobs until he joined the Oxford Fire Department in 1973. Promoted to captain in 1986, Brown retired from firefighting in 1990 in order to pursue full time a writing career that had begun in 1986 with the publication of a collection of short stories, *Facing the Music.* This book was followed by two well-received novels: *Dirty Work* (1989), about two hospitalized Vietnam veterans, and *Joe* (1991), which won the Southern Book Critics' Circle Award for fiction. His latest novel is *Father and Son* (1996). Brown is noted for his harshly realistic stories of the rural South, which focus on working-class characters struggling with dead-end jobs, alcoholism, and family conflict. *On Fire: A Personal Account of Life and Death and Choices* (1994), his only work of nonfiction to date, is a series of diary-like entries looking back at his life as a firefighter. The following selection from that book explains the job of a firefighter in almost clinical detail.

On Fire

You learn early to go in low, that heat and smoke rise into the ceiling, that cooler air is near the floor. You learn to button your collar tightly around your neck, to pull the gauntlets of your gloves up over the cuffs of your coat, that embers can go anywhere skin is exposed. You learn that you are only human flesh, not Superman, and that you can burn like a candle.

You try to go easy on the air that's inside the tank on your back, try to be calm and not overly exert yourself, try and save some of your strength. You learn about exhaustion and giving it all you've got, then having to reach back and pull up some more. Suck it up and go.

You learn eventually not to let your legs tremble when you're pressing hard on the gas or the diesel pedal, when you're driving into something that is unknown.

One day if you make rank you will be promoted to driver or pump operator or lieutenant and you will discover what it feels like to roll up to a burning structure, a house that somebody lives in, or a university dormitory where hundreds of people live, or a business upon whose commerce somebody's livelihood depends. You will change in that moment, stop being a nozzleman and become instead the operator of the apparatus the nozzlemen are pulling lines from, and you will know then that the knowledge pushed into your head at dry training sessions in the fire station must now be applied to practical use, quickly, with no mistakes, because there are men you know whose lives are going to depend on a steady supply of water, at the right pressure, for as long as it takes to put the fire out.

And on that first time you'll probably be like I was, scared shitless.   5
But you can't let that stop you from doing your job.

You learn the difficulty of raising a ladder and pulling the rope and   6
raising the extensions up to a second-floor window, and the difficulty of
climbing that ladder with a charged inch-and-a-half line and then opening it and staying on the ladder without falling.

You learn of ropes and safety belts, insulated gloves to move downed   7
high-voltage lines, nozzle pressure and friction loss and the rule of thumb
for a two-and-a-half-inch nozzle. You learn to check the flow pressure on
a fire hydrant and what burning plastic tastes like, the way it will make
you gag and cough and puke when those fumes get into your lungs and
you know that something very bad has come inside your body. You see
death and hear the sounds of the injured. Some days you look at the fire
phone and have a bad feeling, smoke more cigarettes, glance at the
phone, and sometimes it rings. Sometimes you're wrong and the night
passes without trouble.

You learn to love a job that is not like sacking groceries or working in a   8
factory or painting houses, because everybody watches you when you
come down the street. You wear a blue uniform with silver or brass or gold,
and you get free day-old doughnuts from the bakery shop down the street.
At Christmas people bring in pies, cakes, cookies, ham, smoked sausage,
cheese, half-pints of whiskey. They thank you for your work in a season of
good cheer. One freezing December night the whole department gathers
with eighty steaks and Wally parks his wheeled cooker and dumps in sixty
or seventy pounds of charcoal to cook them and you have drinks and play
Bingo for prizes that businesses in your town have donated, a rechargeable
flashlight from the auto supply, a hot-air popcorn popper from a department store, a case of beer from the grocery down the street.

You lay out hose in the deadly summer heat on a street with no   9
shade, hook it all up, hundreds and hundreds of feet of it, put closed nozzles on the end of the hose, and run the pressure up to three hundred psi
and hold it for five minutes. If a piece bursts and creates a waterstorm on
the street, you remove that section from the line and throw it away. Then
you shut it down and drain it and write down the identification number
of every piece of hose that survived the test and put it all back on the
truck, thirteen hundred feet of it, and you make new bends and turns so
the rubber coating inside it won't kink and start to dry-rot.

You learn the major arteries of the body and the names of the bones   10
and how to splint a leg or an arm, how to tie off and cut an umbilical cord.
You learn to read blood pressure, administer oxygen. You see amounts of
blood that are unbelievable, not realizing until it's actually spilled how
much the human body holds. You crawl up under taxpayers' houses for
their dogs, go inside culverts where snakes may be hiding for their cats.
You learn to do whatever is called for.

No two days are ever the same and you're thankful for that. You   11
dread the winter and the advent of ice. On an August day you pray that

the city will behave and let you lie under the air conditioner and read a good book, draw easy money.

You learn that your muscles and bones and tendons get older and   12 that you cannot remain young forever. You test the pump on the truck every day when you come on duty, make sure it's full of fuel, clean, full of water, that the extinguishers are up. You check that your turnouts* are all together, hanging on the hook that has your name written above it, and that both your gloves are in your coat pocket. You make sure your flashlight works. You test the siren and the lights because everything has to be in readiness. You shut it all down and stand back and look at the deep red Imron paint, the gold leafing and lettering, the chrome valves and caps, the shiny chains and levers, the fluid-filled pressure gauges, the beds filled with woven nylon, the nozzles folded back into layers of hose, the hydrant wrenches snug in their holders, everything on this magnificent machine. You learn every inch of your truck and you know which compartments hold the forcible entry tools, the exhaust fans for removing smoke from a house, the power saws, the portable generator, the pike poles, the scoops, the salvage covers, the boltcutters, the axes, the ropes, the rappelling gear. You look at all of it over and over again and then you go inside the fire station and get a cup of coffee, sit down with a magazine or a newspaper, and once more, you wait for whatever comes your way.

• • •

COMPREHENSION

1. What process does Brown describe?

2. Into what general stages can you group the individual steps in the process?

3. Does Brown seem to consider some steps more important than others? If so, how does he indicate this?

PURPOSE AND AUDIENCE

1. For whom is this essay intended? Firefighters? A general audience? How can you tell?

2. What impressions of firefighting does Brown wish to convey? Do you think he achieves his purpose?

3. Does this essay have an explicitly stated thesis? If so, where is it? Do you think an explicit thesis statement is necessary here?

STYLE AND STRUCTURE

1. What words and phrases are repeated in this essay? Do these repetitions strengthen or weaken the essay? Explain your reasoning.

---

*Eds. note—Firefighter's apparel.

2. In paragraph 1 Brown uses a **simile** when he says that one of the things firefighters learn is that they "can burn like a candle." Where else does he use similes or other **figures of speech?** How does such language enhance the essay?

3. Brown uses a variety of stylistic devices in his essay. Comment on the effectiveness of each of these devices: sentence fragments; contractions; long, rhythmic sentences; the juxtaposition of long and short paragraphs.

4. How do you interpret the essay's title? Do you think Brown intends it to have more than one meaning?

5. Throughout his essay, Brown repeatedly uses the pronoun *you*. Some readers might find this usage too general or too informal for a discussion of such a serious subject. Why do you suppose Brown chooses this pronoun instead of the more usual *I* or *he*? Does *you* refer to his readers? Explain.

6. How is this essay like and unlike the typical process explanation? For example, does it include steps presented in chronological order? A list of materials and equipment? Warnings and cautions? How do you account for any departures from the normal process explanation?

7. Is paragraph 8 a digression, or is it part of the process? Explain.

VOCABULARY PROJECTS

1. Define each of the following words as it is used in this selection.
   gauntlets (1)   culverts (10)   advent (11)   rappelling (12)

2. Brown uses **slang,** professional **jargon,** and impolite language in this essay. Identify one or two examples of each, and explain why it is used instead of a more formal, neutral, or polite term.

JOURNAL ENTRY

Brown clearly has mixed feelings about his job. What conflicting emotions do you see in his essay?

WRITING WORKSHOP

1. Recast "On Fire" as a letter of application for a position with a different fire department or as an application for promotion. Use process to structure the body of the essay, and write in the first person and the present tense. Try to be somewhat less emotional and subjective than Brown, but be sure to stress how valuable an employee you have been.

2. Write a process essay about a difficult job you have (or have had). As you explain your day-to-day routine, try to convey the challenges of your job to readers.

3. Use the material in Brown's essay to help you write a set of instructions directed at firefighter trainees. Be honest about the tasks required, and try to balance the positive and negative aspects of the job.

COMBINING THE PATTERNS

In paragraph 8 Brown comments that firefighting is "a job that is not like sacking groceries or working in a factory or painting houses, because everybody watches you when you come down the street," but he does not go beyond this comment to compare firefighting to other occupations. Do you think this essay would be strengthened if it began or ended with a **comparison-and-contrast** paragraph that explained exactly how different firefighting is from other jobs? How would the addition of such an opening or closing paragraph change the essay?

THEMATIC CONNECTIONS

- "Reading the River" (page 126)
- "Midnight" (page 165)
- "The Men We Carry in Our Minds" (page 387)

JESSICA MITFORD

Jessica Mitford (1917–1996) was born in Batsford Mansion, England, to a wealthy, aristocratic family. She rebelled against her sheltered upbringing, becoming involved in left-wing politics and eventually immigrating to the United States. Mitford wrote two volumes of autobiography, *Daughters and Rebels* (1960), about her eccentric family, and *A Fine Old Conflict* (1976), about her involvement with the Communist party. After leaving the party in the 1950s, she began a career in investigative journalism, which produced the books *The American Way of Death* (1963), on the mortuary business; *Kind and Unusual Punishment: The Prison Business* (1973), on the prison system; *Poison Penmanship: The Gentle Art of Muckraking* (1979), a collection of articles; and *The American Way of Birth* (1992), about the crisis in American obstetrical care. "The Embalming of Mr. Jones" is excerpted from *The American Way of Death*. This book criticized the funeral industry and prompted angry responses from morticians. Here Mitford painstakingly and ironically describes the dual process of embalming and restoring a cadaver. (Late in life Mitford remarked that for her own funeral she wanted "one of those marvelous jobs of embalming that take twenty years off." No one doubted that she was speaking ironically.)

The Embalming of Mr. Jones

Embalming is indeed a most extraordinary procedure, and one must 1 wonder at the docility of Americans who each year pay hundreds of millions of dollars for its perpetuation, blissfully ignorant of what it is all about, what is done, how it is done. Not one in ten thousand has any idea of what actually takes place. Books on the subject are extremely hard to come by. They are not to be found in most libraries or bookshops.

In an era when huge television audiences watch surgical operations 2 in the comfort of their living rooms, when, thanks to the animated cartoon, the geography of the digestive system has become familiar territory even to the nursery school set, in a land where the satisfaction of curiosity about almost all matters is a national pastime, the secrecy surrounding embalming can, surely, hardly be attributed to the inherent gruesomeness of the subject. Custom in this regard has within this century suffered a complete reversal. In the early days of American embalming, when it was performed in the home of the deceased, it was almost mandatory for some relative to stay by the embalmer's side and witness the procedure. Today, family members who might wish to be in attendance would certainly be dissuaded by the funeral director. All others, except apprentices, are excluded by law from the preparation room.

A close look at what does actually take place may explain in large 3 measure the undertaker's intractable reticence concerning a procedure that has become his major *raison d'être*.* Is it possible he fears that public

---

*EDS. NOTE—French expression meaning "reason for being."

information about embalming might lead patrons to wonder if they really want this service? If the funeral men are loath to discuss the subject outside the trade, the reader may, understandably, be equally loath to go on reading at this point. For those who have the stomach for it, let us part the formaldehyde curtain....

The body is first laid out in the undertaker's morgue—or rather, Mr. Jones is reposing in the preparation room—to be readied to bid the world farewell.

The preparation room in any of the better funeral establishments has the tiled and sterile look of a surgery, and indeed the embalmer-restorative artist who does his chores there is beginning to adopt the term "dermasurgeon" (appropriately corrupted by some mortician-writers as "demisurgeon") to describe his calling. His equipment, consisting of scalpels, scissors, augers, forceps, clamps, needles, pumps, tubes, bowls, and basin, is crudely imitative of the surgeon's as is his technique, acquired in a nine- or twelve-month post-high-school course in an embalming school. He is supplied by an advanced chemical industry with a bewildering array of fluids, sprays, pastes, oils, powders, creams, to fix or soften tissue, shrink or distend it as needed, dry it here, restore the moisture there. There are cosmetics, waxes, and paints to fill and cover features, even plaster of Paris to replace entire limbs. There are ingenious aids to prop and stabilize the cadaver: a Vari-Pose Head Rest, the Edwards Arm and Hand Positioner, the Repose Block (to support the shoulders during the embalming), and the Throop Foot Positioner, which resembles an old-fashioned stocks.

Mr. John H. Eckels, president of the Eckels College of Mortuary Science, thus describes the first part of the embalming procedure: "In the hands of a skilled practitioner, this work may be done in a comparatively short time and without mutilating the body other than by slight incision—so slight that it scarcely would cause serious inconvenience if made upon a living person. It is necessary to remove all the blood, and doing this not only helps in the disinfecting, but removes the principal cause of disfigurements due to discoloration."

Another textbook discusses the all-important time element: "The earlier this is done, the better, for every hour that elapses between death and embalming will add to the problems and complications encountered...." Just how soon should one get going on the embalming? The author tells us, "On the basis of such scanty information made available to this profession through its rudimentary and haphazard system of technical research, we must conclude that the best results are to be obtained if the subject is embalmed before life is completely extinct—that is, before cellular death has occurred. In the average case, this would mean within an hour after somatic death." For those who feel that there is something a little rudimentary, not to say haphazard, about this advice, a comforting thought is offered by another writer. Speaking of fears entertained in early days of premature burial, he points out, "One of the effects of embalming by chemical injection, however, has been to dispel fears of live burial." How true; once the blood is removed, chances of live burial are indeed remote.

To return to Mr. Jones, the blood is drained out through the veins and replaced by embalming fluid pumped in through the arteries. As noted in *The Principles and Practices of Embalming,* "every operator has a favorite injection and drainage point—a fact which becomes a handicap only if he fails or refuses to forsake his favorites when conditions demand it." Typical favorites are the carotid artery, femoral artery, jugular vein, subclavian vein. There are various choices of embalming fluid. If Flextone is used, it will produce a "mild, flexible rigidity. The skin retains a velvety softness, the tissues are rubbery and pliable. Ideal for women and children." It may be blended with B. and G. Products Company's Lyf-Lyk tint, which is guaranteed to reproduce "nature's own skin texture . . . the velvety appearance of living tissue." Suntone comes in three separate tints: Suntan; Special Cosmetic Tint, a pink shade "especially indicated for young female subjects"; and Regular Cosmetic Tint, moderately pink.

About three to six gallons of a dyed and perfumed solution of formaldehyde, glycerin, borax, phenol, alcohol, and water is soon circulating through Mr. Jones, whose mouth has been sewn together with a "needle directed upward between the upper lip and gum and brought out through the left nostril," with the corners raised slightly "for a more pleasant expression." If he should be buck-toothed, his teeth are cleaned with Bon Ami and coated with colorless nail polish. His eyes, meanwhile, are closed with flesh-tinted eye caps and eye cement.

The next step is to have at Mr. Jones with a thing called a trocar. This is a long, hollow needle attached to a tube. It is jabbed into the abdomen, poked around the entrails and chest cavity, the contents of which are pumped out and replaced with "cavity fluid." This done, and the hole in the abdomen sewed up, Mr. Jones's face is heavily creamed (to protect the skin from burns which may be caused by leakage of the chemicals), and he is covered with a sheet and left unmolested for a while. But not for long—there is more, much more, in store for him. He has been embalmed, but not yet restored, and the best time to start restorative work is eight to ten hours after embalming, when the tissues have become firm and dry.

The object of all this attention to the corpse, it must be remembered, is to make it presentable for viewing in an attitude of healthy repose. "Our customs require the presentation of our dead in the semblance of normality . . . unmarred by the ravages of illness, disease or mutilation," says Mr. J. Sheridan Mayer in his *Restorative Art.* This is rather a large order since few people die in the full bloom of health, unravaged by illness and unmarked by some disfigurement. The funeral industry is equal to the challenge: "In some cases the gruesome appearance of a mutilated or disease-ridden subject may be quite discouraging. The task of restoration may seem impossible and shake the confidence of the embalmer. This is the time for intestinal fortitude and determination. Once the formative work is begun and affected tissues are cleaned or removed, all doubts of success vanish. It is surprising and gratifying to discover the results which may be obtained."

The embalmer, having allowed an appropriate interval to elapse, returns to the attack, but now he brings into play the skill and equipment of sculptor and cosmetician. Is a hand missing? Casting one in plaster of Paris is a simple matter. "For replacement purposes, only a cast of the back of the hand is necessary; this is within the ability of the average operator and is quite adequate." If a lip or two, a nose or an ear should be missing, the embalmer has at hand a variety of restorative waxes with which to model replacements. Pores and skin texture are simulated by stippling with a little brush, and over this cosmetics are laid on. Head off? Decapitation cases are rather routinely handled. Ragged edges are trimmed, and head joined to torso with a series of splints, wires, and sutures. It is a good idea to have a little something at the neck—a scarf or high collar—when time for viewing comes. Swollen mouth? Cut out tissue as needed from inside the lips. If too much is removed, the surface contour can easily be restored by padding with cotton. Swollen necks and cheeks are reduced by removing tissue through vertical incisions made down each side of the neck. "When the deceased is casketed, the pillow will hide the suture incisions. . . . as an extra precaution against leakage, the suture may be painted with liquid sealer." 12

The opposite condition is more likely to be present itself—that of emaciation. His hypodermic syringe now loaded with massage cream, the embalmer seeks out and fills the hollowed and sunken areas by injection. In this procedure the backs of the hands and fingers and the under-chin area should not be neglected. 13

Positioning the lips is a problem that recurrently challenges the ingenuity of the embalmer. Closed too tightly, they tend to give a stern, even disapproving expression. Ideally, embalmers feel, the lips should give the impression of being ever so slightly parted, the upper lip protruding slightly for a more youthful appearance. This takes some engineering, however, as the lips tend to drift apart. Lip drift can sometimes be remedied by pushing one or two straight pins through the inner margin of the lower lip and then inserting them between the two front upper teeth. If Mr. Jones happens to have no teeth, the pins can just as easily be anchored in his Armstrong Face Former and Denture Replacer. Another method to maintain lip closure is to dislocate the lower jaw, which is then held in its new position by a wire run through holes which have been drilled through the upper jaws at the midline. As the French are fond of saying, *il faut souffrir pour être belle.** 14

---

*EDS. NOTE—It is necessary to suffer in order to be beautiful.

If Mr. Jones has died of jaundice, the embalming fluid will very likely   15
turn him green. Does this deter the embalmer? Not if he has intestinal fortitude. Masking pastes and cosmetics are heavily laid on, burial garments
and casket interiors are color-correlated with particular care, and Jones is
displayed beneath rose-colored lights. Friends will say, "How *well* he
looks." Death by carbon monoxide, on the other hand, can be rather a
good thing from an embalmer's viewpoint: "One advantage is the fact
that this type of discoloration is an exaggerated form of a natural pink
coloration." This is nice because the healthy glow is already present and
needs but little attention.

The patching and filling completed, Mr. Jones is now shaved,   16
washed, and dressed. Cream-based cosmetic, available in pink, flesh,
suntan, brunette, and blonde, is applied to his hands and face, his hair is
shampooed and combed (and, in the case of Mrs. Jones, set), his hands
manicured. For the horny-handed son of toil special care must be taken;
cream should be applied to remove ingrained grime, and the nails
cleaned. "If he were not in the habit of having them manicured in life,
trimming and shaping is advised for better appearance—never questioned by kin."

Jones is now ready for casketing (this is the present participle of the   17
verb "to casket"). In this operation his right shoulder should be de-
pressed slightly "to turn the body a bit to the right and soften the appearance of lying flat on the back." Positioning the hands is a matter of
importance, and special rubber positioning blocks may be used. The
hands should be cupped slightly for a more lifelike, relaxed appearance. Proper placement of the body requires a delicate sense of balance.
It should lie as high as possible in the casket, yet not so high that the
lid, when lowered, will hit the nose. On the other hand, we are cau-
tioned, placing the body too low "creates the impression that the body
is in a box."

Jones is next wheeled into the appointed slumber room where a few   18
last touches may be added—his favorite pipe placed in his hand or, if he
was a great reader, a book propped into position. (In the case of little
Master Jones a Teddy bear may be clutched.) Here he will hold open
house for a few days, visiting hours 10 A.M. to 9 P.M.

• • •

COMPREHENSION

1. How, according to Mitford, has the public's knowledge of embalming
   changed? How does she explain this change?

2. To what other professionals does Mitford liken the embalmer? Are these
   analogies flattering or critical? Explain.

3. What are the major stages in the process of embalming and restoration?

PURPOSE AND AUDIENCE

1. Mitford's purpose in this essay is to convince her audience of something. What is her thesis?

2. Do you think Mitford expects her audience to agree with her thesis? How can you tell?

3. In one of her books, Mitford refers to herself as a *muckraker,* one who informs the public of misconduct. Does she achieve this status here? Cite specific examples.

4. Mitford's tone in this essay is very subjective, even judgmental. What effect does her tone have on you? Does it encourage you to trust her? Should she present her facts in a more objective way? Explain.

STYLE AND STRUCTURE

1. Identify the stylistic features that distinguish this process explanation from a set of instructions.

2. In this selection, as in many process essays, a list of necessary materials comes before the procedure. What additional details does Mitford include in her list in paragraph 5? How do these additions affect you?

3. Go through the essay and locate Mitford's remarks about the language of embalming. How do her comments about euphemisms, newly coined words, and other aspects of language help to support her thesis?

4. Throughout the essay, Mitford quotes various experts. How does she use their remarks to support her thesis?

5. What phrases serve as transitions between the various stages of Mitford's process?

VOCABULARY PROJECTS

1. Define each of the following words as it is used in this selection.

perpetuation (1)	rudimentary (7)	stippling (12)
inherent (2)	haphazard (7)	emaciation (13)
mandatory (2)	entertained (7)	recurrently (14)
dissuaded (2)	pliable (8)	jaundice (15)
intractable (3)	repose (11)	toil (16)
reticence (3)	unravaged (11)	
loath (3)	fortitude (11)	

2. Substitute another word for each of the following.

territory (2)	ingenious (5)	presentable (11)
gruesomeness (2)	jabbed (10)	

What effect does each of your changes have on Mitford's meaning?

3. Reread paragraphs 5–9 very carefully. Then, list all the words in this section of the essay that suggest surgical technique and all the words that suggest cosmetic artistry. What do your lists tell you about Mitford's intent in these paragraphs?

JOURNAL ENTRY

What are your thoughts about the way your religion or culture deals with death and dying? What practices, if any, make you uncomfortable? Why?

WRITING WORKSHOP

1. Rewrite this process explanation as a set of instruction for undertakers, condensing it so that your essay is about five hundred words long. Unlike Mitford, keep your essay objective.

2. In the role of a funeral director, write a letter to Mitford in which you take issue with her essay. Explain the practice of embalming as necessary and practical. Unlike Mitford, design your process explanation to defend the practice.

3. Write an explanation of a process that you personally find disgusting—or delightful. Make your attitude clear in your thesis statement and in your choice of words.

COMBINING THE PATTERNS

Although Mitford structures this essay as a process, many passages rely heavily on subjective **description**. Where is her focus on descriptive details most obvious? What is her purpose in describing particular individuals and objects as she does? How do these descriptive passages help to support her essay's thesis?

THEMATIC CONNECTIONS

- "English Is a Crazy Language" (page 181)
- "My First Conk" (page 218)
- "The Ways We Lie" (page 414)

SHIRLEY JACKSON

Shirley Jackson (1919–1965) was born in California and graduated from Syracuse University in 1940. Jackson is best known for her horror stories exploring human motivation and social behavior and for her suspense novels, macabre tales of loneliness and isolation, which include *The Haunting of Hill House* (1959) and *We Have Always Lived in the Castle* (1962). Jackson also wrote accounts of her life as a wife and the mother of four children in *Life Among the Savages* (1953) and *Raising Demons* (1957). Three posthumous volumes, *The Magic of Shirley Jackson* (1966), *Come Along with Me* (1968), and *Just an Ordinary Day* (1996), collect Jackson's stories, novels, and lectures. "The Lottery," Jackson's best-known story, first appeared in 1948 in the *New Yorker*, where this haunting tale of an annual ritual inspired a flood of letters of protest and outrage as well as praise.

The Lottery

The morning of June 27th was clear and sunny, with the fresh warmth of a full-summer day; the flowers were blossoming profusely and the grass was richly green. The people of the village began to gather in the square, between the post office and the bank, around ten o'clock; in some towns there were so many people that the lottery took two days and had to be started on June 26th, but in this village, where there were only about three hundred people, the whole lottery took less than two hours, so it could begin at ten o'clock in the morning and still be through in time to allow the villagers to get home for noon dinner. 1

The children assembled first, of course. School was recently over for the summer, and the feeling of liberty sat uneasily on most of them; they tended to gather together quietly for a while before they broke into boisterous play, and their talk was still of the classroom and the teacher, of books and reprimands. Bobby Martin had already stuffed his pockets full of stones, and the other boys soon followed his example, selecting the smoothest and roundest stones; Bobby and Harry Jones and Dickie Delacroix—the villagers pronounced his name "Dellacroy"—eventually made a great pile of stones in one corner of the square and guarded it against the raids of the other boys. The girls stood aside, talking among themselves, looking over their shoulders at the boys, and the very small children rolled in the dust or clung to the hands of their older brothers or sisters. 2

Soon the men began to gather, surveying their own children, speaking of planting and rain, tractors and taxes. They stood together, away from the pile of stones in the corner, and their jokes were quiet and they smiled rather than laughed. The women, wearing faded house dresses and sweaters, came shortly after their menfolk. They greeted one another and exchanged bits of gossip as they went to join their husbands. Soon the women, standing by their husbands, began to call to their children, 3 and the children came reluctantly, having to be called four or five times. Bobby Martin ducked under his mother's grasping hand and ran, laughing, back to the pile of stones. His father spoke up sharply, and Bobby came quickly and took his place between his father and his oldest brother.

The lottery was conducted—as were the square dances, the teenage club, the Halloween program—by Mr. Summers, who had time and energy to devote to civic activities. He was a round-faced, jovial man and he ran the coal business, and people were sorry for him, because he had no children and his wife was a scold. When he arrived in the square, carrying the black wooden box, there was a murmur of conversation among the villagers, and he waved and called "Little late today, folks." The postmaster, Mr. Graves, followed him, carrying a three-legged stool, and the stool was put in the center of the square and Mr. Summers set the black box down on it. The villagers kept their distance, leaving a space between themselves and the stool, and when Mr. Summers said, "Some of you fellows want to give me a hand?" there was a hesitation before two men, Mr. Martin and his oldest son, Baxter, came forward to hold the box steady on the stool while Mr. Summers stirred up the papers inside it.

The original paraphernalia for the lottery had been lost long ago, and the black box now resting on the stool had been put into use even before Old Man Warner, the oldest man in town, was born. Mr. Summers spoke frequently to the villagers about making a new box, but no one liked to upset even as much tradition as was represented by the black box. There was a story that the present box had been made with some pieces of the box that had preceded it, the one that had been constructed when the first people settled down to make a village here. Every year, after the lottery, Mr. Summers began talking about a new box, but every year the subject was allowed to fade off without anything's being done. The black box grew shabbier each year; by now it was no longer completely black but splintered badly along one side to show the original wood color, and in some places faded and stained.

Mr. Martin and his oldest son, Baxter, held the black box securely on the stool until Mr. Summers had stirred the papers thoroughly with his hand. Because so much of the ritual had been forgotten or discarded, Mr. Summers had been successful in having slips of paper substituted for the chips of wood that had been used for generations. Chips of wood, Mr. Summers had argued, had been all very well when the village was tiny, but now that the population was more than three hundred and likely to keep on growing, it was necessary to use something that would fit more easily into the black box. The night before the lottery, Mr. Summers and Mr. Graves made up the slips of paper and put them in the box, and it was then taken to the safe of Mr. Summers' coal company and locked up until Mr. Summers was ready to take it to the square the next morning. The rest of the year, the box was put away, sometimes one place, sometimes another; it had spent one year in Mr. Graves' barn and another year underfoot in the post office, and sometimes it was set on a shelf in the Martin grocery and left there.

There was a great deal of fussing to be done before Mr. Summers declared the lottery open. There were the lists to make up—of heads of families, heads of households in each family, members of each household in each family. There was the proper swearing-in of Mr. Summers by the postmaster, as the official of the lottery; at one time, some people remembered, there had been a recital of some sort, performed by the official of the lottery, a perfunctory, tuneless chant that had been rattled off duly each year; some people believed that the official of the lottery used to stand just so when he said or sang it, others believed that he was supposed to walk among the people, but years and years ago this part of the ritual had been allowed to lapse. There had been, also, a ritual salute, which the official of the lottery had had to use in addressing each person who came up to draw from the box, but this also had changed with time, until now it was felt necessary only for the official to speak to each person approaching. Mr. Summers was very good at all this; in his clean white shirt and blue jeans, with one hand resting carelessly on the black box, he seemed very proper and important as he talked interminably to Mr. Graves and the Martins.   7

Just as Mr. Summers finally left off talking and turned to the assembled villagers, Mrs. Hutchinson came hurriedly along the path to the square, her sweater thrown over her shoulders, and slid into place in the back of the crowd. "Clean forgot what day it was," she said to Mrs. Delacroix, who stood next to her, and they both laughed softly. "Thought my old man was out back stacking wood," Mrs. Hutchinson went on, "and then I looked out the window and the kids were gone, and then I remembered it was the twenty-seventh and came a-running." She dried her hands on her apron, and Mrs. Delacroix said, "You're in time, though. They're still talking away up there."   8

Mrs. Hutchinson craned her neck to see through the crowd and found her husband and children standing near the front. She tapped Mrs. Delacroix on the arm as a farewell and began to make her way through the crowd. The people separated good-humoredly to let her through; two or three people said, in voices just loud enough to be heard across the crowd, "Here comes your Missus, Hutchinson," and "Bill, she made it after all." Mrs. Hutchinson reached her husband, and Mr. Summers, who had been waiting, said cheerfully, "Thought we were going to have to get on without you, Tessie." Mrs. Hutchinson said, grinning, "Wouldn't have me leave m'dishes in the sink, now, would you, Joe?" and soft laughter ran through the crowd as the people stirred back into position after Mrs. Hutchinson's arrival.   9

"Well, now," Mr. Summers said soberly, "guess we better get started, get this over with, so's we can go back to work. Anybody ain't here?"   10

"Dunbar," several people said. "Dunbar, Dunbar."   11

Mr. Summers consulted his list. "Clyde Dunbar," he said. "That's right. He's broke his leg, hasn't he? Who's drawing for him?"   12

"Me, I guess," a woman said, and Mr. Summers turned to look at her. "Wife draws for her husband," Mr. Summers said. "Don't you have a   13 grown boy to do it for you, Janey?" Although Mr. Summers and everyone else in the village knew the answer perfectly well, it was the business of the official of the lottery to ask such questions formally. Mr. Summers waited with an expression of polite interest while Mrs. Dunbar answered.

"Horace's not but sixteen yet," Mrs. Dunbar said regretfully. "Guess I   14
gotta fill in for the old man this year."

"Right," Mr. Summers said. He made a note on the list he was hold-   15
ing. Then he asked, "Watson boy drawing this year?"

A tall boy in the crowd raised his hand. "Here," he said. "I'm draw-   16
ing for m'mother and me." He blinked his eyes nervously and ducked his head as several voices in the crowd said things like "Good fellow, Jack," and "Glad to see your mother's got a man to do it."

"Well," Mr. Summers said, "guess that's everyone. Old Man Warner   17
make it?"

"Here," a voice said, and Mr. Summers nodded.   18

A sudden hush fell on the crowd as Mr. Summers cleared his throat   19
and looked at the list. "All ready?" he called. "Now, I'll read the names— heads of families first—and the men come up and take a paper out of the box. Keep the paper folded in your hand without looking at it until everyone has had a turn. Everything clear?"

The people had done it so many times that they only half listened to   20
the directions; most of them were quiet, wetting their lips, not looking around. Then Mr. Summers raised one hand high and said, "Adams." A man disengaged himself from the crowd and came forward. "Hi, Steve," Mr. Summers said, and Mr. Adams said, "Hi, Joe." They grinned at one another humorlessly and nervously. Then Mr. Adams reached into the black box and took out a folded paper. He held it firmly by one corner as he turned and went hastily back to his place in the crowd, where he stood a little apart from his family, not looking down at his hand.

"Allen." Mr. Summers said. "Anderson. . . . Betham."   21

"Seems like there's no time at all between lotteries any more," Mrs.   22
Delacroix said to Mrs. Graves in the back row. "Seems like we got through the last one only last week."

"Time sure goes fast,"Mrs. Graves said.   23

"Clark. . . . Delacroix."   24

"There goes my old man," Mrs. Delacroix said. She held her breath   25
while her husband went forward.

"Dunbar," Mr. Summers said, and Mrs. Dunbar went steadily to the   26
box while one of the women said, "Go on, Janey," and another said, "There she goes."

"We're next," Mrs. Graves said. She watched while Mr. Graves came   27
around from the side of the box, greeted Mr. Summers gravely, and selected a slip of paper from the box. By now, all through the crowd there were men holding the small folded papers in their large hands, turning

them over and over nervously. Mrs. Dunbar and her two sons stood together, Mrs. Dunbar holding the slip of paper.

"Harburt. . . . Hutchinson."

28

"Get up there, Bill," Mrs. Hutchinson said, and the people near her laughed.

29

"Jones."

30

"They do say," Mr. Adams said to Old Man Warner, who stood next to him, "that over in the north village they're talking of giving up the lottery."

31

Old Man Warner snorted. "Pack of crazy fools," he said. "Listening to the young folks, nothing's good enough for *them*. Next thing you know, they'll be wanting to go back to living in caves, nobody work any more, live *that* way for a while. Used to be a saying about 'Lottery in June, corn be heavy soon.' First thing you know, we'd all be eating stewed chickweed and acorns. There's *always* been a lottery," he added petulantly. "Bad enough to see young Joe Summers up there joking with everybody."

32

"Some places have already quit lotteries," Mrs. Adams said.

33

"Nothing but trouble in *that*," Old Man Warner said stoutly. "Pack of young fools."

34

"Martin." And Bobby Martin watched his father go forward. "Overdyke. . . . Percy."

35

"I wish they'd hurry," Mrs. Dunbar said to her older son. "I wish they'd hurry."

36

"They're almost through," her son said.

37

"You get ready to run tell Dad," Mrs. Dunbar said.

38

Mr. Summers called his own name and then stepped forward precisely and selected a slip from the box. Then he called, "Warner."

39

"Seventy-seventh year I been in the lottery," Old Man Warner said as he went through the crowd. "Seventy-seventh time."

40

"Watson." The tall boy came awkwardly through the crowd. Someone said, "Don't be nervous, Jack," and Mr. Summers said, "Take your time, son."

41

"Zanini."

42

After that, there was a long pause, a breathless pause, until Mr. Summers, holding his slip of paper in the air, said, "All right fellows." For a minute, no one moved, and then all the slips of paper were opened. Suddenly, all the women began to speak at once, saying, "Who is it," "Who's got it?," "Is it the Dunbars?," "Is it the Watsons?" Then the voices began to say, "It's Hutchinson. It's Bill," "Bill Hutchinson's got it."

43

"Go tell your father," Mrs. Dunbar said to her older son.

44

People began to look around to see the Hutchinsons. Bill Hutchinson was standing quiet, staring down at the paper in his hand. Suddenly, Tessie Hutchinson shouted to Mr. Summers, "You didn't give him time enough to take any paper he wanted. I saw you. It wasn't fair!"

45

"Be a good sport, Tessie," Mrs. Delacroix called, and Mrs. Graves said, "All of us took the same chance."

46

"Shut up, Tessie," Bill Hutchinson said. [47]

"Well, everyone," Mr. Summers said, "That was done pretty fast, and [48] now we've got to be hurrying a little more to get it done in time." He consulted his next list. "Bill," he said, "you draw for the Hutchinson family. You got any other households in the Hutchinsons?"

"There's Don and Eva," Mrs. Hutchinson yelled. "Make *them* take [49] their chance!"

"Daughters draw with their husbands' families, Tessie," Mr. [50] Summers said gently. "You know that as well as anyone else."

"It wasn't *fair*," Tessie said. [51]

"I guess not, Joe," Bill Hutchinson said regretfully. "My daughter [52] draws with her husband's family, that's only fair. And I've got no other family except the kids."

"Then, as far as drawing for families is concerned, it's you," Mr. [53] Summers said in explanation, "and as far as drawing for households is concerned, that's you, too. Right?"

"Right," Bill Hutchinson said. [54]

"How many kids, Bill?" Mr. Summers asked formally. [55]

"Three," Bill Hutchinson said. "There's Bill, Jr., and Nancy, and little [56] Dave. And Tessie and me."

"All right, then," Mr. Summers said. "Harry, you got their tickets [57] back?"

Mr. Graves nodded and held up the slips of paper. "Put them in the [58] box, then," Mr. Summers directed. "Take Bill's and put it in."

"I think we ought to start over," Mrs. Hutchinson said, as quietly as [59] she could. "I tell you it wasn't *fair*. You didn't give him time enough to choose. *Every*body saw that."

Mr. Graves had selected the five slips and put them in the box, and he [60] dropped all the papers but those onto the ground, where the breeze caught them and lifted them off.

"Listen, everybody," Mrs. Hutchinson was saying to the people [61] around her.

"Ready, Bill?" Mr. Summers asked, and Bill Hutchinson, with one [62] quick glance around at his wife and children, nodded.

"Remember," Mr. Summers said, "take the slips and keep them [63] folded until each person has taken one. Harry, you help little Dave." Mr. Graves took the hand of the little boy, who came willingly with him up to the box. "Take a paper out of the box, Davy," Mr. Summers said. Davy put his hand into the box and laughed. "Take just *one* paper," Mr. Summers said. "Harry, you hold it for him." Mr. Graves took the child's hand and removed the folded paper from the tight fist and held it while little Dave stood next to him and looked up at him wonderingly.

"Nancy next," Mr. Summers said. Nancy was twelve, and her school [64] friends breathed heavily as she went forward, switching her skirt, and took a slip daintily from the box. "Bill, Jr.," Mr. Summers said, and Billy, his face red and his feet over-large, nearly knocked the box over as he got a paper out. "Tessie," Mr. Summers said. She hesitated for a minute, looking around defiantly, and then set her lips and went up to the box. She snatched a paper out and held it behind her.

"Bill," Mr. Summers said, and Bill Hutchinson reached into the box   65
and felt around, bringing his hand out at last with the slip of paper in it.

The crowd was quiet. A girl whispered, "I hope it's not Nancy," and   66
the sound of the whisper reached the edges of the crowd.

"It's not the way it used to be," Old Man Warner said clearly. "People   67
ain't the way they used to be."

"All right," Mr. Summers said. "Open the papers. Harry, you open   68
little Dave's."

Mr. Graves opened the slip of paper and there was a general sigh   69
through the crowd as he held it up and everyone could see that it was blank. Nancy and Bill, Jr., opened theirs at the same time, and both beamed and laughed, turning around to the crowd and holding their slips of paper above their heads.

"Tessie," Mr. Summers said. There was a pause, and then Mr.   70
Summers looked at Bill Hutchinson, and Bill unfolded his paper and showed it. It was blank.

"It's Tessie," Mr. Summers said, and his voice was hushed. "Show us   71
her paper, Bill."

Bill Hutchinson went over to his wife and forced the slip of paper out   72
of her hand. It had a black spot on it, the black spot Mr. Summers had made the night before with the heavy pencil in the coal-company office. Bill Hutchinson held it up, and there was a stir in the crowd.

"All right, folks," Mr. Summers said. "Let's finish quickly."   73

Although the villagers had forgotten the ritual and lost the original   74
black box, they still remembered to use stones. The pile of stones the boys had made earlier was ready; there were stones on the ground with the blowing scraps of paper that had come out of the box. Mrs. Delacroix elected a stone so large she had to pick it up with both hands and turned to Mrs. Dunbar. "Come on," she said. "Hurry up."

Mrs. Dunbar had small stones in both hands, and she said, gasping   75
for breath, "I can't run at all. You'll have to go ahead and I'll catch up with you."

The children had stones already, and someone gave little Davy   76
Hutchinson a few pebbles.

Tessie Hutchinson was in the center of a cleared space by now, and   77
she held her hands out desperately as the villagers moved in on her. "It isn't fair," she said. A stone hit her on the side of the head.

Old Man Warner was saying, "Come on, come on, everyone." Steve   78
Adams was in the front of the crowd of villagers, with Mrs. Graves besides him.

"It isn't fair, it isn't right," Mrs. Hutchinson screamed, and then they   79
were upon her.

• • •

THINKING ABOUT LITERATURE

1. List the stages in the process of the lottery. Then identify passages that explain the reasons behind each step. How logical are these explanations?

2. What is the significance of the fact that the process has continued essentially unchanged for so many years? What does this fact suggest about the people in the town?

3. Do you see this story as an explanation of a brutal process carried out in one particular town, or do you see it as a universal statement about dangerous tendencies in modern society—or in human nature? Explain your reasoning.

JOURNAL ENTRY

What do you think it would take to stop a process like the lottery? What could be done—and who would have to do it?

THEMATIC CONNECTIONS

- "Thirty-Eight Who Saw Murder Didn't Call the Police" (page 86)
- "Shooting an Elephant" (page 91)
- "Samuel" (page 202)

WRITING ASSIGNMENTS FOR PROCESS

1. Both Larry Brown and Jessica Mitford describe the process of doing a job. Write an essay in which you summarize the steps involved in applying for, performing, or quitting a particular job you have held.

2. Write a set of instructions explaining in very objective terms how the lottery Shirley Jackson describes should be conducted. Imagine you are setting these steps down in writing for generations of your fellow townspeople to follow.

3. Write a consumer-oriented article for your school newspaper in which you explain how to apply for financial aid, a work-study job, a student internship, or a permanent job in your field.

4. List the steps in the process you follow when you study for an important exam. Then, interview a friend about how he or she studies, and take notes about his or her customary procedure. Finally, combine the most helpful strategies into a set of instructions aimed at students entering your school.

5. Write a set of instructions explaining how to use a print reference work or an online database with which you are familiar—or, explain how you use the Internet for research.

6. Think of a series of steps in a bureaucratic process, a process you had to go through to accomplish something: registering to vote, getting a driver's license, becoming a U.S. citizen, or applying for financial aid, for instance. Write an essay in which you explain that process, and include a thesis statement that evaluates the efficiency of the process.

7. Imagine you have encountered a visitor from another country (or another planet) who is not familiar with a social ritual you take for granted. Try to outline the steps involved in one such ritual—for instance, choosing sides for a game or pledging a fraternity or sorority.

8. Write a process essay explaining how you went about putting together a collection, a scrapbook, a portfolio, or an album of some kind. Be sure your essay makes clear why you collected or compiled your materials.

9. Explain how a certain ritual or ceremony is conducted in your religion. Make sure someone of another faith will be able to understand the process, and include a thesis statement that explains why the ritual is important to you.

10. Think of a process you believe should be modified or discontinued. Formulate a persuasive thesis that presents your negative feelings, and then explain the process so that you make your objections to it clear to your readers.

COLLABORATIVE ACTIVITY FOR PROCESS

Working with three other students, create an illustrated instructional pamphlet to help new students survive four of your college's first "ordeals"—for example, registering for classes, purchasing textbooks, eating in the cafeteria, and moving into a dorm. Before beginning, decide as a group which processes to write about, whether you want your pamphlet to be practical and serious or humorous and irreverent, and what kind of illustrations it should include. Then decide which of you will write about which process—each student should do one—and who will be responsible for the illustrations. When all of you are ready, assemble your individual efforts into a single piece of writing.

6

CAUSE AND EFFECT

WHAT IS CAUSE AND EFFECT?

Process describes *how* something happens; **cause and effect** analyzes *why* something happens. Cause-and-effect essays examine causes, describe effects, or do both. In the following paragraph, Tom Wicker considers the effects of a technological advance on a village in India:

Cause

Effects

Topic sentence

When a solar-powered water pump was provided for a well in India, the village headman took it over and sold the water, until stopped. The new liquid abundance attracted hordes of unwanted nomads. Village boys who had drawn water in buckets had nothing to do, and some became criminals. The gap between rich and poor widened, since the poor had no land to benefit from irrigation. Finally, village women broke the pump, so they could gather again around the well that had been the center of their social lives. Moral: technological advances have social, cultural, and economic consequences, often unanticipated.

Cause and effect, like narration, links situations and events together in time, with causes preceding effects. But causality involves more than sequence: cause-and-effect analysis explains why something happened—or is happening—and it predicts what probably will happen.

Sometimes many different causes can be responsible for one effect. For example, many elements may contribute to an individual's decision to leave his or her country of origin and come to the United States, as shown in the following diagram:

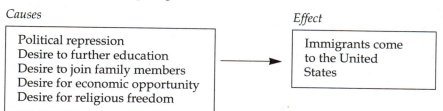

Causes

Political repression
Desire to further education
Desire to join family members
Desire for economic opportunity
Desire for religious freedom

Effect

Immigrants come
to the United
States

Similarly, many different effects can be produced by a single cause. Immigration, for instance, has had a variety of effects on the United States:

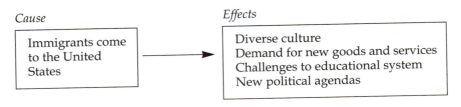

Cause

Immigrants come
to the United
States

Effects

Diverse culture
Demand for new goods and services
Challenges to educational system
New political agendas

Of course, causal relationships are rarely as neat as these boxes suggest. Such relationships are often subtle and complex. As you examine situations that seem suited to cause-and-effect analysis, you will discover that most complex situations involve numerous causes and many different effects.

Consider this example: for more than twenty years, from the 1960s to the 1980s, the college-board scores of high school seniors steadily declined. This decline began soon after television became popular, and therefore many people concluded that the two events were connected. The idea is plausible because children did seem to be reading less in order to watch television more, and because reading comprehension is one of the chief skills the tests evaluate.

But many other elements might have contributed to the lowering of test scores. During the same period, for example, many schools reduced the number of required courses and deemphasized traditional subjects and skills, such as reading. Adults were reading less than they used to, and perhaps they were not encouraging their children to read. Furthermore, during the 1960s and 1970s, many colleges changed their policies and admitted students who previously would not have qualified. These new admission standards encouraged students who would not have taken college boards in earlier years to take the tests. Therefore, the scores may have been lower because they measured the top third of high school seniors rather than the top fifth. In any case, the reason for the lower scores is not clear. Perhaps television was the cause after all, but now—with 1995 SAT verbal scores showing their biggest increase in ten years while television watching remains fairly constant—nobody knows for sure. In such a case, it is easy—too easy—to claim a cause-and-effect relationship without the evidence to support it.

Just as the drop in scores may have had many causes, television watching may have had many effects. For instance, it may have made those same students better observers and listeners, even if they did less well on standardized written tests. It may have encouraged them to have a national or even international outlook instead of a narrow interest in local affairs. In other words, even if watching television did limit people in some ways, it may also have expanded their horizons.

To give a balanced analysis, try to consider all causes and effects, not just the most obvious ones or the first ones you think of. For example, suppose a professional basketball team, recently stocked with the best players money can buy, has had a mediocre season. Because the individual players are talented and were successful under other coaches, fans blame the current coach for the team's losing streak and want him fired. But is the coach alone responsible? Maybe the inability of the players to mesh well as a team is responsible for their poor performance. Perhaps some of the players are suffering from injuries, personal problems, or drug dependency. Or maybe the drop in attendance at games has affected the team's morale. Clearly, other elements besides the new coach could have caused the losing streak. Indeed, the suspected cause of the team's decline—the coach—may actually have saved the team from total collapse by keeping the players from quarreling with one another. When you write about such a situation, you need to carefully identify these complex causes and effects.

Main and Contributory Causes

Even when you have identified several causes of an effect, one—the *main cause*—is always more important than the others—the *contributory causes*. Understanding the distinction between the **main** (most important) cause and the **contributory** (less important) cause is vital for planning a cause-and-effect paper: once you identify the main cause, you can emphasize it in your paper and downplay the other causes. How, then, can you tell which cause is most important? Sometimes the main cause is obvious, but often it is not, as the following example shows.

During one winter a number of years ago, an abnormally large amount of snow accumulated on the roof of the Civic Center Auditorium in Hartford, Connecticut, and the roof fell in. Newspapers reported that the weight of the snow had caused the collapse, and they were partly right. Other buildings, however, had not been flattened by the snow, so the main cause seemed to lie elsewhere. Insurance investigators eventually decided that the design of the roof, not the weight of the snow (which was a contributory cause), was the main cause of the collapse. The cause-and-effect relationships summarized above are shown in this diagram:

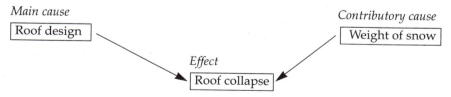

Because the main cause is not always obvious, you should be sure to consider the significance of each cause very carefully as you plan your essay—and continue to evaluate the importance of each cause as you write and revise.

Immediate and Remote Causes

Another important distinction is the difference between an *immediate cause* and a *remote cause*. An **immediate cause** closely precedes an effect and is therefore relatively easy to recognize. A **remote cause** is less obvious, perhaps because it involves something in the past or far away. Assuming that the most obvious cause is always the most important can be dangerous as well as shortsighted.

For example, look again at the Hartford roof collapse. Most people agreed that the snow was the immediate, or most obvious, cause of the roof collapse. But further study by insurance investigators suggested remote causes that were not so apparent. The design of the roof was the most important remote cause of the collapse. In addition, perhaps the materials used in the roof's construction were partly to blame. Maybe maintenance crews had not done their jobs properly, or necessary repairs had not been made. If you were the insurance investigator analyzing the causes of this event, you would want to assess all possible contributing factors rather than just the most obvious. If you did not consider the remote as well as the immediate causes, you would reach an oversimplified and perhaps incorrect conclusion.

This diagram shows the cause-and-effect relationships summarized above:

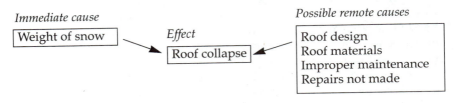

Remote causes can be extremely important. In the roof-collapse situation, as we have seen, a remote cause—the roof design—was the main cause of the accident.

The Causal Chain

Sometimes an effect can also be a cause. This is true in a **causal chain,** where A causes B, B causes C, C causes D, and so on, as shown here:

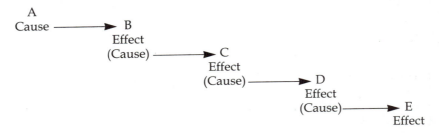

A simple example of a causal chain starts with the conclusion of World War II in 1945. Beginning in 1946, as thousands of American soldiers returned home, the U.S. birth rate began to rise dramatically. As the numbers of births increased, the creation of goods and services to meet the needs of this growing population also increased. As advertisers competed to attract this group's attention to various products, the so-called baby-boom generation became more and more visible. Consequently, baby boomers were perceived as more and more powerful—as voters as well as consumers. As a result, this group's emergence has been a major factor in shaping American political, social, cultural, and economic life.

In a causal chain like this one, the result of one action is the cause of another. Leaving out any link in the chain, or putting any link in improper order, destroys the logic and continuity of the chain.

If your analysis of a situation reveals a causal chain, this discovery can be useful in your writing. The very operation of a causal chain suggests an organizational pattern for a paper, and following the chain helps you to discuss items in their logical order. Be careful, however, to keep your emphasis on the causal connections and not to lapse into narration.

Post Hoc Reasoning

When developing a cause-and-effect paper, you should not assume that just because event A *precedes* event B, event A has *caused* event B. This illogical assumption, called ***post hoc* reasoning,** equates a chronological sequence with causality. When you fall into this trap—assuming, for instance, that you failed an exam because a black cat crossed your path the day before—you are mistaking coincidence for causality.

Consider another example of *post hoc* reasoning. Until the late nineteenth century, many scientists accepted the notion of spontaneous generation—that is, they believed living things could arise directly from nonliving matter. To support their beliefs, they pointed to specific situations. For instance, they observed that maggots, the larvae of the housefly, seemed to arise directly from the decaying flesh of dead animals.

These scientists were confusing sequence with causality, assuming that just because the presence of decaying meat preceded the appearance of maggots, the two were connected in a causal relationship. In fact, because the dead animals were exposed to the air, flies were free to lay eggs in the animals' bodies, and these eggs hatched into maggots. Therefore, the living maggots were not a direct result of the presence of nonliving matter. Although these scientists were applying the best technology and scientific theory of their time, hindsight reveals that their conclusions were not valid.

In your writing as well as in your observations, it is neither logical nor fair to assume that a causal relationship exists unless clear, strong evidence supports the connection. When you revise a cause-and-effect paper, make sure you have not confused words like *because, therefore,* and *consequently*—words that show a causal relationship—with words like *subsequently, later,* and *afterward*—words that show a chronological relationship. When you use a word like *because,* you are signaling to readers that you are telling *why* something happened; when you use a word like *later,* you are only showing *when* it happened.

Being able to identify and analyze cause-and-effect relationships; to distinguish causes from effects and recognize causal chains; and to distinguish immediate from remote, main from contributory, and logical from illogical causes are all skills that will improve your writing. Understanding the nature of the cause-and-effect relationship will help you decide when to use this pattern to structure a paper.

STRUCTURING A CAUSE-AND-EFFECT ESSAY

After you have sorted out the cause-and-effect relationships you will write about, you are ready to plan your paper. You have three basic options: to discuss causes, to discuss effects, or to discuss both causes and effects. Often your assignment will suggest which of these options to use. Here are a few likely topics for cause-and-effect treatment:

Focus on finding causes	Identify some possible causes of collective obsessional behavior. (psychology exam)
	Discuss the factors that have contributed to the declining population of state mental hospitals. (social work paper)
Focus on describing or predicting effects	Evaluate the probable effects of moving elementary school children from a highly structured classroom to a relatively open classroom. (education paper)
	Discuss the impact of World War I on two of Ernest Hemingway's characters. (literature exam)
Focus on both causes and effects	The 1840s were very volatile years in Europe. Choose one social, political, or economic event that occurred during those years, analyze its causes, and briefly note how the event influenced later developments in European history. (history exam)

Of course, a cause-and-effect essay usually does more than just enumerate causes or effects. For example, an economics paper treating the major effects of the Vietnam War on the U.S. economy could be a straightforward presentation of factual information—an attempt to inform readers of the war's economic impact. It is more likely, however, that the paper would indicate the significance of the war's effects, not just list them. In fact, cause-and-effect analysis often requires you to judge various factors so that you can assess their relative significance.

When you formulate a thesis statement, be sure that it identifies the relationships among the specific causes or effects you will discuss. This thesis statement should tell your readers three things: the points you plan to consider, the position you will take, and whether your emphasis is on causes, effects, or both. Your thesis statement may also indicate explicitly or implicitly the cause or effect you consider most important and the order in which you will treat your points.

When deciding on the sequence in which you will present causes or effects, you have several options. One option, of course, is chronological order—you can present causes or effects in the order in which they occurred. Another option is to introduce the main cause first and then contributory causes—or to do just the opposite. If you want to stress positive consequences, begin by briefly discussing the negative ones; if you plan to emphasize negative results, summarize the less important positive effects first. Still another possibility is to begin by dismissing any events that were *not* causes and then explain what the real causes were. This method is especially effective if you think your readers are likely to jump to *post hoc* conclusions. Finally, you can begin with the most obvious causes or effects and move on to more subtle factors—and then to your analysis and conclusion.

Finding Causes

Suppose you are planning the social work paper mentioned earlier: "Discuss the factors that have contributed to the declining population of state mental hospitals." Your assignment specifies an effect—the declining population of state hospitals—and asks you to discuss possible causes, which might include the following:

- An increasing acceptance of mental illness in our society
- Prohibitive costs of in-patient care
- Increasing numbers of mental-health professionals, facilitating treatment outside of hospitals

Many health professionals, however, believe that the most important cause is the development and use of psychotropic drugs, such as chlorpromazine (Thorazine), which can alter behavior. To emphasize this cause in your paper, you could formulate the following thesis statement:

Less important causes	Although society's increasing acceptance of the mentally ill, the high cost of in-patient care, and the rise in the number of health professionals have all been influential
Effect	in reducing the population of state mental hospitals, the
Most important cause	most important cause of this reduction is the development and use of psychotropic drugs.

This thesis statement fully prepares your readers for your essay. It identifies the points you will consider, and it reveals your position—your assessment of the relative significance of the causes you identify. It states the less important causes first and indicates their secondary importance with *although*. In the body of your essay, the less important causes would come first so that the essay could gradually build up to the most convincing material. An informal outline for your paper might look like this:

Introduction:	Thesis statement—Although society's increasing acceptance of the mentally ill, the high cost of in-patient care, and the rise in the number of health professionals have all been influential in reducing the population of state mental hospitals, the most important cause of this reduction is the development and use of psychotropic drugs.
First cause:	Increasing acceptance of the mentally ill
Second cause:	High cost of in-patient care
Third cause:	Rise in the number of health professionals
Fourth (and most important) cause:	Development and use of psychotropic drugs
Conclusion:	Restatement of thesis or summary of key points

Describing or Predicting Effects

Suppose you were planning the education paper mentioned earlier: "Evaluate the probable effects of moving elementary school children from a highly structured classroom to a relatively open classroom." You would use a procedure similar to the preceding one, but you would focus on effects rather than on causes. After brainstorming and deciding which specific points to discuss, you might formulate this thesis statement:

| Cause | Moving children from a highly structured classroom to a relatively open one is desirable because it is likely to encourage more independent play, more flexibility in forming friendship groups, and, ultimately, more creativity. |
| Effects | |

This thesis statement clearly tells readers the stand you will take and the main points your essay will consider; the thesis also clearly specifies that these points are *effects* of the open classroom. After introducing the cause, your essay would treat these three effects in the order in which they are presented in the thesis statement, building up to the most important point. An informal outline of your paper might look like this:

Introduction: Thesis statement—Moving children from a highly
                       structured classroom to a relatively open one is de-
                       sirable because it is likely to encourage more inde-
                       pendent play, more flexibility in forming friendship
                       groups, and, ultimately, more creativity.

First effect: More independent play

Second effect: More flexible friendship groups

Third (and most
important) effect: More creativity

Conclusion: Restatement of thesis or summary of key points

▶ **A STUDENT WRITER: CAUSE AND EFFECT**

The following midterm exam, written for a history class, analyzes
both the causes and effects of the Irish potato famine that occurred during
the 1840s. Notice how the writer, Evelyn Pellicane, concentrates on causes
but also discusses briefly the effects of this tragedy, just as the exam question directs.

Question: The 1840s were very volatile years in Europe. Choose one social, political, or economic event that occurred during those years, analyze its causes, and briefly note how the event influenced later
developments in European history.

The Irish Famine, 1845-1849

Thesis statement   The Irish famine, which brought hardship   1
                       and tragedy to Ireland during the 1840s, was
                       caused and prolonged by four basic factors: the
                       failure of the potato crop, the landlord-tenant
                       system, errors in government policy, and the
                       long-standing prejudice of the British toward
                       Ireland.

First cause   The immediate cause of the famine was the   2
                       failure of the potato crop. In 1845, potato
                       disease struck the crop, and potatoes rotted in
                       the ground. The 1846 crop also failed, and be-
                       fore long people were eating weeds. The 1847
                       crop was healthy, but there were not enough
                       potatoes to go around, and in 1848 the blight
                       struck again, leading to more and more evic-
                       tions of tenants by landlords.

Second cause   The tenants' position on the land had   3
                       never been very secure. Most had no leases and
                       could be turned out by their landlords at any
                       time. If a tenant owed rent, he was evicted--or,

worse, put in prison, leaving his family to starve. The threat of prison caused many tenants to leave their land; those who could leave Ireland did so, sometimes with money provided by their landlords. Some landlords did try to take care of their tenants, but most did not. Many were absentee landlords who spent their rent money abroad.

Third cause   Government policy errors, although not an   4 immediate cause of the famine, played an important role in creating an unstable economy and perpetuating starvation. In 1846, the government decided not to continue selling corn, as it had during the first year of the famine, claiming that low-cost purchases of corn by Ireland had paralyzed British trade by interfering with free enterprise. Therefore, 1846 saw a starving population, angry demonstrations, and panic; even those with money were unable to buy food. Still, the government insisted that if it sent food to Ireland, prices would rise in the rest of the United Kingdom and that this would be unfair to hardworking English and Scots. As a result, no food was sent. Throughout the years of the famine, the British government aggravated an already grave situation: they did nothing to improve agricultural operations, to help people adjust to another crop, to distribute seeds, or to reorder the landlord-tenant system that made the tenants' position so insecure.

Fourth cause   At the root of this poor government policy   5 was the long-standing British prejudice against the Irish. Hostility between the two countries went back some six hundred years, and the British were simply not about to inconvenience themselves to save the Irish. When the Irish so desperately needed grain to replace the damaged potatoes, it was clear that grain had to be im-

ported from England. This meant, however, that
the Corn Laws, which had been enacted to keep
the price of British corn high by taxing imported grain, had to be repealed. The British
were unwilling to repeal the Corn Laws. Even
when they did supply cornmeal, they made no attempt to explain to the Irish how to cook this
unfamiliar food. Moreover, the British government was determined to make Ireland pay for its
own poor, and so it forced the collection of
taxes. Since many landlords just did not have
the tax money, they were forced to evict their
tenants. The British government's callous and
indifferent treatment of the Irish has been
called genocide.

Effects   As a result of this devastating famine,   6
the population of Ireland was reduced from
about nine million to about six and one-half
million. During the famine years, men roamed
the streets looking for work, begging when they
found none. Epidemics of "famine fever" and
dysentery reduced the population drastically.
The most important historical result of the
famine, however, was the massive immigration to
the United States, Canada, and Great Britain of
poor, unskilled people who had to struggle to
fit into a skilled economy and who brought with
them a deep-seated hatred of the British. (This
same hatred remained strong in Ireland itself--
so strong that at the time of World War II,
Ireland, then independent, remained neutral
rather than coming to England's aid.) Irish immigrants faced slums, fever epidemics, jobless-
ness, and hostility--even anti-Catholic and
anti-Irish riots--in Boston, New York, London,
Glasgow, and Quebec. In Ireland itself, poverty
and discontent continued, and by 1848 those em-
igrating from Ireland included a more highly
skilled class of farmer, the ones Ireland
needed to recover and to survive.

Conclusion (includes restatement of thesis)

The Irish famine, one of the great tragedies of the nineteenth century, was a natural disaster compounded by the insensitivity of the British government and the archaic agricultural system of Ireland. Although the deaths that resulted depleted Ireland's resources even more, the men and women who immigrated to other countries permanently enriched those nations.

7

Points for Special Attention

STRUCTURE.   This is a relatively long essay; if it were not so clearly organized, it would be difficult to follow. Because the essay was to focus primarily on causes, Evelyn first introduces the effect—the famine itself—and then considers its causes. After she examines the causes, she moves on to the results of the famine, treating the most important result last. In this essay, then, the famine is first treated as an effect and then, toward the end, as a cause. In fact, it is the central link in a causal chain. Evelyn devotes one paragraph to her introduction and one to each cause; she sums up the famine's results in a separate paragraph and devotes the final paragraph to her conclusion. (Depending on a particular paper's length and complexity, more—or less—than one paragraph may be devoted to each cause or effect.) An informal outline for her paper might look like this:

Introduction (including thesis statement)
First cause: Failure of the potato crop
Second cause: The landlord-tenant system
Third cause: Errors in government policy
Fourth cause: British prejudice
Results of the famine
Conclusion

Because Evelyn sees all the causes as important and interrelated, she does not present them in order of increasing importance. Instead, she begins with the immediate cause of the famine—the failure of the potato crop—and then digs more deeply until she arrives at the most remote cause, British prejudice. The immediate cause is also the main (most important) cause, for the other situations had existed before the famine began.

TRANSITIONS.   The cause-and-effect relationships in this essay are both subtle and complex; Evelyn considers a series of relationships as well as an intricate causal chain. Throughout the essay, many words suggest cause-and-effect connections: *so, therefore, because, as a result, since, led* *to, brought about, caused,* and the like. These are the most effective transitions for such an essay.

ANSWERING AN EXAMINATION QUESTION. Before planning and writing her answer, Evelyn read the exam question very carefully. She noted that it asked for both causes and effects but that its wording directed her to spend more time on causes ("analyze") than on effects ("briefly note"). Consequently, she decided to organize her discussion to conform to these directions and is careful to indicate *explicitly* which are the causes ("government policy . . . played an important role") and which are the effects ("The most important historical result").

Evelyn's purpose is to convey factual information and, in doing so, to demonstrate her understanding of the course material. Rather than waste her limited time choosing a clever opening strategy or making elaborate attempts to engage her audience, Evelyn begins her essay with a direct statement of her thesis.

Evelyn has obviously been influenced by outside sources; the ideas in the essay are not completely her own. Because this is an exam, however, and because the instructor expected that students would base their essays on class notes and assigned readings, Evelyn does not have to document her sources.

Focus on Revision

Because this essay was written as an exam answer, Evelyn had no time—and no need—to revise it further. If she had been preparing this assignment outside of class, however, she might have done more. For example, she could have added a more arresting opening, such as a brief eyewitness account of the famine's effects. Her conclusion—appropriately brief and straightforward for an exam answer—could also have been strengthened, perhaps with the addition of information about the nation's eventual recovery. Finally, the addition of statistics, quotations by historians, or a brief summary of Irish history before the famine could have further enriched the essay.

All the selections that follow focus on cause-and-effect relationships. Some readings focus on causes, others on effects. As these essays illustrate, the cause-and-effect pattern is so versatile that it may be used to examine topics as dissimilar as boxing, television, racial segregation, rural poverty, and a young girl's life.

NORMAN COUSINS

Norman Cousins (1915–1990) was born in Union City, New Jersey, and graduated from Columbia University's Teachers College in 1933. He began his career in journalism writing for the *New York Evening Post* and *Current History*
magazine. In 1940 Cousins joined the *Saturday Review*, where he served as editor from 1942 to 1978. Cousins lectured widely on world affairs, was a social
critic and a strong advocate of nuclear controls, and arranged for victims of
the atomic bombing of Hiroshima to come to the United States for medical
treatment. From 1978 until his death, he was an adjunct professor in the department of psychiatry and biobehavioral science at U.C.L.A. Medical
School. Cousins published numerous books, including many urging a positive outlook to combat illness: *Anatomy of an Illness* (1979), about his own
struggle with a life-threatening form of arthritis; *Human Options: An
Autobiographical Notebook* (1981); *Healing and Belief* (1982); *The Healing Heart:
Antidotes to Panic and Helplessness* (1983); *The Pathology of Power* (1987); and his
last book, about the effect of the emotions on the body's resistance to disease,
Head First: The Biology of Hope (1989). In his 1962 essay "Who Killed Benny
Paret?" Cousins investigates the causes of a boxer's death. In answering the
question posed by his essay's title, Cousins takes a strong stand against vio-
lence in boxing.

Who Killed Benny Paret?

Sometime about 1935 or 1936 I had an interview with Mike Jacobs, 1
the prize-fight promoter. I was a fledgling reporter at that time; my beat
was education but during the vacation season I found myself on varied
assignments, all the way from ship news to sports reporting. In this way I
found myself sitting opposite the most powerful figure in the boxing
world.

There was nothing spectacular in Mr. Jacobs' manner or appearance; 2
but when he spoke about prize fights, he was no longer a bland little man
but a colossus who sounded the way Napoleon must have sounded when
he reviewed a battle. You knew you were listening to Number One. His
saying something made it true.

We discussed what to him was the only important element in success- 3
ful promoting—how to please the crowd. So far as he was concerned,
there was no mystery to it. You put killers in the ring and the people filled
your arena. You hire boxing artists—men who are adroit at feinting, par-
rying, weaving, jabbing, and dancing, but who don't pack dynamite in
their fists—and you wind up counting your empty seats. So you searched
for the killers and sluggers and maulers—fellows who could hit with the
force of a baseball bat.

I asked Mr. Jacobs if he was speaking literally when he said people 4
came out to see the killer.

"They don't come out to see a tea party," he said evenly. "They come out to see the knockout. They come out to see a man hurt. If they think anything else, they're kidding themselves."

Recently, a young man by the name of Benny Paret was killed in the ring. The killing was seen by millions; it was on television. In the twelfth round, he was hit hard in the head several times, went down, was counted out, and never came out of the coma.

The Paret fight produced a flurry of investigations. Governor Rockefeller was shocked by what happened and appointed a committee to assess the responsibility. The New York State Boxing Commission decided to find out what was wrong. The District Attorney's office expressed its concern. One question that was solemnly studied in all three probes concerned the action of the referee. Did he act in time to stop the fight? Another question had to do with the role of the examining doctors who certified the physical fitness of the fighters before the bout. Still another question involved Mr. Paret's manager; did he rush his boy into the fight without adequate time to recuperate from the previous one?

In short, the investigators looked into every possible cause except the real one. Benny Paret was killed because the human fist delivers enough impact, when directed against the head, to produce a massive hemorrhage in the brain. The human brain is the most delicate and complex mechanism in all creation. It has a lacework of millions of highly fragile nerve connections. Nature attempts to protect this exquisitely intricate machinery by encasing it in a hard shell. Fortunately, the shell is thick enough to withstand a great deal of pounding. Nature, however, can protect a man against everything except man himself. Not every blow to the head will kill a man—but there is always the risk of concussion and damage to the brain. A prize fighter may be able to survive even repeated brain concussions and go on fighting, but the damage to his brain may be permanent.

In any event, it is futile to investigate the referee's role and seek to determine whether he should have intervened to stop the fight earlier. That is not where the primary responsibility lies. The primary responsibility lies with the people who pay to see a man hurt. The referee who stops a fight too soon from the crowd's viewpoint can expect to be booed. The crowd wants the knockout; it wants to see a man stretched out on the canvas. This is the supreme moment in boxing. It is nonsense to talk about prize fighting as a test of boxing skills. No crowd was ever brought to its feet screaming and cheering at the sight of two men beautifully dodging and weaving out of each other's jabs. The time the crowd comes alive is when a man is hit hard over the heart or the head, when his mouthpiece flies out, when the blood squirts out of his nose or eyes, when he wobbles under the attack and his pursuer continues to smash at him with pole-axe impact.

Don't blame it on the referee. Don't even blame it on the fight managers. Put the blame where it belongs—on the prevailing mores that re-

gard prize fighting as a perfectly proper enterprise and vehicle of entertainment. No one doubts that many people enjoy prize fighting and will
miss it if it should be thrown out. And that is precisely the point.

• • •

COMPREHENSION

1. Why, according to Mike Jacobs, do people come to see a prizefight? Does
   Cousins agree with him?

2. What was the immediate cause of Paret's death? What remote causes did
   the investigators consider? What, according to Cousins, was the main
   cause? That is, where does the "primary responsibility" (9) lie?

3. Why does Cousins believe that "it is futile to investigate the referee's
   role?" (9)?

4. Cousins ends his essay with "And that is precisely the point." What is the
   "point" to which he refers?

PURPOSE AND AUDIENCE

1. This persuasive essay has a strong thesis. What is it?

2. This essay appeared on May 5, 1962, a month after Paret died. What do
   you suppose its impact was on its audience? Is the impact the same
   today, or has it changed?

3. At whom is this essay aimed—boxing enthusiasts, sportswriters, or a
   general audience? What led you to your conclusion?

4. Does Cousins expect his audience to agree with his thesis? How does he
   try to win sympathy for his position?

STYLE AND STRUCTURE

1. Does Cousins include enough detail to convince readers? Explain.
   Where, if anywhere, might more detail be helpful?

2. Sort out the complex cause-and-effect relationships discussed in paragraph 9.

3. What strategy does Cousins use in his conclusion? Is it effective? Explain
   your reasoning.

VOCABULARY PROJECTS

1. Define each of the following words as it is used in this selection.

promoter (1)	feinting (3)	lacework (8)
fledgling (1)	parrying (3)	encasing (8)
colossus (2)	maulers (3)	intervened (9)

2. The specialized vocabulary of boxing is prominent in this essay, but the facts Cousins presents would apply equally well to any sport in which violence is a potential problem.

    a. Assume that you are writing a similar essay about football, hockey, rugby, or another sport; substitute an appropriate equivalent word for each of the following:

promoter (1)	feinting, parrying, weaving,	knockout (5)
prize fights (2)	jabbing, and dancing (3)	referee (7)
in the ring (3)	killers and sluggers	fighters/fight (7)
boxing artists (3)	and maulers (3)	

    b. Rewrite this sentence so that it suits the sport you have chosen: "The crowd wants the knockout; it wants to see a man stretched out on the canvas. . . . It is nonsense to talk about prize fighting as a test of boxing skills. No crowd was ever brought to its feet screaming and cheering at the sight of two men beautifully dodging and weaving out of each other's jabs" (9).

JOURNAL ENTRY

Do Cousins's graphic descriptions convince you that boxing should be outlawed? Explain.

WRITING WORKSHOP

1. Write a cause-and-effect essay examining how the demands of the public affect a professional sport. (You might examine violence in hockey or football, for example, or the ways in which an individual player cultivates an image for the fans.)

2. Write a cause-and-effect essay about a time when, in response to peer pressure, you encouraged someone to do something you felt was dishonest or unwise. Be sure to identify the causes for your actions.

3. Why do you think a young person might turn to a career in boxing? Write a cause-and-effect essay in which you examine the possible motives.

COMBINING THE PATTERNS

This essay begins with five paragraphs of **narration** that summarize a meeting between Cousins and Mike Jacobs. What function does this narrative introduction serve in this essay? Once Paret's death is mentioned and the persuasive portion of the essay begins, Cousins never resumes the narrative. Do you think he should have returned to this narrative? If so, where might he have continued the story?

THEMATIC CONNECTIONS

- "Thirty-Eight Who Saw Murder Didn't Call the Police" (page 86)
- "Shooting an Elephant" (page 91)
- "The Spider and the Wasp" (page 223)
- "Ex–Basketball Player" (page 364)

MARIE WINN

Marie Winn was born in 1936 in Prague, Czechoslovakia, and came to the United States in 1939. She was educated at Radcliffe College and Columbia University. As a freelance writer, Winn has contributed articles to the *New York Times Magazine*, the *New York Times Book Review, Parade*, and the *Village Voice*. She has written books for children, including *The Sick Book* and *The Baby Reader*, and edited *The Fireside Book of Children's Songs* (1966) and *The Fireside Book of Fun and Game Songs* (1975). Winn also writes books for parents and teachers, including *The Plug-In Drug: Television, Children, and the Family* (1977), where the following selection first appeared; *Children without Childhood* (1983); and *Unplugging the Plug-In Drug* (1987). Her most recent book is *The Secret Life of Central Park (1997)*, an examination of urban wildlife. In "Television: The Plug-In Drug" (originally titled "Family Life"), Winn considers the effects of television on the American family.

Television: The Plug-In Drug

A quarter of a century after the introduction of television into American society, a period that has seen the medium become so deeply ingrained in American life that in at least one state the television set has attained the rank of a legal necessity, safe from repossession in case of debt along with clothes, cooking utensils, and the like, television viewing has become an inevitable and ordinary part of daily life. Only in the early years of television did writers and commentators have sufficient perspective to separate the activity of watching television from the actual content it offers the viewer. In those early days writers frequently discussed the effects of television on family life. However, a curious myopia afflicted those early observers: almost without exception they regarded television as a favorable, beneficial, indeed, wondrous influence upon the family.

"Television is going to be a real asset in every home where there are children," predicts a writer in 1949.

"Television will take over your way of living and change your children's habits, but this change can be a wonderful improvement," claims another commentator.

"No survey's needed, of course, to establish that television has brought the family together in one room," writes *The New York Times* television critic in 1949.

Each of the early articles about television is invariably accompanied by a photograph or illustration showing a family cozily sitting together before the television set, Sis on Mom's lap, Buddy perched on the arm of Dad's chair, Dad with his arm around Mom's shoulder. Who could have guessed that twenty or so years later Mom would be watching a drama in the kitchen, the kids would be looking at cartoons in their room, while Dad would be taking in the ball game in the living room?

Of course television sets were enormously expensive in those early days. The idea that by 1975 more than 60 percent of American families would own two or more sets was preposterous. The splintering of the multiple-set family was something the early writers could not foresee. Nor did anyone imagine the numbers of hours children would eventually devote to television, the common use of television by parents as a child pacifier, the changes television would effect upon child-rearing methods, the increasing domination of family schedules by children's viewing requirements—in short, the *power* of the new medium to dominate family life.   6

After the first years, as children's consumption of the new medium increased, together with parental concern about the possible effects of so much television viewing, a steady refrain helped to soothe and reassure anxious parents. "Television always enters a pattern of influences that already exist: the home, the peer group, the school, the church and culture generally," write the authors of an early and influential study of television's effects on children. In other words, if the child's home life is all right, parents need not worry about the effects of all that television watching.   7

But television does not merely influence the child; it deeply influences that "pattern of influences" that is meant to ameliorate its effects. Home and family life has changed in important ways since the advent of television. The peer group has become television-oriented, and much of the time children spend together is occupied by television viewing. Culture generally has been transformed by television. Therefore it is improper to assign to television the subsidiary role its many apologists (too often members of the television industry) insist it plays. Television is not merely one of a number of important influences upon today's child. Through the changes it has made in family life, television emerges as *the* important influence in children's lives today.   8

Television's contribution to family life has been an equivocal one. For while it has, indeed, kept the members of the family from dispersing, it has not served to bring them *together*. By its domination of the time families spend together, it destroys the special quality that distinguishes one family from another, a quality that depends to a great extent on what a family *does*, what special rituals, games, recurrent jokes, familiar songs, and shared activities it accumulates.   9

"Like the sorcerer of old," writes Urie Bronfenbrenner, "the television set casts its magic spell, freezing speech and action, turning the living into silent statues so long as the enchantment lasts. The primary danger of the television screen lies not so much in the behavior it produces—although there is danger there—as in the behavior it prevents: the talks, the games, the family festivities and arguments through which much of the child's learning takes place and through which his character is formed. Turning on the television set can turn off the process that transforms children into people."   10

Yet parents have accepted a television-dominated family life so completely that they cannot see how the medium is involved in whatever problems they might be having. A first-grade teacher reports: 11

"I have one child in the group who's an only child. I wanted to find   12
out more about her family life because this little girl was quite isolated
from the group, didn't make friends, so I talked to her mother. Well, they
don't have time to do anything in the evening, the mother said. The parents come home after picking up the child at the babysitter's. Then the
mother fixes dinner while the child watches TV. Then they have dinner
and the child goes to bed. I said to this mother. 'Well, couldn't she help
you fix dinner? That would be a nice time for the two of you to talk,' and
the mother said, 'Oh, but I'd hate to have her miss "Zoom." It's such a
good program!'"

Even when families make efforts to control television, too often its   13
very presence counterbalances the positive features of family life. A
writer and mother of two boys aged 3 and 7 described her family's television schedule in an article in *The New York Times:*

> We were in the midst of a full-scale War. Every day was a new battle
> and every program was a major skirmish. We agreed it was a bad scene
> all around and were ready to enter diplomatic negotiations. . . . In
> principle we have agreed on 2 1/2 hours of TV a day, "Sesame Street,"
> "Electric Company" (with dinner gobbled up in between) and two
> half-hour shows between 7 and 8:30, which enables the grown-ups to
> eat in peace and prevents the two boys from destroying one another.
> Their pre-bedtime choice is dreadful, because, as Josh recently
> admitted, "There's nothing much on I really like." So . . . it's "What's
> My Line" or "To Tell the Truth." . . . Clearly there is a need for first-
> rate children's shows at this time. . . .

Consider the "family life" described here: Presumably the father   14
comes home from work during the "Sesame Street"–"Electric Company"
stint. The children are either watching television, gobbling their dinner, or
both. While the parents eat their dinner in peaceful privacy, the children
watch another hour of television. Then there is only a half-hour left before
bedtime, just enough time for baths, getting pajamas on, brushing teeth,
and so on. The children's evening is regimented with an almost military
precision. They watch their favorite programs, and when there is "nothing much on I really like," they watch whatever else is on—because
watching is the important thing. Their mother does not see anything amiss
with watching programs just for the sake of watching; she only wishes
there were some first-rate children's shows on at those times.

Without conjuring up memories of the Victorian era with family   15
games and long, leisurely meals, and large families, the question arises:
isn't there a better family life available than this dismal, mechanized
arrangement of children watching television for however long is allowed
them, evening after evening?

Of course, families today still do *special* things together at times: go   16
camping in the summer, go to the zoo on a nice Saturday, take various

trips and expeditions. But their *ordinary* daily life together is diminished—that sitting around at the dinner table, that spontaneous taking up of an activity, those little games invented by children on the spur of the moment when there is nothing else to do, the scribbling, the chatting, and even the quarreling, all the things that form the fabric of a family, that define a childhood. Instead, the children have their regular schedule of television programs and bedtime, and the parents have their peaceful dinner together.

The author of the article in the *Times* notes that "keeping a family   17
sane means mediating between the needs of both children and adults." But surely the needs of adults are being better met than the needs of the children, who are effectively shunted away and rendered untroublesome, while their parents enjoy a life as undemanding as that of any childless couple. In reality, it is those very demands that young children make upon a family that lead to growth, and it is the way parents accede to those demands that builds the relationships upon which the future of the family depends. If the family does not accumulate its backlog of shared experiences, shared *everyday* experiences that occur and recur and change and develop, then it is not likely to survive as anything other than a caretaking institution.

FAMILY RITUALS

Ritual is defined by sociologists as "that part of family life that the   18
family likes about itself, is proud of and wants formally to continue." Another text notes that "the development of a ritual by a family is an index of the common interest of its members in the family as a group."

What has happened to family rituals, those regular, dependable, re-   19
current happenings that gave members of a family a feeling of *belonging* to a home rather than living in it merely for the sake of convenience, those experiences that act as the adhesive of family unity far more than any material advantages?

Mealtime rituals, going-to-bed rituals, illness rituals, holiday rituals,   20
how many of these have survived the inroads of the television set?

A young woman who grew up near Chicago reminisces about her   21
childhood and gives an idea of the effects of television upon family rituals:

"As a child I had millions of relatives around—my parents both come   22
from relatively large families. My father had nine brothers and sisters. And so every holiday there was this great swoop-down of aunts, uncles, and millions of cousins. I just remember how wonderful it used to be. These thousands of cousins would come and everyone would play and ultimately, after dinner, all the women would be in the front of the house, drinking coffee and talking, all the men would be in the back of the house, drinking and smoking, and all the kids would be all over the place, playing hide and seek. Christmas time was particularly nice be-

cause everyone always brought all their toys and games. Our house had a couple of rooms with go-through closets, so there was always kids running in a great circle route. I remember it was just wonderful.

"And then all of a sudden one year I remember becoming suddenly aware of how different everything had become. The kids were no longer playing Monopoly or Clue or the other games we used to play together. It was because we had a television set which had been turned on for a football game. All of that socializing that had gone on previously had ended. Now everyone was sitting in front of the television set, on a holiday, at a family party! I remember being stunned by how awful that was. Somehow the television had become more attractive." 23

As families have come to spend more and more of their time together engaged in the single activity of television watching, those rituals and pastimes that once gave family life its special quality have become more and more uncommon. Not since prehistoric times when cave families hunted, gathered, ate, and slept, with little time remaining to accumulate a culture of any significance, have families been reduced to such a sameness. 24

REAL PEOPLE

It is not only the activities that a family might engage in together that are diminished by the powerful presence of television in the home. The relationships of the family members to each other are also affected, in both obvious and subtle ways. The hours that the young child spends in a one-way relationship with television people, an involvement that allows for no communication or interaction, surely affect his relationships with real-life people. 25

Studies show the importance of eye-to-eye contact, for instance, in real-life relationships, and indicate that the nature of a person's eye-contact patterns, whether he looks another squarely in the eye or looks to the side or shifts his gaze from side to side, may play a significant role in his success or failure in human relationships. But no eye contact is possible in the child-television relationship, although in certain children's programs people purport to speak directly to the child and the camera fosters this illusion by focusing directly upon the person being filmed. (Mr. Rogers is an example, telling the child "I like you, you're special," etc.) How might such a distortion of real-life relationships affect a child's development of trust, of openness, of an ability to relate well to other *real* people? 26

Bruno Bettelheim writes: 27

Children who have been taught, or conditioned, to listen passively most of the day to the warm verbal communications coming from the TV screen, to the deep emotional appeal of the so-called TV personality, are often unable to respond to real persons because they arouse so much less feeling than the skilled actor. Worse, they lose the ability to learn from reality because life experiences are much more complicated than the ones they see on the screen. . . .

A teacher makes a similar observation about her personal viewing ex-   28
periences:

"I have trouble mobilizing myself and dealing with real people after   29
watching a few hours of television. It's just hard to make that transition
from watching television to a real relationship. I suppose it's because
there was no effort necessary while I was watching, and dealing with real
people always requires a bit of effort. Imagine, then, how much harder it
might be to do the same thing for a small child, particularly one who
watches a lot of television every day."

But more obviously damaging to family relationships is the elimina-   30
tion of opportunities to talk, and perhaps more important, to argue, to air
grievances, between parents and children and brothers and sisters.
Families frequently use television to avoid confronting their problems,
problems that will not go away if they are ignored but will only fester and
become less easily resolvable as time goes on.

A mother reports: 31

"I find myself, with three children, wanting to turn on the TV set   32
when they're fighting. I really have to struggle not to do it because I feel
that's telling them this is the solution to the quarrel—but it's so tempting
that I often do it."

A family therapist discusses the use of television as an avoidance   33
mechanism:

"In a family I know the father comes home from work and turns on   34
the television set. The children come and watch him and the wife serves
them their meal in front of the set. He then goes and takes a shower, or
works on the car or something. She then goes and has her own dinner in
front of the television set. It's a symptom of a deeper-rooted problem,
sure. But it would help them all to get rid of the set. It would be far easier
to work on what the symptom really means without the television. The
television simply encourages a double avoidance of each other. They'd
find out more quickly what was going on if they weren't able to hide behind the TV. Things wouldn't necessarily be better, of course, but they
wouldn't be anesthetized."

The decreased opportunities for simple conversation between par-   35
ents and children in the television-centered home may help explain an
observation made by an emergency room nurse at a Boston hospital.
She reports that parents just seem to sit there these days when they
come in with a sick or seriously injured child, although talking to the
child would distract and comfort him. "They don't seem to know *how* to
talk to their own children at any length," the nurse observes. Similarly, a
television critic writes in *The New York Times:* "I had just a day ago taken
my son to the emergency ward of a hospital for stitches above his left
eye, and the occasion seemed no more real to me than Maalot or 54th
Street, south-central Los Angeles. There was distance and numbness
and an inability to turn off the total institution. I didn't behave at all; I
just watched. . . . "

A number of research studies substantiate the assumption that television interferes with family activities and the formation of family relationships. One survey shows that 78 percent of the respondents indicated no conversation taking place during viewing except at specified times such as commercials. The study notes: "The television atmosphere in most households is one of quiet absorption on the part of family members who are present. The nature of the family social life during a program could be described as 'parallel' rather than interactive, and the set does seem to dominate family life when it is on." Thirty-six percent of the respondents in another study indicated that television viewing was the only family activity participated in during the week.   36

In a summary of research findings on television's effect on family interactions James Gabardino states: "The early findings suggest that television had a disruptive effect upon interaction and thus presumably human development. . . . It is not unreasonable to ask: 'Is the fact that the average American family during the 1950s came to include two parents, two children, and a television set somehow related to the psychosocial characteristics of the young adults of the 1970s?'"   37

UNDERMINING THE FAMILY

In its effect on family relationships, in its facilitation of parental withdrawal from an active role in the socialization of their children, and in its replacement of family rituals and special events, television has played an important role in the disintegration of the American family. But of course it has not been the only contributing factor, perhaps not even the most important one. The steadily rising divorce rate, the increase in the number of working mothers, the decline of the extended family, the breakdown of neighborhoods and communities, the growing isolation of the nuclear family—all have seriously affected the family.   38

As Urie Bronfenbrenner suggests, the sources of family breakdown do not come from the family itself, but from the circumstances in which the family finds itself and the way of life imposed upon it by those circumstances. "When those circumstances and the way of life they generate undermine relationships of trust and emotional security between family members, when they make it difficult for parents to care for, educate, and enjoy their children, when there is no support or recognition from the outside world for one's role as a parent, and when time spent with one's family means frustration of career, personal fulfillment, and peace of mind, then the development of the child is adversely affected," he writes.   39

But while the roots of alienation go deep into the fabric of American social history, television's presence in the home fertilizes them, encourages their wild and unchecked growth. Perhaps it is true that America's commitment to the television experience masks a spiritual vacuum, an empty and barren way of life, a desert of materialism. But it is television's   40 dominant role in the family that anesthetizes the family into accepting its unhappy state and prevents it from struggling to better its condition, to improve its relationships, and to regain some of the richness it once possessed.

Others have noted the role of mass media in perpetuating an unsatis- 41
factory *status quo.* Leisure-time activity, writes Irving Howe, "must provide relief from work monotony without making the return to work too unbearable; it must provide amusement without insight and pleasure without disturbance—as distinct from art which gives pleasure through disturbance. Mass culture is thus oriented towards a central aspect of industrial society: the depersonalization of the individual." Similarly, Jacques Ellul rejects the idea that television is a legitimate means of educating the citizen: "Education . . . takes place only incidentally. The clouding of his consciousness is paramount. . . . "

And so the American family muddles on, dimly aware that some- 42
thing is amiss but distracted from an understanding of its plight by an endless stream of television images. As family ties grow weaker and vaguer, as children's lives become more separate from their parents', as parents' educational role in their children's lives is taken over by television and schools, family life becomes increasingly more unsatisfying for both parents and children. All that seems to be left is Love, an abstraction that family members *know* is necessary but find great difficulty giving each other because the traditional opportunities for expressing love within the family have been reduced or destroyed.

For contemporary parents, love toward each other has increasingly 43
come to mean successful sexual relations, as witnessed by the proliferation of sex manuals and sex therapists. The opportunities for manifesting other forms of love through mutual support, understanding, nurturing, even, to use an unpopular word, *serving* each other, are less and less available as mothers and fathers seek their independent destinies outside the family.

As for love of children, this love is increasingly expressed through 44
supplying material comforts, amusements, and educational opportunities. Parents show their love for their children by sending them to good schools and camps, by providing them with good food and good doctors, by buying them toys, books, games, and a television set of their very own. Parents will even go further and express their love by attending PTA meetings to improve their children's schools, or by joining groups that are acting to improve the quality of their children's television programs.

But this is love at a remove, and is rarely understood by children. 45
The more direct forms of parental love require time and patience, steady, dependable, ungrudgingly given time actually spent *with* a child, reading to him, comforting him, playing, joking, and working with him. But even if a parent were eager and willing to demonstrate that sort of direct love to his children today, the opportunities are diminished. What with school and Little League and piano lessons and, of course, the inevitable television programs, a day seems to offer just enough time for a good-night kiss.

• • •

COMPREHENSION

1. How did early observers view television? How, in general, does Winn's view differ from theirs?

2. How has the nature of family television viewing changed since its inception? How does Winn account for this change?

3. How does television keep families apart? In what sense does Winn see television as a threat to the very nature of the family?

4. How does Winn define "family rituals" (19)? According to Winn, how has television affected these rituals?

5. What other factors besides television does Winn see as having a negative effect on the family?

6. Why does Winn believe today's families have such difficulty expressing love?

PURPOSE AND AUDIENCE

1. Winn states her thesis in paragraph 8. What is it?

2. In paragraphs 10 and 27, Winn quotes two noted psychologists. What effect do you think she expects their words to have on her audience?

3. What effect do you believe the young woman's testimony in paragraphs 22–23 is calculated to have on Winn's readers?

4. In paragraph 24, Winn makes an **analogy** between modern families and cave families. What is her purpose in doing this?

STYLE AND STRUCTURE

1. Winn does not state her thesis until paragraph 8. What does she do in the paragraphs that precede this?

2. The length of Winn's paragraphs varies considerably. What effect do you think short paragraphs such as paragraphs 2, 3, 4, and 20 are likely to have on readers?

3. From what sources does Winn draw the many quotations she uses in this essay? How does the varied nature of these quotations help support her thesis?

4. This essay includes three headings: "Family Rituals," "Real People," and "Undermining the Family." What functions do these headings serve? Could they be omitted? Should they be? Why or why not?

5. Winn's focus in this essay is on the effects of television on the American family. In the last four paragraphs, however, her focus widens, and she touches on television only incidentally. Does this concluding strategy strengthen or weaken her essay? Explain.

VOCABULARY PROJECTS

1. Define each of the following words as it is used in this selection.

myopia (1)	counterbalances (13)	facilitation (38)
ameliorate (8)	regimented (14)	perpetuating (41)
advent (8)	mediating (17)	depersonalization (41)
subsidiary (8)	adhesive (19)	amiss (42)
apologists (8)	fosters (26)	abstraction (42)
equivocal (9)	substantiate (36)	remove (45)

2. One effect of television has been on our vocabulary: television has spawned new words (for example, *sitcom*) and suggested new uses for old words (for instance, *tube*). List as many television-inspired words as you can, and define each.

JOURNAL ENTRY

What effects—positive or negative—do you think television has had on your life? What would your life be like without it?

WRITING WORKSHOP

1. Write an essay in which you consider the effects (including any possible future effects) of one of these inventions on the American family: the cellular phone, the personal computer, the microwave, the calculator, the VCR, the Walkman, Nintendo, the answering machine, the pager.

2. Write a cause-and-effect essay in which you discuss the *positive* effects of television on American society.

3. Winn's essay is more than twenty years old, and both television and viewers have changed considerably since she wrote "The Plug-In Drug." Write a cause-and-effect essay about television in which you consider developments that Winn does not take into account—for example, the availability of cable television, satellite dishes, and pay-per-view broadcasts.

COMBINING THE PATTERNS

Winn's essay relies on several patterns of development besides cause and effect. Where does she use **narration? Definition? Exemplification?** Why does she use each of these patterns?

THEMATIC CONNECTIONS

- "Once More to the Lake" (page 142)
- "The Human Cost of an Illiterate Society" (page 192)
- "It's Just Too Late" (page 294)
- "Frankenstein Must Be Destroyed: Chasing the Monster of TV Violence" (page 591)

LAWRENCE OTIS GRAHAM

Lawrence Otis Graham was born in 1962 into one of the few African-American families then living in an upper-middle-class community in Westchester County, near New York City. A graduate of Princeton University and Harvard Law School, Graham works as a corporate attorney in Manhattan and teaches at Fordham University. He is the author of eleven books, including *Your Ticket to Business School* (1985) and *The Best Companies for Minorities* (1993). Graham received considerable attention for "Invisible Man," an article recounting his experiences when he took a temporary leave from his job as an attorney to work as a busboy at a century-old country club in Greenwich, Connecticut ("the only way a black man like me could get in"). The article, which examined the institutional racism of such restricted "private associations," was included in the *Best American Essays* series. "Invisible Man" and the following essay, originally published in the *New York Times,* are included in Graham's latest book, *Member of the Club: Reflections on Life in a Racially Polarized Society* (1995). In "The 'Black Table' Is Still There," Graham returns to his largely white junior high school and discovers to his dismay how little has changed since the 1970s.

The "Black Table" Is Still There

During a recent visit to my old junior high school in Westchester County, I came upon something that I never expected to see again, something that was a source of fear and dread for three hours each school morning of my early adolescence: the all-black lunch table in the cafeteria of my predominantly white suburban junior high school. 1

As I look back on 27 years of often being the first and only black person integrating such activities and institutions as the college newspaper, the high school tennis team, summer music camps, our all-white suburban neighborhood, my eating club at Princeton, or my private social club at Harvard Law School, the one scenario that puzzled me the most then and now is the all-black lunch table. 2

Why was it there? Why did the black kids separate themselves? What did the table say about the integration that was supposedly going on in home rooms and gym classes? What did it say about the black kids? The white kids? What did it say about me when I refused to sit there, day after day, for three years? 3

Each afternoon, at 12:03 P.M., after the fourth period ended, I found myself among 600 12-, 13-, and 14-year-olds who marched into the brightly-lit cafeteria and dashed for a seat at one of the 27 blue formica lunch tables. 4

No matter who I walked in with—usually a white friend—no matter what mood I was in, there was one thing that was certain: I would not sit at the black table. 5

I would never consider sitting at the black table.   6

What was wrong with me? What was I afraid of?   7

I would like to think that my decision was a heroic one, made in   8
order to express my solidarity with the theories of integration that my
community was espousing. But I was just 12 at the time, and there was
nothing heroic in my actions.

I avoided the black table for a very simple reason: I was afraid that by   9
sitting at the black table I'd lose all my white friends. I thought that by sitting there I'd be making a racist, anti-white statement.

Is that what the all-black table means? Is it a rejection of white peo-   10
ple? I no longer think so.

At the time, I was angry that there was a black lunch table. I believed   11
that the black kids were the reason why other kids didn't mix more. I was
ready to believe that their self-segregation was the cause of white bigotry.

Ironically, I even believed this after my best friend (who was white)   12
told me I probably shouldn't come to his bar mitzvah because I'd be the
only black and people would feel uncomfortable. I even believed this after
my Saturday afternoon visit, at age 10, to a private country club pool
prompted incensed white parents to pull their kids from the pool in terror.

In the face of this blatantly racist (anti-black) behavior I still somehow   13
managed to blame only the black kids for being the barrier to integration
in my school and my little world. What was I thinking?

I realize now how wrong I was. During that same time, there were   14
at least two tables of athletes, an Italian table, a Jewish girls' table, a
Jewish boys' table (where I usually sat), a table of kids who were into
heavy metal music and smoking pot, a table of middle-class Irish kids.
Weren't these tables just as segregationist as the black table? At the time,
no one thought so. At the time, no one even acknowledged the segregated
nature of these other tables.

Maybe it's the color difference that makes all-black tables or all-black   15
groups attract the scrutiny and wrath of so many people. It scares and
angers people; it exasperates. It did those things to me, and I'm black.

As an integrating black person, I know that my decision *not* to join the   16
black lunch table attracted its own kinds of scrutiny and wrath from my
classmates. At the same time that I heard angry words like "Oreo" and
"white boy" being hurled at me from the black table, I was also dodging
impatient questions from white classmates: "Why do all those black kids
sit together?" or "Why don't you ever sit with the other blacks?"

The black lunch table, like those other segregated tables, is a comment   17
on the superficial inroads that integration has made in society. Perhaps I
should be happy that even this is a long way from where we started. Yet, I
can't get over the fact that the 27th table in my junior high school cafeteria
is still known as the "black table"—14 years after my adolescence.

•   •   •

COMPREHENSION

1. What exactly is the "black table"?

2. In paragraph 1 Graham says that on a recent visit to his old junior high school he "came upon something that [he] never expected to see again." Why do you think the sight of the all-black lunch table was such a surprise to him?

3. In Graham's junior high school, what factors determined where students sat?

4. Why didn't Graham sit at the black table when he was in junior high?

5. When he was a junior high school student, whom did Graham blame for the existence of the exclusively black lunch table? Who or what does he now see as the cause of the table's existence?

PURPOSE AND AUDIENCE

1. What is Graham's thesis?

2. Rather than introducing outside supporting information—such as statistics, interviews with educators, or sociological studies—Graham relies on his own opinions and anecdotal evidence to support his thesis. Do you think this is enough? Explain.

3. What is Graham's purpose in giving background information about himself in this essay—for example, in paragraphs 2 and 12? How does this information affect your reaction to him as a person? To his essay? Do you think he needs to supply additional information about himself or his school? If so, what kind of information would be helpful?

4. Do you think Graham's primary purpose is to criticize a system he despises, to change his audience's views about segregated lunch tables, or to justify his own behavior? Explain your conclusion.

5. In paragraph 5 Graham tells readers that he usually entered the cafeteria with a white friend; in paragraph 12 he reveals that his best friend was white. Why do you suppose he wants his audience to know these facts?

STYLE AND STRUCTURE

1. Throughout his essay Graham asks **rhetorical questions.** Identify as many of these questions as you can. Are they necessary? Provocative? Distracting? Explain.

2. In paragraph 16 Graham quotes his long-ago classmates. What do these quotations reveal? Should he have included more of them?

3. Is Graham's focus on finding causes, describing effects, or both? Explain.

4. Graham's essay uses first-person pronouns and contractions. Do you think Graham would have more credibility if he used a style that was less personal and more formal? Why or why not?

VOCABULARY PROJECTS

1. Define each of the following words as it is used in this selection.

   scenario (2)   incensed (12)   scrutiny (15)
   espousing (8)   blatantly (13)   inroads (17)

2. Does the phrase *black table* have a negative connotation for you? Do you think this is Graham's intention? What other names could he give to the table that might present it in a more neutral, even positive, light? What names could he give to the other tables he lists in paragraph 14?

JOURNAL ENTRY

Graham sees the continued presence of the black table as a serious problem. Do you agree?

WRITING WORKSHOP

1. In paragraph 14 Graham mentions other lunch tables that were limited to certain groups and asks, "Weren't these tables just as segregationist as the black table?" Answer his question in a cause-and-effect essay that explains why you believe black tables exist.

2. In addition to self-segregated lunch tables, many schools also have single-race social clubs, dormitories, fraternities, and even graduation ceremonies. Do you see such self-segregation as something that divides our society (that is, as a cause) or as something that reflects divisions that already exist (that is, as an effect)? Write an essay in which you discuss this issue, supporting your thesis with examples from your own experience.

3. Do the people in your school or workplace tend to segregate themselves according to race, gender, or some other principle? Do you see a problem in such behavior? Write a memo to your school's dean of students or to your employer explaining what you believe causes this pattern and what effects, positive or negative, you have observed.

COMBINING THE PATTERNS

In paragraph 14 Graham uses **classification and division.** What is he categorizing? What categories does he identify? What other categories might he include? Why is this pattern of development particularly appropriate for this essay?

THEMATIC CONNECTIONS

- "Just Walk On By" (page 186)
- "Aria: A Memoir of a Bilingual Childhood" (page 357)
- "College Pressures" (page 378)
- "The Ways We Lie" (page 414)

MELANIE SCHELLER

Melanie Scheller (1953–   ) grew up in rural North Carolina, one of six children of a widowed mother. Her escape from the hardships of poverty that
marked much of her early life came in the form of a college scholarship from
the University of North Carolina at Chapel Hill. She eventually earned degrees in education and public health administration. The author of many
magazine and journal articles on health and wellness topics, Scheller also
writes fiction and nonfiction for children; her illustrated children's book *My
Grandfather's Hat* was published in 1992. In the following essay, Scheller recalls the shame she felt growing up in dilapidated, rented farmhouses that
had no indoor plumbing and remembers how her early experiences defined
her view of herself for many years afterward. When "On the Meaning of
Plumbing and Poverty" (1990) first appeared in the *Independent Weekly,* a
newspaper published in Durham, North Carolina, it won the North Carolina
Writers' Network Creative Journalism Award.

On the Meaning of Plumbing
and Poverty

Several years ago I spent some time as a volunteer on the geriatric   1
ward of a psychiatric hospital. I was fascinated by the behavior of one of
the patients, an elderly woman who shuffled at regular intervals to the
bathroom, where she methodically flushed the toilet. Again and again she
carried out her sacred mission as if summoned by some supernatural
force, until the flush of the toilet became a rhythmic counterpoint for the
ward's activity. If someone blocked her path or if, God forbid, the bathroom was in use when she reached it, she became agitated and confused.

Obviously, that elderly patient was a sick woman. And yet I felt a cer-   2
tain kinship with her, for I too have suffered from an obsession with toilets. I spent much of my childhood living in houses without indoor
plumbing, and while I don't feel compelled to flush a toilet at regular intervals, I sometimes feel that toilets, or the lack thereof, have shaped my
identity in ways that are painful to admit.

I'm not a child of the Depression, but I grew up in an area of the   3
South that had changed little since the days of the New Deal.* My mother
was a widow with six children to support, not an easy task under any circumstances, but especially difficult in rural North Carolina during the
1960s. To her credit, we were never seriously in danger of going hungry.
Our vegetable garden kept us stocked with tomatoes and string beans.

---

*EDS. NOTE—The policies instituted by President Franklin Roosevelt to provide
various forms of government assistance to people during the Great Depression of the
1930s were collectively referred to as the "New Deal."

We kept a few chickens and sometimes a cow. Blackberries were free for the picking in the fields nearby. Neighbors did their good Christian duty by bringing us donations of fresh fruit and candy at Christmastime. But a roof over our heads—that wasn't so easily improvised.

Like rural Southern gypsies, we moved from one dilapidated 4 Southern farmhouse to another in a constant search for a decent place to live. Sometimes we moved when the rent increased beyond the 30 or 40 dollars my mother could afford. Or the house burned down, not an unusual occurrence in substandard housing. One year when we were gathered together for Thanksgiving dinner, a stranger walked in without knocking and announced that we were being evicted. The house had been sold without our knowledge and the new owner wanted to start remodeling immediately. We tried to finish our meal with an attitude of thanksgiving while he worked around us with his tape measure.

Usually we rented from farm families who'd moved from the old 5 home place to one of the brick boxes that are now the standard in rural Southern architecture. The old farmhouse wasn't worth fixing up with a septic tank and flush toilet, but it was good enough to rent for a few dollars a month to families like mine. The idea of tenants' rights hadn't trickled down yet from the far reaches of the liberal North. It never occurred to us to demand improvements in the facilities. The ethic of the land said we should take what we could get and be grateful for it.

Without indoor plumbing, getting clean is a tiring and time-consum- 6 ing ritual. At one point I lived in a five-room house with six or more people, all of whom congregated in the one heated room to eat, do homework, watch television, dress and undress, argue, wash dishes. During cold weather we dragged mattresses from the unheated rooms and slept huddled together on the floor by the woodstove. For my bathing routine, I first pinned a sheet to a piece of twine strung across the kitchen. That gave me some degree of privacy from the six other people in the room. At that time our house had an indoor cold-water faucet, from which I filled a pot of water to heat on the kitchen stove. It took several pots of hot water to fill the metal washtub we used.

Since I was a teenager and prone to sulkiness if I didn't get special 7 treatment, I got to take the first bath while the water was still clean. The others used the water I left behind, freshened up with hot water from the pot on the stove. Then the tub had to be dragged to the door and the bath water dumped outside. I longed to be like the woman in the Calgon bath oil commercials, luxuriating in a marble tub full of scented water with bubbles piled high and stacks of thick, clean towels nearby.

People raised in the land of the bath-and-a-half may wonder why I 8 make such a fuss about plumbing. Maybe they spent a year in the Peace Corps, or they back-packed across India, or they worked at a summer camp and, gosh, using a latrine isn't all that bad. And of course it's *not* that bad. Not when you can catch the next plane out of the country, or pick up your duffel bag and head for home, or call mom and dad to come and get you when things get too tedious. A sojourn in a Third World country, where everyone shares the same primitive facilities, may cause some temporary discomfort, but the experience is soon converted into amusing anecdotes for cocktail-party conversation. It doesn't corrode your self-esteem with a sense of shame the way a childhood spent in chronic, unrelenting poverty can.

In the South of my childhood, not having indoor plumbing was the   9
indelible mark of poor white trash. The phrase "so poor they didn't have a pot to piss in" said it all. Poor white trash were viciously stereotyped, and never more viciously than on the playground. White-trash children had cooties—everybody knew that. They had ringworm and pinkeye—don't get near them or you might catch it. They picked their noses. They messed in their pants. If a white-trash child made the mistake of catching a softball during recess, the other children made an elaborate show of wiping it clean before they would touch it.

Once a story circulated at school about a family whose infant daugh-   10
ter had fallen into the "slop jar" and drowned. When I saw the smirks and heard the laughter with which the story was told, I felt sick and afraid in the pit of my stomach. A little girl had died, but people were laughing. What had she done to deserve that laughter? I could only assume that using a chamber pot was something so disgusting, so shameful, that it made a person less than human.

My family was visibly and undeniably poor. My clothes were obvi-   11
ously hand-me-downs. I got free lunches at school. I went to the health department for immunizations. Surely it was equally obvious that we didn't have a flush toilet. But like an alcoholic who believes no one will know he has a problem as long as he doesn't drink in public, I convinced myself that no one knew my family's little secret. It was a form of denial that would color my relationships with the outside world for years to come.

Having a friend from school spend the night at my house was out of   12
the question. Better to be friendless than to have my classmates know my shameful secret. Home visits from teachers or ministers left me in a dither of anticipatory anxiety. As they chattered on and on with Southern small talk about tomato plants and relish recipes, I sat on the edge of my seat, tensed against the dreaded words, "May I use your bathroom, please?" When I began dating in high school, I'd lie in wait behind the front door, ready to dash out as soon as my date pulled in the driveway, never giving him a chance to hear the call of nature while on our property.

With the help of a scholarship I was able to go away to college, where   13
I could choose from dozens of dormitory toilets and take as many hot showers as I wanted, but I could never openly express my joy in using the facilities. My roommates, each a pampered only child from a well-to-do family, whined and complained about having to share a bathroom. I knew that if I expressed delight in simply having a bathroom, I would im-

mediately be labeled as a hick. The need to conceal my real self by stifling my emotions created a barrier around me and I spent my college years in a vacuum of isolation.

Almost 20 years have passed since I first tried to leave my family's chamber pot behind. For many of those years it followed behind me—the ghost of chamber pots past—clanging and banging and threatening to spill its humiliating contents at any moment. I was convinced that everyone could see it, could smell it even. No college degree or job title seemed capable of banishing it.   14

If finances had permitted, I might have become an Elvis Presley or a Tammy Faye Bakker, easing the pain of remembered poverty with gold-plated bathtub fixtures and leopard-skinned toilet seats. I feel blessed that gradually, ever so gradually, the shame of poverty has begun to fade. The pleasures of the present now take priority over where a long-ago bowel movement did or did not take place. But for many Southerners, chamber pots and outhouses are more than just memories.   15

In North Carolina alone, 200,000 people still live without indoor plumbing. People who haul their drinking water home from a neighbor's house or catch rainwater in barrels. People who can't wash their hands before handling food, the way restaurant employees are required by state law to do. People who sneak into public restrooms every day to wash, shave, and brush their teeth before going to work or to school. People who sacrifice their dignity and self-respect when forced to choose between going homeless and going to an outhouse. People whose children think they deserve the conditions in which they live and hold their heads low to hide the shame. But they're not the ones who should feel ashamed. No, they're not the ones who should feel ashamed.   16

•　•　•

COMPREHENSION

1. What practical disadvantages of life without indoor plumbing does Scheller identify?

2. During Scheller's childhood and afterward, what social problems did her family's lack of indoor plumbing cause for her? Identify as many specific problems as you can.

3. What negative effects of poverty does Scheller discuss?

4. In her essay's last line, Scheller suggests that someone or something should be blamed for the hardships she describes. Who or what do you think she believes is at fault?

5. What do you think Scheller means to suggest by her title? Exactly what does she see as the relationship between plumbing and poverty?

PURPOSE AND AUDIENCE

1. How familiar do you think Scheller expects her readers to be with the situation she describes? Explain your reasoning.

2. In paragraph 2 Scheller states her thesis: "I sometimes feel that toilets, or the lack thereof, have shaped my identity in ways that are painful to admit." List several specific points that support this thesis. Does Scheller include enough examples to convince her readers? Explain.

3. In paragraph 8 Scheller seems to be anticipating and refuting her audience's possible criticism of her essay. Does her assessment of her audience's reaction seem accurate, or does she seem overly defensive? Is her refutation convincing? Why or why not?

STYLE AND STRUCTURE

1. Why does Scheller begin her essay with the anecdote about the elderly woman? Is this an effective opening strategy? How else might she introduce her essay?

2. In much of this essay, Scheller maintains a matter-of-fact tone. At times, though, her tone seems self-pitying, even bitter. Identify passages that convey neutral, angry, and self-pitying tones. Which kind of tone do you see as most effective? Why?

3. Is the anecdote in paragraph 10 necessary to the essay? Why or why not?

4. How does Scheller's use of terms like *poor white trash* (9) and *hick* (13) in reference to herself affect your feelings about her? Do such terms make you more or less sympathetic to her? Why?

5. Although Scheller's essay is highly personal, in the last paragraph she moves beyond her own life to take a position on poverty and plumbing as a social and political issue. Do you think this is an appropriate closing strategy? What other strategy might work?

VOCABULARY PROJECTS

1. Define each of the following words as it is used in this selection.

   geriatric (1)   ethic (5)   indelible (9)
   counterpoint (1)   sojourn (8)

2. Scheller's self-described "obsession with toilets" (2) manifests itself in this essay in her use of many words associated with plumbing. List as many of these words as you can. Would you describe Scheller's use of such words as generally direct and straightforward, overly polite and euphemistic, or distasteful? Do you think her choice of the word *obsession* is accurate in this context?

JOURNAL ENTRY

Scheller tried very hard to keep her family's secret. Do you think she was right to do so? Or, do you think she should have been honest about her status despite the risk of public humiliation?

WRITING WORKSHOP

1. In what ways is a person whose home lacks indoor plumbing at a disadvantage in today's society? Considering the world of work and school as well as your personal world, write a cause-and-effect essay that discusses how a lack of indoor bathing and toilet facilities would affect your life.

2. What should be done to improve the situation Scheller describes in her essay? Write a letter to the editor of a North Carolina newspaper (or a newspaper in another state) in which you discuss the positive results of installing indoor plumbing in every home in the state.

3. Has your life, like Scheller's, been shaped by the *lack* of something most other people have? Write a cause-and-effect essay in which you explain how the lack of something material, emotional, or spiritual has affected who you are.

COMBINING THE PATTERNS

In paragraphs 6 and 7 Scheller uses **process** to explain a "tiring and time-consuming ritual." List the steps in this process. Do you consider these process paragraphs essential to the essay? Explain.

THEMATIC CONNECTIONS

- "My Mother Never Worked" (page 81)
- "The Human Cost of an Illiterate Society" (page 192)
- "The Men We Carry in Our Minds" (page 387)
- "The Ways We Lie" (page 414)

CALVIN TRILLIN

Calvin Trillin was born in 1935 in Kansas City, Missouri, and graduated from Yale University in 1957. He has written investigative journalism, humor columns, short stories, a novel, and social and political commentary for several magazines. Trillin was a staff writer for the *New Yorker* for almost twenty years. Some of his pieces from that magazine are collected in *U.S. Journals* (1971), about the conflicts of ordinary people in small towns; *Killings* (1984), on the ways Americans are killed; and *American Stories* (1991). Trillin's writings on American food, prompted by his extensive travels as a journalist, are collected in *American Fried* (1974); *Alice, Let's Eat* (1978); and *Third Helpings* (1983). His humor columns, written originally for the *Nation* and since 1986 for newspaper syndication, have been published in several collections, including *Too Soon to Tell* (1995). He also writes humorous verse, most recently collected in *Deadline Poet: My Life as a Doggeralist* (1994). Trillin's most recent book is *Messages from My Father* (1996), a memoir in which he explores his father's influence on his life. "It's Just Too Late," which comes from *Killings*, examines the events leading up to a fatal car accident.

It's Just Too Late

—KNOXVILLE, TENNESSEE
March 1979

Until she was sixteen, FaNee Cooper was what her parents some- 1
times called an ideal child. "You'd never have to correct her," FaNee's mother has said. In sixth grade, FaNee won a spelling contest. She played the piano and the flute. She seemed to believe what she heard every Sunday at the Beaver Dam Baptist Church about good and evil and the hereafter. FaNee was not an outgoing child. Even as a baby, she was uncomfortable when she was held and cuddled. She found it easy to tell her parents she loved them but difficult to confide in them. Particularly compared to her sister, Kristy, a cheerful, open little girl two and a half years younger, she was reserved and introspective. The thoughts she kept to herself, though, were apparently happy thoughts. Her eighth-grade essay on Christmas—written in a remarkably neat hand—talked of the joys of helping put together toys for her little brother, Leo, Jr., and the importance of her parents' reminder that Christmas is the birthday of Jesus. Her parents were the sort of people who might have been expected to have an ideal child. As a boy, Leo Cooper had been called "one of the greatest high-school basketball players ever developed in Knox County." He went on to play basketball at East Tennessee State, and he married the homecoming queen, JoAnn Henson. After college, Cooper became a high-school basketball coach and teacher and, eventually, an administrator. By the time FaNee turned thirteen, in 1973, he was in his third year as the principal of Gresham Junior High School, in Fountain City—a small Knox

County town that had been swallowed up by Knoxville when the suburbs began to move north. A tall man with curly black hair going on gray,
Leo Cooper has an elaborate way of talking ("Unless I'm very badly mistaken, he has never related to me totally the content of his conversation")
and a manner that may come from years of trying to leave errant junior-
high-school students with the impression that a responsible adult is mag-
nanimous, even humble, about invariably being in the right. His wife, a
high-school art teacher, paints and does batik, and created the name
FaNee because she liked the way it looked and sounded—it sounds like
"Fawn*ee*" when the Coopers say it—but the impression she gives is not of
artiness but of soft-spoken small-town gentility. When she found, in the
course of cleaning up FaNee's room, that her ideal thirteen-year-old had
been smoking cigarettes, she was, in her words, crushed. "FaNee was
such a perfect child before that," JoAnn Cooper said some time later. "She
was angry that we found out. She knew we knew that she had done
something we didn't approve of, and then the rebellion started. I was
hurt. I was very hurt. I guess it came through as disappointment."

Several months later, FaNee's grandmother died. FaNee had been devoted to her grandmother. She wrote a poem in her memory—an almost
joyous poem, filled with Christian faith in the afterlife ("Please don't
grieve over my happiness/Rejoice with me in the presence of the Angels
of Heaven"). She also took some keepsakes from her grandmother's
house, and was apparently mortified when her parents found them and
explained that they would have to be returned. By then, the Coopers were
aware that FaNee was going to have a difficult time as a teenager. They
thought she might be self-conscious about the double affliction of glasses
and braces. They thought she might be uncomfortable in the role of the
principal's daughter at Gresham. In ninth grade, she entered Halls High
School, where JoAnn Cooper was teaching art. FaNee was a loner at first.
Then she fell in with what could only be considered a bad crowd.

Halls, a few miles to the north of Fountain City, used to be known as
Halls Crossroads. It is what Knoxville people call "over the ridge"—on
the side of Black Oak Ridge that has always been thought of as rural.
When FaNee entered Halls High, the Coopers were already in the process
of building a house on several acres of land they had bought in Halls, in a
sparsely settled area along Brown Gap road. Like two or three other
houses along the road, it was to be constructed basically of huge logs
taken from old buildings—a house that Leo Cooper describes as being,
like the name FaNee, "just a little bit different." Ten years ago, Halls
Crossroads was literally a crossroads. Then some of the Knoxville expansion that had swollen Fountain City spilled over the ridge, planting subdivisions here and there on roads that still went for long stretches with
nothing but an occasional house with a cow or two next to it. The increase
in population did not create a town. Halls has no center. Its commercial
area is a series of two or three shopping centers strung together on the
Maynardville Highway, the four-lane that leads north into Union

County—a place almost synonymous in east Tennessee with mountain poverty. Its restaurant is the Halls Freezo Drive-In. The gathering place for the group FaNee Cooper eventually found herself in was the Maynardville Highway Exxon station.

At Halls High School, the social poles were represented by the Jocks   4 and the Freaks. FaNee found her friends among the Freaks. "I am truly enlighted upon irregular trains of thought aimed at strange depots of mental wards," she wrote when she was fifteen. "Yes! Crazed farms for the mental off—Oh! I walked through the halls screams & loud laughter fill my ears—Orderlys try to reason with me—but I am unreasonable! The joys of being a FREAK in a circus of imagination." The little crowd of eight or ten young people that FaNee joined has been referred to by her mother as "the Union County group." A couple of the girls were from backgrounds similar to FaNee's, but all the boys had the characteristics, if not the precise addresses, that Knoxville people associate with the poor whites of Union County. They were the sort of boys who didn't bother to finish high school, or finished it in a special program for slow learners, or get ejected from it for taking a swing at the principal.

"I guess you can say they more or less dragged us down to their level   5 with the drugs," a girl who was in the group—a girl who can be called Marcia—said recently. "And somehow we settled for it. It seems like we had to get ourselves in the pit before we could look out." People in the group used marijuana and Valium and LSD. They sneered at the Jocks and the "prim and proper little ladies" who went with Jocks. "We set ourselves aside," Marcia now says. "We put ourselves above everyone. How we did that I don't know." In a Knox County high school, teenagers who want to get themselves in the pit need not mainline heroin. The Jocks they mean to be compared to do not merely show up regularly for classes and practice football and wear clean clothes; they watch their language and preach temperance and go to prayer meetings on Wednesday nights and talk about having a real good Christian witness. Around Knoxville, people who speak of well-behaved high-school kids often seem to use words like "perfect," or even "angels." For FaNee's group, the opposite was not difficult to figure out. "We were into wicked things, strange things," Marcia says. "It was like we were on some kind of devil trip." FaNee wrote about demons and vultures and rats. "Slithering serpents eat my sanity and bite my ass," she wrote in an essay called "The Lovely Road of Life," just after she turned sixteen, "while tornadoes derail and ever so swiftly destroy every car in my train of thought." She wrote a lot about death.

FaNee's girl friends spoke of her as "super-intelligent." Her English   6 teacher found some of her writing profound—and disturbing. She was thought to be not just super-intelligent but super-mysterious, and even, at times, super-weird—an introverted girl who stared straight ahead with deep-brown, nearly black eyes and seemed to have thoughts she couldn't share. Nobody really knew why she had chosen to run with the Freaks— whether it was loneliness or rebellion or simple boredom. Marcia thought it might have had something to do with a feeling that her parents had settled on Kristy as their perfect child. "I guess she figured she couldn't be the best," Marcia said recently. "So she decided she might as well be the worst."

Toward the spring of FaNee's junior year at Halls, her problems 7
seemed to deepen. Despite her intelligence, her grades were sliding. She was what her mother called "a mental dropout." Leo Cooper had to visit Halls twice because of minor suspensions. Once, FaNee had been caught smoking. Once, having ducked out of a required assembly, she was spotted by a favorite teacher, who turned her in. At home, she exchanged little more than short, strained formalities with Kristy, who shared their parents' opinion of FaNee's choice of friends. The Coopers had finished their house—a large house, its size accentuated by the huge old logs and a great stone fireplace and outsize "Paul Bunyan"-style furniture—but FaNee spent most of her time there in her own room, sleeping or listening to rock music through earphones. One night, there was a terrible scene when FaNee returned from a concert in a condition that Leo Cooper knew had to be the result of marijuana. JoAnn Cooper, who ordinarily strikes people as too gentle to raise her voice, found herself losing her temper regularly. Finally, Leo Cooper asked a counselor he knew, Jim Griffin, to stop in at Halls High School and have a talk with FaNee—unofficially.

Griffin—a young man with a warm, informal manner—worked for 8
the Juvenile Court of Knox County. He had a reputation for being able to reach teenagers who wouldn't talk to their parents or to school administrators. One Friday in March of 1977, he spent an hour and a half talking to FaNee Cooper. As Griffin recalls the interview, FaNee didn't seem alarmed by his presence. She seemed to him calm and controlled— Griffin thought it was something like talking to another adult—and, unlike most teenagers he dealt with, she looked him in the eye the entire time. Griffin, like some of FaNee's friends, found her eyes unsettling— "the coldest, most distant, but, at the same time, the most knowing eyes I'd ever seen." She expressed affection for her parents, but she didn't seem interested in exploring ways of getting along better with them. The impression she gave Griffin was that they were who they were, and she was who she was, and there didn't happen to be any connection. Several times, she made the same response to Griffin's suggestions: "It's too late."

That weekend, neither FaNee nor her parents brought up the subject 9
of Griffin's visit. Leo Cooper has spoken of the weekend as being particularly happy; a friend of FaNee's who stayed over remembers it as particularly strained. FaNee stayed home from school on Monday because of a bad headache—she often had bad headaches—but felt well enough on Monday evening to drive to the library. She was to be home at nine. When she wasn't, Mrs. Cooper began to phone her friends. Finally, around ten, Leo Cooper got into his other car and took a swing around Halls—past the teenage hangouts like the Exxon station and the Pizza Hut and the Smoky Mountain Market. Then he took a second swing. At eleven, FaNee was still not home.

She hadn't gone to the library. She had picked up two girl friends and   10
driven to the home of a third, where everyone took five Valium tablets.
Then the four girls drove over to the Exxon station, where they met four
boys from their crowd. After a while, the group bought some beer and
some marijuana and reassembled at Charlie Stevens's trailer. Charlie
Stevens was five or six years older than everyone else in the group—a
skinny, slow-thinking young man with long black hair and a sparse
beard. He was married and had a child, but he and his wife had separated; she was back in Union County with the baby. Stevens had remained in their trailer—parked in the yard near his mother's house, in a
back-road area of Knox County dominated by decrepit, unpainted sheds
and run-down trailers and rusted-out automobiles. Stevens had picked
up FaNee at home once or twice—apparently, more as a driver for the
group than as a date—and the Coopers, having learned that his unsuit-
ability extended to being married, had asked her not to see him.

In Charlie's trailer, which had no heat or electricity, the group drank   11
beer and passed around joints, keeping warm with blankets. By eleven or
so, FaNee was what one of her friends has called "super-messed-up." Her
speech was slurred. She was having trouble keeping her balance. She had
decided not to go home. She had apparently persuaded herself that her
parents intended to send her away to some sort of home for incorrigibles.
"It's too late," she said to one of her friends. "It's just too late." It was decided that one of the boys, David Munsey, who was more or less the
leader of the group, would drive the Coopers' car to FaNee's house,
where FaNee and Charlie Stevens would pick him up in Stevens's car—a
worn Pinto with four bald tires, one light, and a dragging muffler. FaNee
wrote a note to her parents, and then, perhaps because her handwriting
was suffering the effects of beer and marijuana and Valium, asked
Stevens to rewrite it on a large piece of paper, which would be left on the
seat of the Coopers' car. The Stevens version was just about the same as
FaNee's, except that Stevens left out a couple of sentences about trying to
work things out ("I'm willing to try") and, not having won any spelling
championship himself, he misspelled a few words, like "tomorrow." The
note said, "Dear Mom and Dad. Sorry I'm late. Very late. I left your car
because I thought you might need it tomorrow. I love you all, but this is
something I just had to do. The man talked to me privately for one and a
half hours and I was really scared, so this is something I just had to do,
but don't worry. I'm with a very good friend. Love you all. FaNee. P.S.
Please try to understand I love you all very much, really I do. Love me if
you have a chance."

At eleven-thirty or so, Leo Cooper was sitting in his living room,   12
looking out the window at his driveway—a long gravel road that runs almost four hundred feet from the house to Brown Gap Road. He saw the
car that FaNee had been driving pull into the driveway. "She's home," he
called to his wife, who had just left the room. Cooper walked out on the
deck over the garage. The car had stopped at the end of the driveway, and

the lights had gone out. He got into his other car and drove to the end of the driveway. David Munsey had already joined Charlie Stevens and FaNee, and the Pinto was just leaving, travelling at a normal rate of speed. Leo Cooper pulled out on the road behind them.

Stevens turned left on Crippen Road, a road that has a field on one   13 side and two or three small houses on the other, and there Cooper pulled his car in front of the Pinto and stopped, blocking the way. He got out and walked toward the Pinto. Suddenly, Stevens put the car in reverse, backed into a driveway a hundred yards behind him, and sped off. Cooper jumped in his car and gave chase. Stevens raced back to Brown Gap Road, ran a stop sign there, ran another stop sign at Maynardville Highway, turned north, veered off onto the old Andersonville Pike, a nearly abandoned road that runs parallel to the highway, and then crossed back over the highway to the narrow, dark country roads on the other side. Stevens sometimes drove with his lights out. He took some of the corners by suddenly applying his hand brake to make the car swerve around in a ninety-degree turn. He was in familiar territory—he actually passed his trailer—and Cooper had difficulty keeping up. Past the trailer, Stevens swept down a hill into a sharp left turn that took him onto Foust Hollow Road, a winding, hilly road not much wider than one car.

At a fork, Cooper thought he had lost the Pinto. He started to go right   14 and then saw what seemed to be a spark from Stevens's dragging muffler off to the left, in the darkness. Cooper took the left fork, down Salem Church Road. He went down a hill and then up a long, curving hill to a crest, where he saw the Stevens car ahead. "I saw the car airborne. Up in the air," he later testified. "It was up in the air. And then it completely rolled over one more time. It started to make another flip forward, and just as it started to flip to the other side it flipped back this way, and my daughter's body came out."

Cooper slammed on his brakes and skidded to a stop up against the   15 Pinto. "Book!" Stevens shouted—the group's equivalent of "Scram!" Stevens and Munsey disappeared into the darkness. "It was dark, no one around, and so I started yelling for FaNee," Cooper had testified. "I thought it was an eternity before I could find her body, wedged under the back end of that car. . . . I tried everything I could, and saw that I couldn't get her loose. So I ran to a trailer back up to the top of the hill back up there to try to get that lady to call to get me some help, and then apparently she didn't think that I was serious. . . . I took the jack out of my car and got under, and it was dark, still couldn't see too much what was going on . . . and started prying and got her loose, and I don't know how. And then I dragged her over to the side, and, of course, at the time I felt reasonably assured that she was gone, because her head was completely—on one side just as if you had taken a sledgehammer and just hit it and bashed it in. And I did have the pleasure of one thing. I had the pleasure of listening to her breathe about the last three times she ever breathed in her life."

David Munsey did not return to the wreck that night, but Charlie   16
Stevens did. Leo Cooper was kneeling next to his daughter's body.
Cooper insisted that Stevens come close enough to see FaNee. "He was
kneeling down next to her," Stevens later testified. "And he said, 'Do you
know what you've done? Do you really know what you've done?' Like
that. And I just looked at her, and I said, 'Yes,' and just stood there.
Because I couldn't say nothing." There was, of course, a legal decision to
be made about who was responsible for FaNee Cooper's death. In a de-
position, Stevens said he had been fleeing for his life. He testified that
when Leo Cooper blocked Crippen Road, FaNee had said that her father
had a gun and intended to hurt them. Stevens was bound over and eventually indicted for involuntary manslaughter. Leo Cooper testified that
when he approached the Pinto on Crippen Road, FaNee had a strange expression that he had never seen before. "It wasn't like FaNee, and I knew
something was wrong," he said. "My concern was to get FaNee out of the
car." The district attorney's office asked that Cooper be bound over for
reckless driving, but the judge declined to do so. "Any father would have
done what he did," the judge said. "I can see no criminal act on the part of
Mr. Cooper."

Almost two years passed before Charlie Stevens was brought to trial.   17
Part of the problem was assuring the presence of David Munsey, who had
joined the Navy but seemed inclined to assign his own leaves. In the
meantime, the Coopers went to court with a civil suit—they had "unin-
sured-motorist coverage," which requires their insurance company to
cover any defendant who has no insurance of his own—and they won a
judgment. There were ways of assigning responsibility, or course, which
had nothing to do with the law, civil or criminal. A lot of people in
Knoxville thought that Leo Cooper had, in the words of his lawyer, "done
what any daddy worth his salt would have done." There were others who
believed that FaNee Cooper had lost her life because Leo Cooper had lost
his temper. Leo Cooper was not among those who expressed any doubts
about his actions. Unlike his wife, whose eyes filled with tears at almost
any mention of FaNee, Cooper seemed able, even eager to go over the details of the accident again and again. With the help of a school-board security man, he conducted his own investigation. He drove over the route
dozens of times. "I've thought about it every day, and I guess I will the rest
of my life," he said as he and his lawyer and the prosecuting attorney went
over the route again the day before Charlie Stevens's trial finally began.
"But I can't tell any alternative for a father. I simply wanted her out of that
car. I'd have done the same thing again, even at the risk of losing her."

Tennessee law permits the family of a victim to hire a special prosecu-   18
tor to assist the district attorney. The lawyer who acted for the Coopers in
the civil case helped prosecute Charlie Stevens. Both he and the district
attorney assured the jurors that the presence of a special prosecutor was
not to be construed to mean that the Coopers were vindictive. Outside the

courtroom, Leo Cooper said that the verdict was of no importance to him—that he felt sorry, in a way, for Charlie Stevens. But there were people in Knoxville who thought Cooper had a lot riding on the prosecution of Charlie Stevens. If Stevens was not guilty of FaNee Cooper's death—found so by twelve of his peers—who was?

At the trial, Cooper testified emotionally and remarkably graphically   19
about pulling FaNee out from under the car and watching her die in his arms. Charlie Stevens had shaved his beard and cut his hair, but the effort did not transform him into an impressive witness. His lawyer—trying to argue that it would have been impossible for Stevens to concoct the story about FaNee's having mentioned a gun, as the prosecution strongly implied—said, "His mind is such that if you ask him a question you can hear his mind go around, like an old mill creaking." Stevens did not deny the recklessness of his driving or the sorry condition of his car. It happened to be the only car he had available to flee in, he said, and he had fled in fear for his life.

The prosecution said that Stevens could have let FaNee out of the car   20
when her father stopped them, or could have gone to the commercial strip on the Maynardville Highway for protection. The prosecution said that Leo Cooper had done what he might have been expected to do under the circumstances—alone, late at night, his daughter in danger. The defense said precisely the same about Stevens: he had done what he might have been expected to do when being pursued by a man he had reason to be afraid of. "I don't fault Mr. Cooper for what he did, but I'm sorry he did it," the defense attorney said. "I'm sorry the girl said what she said." The jury deliberated for eighteen minutes. Charlie Stevens was found guilty. The jury recommended a sentence of from two to five years in the state penitentiary. At the announcement, Leo Cooper broke down and cried, JoAnn Cooper's eyes filled with tears; she blinked them back and continued to stare straight ahead.

In a way, the Coopers might still strike a casual visitor as an ideal   21
family—handsome parents, a bright and bubbly teenage daughter, a little boy learning the hook shot from his father, a warm house with some land around it. FaNee's presence is there, of course. A picture of her, with a small bouquet of flowers over it, hangs in the living room. One of her poems is displayed in a frame on a table. Even if Leo Cooper continues to think about that night for the rest of his life, there are questions he can never answer. Was there a way that Leo and JoAnn Cooper could have prevented FaNee from choosing the path she chose? Would she still be alive if Leo Cooper had not jumped into his car and driven to the end of the driveway to investigate? Did she in fact tell Charlie Stevens that her father would hurt them—or even that her father had a gun? Did she want to get away from her family even at the risk of tearing around dark country roads in Charlie Stevens's dismal Pinto? Or did she welcome the risk? The poem of FaNee's that the Coopers have displayed is one she wrote a week before her death:

I think I'm going to die
And I really don't know why.
But look in my eye
When I tell you good-bye.
I think I'm going to die.

           •   •   •

COMPREHENSION

1. What early signs suggested that FaNee was not really an "ideal child" (1)?

2. During her high school years, what specific kinds of behavior caused FaNee's parents to worry about her?

3. In what ways, if at all, do FaNee's parents contribute to her problems? Consider their backgrounds, their personalities, and their positions in the town. What other factors might have caused her problems?

4. In what ways did the social structure of the town of Halls—and, in particular, of Halls High School—lead FaNee to become a "Freak" (4)?

5. Identify the immediate cause of FaNee's death. What other, more remote, causes do you see as significant?

6. In what sense might FaNee's decline be described as a causal chain?

7. What do you think Trillin means when he says, in paragraph 17, "There were ways of assigning responsibility . . . which had nothing to do with the law, civil or criminal"?

8. What do you think FaNee means by the statement "It's just too late" (8, 11)? What do you think Trillin means to suggest by using this statement as his essay's title?

PURPOSE AND AUDIENCE

1. Do you believe Trillin's primary purpose in this essay is to report information about FaNee and her family in a case study, or to suggest that her story has wider social or even moral implications for readers? Explain your conclusion.

2. In paragraph 5 Trillin says, "In a Knox County high school, teenagers who want to get themselves in the pit need not mainline heroin. The Jocks they mean to be compared to do not merely show up regularly for classes and practice football and wear clean clothes; they watch their language and preach temperance and go to prayer meetings on Wednesday nights and talk about having a real good Christian witness." Why do you think Trillin finds it necessary to include this explanation? What does it suggest about his view of his audience?

3. "It's Just Too Late" does not have an explicitly stated thesis. What do you think the essay's main idea is? State it in a single sentence. Why do you think Trillin chose not to include a thesis statement?

STYLE AND STRUCTURE

1. Trillin's essay might be divided into three parts: background (1–8); the events of the night FaNee dies (9–16); and the aftermath of that night, including the trial (17–21). How does Trillin signal movement from one part of the story to the next? Do you think he needs to make these signals more explicit? Would internal headings be useful? Explain.

2. What do you think Trillin hopes to accomplish by quoting FaNee's writing in paragraphs 2, 4, 5, 11, and 21? Is he successful? Explain.

3. What do the quotations from FaNee's parents, her friend Marcia, Jim Griffin, and others add to the essay? What other voices would you like to hear?

4. Trillin is a reporter, and his writing is both detailed and objective. Why is this level of detail and objectivity so important here? Where, if anywhere, does he reveal his own opinions?

5. In the last paragraph of his essay, Trillin asks (but does not answer) a series of questions. What do you think he hopes these **rhetorical questions** will suggest to readers?

VOCABULARY PROJECTS

1. Define each of the following words as it is used in this selection.

introspective (1)	affliction (2)	graphically (19)
errant (1)	temperance (5)	
magnanimous (1)	bald (11)	

2. "At Halls High School," Trillin explains, "the social poles were represented by the Jocks and the Freaks" (4). Write one-sentence definitions of *jock* and *freak*. Then, suggest a few alternate names for each group, being careful to choose words that convey the same meanings as the original terms.

JOURNAL ENTRY

Who, if anyone, do you think could have "saved" FaNee? Or do you believe it was really "just too late"? Discuss.

WRITING WORKSHOP

1. Write an essay in which you consider the possible effects of FaNee's death on those who knew her—her parents, her teachers, her friends.

2. Who or what do you see as responsible for FaNee's death? Write an essay in which you consider both the main cause of her death and the contributory causes.

3. Taking the point of view of a school counselor, write a report in which you make specific recommendations for addressing FaNee's needs and problems. In your report, explain the beneficial results of the plan you propose.

COMBINING THE PATTERNS

Paragraphs 4 and 5 of "It's Just Too Late" develop a **comparison and contrast** between the Jocks and the Freaks. How do these two groups differ? Why is the sharp contrast revealed in these paragraphs so important in Trillin's profile of FaNee? Do you think Trillin should have expanded this discussion? Why or why not?

THEMATIC CONNECTIONS

- "Samuel" (page 202)
- "Television: The Plug-In Drug" (page 274)
- "Suicide Note" (page 305)

JANICE MIRIKITANI

Janice Mirikitani, born in 1942, is a Japanese-American poet, editor, and community activist in San Francisco. Her book *Shedding Silence* (1987) is a collection of poetry and prose addressing racism in the United States—how it affects Asians and Asian-Americans, and particularly how it affected the thousands of Japanese-Americans held in internment camps during World War II. She is also the author of *Awake in the River* (1978), another collection of poetry and prose, and *We Are the Dangerous: Selected Poems* (1995); the editor of *Time to Greez! Incantations from the Third World* (1975) and *Ayumi: A Japanese American Anthology* (1980); and the coeditor of *I Have Something to Say about This Big Trouble: Children of the Tenderloin Speak Out* (1989), a collection of drawings, poems, and prose by children of the underclass in San Francisco's Tenderloin neighborhood. In "Suicide Note," which appears in *Shedding Silence,* a note of apology from a young Asian-American college student to her parents reveals the extreme pressure to excel placed on her by her parents and her culture.

Suicide Note

How many notes written . . .
ink smeared like birdprints in snow.

not good enough   not pretty enough   not smart enough

dear mother and father.
I apologize
for disappointing you.   5
I've worked very hard,

                              not good enough

harder, perhaps to please you.
If only I were a son, shoulders broad   10
as the sunset threading through pine,
I would see the light in my mother's
eyes, or the golden pride reflected
in my father's dream
of my wide, male hands worthy of work   15
and comfort.
I would swagger through life
muscled and bold and assured,
drawing praises to me
like currents in the bed of wind, virile   20
with confidence.

      not good enough   not strong enough   not good enough
I apologize.
Tasks do not come easily.
Each failure, a glacier.   25
Each disapproval, a bootprint.
Each disappointment,
ice above my river.
So I have worked hard.
                       not good enough   30

My sacrifice I will drop
bone by bone, perched
on the ledge of my womanhood,
fragile as wings.
                       not strong enough   35

It is snowing steadily
surely not good weather
for flying—this sparrow
sillied and dizzied by the wind
on the edge.   40
                       not smart enough
I make this ledge my altar
to offer penance.
This air will not hold me,
the snow burdens my crippled wings,   45
my tears drop like bitter cloth
softly into the gutter below.
      not good enough   not strong enough   not smart enough

                       Choices thin as shaved
                       ice. Notes shredded   50
                       drift like snow

on my broken body,
covers me like whispers
of sorries
sorries.   55
Perhaps when they find me
they will bury
my bird bones beneath
a sturdy pine
and scatter my feathers like   60
unspoken song
over this white and cold and silent
breast of earth.

• • •

THINKING ABOUT LITERATURE

1. An author's note that originally introduced this poem explained the main cause of the student's death:

   An Asian American college student was reported to have jumped to her death from her dormitory window. Her body was found two days later under a deep cover of snow. Her suicide note contained an apology to her parents for having received less than a perfect four point grade average. . . .

   What other causes might have contributed to her suicide?

2. Why does the speaker believe her life would be happier if she were male? Do you think she is correct?

3. What words, phrases, and images are repeated in this poem? What effect do these repetitions have on you?

JOURNAL ENTRY

Whom (or what) do you blame for teenage suicides such as the one the poem describes? How might the causes of such deaths be eliminated?

THEMATIC CONNECTIONS

- "Only Daughter" (page 70)
- "College Pressures" (page 378)
- "The Company Man" (page 465)

WRITING ASSIGNMENTS FOR CAUSE AND EFFECT

1. "Who Killed Benny Paret?" (page 270), "On Dumpster Diving" (page 609), and "Thirty-Eight Who Saw Murder Didn't Call the Police" (page 86) all encourage readers, either directly or indirectly, to take action rather than remaining uninvolved. Using information gleaned from these essays (or others in the text) as support for your thesis, write an essay in which you explore the possible consequences of apathy.

2. Write an updated version of one of this chapter's essays. For example, you might reconsider Winn's points in light of the increasing influence of cable television in the twenty years since "Television: The Plug-In Drug" was written or explore the kinds of pressure that Lawrence Otis Graham ("The 'Black Table' Is Still There") might face as a junior high school student today.

3. Various technological and social developments have contributed to the decline of formal letter writing. One of these is the telephone. Consider some other possible causes, and write an essay explaining why letter writing has become less popular. You may also consider the *effects* of this decline.

4. How do you account for the popularity of one of the following phenomena: shopping malls, MTV, fast food, e-mail, heavy metal or rap music, soap operas, sensationalist tabloids like the *Star*? Write an essay in which you consider remote as well as immediate causes for the success of the phenomenon you choose.

5. Between 1946 and 1964, the birth rate increased considerably. Some of the effects attributed to this baby boom include the 1960s antiwar movement, the increase in the crime rate, and the development of the women's movement. Write an essay in which you explore some possible effects of the baby-boom generation's growing older. What trends would you expect to find as most baby boomers reach middle age? When they reach retirement?

6. Write an essay in which you trace a series of events from your life that constitutes a causal chain. Indicate clearly both the sequence of events and the causal connections among them.

7. Consider the effects, or possible effects, of one of these scientific developments on your life and/or on the lives of your contemporaries: genetic engineering, space exploration, the Internet, human cloning. Consider negative as well as positive effects.

8. Currently almost half of American marriages end in divorce. To what do you attribute this high divorce rate? Be as specific as possible, citing "case studies" of families with which you are familiar.

9. What do you see as the major cause of any *one* of these problems: acquaintance rape, alcohol or drug abuse among college students, academic cheating? Based on your identification of its causes, formulate some specific solutions for the problem you select.

10. Write an essay in which you consider the likely effects of a severe, protracted shortage of one of the following commodities: food, rental housing, medical care, computer hardware, reading matter. You may consider a community-, city-, or statewide shortage or a nation- or worldwide crisis.

COLLABORATIVE ACTIVITY FOR CAUSE AND EFFECT

Working in groups of four, discuss your thoughts about the increasing homeless population, and then list four *effects* the presence of homeless people is having on you, your community, and our nation. Assign each member of your group to write a paragraph explaining one of the effects the group identifies. Then, arrange the paragraphs in order of increasing importance, moving from the least to the most significant consequence. Finally, work together to turn your individual paragraphs into an essay: write an introduction, a conclusion, and transitions between paragraphs, and include a thesis statement in paragraph 1.

7

COMPARISON AND CONTRAST

WHAT IS COMPARISON AND CONTRAST?

In the narrowest sense, *comparison* shows how two or more things are similar, and *contrast* shows how they are different. In most writing situations, however, you use the two related processes of **comparison and contrast** to consider both similarities and differences. In the following paragraph from *Disturbing the Universe,* scientist Freeman Dyson compares and contrasts two different styles of human endeavor, which he calls "the gray and the green":

Topic
sentence
(outlines
elements of
comparison)

Point-by-point
comparison

In everything we undertake, either on earth or in the sky, we have a choice of two styles, which I call the gray and the green. The distinction between the gray and green is not sharp. Only at the extremes of the spectrum can we say without qualification, this is green and that is gray. The difference between green and gray is better explained by examples than by definitions. Factories are gray, gardens are green. Physics is gray, biology is green. Plutonium is gray, horse manure is green. Bureaucracy is gray, pioneer communities are green. Self-reproducing machines are gray, trees and children are green. Human technology is gray, God's technology is green. Clones are gray, clades* are green. Army field manuals are gray, poems are green.

A special form of comparison, called **analogy,** looks for similarities between two essentially dissimilar things. An analogy explains one thing by comparing it to a second thing that is more familiar than the first. In the following paragraph from *The Shopping Mall High School,* Arthur G. Powell, Eleanor Farrar, and David K. Cohen use analogy to shed light on the nature of American high schools:

---

*EDS. NOTE—A group of organisms that evolved from a common ancestor.

If Americans want to understand their high schools at work, they should imagine them as shopping malls. Secondary education is another consumption experience in an abundant society. Shopping malls attract a broad range of customers with different tastes and purposes. Some shop at Sears, others at Woolworth's or Bloomingdale's. In high schools a broad range of students also shop. They too can select from an astonishing variety of products and services conveniently assembled in one place with ample parking. Furthermore, in malls and schools many different kinds of transactions are possible. Both institutions bring hopeful purveyors and potential purchasers together. The former hope to maximize sales but can take nothing for granted. Shoppers have a wide discretion not only about what to buy but also about whether to buy.

Throughout our lives we are bombarded with countless bits of information from newspapers, television, radio, the Internet, and personal experience: the police strike in Memphis; city workers walk out in Philadelphia; the Senate debates government spending; taxes are lowered in New Jersey. Somehow we must make sense of the jumbled facts and figures that surround us. One way we have of understanding information like this is to put it side by side with other data and then to compare and contrast. Do the police in Memphis have the same complaints as the city workers in Philadelphia? What are the differences between the two situations? Is the national debate on spending analogous to the New Jersey debate on taxes? How do they differ? We make similar distinctions every day about matters that directly affect us. When we make personal decisions, we consider alternatives, asking ourselves whether one option seems better than another. Should I buy a car with manual or automatic transmission? Should I major in history or business? What job opportunities will each major offer me? Should I register as a Democrat or a Republican, or should I join a third party? What are the positions of each on government spending, welfare, and taxes?

Because this way of thinking is central to our understanding of the world, comparison and contrast is often called for in papers and on essay examinations:

> Compare and contrast the attitudes toward science and technology expressed in Fritz Lang's *Metropolis* and George Lucas's *Star Wars*. (film)
>
> What are the similarities and differences between mitosis and meiosis? (biology)
>
> Discuss the relative merits of establishing a partnership or a corporation. (business law)
>
> Discuss the advantages and disadvantages of the heterogeneous grouping of pupils. (education)

Using Comparison and Contrast

You are not likely to sit down and say to yourself, "I think I'll write a comparison-and-contrast essay today. Now what can I write about?"

Instead, you will use comparison and contrast because your assignment suggests that you do so or because you decide it suits your purpose. In the preceding examples, for instance, the instructors have phrased their questions to tell students how to treat the material. When you read the questions, certain key words and phrases—*compare and contrast, similarities and differences, relative merits, advantages and disadvantages*—indicate that you should use a comparison-and-contrast pattern to organize your essay. Sometimes you may not even need a key phrase. Consider the question, "Which of the two Adamses, John or Samuel, had the greater influence on the timing and course of the American Revolution?" Here the word *greater* is enough to suggest a contrast.

Even when your assignment is not worded to suggest comparison and contrast, your purpose may point to this pattern of development. For instance, when you evaluate, you frequently use comparison and contrast. If, as a student in a management course, you are asked to evaluate two health-care systems, you can begin by researching the standards experts use in their evaluations. You can then compare each system's performance with those standards and contrast the systems with each other, concluding perhaps that both systems meet minimum standards but that one is more cost-efficient than the other. Or if you are evaluating two of this year's new cars for a consumer newsletter, you might establish some criteria—fuel economy, handling, comfort, safety features, style—and compare and contrast the cars with respect to each criterion. If each of the cars is better in different categories, your readers will have to decide which features matter most to them.

Establishing a Basis of Comparison

Before you can compare and contrast two things, you must be sure a **basis of comparison** exists—that is, that the things share some significant characteristics. For example, although cats and dogs are very different, they share several common elements: they are mammals, they make good pets, and so forth. Without at least one common element, there would be no basis for analysis, and no comparison would be possible.

A comparison should lead you beyond the obvious. For instance, at first the idea of a comparison-and-contrast essay based on an analogy between bees and people might seem absurd: after all, these two creatures differ in species, physical structure, and intelligence. In fact, their differences are so obvious that an essay based on them might seem pointless. But after further analysis, you might decide that bees and people have quite a few similarities. Both are social animals that live in complex social structures, and both have tasks to perform and roles to fulfill in their respective societies. Therefore, you *could* write about them, but you would focus on the common elements that seem most provocative—social structures and roles—rather than on dissimilar elements. If you tried to draw an analogy between bees and Jeeps or humans and golf tees, however, you would run into trouble. Although some points of comparison could be found, they would be trivial. Why bother to point out that both bees and Jeeps travel great distances or that both people and tees are needed to play golf? Neither statement establishes a significant basis of comparison.

When two subjects are very similar, it is the contrast that may be worth writing about. And when two subjects are not very much alike, you may find their similarities enlightening.

Selecting Points for Discussion

After you decide which subjects to compare and contrast, you need to select the points you want to discuss. You do this by determining your emphasis—on similarities, differences, or both—and the major focus of your paper. If your purpose for comparing two types of house plants is to explain that one is easier to grow than the other, you would contrast points having to do with plant care, not those having to do with plant biology.

When you compare and contrast, make sure you treat the same, or at least similar, elements for each subject you discuss. For instance, if you were going to compare and contrast two novels, you might consider the following elements in both works:

Novel A	*Novel B*
Major characters	Major characters
Minor characters	Minor characters
Themes	Themes

Try to avoid the common error of discussing entirely different elements for each subject. Such an approach obscures any basis of comparison that might exist. The two novels, for example, could not be meaningfully compared or contrasted if you discussed dissimilar elements:

Novel A	*Novel B*
Major characters	Plot
Minor characters	Author's life
Themes	Symbolism

Formulating a Thesis Statement

After you decide on the points you want to discuss, you are ready to formulate your thesis statement. This thesis statement should tell your readers what to expect in your essay, identifying not only the subjects to be compared and contrasted but also the points you will make about them. Your thesis statement should also indicate whether you will concentrate on similarities or differences or whether you will balance the two. In addition, it may list the points of comparison and contrast in the order in which they will be discussed in the essay.

The structure of your thesis statement can indicate the focus of your essay. As the following sentences illustrate, a thesis statement can high-light the central concern of the essay by presenting it in the independent, rather than the dependent, clause of the sentence. The structure of the first sentence emphasizes similarities, and the structure of the second highlights differences:

> Despite the fact that television and radio are distinctly different media, they use similar strategies to appeal to their audiences.

> Although Melville's *Moby-Dick* and London's *The Sea Wolf* are both about the sea, minor characters, major characters, and themes of *Moby-Dick* establish its greater complexity.

STRUCTURING A COMPARISON-AND-CONTRAST ESSAY

Like every other type of essay examined in this book, a comparison-and-contrast essay has an introduction, several body paragraphs, and a conclusion. Within the body of your paper, you can use either of two basic comparison-and-contrast patterns—*subject by subject* or *point by point*. As you might expect, each organizational pattern has advantages and disadvantages that you should consider before choosing one. In general, you should use subject-by-subject comparison when your purpose is to emphasize overall similarities or differences, and you should use point-by-point comparison when your purpose is to emphasize individual points of similarity or difference.

Using Subject-by-Subject Comparison

In a **subject-by-subject comparison,** you essentially write a separate essay about each subject, but you discuss the same points for both subjects. In discussing each subject, you use the same basis of comparison to guide your selection of supporting points, and you arrange these points in some logical order, usually in order of their increasing significance. The following informal outline illustrates a subject-by-subject comparison:

Introduction:	Thesis statement—Despite the fact that television and radio are distinctly different media, they use similar strategies to appeal to their audiences.
Television audiences	
Point 1:	Men
Point 2:	Women
Point 3:	Children
Radio audiences	
Point 1:	Men
Point 2:	Women
Point 3:	Children
Conclusion:	Restatement of thesis or review of key points

Subject-by-subject comparisons are most appropriate for short, un-complicated papers. In longer papers, where many points are made about each subject, this organizational pattern puts too many demands on your readers, requiring them to keep track of all your points throughout your paper. In addition, because of the length of each section, your paper may seem like two separate essays weakly connected by a transitional phrase. For longer or more complex papers, then, it is usually best to use point-by-point comparison.

Using Point-by-Point Comparison

When you write a **point-by-point comparison,** you first make a point about one subject and then follow it with a comparable point about the other. This alternating pattern continues throughout the body of your essay until all your comparisons or contrasts have been made. The following informal outline illustrates a point-by-point comparison:

Introduction:	Thesis statement—Although Melville's *Moby-Dick* and London's *The Sea Wolf* are both about the sea, the minor characters, major characters, and themes of *Moby-Dick* establish its greater complexity.
Minor characters	
Book 1:	*The Sea Wolf*
Book 2:	*Moby-Dick*
Major characters	
Book 1:	*The Sea Wolf*
Book 2:	*Moby-Dick*
Themes	
Book 1:	*The Sea Wolf*
Book 2:	*Moby-Dick*
Conclusion	Restatement of thesis or review of key points

Point-by-point comparisons are especially useful for longer, more complicated essays in which you discuss many different points. (If you treat only one or two points of comparison, you should consider a sub-ject-by-subject organization.) In a point-by-point essay, readers can easily follow comparisons or contrasts and do not have to wait several para-graphs to find out, for example, the differences between minor characters in *Moby-Dick* and *The Sea Wolf* or to remember on page six what was said on page three. Nevertheless, it is easy to fall into a monotonous, back-and-forth movement between points when you write a point-by-point comparison. To avoid this problem, use clear transitions, and vary sen-tence structure as you move from point to point.

Supplying Clear Transitions

Transitions are especially important in comparison-and-contrast es-says because you must supply readers with clear signals that indicate whether you are discussing similarities or differences. Without these cues, readers will have trouble following your train of thought and may lose track of the significance of the points you are making. (Some transitions indicating comparison and contrast are shown in the box below.)

☑ **USEFUL TRANSITIONS FOR COMPARISON AND CONTRAST**

COMPARISON

just as . . . so	in comparison
like	similarly
likewise	in the same way

CONTRAST

although	nevertheless
but	nonetheless
conversely	on the contrary
despite	on the one hand . . . on the other hand . . .
even though	still
however	unlike
in contrast	whereas
instead	yet

Longer essays frequently contain *transitional paragraphs* that connect one part of an essay to another. A transitional paragraph can be a single sentence that signals a shift in focus or a longer paragraph that provides a concise summary of what was said before. In both cases, transitional paragraphs enable readers to pause and consider what has already been said before moving on to a new point.

▶ STUDENT WRITERS: COMPARISON AND CONTRAST

Both of the following essays illustrate comparison and contrast. The first, by Mark Cotharn, is a subject-by-subject comparison. The second, by Margaret Depner, is a point-by-point comparison. Both were written for a composition class in which the instructor asked students to write an essay comparing two experiences with education.

Brains versus Brawn

Introduction   When people think about discrimination,   1
they usually associate it with prejudice and
connect it with race or gender. But discrimination can take another form. For example, a
person can gain an unfair advantage at a job
interview by being attractive or knowing someone who works at the company or by being able
to talk about something that has nothing to do
with the job, like sports. Certainly, the peo-

ple who do not get the job would claim that they were discriminated against, and to some extent they would be right. As a high school athlete, I experienced both types of discrimination. When I was a sophomore in high school, I benefited from discrimination. When I was a junior, however, I was penalized by it, treated as if there were no place for me in a classroom. As a result, I learned that discrimination, whether it helps you or hinders you, is wrong.

Thesis statement (emphasizing differences)

First subject: Mark helped by discrimination

At my high school, football was everything, and the entire town supported the local team. In the summer, merchants would run special football promotions. Adults would wear shirts with the team's logo, students would collect money to buy equipment, and everyone would go to the games and cheer the team on. Coming out of junior high school, I was considered an exceptional athlete who was eventually going to start as the varsity quarterback. Because of my status, I was welcomed with open arms by the high school. Before I entered the school, the varsity coach even visited my home, and the principal called my parents and told them how well I was going to do.

Status of football

2

I knew that high school would be different from junior high, but I wasn't prepared for the treatment I received from teachers. Many of them talked to me as if I were their friend, not their student. My math teacher used to keep me after class just to talk football; he would even give me a note so I could be late for my next class. My biology teacher told me I could skip the afternoon labs so I would have some time for myself before practice. Several of my teachers told me that during football season I didn't have to hand in homework because it might distract me during

Treatment by teachers

3

practice. My Spanish teacher even told me that if I didn't do well on a test, I could take it over after the season. Everything I did seemed to be perfect.

Mark's reaction to treatment

In spite of this favorable treatment, I continued to study hard. I knew that if I wanted to go to a good college, I would have to get good grades, and I resented the implication that the only way I could get good grades was by getting special treatment. I had always been a good student, and I had no intention of changing my study habits. Each night after practice, I would stay up late outlining my notes and completing my class assignments. Any studying I couldn't do during the week, I would complete on the weekends. Of course my social life suffered, but I didn't care. I took pride in the fact that I never had to take advantage of the special treatment my teachers were offering me.

4

Transitional paragraph: signals shift from one subject to another

Then one day the unthinkable happened. The township redrew the district lines, and I suddenly found myself assigned to a new high school--one that was academically more demanding than the one I attended, and, what was worse, one that had a weak football team. When my parents appealed to the school board to let me stay at my current school, they were told that no exceptions could be made. If the board made a change for me, it would have to make changes for others, and that would lead to chaos. My principal and my coach also tried to get the board to change its decision, but they got the same response. So in my junior year, at the height of my career, I changed schools.

5

Second subject: Mark hurt by discrimination

Unlike the people at my old school, no one at my new school seemed to care much about high school football. Many of the students attended the games, but their primary

6

focus was on getting into a good college. If they talked about football at all, they usually discussed the regional college teams. As a result, I didn't have the status I had when I attended my former school. When I met with **Status of football** the coach before school started, he told me the football team was weak. He also told me that his main goal was to make sure everyone on the team had a chance to play. So, even though I would start, I would have to share the quarterback position with two seniors whom he wanted to give a chance to play. Later that day I saw the principal, who told me that although sports were an important part of school, academic achievement was more important. He made it clear that I would play football only as long as my grades did not suffer.

Treatment by teachers Unlike the teachers at my old school, the teachers at my new school did not give any special treatment to athletes. When I entered my new school, I was ready for the challenge. What I was not ready for was the hostility of most of my new teachers. From the first day, in just about every class, my teachers made it obvious they had already made up their minds about what kind of student I was going to be. Some teachers told me I shouldn't expect any special consideration just because I was the team's quarterback. One even said in front of the class that I would have to study as hard as the other students if I expected to pass. I was hurt and embarrassed by these comments. I didn't expect anyone to give me anything, and I was ready to get the grades I deserved. After all, I had gotten good grades up to this point, and I had no reason to think that the situation would **Mark's reaction to treatment** change. Even so, my teachers' preconceived ideas upset me.

7

Just as I had in my old school, I studied   8
hard, but I didn't know how to deal with the
prejudice I faced. At first, it really bothered me and even affected my performance on
the football field. However, after I thought
about it awhile, I realized that the best way
to show my teachers that I was not the stereotypical jock was to prove to them what kind of
student I really was. In the long run, far
from discouraging me, their treatment motivated me, and I decided to work even harder in
the classroom than I did on the football
field. I didn't care if the football team lost
every game as long as I did my best in every
class I had. By the end of high school, not
only had the team won half of their games (a
record season), but I had proved to my teachers that I was a good student as well as an
athlete. (I still remember the surprised look
on the face of my chemistry teacher when she
handed my final exam back to me and told me I
had received the second highest grade in the
class.)

Conclusion   Before I graduated, I talked to the   9
teachers about how they had treated me during
my junior year. Some admitted they had been
harder on me than on the rest of the students, but others denied they had ever discriminated against me. After awhile, I realized they would never understand what they
had done. Even so, my experience did have
some positive effects. I learned that you
should judge people on their merits, not by
some preconceived standard. In addition, I
Restatement learned that although some people are talented
of thesis intellectually, others possess special skills
that should also be valued. And, as I found
out, discriminatory treatment, whether it
helps you or hinders you, is no substitute
for fairness.

Points for Special Attention

BASIS OF COMPARISON.   Mark knew he could easily compare his two experiences. Both involved high school, and both focused on the treatment he had received as a high school athlete. In one case, Mark was treated better than other students because he was the team's quarterback; in the other, he was stereotyped as a "dumb jock" because he was a football player. Mark also knew that his comparison would make an interesting point—that discrimination is unfair, even when it gives a person an advantage.

SELECTING POINTS FOR COMPARISON.   Mark wanted to make certain that he would discuss the same (or at least similar) points for the two experiences he was going to compare. As he planned his essay, Mark consulted his brainstorming notes and made the following informal outline:

Experience 1 (*gained an advantage*)	**Experience 2** (*was put at a disadvantage*)
Status of football	Status of football
Treatment by teachers	Treatment by teachers
My reaction	My reaction

STRUCTURE.   Mark's essay makes three points about each of the two experiences he compares. Because his purpose was to convey overall differences between the two experiences, he decided on a subject-by-subject strategy. In addition, Mark thought he could make his case more convincingly if he discussed the first experience fully before moving on to the next one, and he believed readers would have no trouble keeping his individual points in mind as they read. Of course, Mark could have decided to do a point-by-point comparison. He rejected this strategy, though, because he thought that shifting back and forth between subjects would distract readers from his main point.

In Mark's case, a subject-by-subject comparison made more sense than a point-by-point comparison. Often, however, the choice is a matter of preference—a writer might simply like one strategy better than the other.

TRANSITIONS.   Without adequate transitions, a subject-by-subject comparison can read like two separate essays. Notice that in Mark's essay, paragraph 5 functions as a transitional paragraph that connects the two sections of the essay. In it, Mark sets up the comparison by telling how he suddenly found himself assigned to another high school.

In addition to connecting the sections of an essay, transitional words and phrases can identify similarities and differences for readers. Notice, for example, how the transitional word *however* emphasizes the contrast between the following sentences from paragraph 1:

Without transitions

When I was a sophomore in high school, I benefited from discrimination. When I was a junior, I was penalized by it. . . .

With transitions

When I was a sophomore in high school, I benefited from discrimination. When I was a junior, *however,* I was penalized by it. . . .

TOPIC SENTENCES.   Like transitional phrases, topic sentences help to guide readers through an essay. When reading a comparison-and-contrast essay, readers can easily forget the points that are being compared, especially if the paper is long or complex. Direct, clearly stated topic sentences act as guideposts, alerting readers to the comparisons and contrasts you are making. For example, Mark's straightforward topic sentence at the beginning of paragraph 5 dramatically signals the movement from one experience to the other ("Then one day the unthinkable happened"). In addition, as in any effective comparison-and-contrast essay, each point discussed in connection with one subject is also discussed in connection with the other. Mark's topic sentences reinforce this balance:

First subject

At my high school, football was everything.

Second subject

Unlike the people at my old school, no one at my new school seemed to care much about high school football.

Focus on Revision

Mark's peer critics thought he could have spent more time talking about what he did to counter the preconceptions about athletes that teachers in *both* his schools had. One student pointed out that the teachers at both schools seemed to think athletes were weak students. The only difference was that the teachers at Mark's first school were willing to make allowances for athletes, while the teachers at his second school were not. The student thought that although Mark alluded to this fact, he should have made his point more explicitly. After rereading his essay along with his classmates' comments, Mark decided to add information about how demanding football practice was. Without this information, readers would have a hard time understanding just how difficult it was for him to keep up with his studies. He also thought he should mention that some student athletes do fit the teachers' stereotypes, although many do not. This information would reinforce his thesis and help him demonstrate how unfair his treatment was.

Unlike the preceding essay, Margaret Depner's paper is a point-by-point comparison.

The Big Move

Introduction

The adjustment began when I was a sophomore in high school. I was fifteen--a typical American teenager. I lived to talk on the telephone, hang out at the mall, watch lots of television, and go to the movies. Everything about my life seemed satisfying. I loved my neighborhood, my school, and my friends. But suddenly everything changed. One night my parents told me that my father had been transferred and that we were going to move to England. I felt as if everything I had grown to love was being torn away from me. I was going to have to start over, and I did not want to go. My parents ignored my pleas and told me in no uncertain terms that I had no choice in the matter. My fate was sealed. When we finally arrived in England I was so frightened that I felt sick. Not only would I have **Thesis statement (emphasizing differences)** to get used to a new neighborhood and a new school, but I would also have to get used to a new way of life.

First point: adjusting to a new neighborhood

The first thing I had to adjust to was living in a new neighborhood. The Boston suburb we had left was a known quantity, and perhaps for this reason, I liked it. At home we lived in a new development that was just starting to get built up. There were houses everywhere with a few small trees scattered in between. Our house had a large lawn that my brother and I tried to avoid cutting whenever **Neighborhood in U.S.** we could. Moms carting children around in minivans was a common sight. My dad belonged to a neighborhood watch program and coached a girls' soccer team. My mom had a part-time job and rushed around on weekends catching up on all the things she could not do during the

1

2

week. Every fall kids came to the door selling Girl Scout cookies or raising money to fight heart disease. Every spring and summer lawn-mowers hummed away on Saturday mornings, and everyone went to church on Sunday. Everything was familiar . . . almost predictable.

Neighborhood in England

Our neighborhood outside of London, however, was far different from what I was used to. The house we lived in was cozy but much smaller than the house we had left in the United States. It had a cute little lawn in front--which my brother and I still argued about cutting--and was exactly like the house next door. Near our house was a forest in which outlaws were said to have lived several hundred years ago. Most of the women in this area worked full time to supplement their husbands' income, and my mother was no exception. She got a job with my father's company and was very busy most of the time. There was no need for a neighborhood watch program because there was almost no crime. (The only crimes I ever heard about were a parked car that was side-swiped and a cat that had allegedly been stolen.) Although there was a soccer team, girls weren't allowed to play on it. (In England soccer is considered a boy's game, like tackle football.) Some things were the same, however. Just as they did at home, people cut their lawns on Saturday--with a push mower, not a power mower--and went to church every Sunday.

3

Second point: adjusting to a new school

The next thing I had to adjust to was attending a new school. In the United States I had attended a large suburban public high school. It had been built in the 1970s and held almost two thousand students. Sweatshirts and jeans were the most common articles of clothing for the students, and informality was a way of life. Several of my teachers even

4

encouraged students to call them by their first
names and to talk whenever they had something
to say. I was able to choose from a long list
of classes and take almost any course I wanted
to. Classes had a relaxed atmosphere, to say
the least. Some students had private conversations during class and paid little attention to
the teacher. The only time they focused on the
class was when the teacher called on them or
when they made a funny comment or a sarcastic
remark. We frequently had no homework, and we
didn't study much, except for a test. Although
most of us wanted to go on to college, none of
us seemed to take learning seriously. If anyone
did, he or she was usually teased by the rest
of us.

School in U.S.

School in England

The school I attended in England was   5
quite different from the one I attended in the
United States. It was small even by English
standards--only four hundred students--and the
building was over three hundred years old. All
the students wore uniforms--a black blazer, a
freshly ironed white shirt, and a pleated
skirt if you were female or black pants if you
were male. The teachers were the epitome of
formality. You called them "Sir" or "Ma'am"
and always showed respect. I never dreamed of
using their first names. The atmosphere in the
classroom was also quite formal. Students
worked quietly and spoke to the teachers only
when they were called on. When we were called
on, our teachers expected us to respond intel-
ligently. No one joked or made sarcastic
remarks. All of us were serious about our
work. I spent hours studying each night and
wrote a thousand-word essay each week. I
always had papers to hand in or a tutorial to
prepare for. Eventually, I got used to the
workload and was able to budget my time so I
could go out on the weekends.

Third point:
adjusting to
a new way
of life

My greatest challenge, however, was 6
adjusting to a new way of life. In the
United States my social life was predictable,
if not very interesting. Most of my friends
lived in my neighborhood within walking distance of my house. I spent hours talking on
Life in U.S.
the phone each night. Every Friday my friends
and I would hang out at the local mall or go
to the movies. On Saturday we would get
together at someone's house and watch TV or
rent a movie. Sometimes we would go to a party
or take a train into the city and go to Quincy
Market. During the summer my friends and I
would go to the beach or just lie around the
house complaining that we had nothing to do.
Although occasionally I would volunteer to
help a teacher, my friends and I did not consider it acceptable to be too involved with
school. Once, when I tried out for a school
play, they teased me for weeks.

Life in
England

In England my social life was quite dif- 7
ferent. Most of my friends lived almost an
hour away. There were no malls to hang out in,
we never went to the movies, and I spent little time on the phone. At first, my whole life
seemed upside down, but gradually I grew to
like it. I found new things to do. I got
interested in sports and other school activities. I became involved in community service,
joined the debating team, and was elected to
student council. Instead of hanging out at the
mall, my friends and I went to plays and con-
certs in London. During the summer, I went on
trips to Spain and to the Isle of Wight.
Perhaps the most interesting thing I did was
meet people from all over the world and find
out about their customs. And I don't ever
remember sitting around the house wondering
what to do.

Conclusion
In my one year in England, I accomplished   8
more than I had dreamed I would before I left
the United States. It was hard to give up
everything that was familiar to me, but for
the first time I understood what my mother had
meant when she said, "Sometimes, you need to
lose something to gain something." By the end
of the year, when we returned home, I knew
that year had changed me and that I would
never be the same person I had been before.

Points for Special Attention

STRUCTURE. Margaret's purpose in writing this essay was to high-light several specific differences between her two educational experiences. As a result she chose to write a point-by-point comparison. She introduces three points of contrast between her two subjects, and she is careful to present these three points in the same order for both subjects. With this method of organization she can be sure her readers will easily understand the specific differences between her life in the United States and her life in England. Had Margaret used a subject-by-subject comparison, her readers would have had to keep turning back to match points she made about the second subject to those she made about the first.

TOPIC SENTENCES. Without clear transitions, Margaret's readers would have a difficult time determining where each discussion of life in the United States ended and one about life in England began. Margaret makes sure that her readers can follow her discussion by distinguishing the two subjects of her comparison with topic sentences that make the contrast between them clear:

> The Boston suburb we had left was a known quantity, and perhaps for this reason, I liked it.
> Our neighborhood outside of London, however, was far different from what I was used to.

> In the United States I had attended a large suburban public high school. The school I attended in England was quite different from the one I attended in the United States.

> In the United States, my social life was predictable, if not very interesting. In England my social life was quite different.

TRANSITIONS. In addition to the clear and straightforward topic sentences, Margaret also includes transitional sentences that help readers move through the essay. Notice that by establishing a parallel structure, these sentences form a pattern that reinforces the essay's thesis:

> The first thing I had to adjust to was living in England.
> The next thing I had to adjust to was attending a new school.
> My greatest challenge, however, was adjusting to a new way of life.

Focus on Revision

Margaret's peer critics thought the biggest strength of her essay was its use of detail, which made the contrast between the United States and England clear. One student, however, thought that even more detail would improve her essay. For example, in paragraph 3 Margaret could describe her London suburb more precisely than she does. In paragraph 7 she could provide insight into how her English friends were different from her friends in the United States. Margaret agreed with these suggestions and also thought she could improve her conclusion. After rereading it, she decided it was little more than a loose collection of ideas that added little to the discussion. An anecdote that summed up her feelings about leaving England would be an improvement. So would a summary of how her experience changed her life once she returned to the United States.

The selections that follow illustrate both point-by-point and subject-by-subject comparison. Each uses transitional elements and topic sentences to enhance clarity and reinforce the comparisons and contrasts being made. Although the reading selections vary in their organization, length, and complexity, each is primarily concerned with the similarities and differences between its subjects.

▶▶▶▶▶▶▶▶▶▶▶▶▶▶▶▶▶▶

BRUCE CATTON

Bruce Catton (1899–1978) was born in Petoskey, Michigan, and attended Oberlin College. His studies were interrupted by his service in World War I, after which he worked as a journalist and then as a public official for various government agencies. Catton edited *American Heritage* magazine from 1954 until his death. His first book, *The War Lords of Washington* (1948), grew out of his service with the War Production Board during World War II. Catton was an authority on the Civil War, and among his many books on the subject are *Mr. Lincoln's Army* (1951); *Glory Road* (1952); *A Stillness at Appomattox* (1953), which won both a Pulitzer Prize and a National Book Award; *This Hallowed Ground* (1956); *Terrible Swift Sword* (1963); and *Gettysburg: The Final Fury* (1974). He also wrote a memoir, *Waiting for the Morning Train* (1972), in which he recalls listening as a young boy to the memories of Union Army veterans. A book based on tape recordings that Catton had made for educational purposes, *Reflections on the Civil War* (1981, edited by John Leekley), was published posthumously. "Grant and Lee: A Study in Contrasts" first appeared in a collection of historical essays entitled *The American Story*. This essay identifies not only differences but also important similarities between the two generals who headed the opposing armies of the Civil War.

Grant and Lee: A Study in Contrasts

When Ulysses S. Grant and Robert E. Lee met in the parlor of a modest house at Appomattox Court House, Virginia, on April 9, 1865, to work out the terms for the surrender of Lee's Army of Northern Virginia, a great chapter in American life came to a close, and a great new chapter began. 1

These men were bringing the Civil War to its virtual finish. To be sure, other armies had yet to surrender, and for a few days the fugitive Confederate government would struggle desperately and vainly, trying to find some way to go on living now that its chief support was gone. But in effect it was all over when Grant and Lee signed the papers. And the little room where they wrote out the terms was the scene of one of the poignant, dramatic contrasts in American history. 2

They were two strong men, these oddly different generals, and they represented the strengths of two conflicting currents that, through them, had come into final collision. 3

Back of Robert E. Lee was the notion that the old aristocratic concept might somehow survive and be dominant in American life. 4

Lee was tidewater Virginia, and in his background were family, culture, and tradition . . . the age of chivalry transplanted to a New World which was making its own legends and its own myths. He embodied a way of life that had come down through the age of knighthood and the English country squire. America was a land that was beginning all over again, dedicated to nothing much more complicated than the rather hazy belief that all men had equal rights and should have an equal chance in 5 the world. In such a land Lee stood for the feeling that it was somehow of advantage to human society to have pronounced inequality in the social structure. There should be a leisure class, backed by ownership of land; in turn, society itself should be keyed to the land as the chief source of wealth and influence. It would bring forth (according to this deal) a class of men with a strong sense of obligation to the community; men who lived not to gain advantage for themselves, but to meet the solemn obligations which had been laid on them by the very fact that they were privileged. From them the country would get its leadership; to them it could look for the higher values—of thought, of conduct, of personal deportment—to give it strength and virtue.

Lee embodied the noblest elements of this aristocratic ideal. Through him, the landed nobility justified itself. For four years, the Southern states had fought a desperate war to uphold the ideals for which Lee stood. In the end, it almost seemed as if the Confederacy fought for Lee; as if he himself was the Confederacy . . . the best thing that the way of life for which the Confederacy stood could ever have to offer. He had passed into legend before Appomattox. Thousands of tired, underfed, poorly clothed Confederate soldiers, long since past the simple enthusiasm of the early days of the struggle, somehow considered Lee the symbol of everything for which they had been willing to die. But they could not quite put this feeling into words. If the Lost Cause, sanctified by so much heroism and so many deaths, had a living justification, its justification was General Lee.   6

Grant, the son of a tanner on the Western frontier, was everything Lee was not. He had come up the hard way and embodied nothing in particular except the eternal toughness and sinewy fiber of the men who grew up beyond the mountains. He was one of a body of men who owed reverence and obeisance to no one, who were self-reliant to a fault, who cared hardly anything for the past but who had a sharp eye for the future.   7

These frontier men were the precise opposites of the tidewater aristocrats. Back of them, in the great surge that had taken people over the Alleghenies and into the opening Western country, there was a deep, implicit dissatisfaction with a past that had settled into grooves. They stood for democracy, not from any reasoned conclusion about the proper ordering of human society, but simply because they had grown up in the middle of democracy and knew how it worked. Their society might have privileges, but they would be privileges each man had won for himself. Forms and patterns meant nothing. No man was born to anything, except perhaps to a chance to show how far he could rise. Life was competition.   8

Yet along with this feeling had come a deep sense of belonging to a national community. The Westerner who developed a farm, opened a shop, or set up in business as a trader, could hope to prosper only as his own community prospered—and his community ran from the Atlantic to the Pacific and from Canada down to Mexico. If the land was settled, with towns and highways and accessible markets, he could better himself. He saw his fate in terms of the nation's own destiny. As its horizons ex-   9 panded, so did his. He had, in other words, an acute dollars-and-cents stake in the continued growth and development of his country.

And that, perhaps, is where the contrast between Grant and Lee becomes most striking. The Virginia aristocrat, inevitably, saw himself in relation to his own region. He lived in a static society which could endure almost anything except change. Instinctively, his first loyalty would go to the locality in which that society existed. He would fight to the limit of endurance to defend it, because in defending it he was defending everything that gave his own life its deepest meaning. 10

The Westerner, on the other hand, would fight with an equal tenacity for the broader concept of society. He fought so because everything he lived by was tied to growth, expansion, and a constantly widening horizon. What he lived by would survive or fall with the nation itself. He could not possibly stand by unmoved in the face of an attempt to destroy the Union. He would combat it with everything he had, because he could only see it as an effort to cut the ground out from under his feet. 11

So Grant and Lee were in complete contrast, representing two diametrically opposed elements in American life. Grant was the modern man emerging; beyond him, ready to come on the stage, was the great age of steel and machinery, of crowded cities and a restless burgeoning vitality. Lee might have ridden down from the old age of chivalry, lance in hand, silken banner fluttering over his head. Each man was the perfect champion of his cause, drawing both his strengths and his weaknesses from the people he led. 12

Yet it was not all contrast, after all. Different as they were—in background, in personality, in underlying aspiration—these two great soldiers had much in common. Under everything else, they were marvelous fighters. Furthermore, their fighting qualities were really very much alike. 13

Each man had, to begin with, the great virtue of utter tenacity and fidelity. Grant fought his way down the Mississippi Valley in spite of acute personal discouragement and profound military handicaps. Lee hung on in the trenches at Petersburg after hope itself had died. In each man there was an indomitable quality . . . the born fighter's refusal to give up as long as he can still remain on his feet and lift his two fists. 14

Daring and resourcefulness they had, too; the ability to think faster and move faster than the enemy. These were the qualities which gave Lee the dazzling campaigns of Second Manassas and Chancellorsville and won Vicksburg for Grant. 15

Lastly, and perhaps greatest of all, there was the ability, at the end, to turn quickly from war to peace once the fighting was over. Out of the way these two men behaved at Appomattox came the possibility of a peace of reconciliation. It was a possibility not wholly realized, in the years to come, but which did, in the end, help the two sections to become one nation again . . . after a war whose bitterness might have seemed to make such a reunion wholly impossible. No part of either man's life became him more than the part he played in this brief meeting in the McLean 16

house at Appomattox. Their behavior there put all succeeding generations of Americans in their debt. Two great Americans, Grant and Lee—
very different, yet under everything very much alike. Their encounter at
Appomattox was one of the great moments of American history.

• • •

COMPREHENSION

1. What took place at Appomattox Court House on April 9, 1865? Why did
   the meeting at Appomattox signal the closing of "a great chapter in
   American life" (1)?

2. How does Robert E. Lee represent aristocracy? How does Ulysses S.
   Grant represent Lee's opposite?

3. According to Catton, where is it that "the contrast between Grant and
   Lee becomes most striking" (10)?

4. What similarities does Catton see between the two men?

5. Why, according to Catton, are "succeeding generations of Americans"
   (16) in debt to Grant and Lee?

PURPOSE AND AUDIENCE

1. Catton's purpose in contrasting Grant and Lee is to make a general statement about the differences between two currents in American history.
   Summarize these differences. Do you think the differences still exist
   today? Explain.

2. Is Catton's purpose in comparing Grant and Lee the same as his purpose
   in contrasting them? That is, do their similarities also make a statement
   about U.S. history? Explain.

3. State the essay's thesis in your own words.

STYLE AND STRUCTURE

1. Does Catton use subject-by-subject or point-by-point comparison? Why
   do you think he chooses the structure he does?

2. In this essay, topic sentences are extremely helpful to the reader. Explain
   the functions of the following sentences: "Grant . . . was everything Lee
   was not" (7); "So Grant and Lee were in complete contrast . . . " (12);
   "Yet it was not all contrast, after all" (13); "Lastly, and perhaps greatest of
   all . . . " (16).

3. Catton uses transitions skillfully in his essay. Identify the transitional
   words or expressions that link each paragraph to the preceding one.

4. Why do you suppose Catton provides the background for the meeting
   at Appomattox but presents no information about the dramatic meeting
   itself?

VOCABULARY PROJECTS

1. Define each of the following words as it is used in this selection.

poignant (2)	obeisance (7)	tenacity (14)
chivalry (5)	implicit (8)	fidelity (14)
deportment (5)	inevitably (10)	indomitable (14)
sanctified (6)	diametrically (12)	reconciliation (16)
embodied (7)	burgeoning (12)	
sinewy (7)	aspiration (13)	

2. Look up **synonyms** for each of the following words and determine which synonyms would and would not be as effective as the word used in this essay. Explain your choices.

deportment (5)	obeisance (7)	indomitable (14)
sanctified (6)	diametrically (12)	

JOURNAL ENTRY

Compare your attitudes about the United States to those held by Grant and Lee. With which man do you agree?

WRITING WORKSHOP

1. Write a "study in contrasts" about two people you know well—two teachers, your parents, two relatives, two friends—or about two fictional characters with whom you are very familiar. Be sure to include a thesis statement.

2. Write a dialogue between two people you know that reveals their contrasting attitudes toward school, work, or any other subject.

3. Write an essay about two individuals from a period of American history other than the Civil War to make the same points Catton makes. Do some research if necessary.

COMBINING THE PATTERNS

In several places, Catton uses **exemplification** to structure a paragraph. For instance, in paragraph 7 he uses examples to support the topic sentence "Grant, the son of a tanner on the Western frontier, was everything Lee was not." Identify three paragraphs that use examples to support the topic sentence, and bracket the examples. In what ways do these examples in these paragraphs reinforce the similarities and differences between Grant and Lee?

THEMATIC CONNECTIONS

- "Aria: A Memoir of a Bilingual Childhood" (page 357)
- "The Declaration of Independence" (page 507)
- "Letter from Birmingham Jail" (page 513)

▓▓▓▓▓▓▓▓▓▓▓▓▓▓▓▓

EDWARD MENDELSON

Edward Mendelson was born in 1946 in New York City. He graduated from the University of Rochester and received a Ph.D. in English literature from Johns Hopkins University. He began his teaching career at Yale University and has been on the faculty of Columbia University since 1979. Literary executor of the estate of the English poet W. H. Auden, Mendelson is the author of *The English Auden* (1979) and *Early Auden* (1981) as well as the editor of *The Complete Works of W. H. Auden* (1988–   ). He also edited the anthologies *Homer to Brecht* (1977) and *Pynchon: A Collection of Critical Essays* (1978). Mendelson writes extensively about computer technology and is a contributing editor at *PC Magazine*. In the following essay, which originally appeared in the *New York Times Book Review* in 1996, Mendelson compares the hyperlinks of the World Wide Web to the cross-references created for medieval translations of the Bible.

The Word and the Web

When the Benedictine monks at the Monastery of Christ in the Desert, in New Mexico, created a Web site on the Internet, they claimed to be reviving a tradition that began when monastic scribes created the first illuminated manuscripts. One of the monks told a reporter for the *New York Times* that their work "goes back to the ancient tradition of the scribes, taking information and making it beautiful, into art." But the relation between modern Web sites and medieval scriptoria, or writing rooms, is even closer than these monks may have guessed. The technology that connects all the millions of pages on the World Wide Web derives ultimately from techniques invented by the scribes and scholars who copied out the Bible more than a thousand years ago.

The pages of the Web are connected by a system of hyperlinks—words, phrases, or pictures that, when you click on one with a mouse, will summon up another page to your computer screen, perhaps a page on a computer thousands of miles away. Medieval manuscripts of the Bible were the first books to be interconnected by a system of cross-references—marginal notes that directed a reader from one biblical passage to another, perhaps to a passage written at a distance of hundreds of years from the first. The marginal references to the Bible and the hyperlinks of the World Wide Web may be the only two systems ever invented that give concrete expression to the idea that everything in the world holds together, that every event, every fact, every datum is connected to every other. Where the two systems differ drastically is in what their connections mean.

A tenth-century monk reading a manuscript of the Book of Exodus might find a line under the verse "And the Lord went before them by day in a pillar of a cloud, to lead them the way." A note in the margin would refer him to a verse in another manuscript that included Paul's First Letter to the Corinthians: "Our fathers were under the cloud, and all passed through the sea; and were all baptized unto Moses in the cloud and in the sea." This gives a new meaning to the verse from Exodus, but also gives new meaning to verses in the Gospels about baptism, verses that the monk could find by tracing further cross-references in the margin of Paul's letters.

The system of hyperlinks connecting the pages of the World Wide Web suggests a world where connections are everywhere but are mostly meaningless, transient, fragile, and unstable. A would-be monk in the twentieth century who visits the Web page of the Monastery of Christ in the Desert will find the exhortation "Don't miss our Thanks page." A few clicks, and he arrives at an image by a local artist, which will be replaced on screen automatically and randomly in a few seconds by another, and then another. You can create a link between your own Web page—the "home page" that acts as a table of contents for all the pages linked to it—and someone else's home page, but you have no assurance that the other person's page will display the same content from one day to the next. 4

In a world without tangible bodies or enduring memories, no one can keep promises. No one can even remember why they might be worth keeping. In the Bible, the connections between early and later books signify covenants that a personal God has already kept and promises that will be kept in the future. The connections between pages on the World Wide Web exist independently of space or time. The World Wide Web is touted by its evangelists as a force that will transform society in ways that no political revolution could ever accomplish. Until now the Web's main social achievement has been to provide a cure for spare time. 5

Another claim for the Web is that it is uniquely nonhierarchical, that it has no beginning and no end, no top or bottom, that it can be entered anywhere and traveled in any direction. In a strictly technical sense, all this is true, but in all practical and social senses, the Web dutifully reproduces all the hierarchies and inequalities of the world outside. Thousands of links point toward Web sites backed by fame, money, and power. Far fewer scattered links point toward sites posted by the obscure and impoverished. A thousand students can insert in their home pages a link to the page dedicated to a rock group like Sonic Youth, but Sonic Youth's home page contains no link to any of the students' pages. 6

Biblical cross-references, unlike most of the links on the World Wide Web, always point in both directions. A link from the Old Testament to the New is mirrored by a link from the New to the Old. Some parts of the Bible are more densely cross-referenced than others—the margins of the dietary laws in Leviticus are mostly blank—but the annotators of the Bible believed that every word was equally inspired, that it was their own fault if they had not yet found all the connections that the Bible contained. Some passages of the Bible were more difficult than others, but all were available to be read and studied. The Web, on the other hand, has secret 7 pages accessible only to those who know a password, and others accessible only to those willing to pay.

The vision of coherence and connectedness that gave rise to biblical cross-references can plausibly be credited with one of the greatest social transformations of all time: the nineteenth-century abolition of slavery. The movement to ban first the slave trade and then slavery itself in the British Empire came from Quakers and other religious-minded men and women who understood the link between Exodus and Corinthians to mean that they were morally obliged to repeat the work of Moses as long as any individual people were enslaved, that every individual—not only one or another group of people—had been promised liberation by God. The slaves themselves, in their campaign for freedom, found in this connection both a promise of deliverance and an unanswerable rebuke to the slaveholders, who so manifestly failed to practice the religion they professed. To accept slavery was to sign up with Pharaoh. To fight against it was to obey the same imperatives that Moses obeyed.   8

The annotators who marked biblical cross-references in medieval manuscripts and early printed editions were more interested in the text of the Bible than in their marginal commentary on it. No scholar has studied the history of the references. No one seems to have given much thought to them as a form or a medium. The one notably eccentric exception was the Rev. C. I. Scofield, who announced on the title page of Scofield Reference Bible, first published in 1909, that he had included "a new system of connected topical references to all the greater themes of Scripture," and then devoted much of his introduction to the merits of his new system.   9

The World Wide Web, from the start, has been obsessed with the visual display and invisible technology of its hyperlinks, and the heaviest traffic on the Web seems to consist of computer users in search of new versions of their favorite navigation software. As Kierkegaard* wrote in 1839: "It is characteristic of the present time always to be conscious of the medium. It is almost bound to end in madness, like a man who whenever he looked at the sun and the stars was conscious of the world going round."   10

But the greatest difference between the cross-references in the Bible and the links on the World Wide Web is the difference between words written on parchment or paper in books that were meant to last forever and words written on the transient phosphorescence of a computer screen, where they will soon be effaced by others. This may or may not be the same contrast, written down 1,900 years ago, between the wise man who built his house upon rock and the foolish man who built his house upon sand.   11

---

*EDS. NOTE—Søren Kierkegaard (1813–1855), a Danish philosopher and religious thinker who had a major influence on twentieth-century philosophy and Protestant theology.

• • •

COMPREHENSION

1. What are hyperlinks? How do they connect pages of the World Wide Web?

2. In what ways are hyperlinks and biblical cross-references alike? How are they different?

3. What is Mendelson's justification for saying in paragraph 8 that biblical cross-references can be given credit for abolishing slavery?

4. What does Mendelson mean when he says that the Web is "obsessed with the visual display and invisible technology of its hyperlinks" (10)?

5. According to Mendelson, what is the greatest difference between biblical cross-references and Web hyperlinks?

PURPOSE AND AUDIENCE

1. Mendelson is a professor of English at Columbia University. Is he writing this essay for other professors or for a more general audience? On what do you base your conclusions?

2. What is the essay's thesis? Why do you think Mendelson places it at the beginning of the essay?

3. What general knowledge about computers and the Web does Mendelson have? How can you tell? What preconceived ideas about computers and the Web does he seem to have? Do you think he expects his readers to share his views?

4. What purpose do you think Mendelson has for writing this essay? Is he trying to change readers' minds, or is he simply informing them?

STYLE AND STRUCTURE

1. Is this a subject-by-subject or a point-by-point comparison? Why do you think Mendelson chose this strategy?

2. What basis of comparison exists between biblical cross-references and Web hyperlinks? Is the basis of comparison significant enough to justify a comparison-and-contrast essay?

3. Does Mendelson emphasize similarities, differences, or both? Explain.

4. Do you think Mendelson discusses too many points? Should he have concentrated on fewer points and discussed them in more depth?

5. What point does Mendelson choose to emphasize in his conclusion? Why do you think he chooses this point? What other strategy could he use for his conclusion?

VOCABULARY PROJECTS

1. Define each of the following words as it is used in this selection.

   monastic (1)
   scribes (1)
   illuminated (1)
   datum (2)
   exhortation (4)
   touted (5)
   evangelists (5)

   hierarchies (6)
   annotators (7)
   eccentric (9)
   transient (11)
   phosphorescence (11)
   effaced (11)

2. What adjectives does Mendelson use when he discusses the Bible and the Web. How do these adjectives differ? If you can, explain the reasons for the differences.

JOURNAL ENTRY

Should Mendelson have spent more time discussing the social context of the Web? In other words, what are the consequences of certain groups having access to the Web and other groups not having access?

WRITING WORKSHOP

1. Write an essay in which you compare your opinion of the Web with Mendelson's. Be specific, and use examples from your own experience to support your points.

2. According to Mendelson, the World Wide Web is "obsessed with the visual display . . . of its hyperlinks" (10). If you have access to the Internet, call up two Web pages. List the similarities and differences between them. Then, write an essay comparing the ways in which the two Web pages present information—for example, their use of color, graphics, and layout. Make sure your thesis statement indicates how the features you discuss affect your response to the pages.

3. On a piece of paper, sketch your own personal Web page. Insert all the information you want to present on your Web page, including the hyperlinks that would connect your Web page to other Web pages. Then, write an essay in which you discuss the advantages or disadvantages of presenting yourself by means of words, graphics, and hyperlinks as opposed to presenting yourself in a letter or a résumé.

COMBINING THE PATTERNS

Paragraph 8 of the essay uses a *cause-and-effect* pattern of organization. What is the main point of this discussion? How does it help Mendelson support his thesis? Why do you think he uses a cause-and-effect paragraph at this particular place in his essay?

THEMATIC CONNECTIONS

- "The Human Cost of an Illiterate Society" (page 192)
- "Television: The Plug-In Drug" (page 274)

![decorative banner]

BHARATI MUKHERJEE

Born in 1940 in Calcutta, India, novelist Bharati Mukherjee attended the University of Calcutta before immigrating to the United States in 1961. After receiving an M.F.A. from the University of Iowa, she moved with her husband to Canada, where she taught at McGill University. Now a naturalized U.S. citizen, she teaches at Skidmore College. Mukherjee's novels include *Tiger's Daughter* (1972), *Wife* (1975), *Jasmine* (1989), and *The Holder of the World* (1993); her story collections are *Darkness* (1975) and *The Middleman and Other Stories* (1988), for which she won the National Book Critics Award. Her fiction, often based on her own experiences, explores the tensions between the traditional role of women in Indian society and their very different role in the United States as well as the racism often faced by immigrants from India. Of her adopted country she has said, "I've lived everywhere, [and] I'm truly touched and moved by the idea of America. It *includes* you and is curious about other people." This essay, originally published on the *New York Times* Op-Ed page in 1996, was written following proposals to enact legislation to deny government benefits to resident aliens. In it Mukherjee considers the differences between herself, who chose to become a U.S. citizen, and her sister, who remains a resident alien.

Two Ways to Belong in America

This is a tale of two sisters from Calcutta, Mira and Bharati, who have lived in the United States for some 35 years, but who find themselves on different sides in the current debate over the status of immigrants. I am an American citizen and she is not. I am moved that thousands of long-term residents are finally taking the oath of citizenship. She is not.

Mira arrived in Detroit in 1960 to study child psychology and pre-school education. I followed her a year later to study creative writing at the University of Iowa. When we left India, we were almost identical in appearance and attitude. We dressed alike, in saris; we expressed identical views on politics, social issues, love, and marriage in the same Calcutta convent-school accent. We would endure our two years in America, secure our degrees, then return to India to marry the grooms of our father's choosing.

Instead, Mira married an Indian student in 1962 who was getting his business administration degree at Wayne State University. They soon acquired the labor certifications necessary for the green card of hassle-free residence and employment.

Mira still lives in Detroit, works in the Southfield, Mich., school system, and has become nationally recognized for her contributions in the fields of pre-school education and parent-teacher relationships. After 36 years as a legal immigrant in this country, she clings passionately to her Indian citizenship and hopes to go home to India when she retires.

In Iowa City in 1963, I married a fellow student, an American of   5
Canadian parentage. Because of the accident of his North Dakota birth, I
bypassed labor-certification requirements and the race-related "quota"
system that favored the applicant's country of origin over his or her
merit. I was prepared for (and even welcomed) the emotional strain that
came with marrying outside my ethnic community. In 33 years of marriage, we have lived in every part of North America. By choosing a husband who was not my father's selection, I was opting for fluidity,
self-invention, blue jeans and T-shirts, and renouncing 3,000 years (at
least) of case-observant, "pure culture" marriage in the Mukherjee family.
My books have often been read as unapologetic (and in some quarters
overenthusiastic) texts for cultural and psychological "mongrelization."
It's a word I celebrate.

Mira and I have stayed sisterly close by phone. In our regular Sunday   6
morning conversations, we are unguardedly affectionate. I am her only
blood relative on this continent. We expect to see each other through the
looming crises of aging and ill heath without being asked. Long before
Vice President Gore's "Citizenship U.S.A." drive, we'd had our polite arguments over the ethics of retaining an overseas citizenship while expect-
ing the permanent protection and economic benefits that come with
living and working in America.

Like well-raised sisters, we never said what was really on our minds,   7
but we probably pitied one another. She, for the lack of structure in my
life, the erasure of Indianness, the absence of an unvarying daily core. I,
for the narrowness of her perspective, her uninvolvement with the
mythic depths or the superficial pop culture of this society. But, now, with
the scapegoatings of "aliens" (documented or illegal) on the increase, and
the targeting of long-term legal immigrants like Mira for new scrutiny
and new self-consciousness, she and I find ourselves unable to maintain
the same polite discretion. We were always unacknowledged adversaries,
and we are now, more than ever, sisters.

"I feel used," Mira raged on the phone the other night. "I feel manip-   8
ulated and discarded. This is such an unfair way to treat a person who
was invited to stay and work here because of her talent. My employer
went to the I.N.S. and petitioned for the labor certification. For over 30
years, I've invested my creativity and professional skills into the improvement of *this* country's pre-school system. I've obeyed all the rules,
I've paid my taxes, I love my work, I love my students, I love the friends
I've made. How dare America now change its rules in midstream? If
America wants to make new rules curtailing benefits of legal immigrants,
they should apply only to immigrants who arrive after those rules are already in place."

To my ears, it sounded like the description of a long-enduring, com-   9
fortable yet loveless marriage, without risk or recklessness. Have we the
right to demand, and to expect, that we be loved? (That, to me, is the sub-
text of the arguments by immigration advocates.) My sister is an expatri-

ate, professionally generous and creative, socially courteous and gracious, and that's as far as her Americanization can go. She is here to maintain an identity, not to transform it.

I asked her if she would follow the example of others who have decided to become citizens because of the anti-immigration bills in Congress. And here, she surprised me. "If America wants to play the manipulative game, I'll play it, too," she snapped. "I'll become a U.S. citizen for now, then change back to India when I'm ready to go home. I feel some kind of irrational attachment to India that I don't to America. Until all this hysteria against legal immigrants, I was totally happy. Having my green card meant I could visit any place in the world I wanted to and then come back to a job that's satisfying and that I do very well." 10

In one family, from two sisters alike as peas in a pod, there could not be a wider divergence of immigrant experience. America spoke to me—I married it—I embraced the demotion from expatriate aristocrat to immigrant nobody, surrendering those thousands of years of "pure culture," the saris, the delightfully accented English. She retained them all. Which of us is the freak? 11

Mira's voice, I realize, is the voice not just of the immigrant South Asian community but of an immigrant community of the millions who have stayed rooted in one job, one city, one house, one ancestral culture, one cuisine, for the entirety of their productive years. She speaks for greater numbers than I possibly can. Only the fluency of her English and the anger, rather than fear, born of confidence from her education, differentiate her from the seamstresses, the domestics, the technicians, the shop owners, the millions of hard-working but effectively silenced documented immigrants as well as their less fortunate "illegal" brothers and sisters. 12

Nearly 20 years ago, when I was living in my husband's ancestral homeland of Canada, I was always well-employed but never allowed to feel part of the local Quebec or larger Canadian society. Then, through a Green Paper that invited a national referendum on the unwanted side effects of "nontraditional" immigration, the Government officially turned against its immigrant communities, particularly those from South Asia. 13

I felt then the same sense of betrayal that Mira feels now. I will never forget the pain of that sudden turning, and the casual racist outbursts the Green Paper elicited. That sense of betrayal had its desired effect and drove me, and thousands like me, from the country. 14

Mira and I differ, however, in the ways in which we hope to interact with the country that we have chosen to live in. She is happier to live in America as expatriate Indian than as an immigrant American. I need to feel like a part of the community I have adopted (as I tried to feel in Canada as well). I need to put roots down, to vote and make the difference that I can. The price that the immigrant willingly pays, and that the exile avoids, is the trauma of self-transformation. 15

•   •   •

COMPREHENSION

1. At first, how long did Mukherjee and her sister intend to stay in America? Why did they change their plans?

2. What does Mukherjee mean when she says she welcomed the "emotional strain" of "marrying outside [her] ethnic community" (5)?

3. In what ways is Mukherjee different from her sister? What kind of relationship do they have?

4. Why does Mukherjee's sister feel used? Why does she think America has changed "its rules in midstream" (8)?

5. According to Mukherjee, how is her sister like all immigrants who "have stayed rooted in one job, one city, one house, one ancestral culture, one cuisine, for the entirety of their productive years" (12)?

PURPOSE AND AUDIENCE

1. What is Mukherjee's thesis? At what point does she state it?

2. At whom is Mukherjee is aiming her remarks? Immigrants like herself? Immigrants like her sister? General readers? Explain.

3. What is Mukherjee's purpose? Is she trying to inform? To move readers to action? To accomplish something else? Explain.

STYLE AND STRUCTURE

1. What basis of comparison exists between Mukherjee and her sister? Where in the essay does Mukherjee establish this basis of comparison?

2. Is this essay a point-by-point or a subject-by-subject comparison? Why do you think Mukherjee chose the option she did?

3. What points does Mukherjee discuss for each subject? Should she have discussed any other points?

4. What transitional words and phrases does Mukherjee use to signal shifts from one point to another?

5. How effective is Mukherjee's conclusion? Does it summarize the major points of the essay? Would another strategy be more effective? Explain.

VOCABULARY PROJECTS

1. Define each of the following words as it is used in this selection.

certifications (3)	superficial (7)
mongrelization (5)	scrutiny (7)
perspective (7)	discretion (7)
mythic (7)	curtailing (8)

divergence (11)   saris (11)
expatriate (11)   trauma (15)

2. What, according to Mukherjee, is the difference between an *immigrant* and an *exile* (15)? What are the connotations of these two words? Do you think the distinction Mukherjee makes is valid?

JOURNAL ENTRY

Do you think Mukherjee respects her sister's decision? From your perspective, which sister has made the right decision?

COMBINING THE PATTERNS

Do you think Mukherjee should have used **cause and effect** to structure a section explaining why she and her sister are so different? Explain what such a section would add to or take away from the essay.

WRITING WORKSHOP

1. Assume that the sister, Mira, has just read Mukherjee's essay and wants to respond to it. Write a letter from Mira in which you compare her position about assimilation to that of Mukherjee. Make sure you explain Mira's position and address Mukherjee's points about assimilation.

2. Have you ever moved from one town or city to another? Write an essay in which you compare the two places. Your thesis statement should indicate whether you are emphasizing similarities or differences and convey your opinion of the new area to which you moved. (If you have never moved, write an essay comparing two places you are familiar with—college and your high school, for example.)

3. Assume you had to move to another country. Where would you move? Would you, like Mukherjee, assimilate into your new culture, or, like her sister, retain your own cultural values? Write an essay in which you compare life in your new country to life in the United States. Make sure your thesis reflects your attitude toward assimilation. If you have already moved from another country, compare your life in the United States with your life in your country of origin.

THEMATIC CONNECTIONS

- "Only Daughter" (page 70)
- "The Way to Rainy Mountain" (page 136)
- "The Big Move" (page 324)
- "Aria: A Memoir of a Bilingual Childhood" (page 357)
- "The Untouchable" (page 448)
- "Five Myths about Immigration" (page 541)

CHRISTOPHER B. DALY

Born in Boston, Christopher B. Daly (1954–   ) received a B.A. from Harvard and an M.A. in history from the University of North Carolina at Chapel Hill. He is the coauthor of *Like a Family* (1987), a prize-winning social history of the industrialization of the South. A veteran journalist, Daly spent ten years working at the Associated Press and another seven years covering New England for the *Washington Post.* He has taught journalism and writing at Harvard, Brandeis, and Boston University and currently divides his time between teaching and freelance writing. His work has appeared in a variety of magazines and journals, including the *Atlantic Monthly,* the *Columbia Journalism Review,* and *New England Monthly.* In the following essay, which originally appeared in the *Atlantic* in 1995, Daly remembers the boyhood pleasure of ice skating on a local pond—"once the heart of winter in New England"—and contrasts his memories with his view of the present.

How the Lawyers Stole Winter

When I was a boy, my friends and I would come home from school each day, change our clothes (because we were not allowed to wear "play clothes" to school), and go outside until dinnertime. In the early 1960s in Medford, a city on the outskirts of Boston, that was pretty much what everybody did. Sometimes there might be flute lessons, or an organized Little League game, but usually not. Usually we kids went out and played. 1

In winter, on our way home from the Gleason School, we would go past Brooks Pond to check the ice. By throwing heavy stones on it, hammering it with downed branches, and, finally, jumping on it, we could figure out if the ice was ready for skating. If it was, we would hurry home to grab our skates, our sticks, and whatever other gear we had, and then return to play hockey for the rest of the day. When the streetlights came on, we knew it was time to jam our cold, stiff feet back into our green rubber snow boots and get home for dinner. 2

I had these memories in mind recently when I moved, with my wife and two young boys, into a house near a lake even closer to Boston, in the city of Newton. As soon as Crystal Lake froze over, I grabbed my skates and headed out. I was not the first one there, though: the lawyers had beaten me to the lake. They had warned the town recreation department to put it off limits. So I found a sign that said DANGER, THIN ICE. NO SKATING. 3

Knowing a thing or two about words myself, I put my own gloss on the sign. I took it to mean *When the ice is thin, there is danger and there should be no skating.* Fair enough, I thought, but I knew that the obverse was also true: *When the ice is thick, it is safe and there should be skating.* Finding the ice plenty thick, I laced up my skates and glided out onto the miraculous glassy surface of the frozen lake. My wife, a native of Manhattan, would not let me take our two boys with me. But for as long as I could, I enjoyed 4 the free, open-air delight of skating as it should be. After a few days others joined me, and we became an outlaw band of skaters.

What we were doing was once the heart of winter in New England— and a lot of other places, too. It was clean, free exercise that needed no StairMasters, no health clubs, no appointments, and hardly any gear. Sadly, it is in danger of passing away. Nowadays it seems that every city and town and almost all property holders are so worried about liability and lawsuits that they simply throw up a sign or a fence and declare that henceforth there shall be no skating, and that's the end of it.

As a result, kids today live in a world of leagues, rinks, rules, uni- 6 forms, adults, and rides—rides here, rides there, rides everywhere. It is not clear that they are better off; in some ways they are clearly *not* better off.

When I was a boy skating on Brooks Pond, there were no grown-ups 7 around. Once or twice a year, on a weekend day or a holiday, some parents might come by with a thermos of hot cocoa. Maybe they would build a fire (which we were forbidden to do), and we would gather round.

But for the most part the pond was the domain of children. In the ab- 8 sence of adults, we made and enforced our own rules. We had hardly any gear—just some borrowed hockey gloves, some hand-me-down skates, maybe an elbow pad or two—so we played a clean form of hockey, with no high-sticking, no punching, and almost no checking. A single fight could ruin the whole afternoon. Indeed, as I remember it, thirty years later, it was the purest form of hockey I ever saw—until I got to see the Russian national team play the game.

But before we could play, we had to check the ice. We became serious 9 junior meteorologists, true connoisseurs of cold. We learned that the best weather for pond skating is plain, clear cold, with starry nights and no snow. (Snow not only mucks up the skating surface but also insulates the ice from the colder air above.) And we learned that moving water, even the gently flowing Mystic River, is a lot less likely to freeze than standing water. So we skated only on the pond. We learned all the weird whooping and cracking sounds that ice makes as it expands and contracts, and thus when to leave the ice.

Do kids learn these things today? I don't know. How would they? We 10 don't let them. Instead we post signs. Ruled by lawyers, cities and towns everywhere try to eliminate their legal liability. But try as they might, they cannot eliminate the underlying risk. Liability is a social construct; risk is a natural fact. When it is cold enough, ponds freeze. No sign or fence or ordinance can change that.

In fact, by focusing on liability and not teaching our kids how to take 11 risks, we are making their world more dangerous. When we were children, we had to learn to evaluate risks and handle them on our own. We had to learn, quite literally, to test the waters. As a result, we grew up to be savvier about ice and ponds than any kid could be who has skated only under adult supervision on a rink.

When I was a boy, despite the risks we took on the ice no one I knew   12
ever drowned. The only people I heard about who drowned were graduate students at Harvard or MIT who came from the tropics and were living through their first winters. No knowing (after all, how could they?)
about ice on moving water, they would innocently venture out onto the
half-frozen Charles River, fall through, and die. They were literally out of
their element.

Are we raising a generation of children who will be out of their ele-   13
ment? And if so, what can we do about it? We cannot just roll back the
calendar. I cannot tell my six-year-old to head down to the lake by himself to play all afternoon—if for no other reason than that he would not
find twenty or thirty other kids there, full of the collective wisdom about
cold and ice that they had inherited, along with hockey equipment, from
their older brothers and sisters. Somewhere along the line that link got
broken.

The whole setting of childhood has changed. We cannot change it   14
again overnight. I cannot send my children out by themselves yet, but
at least some of the time I can go out there with them. Maybe that is a
start.

As for us, last winter was a very unusual one. We had ferocious cold   15
(near-zero temperatures on many nights) and tremendous snows (about a
hundred inches in all). Eventually a strange thing happened. The town
gave in—sort of. Sometime in January the recreation department
"opened" a section of the lake, and even dispatched a snowplow truck to
clear a good-sized patch of ice. The boys and I skated during the rest of
winter. Ever vigilant, the town officials kept the THIN ICE signs up, even
though their own truck could safely drive on the frozen surface. And they
brought in "lifeguards" and all sorts of rules about the hours during
which we could skate and where we had to stay.

But at least we were able to skate in the open air, on real ice.   16
And it was still free.   17

• • •

COMPREHENSION

1. What did Daly and his friends do when they came home from school in
   the 1960s?

2. According to Daly, why is winter "in danger of passing away" (5)?

3. During the 1960s, how did children make sure the ice was safe to skate
   on? Why don't children learn these things today?

4. According to Daly, in what ways has "the whole setting of childhood"
   changed? What does he propose to do about this situation?

5. What does Daly mean when he says that "by focusing on liability and not
   teaching our kids to take risks, we are making their world more dangerous" (11)?

PURPOSE AND AUDIENCE

1. At what point does Daly state his thesis? Why does he wait so long to state it? Should he have stated it sooner?

2. What is Daly's purpose in writing his essay? What does he hope to accomplish?

3. Does Daly think his readers will be sympathetic, neutral, or hostile to his ideas? How can you tell?

4. How would you expect an audience of Daly's contemporaries to react to his essay? Would an audience of Daly's children and their friends have a different reaction?

5. What is Daly's purpose in mentioning StairMasters and health clubs in paragraph 5? How might he expect his audience of fairly affluent, well-educated adults to react?

STYLE AND STRUCTURE

1. How does the introduction of this essay prepare readers for the discussion that follows?

2. Does Daly use a subject-by-subject or a point-by-point method of comparison, or a combination of the two? What is the advantage of the strategy he uses?

3. Daly refers to THIN ICE signs at the beginning and end of his essay. Why does he refer to the signs at these key points in his essay? Do the words *thin ice* suggest any meaning beyond the literal one? Explain.

4. What transitional words and phrases indicate that Daly is shifting from one subject to another? From one point to another? Does the essay need more transitions? If so, where?

5. Daly's essay has a one-sentence conclusion. Should it be expanded? If so, how? If not, why not?

VOCABULARY PROJECTS

1. Define each of the following words as it is used in this selection.

   gloss (4)   domain (8)
   liability (5)   connoisseurs (9)

2. Underline all the uses of the words *risk* and *liability* in Daly's essay. Do these words have the same meaning each time he uses them?

JOURNAL ENTRY

Do you agree with Daly's assertion that because of the threat of lawsuits and liability, children are being raised not to take risks? Are there other explanations for the rules and uniforms Daly observes?

WRITING WORKSHOP

1. Write an essay comparing how you performed a particular activity when you were a child with how you perform the same activity now. Make sure you focus on the differences and, like Daly, draw some conclusion about the present.

2. Write a letter to Daly in which you compare his memories of winter with your own. In your essay, address Daly's contention that children today are brought up not to take risks.

3. Write an essay in which you compare your own willingness to take risks with that of one of your friends or family members.

COMBINING THE PATTERNS

Daly ends his essay with a **narrative** about a particularly cold winter. Does the narrative contain enough detail? Would more detail make this paragraph more effective? Explain.

THEMATIC CONNECTIONS

- "Reading the River" (page 126)
- "The Way to Rainy Mountain" (page 136)
- "Once More to the Lake" (page 142)
- "Television: The Plug-In Drug" (page 274)
- "It's Just Too Late" (page 294)

DEBORAH TANNEN

Deborah Tannen was born in Brooklyn, New York, in 1945. She graduated from the State University of New York at Binghamton, was awarded a doctorate from the University of California at Berkeley, and currently teaches at Georgetown University. Tannen has written and edited several scholarly books on the problems of communication across cultural, class, ethnic, and sexual divides. She has also presented her research to the general public in newspapers and magazines, including the *New York Times Magazine* and *Newsweek*; in her best-selling books *That's Not What I Meant! How Conversational Style Makes or Breaks Relationships* (1986), *You Just Don't Understand: Women and Men in Conversation* (1990), and *Talking from 9 to 5* (1994); and through appearances on television news and talk shows. In 1992, Tannen conducted a seminar on gender dynamics for members of the Senate in the wake of the hearings into Anita Hill's charges of sexual harassment against Supreme Court nominee Clarence Thomas. "Sex, Lies, and Conversation," which appeared in the *Washington Post* in 1990, presents Tannen's views on conversational differences between women and men.

Sex, Lies, and Conversation

I was addressing a small gathering in a suburban Virginia living room—a women's group that had invited men to join them. Throughout the evening, one man had been particularly talkative, frequently offering ideas and anecdotes, while his wife sat silently beside him on the couch. Toward the end of the evening, I commented that women frequently complain that their husbands don't talk to them. This man quickly concurred. He gestured toward his wife and said, "She's the talker in our family." The room burst into laughter; the man looked puzzled and hurt. "It's true," he explained. "When I come home from work I have nothing to say. If she didn't keep the conversation going, we'd spend the whole evening in silence."

This episode crystallizes the irony that although American men tend to talk more than women in public situations, they often talk less at home. And this pattern is wreaking havoc with marriage.

The pattern was observed by political scientist Andrew Hacker in the late '70s. Sociologist Catherine Kohler Riessman reports in her new book *Divorce Talk* that most of the women she interviewed—but only a few of the men—gave lack of communication as the reason for their divorces. Given the current divorce rate of nearly 50 percent, that amounts to millions of cases in the United States every year—a virtual epidemic of failed conversation.

In my own research, complaints from women about their husbands most often focused not on tangible inequities such as having given up the chance for a career to accompany a husband to his, or doing far more than their share of daily life-support work like cleaning, cooking, social arrangements, and errands. Instead, they focused on communication: "He doesn't listen to me," "He doesn't talk to me." I found, as Hacker observed years before, that most wives want their husbands to be, first and foremost, conversational partners, but few husbands share this expectation of their wives.

In short, the image that best represents the current crisis is the stereo-   5
typical cartoon scene of a man sitting at the breakfast table with a newspaper held up in front of his face, while a woman glares at the back of it, wanting to talk.

LINGUISTIC BATTLE OF THE SEXES

How can women and men have such different impressions of com-   6
munication in marriage? Why the widespread imbalance in their interests and expectations?

In the April issue of *American Psychologist,* Stanford University's   7
Eleanor Maccoby reports the results of her own and others' research showing that children's development is most influenced by the social structure of peer interactions. Boys and girls tend to play with children of their own gender, and their sex-separate groups have different organizational structures and interactive norms.

I believe these systematic differences in childhood socialization make   8
talk between women and men like cross-cultural communication, heir to all the attraction and pitfalls of that enticing but difficult enterprise. My research on men's and women's conversations uncovered patterns similar to those described for children's groups.

For women, as for girls, intimacy is the fabric of relationships, and talk   9
is the thread from which it is woven. Little girls create and maintain friendships by exchanging secrets; similarly, women regard conversation as the cornerstone of friendship. So a woman expects her husband to be a new and improved version of a best friend. What is important is not the individual subjects that are discussed but the sense of closeness, of a life shared, that emerges when people tell their thoughts, feelings, and impressions.

Bonds between boys can be as intense as girls', but they are based less   10
on talking, more on doing things together. Since they don't assume talk is the cement that binds a relationship, men don't know what kind of talk women want, and they don't miss it when it isn't there.

Boys' groups are larger, more inclusive, and more hierarchical, so boys   11
must struggle to avoid the subordinate position in the group. This may play a role in women's complaints that men don't listen to them. Some men really don't like to listen, because being the listener makes them feel one-down, like a child listening to adults or an employee to a boss.

But often when women tell men, "You aren't listening," and the men   12
protest, "I am," the men are right. The impression of not listening results

from misalignments in the mechanics of conversation. The misalignment begins as soon as a man and a woman take physical positions. This became clear when I studied videotapes made by psychologist Bruce Dorval of children and adults talking to their same-sex best friends. I found that at every age, the girls and women faced each other directly, their eyes anchored on each other's faces. At every age, the boys and men sat at angles to each other and looked elsewhere in the room, periodically glancing at each other. They were obviously attuned to each other, often mirroring each other's movements. But the tendency of men to face away can give women the impression they aren't listening even when they are. A young woman in college was frustrated: Whenever she told her boyfriend she wanted to talk to him, he would lie down on the floor, close his eyes, and put his arm over his face. This signaled to her, "He's taking a nap." But he insisted he was listening extra hard. Normally, he looks around the room, so he is easily distracted. Lying down and covering his eyes helped him concentrate on what she was saying.

Analogous to the physical alignment that women and men take in 13 conversation is their topical alignment. The girls in my study tended to talk at length about one topic, but the boys tended to jump from topic to topic. The second-grade girls exchanged stories about people they knew. The second-grade boys teased, told jokes, noticed things in the room, and talked about finding games to play. The sixth-grade girls talked about problems with a mutual friend. The sixth-grade boys talked about 55 different topics, none of which extended over more than a few turns.

LISTENING TO BODY LANGUAGE

Switching topics is another habit that gives women the impression 14 men aren't listening, especially if they switch to a topic about themselves. But the evidence of the 10th-grade boys in my study indicates otherwise. The 10th-grade boys sprawled across their chairs with bodies parallel and eyes straight ahead, rarely looking at each other. They looked as if they were riding in a car, staring out the windshield. But they were talking about their feelings. One boy was upset because a girl had told him he had a drinking problem, and the other was feeling alienated from all his friends.

Now, when a girl told a friend about a problem, the friend responded 15 by asking probing questions and expressing agreement and understanding. But the boys dismissed each other's problems. Todd assured Richard that his drinking was "no big problem" because "sometimes you're funny when you're off your butt." And when Todd said he felt left out, Richard responded, "Why should you? You know more people than me."

Women perceive such responses as belittling and unsupportive. But 16 the boys seemed satisfied with them. Whereas women reassure each other by implying, "You shouldn't feel bad because I've had similar experiences," men do so by implying, "You shouldn't feel bad because your problems aren't so bad."

There are even simpler reasons for women's impression that men don't   17
listen. Linguist Lynette Hirschman found that women make more listener-noise, such as "mhm," "uhuh," and "yeah," to show "I'm with you." Men, she found, more often give silent attention. Women who expect a stream of listener-noise interpret silent attention as no attention at all.

Women's conversational habits are as frustrating to men as men's are   18
to women. Men who expect silent attention interpret a stream of listener-noise as overreaction or impatience. Also, when women talk to each other in a close, comfortable setting, they often overlap, finish each other's sentences, and anticipate what the other is about to say. This practice, which I call "participatory listenership," is often perceived by men as interruption, intrusion, and lack of attention.

A parallel difference caused a man to complain about his wife, "She   19
just wants to talk about her own point of view. If I show her another view, she gets mad at me." When most women talk to each other, they assume a conversationalist's job is to express agreement and support. But many men see their conversational duty as pointing out the other side of an argument. This is heard as disloyalty by women, and refusal to offer the requisite support. It is not that women don't want to see other points of view, but that they prefer them phrased as suggestions and inquiries rather than as direct challenges.

In his book *Fighting for Life,* Walter Ong points out that men use "ago-   20
nistic" or warlike, oppositional formats to do almost anything; thus discussion becomes debate, and conversation a competitive sport. In contrast, women see conversation as a ritual means of establishing rapport. If Jane tells a problem and June says she has a similar one, they walk away feeling closer to each other. But this attempt at establishing rapport can backfire when used with men. Men take too literally women's ritual "troubles talk," just as women mistake men's ritual challenges for real attack.

THE SOUNDS OF SILENCE

These differences begin to clarify why women and men have such   21
different expectations about communication in marriage. For women, talk creates intimacy. Marriage is an orgy of closeness: you can tell your feelings and thoughts, and still be loved. Their greatest fear is being pushed away. But men live in a hierarchical world, where talk maintains independence and status. They are on guard to protect themselves from being put down and pushed around.

This explains the paradox of the talkative man who said of his silent   22
wife, "She's the talker." In the public setting of a guest lecture, he felt challenged to show his intelligence and display his understanding of the lecture. But at home, where he has nothing to prove and no one to defend

against, he is free to remain silent. For his wife, being home means she is free from the worry that something she says might offend someone, or spark disagreement, or appear to be showing off; at home she is free to talk.

The communication problems that endanger marriage can't be fixed by mechanical engineering. They require a new conceptual framework about the role of talk in human relationships. Many of the psychological explanations that have become second nature may not be helpful, because they tend to blame either women (for not being assertive enough) or men (for not being in touch with their feelings). A sociolinguistic approach by which male-female conversation is seen as cross-cultural communication allows us to understand the problem and forge solutions without blaming either party. 23

Once the problem is understood, improvement comes naturally, as it did to the young woman and her boyfriend who seemed to go to sleep when she wanted to talk. Previously, she had accused him of not listening, and he had refused to change his behavior, since that would be admitting fault. But then she learned about and explained to him the differences in women's and men's habitual ways of aligning themselves in conversation. The next time she told him she wanted to talk, he began, as usual, by lying down and covering his eyes. When the familiar negative reaction bubbled up, she reassured herself that he really was listening. But then he sat up and looked at her. Thrilled, she asked why. He said, "You like me to look at you when we talk, so I'll try to do it." Once he saw their differences as cross-cultural rather than right and wrong, he independently altered his behavior. 24

Women who feel abandoned and deprived when their husbands won't listen to or report daily news may be happy to discover their husbands trying to adapt once they understand the place of small talk in women's relationships. But if their husbands don't adapt, the women may still be comforted that for men, this is not a failure of intimacy. Accepting the difference, the wives may look to their friends or family for that kind of talk. And husbands who can't provide it shouldn't feel their wives have made unreasonable demands. Some couples will still decide to divorce, but at least their decisions will be based on realistic expectations. 25

In these times of resurgent ethnic conflicts, the world desperately needs cross-cultural understanding. Like charity, successful cross-cultural communication should begin at home. 26

• • •

COMPREHENSION

1. What pattern of communication does Tannen identify at the beginning of her essay?

2. According to Tannen, what do women complain about most in their marriages?

3. What gives women the impression that men do not listen?

4. What characteristics of women's speech do men find frustrating?

5. According to Tannen, what can men and women do to remedy the communication problems that exist in most marriages?

PURPOSE AND AUDIENCE

1. What is Tannen's thesis?

2. What is Tannen's purpose in writing this essay? Do you think she wants to inform or to persuade? On what do you base your conclusion?

3. Is Tannen writing to an expert audience or an audience of general readers? To men, women, or both? How can you tell?

STYLE AND STRUCTURE

1. What does Tannen gain by stating her thesis in paragraph 2 of the essay? Would there be any advantage in postponing the thesis statement until the end? Explain.

2. Is this essay a subject-by-subject or a point-by-point comparison? What does Tannen gain by organizing her essay the way she does?

3. Throughout her essay, Tannen cites scholarly studies and quotes statistics. How effectively does this information support her points? Could she have made a strong case without this material? Why or why not?

4. Would you say Tannen's tone is hopeful, despairing, sarcastic, angry, or something else? Explain.

5. Tannen concludes her essay with a far-reaching statement. What do you think she hopes to accomplish with this conclusion? Is she successful? Explain your reasoning.

VOCABULARY PROJECTS

1. Define each of the following words as it is used in this selection.

concurred (1)	pitfalls (8)	rapport (20)
crystallizes (2)	subordinate (11)	ritual (20)
inequities (4)	misalignment (12)	orgy (21)
imbalance (6)	analogous (13)	sociolinguistic (23)
peer (7)	alienated (14)	forge (23)
organizational (7)	intrusion (18)	

2. Where does Tannen use professional **jargon** in this essay? Would the essay be more or less effective without these words? Explain.

JOURNAL ENTRY

Based on your own observations of male-female communication, how accurate is Tannen's analysis? Can you relate an anecdote from your own life that illustrates (or contradicts) her thesis?

WRITING WORKSHOP

1. In another essay, Tannen contrasts the communication patterns of male and female students in classroom settings. After observing a few of your own classes, write an essay in which you, too, draw a comparison between the communication patterns of your male and female classmates.

2. Write an essay in which you compare the way male and female characters speak in films or on television. Use examples to support your points.

3. Write an essay in which you compare the vocabulary used in two different sports. Does one sport use more violent language than the other? For example, baseball uses the terms *bunt* and *sacrifice,* and football uses the terms *blitz* and *bomb.* Use as many examples as you can to support your points.

COMBINING THE PATTERNS

Tannen begins her essay with an anecdote. Why does she begin with a paragraph of **narration?** How does this story set the tone for the rest of the essay?

THEMATIC CONNECTIONS

- "The Grave" (page 149)
- "Aria: A Memoir of a Bilingual Childhood" (page 357)
- "Sexism in English: A 1990s Update" (page 401)
- "I Want a Wife" (page 461)

RICHARD RODRIGUEZ

Born in San Francisco in 1944 to Mexican immigrants, Richard Rodriguez learned to speak English as an elementary school student in Sacramento, California. He graduated from Stanford University in 1967, received a master's degree from Columbia University, and later earned a doctorate in English Renaissance literature from the University of California at Berkeley, where he taught for a time before devoting himself solely to writing. He is now an editor for the Pacific News Service. Rodriguez's essays and articles have appeared in the *American Scholar, College English, Change,* and *Harper's.* In a series of autobiographical essays collected in the book *Hunger of Memory: The Education of Richard Rodriguez* (1982), he explores his ambivalent feelings about what he gained—and lost—by leaving his immigrant culture and entering American society. Another collection of essays, *Days of Obligation: An Argument with My Mexican Father* (1992), focuses on the conflicts Rodriguez sees, within himself and elsewhere, between Mexican fatalism and American optimism. In "Aria: A Memoir of a Bilingual Childhood," originally published in the *American Scholar* in 1981 and later collected in *Hunger of Memory,* Rodriguez compares the conflicting pulls of home and school, family and outsiders, Spanish and English.

Aria: A Memoir of a Bilingual Childhood

I remember to start with that day in Sacramento—a California now nearly thirty years past—when I first entered a classroom, able to understand some fifty stray English words. 1

The third of four children, I had been preceded to a neighborhood Roman Catholic school by an older brother and sister. But neither of them had revealed very much about their classroom experiences. Each afternoon they returned, as they left in the morning, always together, speaking in Spanish as they climbed the five steps of the porch. And their mysterious books, wrapped in shopping-bag paper, remained on the table next to the door, closed firmly behind them. 2

An accident of geography sent me to a school where all my classmates were white, many the children of doctors and lawyers and business executives. All my classmates certainly must have been uneasy on that first day of school—as most children are uneasy—to find themselves apart from their families in the first institution of their lives. But I was astonished. 3

The nun said, in a friendly but oddly impersonal voice, "Boys and girls, this is Richard Rodriguez." (I heard her sound out: *Richard Road-ree-guess.*) It was the first time I had heard anyone name me in English. "Richard," the nun repeated more slowly, writing my name down in her black leather book. Quickly I turned to see my mother's face dissolve in a watery blur behind the pebbled glass door. 4

Many years later there is something called bilingual education—a
scheme proposed in the late 1960s by Hispanic-American social activists, later endorsed by a congressional vote. It is a program that seeks
to permit non-English-speaking children, many from lower-class
homes, to use their family language as the language of school. (Such is
the goal its supporters announce.) I hear them and am forced to say no:
It is not possible for a child–any child—ever to use his family's language in school. Not to understand this is to misunderstand the public
uses of schooling and to trivialize the nature of intimate life—a family's
"language."

Memory teaches me what I know of these matters; the boy reminds
the adult. I was a bilingual child, a certain kind—socially disadvantaged—the son of working-class parents, both Mexican immigrants.

In the early years of my boyhood, my parents coped very well in
America. My father had steady work. My mother managed at home.
They were nobody's victims. Optimism and ambition led them to a house
(our home) many blocks from the Mexican south side of town. We lived
among *gringos* and only a block from the biggest, whitest houses. It never
occurred to my parents that they couldn't live wherever they chose. Nor
was the Sacramento of the fifties bent on teaching them a contrary lesson.
My mother and father were more annoyed than intimidated by those two
or three neighbors who tried initially to make us unwelcome. ("Keep
your brats away from my sidewalk!") But despite all they achieved, perhaps because they had so much to achieve, any deep feeling of ease, the
confidence of "belonging" in public was withheld from them both. They
regarded the people at work, the faces in crowds, as very distant from us.
They were the others, *los gringos*. That term was interchangeable in their
speech with another, even more telling, *los americanos*.

I grew up in a house where the only regular guests were my relations.
For one day, enormous families of relatives would visit and there would
be so many people that the noise and the bodies would spill out to the
backyard and front porch. Then, for weeks, no one came by. (It was usually a salesman who rang the doorbell.) Our house stood apart. A gaudy
yellow in a row of white bungalows. We were the people with the noisy
dog. The people who raised pigeons and chickens. We were the foreigners on the block. A few neighbors smiled and waved. We waved back. But
no one in the family knew the names of the old couple who lived next
door; until I was seven years old, I did not know the names of the kids
who lived across the street.

In public, my father and mother spoke a hesitant, accented, not always grammatical English. And they would have to strain—their bodies
tense—to catch the sense of what was rapidly said by *los gringos*. At home
they spoke Spanish. The language of their Mexican past sounded in counterpoint to the English of public society. The words would come quickly,
with ease. Conveyed through those sounds was the pleasing, soothing,
consoling reminder of being at home.

During those years when I was first conscious of hearing, my mother   10
and father addressed me only in Spanish; in Spanish I learned to reply. By
contrasts, English (*inglés*), rarely heard in the house, was the language I
came to associate with *gringos*. I learned my first words of English over-
hearing my parents speak to strangers. At five years of age, I knew just
enough English for my mother to trust me on errands to stores one block
away. No more.

I was a listening child, careful to hear the very different sounds of   11
Spanish and English. Wide-eyed with hearing, I'd listen to sounds more
than words. First, there were English (*gringo*) sounds. So many words
were still unknown that when the butcher or the lady at the drugstore said
something to me, exotic polysyllabic sounds would bloom in the midst of
their sentences. Often the speech of people in public seemed to me very
loud, booming with confidence. The man behind the counter would literally ask, "What can I do for you?" But by being so firm and so clear, the
sound of his voice said that he was a *gringo*; he belonged in public society.

I would also hear then the high nasal notes of middle-class American   12
speech. The air stirred with sound. Sometimes, even now, when I have
been traveling abroad for several weeks, I will hear what I heard as a boy.
In hotel lobbies or airports, in Turkey or Brazil, some Americans will pass,
and suddenly I will hear it again—the high sound of American voices.
For a few seconds I will hear it with pleasure, for it is now the sound of
my society—a reminder of home. But inevitably—already on the flight
headed for home—the sound fades with repetition. I will be unable to
hear it anymore.

When I was a boy, things were different. That accent of *los gringos* was   13
never pleasing nor was it hard to hear. Crowds at Safeway or at bus stops
would be noisy with sound. And I would be forced to edge away from
the chirping chatter above me.

I was unable to hear my own sounds, but I knew very well that I   14
spoke English poorly. My words could not stretch far enough to form
complete thoughts. And the words I did speak I didn't know well enough
to make into distinct sounds. (Listeners would usually lower their heads,
better to hear what I was trying to say.) But it was one thing for *me* to
speak English with difficulty. It was more troubling for me to hear my
parents speak in public: their high-whining vowels and guttural conso-
nants; their sentences that got stuck with "eh" and "ah" sounds; the confused syntax; the hesitant rhythm of sounds so different from the way
gringos spoke. I'd notice, moreover, that my parents' voices were softer
than those of *gringos* we'd meet.

I am tempted now to say that none of this mattered. In adulthood I   15
am embarrassed by childhood fears. And, in a way, it didn't matter very
much that my parents could not speak English with ease. Their linguistic
difficulties had no serious consequences. My mother and father made
themselves understood at the county hospital clinic and at government
offices. And yet, in another way, it mattered very much—it was unsettling

to hear my parents struggle with English. Hearing them, I'd grow nervous, my clutching trust in their protection and power weakened.

There were many times like the night at a brightly lit gasoline station   16
(a blaring white memory) when I stood uneasily, hearing my father. He was talking to a teenaged attendant. I do not recall what they were saying, but I cannot forget the sounds my father made as he spoke. At one point his words slid together to form one word—sounds as confused as the threads of blue and green oil in the puddle next to my shoes. His voice rushed through what he had left to say. And, toward the end, reached falsetto notes, appealing to his listener's understanding. I looked away to the lights of passing automobiles. I tried not to hear anymore. But I heard only too well the calm, easy tones in the attendant's reply. Shortly afterward, walking toward home with my father, I shivered when he put his hand on my shoulder. The very first chance that I got, I evaded his grasp and ran on ahead into the dark, skipping with feigned boyish exuberance.

But then there was Spanish. *Español:* my family's language. *Español:*   17
the language that seemed to me a private language. I'd hear strangers on the radio and in the Mexican Catholic church across town speaking in Spanish, but I couldn't really believe that Spanish was a public language, like English. Spanish speakers, rather, seemed related to me, for I sensed that we shared—through our language—the experience of feeling apart from *los gringos.* It was thus a ghetto Spanish that I heard and I spoke. Like those whose lives are bound by a barrio, I was reminded by Spanish of my separateness from *los otros, los gringos* in power. But more intensely than for most barrio children—because I did not live in a barrio—Spanish seemed to me the language of home. (Most days it was only at home that I'd hear it.) It became the language of joyful return.

A family member would say something to me and I would feel my-   18
self specially recognized. My parents would say something to me and I would feel embraced by the sounds of their words. Those sounds said: *I am speaking with ease in Spanish. I am addressing you in words I never use with* los gringos. *I recognize you as someone special, close, like no one outside. You belong with us. In the family.*

(Ricardo.)   19

At the age of five, six, well past the time when most other children no   20
longer easily notice the difference between sounds uttered at home and word spoken in public, I had a different experience. I lived in a world magically compounded of sounds. I remained a child longer than most; I lingered too long, poised at the edge of language—often frightened by the sounds of *los gringos,* delighted by the sounds of Spanish at home. I shared with my family a language that was startlingly different from that used in the great city around us.

For me there were none of the gradations between public and private   21
society so normal to a maturing child. Outside the house was public society; inside the house was private. Just opening or closing the screen door

behind me was an important experience. I'd rarely leave home all alone or without reluctance. Walking down the sidewalk, under the canopy of tall trees, I'd warily notice the—suddenly—silent neighborhood kids who stood warily watching me. Nervously, I'd arrive at the grocery store to hear there the sounds of the *gringo*—foreign to me—reminding me that in this world so big, I was a foreigner. But then I'd return. Walking back toward our house, climbing the steps from the sidewalk, when the front door was open in summer, I'd hear voices beyond the screen door talking in Spanish. For a second or two, I'd stay, linger there listening. Smiling, I'd hear my mother call out, saying in Spanish (words): "Is that you, Richard?" All the while her sounds would assure me: *You are home now; come closer; inside. With us.*

"Si," I'd reply.   22

Once more inside the house I would resume (assume) my place in the   23 family. The sounds would dim, grow harder to hear. Once more at home, I would grow less aware of that fact. It required, however, no more than the blurt of the doorbell to alert me to listen to sounds all over again. The house would turn instantly still while my mother went to the door. I'd hear her hard English sounds. I'd wait to hear her voice return to soft-sounding Spanish, which assured me, as surely as did the clicking tongue of the lock on the door, that the stranger was gone.

Plainly, it is not healthy to hear such sounds so often. It is not healthy   24 to distinguish public words from private sounds so easily. I remained cloistered by sounds, timid and shy in public, too dependent on voices at home. And yet it needs to be emphasized: I was an extremely happy child at home. I remember many nights when my father would come back from work, and I'd hear him call out to my mother in Spanish, sounding relieved. In Spanish, he'd sound light and free notes he never could manage in English. Some nights I'd jump up just at hearing his voice. With *mis hermanos* I would come running into the room where he was with my mother. Our laughing (so deep was the pleasure!) became screaming. Like others who know the pain of public alienation, we transformed the knowledge of our public separateness and made it consoling—the reminder of intimacy. Excited, we joined our voices in a celebration of sounds. *We are speaking now the way we never speak out in public. We are alone—together,* voices sounded, surrounded to tell me. Some nights, no one seemed willing to loosen the hold sounds had on us. At dinner, we invented new words. (Ours sounded Spanish, but made sense only to us.) We pieced together new words by taking, say, an English verb and giving it Spanish endings. My mother's instructions at bedtime would be lacquered with mock-urgent tones. Or a word like *si* would become, in several notes, able to convey added measures of feeling. Tongues explored the edges of words, especially the fat vowels. And we happily sounded that military drum roll, the twirling roar of the Spanish *r.* Family language: my family's sounds. The voices of my parents and sisters and brother. Their voices insisting: *You belong here. We are family members.*

Related. Special to one another. Listen! Voices singing and sighing, rising, straining, then surging, teeming with pleasure that burst syllables into fragments of laughter. At times it seemed there was steady quiet only when, from another room, the rustling whispers of my parents faded and I moved closer to sleep.

• • •

COMPREHENSION

1. What things made Rodriguez ill at ease on his first day of school? In what ways was he different from the other children?

2. To the young Rodriguez, how did the sounds of English differ from the sounds of Spanish? Why did Spanish seem to be a private language?

3. What does Rodriguez mean in paragraph 24 when he says, "It is not healthy to distinguish public words from private sounds so easily"?

4. In addition to the differences between public and private language, what other oppositions does Rodriguez encounter?

5. Does Rodriguez consider his experiences similar to or different from those facing other Mexican-American children? What statements in the essay lead you to your conclusion?

PURPOSE AND AUDIENCE

1. What is Rodriguez's thesis? Where does he state it?

2. Is Rodriguez writing this essay to enlighten? Persuade? Debunk? Educate? Entertain? Or does he have some other, more personal, purpose? Explain.

3. This essay is addressed to a well-educated audience largely made up of *los gringos.* What concessions does Rodriguez make to his audience?

4. Does Rodriguez consider his audience hostile or friendly? Well informed or misinformed? Explain your answer.

STYLE AND STRUCTURE

1. Why are some passages italicized?

2. Rodriguez's essay does not move in a straight line from one time period or episode to the next; different periods blend together. How is this indefinite sense of time consistent with the aims of the essay? What would Rodriguez have gained or lost by presenting events in chronological order?

3. What transitional words and phrases does Rodriguez use to indicate what he is comparing?

4. In the first four paragraphs, Rodriguez uses a flashback to highlight an episode that occurred when he is a child. How does this flashback set the stage for his thesis?

5. Does Rodriguez present his ideas objectively or subjectively? Could he be accused of sentimentalizing the nature of family life and its reliance on a "private language" (17)? Explain.

VOCABULARY PROJECTS

1. Define each of the following words as it is used in this selection.

   bilingual (5)   guttural (14)
   polysyllabic (11)   barrio (17)

2. What Spanish words does Rodriguez use in this essay? Doe he make sure that his English-speaking readers understand the meaning of the words? What effect does he achieve by including them? Write a paragraph in which you explain your reaction to their use.

JOURNAL ENTRY

Do you agree with Rodriguez's comments about bilingual education? Do you think it is desirable for children who speak no English to be taught in their native language?

WRITING WORKSHOP

1. Think of a time when you felt like an outsider. Write an essay in which you compare your actions to those of the members of the group from which you felt estranged.

2. Has anyone you know come from a family whose private language, unique culture, or special customs set them apart from you and your family? Write an essay in which you compare your family to the person you know and explain how these differences manifested themselves.

3. Write an essay in which you respond to Rodriguez's thesis that it is not possible for a child to use his or her private language in school. Compare your own ideas about the public uses of language to the ideas Rodriguez expresses in paragraph 5.

COMBINING THE PATTERNS

In paragraph 5 Rodriguez includes a passage of **definition.** Is this definition necessary? What function does it serve? Should Rodriguez have defined *bilingual education* in more detail? If so, what should he have added?

THEMATIC CONNECTIONS

- "Finishing School" (page 75)
- "Words Left Unspoken" (page 121)
- "Two Ways to Belong in America" (page 340)
- "Mother Tongue" (page 393)
- "Let's Tell the Story of All America's Cultures" (page 552)

JOHN UPDIKE

John Updike was born in 1932 in Shillington, Pennsylvania. After graduating from Harvard University in 1954, he attended the Ruskin School of Drawing and Fine Arts in England for a year and then worked for several years as a staff writer for the *New Yorker* magazine, to which he has continued to contribute poems, short stories, essays, and book reviews. Updike is the author of numerous books of poetry, fiction, and criticism. His most recent works include *Collected Poems 1953–1993* (1993); *The Afterlife and Other Stories* (1994); the essay collection *Odd Jobs* (1991); and two novels, *Brazil* (1994) and *In the Beauty of the Lilies* (1996). Updike received Pulitzer Prizes for *Rabbit Is Rich* (1981) and *Rabbit at Rest* (1990), the last two of four novels that chronicle the changes in American society from the 1950s through the 1980s as reflected in the life of a man of Updike's generation. "Ex–Basketball Player," published in *The Carpentered Hen and Other Tame Creatures* (1958), looks back at the talents and accomplishments of a young athlete through a description of what his life has become.

Ex–Basketball Player

Pearl Avenue runs past the high-school lot,
Bends with the trolley tracks, and stops, cut off
Before it has a chance to go two blocks.
At Colonel McComsky Plaza, Berth's Garage
Is on the corner facing west, and there,   5
Most days, you'll find Flick Webb, who helps Berth out.

Flick stands tall among the idiot pumps—
Five on a side, the old bubble-head style,
Their rubber elbows hanging loose and low.
One's nostrils are two S's, and his eyes   10
An E and O. And one is squat, without
A head at all—more of a football type.

Once Flick played for the high-school team, the Wizards.
He was good: in fact, the best. In '46
He bucketed three hundred ninety points,   15
A county record still. The ball loved Flick.
I saw him rack up thirty-eight or forty
In one home game. His hands were like wild birds.

He never learned a trade, he just sells gas,
Checks oil, and changes flats. Once in a while,   20
As a gag, he dribbles an inner tube,
But most of us remember anyway.
His hands are fine and nervous on the lug wrench.
It makes no difference to the lug wrench, though.

Off work, he hangs around Mae's luncheonette.   25
Grease-gray and kind of coiled, he plays pinball,
Smokes those thin cigars, nurses lemon phosphates.
Flick seldom says a word to Mae, just nods
Beyond her face toward bright applauding tiers
Of Necco Wafers, Nibs, and Juju Beads.   30

• • •

THINKING ABOUT LITERATURE

1. What two things are being compared in the poem? What strategies does the speaker use to let readers know when he is shifting from one subject to another?

2. Do you know any people like Flick? How accurate do you think the speaker's characterization is? Do you think the speaker is stereotyping Flick? Explain.

3. What comment is the poem making about the role of sports in our society? About the relationship between education and sports?

JOURNAL ENTRY

What do you think went wrong with Flick's sports career? Why is Flick not a success today?

THEMATIC CONNECTIONS

- "The Human Cost of an Illiterate Society" (page 192)
- "Who Killed Benny Paret?" (page 270)
- "Brains versus Brawn" (page 317)
- "The Men We Carry in Our Minds" (page 387)

WRITING ASSIGNMENTS FOR COMPARISON AND CONTRAST

1. Find a description of the same event in two different magazines or newspapers. Write a comparison-and-contrast essay in which you discuss the similarities and differences between these two stories.

2. Go to the library and locate two children's books on the same subject, one written in the 1950s and one written today. Write an essay discussing which elements are the same and which are different. Include a thesis statement that makes a point about the significance of the differences between the two books.

3. Write a comparison-and-contrast essay in which you show how your knowledge of an academic subject has either increased or decreased your enthusiasm for it. If you like, you can refer to "Reading the River" (page 126).

4. Write an essay about a relative or friend you knew when you were a child. Consider in what respects your opinion of this person has changed and in what sense it has remained the same.

5. Are the academic standards for athletes different from the standards applied to other students at your school? Compare the academic requirements and other expectations for athletes and nonathletes. Include a thesis that states your opinion about any discrepancies you identify.

6. Since you started college, how have you changed and how have you stayed the same? Write an essay that answers this question.

7. Watch a local television news program and then a national news broadcast. Write an essay in which you compare the two programs, paying particular attention to the news content and to the broadcasting styles of the journalists.

8. Write an essay in which you compare your own early memories of school with those of Richard Rodriguez.

9. Do students who work to finance their own education have different attitudes toward that education than students who do not? If so, why? Your thesis statement should explain why you believe a difference exists (or does not exist).

10. Write an essay in which you compare any two groups that have divergent values: vegetarians and meat eaters or smokers and nonsmokers, for example.

COLLABORATIVE ACTIVITY FOR COMPARISON AND CONTRAST

Form groups of four students. Assume you are consultants who have been asked by your college to suggest solutions for several problems students have been complaining about. Select the three areas—food, campus safety, and class scheduling for example—that you think are most in need of improvement. Then, as a group, write a short report to your college in which you describe the present conditions in these areas and compare them to the improvements you envision. (Be sure to organize your report as a comparison-and-contrast essay.) Finally, have one person from each group read the group's report to the class, and then decide as a class which group has the best suggestion.

8

CLASSIFICATION AND DIVISION

WHAT IS CLASSIFICATION AND DIVISION?

Division is the process of breaking a whole into parts; **classification** is the process of sorting individual items into categories. In the following paragraph from "Fans," Paul Gallico divides sports fans into categories based on the different sports they watch:

<table>
<tr>
<td>Parts: kinds of sports fans</td>
<td>The fight crowd is a beast that lurks in the darkness behind the fringe of white light shed over the first six rows by the incandescents atop the ring, and is not to be trusted with pop bottles or other hardware. The tennis crowd is the pansy of all the great sports mobs and is always preening and shushing itself. The golf crowd is the most unwieldy and most sympathetic, and is the only horde given to mass production of that absurd noise written generally as "tsk tsk tsk tsk," and made between tongue and teeth with head-waggings to denote extreme commiseration. The baseball crowd is the most hysterical, the football crowd the best-natured, and the polo crowd the most aristocratic. Racing crowds are the most restless, wrestling crowds the most tolerant, and soccer crowds the most easily incitable to riot and disorder.</td>
</tr>
<tr>
<td>Topic sentence identifies whole (sports fans)</td>
<td>Every sports crowd takes on the characteristics of the individuals who compose it. Each has its particular note of hysteria, its own little cruelties, mannerisms, and bad mannerisms, its own code of sportsmanship, and its own method of expressing its emotions.</td>
</tr>
</table>

Through **classification and division,** we can make sense of seemingly random ideas by putting scattered bits of information into useful, coherent order. By breaking a large group into smaller categories and assigning individual items to larger categories, we are able to identify relationships between a whole and its parts and among the parts themselves. (Remember, though, that classification involves more than simply enumerating examples; when you classify, you sort examples into categories according to a particular principle.)

In countless practical situations, classification and division brings order to chaos. Items in a Sunday newspaper are *classified* in clearly defined sections—international news, sports, travel, entertainment, comics, and so on—so that hockey scores, for example, are not mixed up with real estate listings. Similarly, department stores are *divided* into different departments so that managers can assign merchandise to particular areas and shoppers can know where to look for a particular item. Without such organization, an item might be anywhere in a store. Thus, order is brought to newspapers and department stores—and to supermarkets, biological hierarchies, and libraries—when a whole is divided into categories or sections and individual items are assigned to one or another of these subgroups.

Understanding Classification and Division

Even though the interrelated processes of classification and division invariably occur together, they are two separate operations. When you *classify*, you begin with individual items and sort them into categories. Since most things have several different attributes, they can be classified in several different ways. Take as an example the students who attend your school. The most obvious way to classify these individuals might be according to their year in college. But you could also classify students according to their major, racial or ethnic background, home state, grade-point average, or any number of other principles. The **principle of classification** you choose—the quality your items have in common—would depend on how you wished to approach the members of this large and diverse group.

Division is the opposite of classification. When you *divide*, you start with a whole (an entire class) and break it into its individual parts—smaller, more specific classes, called *subclasses*. For example, you might start with the large general class *television shows* and divide it into smaller subclasses: *comedy, drama, action/adventure,* and so forth. You could then divide each of these subclasses still further. *Action/adventure programs,* for example, might include *Westerns, police shows,* and so on—and each of these subclasses could be divided as well. Eventually you would need to determine a particular principle to help you assign specific programs to one category or another—that is, to classify them. The guidelines on page 369 will help you understand the processes of classification and division.

Uses of Classification and Division

Whenever you write an essay, you use classification and division to bring order to the invention stage of the writing process. For example, when you brainstorm, as Chapter 1 explains, you begin with your

☑ **GUIDELINES FOR CLASSIFICATION AND DIVISION**

- *All the categories should result from the same principle.* If you decide to divide *television shows* into *soap operas, police shows,* and the like, it is not logical to include the subclass *children's programs,* for this subclass results from one principle (target audience) while the others result from another principle (genre). Similarly, if you were classifying undergraduates at your school according to their year, you would not include the subclass *students receiving financial aid.*

- *All the subclasses should be on the same level.* In the series *comedy, drama, action/adventure,* and *Westerns,* the last item, *Westerns,* does not belong because it is on a lower level—that is, it is a subclass of *action/adventure.* Likewise, *sophomores* (a subclass of *undergraduates*) does not belong in the series *undergraduates, graduate students, continuing education students.*

- *You should treat all subclasses that are significant and relevant to your discussion.* Include enough subclasses to make your point, with no important omissions and no overlapping categories. In a review of a network's fall television lineup, the series *sitcoms, soap operas, police shows,* and *detective shows* is incomplete because it omits important subclasses like *news programs, game shows, talk shows,* and *documentaries;* moreover, *detective shows* may overlap with *police shows.* In the same way, the series *freshmen, sophomores, juniors,* and *transfers* is illogical: the important group *seniors* has been omitted, and *transfers* may include *freshmen, sophomores,* and *juniors.*

paper's topic and list all the related points you can think of. Next, you *divide* your topic into logical categories and *classify* the items in your brainstorming notes into one category or another, perhaps narrowing, expanding, or eliminating some categories—or some points—as you go along. This picking and choosing, sorting and grouping, enables you to condense your material until it eventually suggests a thesis and the main points of your essay.

In addition, certain topics and questions, because of the way they are worded, immediately suggest a classification-and-division pattern. Suppose, for example, you are asked, "What kinds of policies can be used to direct and control the national economy?" Here the word *kinds* suggests classification and division. Other words, such as *types, varieties, aspects,* and *categories,* can also serve as clues.

STRUCTURING A CLASSIFICATION-AND-DIVISION ESSAY

Once you decide to use a classification-and-division pattern, you need to identify a principle of classification. Every group of people, things, or ideas can be categorized in many ways. When you are at your college bookstore with only thirty dollars, the cost of different books may be the only principle of classification you use to decide what to buy. As you consider which books to carry across campus, however, weight may matter more. Finally, as you study and read, the usefulness of the books will determine which ones you concentrate on. Similarly, when you organize an essay, your principle of classification and division is determined by your writing situation—your assignment, your purpose, your audience, and your special knowledge and interests.

Selecting and Arranging Categories

After you define your principle of classification and apply it to your topic, you should select your categories by dividing a whole class into parts and grouping a number of different items together within each part. Next, you should decide how you will treat the categories in your essay. Just as a comparison-and-contrast essay makes comparable points about its subjects, so your classification-and-division essay should treat all categories similarly. When you discuss comparable points for each category, your readers are able to understand your distinctions among categories as well as your definition of each category.

Finally, you should arrange your categories in some logical order, so that readers can see how the categories are related and how significant each is. Whatever order you choose, it should be consistent with your purpose and support your thesis.

Formulating a Thesis Statement

Like other kinds of essays, a classification-and-division essay must have a thesis. Your thesis statement should identify your subject, present the categories you will discuss, and perhaps show readers the relationships of your categories to one another and to the subject as a whole. In addition, your thesis statement should tell your readers why your categories are significant or establish their relative value. For example, listing different kinds of investments would be pointless if you did not evaluate their strengths and weaknesses and then make recommendations based on your assessment. Similarly, a term paper about a writer's major works would accomplish little if it merely categorized his or her writings. Instead, your thesis statement should communicate your evaluation of these works, perhaps demonstrating that some deserve higher public regard than others.

Planning and Outlining Your Essay

Once you have formulated your essay's thesis and established your subclasses, you should plan your classification-and-division essay around the same three major sections that other essays have: introduction, body, and conclusion. Your *introduction* should orient your readers by mentioning your topic, the principle by which your material is divided and classified, and the individual subclasses you plan to discuss; your thesis is also usually stated in the introduction. In the subsequent *body paragraphs,* you should treat the categories one by one in the order in which your introduction presents them. Finally, your *conclusion* should restate your thesis, summing up the points you have made and perhaps considering their implications.

Suppose you are preparing a term paper on Mark Twain's nonfiction works for an American literature course. You have read *Roughing It, Life on the Mississippi,* and *The Innocents Abroad.* Besides these travel narratives, you have read Twain's autobiography as well as some of his correspondence and essays. When you realize that the works you have studied can easily be classified as four different types of Twain's nonfiction—travel narratives, essays, letters, and autobiography—you decide to use classification and division to structure your essay. Therefore, you first divide the large class *Twain's nonfiction prose* into major subclasses—his travel narratives, essays, autobiography, and letters. Then you classify the individual works—that is, assign the works to these subclasses, which you plan to discuss one at a time. Your purpose is to persuade readers to reconsider the reputations of some of these works, and you formulate your thesis accordingly. You might then prepare a formal outline like this one for the body of your paper:

> *Thesis statement:* Most readers know Mark Twain as a writer of novels, such as *Huckleberry Finn,* but his nonfiction works—his travel narratives, essays, letters, and especially his autobiography—deserve more attention.

I. Travel narratives
   A. *Roughing It*
   B. *The Innocents Abroad*
   C. *Life on the Mississippi*

II. Essays
   A. "Fenimore Cooper's Literary Offenses"
   B. "How to Tell a Story"
   C. "The Awful German Language"

III. Letters
   A. To W. D. Howells
   B. To his family

IV. Autobiography

Because this will be a long term paper, each of the outline's divisions will have several subdivisions, and each subdivision might require several paragraphs.

This outline illustrates all the characteristics of an effective classification-and-division essay. To begin with, Twain's nonfiction works are classified according to a single principle of classification—literary genre. Depending on your purpose, of course, another principle—such as theme or subject matter—could work just as well. (If you were writing your term paper for a political science course, you might have decided to examine Twain as a social critic by classifying his works according to the kind of political commentary in each.) Literary genre, however, is an appropriate principle of classification for the writing situation at hand. In addition to illustrating a single principle of classification, the outline reveals that the paper's subclasses are on the same level (each is a different literary genre) and that all relevant subclasses are included. Had you left out the subclass *essays,* for example, you would have been unable to classify several significant works of nonfiction.

This outline also arranges the four subclasses so they will support your thesis most effectively. Because you believe Twain's travel narratives are somewhat overrated, you plan to discuss them early in your paper. Similarly, because you think the autobiography would make your best case for the merit of the nonfiction works as a whole, you decide it should be placed last. (Of course, you could arrange your categories in several other orders, such as shorter to longer works or least to most popular, depending on the thesis your paper will support.)

Finally, this outline helps you to treat all categories comparably in your paper. Now, you should identify each main point in your rough draft and cross-check the order of points from category to category. Your case would be weakened if, for example, you inadvertently skipped style in your discussion of Twain's letters while discussing style for every other category. This omission might lead your readers to suspect that you had not done enough research on the letters or that you had ignored them because the style of Twain's letters did not measure up to the style of his other works.

▶ **A STUDENT WRITER: CLASSIFICATION AND DIVISION**

The following classification-and-division essay was written by Roger Bauer for a course in American literature. The essay *divides* a whole entity—fiction of the American West—into four parts, or elements, using a principle of division common in literary analysis. In addition, it *classifies* material—details about fiction of the American West—into categories.

The Western: More Than Just

"Popular" Literature

Introduction   Works of popular fiction--detective sto-   1
ries, Gothic novels, and Westerns, for exam-
ple--are usually not regarded very highly by
literary critics. This evaluation is justified
in most cases. All too often in popular fiction characters are familiar stereotypes, plot
devices are predictable (and sometimes improb-

able), settings are overly familiar or only vaguely described, and themes are simplistic or undeveloped. To some extent, these characteristics apply to fiction of the American West--not only to contemporary Westerns, but also to those novels and stories that have

Thesis (identifies four elements to be discussed)

achieved status as classics. Still, although clichéd characters and trite plots dominate even classic Westerns, a strong sense of place and timeless themes give the Western the power to transcend the "popular fiction" category.

First element: characters

Readers encounter familiar characters in novels and short stories with western settings. The cast of characters is likely to include at least a few of the following: the cowboy, the dance hall girl, the sheriff, the deputy, the madam, the miner, the schoolmarm, the easterner, the gambler, the rancher, the hired hand, the merchant, the preacher, the traveling salesman, and assorted cavalry soldiers, cattle rustlers, Indians, and Mexicans. These people are seldom fully developed; rather, they are stock characters who play exactly the roles readers expect them to play. Some classic stories, such as "The Outcasts of Poker Flat" and "Stage to Lordsburg," gather an assortment of these characters together in an isolated setting, playing them off against one another in a way that emphasizes their status as types rather than as individuals.

2

Second element: plot

The plot elements are just as predictable. Often a gang terrorizes innocent settlers or ranchers or townspeople, as in Shane; just as often a desperado is on the loose, as in "The Bride Comes to Yellow Sky." Other common elements are a showdown on a dusty street, as in "The Tin Star," or an ambush, as in "Stage to Lordsburg." Scenes of chase and capture are staples from James

3

Fenimore Cooper to Louis L'Amour, and standard boy-meets-girl plots can be traced from The Virginian to current popular novels.

Third element: setting

But the Western has the potential to transcend the limits of these familiar materials. A particular strength is its geographical setting, which includes an unusually varied landscape and some magnificent scenery. The setting in Western fiction is special for a variety of reasons. First, the West is beautiful and exotic. Second, the West is huge: towns are widely separated, and characters travel great distances. As a result, a sense of loneliness and isolation pervades the Western. Third, the West is frightening and unpredictable, characterized by untamed landscapes, wild animals, and terrifying extremes of weather. The harshness and unpredictability of the climate are especially frightening to newcomers to the West (and to readers). Still, the very extreme conditions (tornadoes, blizzards, desert sun) and unfamiliar topography (mesas, plains, canyons) that are so disturbing are also fascinating. Ultimately, the setting can be friend or enemy: Zane Grey's Riders of the Purple Sage ends with its lovers isolated in a canyon by a rock slide; in Max Brand's "Wine on the Desert," a man dies of thirst in the hostile sun. In these and other Western stories, the setting is a powerful presence that is always strongly felt.

4

Fourth element: theme

Perhaps even more powerful than the setting are the themes of the Western--themes found in all great literature. Each of these themes adds interest to the Western, giving it substance and stature. One such theme is the classic conflict between East and West, civilization and the wilderness, illustrated in

5

novels as diverse as Cooper's <u>The Prairie</u> and Wister's <u>The Virginian</u>. (In <u>The Virginian</u>, as in Crane's "The Bride Comes to Yellow Sky," it is the woman who is the symbol of civilization.) Typically, the East is portrayed as rigid, sterile, and limiting, while the West is natural and spontaneous, untamed and beautiful. Another classic theme frequently seen in Western literature is the initiation theme. Here a young man or a boy (or, occasionally, a girl) is initiated into the mysteries of adulthood through participation in a physical test of his courage--for example, a fistfight, a gun battle, or a feat of strength. This theme is developed in "The Tin Star" as well as in the 1952 film <u>High Noon</u>. A third theme frequently explored in Western fiction is the journey or search. The vast spaces and dangerous climate and topography of the West make it an ideal setting for this theme. In works as diverse as Charles Portis's <u>True Grit</u>, Louis L'Amour's <u>Down the Long Hills</u>, and the classic John Ford film <u>The Searchers</u>, the journey figures prominently. Whether the quest is for a long-lost relative, for land or gold or silver, or for knowledge or experience, the search theme dominates many works of Western literature, particularly longer works.

Conclusion (restates thesis)

Balancing the familiar plot elements and stereotypical characters of Western fiction are two other elements, setting and theme, that set it apart from other kinds of popular fiction. In addition to its vivid settings and universal themes, the Western also boasts a strong sense of history and an identity as a uniquely American genre. These two qualities should give it a lasting importance consistent with its continuing popularity.

Points for Special Attention

THESIS AND SUPPORT.   Roger Bauer's purpose in writing this essay was not just to describe the fiction of the American West but also to evaluate it. Consequently, his thesis statement presents his assessment of the genre's literary value, and his body paragraphs support his position with analysis and examples.

ORGANIZATION.   Roger planned his essay carefully, and his organization scheme keeps the four elements he discusses distinct; in addition, both the space he allots to each element and the order in which he presents them convey his emphasis to his readers. Thus, paragraph 2 combines a discussion of the two elements Roger does not consider to be particularly noteworthy; in paragraphs 3 and 4 he goes on to give fuller treatment to his two main topics, setting and theme. Because he considers some elements to be more important than others, his treatment of the four categories is necessarily unequal. Still, Roger is careful to provide specific examples from various works of Western literature in all four cases.

TRANSITION BETWEEN CATEGORIES.   Roger uses clear transitional sentences to introduce each element of literature he discusses: "Readers encounter familiar characters in novels and short stories with Western settings"; "The plot elements are just as predictable"; "A particular strength is its geographical setting, which provides it with an unusually varied landscape and some magnificent scenery"; and "Perhaps even more powerful than the setting are the themes of the Western—themes found in all great literature." To indicate his shift from less important elements to more significant ones, Roger uses another strong transition: "But the Western has the potential to transcend the limits of these familiar materials." Each of these transitional sentences not only distinguishes the four elements from one another but also conveys Roger's direction and emphasis.

WRITING ABOUT LITERATURE.   Because he is writing for a course in American literature, Roger pays special attention to certain conventions that apply to writing about literature. He uses present tense when referring to literary works, and he places titles of short stories within quotation marks and underlines titles of novels and films to indicate italics. Also, he presents his interpretations and evaluations straightforwardly, without using unnecessary phrases like *In my opinion* and *I think*.

Focus on Revision

One student who did a peer critique of this essay thought Roger could make a stronger case for the value of the fiction of the American West if he condensed paragraph 2, which deals with the formulaic aspects of such fiction, and expanded the paragraphs about setting and theme. Another student suggested that quotations from a few of the works Roger mentions might add interest to his essay. Roger liked both of these suggestions and decided to follow up on them when he revised his paper. Of course, if he were writing a longer paper, Roger could provide brief plot summaries of the works he mentions in order to accommodate readers who might not be familiar with them. In a longer essay, additional examples—particularly from modern Westerns, which apply the conventions of the genre somewhat differently—would also be helpful.

Each of the following reading selections is developed by means of classification and division. In some cases, the pattern is used to explain ideas; in others, it is used to persuade the reader.

WILLIAM ZINSSER

Born in 1922 in New York City, William Zinsser graduated from Princeton University in 1944. He worked at the *New York Herald Tribune* as a feature and editorial writer, drama editor, and film critic, and he was a columnist for *Life* magazine and the *New York Times*. Zinsser has also taught English at Yale University and served as general editor for the Book-of-the-Month Club. He is the author of several books on writing, including five editions of *On Writing Well: An Informal Guide to Writing Nonfiction* (fifth edition, 1994) and *Writing to Learn* (1988). He has also written works on American culture, including *Spring Training* (1989), about the culture of baseball as Zinsser observed it at the Pittsburgh Pirates' training camp, and most recently *American Places: A Writer's Pilgrimage to 15 of This Country's Most Visited and Cherished Sites* (1992). In "College Pressures" written for *Country Journal* magazine in 1979, Zinsser analyzes the different forces contributing to the anxiety of students at Yale.

College Pressures

Dear Carlos: I desperately need a dean's excuse for my chem midterm which will begin in about 1 hour. All I can say is that I totally blew it this week. I've fallen incredibly, inconceivably behind. 1

Carlos: Help! I'm anxious to hear from you. I'll be in my room and won't leave it until I hear from you. Tomorrow is the last day for.... 2

Carlos: I left town because I started bugging out again. I stayed up all night to finish a take home make-up exam and am typing it to hand in on the 10th. It was due on the 5th. P.S. I'm going to the dentist. Pain is pretty bad. 3

Carlos: Probably by Friday I'll be able to get back to my studies. Right now I'm going to take a long walk. This whole thing has taken a lot out of me. 4

Carlos: I'm really up the proverbial creek. The problem is I really *bombed* the history final. Since I need that course for my major.... 5

Carlos: Here follows a tale of woe. I went home this weekend, had to help my Mom, & caught a fever so didn't have much time to study. My professor.... 6

Carlos: Aargh! Nothing original but everything's piling up at once. To be brief, my job interview.... 7

Hey Carlos, good news! I've got mononucleosis. 8

Who are these wretched supplicants, scribbling notes so laden with anxiety, seeking such miracles of postponement and balm? They are men and women who belong to Bradford College, one of the twelve residen- 9 tial colleges at Yale University, and the messages are just a few of the hundreds that they left for their dean, Carlos Hortas—often slipped under his door at 4 A.M.—last year.

But students like the ones who wrote those notes can also be found on campuses from coast to coast—especially in New England and at many other private colleges across the country that have high academic standards and highly motivated students. Nobody could doubt that the notes are real. In their urgency and their gallows humor they are authentic voices of a generation that is panicky to succeed.

My own connection with the message writers is that I am master of Bradford College. I live in its Gothic quadrangle and know the students well. (We have 485 of them.) I am privy to their hopes and fears—and also to their stereo music and their piercing cries in the dead of night ("Does anybody *ca-a-are?*"). If they went to Carlos to ask how to get through tomorrow, they come to me to ask how to get through the rest of their lives.

Mainly I try to remind them that the road ahead is a long one and that it will have more unexpected turns than they think. There will be plenty of time to change jobs, change careers, change whole attitudes and approaches. They don't want to hear such liberating news. They want a map—right now—that they can follow unswervingly to career security, financial security, Social Security, and, presumably, a prepaid grave.

What I wish for all students is some release from the clammy grip of the future. I wish them a chance to savor each segment of their education as an experience in itself and not as a grim preparation for the next step. I wish them the right to experiment, to trip and fall, to learn that defeat is as instructive as victory and is not the end of the world.

My wish, of course, is naive. One of the few rights that America does not proclaim is the right to fail. Achievement is the national god, venerated in our media—the million-dollar athlete, the wealthy executive—and glorified in our praise of possessions. In the presence of such a potent state religion, the young are growing up old.

I see four kinds of pressure working on college students today: economic pressure, parental pressure, peer pressure, and self-induced pressure. It is easy to look around for villains—to blame the colleges for charging too much money, the professors for assigning too much work, the parents for pushing their children too far, the students for driving themselves too hard. But there are no villains, only victims.

"In the late 1960s," one dean told me, "the typical question that I got from students was 'Why is there so much suffering in the world?' or 'How can I make a contribution?' Today it's 'Do you think it would look better for getting into law school if I did a double major in history and political science, or just majored in one of them?'" Many other deans confirmed this pattern. One said: "They're trying to find an edge—the intangible something that will look better on paper if two students are about equal."

Note the emphasis on looking better. The transcript has become a sacred document, the passport to security. How one appears on paper is more important than how one appears in person. *A* is for Admirable and *B* is for Borderline, even though, in Yale's official system of grading, *A* means "excellent" and *B* means "very good." Today, looking very good is no longer good enough, especially for students who hope to go on to law school or medical school. They know that entrance into the better schools will be an entrance into the better law firms and better medical practices where they will make a lot of money. They also know that the odds are harsh. Yale Law School for instance, matriculates 170 students from an applicant pool of 3,700; Harvard enrolls 550 from a pool of 7,000.

It's all very well for those of us who write letters of recommendation 18 for our students to stress the qualities of humanity that will make them good lawyers or doctors. And it's nice to think that admission officers are really reading our letters and looking for the extra dimension of commitment or concern. Still, it would be hard for a student not to visualize these officers shuffling so many transcripts studded with *A*s that they regard a *B* as positively shameful.

The pressure is almost as heavy on students who just want to gradu- 19 ate and get a job. Long gone are the days of the "gentleman's C," when students journeyed through college with a certain relaxation, sampling a wide variety of courses—music, art, philosophy, classics, anthropology, poetry, religion—that would send them out as liberally educated men and women. If I were an employer I would rather employ graduates who have this range and curiosity than those who narrowly pursued safe subjects and high grades. I know countless students whose inquiring minds exhilarate me. I like to hear the play of their ideas. I don't know if they're getting *A*s or *C*s, and I don't care. I also like them as people. The country needs them, and they will find satisfying jobs. I tell them to relax. They can't.

Nor can I blame them. They live in a brutal economy. Tuition, room, 20 and board at most private colleges now comes to at least $7,000, not counting books and fees.* This might seem to suggest that the colleges are getting rich. But they are equally battered by inflation. Tuition covers only 60 percent of what it costs to educate a student, and ordinarily the remainder comes from what colleges receive in endowments, grants, and gifts. Now the remainder keeps being swallowed by cruel costs—higher every year—of just opening the doors. Heating oil is up. Insurance is up. Postage is up. Health-premium costs are up. Everything is up. Deficits are up. We are witnessing in America the creation of a brotherhood of paupers—colleges, parents, and students, joined by the common bond of debt.

Today it is not unusual for a student, even if he works part time at 21 college and full time during the summer, to accrue $5,000 in loans after four years—loans that he must start to repay within one year after graduation. Exhorted at commencement to go forth into the world, he is already behind as he goes forth. How could he not feel under pressure throughout college to prepare for this day of reckoning? I have used "he"

---

*EDS. NOTE—Zinsser's essay was published in 1979; the figures quoted for tuition and other expenses would be much higher today.

incidentally, only for brevity. Women at Yale are under no less pressure to justify their expensive education to themselves, their parents, and society. In fact, they are probably under more pressure. For although they leave college superbly equipped to bring fresh leadership to traditionally male jobs, society hasn't yet caught up with this fact.

Along with economic pressure goes parental pressure. Inevitably, the two are deeply intertwined. 22

I see many students taking pre-medical courses with joyless tenacity. They go off to their labs as if they were going to the dentist. It saddens me because I know them in other corners of their life as cheerful people. 23

"Do you want to go to medical school?" I ask them. 24

"I guess so," they say, without conviction, or "Not really." 25

"Then why are you going?" 26

"Well, my parents want me to be a doctor. They're paying all this money and..." 27

Poor students, poor parents. They are caught in one of the oldest webs of love and duty and guilt. The parents mean well; they are trying to steer their sons and daughters toward a secure future. But the sons and daughters want to major in history or classics or philosophy—subjects with no "practical" value. Where's the payoff on the humanities? It's not easy to persuade such loving parents that the humanities do indeed pay off. The intellectual faculties developed by studying subjects like history and classics—an ability to synthesize and relate, to weigh cause and effect, to see events in perspective—are just the faculties that make creative leaders in business or almost any general field. Still, many fathers would rather put their money on courses that point toward a specific profession—courses that are pre-law, pre-medical, pre-business, or, as I sometimes heard it put, "pre-rich." 28

But the pressure on students is severe. They are truly torn. One part of them feels obliged to fulfill their parents' expectations, after all, their parents are older and presumably wiser. Another part tells them that the expectations that are right for their parents are not right for them. 29

I know a student who wants to be an artist. She is very obviously an artist and will be a good one—she has already had several modest exhibits. Meanwhile she is growing as a well-rounded person and taking humanistic subjects that will enrich the inner resources out of which her art will grow. But her father is strongly opposed. He thinks that an artist is a "dumb" thing to be. The student vacillates and tries to please everybody. She keeps up with her art somewhat furtively and takes some of the "dumb" courses her father wants her to take—at least they are dumb courses for her. She is a free spirit on a campus of tense students—no small achievement in itself— and she deserves to follow her muse. 30

Peer pressure and self-induced pressure are also intertwined, and they begin almost at the beginning of freshman year. 31

"I had a freshman student I'll call Linda," one dean told me, "who came in and said she was under terrible pressure because her roommate, Barbara, was much brighter and studied all the time. I couldn't tell her that Barbara had come in two hours earlier to say the same thing about Linda." 32

The story is almost funny—except that it's not. It's symptomatic of all   33
the pressures put together. When every student thinks every other student is working harder and doing better, the only solution is to study
harder still. I see students going off to the library every night after dinner
and coming back when it closes at midnight. I wish they could sometimes
forget about their peers and go to a movie. I hear the clacking of typewrit-
ers in the hours before dawn. I see the tension in their eyes when exams
are approaching and papers are due: *"Will I get everything done?"*

Probably they won't. They will get sick. They will get "blocked."   34
They will sleep. They will oversleep. They will bug out. *Hey Carlos, help!*

Part of the problem is that they do more than they are expected to do.   35
A professor will assign five-page papers. Several students will start writing ten-page papers to impress him. Then more students will write ten-
page papers, and a few will raise the ante to fifteen. Pity the poor student
who is still just doing the assignment.

"Once you have twenty or thirty percent of the student population   36
deliberating overexerting," one dean points out, "it's bad for everybody.
When a teacher gets more and more effort from his class, the student who
is doing normal work can be perceived as not doing well. The tactic
works, psychologically."

Why can't the professor just cut back and not accept longer papers?   37
He can, and he probably will. But by then the term will be half over and
the damage done. Grade fever is highly contagious and not easily reversed. Besides, the professor's main concern is with his course. He
knows his students only in relation to the course and doesn't know that
they are also overexerting in their other courses. Nor is it really his business. He didn't sign up for dealing with the student as a whole person
and with all the emotional baggage the student brought along from
home. That's what deans, masters, chaplains, and psychiatrists are for.

To some extent this is nothing new: a certain number of professors   38
have always been self-contained islands of scholarship and shyness, more
comfortable with books than with people. But the new pauperism has
widened the gap still further, for professors who actually like to spend
time with students don't have as much time to spend. They also are
overexerting. If they are young, they are busy trying to publish in order
not to perish, hanging by their fingernails onto a shrinking profession. If
they are old and tenured, they are buried under the duties of administering departments—as departmental chairmen or members of committees—that have been thinned out by the budgetary axe.

Ultimately it will be the students' own business to break the circles in   39
which they are trapped. They are too young to be prisoners of their parents' dreams and their classmates' fears. They must be jolted into believing in themselves as unique men and women who have the power to
shape their own future.

"Violence is being done to the undergraduate experience," says   40
Carlos Hortas. "College should be open-ended: at the end it should open

many, many roads. Instead, students are choosing their goal in advance, and their choices narrow as they go along. It's almost as if they think that the country has been codified in the type of jobs that exist—that they've got to fit into certain slots. Therefore, fit into the best-paying slot.

"They ought to take chances. Not taking chances will lead to a life of   41
colorless mediocrity. They'll be comfortable. But something in the spirit will be missing."

I have painted too drab a portrait of today's students, making them   42
seem a solemn lot. That is only half of their story; if they were so dreary I wouldn't so thoroughly enjoy their company. The other half is that they are easy to like. They are quick to laugh and to offer friendship. They are not introverts. They are usually kind and are more considerate of one another than any student generation I have known.

Nor are they so obsessed with their studies that they avoid sports and   43
extracurricular activities. On the contrary, they juggle their crowded hours to play on a variety of teams, perform with musical and dramatic groups, and write for campus publications. But this in turn is one more cause of anxiety. There are too many choices. Academically, they have 1,300 courses to select from; outside class they have to decide how much spare time they can spare and how to spend it.

This means that they engage in fewer extracurricular pursuits than   44
their predecessors did. If they want to row on the crew and play in the symphony they will eliminate one; in the '60s they would have done both. They also tend to choose activities that are self-limiting. Drama, for instance, is flourishing in all twelve of Yale's residential colleges as it never has before. Students hurl themselves into these productions—as actors, directors, carpenters, and technicians—with a dedication to create the best possible play, knowing that the day will come when the run will end and they can get back to their studies.

They also can't afford to be the willing slave of organizations like the   45
Yale Daily News. Last spring at the one-hundredth anniversary banquet of that paper—whose past chairmen include such once and future kings as Potter Stewart, Kingman Brewster, and William F. Buckley, Jr.*—much was made of the fact that the editorial staff used to be small and totally committed and that "newsies" routinely worked fifty hours a week. In effect they belonged to a club; Newsies is how they defined themselves at Yale. Today's student will write one or two articles a week, when he can, and he defines himself as a student. I've never heard the word Newsie except at the banquet.

If I have described the modern undergraduate primarily as a driven   46
creature who is largely ignoring the blithe spirit inside who keeps trying to come out and play, it's because that's where the crunch is, not only at Yale but throughout American education. It's why I think we should all

---

*EDS. NOTE—Stewart is a former U.S. Supreme Court Justice; Brewster is a former president of Yale; and Buckley is a conservative editor and columnist.

be worried about the values that are nurturing a generation so fearful of risk and so goal-obsessed at such an early age.

I tell students that there is no one "right" way to get ahead—that each of them is a different person, starting from a different point and bound for a different destination. I tell them that change is a tonic and that all the slots are not codified nor the frontiers closed. One of my ways of telling them is to invite men and women who have achieved success outside the academic world to come and talk informally with my students during the year. They are heads of companies or ad agencies, editors of magazines, politicians, public officials, television magnates, labor leaders, business executives, Broadway producers, artists, writers, economists, photographers, scientists, historians—a mixed bag of achievers.   47

I ask them to say a few words about how they got started. The students assume that they started in their present profession and knew all along that it was what they wanted to do. Luckily for me, most of them got into their field by a circuitous route, to their surprise, after many detours. The students are startled. They can hardly conceive of a career that was not pre-planned. They can hardly imagine allowing the hand of God or chance to nudge them down some unforeseen trail.   48

•   •   •

COMPREHENSION

1. What advice does Zinsser give students when they bring their problems to him?

2. What does Zinsser wish for his students? Why does he believe his wish is naive?

3. What four kinds of pressures does Zinsser identify?

4. Whom does Zinsser blame for the existence of the pressures? Explain.

5. How, according to Zinsser, is his evaluation of students different from their own and from their potential employers' assessments?

6. Why does Zinsser believe that women are probably under even more pressure than men?

7. How does what Zinsser calls the "new pauperism" (38) affect professors?

8. Who, according to Zinsser, is ultimately responsible for eliminating college pressures? Explain.

9. In what sense are sports and other extracurricular activities another source of anxiety for students? How do they adapt to this pressure?

PURPOSE AND AUDIENCE

1. In your own words, state Zinsser's thesis. Is his intent in this essay simply to expose a difficult situation or to effect change? Explain.

2. On what kind of audience do you think this essay would have the most significant impact: students, teachers, parents, potential employers, graduate school admissions committees, or college administrators? Why?

3. What do you think Zinsser hopes to accomplish in paragraphs 42–46? How might the essay be different without this section?

4. What assumptions does Zinsser make about his audience? Do you think these assumptions are valid? Explain.

STYLE AND STRUCTURE

1. Evaluate the essay's introductory strategy. What impact do you think the notes to Carlos are likely to have on readers?

2. Identify the boundaries of Zinsser's actual classification. How does he introduce the first category? How does he indicate that his treatment of the final category is complete?

3. What function do paragraphs 22 and 31 serve in the essay?

4. Zinsser is careful to explain that when he refers to students as *he,* he includes female students as well. However, he also refers to professors as *he* (for example, in paragraphs 35–37). Assuming that not all professors at Yale are male, what other stylistic options does Zinsser have in this situation?

5. At various points in the essay Zinsser quotes deans and students at Yale. What is the effect of these quotations?

6. Zinsser notes that his categories are "intertwined" (22, 31). In what ways do the categories overlap? Does this overlap weaken the essay? Explain.

7. What, if anything, seems to determine the order in which Zinsser introduces his categories? Is this order effective? Why or why not?

VOCABULARY PROJECTS

1. Define each of the following words as it is used in this selection.

proverbial (5)	intangible (16)	blithe (46)
supplicants (9)	accrue (21)	tonic (47)
balm (9)	exhorted (21)	codified (47)
privy (11)	tenacity (23)	
venerated (14)	faculties (28)	

2. At times Zinsser uses religious language—*national god, sacred document*—to describe the students' quest for success. Identify other examples of such language, and explain why it is used.

JOURNAL ENTRY

Which of the pressures Zinsser identifies has the strongest impact on you? Why? Do you have any other pressures that Zinsser does not mention?

WRITING WORKSHOP

1. Zinsser describes problems faced by students at an elite private college in the late 1970s. Are the pressures you experience as a college student similar to or different from the ones Zinsser identifies? Classify your own college pressures, and write an essay with a thesis statement that takes a strong stand against the forces responsible for the pressures.

2. Write a classification essay in which you support a thesis about college students' drive for success. Categorize students you know either by the degree of their need to succeed or by the different ways in which they wish to succeed.

3. Zinsser takes a negative view of the college pressures he identifies. Using his four categories, write an essay that argues that in the long run, these pressures are not only necessary but valuable.

COMBINING THE PATTERNS

Exemplification is an important secondary pattern in this classification-and-division essay. Identify as many passages of exemplifications as you can. What do these examples add to Zinsser's essay? What other examples might be helpful to readers?

THEMATIC CONNECTIONS

- "The 'Black Table' Is Still There" (page 284)
- "Suicide Note" (page 305)
- "The Company Man" (page 465)

SCOTT RUSSELL SANDERS

Scott Russell Sanders, born in 1945, is a professor of English at Indiana University and has written science fiction, folktales, children's stories, essays, and novels. His books include *Stone Country* (1985), a documentary narrative about Indiana's limestone region; *The Paradise of Bombs* (1987), a collection of essays; *The Invisible Company* (1989), a novel; two essay collections, *Secrets of the Universe: Scenes from the Journey Home* (1991) and *Staying Put: Making a Home in a Restless World* (1993); a book for young adults, *Writing from the Inside* (1995); and his latest work, *Terrarium* (1996). In "The Men We Carry in Our Minds," from *The Paradise of Bombs*, Sanders explains why as a man from a poor rural background he sees the men from his childhood community as very far from the positions of power that some women from more privileged circumstances think of and envy as typically male.

The Men We Carry in Our Minds

The first men, besides my father, I remember seeing were black convicts and white guards, in the cottonfield across the road from our farm on the outskirts of Memphis. I must have been three or four. The prisoners wore dingy gray-and-black zebra suits, heavy as canvas, sodden with sweat. Hatless, stooped, they chopped weeds in the fierce heat, row after row, breathing the acrid dust of boll-weevil poison. The overseers wore dazzling white shirts and broad shadowy hats. The oiled barrels of their shotguns flashed in the sunlight. Their faces in memory are utterly blank. Of course those men, white and black, have become for me an emblem of racial hatred. But they have also come to stand for the twin poles of my early vision of manhood—the brute toiling animal and the boss. 1

When I was a boy, the men I knew labored with their bodies. They were marginal farmers, just scraping by, or welders, steel workers, carpenters; they swept floors, dug ditches, mined coal, or drove trucks, their forearms ropy with muscle; they trained horses, stoked furnaces, built tires, stood on assembly lines wrestling parts onto cars and refrigerators. They got up before light, worked all day long whatever the weather, and when they came home at night they looked as though somebody had been whipping them. In the evenings and on weekends they worked on their own places, tilling gardens that were lumpy with clay, fixing broken-down cars, hammering on houses that were always too drafty, too leaky, too small. 2

The bodies of the men I knew were twisted and maimed in ways visible and invisible. The nails of their hands were black and split, the hands tattooed with scars. Some had lost fingers. Heavy lifting had given many of them finicky backs and guts weak from hernias. Racing against conveyor belts had given them ulcers. Their ankles and knees ached from years of standing on concrete. Anyone who had worked for long around 3 machines was hard of hearing. They squinted, and the skin of their faces was creased like the leather of old work gloves. There were times, studying them, when I dreaded growing up. Most of them coughed, from dust or cigarettes, and most of them drank cheap wine or whiskey, so their eyes looked bloodshot and bruised. The fathers of my friends always seemed older than the mothers. Men wore out sooner. Only women lived into old age.

As a boy I also knew another sort of men, who did not sweat and   4
break down like mules. They were soldiers, and so far as I could tell they scarcely worked at all. During my early school years we lived on a military base, an arsenal in Ohio, and every day I saw GIs in the guardshacks, on the stoops of barracks, at the wheels of olive drab Chevrolets. The chief fact of their lives was boredom. Long after I left the Arsenal I came to recognize the sour smell the soldiers gave off as that of souls in limbo. They were all waiting—for wars, for transfers, for leaves, for promotions, for the end of their hitch—like so many braves waiting for the hunt to begin. Unlike the warriors of older tribes, however, they would have no say about when the battle would start or how it would be waged. Their waiting was broken only when they practiced for war. They fired guns at targets, drove tanks across the churned-up fields of the military reservation, set off bombs in the wrecks of old fighter planes. I knew this was all play. But I also felt certain that when the hour for killing arrived, they would kill. When the real shooting started, many of them would die. This was what soldiers were *for*, just as a hammer was for driving nails.

Warriors and toilers: those seemed, in my boyhood vision, to be the   5
chief destinies for men. They weren't the only destinies, as I learned from having a few male teachers, from reading books, and from watching television. But the men on television—the politicians, the astronauts, the generals, the savvy lawyers, the philosophical doctors, the bosses who gave orders to both soldiers and laborers—seemed as remote and unreal to me as the figures in tapestries. I could no more imagine growing up to become one of these cool, potent creatures than I could imagine becoming a prince.

A nearer and more hopeful example was that of my father, who had   6
escaped from a red-dirt farm to a tire factory, and from the assembly line to the front office. Eventually he dressed in a white shirt and tie. He carried himself as if he had been born to work with his mind. But his body, remembering the earlier years of slogging work, began to give out on him in his fifties, and it quit on him entirely before he turned sixty-five. Even such a partial escape from man's fate as he had accomplished did not seem possible for most of the boys I knew. They joined the Army, stood in line for jobs in the smoky plants, helped build highways. They were bound to work as their fathers had worked, killing themselves or preparing to kill others.

A scholarship enabled me not only to attend college, a rare enough   7
feat in my circle, but even to study in a university meant for the children of the rich. Here I met for the first time young men who had assumed

from birth that they would lead lives of comfort and power. And for the first time I met women who told me that men were guilty of having kept all the joys and privileges of the earth for themselves. I was baffled. What privileges? What joys? I thought about the maimed, dismal lives of most of the men back home. What had they stolen from their wives and daughters? The right to go five days a week, twelve months a year, for thirty or forty years to a steel mill or a coal mine? The right to drop bombs and die in war? The right to feel every leak in the roof, every gap in the fence, every cough in the engine, as a wound they must mend? The right to feel, when the layoff comes or the plant shuts down, not only afraid but ashamed?

I was slow to understand the deep grievances of women. This was   8
because, as a boy, I had envied them. Before college, the only people I had ever known who were interested in art or music or literature, the only ones who read books, the only ones who ever seemed to enjoy a sense of ease and grace were the mothers and daughters. Like the menfolk, they fretted about money, they scrimped and made-do. But, when the pay stopped coming in, they were not the ones who had failed. Nor did they have to go to war, and that seemed to me a blessed fact. By comparison with the narrow, ironclad days of fathers, there was an expansiveness, I thought, in the days of mothers. They went to see neighbors, to shop in town, to run errands at school, at the library, at church. No doubt, had I looked harder at their lives, I would have envied them less. It was not my fate to become a woman, so it was easier for me to see the graces. Few of them held jobs outside the home, and those who did filled thankless roles as clerks and waitresses. I didn't see, then, what a prison a house could be, since houses seemed to me brighter, handsomer places than any factory. I didn't realize—because such things were never spoken of—how often women suffered from men's bullying. I did learn about the wretchedness of abandoned wives, single mothers, widows; but I also learned about the wretchedness of lone men. Even then I could see how exhausting it was for a mother to cater all day to the needs of young children. But if I had been asked, as a boy, to choose between tending a baby and tending a machine, I think I would have chosen the baby. (Having now tended both, I know I would choose the baby.)

So I was baffled when the women at college accused me and my sex   9
of having cornered the world's pleasures. I think something like my bafflement has been felt by other boys (and by girls as well) who grew up in dirt-poor farm country, in mining country, in black ghettos, in Hispanic barrios, in the shadows of factories, in Third World nations—any place where the fate of men is as grim and bleak as the fate of women. Toilers and warriors. I realize now how ancient these identities are, how deep the tug they exert on men, the undertow of a thousand generations. The miseries I saw, as a boy, in the lives of nearly all men I continue to see in the lives of many—the body-breaking toil, the tedium, the call to be tough, the humiliating powerlessness, the battle for a living and for territory.

When the women I met at college thought about the joys and privi- 10
leges of men, they did not carry in their minds the sort of men I had
known in my childhood. They thought of their fathers, who were
bankers, physicians, architects, stockbrokers, the big wheels of the big
cities. These fathers rode the train to work or drove cars that cost more
than any of my childhood houses. They were attended from morning to
night by female helpers, wives and nurses and secretaries. They were
never laid off, never short of cash at month's end, never lined up for
welfare. These fathers made decisions that mattered. They ran the
world.

The daughters of such men wanted to share in this power, this glory. 11
So did I. They yearned for a say over their future, for jobs worthy of
their abilities, for the right to live at peace, unmolested, whole. Yes, I
thought, yes yes. The difference between me and these daughters was
that they saw me, because of my sex, as destined from birth to become
like their fathers, and therefore as an enemy to their desires. But I knew
better. I wasn't an enemy, in fact or in feeling. I was an ally. If I had
known, then, how to tell them so, would they have believed me? Would
they now?

•   •   •

COMPREHENSION

1. What does Sanders mean in paragraph 1 when he characterizes the black
   convicts and white guards as "an emblem of racial hatred"? In what
   sense do they represent "the twin poles of [his] early vision of manhood"?

2. When he was a child, what did Sanders expect to become when he grew
   up? Why? How did he escape this destiny?

3. What advantages did Sanders initially attribute to women? Why? What
   challenged his assumptions?

4. What kind of men did the women Sanders met in college carry in their
   minds? Why did the women see Sanders as "an enemy to their desires"
   (11)? How did he defend himself against their charges?

PURPOSE AND AUDIENCE

1. What purpose do you think Sanders had in mind when he wrote this
   essay? Is his essay intended as a personal memoir, or does he have another agenda? Explain.

2. What is the essay's thesis?

3. Is this essay directed primarily at workers like the ones Sanders grew up
   watching or at the "children of the rich" (7)? At men or at women? On
   whom would you expect it to have the greatest impact? Explain.

STYLE AND STRUCTURE

1. What is Sanders categorizing in this essay? What categories does he name? What other, unnamed categories does he identify?

2. What principle of classification determines the categories Sanders discusses?

3. What, if anything, determines the order in which Sanders discusses his categories?

4. Is the treatment of the various categories in this essay balanced, or does Sanders give more attention to some than to others? If some categories are given more attention, does this weaken the essay? Explain.

VOCABULARY PROJECTS

1. Define each of the following words as it is used in this selection.

acrid (1)	finicky (3)	expansiveness (8)
boll weevil (1)	slogging (6)	undertow (9)
overseers (1)	fretted (8)	unmolested (11)
maimed (3)	ironclad (8)	

2. Invent descriptive titles for the categories Sanders does not name. Be sure to include categories that cover women's roles as well as men's, and be sure your categories do not overlap.

JOURNAL ENTRY

Do you agree with Sanders when he suggests that men have harder lives than women do? What is your reaction to his parenthetical comment at the end of paragraph 8?

WRITING WORKSHOP

1. Imagine the possible kinds of work available to you in the field you expect to study. Write a classification-and-division essay in which you discuss several categories of possible future employment, arranging them from least to most desirable.

2. Consider the adult workers you know best—your relatives, friends' parents, employers, teachers—and other workers with whom you come in contact on a regular basis (merchants, for example). Write a classification-and-division essay in which you devise categories that distinguish different types of workers. Then, discuss these categories of workers in terms of how fortunate (or unfortunate) they are. Consider income level, job security, working conditions, prestige, and job satisfaction in your discussion of each category. In your essay's introduction and conclusion, consider how the employment categories you have devised are like or unlike Sanders's.

3. What kinds of jobs do you see as "dream jobs"? Why? List as many of these ideal jobs as you can, and group them into logical categories according to a single principle of classification. Then, write an essay with a thesis statement that expresses the value you see in these jobs.

COMBINING THE PATTERNS

After he establishes his categories, Sanders uses **description** to characterize workers and distinguish them from one another. Identify and evaluate the passages that serve these two purposes. Is any category of worker identified but not described? Explain.

THEMATIC CONNECTIONS

- "Midnight" (page 165)
- "On Fire" (page 235)
- "On the Meaning of Plumbing and Poverty" (page 288)
- "Ex–Basketball Player" (page 364)

AMY TAN

Amy Tan (1952–) was born in Oakland, California, the daughter of recent Chinese immigrants. Her parents had high ambitions for her; in fact, Tan has quipped, her mother expected her to become both a neurosurgeon and a world-famous classical pianist. Instead, she studied linguistics at San Francisco State University and began a career as a corporate communications specialist. In 1984, at the suggestion of a counselor she was seeing for her workaholism, Tan began to write stories as a sort of do-it-yourself therapy. At about the same time, a visit to China with her mother helped focus her thinking on her parents' traditional life in China and on the internal contradictions she faced in her role as both their daughter and a highly Americanized Chinese-American. Three years later she published her first novel, *The Joy Luck Club* (1987), a critically acclaimed look at the impact of past generations on the present, told through the stories of four immigrant Chinese women and their American-born daughters. Later works include *The Kitchen God's Wife* (1991) and *The Hundred Secret Senses* (1995) as well as two children's books, *The Moon Lady* (1992) and *The Chinese Siamese Cat* (1994). In the following essay Tan explores the different "Englishes" she uses, particularly in relation to her mother.

Mother Tongue

I am not a scholar of English or literature. I cannot give you much more than personal opinions on the English language and its variations in this country or others.

I am a writer. And by that definition, I am someone who has always loved language. I am fascinated by language in daily life. I spend a great deal of my time thinking about the power of language—the way it can evoke an emotion, a visual image, a complex idea, or a simple truth. Language is the tool of my trade. And I use them all—all the Englishes I grew up with.

Recently, I was made keenly aware of the different Englishes I do use. I was giving a talk to a large group of people, the same talk I had already given to half a dozen other groups. The nature of the talk was about my writing, my life, and my book, *The Joy Luck Club*. The talk was going along well enough, until I remembered one major difference that made the whole talk sound wrong. My mother was in the room. And it was perhaps the first time she had heard me give a lengthy speech, using the kind of English I have never used with her. I was saying things like, "The intersection of memory upon imagination" and "There is an aspect of my fiction that relates to thus-and-thus"—a speech filled with carefully wrought grammatical phrases, burdened, it suddenly seemed to me, with nominalized forms, past perfect tenses, conditional phrases, all the forms of standard English that I had learned in school and through books, the forms of English I did not use at home with my mother.

Just last week, I was walking down the street with my mother, and I   4
again found myself conscious of the English I was using, and the English
I do use with her. We were talking about the price of new and used furniture and I heard myself saying this: "Not waste money that way." My
husband was with us as well, and he didn't notice any switch in my
English. And then I realized why. It's because over the twenty years
we've been together I've often used that same kind of English with him,
and sometimes he even uses it with me. It has become our language of intimacy, a different sort of English that relates to family talk, the language I
grew up with.

So you'll have some idea of what this family talk I heard sounds like,   5
I'll quote what my mother said during a recent conversation which I
videotaped and then transcribed. During this conversation my mother
was talking about a political gangster in Shanghai who had the same last
name as her family's, Du, and how the gangster in his early years wanted
to be adopted by her family, which was rich by comparison. Later, the
gangster became more powerful, far richer than my mother's family, and
one day showed up at my mother's wedding to pay his respects. Here's
what she said in part:

"Du Yusong having business like fruit stand. Like off the street kind.   6
He is Du like Du Zong—but not Tsung-ming Island people. The local people call putong, the river east side, he belong to that side local people. The
man want to ask Du Zong father take him in like become own family. Du
Zong father wasn't looking down on him, but didn't take seriously, until
that man big like become a mafia. Now important person very hard to
inviting him. Chinese way, come only to show respect, don't stay for dinner. Respect for making big celebration, he shows up. Mean gives lots of respect. Chinese custom. Chinese social life that way. If too important won't
have to stay too long. He come to my wedding. I didn't see. I heard it. I
gone to boy's side, they have YMCA dinner. Chinese age I was nineteen."

You should know that my mother's expressive command of English   7
belies how much she actually understands. She reads the *Forbes* report,
listens to *Wall Street Week*, converses daily with her stockbroker, reads all
of Shirley MacLaine's books with ease—all kinds of things I can't begin to
understand. Yet some of my friends tell me they understand 50 percent of
what my mother says. Some say they understand 80 to 90 percent. Some
say they understand none of it, as if she were speaking pure Chinese. But
to me, my mother's English is perfectly clear, perfectly natural. It's my
mother's tongue. Her language, as I hear it, is vivid, direct, full of observation and imagery. This was the language that helped shape the way I
saw things, expressed things, made sense of the world.

Lately, I've been giving more thought to the kind of English my   8
mother speaks. Like others, I have described it to people as "broken" or
"fractured" English. But I wince when I say that. It has always bothered
me that I can think of no way to describe it other than "broken," as if it

were damaged and needed to be fixed, as if it lacked a certain wholeness and soundness. I've heard other terms used, "limited English," for example. But they seem just as bad, as if everything is limited, including people's perceptions of the limited English speaker.

I know this for a fact, because when I was growing up, my mother's 9 "limited" English limited *my* perception of her. I was ashamed of her English. I believed that her English reflected the quality of what she had to say. That is, because she expressed them imperfectly her thoughts were imperfect. And I had plenty of empirical evidence to support me: the fact that people in department stores, at banks, and at restaurants did not take her seriously, did not give her good service, pretended not to understand her, or even acted as if they did not hear her.

My mother has long realized the limitations of her English as well. 10 When I was fifteen, she used to have me call people on the phone to pretend I was she. In this guise, I was forced to ask for information or even complain and yell at people who had been rude to her. One time it was a call to her stockbroker in New York. She had cashed out her small portfolio and it just so happened we were going to go to New York the next week, our very first trip outside California. I had to get on the phone and say in an adolescent voice that was not very convincing, "This is Mrs. Tan."

And my mother was standing in the back whispering loudly, "Why 11 he don't send me check, already two weeks late. So mad he lie to me, losing me money."

And then I said in perfect English, "Yes, I'm getting rather concerned. 12 You had agreed to send the check two weeks ago, but it hasn't arrived."

Then she began to talk more loudly. "What he want, I come to New 13 York tell him front of his boss, you cheating me?" And I was trying to calm her down, make her be quiet, while telling the stockbroker, "I can't tolerate any more excuses. If I don't receive the check immediately I am going to have to speak to your manager when I'm in New York next week." And sure enough, the following week there we were in front of this astonished stockbroker, and I was sitting there red-faced and quiet, and my mother, the real Mrs. Tan, was shouting at his boss in her impeccable broken English.

We used a similar routine just five days ago, for a situation that was 14 far less humorous. My mother had gone to the hospital for an appointment, to find out about a benign brain tumor a CAT scan had revealed a month ago. She said she had spoken very good English, her best English, no mistakes. Still, she said, the hospital did not apologize when they said they had lost the CAT scan and she had come for nothing. She said they did not seem to have any sympathy when she told them she was anxious to know the exact diagnosis, since her husband and son had both died of brain tumors. She said they would not give her any more information until the next time and she would have to make another appointment for that. So she said she would not leave until the doctor called her daughter. She wouldn't budge. And when the doctor finally called her daughter, me, who spoke in perfect English—lo and behold—we had assurances the CAT scan would be found, promises that a conference call on Monday would be held, and apologies for any suffering my mother had gone through for a most regrettable mistake.

I think my mother's English almost had an effect on limiting my pos- 15 sibilities in life as well. Sociologists and linguists probably will tell you that a person's developing language skills are more influenced by peers. But I do think that the language spoken in the family, especially in immi- grant families which are more insular, plays a large role in shaping the language of the child. And I believe that it affected my results on achieve- ment tests, IQ tests, and the SAT. While my English skills were never judged as poor, compared to math, English could not be considered my strong suit. In grade school I did moderately well, getting perhaps B's, sometimes B-pluses, in English and scoring perhaps in the sixtieth or sev- entieth percentile on achievement tests. But those scores were not good enough to override the opinion that my true abilities lay in math and sci- ence, because in those areas I achieved A's and scored in the ninetieth per- centile or higher.

This was understandable. Math is precise; there is only one correct 16 answer. Whereas, for me at least, the answers on English tests were al- ways a judgment call, a matter of opinion and personal experience. Those tests were constructed around items like fill-in-the-blank sentence com- pletion, such as "Even though Tom was _____, Mary thought he was _____." And the correct answer always seemed to be the most bland combinations of thoughts, for example, "Even though Tom was shy, Mary thought he was charming," with the grammatical structure "even though" limiting the correct answer to some sort of semantic opposites, so you wouldn't get answers like, "Even though Tom was foolish, Mary thought he was ridiculous." Well, according to my mother, there were very few limitations as to what Tom could have been and what Mary might have thought of him. So I never did well on tests like that.

The same was true with word analogies, pairs of words in which you 17 were supposed to find some sort of logical, semantic relationship—for ex- ample, "*Sunset* is to *nightfall* as _____ is to _____." And here you would be presented with a list of four possible pairs, one of which showed the same kind of relationship: *red* is to *stoplight*, *bus* is to *arrival*, *chills* is to *fever*, *yawn* is to *boring*. Well, I could never think that way. I knew what the tests were asking, but I could not block out of my mind the images already created by the first pair, "*sunset* is to *nightfall*"—and I would see a burst of colors against a darkening sky, the moon rising, the lowering of a curtain of stars. And all the other pairs of words—red, bus, stoplight, boring—just threw up a mass of confusing images, making it impossible for me to sort out something as logical as saying: "A sunset precedes nightfall" is the same as "a chill precedes a fever." The only way I would have gotten that answer right would have been to imagine an as- sociative situation, for example, my being disobedient and staying out past sunset, catching a chill at night, which turns into feverish pneumonia as punishment, which indeed did happen to me.

I have been thinking about all this lately, about my mother's English,   18
about achievement tests. Because lately I've been asked, as a writer, why there are not more Asian Americans represented in American literature. Why are there few Asian Americans enrolled in creative writing programs? Why do so many Chinese students go into engineering? Well, these are broad sociological questions I can't begin to answer. But I have noticed in surveys—in fact, just last week—that Asian students, as a whole, always do significantly better on math achievement tests than in English. And this makes me think that there are other Asian-American students whose English spoken in the home might also be described as "broken" or "limited." And perhaps they also have teachers who are steering them away from writing and into math and science, which is what happened to me.

Fortunately, I happen to be rebellious in nature and enjoy the chal-   19
lenge of disproving assumptions made about me. I became an English major my first year in college, after being enrolled as pre-med. I started writing nonfiction as a freelancer the week after I was told by my former boss that writing was my worst skill and I should hone my talents toward account management.

But it wasn't until 1985 that I finally began to write fiction. And at   20
first I wrote using what I thought to be wittily crafted sentences, sentences that would finally prove I had mastery over the English language. Here's an example from the first draft of a story that later made its way into *The Joy Luck Club*, but without this line: "That was my mental quandary in its nascent state." A terrible line, which I can barely pronounce.

Fortunately, for reasons I won't get into today, I later decided I should   21
envision a reader for the stories I would write. And the reader I decided upon was my mother because these were stories about mothers. So with this reader in mind—and in fact she did read my early drafts—I began to write stories using all the Englishes I grew up with: the English I spoke to my mother, which for lack of a better term might be described as "simple"; the English she used with me, which for lack of a better term might be described as "broken"; my translation of her Chinese, which could certainly be described as "watered down"; and what I imagined to be her translation of her Chinese if she could speak in perfect English, her internal language, and for that I sought to preserve the essence, but neither an English nor a Chinese structure. I wanted to capture what language ability tests can never reveal: her intent, her passion, her imagery, the rhythms of her speech and the nature of her thoughts.

Apart from what any critic had to say about my writing, I knew I had   22
succeeded where it counted when my mother finished reading my book and gave me her verdict: "So easy to read."

• • •

COMPREHENSION

1. What is Tan classifying in this essay? What individual categories does she identify?

2. Where does Tan identify the different categories she discusses in "Mother Tongue"? Should she have identified these categories earlier? Why or why not?

3. Does Tan illustrate each category she identifies? Does she treat all categories equally? If she does not, do you see this as a problem? Explain.

4. In what specific situations does Tan say her mother's "limited English" was a handicap? In what other situations might Mrs. Tan face difficulties?

5. How did her mother's English affect Tan's life?

6. How does Tan account for the difficulty she had in answering questions on achievement tests, particularly word analogies? Do you think her problems in this area can be explained by the level of her family's language skills, or might other factors have contributed to the problem? Explain.

7. In paragraph 18 Tan considers the possible reasons for the lack of Asian-Americans in the fields of language and literature. What explanations does she offer? What other explanations can you think of?

PURPOSE AND AUDIENCE

1. Why do you suppose Tan opens her essay by explaining her qualifications? Why, for example, does she tell her readers that she is "not a scholar of English or literature" (1) but rather a writer who is "fascinated by language in daily life" (2)?

2. Do you think Tan expects most of her readers to be Asian-American? To be familiar with Asian-American languages and culture? Explain your reasoning.

3. Is Tan's primary focus in this essay on language or on her mother? Explain your conclusion.

STYLE AND STRUCTURE

1. This essay is relatively informal. For example, Tan uses *I* to refer to herself and addresses her readers as *you*. Identify other features that characterize her style as informal. Do you think Tan would increase her credibility if she were to use a more formal style? Explain your reasoning.

2. In paragraph 6 Tan quotes a passage of her mother's speech. What purpose does Tan say is served by this quotation? What impression does it give of her mother? Do you think this effect is what Tan intended? Explain.

3. In paragraphs 10 through 13 Tan juxtaposes her mother's English with her own. What point do these quoted passages make?

4. The expression used in Tan's title, "Mother Tongue," is also used in paragraph 7. What does this expression generally mean? What does it seem to mean in this essay?

5. In paragraph 20 Tan quotes a "terrible line" from an early draft of part of her novel *The Joy Luck Club*. Why do you suppose she quotes this line? How is it different from the style she uses in "Mother Tongue"?

VOCABULARY PROJECTS

1. Define each of the following words as it is used in this selection.

nominalized (3)	guise (10)	semantic (16)
belies (7)	impeccable (13)	quandary (20)
empirical (9)	insular (15)	nascent (20)

2. In paragraph 8 Tan discusses the different words that might be used to describe her mother's spoken English. Which term seems most accurate? Do you agree with Tan that these words are unsatisfactory? What other term for her mother's English would be both neutral and accurate?

JOURNAL ENTRY

In paragraph 9 Tan says that when she was growing up she was sometimes ashamed of her mother because of her limited English proficiency. Have you ever felt ashamed of one of your parents because of their inability to "fit in" in some way? How do you feel now about your earlier reaction?

WRITING WORKSHOP

1. What different "Englishes" (or other languages) do you use in your day-to-day life as a student, employee, friend, and family member? Write a classification-and-division essay in which you identify, describe, and illustrate each kind of language and explain the purpose it serves.

2. What kinds of problems are faced today by a person whose English is as limited as that of Mrs. Tan? Write a classification-and-division essay that identifies and explains the kinds of problems you might encounter if your spoken English were comparable to hers.

3. Tan's essay focuses on spoken language, but people also use different kinds of *written* language in different situations. Write a classification-and-division essay that identifies three different kinds of written English: one appropriate for your parents, one for a teacher or employer, and one for a friend. Illustrate each kind of language with an extended example in which you write about your plans for your future. Then analyze the language used in each piece of writing. In your thesis statement, explain why you need all three kinds of language.

COMBINING THE PATTERNS

Tan develops her essay with a series of anecdotes about her mother and about herself. How does this use of **narration** strengthen her essay? Could she have made her point about the use of different "Englishes" without these anecdotes? What other strategy could she have used?

THEMATIC CONNECTIONS

- "Only Daughter" (page 70)
- "Words Left Unspoken" (page 121)
- "English Is a Crazy Language" (page 181)
- "The Human Cost of an Illiterate Society" (page 192)
- "Aria: A Memoir of a Bilingual Childhood" (page 357)

ALLEEN PACE NILSEN

Alleen Pace Nilsen was born in 1936 in Phoenix, Arizona, and graduated from Brigham Young University in 1958. She received her doctorate from the University of Iowa in 1973, writing her dissertation on the effect of sexist language in children's literature. In 1975 Nilsen began teaching at Arizona State University, where she became professor of education and assistant dean of the graduate college and is currently professor of English. Nilsen writes articles on young adult literature for several scholarly journals. She has also written, coauthored, or edited several books, including *Sexism and Language* (1977), a collection of scholarly essays; *Presenting M. E. Kerr* (1986), a study of Kerr's young adult fiction; and the fourth edition of *Literature for Today's Young Adults* (1995). The original version of the following essay was titled "Sexism in English: A Feminist View" and appeared in a collection published in 1972. In this version, written in 1990, Nilsen brings up to date her examination of how language, in particular the terms used for women and men, reveals much about social attitudes and assumptions.

Sexism in English: A 1990s Update

Twenty years ago I embarked on a study of the sexism inherent in American English. I had just returned to Ann Arbor, Michigan, after living for two years (1967–69) in Kabul, Afghanistan, where I had begun to look critically at the role society assigned to women. The Afghan version of the *chaderi** prescribed for Moslem women was particularly confining. Afghan jokes and folklore were blatantly sexist, such as this proverb: "If you see an old man, sit down and take a lesson; if you see an old woman, throw a stone."

But it wasn't only the native culture that made me question women's roles, it was also the American community.

Most of the American women were like myself—wives and mothers whose husbands were either career diplomats, employees of USAID, or college professors who had been recruited to work on various contract teams. We were suddenly bereft of our traditional roles: some of us became alcoholics, others got very good at bridge while still others searched desperately for ways to contribute either to our families or to the Afghans. The local economy provided few jobs for women and certainly none for foreigners; we were isolated from former friends and the social goals we had grown up with.

When I returned in the fall of 1969 to the University of Michigan in Ann Arbor, I was surprised to find that many other women were also questioning the expectations they had grown up with. In the spring of

1

2

3

4

---

*EDS. NOTE—Full-length outer garment traditionally worn by Muslim women in public.

1970, a women's conference was announced. I hired a baby-sitter and attended, but I returned home more troubled than ever. The militancy of these women frightened me. Since I wasn't ready for a revolution, I decided I would have my own feminist movement. I would study the English language and see what it could tell me about sexism. I started reading a desk dictionary and making notecards on every entry that seemed to tell something about male and female. I soon had a dog-eared dictionary, along with a collection of notecards filling two shoe boxes.

Ironically, I started reading the dictionary because I wanted to avoid   5
getting involved in social issues, but what happened was that my notecards brought me right back to looking at society. Language and society are as intertwined as a chicken and an egg. The language a culture uses is telltale evidence of the values and beliefs of that culture. And because there is a lag in how fast a language changes—new words can easily be introduced, but it takes a long time for old words and usages to disappear—a careful look at English will reveal the attitudes that our ancestors held and that we as a culture are therefore predisposed to hold. My notecards revealed three main points. Friends have offered the opinion that I didn't need to read the dictionary to learn such obvious facts. Nevertheless, it was interesting to have linguistic evidence of sociological observations.

WOMEN ARE SEXY; MEN ARE SUCCESSFUL

First, in American culture a woman is valued for the attractiveness   6
and sexiness of her body, while a man is valued for his physical strength and accomplishments. A woman is sexy. A man is successful.

A persuasive piece of evidence supporting this view are the eponyms   7
—words that have come from someone's name—found in English. I had a two-and-a-half-inch stack of cards taken from men's names but less than a half-inch stack from women's names, and most of those came from Greek mythology. In the words that came into American English since we separated from Britain, there are many eponyms based on the names of famous American men: *Bartlett pear, boysenberry, diesel engine, Franklin stove, Ferris wheel, Gatling gun, mason jar, sideburns, sousaphone, Schick test,* and *Winchester rifle.* The only common eponyms taken from American women's names are *Alice blue* (after Alice Roosevelt Longworth), *bloomers* (after Amelia Jenks Bloomer), and *Mae West jacket* (after the buxom actress). Two out of the three feminine eponyms relate closely to a woman's physical anatomy, while the masculine eponyms (except for *sideburns* after General Burnsides) have nothing to do with the namesake's body but, instead, honor the man for an accomplishment of some kind.

Although in Greek mythology women played a bigger role than they   8
did in the biblical stories of the Judeo-Christian cultures and so the names of goddesses are accepted parts of the language in such place names as

Pomona from the goddess of fruit and *Athens* from Athena and in such common words as *cereal* from Ceres, *psychology* from Psyche, and *arachnoid* from Arachne, the same tendency to think of women in relation to sexuality is seen in the eponyms *aphrodisiac* from Aphrodite, the Greek name for the goddess of love and beauty, and *venereal disease* from Venus, the Roman name for Aphrodite.

Another interesting word from Greek mythology is *Amazon.* 9
According to Greek folk etymology, the *a* means "without" as in *atypical* or *amoral,* while *mazon* comes from *mazos* meaning "breast" as still seen in *mastectomy.* In the Greek legend, Amazon women cut off their right breasts so that they could better shoot their bows. Apparently, the storytellers had a feeling that for women to play the active, "masculine" role the Amazons adopted for themselves, they had to trade in part of their femininity.

This preoccupation with women's breasts is not limited to ancient 10
stories. As a volunteer for the University of Wisconsin's *Dictionary of American Regional English (DARE),* I read a western trapper's diary from the 1930s. I was to make notes of any unusual usages or language patterns. My most interesting finding was that the trapper referred to a range of mountains as *The Teats,* a metaphor based on the similarity between the shapes of mountains and women's breasts. Because today we use the French wording, *The Grand Tetons,* the metaphor isn't as obvious, but I wrote to mapmakers and found the following listings: *Nippletop* and *Little Nipple Top* near Mount Marcy in the Adirondacks; *Nipple Mountain* in Archuleta County, Colorado; *Nipple Peak* in Coke County, Texas; *Nipple Butte* in Pennington, South Dakota; *Squaw Peak* in Placer County, California (and many other locations); *Maiden's Peak* and *Squaw Tit* (they're the same mountain) in the Cascade Range in Oregon; *Mary's Nipple* near Salt Lake City, Utah; and *Jane Russell Peaks* near Stark, New Hampshire.

Except for the movie star Jane Russell, the women being referred to 11
are anonymous—it's only a sexual part of their body that is mentioned. When topographical features are named after men, it's probably not going to be to draw attention to a sexual part of their bodies but instead to honor individuals for an accomplishment. For example, no one thinks of a part of the male body when hearing a reference to Pike's Peak, Colorado, or Jackson Hole, Wyoming.

Going back to what I learned from my dictionary cards, I was sur- 12
prised to realize how many pairs of words we have in which the feminine word has acquired sexual connotations while the masculine word retains a serious businesslike aura. For example, a *callboy* is the person who calls actors when it is time for them to go on stage, but a *callgirl* is a prostitute. Compare *sir* and *madam. Sir* is a term of respect, while *madam* has acquired the specialized meaning of a brothel manager. Something similar has happened to *master* and *mistress.* Would you rather have a painting by an *old master* or an *old mistress*?

It's because the word *woman* had sexual connotations, as in "She's his   13
woman," that people began avoiding its use, hence such terminology as
ladies' room, lady of the house, and *girls' school* or *school for young ladies.*
Feminists, who ask that people use the term *woman* rather than *girl* or *lady,*
are rejecting the idea that *woman* is primarily a sexual term. They have
been at least partially successful in that today *woman* is commonly used to
communicate gender without intending implications about sexuality.

I found two hundred pairs of words with masculine and feminine   14
forms, e.g., *heir-heiress, hero-heroine, steward-stewardess, usher-usherette.* In
nearly all such pairs, the masculine word is considered the base, with
some kind of feminine suffix being added. The masculine form is the one
from which compounds are made, e.g., from *king-queen* comes *kingdom*
but not *queendom,* from *sportsman-sportslady* comes *sportsmanship* but not
sportsladyship. There is one—and only one—semantic area in which the
masculine word is not the base or more powerful word. This is the area
dealing with sex and marriage. When someone refers to a *virgin,* a listener
will probably think of a female, unless the speaker specifies *male* or uses a
masculine pronoun. The same is true for *prostitute.*

In relation to marriage, there is much linguistic evidence showing   15
that weddings are more important to women than to men. A woman
cherishes the wedding and is considered a bride for a whole year, but a
man is referred to as a groom only on the day of the wedding. The word
bride appears in *bridal attendant, bridal gown, bridesmaid, bridal shower,* and
even *bridegroom. Groom* comes from the Middle English *grom,* meaning
"man," and in the sense is seldom used outside of the wedding. With
most pairs of male/female words, people habitually put the masculine
word first, *Mr. and Mrs., his and hers, boys and girls, men and women, kings
and queens, brothers and sisters, guys and dolls,* and *host and hostess,* but it is
the *bride and groom* who are talked about, not the *groom and bride.*

The importance of marriage to a woman is also shown by the fact that   16
when a marriage ends in death, the woman gets the title of *widow.* A man
gets the derived title of *widower.* This term is not used in other phrases or
contexts, but *widow* is seen in *widowhood, widow's peak,* and *widow's walk.* A
widow in a card game is an extra hand of cards, while in typesetting it is
an extra line of type.

How changing cultural ideas bring changes to language is clearly vis-   17
ible in this semantic area. The feminist movement has caused the differences between the sexes to be downplayed, and since I did my dictionary
study two decades ago, the word *singles* has largely replaced such sex
specific and value-laden terms as *bachelor, old maid, spinster, divorcee,
widow,* and *widower.* And in 1970 I wrote that when a man is called *a professional* he is thought to be a doctor or a lawyer, but when people hear a
woman referred to as *a professional* they are likely to think of a prostitute.
That's not as true today because so many women have become doctors
and lawyers that it's no longer incongruous to think of women in those
professional roles.

Another change that has taken place is in wedding announcements.   18
They used to be sent out from the bride's parents and did not even give
the name of the groom's parents. Today, most couples choose to list either
all or none of the parents' names. Also it is now much more likely that
both the bride and groom's picture will be in the newspaper, while a
decade ago only the bride's picture was published on the "Women's" or
the "Society" page. Even the traditional wording of the wedding ceremony is being changed. Many officials now pronounced the couple "husband and wife" instead of the old "man and wife," and they ask the bride
if she promises "to love, honor, and cherish," instead of "to love, honor,
and obey."

WOMEN ARE PASSIVE; MEN ARE ACTIVE

The wording of the wedding ceremony also relates to the second   19
point that my cards showed, which is that women are expected to play a
passive or weak role while men play an active or strong role. In the traditional ceremony, the official asks, "Who gives the bride away?" and the
father answers, "I do," Some fathers answer, "Her mother and I do," but
that doesn't solve the problem inherent in the question. The idea that a
bride is something to be handed over from one man to another bothers
people because it goes back to the days when a man's servants, his children, and his wife were all considered to be his property. They were
known by his name because they belonged to him, and he was responsible for their actions and their debts.

The grammar used in talking or writing about weddings as well as   20
other sexual relationships shows the expectation of men playing the active role. Men *wed* women while women *become* brides of men. A man *pos-
sesses* a woman; he *deflowers* her; he *performs*; he *scores*; he *takes away* her
virginity. Although a woman can *seduce* a man, she cannot offer him her
virginity. When talking about virginity, the only way to make the woman
the actor in the sentence is to say that "She lost her virginity," but people
lose things by accident rather than by purposeful actions, and so she's
only the grammatical, not the real-life, actor.

The reason that women tried to bring the term *Ms.* into the language   21
to replace *Miss* and *Mrs.* relates to this point. Married women resent
being identified only under their husband's names. For example, when
Susan Glascoe did something newsworthy, she would be identified in the
newspaper only as Mrs. John Glascoe. The dictionary cards showed what
appeared to be an attitude on the part of the editors that it was almost in-
decent to let a respectable woman's name march unaccompanied across
the pages of a dictionary. Women were listed with male names whether or
not the male contributed to the woman's reason for being in the dictionary or in his own right was as famous as the women. For example,
Charlotte Brontë was identified as Mrs. Arthur B. Nicholls, Amelia

Earhart as Mrs. George Palmer Putman, Helen Hayes as Mrs. Charles MacArthur, Jenny Lind as Mme. Otto Goldschmit, Cornelia Otis Skinner as the daughter of Otis, Harriet Beecher Stowe as the sister of Henry Ward Beecher, and Edith Sitwell as the sister of Osbert and Sacheverell.* A very small number of women got into the dictionary without the benefit of a masculine escort. They were rebels and crusaders: temperance leaders Frances Elizabeth Caroline Willard and Carry Nation, women's rights leaders Carrie Chapman Catt and Elizabeth Cady Stanton, birth control educator Margaret Sanger, religious leader Mary Baker Eddy, and slaves Harriet Tubman and Phillis Wheatley.

Etiquette books used to teach that if a woman had *Mrs.* in front of her   22
name, then the husband's name should follow because *Mrs.* is an abbreviated form of *Mistress* and a woman couldn't be a mistress of herself. As with many arguments about "correct" language usage, this isn't very logical because *Miss* is also an abbreviation of *Mistress.* Feminists hoped to simplify matters by introducing *Ms.* as an alternative to both *Mrs.* and *Miss*, but what happened is that *Ms.* largely replaced *Miss*, to become a catch-all business title for women. Many married women still prefer the title *Mrs.*, and some resent being addressed with the term *Ms.* As one frustrated newspaper reporter complained, "Before I can write about a woman, I have to know not only her marital status but also her political philosophy." The result of such complications may contribute to the demise of titles, which are already being ignored by many computer programmers who find it more efficient to simply use names, for example in a business letter: "Dear Joan Garcia," instead of Dear Mrs. Joan Garcia," "Dear Ms. Garcia," or "Dear Mrs. Louis Garcia."

The titles given to royalty provide an example of how males can be   23
disadvantaged by the assumption that they are always to play the more powerful role. In British royalty, when a male holds a title, his wife is automatically given the feminine equivalent. But the reverse is not true. For example, a *count* is a high political officer with a *countess* being his wife. The same is true for a *duke* and a *duchess* and a *king* and a *queen.* But when a female holds the royal title, the man she marries does not automatically acquire the matching title. For example, Queen Elizabeth's husband has the title of *prince* rather than *king....* The reasoning appears to be that since masculine words are stronger, they are reserved for true heirs and withheld from males coming into the royal family by marriage. If Prince Phillip were called *King Phillip*, it would be much easier for British subjects to forget where the true power lies.

---

*EDS. NOTE—Charlotte Brontë (1816–1855), author of *Jane Eyre;* Amelia Earhart (1898–1937), first woman to fly over the Atlantic; Helen Hayes (1900–1993), actress; Jenny Lind (1820–1887), Swedish soprano known as the "Swedish nightingale"; Cornelia Otis Skinner (1901–1979), actress and writer; Harriet Beecher Stowe (1811–1896), author of *Uncle Tom's Cabin;* and Edith Sitwell (1877–1964), English poet and critic.

The names that people give their children show the hopes and dreams they have for them, and when we look at the differences between male and female names in a culture, we can see the cumulative expectations of that culture. In our culture girls often have names taken from small, aesthetically pleasing items, e.g., *Ruby, Jewel,* and *Pearl. Esther* and *Stella* mean "star," *Ada* means "ornament," and *Vanessa* means "butterfly." Boys are more likely to be given names with meanings of power and strength, e.g., *Neil* means "champion," *Martin* is from Mars, the God of War, *Raymond* means "wise protection," *Harold* means "strong king." 24

We see similar differences in food metaphors. Food is a passive substance just sitting there waiting to be eaten. Many people have recognized this and so no longer feel comfortable describing women as "delectable morsels." However, when I was a teenager, it was considered a compliment to refer to a girl (we didn't call anyone a *woman* until she was middle-aged) as a *cute tomato,* a *peach,* a *dish,* a *cookie, honey, sugar,* or *sweetie-pie.* When being affectionate, women will occasionally call a man *honey* or *sweetie,* but in general, food metaphors are used much less often with men than with women. If a man is called *a fruit,* his masculinity is being questioned. But it's perfectly acceptable to use a food metaphor if the food is heavier and more substantive than that used for women. For example pin-up pictures of women have long been known as *cheesecake,* but when Burt Reynolds posed for a nude centerfold the picture was immediately dubbed *beefcake,* c.f., *a hunk of meat.* That such sexual references to men have come into the language is another reflection of how society is beginning to lessen the differences between their attitudes toward men and women. 25

Something similar to the *fruit* metaphor happens with references to plants. We insult a man by calling him a *pansy,* but it wasn't considered particularly insulting to talk about a girl being a *wallflower,* a *clinging vine,* or a *shrinking violet,* or to give girls such names as *Ivy, Rose, Lily, Iris, Daisy, Camellia, Heather,* and *Flora.* A plant metaphor can be used with a man if the plant is big and strong, for example, Andrew Jackson's nickname of *Old Hickory.* Also, the phrases *blooming idiots* and *budding geniuses* can be used with either sex, but notice how they are based on the most active thing a plant can do, which is to bloom or bud. 26

Animal metaphors also illustrate the different expectations for males and females. Men are referred to as *studs, bucks,* and *wolves* while women are referred to with such metaphors as *kitten, bunny, beaver, bird, chick,* and *lamb.* In the 1950s we said that boys went *tomcatting,* but today it's just *catting around* and both boys and girls do it. When the term *foxy,* meaning that someone was sexy, first became popular it was used only for girls, but now someone of either sex can be described as *a fox.* Some animal metaphors that are used predominantly with men have negative connotations based on the size and/or strength of the animals, e.g., *beast, bullheaded, jackass, rat, loanshark,* and *vulture.* Negative metaphors used with women are based on smaller animals, e.g., *social butterfly, mousy, catty,* and 27 *vixen.* The feminine terms connote action, but not the same kind of large scale action as with the masculine terms.

WOMEN ARE CONNECTED WITH NEGATIVE CONNOTATIONS; MEN WITH POSITIVE CONNOTATIONS

The final point that my notecards illustrated was how many positive connotations are associated with the concept of masculine, while there are either trivial or negative connotations connected with the corresponding feminine concept. An example from the animal metaphors makes a good illustration. The word *shrew* taken from the name of a small but especially vicious animal was defined in my dictionary as "an ill-tempered scolding woman," but the word *shrewd* taken from the same root was defined as "marked by clever, discerning awareness" and was illustrated with the phrase "a shrewd businessman." 28

Early in life, children are conditioned to the superiority of the masculine role. As child psychologists point out, little girls have much more freedom to experiment with sex roles than do little boys. If a little girl acts like a *tomboy,* most parents have mixed feelings, being at least partially proud. But if their little boy acts like a *sissy* (derived from *sister*), they call a psychologist. It's perfectly acceptable for a little girl to sleep in the crib that was purchased for her brother, to wear his hand-me-down jeans and shirts, and to ride the bicycle that he has outgrown. But few parents would put a boy baby in a white and gold crib decorated with frills and lace, and virtually no parents would have their boys wear his sister's hand-me-down dresses, nor would they have their son ride a girl's pink bicycle with a flower-bedecked basket. The proper names given to girls and boys show this same attitude. Girls can have "boy" names—*Cris, Craig, Jo, Kelly, Shawn, Teri, Toni* and *Sam*—but it doesn't work the other way around. A couple of generations ago, *Beverley, Francis, Hazel, Marion,* and *Shirley* were common boys' names. As parents gave these names to more and more girls, they fell into disuse for males, and some older men who have these names prefer to go by their initials or by such abbreviated forms as *Haze* or *Shirl.* 29

When a little girl is told to *be a lady,* she is being told to sit with her knees together and to be quiet and dainty. But when a little boy is told to *be a man* he is being told to be noble, strong, and virtuous—to have all the qualities that the speaker looks on as desirable. The concept of manliness has such positive connotations that it used to be a compliment to call someone a *he-man,* to say that he was doubly a man. Today many people are more ambivalent about this term and respond to it much as they do to the word *macho.* But calling someone a *manly man* or a *virile man* is nearly always meant as a compliment. *Virile* comes from the Indo-European *vir* meaning "man," which is also the basis for *virtuous.* Contrast the positive connotations of both *virile* and *virtuous* with the negative connotations of 30 *hysterical.* The Greeks took this latter word from their name for *uterus* (as still seen in *hysterectomy*). They thought that women were the only ones who experienced uncontrolled emotional outbursts, and so the condition must have something to do with a part of the body that only women have.

Differences in the connotations between positive male and negative female can be seen in several pairs of words that differ denotatively only in the matter of sex. *Bachelor* as compared to *spinster* or *old maid* has such positive connotations that women try to adopt them by using the term *bachelorgirl* or *bachelorette*. *Old maid* is so negative that it's the basis for metaphors: pretentious and fussy old men are called *old maids*, as are the leftover kernels of unpopped popcorn, and the last card in a popular children's game. 31

Patron and *matron* (Middle English for *father* and *mother*) have such different levels of prestige that women try to borrow the more positive masculine connotations with the word *patroness*, literally "female father." Such a peculiar term came about because of the high prestige attached to *patron* in such phrases as *a patron of the arts* or *a patron saint*. *Matron* is more apt to be used in talking about a woman in charge of a jail or a public restroom. 32

When men are doing jobs that women often do, we apparently try to pay the men extra by giving them fancy titles; for example, a male cook is more likely to be called a *chef* while a male seamstress will get the title of *tailor*. The armed forces have a special problem in that they recruit under such slogans as "The Marine Corps builds men!" and "Join the Army! Become a Man." Once the recruits are enlisted, they find themselves doing much of the work that has been traditionally thought of a "women's work." The solution to getting the work done and not insulting anyone's masculinity was to change the titles as shown below: 33

waitress	orderly
nurse	medic or corpsman
secretary	clerk-typist
assistant	adjutant
dishwasher or kitchen helper	KP (kitchen police)

Compare *brave* and *squaw.* Early settlers in America truly admired Indian men and hence named them with a word that carried connotations of youth, vigor, and courage. But they used the Algonquin's name for "woman" and over the years it developed almost opposite connotations to those of *brave. Wizard* and *witch* contrast almost as much. The masculine *wizard* implies skill and wisdom combined with magic, while the feminine *witch* implies evil intentions combined with magic. Part of the unattractiveness of both *witch* and *squaw* is that they have been used so often to refer to old women, something with which our culture is particularly uncomfortable, just as the Afghans were. Imagine my surprise when I ran across the phrases *grandfatherly advice* and *old wives' tales* and realized that the underlying implication is the same as the Afghan proverb about old men being worth listening to while old women talk only foolishness. 34

Other terms that show how negatively we view old women as com-   35
pared to young women are *old nag* as compared to *filly, old crow* or *old bat*
as compared to *bird,* and being *catty* as compared to being *kittenish.* There
is no matching set of metaphors for men. The chicken metaphor tells the
whole story of a woman's life. In her youth she is a *chick.* Then she marries and begins *feathering her nest.* Soon she begins feeling *cooped up,* so she
goes to *hen parties* where she *cackles* with her friends. Then she has her
brood, begins to *henpeck* her husband, and finally turns into an *old biddy.*

I embarked on my study of the dictionary not with the intention of   36
prescribing language change but simply to see what the language would
tell me about sexism. Nevertheless I have been both surprised and
pleased as I've watched the changes that have occurred over the past two
decades. I'm one of those linguists who believes that new language customs will cause a new generation of speakers to grow up with different
expectations. That is why I'm happy about people's efforts to use inclusive language, to say *he or she* or *they* when speaking about individuals
whose names they do not know. I'm glad that leading publishers have developed guidelines to help writers use language that is fair to both sexes,
and I'm glad that most newspapers and magazines list women by their
own names instead of only by their husbands' names and that educated
and thoughtful people no longer begin their business letters with "Dear
Sir" or "Gentlemen," but instead use a memo form or begin with such
salutations as "Dear Colleagues," "Dear Reader," or "Dear Committee
Members." I'm also glad that such words as *poetess, authoress, conductress,*
and *aviatrix* now sound quaint and old-fashioned and that *chairman* is
giving way to *chair* or *head, mailman* to *mail carrier, clergyman* to *clergy,* and
stewardess to *flight attendant.* I was also pleased when the National
Oceanic and Atmospheric Administration bowed to feminist complaints
and in the late 1970s began to alternate men's and women's names for
hurricanes. However, I wasn't so pleased to discover that the change did
not immediately erase sexist thoughts from everyone's mind, as shown
by a headline about Hurricane David in a 1979 New York tabloid, "David
Rapes Virgin Islands." More recently a similar metaphor appeared in a
headline in the *Arizona Republic* about Hurricane Charlie, "Charlie Quits
Carolinas, Flirts with Virginia."

What these incidents show is that sexism is not something existing in-   37
dependently in American English or in the particular dictionary that I
happened to read. Rather, it exists in people's minds. Language is like an
X-ray in providing visible evidence of invisible thoughts. The best thing
about people being interested in and discussing sexist language is that as
they make conscious decisions about what pronouns they will use, what
jokes they will tell or laugh at, how they will write their names, or how
they will begin their letters, they are forced to think about the underlying
issue of sexism. This is good because as a problem that begins in people's
assumptions and expectations, it's a problem that will be solved only
when a great many people have given it a great deal of thought.

• • •

COMPREHENSION

1. Why did Nilsen first decide to study the English language? Why does she now see **irony** in her motive?

2. What are some of the examples Nilsen uses to support the idea that language portrays women as sexy and men as successful?

3. How, according to Nilsen, does language suggest "weddings are more important to women than to men" (15)?

4. According to Nilsen, how have marriage customs changed since she wrote her original essay?

5. What are some of the examples Nilsen uses to support the idea that language casts women as weak and passive?

6. Why was the term *Ms.* introduced into the language? Does Nilsen believe it has solved the problems feminists hoped it would? Explain.

7. What are some of the examples Nilsen uses to support the idea that men are associated with positive connotations while women are associated with negative connotations?

8. Does Nilsen still see the English language as sexist, or does she believe that changes in language customs have largely eliminated such bias?

PURPOSE AND AUDIENCE

1. Is the primary purpose of this essay to inform or to persuade? Explain your conclusion.

2. What is Nilsen's thesis? Do you think the thesis should take a more argumentative stance—for example, suggesting the dangers of sexist language? Explain your conclusion.

3. This essay updates an essay Nilsen published twenty years earlier. Would you expect audience reaction in the 1970s to be different from audience reaction today? If so, how? If not, why not?

STYLE AND STRUCTURE

1. Into what three categories does Nilsen divide sexist language?

2. Where, if anywhere, do Nilsen's categories overlap? Is this overlap to be expected, or does it reveal a flaw in Nilsen's classification system? Explain.

3. Nilsen uses headings to identify her categories. Are these headings helpful? Necessary? Misleading? Distracting? Does she need additional headings? Subheadings? Explain.

4. What function does the essay's introduction (1–5) serve? Do you think it could be condensed? How much of it do you consider essential to your understanding and appreciation of the essay that follows?

5. Which paragraph or paragraphs constitute Nilsen's conclusion? Should the conclusion be expanded? If so, what could be added?

6. Does Nilsen include enough examples to convince readers that sexism exists in English? Explain.

7. Nilsen's use of contractions and first-person pronouns in her essay gives it an informal, even conversational, style. Is this style appropriate for her subject matter? Explain.

8. Are paragraphs 15–18 a digression, or do they illustrate the statement "Women are sexy; men are successful"? Do any other paragraphs strike you as digressions? Explain.

VOCABULARY PROJECTS

1. Define each of the following words as it is used in this selection.

   inherent (1)   buxom (7)   ambivalent (30)
   blatantly (1)   semantic (14)
   bereft (3)   connote (27)

2. List as many additional examples of your own as you can of words that illustrate each of Nilsen's three points.

3. Even though Nilsen has updated her essay for the 1990s, some of the usages she describes may no longer be current. Identify any words that you believe are no longer used as Nilsen says they are.

JOURNAL ENTRY

In recent years, some feminists began spelling the word *woman* as *womyn* so it will not include the word *man*. What is your reaction to this practice?

WRITING WORKSHOP

1. What special kinds of language are used in sports—for example, by players, fans, and sportswriters? How do various sports differ in their idioms? Answer these questions in a classification-and-division essay about the language of sports. (How you organize your essay will depend on whether you write about one particular sport or several different ones.)

2. How does today's advertising portray women? Using Nilsen's general categories (and her headings if you like), collect examples to support the thesis that advertising, like language, has a sexist bias.

3. Many people believe that the English language reflects not only the sexism in people's minds but also the racism. Write an essay called "Racism in English." Begin by listing individual words and usage patterns you consider racist. Then divide your list into categories determined by a sin-

gle principle of classification—for example, kinds of racist language, kinds of language applied to different racial groups, or different motives for using racist language. Your thesis can simply sum up current practices or take a stand against them. Reading (or rereading) some of the essays on this topic that appear in other chapters, such as "'What's in a Name?'" "The 'Black Table' Is Still There," and "Finishing School," might help you plan your paper.

COMBINING THE PATTERNS

Many of the paragraphs in this essay are developed by means of **exemplification.** Identify several of these paragraphs. How does Nilsen use topic sentences to unify the examples in each paragraph? What transitional words and expressions does she use to link the individual examples within each of these paragraphs?

THEMATIC CONNECTIONS

- "My Field of Dreams" (page 65)
- "Only Daughter" (page 70)
- "English Is a Crazy Language" (page 181)
- "Sex, Lies, and Conversation" (page 350)
- "The Catbird Seat" (page 474)

▷▷▷▷▷▷▷▷▷▷▷▷▷▷▷▷▷▷

STEPHANIE ERICSSON

Stephanie Ericsson (1953–   ) grew up in San Francisco and began writing as a teenager. She has worked as a screenwriter and an advertising copywriter and has published several books based on her own life. *Shamefaced: The Road to Recovery* and *Women of AA: Recovering Together* (both 1985) focus on her experiences with substance abuse; *Companion through the Darkness: Inner Dialogues on Grief* (1993) deals with the sudden death of her husband. "The Ways We Lie" is from Ericsson's most recent book, *Companion into the Dawn: Inner Dialogues on Loving* (1994). In this piece, originally published in the *Utne Reader* in 1992, Ericsson looks at the many ways we deceive ourselves and others.

The Ways We Lie

The bank called today and I told them my deposit was in the mail, even though I hadn't written a check yet. It'd been a rough day. The baby I'm pregnant with decided to do aerobics on my lungs for two hours, our three-year-old daughter painted the living-room couch with lipstick, the IRS put me on hold for an hour, and I was late to a business meeting because I was tired.   1

I told my client the traffic had been bad. When my partner came home, his haggard face told me his day hadn't gone any better than mine, so when he asked, "How was your day?" I said, "Oh, fine," knowing that one more straw might break his back. A friend called and wanted to take me to lunch. I said I was busy. Four lies in the course of a day, none of which I felt the least bit guilty about.   2

We lie. We all do. We exaggerate, we minimize, we avoid confrontation, we spare people's feelings, we conveniently forget, we keep secrets, we justify lying to the big-guy institutions. Like most people, I indulge in small falsehoods and still think of myself as an honest person. Sure I lie, but it doesn't hurt anything. Or does it?   3

I once tried going a whole week without telling a lie, and it was paralyzing. I discovered that telling the truth all the time is nearly impossible. It means living with some serious consequences: The bank charges me $60 in overdraft fees, my partner keels over when I tell him about my travails, my client fires me for telling her I didn't feel like being on time, and my friend takes it personally when I say I'm not hungry. There must be some merit to lying.   4

But if I justify lying, what makes me any different from slick politicians or the corporate robbers who raided the S&L industry? Saying it's okay to lie one way and not another is hedging. I cannot seem to escape the voice deep inside me that tells me: When someone lies, someone loses.   5

What far-reaching consequences will I, or others, pay as a result of my lie? Will someone's trust be destroyed? Will someone else pay *my* penance because I ducked out? We must consider the *meaning of our*   6 *actions.* Deception, lies, capital crimes, and misdemeanors all carry meanings. *Webster's* definition of *lie* is specific:

> 1: a false statement or action especially made with the intent to deceive;
> 2: anything that gives or is meant to give a false impression.

A definition like this implies that there are many, many ways to tell a lie. Here are just a few. 7

THE WHITE LIE

> A man who won't lie to a woman has very little consideration
> for her feelings.
>
> —BERGEN EVANS

The white lie assumes that the truth will cause more damage than a 8 simple, harmless untruth. Telling a friend he looks great when he looks like hell can be based on a decision that the friend needs a compliment more than a frank opinion. But, in effect, it is the liar deciding what is best for the lied to. Ultimately, it is a vote of no confidence. It is an act of subtle arrogance for anyone to decide what is best for someone else.

Yet not all circumstances are quite so cut-and-dried. Take, for instance, the sergeant in Vietnam who knew one of his men was killed in action but listed him as missing so that the man's family would receive indefinite compensation instead of the lump-sum pittance the military gives widows and children. His intent was honorable. Yet for twenty years this family kept their hopes alive, unable to move on to a new life. 9

FACADES

> Et tu, Brute?
> —CAESAR*

We all put up facades to one degree or another. When I put on a suit 10 to go to see a client, I feel as though I am putting on another face, obeying the expectation that serious businesspeople wear suits rather than sweatpants. But I'm a writer. Normally, I get up, get the kid off to school, and sit at my computer in my pajamas until four in the afternoon. When I answer the phone, the caller thinks I'm wearing a suit (though the UPS man knows better).

But facades can be destructive because they are used to seduce others 11 into an illusion. For instance, I recently realized that a former friend was a

---

*EDS. NOTE—"And you, Brutus?" In Shakespeare's play *Julius Caesar,* Caesar asks this question when he sees Brutus, whom he has believed to be his friend, among the conspirators who are stabbing him.

liar. He presented himself with all the right looks and the right words and offered lots of new consciousness theories, fabulous books to read, and fascinating insights. Then I did some business with him, and the time came for him to pay me. He turned out to be all talk and no walk. I heard a plethora of reasonable excuses, including in-depth descriptions of the big break around the corner. In six months of work, I saw less than a hundred bucks. When I confronted him, he raised both eyebrows and tried to convince me that I'd heard him wrong, that he'd made no commitment to me. A simple investigation into his past revealed a crowded graveyard of disenchanted former friends.

IGNORING THE PLAIN FACTS

> Well, you must understand that Father Porter is only human....
> —A MASSACHUSETTS PRIEST

In the '60s, the Catholic Church in Massachusetts began hearing complaints that Father James Porter was sexually molesting children. Rather than relieving him of his duties, the ecclesiastical authorities simply moved him from one parish to another between 1960 and 1967, actually providing him with a fresh supply of unsuspecting families and innocent children to abuse. After treatment in 1967 for pedophilia, he went back to work, this time in Minnesota. The new diocese was aware of Father Porter's obsession with children, but they needed priests and recklessly believed treatment had cured him. More children were abused until he was relieved of his duties a year later. By his own admission, Porter may have abused as many as a hundred children.   12

Ignoring the facts may not in and of itself be a form of lying, but consider the context of this situation. If a lie is *a false action done with the intent to deceive,* then the Catholic Church's conscious covering for Porter created irreparable consequences. The church became a co-perpetrator with Porter.   13

DEFLECTING

> When you have no basis for an argument, abuse the plaintiff.
> —CICERO

I've discovered that I can keep anyone from seeing the true me by being selectively blatant. I set a precedent of being up-front about intimate issues, but I never bring up the things I truly want to hide; I just let people assume I'm revealing everything. It's an effective way of hiding.   14

Any good liar knows that the way to perpetuate an untruth is to deflect attention from it. When Clarence Thomas exploded with accusations that the Senate hearings were a "high-tech lynching," he simply switched   15 the focus from a highly charged subject to a radioactive subject. Rather than defending himself, he took the offensive and accused the country of racism. It was a brilliant maneuver. Racism is now politically incorrect in official circles—unlike sexual harassment, which still rewards those who can get away with it.

Some of the most skillful deflectors are passive-aggressive people   16
who, when accused of inappropriate behavior, refuse to respond to the accusations. This you-don't-exist stance infuriates the accuser, who, understandably, screams something obscene out of frustration. The trap is sprung and the act of deflection successful, because now the passive-aggressive person can indignantly say, "Who can talk to someone as unreasonable as you?" The real issue is forgotten and the sins of the original victim become the focus. Feeling guilty of name-calling, the victim is fully tamed and crawls into a hole, ashamed. I have watched this fighting technique work thousands of times in disputes between men and women, and what I've learned is that the real culprit is not necessarily the one who swears the loudest.

OMISSION

The cruelest lies are often told in silence.
          —R. L. STEVENSON

Omission involves telling most of the truth minus one or two key   17
facts whose absence changes the story completely. You break a pair of glasses that are guaranteed under normal use and get a new pair, without mentioning that the first pair broke during a rowdy game of basketball. Who hasn't tried something like that? But what about omission of information that could make a difference in how a person lives his or her life?

For instance, one day I found out that rabbinical legends tell of an-   18
other woman in the Garden of Eden before Eve. I was stunned. The omission of the Sumerian goddess Lilith from Genesis—as well as her demonization by ancient misogynists as an embodiment of female evil—felt like spiritual robbery. I felt like I'd just found out my mother was really my stepmother. To take seriously the tradition that Adam was created out of the same mud as his equal counterpart, Lilith, redefines all of Judeo-Christian history.

Some renegade Catholic feminists introduced me to a view of Lilith   19
that had been suppressed during the many centuries when this strong goddess was seen only as a spirit of evil. Lilith was a proud goddess who defied Adam's need to control her, attempted negotiations, and when this failed, said adios and left the Garden of Eden.

This omission of Lilith from the Bible was a patriarchal strategy to   20
keep women weak. Omitting the strong-woman archetype of Lilith from Western religions and starting the story with Eve the Rib has helped keep

Christian and Jewish women believing they were the lesser sex for thousands of years.

STEREOTYPES AND CLICHÉS

> Where opinion does not exist, the status quo becomes stereotyped and all originality is discouraged.
> —BERTRAND RUSSELL

Stereotype and cliché serve a purpose as a form of shorthand. Our   21
need for vast amounts of information in nanoseconds has made the
stereotype vital to modern communication. Unfortunately, it often
shuts down original thinking, giving those hungry for the truth a
candy bar of misinformation instead of a balanced meal. The stereotype explains a situation with just enough truth to seem unquestionable.

All the "isms"—racism, sexism, ageism, et al.—are founded on and   22
fueled by the stereotype and the cliché, which are lies of exaggeration,
omission, and ignorance. They are always dangerous. They take a single
tree and make it a landscape. They destroy curiosity. They close minds
and separate people. The single mother on welfare is assumed to be
cheating. Any black male could tell you how much of his identity is obliterated daily by stereotypes. Fat people, ugly people, beautiful people, old
people, large-breasted women, short men, the mentally ill, and the homeless all could tell you how much more they are like us than we want to
think. I once admitted to a group of people that I had a mouth like a truck
driver. Much to my surprise, a man stood up and said, "I'm a truck driver, and I never cuss." Needless to say, I was humbled.

GROUPTHINK

> Who is more foolish, the child afraid of the dark, or the man
> afraid of the light?
> —MAURICE FREEHILL

Irving Janis, in *Victims of GroupThink,* defines this sort of lie as a psy-   23
chological phenomenon within decision-making groups in which loyalty
to the group has become more important than any other value, with the
result that dissent and the appraisal of alternatives are suppressed. If
you've ever worked on a committee or in a corporation, you've encountered groupthink. It requires a combination of other forms of lying—
ignoring facts, selective memory, omission, and denial, to name a few.

The textbook example of groupthink came on December 7, 1941.   24
From as early as the fall of 1941, the warnings came in, one after another,
that Japan was preparing for a massive military operation. The Navy
command in Hawaii assumed Pearl Harbor was invulnerable—the

Japanese weren't stupid enough to attack the United States' most important base. On the other hand, racist stereotypes said the Japanese weren't
smart enough to invent a torpedo effective in less than 60 feet of water
(the fleet was docked in 30 feet); after all, U.S. technology hadn't been
able to do it.

On Friday, December 5, normal weekend leave was granted to all the   25
commanders at Pearl Harbor, even though the Japanese consulate in
Hawaii was busy burning papers. Within the tight, good-ole-boy cohe-
siveness of the U.S. command in Hawaii, the myth of invulnerability
stayed well entrenched. No one in the group considered the alternatives.
The rest is history.

OUT-AND-OUT LIES

> The only form of lying that is beyond reproach is lying for its
> own sake.
>
> —OSCAR WILDE

Of all the ways to lie, I like this one the best, probably because I get   26
tired of trying to figure out the real meanings behind things. At least I can
trust the bald-faced lie. I once asked my five-year-old nephew, "Who
broke the fence?" (I had seen him do it.) He answered, "The murderers."
Who could argue?

At least when this sort of lie is told it can be easily confronted. As the   27
person who is lied to, I know where I stand. The bald-faced lie doesn't toy
with my perceptions—it argues with them. It doesn't try to refashion reality, it tries to refute it. *Read my lips.* . . . No sleight of hand. No guessing. If
this were the only form of lying, there would be no such thing as floating
anxiety or the adult-children of alcoholics movement.

DISMISSAL

> Pay no attention to that man behind the curtain! I am the Great Oz!
> —THE WIZARD OF OZ

Dismissal is perhaps the slipperiest of all lies. Dismissing feelings,   28
perceptions, or even the raw facts of a situation ranks as a kind of lie that
can do as much damage to a person as any other kind of lie.

The roots of many mental disorders can be traced back to the dis-   29
missal of reality. Imagine that a person is told from the time she is a tot
that her perceptions are inaccurate. *"Mommy, I'm scared."* "No, you're not,
darling." *"I don't like that man next door, he makes me feel icky."* "Johnny,
that's a terrible thing to say, of course you like him. You go over there
right now and be nice to him."

I've often mused over the idea that madness is actually a sane reaction   30
to an insane world. Psychologist R. D. Laing supports this hypothesis in

Sanity, Madness & the Family, an account of his investigations into families of schizophrenics. The common thread that ran through all of the families he studied was a deliberate, staunch dismissal of the patient's perceptions from a very early age. Each of the patients started out with an accurate grasp of reality, which, through meticulous and methodical dismissal, was demolished until the only reality the patient could trust was catatonia.

Dismissal runs the gamut. Mild dismissal can be quite handy for for-   31
giving the foibles of others in our day-to-day lives. Toddlers who have just learned to manipulate their parents' attention sometimes are dismissed out of necessity. Absolute attention from the parents would require so much energy that no one would get to eat dinner. But we must be careful and attentive about how far we take our "necessary" dismissals. Dismissal is a dangerous tool, because it's nothing less than a lie.

DELUSION

We lie loudest when we lie to ourselves.
—ERIC HOFFER

I could write the book on this one. Delusion, a cousin of dismissal, is   32
the tendency to see excuses as facts. It's a powerful lying tool because it filters out information that contradicts what we want to believe. Alcoholics who believe that the problems in their lives are legitimate reasons for drinking rather than results of the drinking offer the classic example of deluded thinking. Delusion uses the mind's ability to see things in myriad ways to support what it wants to be the truth.

But delusion is also a survival mechanism we all use. If we were to   33
fully contemplate the consequences of our stockpiles of nuclear weapons or global warming, we could hardly function on a day-to-day level. We don't want to incorporate that much reality into our lives because to do so would be paralyzing.

Delusion acts as an adhesive to keep the status quo intact. It shame-   34
lessly employs dismissal, omission, and amnesia, among other sorts of lies. Its most cunning defense is that it cannot see itself.

The liar's punishment...is that he cannot believe anyone else.
—GEORGE BERNARD SHAW

These are only a few of the ways we lie. Or are lied to. As I said ear-   35
lier, it's not easy to entirely eliminate lies from our lives. No matter how pious we may try to be, we will still embellish, hedge, and omit to lubricate the daily machinery of living. But there is a world of difference between telling functional lies and living a lie. Martin Buber* once said, "The lie is the spirit committing treason against itself." Our acceptance of

---

*EDS. NOTE—Austrian-born Judaic philosopher (1878–1965).

lies becomes a cultural cancer that eventually shrouds and reorders reality until moral garbage becomes as invisible to us as water is to a fish.

How much do we tolerate before we become sick and tired of being 36 sick and tired? When will we stand up and declare our *right* to trust? When do we stop accepting that the real truth is in the fine print? Whose lips do we read this year when we vote for president? When will we stop being so reticent about making judgments? When do we stop turning over our personal power and responsibility to liars?

Maybe if I don't tell the bank the check's in the mail I'll be less toler- 37 ant of the lies told me every day. A country song I once heard said it all for me: "You've got to stand for something or you'll fall for anything."

• • •

COMPREHENSION

1. List and define each of the ten kinds of lies Ericsson identifies.

2. Why, in Ericsson's view, is each kind of lie necessary?

3. According to Ericsson, what is the danger of each kind of lie?

4. Why does Ericsson like "out-and-out lies" (26–27) best?

5. Why is dismissal the "slipperiest of all lies" (28)?

PURPOSE AND AUDIENCE

1. Is Ericsson's thesis simply that "there are many, many ways to tell a lie" (7)? Or is she defending—or attacking—the process of lying? Try to state her thesis in a single sentence.

2. Do you think Ericsson's choice of examples reveals a political bias? If so, do you think she expects her intended audience to share this bias? Explain.

STYLE AND STRUCTURE

1. Despite the seriousness of her subject matter, Ericsson's essay is informal; her opening paragraphs are especially personal and breezy. Why do you think she uses this kind of opening? Do you think her decision makes sense? Why or why not?

2. Ericsson introduces each category of lie with a quotation. What function do these quotations serve? Would the essay be more or less effective without them? Explain your conclusion.

3. In addition to a heading and a quotation, what other elements does Ericsson include in her discussion of each kind of lie? Are all the discussions parallel—that is, does each include *all* the standard elements, and *only* those elements? If not, do you think this lack of balance is a problem? Explain.

4. What, if anything, determines the order in which Ericsson arranges her categories? Should any category be relocated? Explain.

5. Throughout her essay, Ericsson uses **rhetorical questions.** Why do you suppose she uses this stylistic device?

6. Ericsson occasionally cites the views of experts. Why does she do so? If she wished to cite additional experts, what professional backgrounds or fields of study do you think they should represent? Why?

7. In paragraph 29 Ericsson says, "Imagine that a person is told from the time she is a tot...." Does she use *she* in similar contexts elsewhere in the essay? Do you find the feminine form of the personal pronoun appropriate or distracting? Explain.

8. Paragraphs 35–37 constitute Ericsson's conclusion. How does this conclusion parallel the essay's introduction in terms of style, structure, and content?

VOCABULARY PROJECTS

1. Define each of the following words as it is used in this selection.

travails (4)	deflectors (16)	staunch (30)
hedging (5)	passive-aggressive (16)	catatonia (30)
pittance (9)	misogynists (18)	gamut (31)
facades (10)	counterpart (18)	foibles (31)
plethora (11)	archetype (20)	reticent (36)
pedophilia (12)	nanoseconds (21)	
blatant (14)	obliterated (22)	

2. Ericsson uses many **colloquialisms** in this essay—for example, "I could write the book on this one" (32). Identify as many of these expressions as you can. Why do you think she uses colloquialisms instead of more formal expressions? Do they have a positive or negative effect on your reaction to her ideas? Explain.

JOURNAL ENTRY

In paragraph 3 Ericsson says, "We lie. We all do." Later in the paragraph she comments, "Sure I lie, but it doesn't hurt anything. Or does it?" Answer her question.

WRITING WORKSHOP

1. Choose three or four of Ericsson's categories and write a classification-and-division essay called "The Ways I Lie." Base your essay on personal experience, and include an explicit thesis statement that defends these lies—or is sharply critical of their use.

2. In paragraph 22 Ericsson condemns stereotypes. Write a classification-and-division essay with the following thesis statement: "Stereotypes are sometimes inaccurate, often negative, and always dangerous." In your

essay, consider the stereotypes applied to four of the following groups: the disabled, the overweight, the elderly, teenagers, welfare recipients, housewives, immigrants.

3. Using the same thesis suggested in question 2, write a classification-and-division essay that considers the stereotype applied to four of the following occupations: police officers, librarians, used-car dealers, flight attendants, lawyers, construction workers, rock musicians.

COMBINING THE PATTERNS

A dictionary **definition** is a familiar—even tired—strategy for an essay's introduction. Would you advise Ericsson to delete the definition in paragraph 6 for this reason, or do you believe it is necessary? Explain.

THEMATIC CONNECTIONS

- "'What's in a Name?'" (page 5)
- "Thirty-Eight Who Saw Murder Didn't Call the Police" (page 86)
- "The Lottery" (page 247)

FLANNERY O'CONNOR

Flannery O'Connor (1925–1964) was born in Savannah and lived with her mother in Milledgeville, Georgia, for most of her life. She graduated from Georgia State College for Women in 1945 and received an M.F.A. from the University of Iowa in 1947. In spite of suffering from the debilitating effects of lupus, O'Connor was able to write, travel, and lecture until she died at the age of thirty-nine. She wrote two novels, *Wise Blood* (1952) and *The Violent Bear It Away* (1960), and many short stories, which are collected in *A Good Man Is Hard to Find* (1966) and *Everything That Rises Must Converge* (1965). Her other writings are collected in *Mystery and Manners: Occasional Prose* (1969), *The Habit of Being: Letters of Flannery O'Connor* (1979), and *The Presence of Grace and Other Book Reviews* (1983). Her *Complete Stories* was published in 1971 and her *Collected Works* in 1988. In "Revelation," O'Connor describes the unraveling of a woman's rigidly organized view of the world.

Revelation

The doctor's waiting room, which was very small, was almost full 1 when the Turpins entered and Mrs. Turpin, who was very large, made it look even smaller by her presence. She stood looming at the head of the magazine table set in the center of it, a living demonstration that the room was inadequate and ridiculous. Her little bright black eyes took in all the patients as she sized up the seating situation. There was one vacant chair and a place on the sofa occupied by a blond child in a dirty blue romper who should have been told to move over and make room for the lady. He was five or six, but Mrs. Turpin saw at once that no one was going to tell him to move over. He was slumped down in the seat, his arms idle at his sides and his eyes idle in his head; his nose ran unchecked.

Mrs. Turpin put a firm hand on Claud's shoulder and said in a voice 2 that included everyone that wanted to listen, "Claud, you sit in that chair there," and gave him a push down into the vacant one. Claud was florid and bald and sturdy, somewhat shorter than Mrs. Turpin, but he sat down as if he were accustomed to doing what she told him to.

Mrs. Turpin remained standing. The only man in the room besides 3 Claud was a lean stringy old fellow with a rusty hand spread out on each knee, whose eyes were closed as if he were asleep or dead or pretending to be so as not to get up and offer her his seat. Her gaze settled agreeably on a well-dressed grey-haired lady whose eyes met hers and whose expression said: if that child belonged to me, he would have some manners and move over—there's plenty of room there for you and him too.

Claud looked up with a sigh and made as if to rise. 4

"Sit down," Mrs. Turpin said. "You know you're not supposed to 5 stand on that leg. He has an ulcer on his leg." she explained.

Claud lifted his foot onto the magazine table and rolled his trouser   6
leg up to reveal a purple swelling on a plump marble-white calf.

"My!" the pleasant lady said. "How did you do that?"   7

"A cow kicked him," Mrs. Turpin said.   8

"Goodness!" said the lady.   9

Claud rolled his trouser leg down.   10

"Maybe the little boy would move over," the lady suggested, but the   11
child did not stir.

"Somebody will be leaving in a minute," Mrs. Turpin said. She could   12
not understand why a doctor—with as much money as they made charging five dollars a day just to stick their head in the hospital door and look
at you—couldn't afford a decent-sized waiting room. This one was hardly
bigger than a garage. The table was cluttered with limp-looking magazines and at one end of it there was a big green glass ash tray full of ciga-
ret butts and cotton wads with little blood spots on them. If she had
anything to do with the running of the place, that would have been emptied every so often. There were no chairs against the wall at the head of
the room. It had a rectangular-shaped panel in it that permitted a view of
the office where the nurse came and went and the secretary listened to the
radio. A plastic fern in a gold pot sat in the opening and trailed its fronds
down almost to the floor. The radio was softly playing gospel music.

Just then the inner door opened and a nurse with the highest stack of   13
yellow hair Mrs. Turpin had ever seen put her face in the crack and called
for the next patient. The woman sitting beside Claud grasped the two
arms of her chair and hoisted herself up; she pulled her dress free from her
legs and lumbered through the door where the nurse had disappeared.

Mrs. Turpin eased into the vacant chair, which held her tight as a   14
corset. "I wish I could reduce," she said, and rolled her eyes and gave a
comic sigh.

"Oh, *you* aren't fat," the stylish lady said.   15

"Ooooo I am too," Mrs. Turpin said. "Claud he eats all he wants to   16
and never weighs over one hundred and seventy-five pounds, but me I
just look at something good to eat and I gain weight," and her stomach
and shoulders shook with laughter. "You can eat all you want to, can't
you, Claud?" she asked turning to him.

Claud only grinned.   17

"Well, as long as you have such a good disposition," the stylish lady   18
said, "I don't think it makes a bit of difference what size you are. You just
can't beat a good disposition."

Next to her was a fat girl of eighteen or nineteen, scowling into a   19
thick blue book which Mrs. Turpin saw was titled *Human Development*.
The girl raised her head and directed her scowl at Mrs. Turpin as if she
did not like her looks. She appeared annoyed that anyone should speak
while she tried to read. The poor girl's face was blue with acne and Mrs.
Turpin thought how pitiful it was to have a face like that at that age. She
gave the girl a friendly smile but the girl only scowled the harder. Mrs.

Turpin herself was fat but she had always had good skin, and, though she was forty-seven years old, there was not a wrinkle in her face except around her eyes from laughing too much.

Next to the ugly girl was the child, still in exactly the same position, and next to him was a thin leathery old woman in a cotton print dress. She and Claud had three sacks of chicken feed in their pump house that were in the same print. She had seen from the first that the child belonged with the old woman. She could tell by the way they sat—kind of vacant and white-trashy, as if they would sit there until Doomsday if nobody called and told them to get up. And at right angles but next to the well-dressed pleasant lady was a lank-faced woman who was certainly the child's mother. She had on a yellow sweat shirt and wine-colored slacks, both gritty-looking, and the rims of her lips were stained with snuff. Her dirty yellow hair was tied behind with a piece of red paper ribbon. Worse than niggers any day, Mrs. Turpin thought.   20

The gospel hymn playing was, "When I looked up and He looked down," and Mrs. Turpin, who knew it, supplied the last line mentally, "And wona these days I know I'll we-eara crown."   21

Without appearing to, Mrs. Turpin always noticed people's feet. The well-dressed lady had on red and grey suede shoes to match her dress. Mrs. Turpin had on her good black patent leather pumps. The ugly girl had on Girl Scout shoes and heavy socks. The old woman had on tennis shoes and the white-trashy mother had on what appeared to be bedroom slippers, black straw with gold braid threaded through them—exactly what you would have expected her to have on.   22

Sometimes at night when she couldn't go to sleep, Mrs. Turpin would occupy herself with the question of who she would have chosen to be if she couldn't have been herself. If Jesus had said to her before he made her, "There's only two places available for you. You can either be a nigger or white-trash," what would she have said? "Please, Jesus, please," she would have said, "just let me wait until there's another place available," and he would have said, "No, you have to go right now and I have only those two places so make up your mind." She would have wiggled and squirmed and begged and pleaded but it would have been no use and finally she would have said, "All right, make me a nigger then—but that don't mean a trashy one." And he would have made her a neat clean respectable Negro woman, herself but black.   23

Next to the child's mother was a red-headed youngish woman, reading one of the magazines and working a piece of chewing gum, hell for leather, as Claud would say. Mrs. Turpin could not see the woman's feet. She was not white-trash, just common. Sometimes Mrs. Turpin occupied herself at night naming the classes of people. On the bottom of the heap were most colored people, not the kind she would have been if she had been one, but most of them; then next to them—not above, just away from—were the white-trash; then above them were the home-owners, and above them the home-and-land owners, to which she and   24

Claud belonged. Above she and Claud were people with a lot of money and much bigger houses and much more land. But here the complexity of it would begin to bear in on her, for some of the people with a lot of money were common and ought to be below she and Claud and some of the people who had good blood had lost their money and had to rent and then there were colored people who owned their homes and land as well. There was a colored dentist in town who had two red Lincolns and a swimming pool and a farm with registered white-face cattle on it. Usually by the time she had fallen asleep all the classes of people were moiling and roiling around in her head, and she would dream they were all crammed in together in a box car, being ridden off to be put in a gas oven.

"That's a beautiful clock," she said and nodded to her right. It was a big wall clock, the face encased in a brass sunburst.   25

"Yes, it's very pretty," the stylish lady said agreeably. "And right on the dot too," she added, glancing at her watch.   26

The ugly girl beside her cast an eye upward at the clock, smirked, then looked directly at Mrs. Turpin and smirked again. Then she returned her eyes to her book. She was obviously the lady's daughter because, although they didn't look anything alike as to disposition, they both had the same shape of face and same blue eyes. On the lady they sparkled pleasantly but in the girl's seared face they appeared alternately to smolder and to blaze.   27

What if Jesus had said, "All right, you can be white-trash or a nigger or ugly!"   28

Mrs. Turpin felt an awful pity for the girl, though she thought it was one thing to be ugly and another to act ugly.   29

The woman with the snuff-stained lips turned around in her chair and looked up at the clock. Then she turned back and appeared to look a little to the side of Mrs. Turpin. There was a cast in one of her eyes. "You want to know wher you can get one of themther clocks?" she asked in a loud voice.   30

"No, I already have a nice clock," Mrs. Turpin said. Once somebody like her got a leg in the conversation, she would be all over it.   31

"You can get you one with green stamps," the woman said. "That's most likely wher he got hisn. Save you up enough, you can get you most anythang. I got me some joo'ry."   32

Ought to have got you a wash rag and some soap, Mrs. Turpin thought.   33

"I get contour sheets with mine," the pleasant lady said.   34

The daughter slammed her book shut. She looked straight in front of her, directly through Mrs. Turpin and on through the yellow curtain and the plate glass window which made the wall behind her. The girl's eyes seemed lit all of a sudden with a peculiar light, an unnatural light like night road signs give. Mrs. Turpin turned her head to see if there was anything going on outside that she should see, but she could not see any-   35 thing. Figures passing cast only a pale shadow through the curtain. There was no reason the girl should single her out for her ugly looks.

"Miss Finley," the nurse said, cracking the door. The gum-chewing 36 woman got up and passed in front of her and Claud and went into the office. She had on red high-heeled shoes.

Directly across the table, the ugly girl's eyes were fixed on Mrs. 37 Turpin as if she had some very special reason for disliking her.

"This is wonderful weather, isn't it?" the girl's mother said. 38

"It's good weather for cotton if you can get the niggers to pick it," 39 Mrs. Turpin said, "but niggers don't want to pick cotton any more. You can't get the white folks to pick it and now you can't get the niggers—because they got to be right up there with the white folks."

"They gonna *try* anyways," the white-trash woman said, leaning 40 forward.

"Do you have one of those cotton-picking machines?" the pleasant 41 lady asked.

"No," Mrs. Turpin said, "they leave half the cotton in the field. We 42 don't have much cotton anyway. If you want to make it farming now, you have to have a little of everything. We got a couple of acres of cotton and a few hogs and chickens and just enough white-face that Claud can look after them himself."

"One thang I don't want," the white-trash woman said, wiping her 43 mouth with the back of her hand. "Hogs. Nasty stinking things, a-gruntin and a-rootin all over the place."

Mrs. Turpin gave her the merest edge of her attention. "Our hogs are 44 not dirty and they don't stink," she said. "They're cleaner than some children I've seen. Their feet never touch the ground. We have a pig-parlor—that's where you raise them on concrete," she explained to the pleasant lady, "and Claud scoots them down with the hose every afternoon and washes off the floor." Cleaner by far than that child right there, she thought. Poor nasty little thing. He had not moved except to put the thumb of his dirty hand into his mouth.

The woman turned her face away from Mrs. Turpin. "I know I 45 wouldn't scoot down no hog with no hose," she said to the wall.

You wouldn't have no hog to scoot down, Mrs. Turpin said to herself. 46

"A-gruntin and a-rootin and a-groanin," the woman muttered. 47

"We got a little of everything," Mrs. Turpin said to the pleasant lady. 48 "It's no use in having more than you can handle yourself with help like it is. We found enough niggers to pick our cotton last year but Claud he has to go after them and take them home again in the evening. They can't walk that half a mile. No they can't. I tell you," she said and laughed merrily, "I sure am tired of buttering up niggers, but you got to love em if you want em to work for you. When they come in the morning, I run out and I say, 'Hi, yawl this morning?' and when Claud drives them off to the field I just wave to beat the band and they just wave back." And she waved her hand rapidly to illustrate.

"Like you read out of the same book," the lady said, showing she understood perfectly.   49

"Child, yes," Mrs. Turpin said. "And when they come in from the field, I run out with a bucket of icewater. That's the way it's going to be from now on," she said. "You may as well face it."   50

"One thang I know," the white-trash woman said. "Two thangs I ain't going to do: love no niggers or scoot down no hog with no hose." And she let out a bark of contempt.   51

The look that Mrs. Turpin and the pleasant lady exchanged indicated they both understood that you had to *have* certain things before you could *know* certain things. But every time Mrs. Turpin exchanged a look with the lady, she was aware that the ugly girl's peculiar eyes were still on her, and she had trouble bringing her attention back to the conversation.   52

"When you got something," she said, "you got to look after it." And when you ain't got a thing but breath and britches, she added to herself, you can afford to come to town every morning and just sit on the Court House coping and spit.   53

A grotesque revolving shadow passed across the curtain behind her and was thrown palely on the opposite wall. Then a bicycle clattered down against the outside of the building. The door opened and a colored boy glided in with a tray from the drug store. It had two large red and white paper cups on it with tops on them. He was a tall, very black boy in discolored white pants and a green nylon shirt. He was chewing gum slowly, as if to music. He set the tray down in the office opening next to the fern and stuck his head through to look for the secretary. She was not in there. He rested his arms on the ledge and waited, his narrow bottom stuck out, swaying slowing to the left and right. He raised a hand over his head and scratched the base of his skull.   54

"You see that button there, boy?" Mrs. Turpin said. "You can punch that and she'll come. She's probably in the back somewhere."   55

"Is that right?" the boy said agreeably, as if he had never seen the button before. He leaned to the right and put his finger on it. "She sometime out," he said and twisted around to face his audience, his elbows behind him on the counter. The nurse appeared and he twisted back again. She handed him a dollar and he rooted in his pocket and made the change and counted it out to her. She gave him fifteen cents for a tip and he went out with the empty tray. The heavy door swung to slowly and closed at length with the sound of suction. For a moment no one spoke.   56

"They ought to send all them niggers back to Africa," the white-trash woman said. "That's wher they come from in the first place."   57

"Oh, I couldn't do without my good colored friends," the pleasant lady said.   58

"There's a heap of things worse than a nigger," Mrs. Turpin agreed. "It's all kinds of them just like it's all kinds of us."   59

"Yes, and it takes all kinds to make the world go round," the lady said in her musical voice.   60

As she said it, the raw-complexioned girl snapped her teeth together. 61
Her lower lip turned downwards and inside out, revealing the pale pink
inside of her mouth. After a second it rolled back up. It was the ugliest
face Mrs. Turpin had ever seen anyone make and for a moment she was
certain that the girl had made it at her. She was looking at her as if she
had known and disliked her all her life—all of Mrs. Turpin's life, it
seemed too, not just all the girl's life. Why, girl, I don't even know you,
Mrs. Turpin said silently.

She forced her attention back to the discussion. "It wouldn't be prac-   62
tical to send them back to Africa," she said. "They wouldn't want to go.
They got it too good here."

"Wouldn't be what they wanted—if I had anythang to do with it," the   63
woman said.

"It wouldn't be a way in the world you could get all the niggers back   64
over there," Mrs. Turpin said. "They'd be hiding out and lying down and
turning sick on you and wailing and hollering and raring and pitching. It
wouldn't be a way in the world to get them over there."

"They got over here," the trashy woman said. "Get back like they got   65
over."

"It wasn't so many of them then," Mrs. Turpin explained.   66

The woman looked at Mrs. Turpin as if here was an idiot indeed but   67
Mrs. Turpin was not bothered by the look, considering where it came from.

"Nooo," she said, "they're going to stay here where they can go to   68
New York and marry white folks and improve their color. That's what
they all want to do, every one of them, improve their color."

"You know what comes of that, don't you?" Claud asked.   69

"No, Claud, what?" Mrs. Turpin said.   70

Claud's eyes twinkled. "White-faced niggers," he said with never a smile.   71

Everybody in the office laughed except the white-trash and the ugly girl.   72
The girl gripped the book in her lap with white fingers. The trashy woman
looked around her from face to face as if she thought they were all idiots. The
old woman in the feed sack dress continued to gaze expressionless across the
floor at the high-top shoes of the man opposite her, the one who had been
pretending to be asleep when the Turpins came in. He was laughing heartily,
his hands still spread out on his knees. The child had fallen to the side and
was lying now almost face down in the old woman's lap.

While they recovered from their laughter, the nasal chorus on the   73
radio kept the room from silence.

> You go to blank blank
> And I'll go to mine
> But we'll all blank along
> To-geth-ther,
> And all along the blank
> We'll hep each other out
> Smile-ling in any kind of
> Weath-ther!

Mrs. Turpin didn't catch every word but she caught enough to agree with the spirit of the song and it turned her thoughts sober. To help anybody out that needed it was her philosophy of life. She never spared herself when she found somebody in need, whether they were white or black, trash or decent. And of all she had to be thankful for, she was most thankful that this was so. If Jesus had said, "You can be high society and have all the money you want and be thin and svelte-like, but you can't be a good woman with it," she would have had to say, "Well don't make me that then. Make me a good woman and it don't matter what else, how fat or how ugly or how poor!" Her heart rose. He had not made her a nigger or white-trash or ugly! He had made her herself and given her a little of everything. Jesus, thank you! she said. Thank you thank you thank you! Whenever she counted her blessing she felt as buoyant as if she weighed one hundred and twenty-five pounds instead of one hundred and eighty.

"What's wrong with your little boy?" the pleasant lady asked the white-trashy woman.   74

"He has an ulcer," the woman said proudly. "He ain't give me a minute's peace since he was born. Him and her are just alike," she said, nodding at the old woman, who was running her leathery fingers through the child's pale hair. "Look like I can't get nothing down them two but Co' Cola and candy."   75

That's all you try to get down em, Mrs. Turpin said to herself. Too lazy to light the fire. There was nothing you could tell her about people like them that she didn't know already. And it was not just that they didn't have anything. Because if you gave them everything, in two weeks it would all be broken or filthy or they would have chopped it up for lightwood. She knew all this from her own experience. Help them you must, but help them you couldn't.   76

All at once the ugly girl turned her lips inside out again. Her eyes were fixed like two drills on Mrs. Turpin. This time there was no mistaking that there was something urgent behind them.   77

Girl, Mrs. Turpin explained silently, I haven't done a thing to you! The girl might be confusing her with somebody else. There was no need to sit by and let herself be intimidated. "You must be in college," she said boldly, looking directly at the girl. "I see you reading a book there."   78

The girl continued to stare and pointedly did not answer.   79

Her mother blushed at this rudeness. "The lady asked you a question, Mary Grace," she said under her breath.   80

"I have ears," Mary Grace said.   81

The poor mother blushed again. "Mary Grace goes to Wellesley College," she explained. She twisted one of the buttons on her dress. "In Massachusetts," she added with a grimace. "And in the summer she just keeps right on studying. Just reads all the time, a real book worm. She's done real well at Wellesley; she's taking English and Math and History and Psychology and Social Studies," she rattled on, "and I think it's too much. I think she ought to get out and have fun."   82

The girl looked as if she would like to hurl them all through the plate   83
glass window.

"Way up north," Mrs. Turpin murmured and thought, well, it hasn't   84
done much for her manners.

"I'd almost rather to have him sick," the white-trash woman said,   85
wrenching the attention back to herself. "He's so mean when he ain't. Look
like some children just take natural to meanness. It's some gets bad when
they get sick but he was the opposite. Took sick and turned good. He don't
give me no trouble now. It's me waitin to see the doctor," she said.

If I was going to send anybody back to Africa, Mrs. Turpin thought, it   86
would be your kind, woman. "Yes, indeed," she said aloud, but looking
up at the ceiling, "it's a heap of things worse than a nigger." And dirtier
than a hog, she added to herself.

"I think people with bad dispositions are more to be pitied than any-   87
one on earth," the pleasant lady said in a voice that was decidedly thin.

"I thank the Lord he has blessed me with a good one," Mrs. Turpin said.   88
"The day has never dawned that I couldn't find something to laugh at."

"Not since she married me anyways," Claud said with a comical   89
straight face.

Everybody laughed except the girl and the white-trash.   90

Mrs. Turpin's stomach shook. "He's such a caution," she said, "that I   91
can't help but laugh at him."

The girl made a loud ugly noise through her teeth.   92

Her mother's mouth grew thin and tight. "I think the worst thing in   93
the world," she said, "is an ungrateful person. To have everything and
not appreciate it. I know a girl," she said, "who has parents who would
give her anything, a little brother who loves her dearly, who is getting a
good education, who wears the best clothes, but who can never say a
kind word to anyone, who never smiles, who just criticizes and com-
plains all day long."

"Is she too old to paddle?" Claud asked.   94

The girl's face was almost purple.   95

"Yes," the lady said, "I'm afraid there's nothing to do but leave her to   96
her folly. Some day she'll wake up and it'll be too late."

"It never hurt anyone to smile," Mrs. Turpin said. "It just makes you   97
feel better all over."

"Of course," the lady said sadly, "but there are just some people you   98
can't tell anything to. They can't take criticism."

"If it's one thing I am," Mrs. Turpin said with feeling, "it's grateful.   99
When I think who all I could have been besides myself and what all I
got, a little of everything, and a good disposition besides, I just feel like
shouting, 'Thank you, Jesus, for making everything the way it is!' It
could have been different!" For one thing, somebody else could have got
Claud. At the thought of this, she was flooded with gratitude and a terrible pang of joy ran through her. "Oh thank you, Jesus, Jesus, thank you!"
she cried aloud.

The book struck her directly over her left eye. It struck almost at the same instant that she realized the girl was about to hurl it. Before she could utter a sound, the raw face came crashing across the table toward her, howling. The girl's fingers sank like claws into the soft flesh of her neck. She heard the mother cry out and Claud shout, "Whoa!" There was an instant when she was certain that she was about to be in an earthquake.   100

All at once her vision narrowed and she saw everything as if it were happening in a small room far away, or as if she were looking at it through the wrong end of a telescope. Claud's face crumpled and fell out of sight. The nurse ran in, then out, then in again. Then the gangling figure of the doctor rushed out of the inner door. Magazines flew this way and that as the table turned over. The girl fell with a thud and Mrs. Turpin's vision suddenly reversed itself and she saw everything large instead of small. The eyes of the white-trashy woman were staring hugely at the floor. There the girl, held down on one side by the nurse and on the other by her mother, was wrenching and turning in their gasp. The doctor was kneeling astride her, trying to hold her arm down. He managed after a second to sink a long needle into it.   101

Mrs. Turpin felt entirely hollow except for her heart which swung from side to side as if it were agitated in a great empty drum of flesh.   102

"Somebody that's not busy call for the ambulance," the doctor said in the off-hand voice young doctors adopt for terrible occasions.   103

Mrs. Turpin could not have moved a finger. The old man who had been sitting next to her skipped nimbly into the office and made the call, for the secretary still seemed to be gone.   104

"Claud!" Mrs. Turpin called.   105

He was not in his chair. She knew she must jump up and find him but she felt like someone trying to catch a train in a dream, when everything moves in slow motion and the faster you try to run the slower you go.   106

"Here I am," a suffocated voice, very unlike Claud's, said.   107

He was doubled up in the corner on the floor, pale as paper, holding his leg. She wanted to get up and go to him but she could not move. Instead, her gaze was drawn slowly downward to the churning face on the floor, which she could see over the doctor's shoulder.   108

The girl's eyes stopped rolling and focused on her. They seemed a much lighter blue than before, as if a door that had been tightly closed behind them was now open to admit light and air.   109

Mrs. Turpin's head cleared and her power of motion returned. She leaned forward until she was looking directly into the fierce brilliant eyes. There was no doubt in her mind that the girl did know her, knew her in some intense and personal way, beyond time and place and condition. "What you got to say to me?" she asked hoarsely and held her breath, waiting, as for a revelation.   110

The girl raised her head. Her gaze locked with Mrs. Turpin's. "Go back to hell where you came from, you old wart hog," she whispered.   111

Her voice was low but clear. Her eyes burned for a moment as if she saw with pleasure that her message had struck its target.

Mrs. Turpin sank back into her chair.   112

After a moment the girl's eyes closed and she turned her head   113
wearily to the side.

The doctor rose and handed the nurse the empty syringe. He leaned   114
over and put both hands for a moment on the mother's shoulders, which
were shaking. She was sitting on the floor, her lips pressed together, holding Mary Grace's hand in her lap. The girl's fingers were gripped like a
baby's around her thumb. "Go on to the hospital," he said. "I'll call and
make the arrangements."

"Now, let's see that neck," he said in a jovial voice to Mrs. Turpin. He   115
began to inspect her neck with his two fingers. Two little moonshaped
lines like pink fish bones were indented over her windpipe. There was
the beginning of an angry red swelling above her eye. His fingers passed
over this also.

"Let me be," she said thickly and shook him off. "See about Claud.   116
She kicked him."

"I'll see about him in a minute," he said and felt her pulse. He was a   117
thin grey-haired man, given to pleasantries. "Go home and have yourself
a vacation the rest of the day," he said and patted her on the shoulder.

Quit your pattin me, Mrs. Turpin growled to herself.   118

"And put an ice pack over that eye," he said. Then he went and squat-   119
ted down beside Claud and looked at his leg. After a moment he pulled
him up and Claud limped after him into the office.

Until the ambulance came, the only sounds in the room were the   120
tremulous moans of the girl's mother, who continued to sit on the floor.
The white-trash woman did not take her eyes off the girl. Mrs. Turpin
looked straight ahead at nothing. Presently the ambulance drew up, a long
dark shadow, behind the curtain. The attendants came in and set the
stretcher down beside the girl and lifted her expertly onto it and carried
her out. The nurse helped the mother gather up her things. The shadow of
the ambulance moved silently away and the nurse came back in the office.

"That ther girl is going to be a lunatic, ain't she?" the white-trash   121
woman asked the nurse, but the nurse kept on to the back and never answered her.

"Yes, she's going to be a lunatic," the white-trash woman said to the   122
rest of them.

"Po' critter," the old woman murmured. The child's face was still in   123
her lap. His eyes looked idly over her knees. He had not moved during
the disturbance except to draw one leg up under him.

"I thank Gawd," the white-trash woman said fervently, "I ain't a lunatic."   124

Claud came limping out and the Turpins went home.   125

As their pick-up truck turned into their own dirt road and made the   126
crest of the hill, Mrs. Turpin gripped the window ledge and looked out
suspiciously. The land sloped gracefully down through a field dotted

with lavender weeds and at the start of the rise their small yellow frame house, with its little flower beds spread out around it like a fancy apron, sat primly in its accustomed place between two giant hickory trees. She would not have been startled to see a burnt wound between two blackened chimneys.

Neither of them felt like eating so they put on their house clothes and lowered the shade in the bedroom and lay down, Claud with his leg on a pillow and herself with a damp washcloth over her eye. The instant she was flat on her back, the image of a razor-backed hog with warts on its face and horns coming out behind its ears snorted into her head. She moaned, a low quiet moan.   127

"I am not," she said tearfully, "a wart hog. From hell." But the denial had no force. The girl's eyes and her words, even the tone of her voice, low but clear, directed only to her, brooked no repudiation. She had been singled out for the message, though there was trash in the room to whom it might justly have been applied. The full force of this fact struck her only now. There was a woman there who was neglecting her own child but she had been overlooked. The message had been given to Ruby Turpin, a respectable, hard-working, church-going woman. The tears dried. Her eyes began to burn instead with wrath.   128

She rose on her elbow and the washcloth fell into her hand. Claud was lying on his back, snoring. She wanted to tell him what the girl had said. At the same time, she did not wish to put the imaging of herself as a wart hog from hell into his mind.   129

"Hey, Claud," she muttered and pushed his shoulder.   130

Claud opened one pale baby blue eye.   131

She looked into it warily. He did not think about anything. He just went his way.   132

"Wha, whasit?" he said and closed the eye again.   133

"Nothing," she said. "Does your leg pain you?"   134

"Hurts like hell," Claud said.   135

"It'll quit terreckly," she said and lay back down. In a moment Claud was snoring again. For the rest of the afternoon they lay there. Claud slept. She scowled at the ceiling. Occasionally she raised her fist and made a small stabbing motion over her chest as if she was defending her innocence to invisible guests who were like the comforters of Job, reasonable-seeming but wrong.   136

About five-thirty Claud stirred. "Got to go after those niggers," he sighed, not moving.   137

She was looking straight up as if there were unintelligible handwriting on the ceiling. The protuberance over her eye had turned a greenish-blue. "Listen here," she said.   138

"What?"   139

"Kiss me."   140

Claud leaned over and kissed her loudly on the mouth. He pinched her side and their hands interlocked. Her expression of ferocious concen-   141 tration did not change. Claud got up, groaning and growling, and limped off. She continued to study the ceiling.

She did not get up until she heard the pick-up truck coming back   142
with the Negroes. Then she rose and thrust her feet in her brown oxfords, which she did not bother to lace, and stumped out onto the back porch and got her red plastic bucket. She emptied a tray of ice cubes into it and filled it half full of water and went out into the back yard. Every afternoon after Claud brought the hands in, one of the boys helped him put out hay and the rest waited in the back of the truck until he was ready to take them home. The truck was parked in the shade under one of the hickory trees.

"Hi yawl this evening?" Mrs. Turpin asked grimly, appearing with the   143
bucket and the dipper. There were three women and a boy in the truck.

"Us doin nicely," the oldest woman said. "Hi you doin?" and her   144
gaze struck immediately on the dark lump on Mrs. Turpin's forehead. "You done fell down, ain't you?" she asked in a solicitous voice. The old woman was dark and almost toothless. She had on an old felt hat of Claud's set back of her head. The other two women were younger and lighter and they both had new bright green sun hats. One of them had hers on her head; the other had taken hers off and the boy was grinning beneath it.

Mrs. Turpin set the bucket down on the floor of the truck. "Yawl hep   145
yourselves," she said. She looked around to make sure Claud had gone. "No. I didn't fall down." she said, folding her arms. "It was something worse than that."

"Ain't nothing bad happen to you!" the old woman said. She said it as   146
if they all knew that Mrs. Turpin was protected in some special way by Divine Providence. "You just had you a little fall."

"We were in town at the doctor's office for where the cow kicked Mr.   147
Turpin," Mrs. Turpin said in a flat tone that indicated they could leave off their foolishness. "And there was a girl there. A big fat girl with her face all broke out. I could look at that girl and tell she was peculiar but I couldn't tell how. And me and her mama were just talking and going along and all of a sudden WHAM! She throws this big book she was reading at me and...."

"Naw!" the old woman cried out.   148

"And then she jumps over the table and commences to choke me."   149

"Naw!" they all exclaimed, "naw!"   150

"Hi come she do that?" the old woman asked. "What ail her?"   151

Mrs. Turpin only glared in front of her.   152

"Somethin ail her," the old woman said.   153

"They carried her off in an ambulance." Mrs. Turpin continued, "but   154
before she went she was rolling on the floor and they were trying to hold her down to give her a shot and she said something to me." She paused. "You know what she said to me?"

"What she say?" they asked.   155

"She said," Mrs. Turpin began, and stopped, her face very dark and   156
heavy. The sun was getting whiter and whiter, blanching the sky overhead so that the leaves of the hickory tree were black in the face of it. She
could not bring forth the words. "Something real ugly," she muttered.

"She sho shouldn't said nothin ugly to you." the old woman   157
said."You so sweet. You the sweetest lady I know."

"She pretty too," the one with the hat on said.   158

"And stout," the .other one said. "I never known no sweeter white   159
lady."

"That's the truth befo' Jesus," the old woman said. "Amen! You jes as   160
sweet and pretty as you can be."

Mrs. Turpin knew just exactly how much Negro flattery was worth   161
and it added to her rage. "She said," she began again and finished this
time with a fierce rush of breath, "that I was an old wart hog from hell."

There was an astounded silence.   162

"Where she at?" the youngest woman cried in a piercing voice.   163

"Lemme see her. I'll kill her!"   164

"I'll kill her with you!" the other one cried.   165

"She b'long in the sylum," the old woman said emphatically. "You   166
the sweetest white lady I know."

"She pretty too," the other two said. "Stout as she can be and sweet.   167
Jesus satisfied with her!"

"Deed he is," the old woman declared.   168

Idiots! Mrs. Turpin growled to herself. You could never say anything   169
intelligent to a nigger. You could talk at them but not with them. "Yawl
ain't drunk your water," she said shortly. "Leave the bucket in the truck
when you're finished with it. I got more to do than just stand around and
pass the time of day," and she moved off and into the house.

She stood for a moment in the middle of the kitchen. The dark protu-   170
berance over her eye looked like a miniature tornado cloud which might
any moment sweep across the horizon of her brow. Her lower lip pro-
truded dangerously. She squared her massive shoulders. Then she
marched into the front of the house and out the side door and started
down the road to the pig parlor. She had the look of a woman going single-handed, weaponless, into battle.

The sun was a very deep yellow now like a harvest moon and was   171
rising westward very fast over the far tree line as if it meant to reach the
hogs before she did. The road was rutted and she kicked several good-
sized stones out of her path as she strode along. The pig parlor was on a
little knoll at the end of a lane that ran off from the side of the barn. It was
a square of concrete as large as a small room, with a board fence about
four feet high around it. The concrete floor sloped slightly so that the hog
wash could drain off into a trench where it was carried to the field for fer-
tilizer. Claud was standing on the outside, on the edge of the concrete,
hanging onto the top board, hosing down the floor inside. The hose was
connected to the faucet of a water trough nearby.

Mrs. Turpin climbed up beside him and glowered down at the hogs   172
inside. There were seven long-snouted bristly shoats in it—tan with liver-
colored spots—and an old sow a few weeks off from farrowing. She was
laying on her side grunting. The shoats were running about shaking
themselves like idiot children, their little slit pig eyes searching the floor
for anything left. She had read pigs were the most intelligent animal. She
doubted it. They were supposed to be smarter than dogs. There had even
been a pig astronaut. He had performed his assignment perfectly but died
of a heart attack afterward because they left him in his electric suit, sitting
upright throughout his examination when naturally a hog should be on
all fours.

A-gruntin and a-rooting and a-groanin.   173

"Gimme that hose," she said, yanking it away from Claud. "Go on   174
and carry them niggers home and then get off that leg."

"You look like you might have swallowed a mad dog," Claud observed,   175
but he got down and limped off. He paid no attention to her humors.

Until he was out of earshot, Mrs. Turpin stood on the side of the   176
pen, holding the hose and pointing the stream of water at the hind quarters of any shoat that looked as if it might try to lie down. When he had
had time to get over the hill, she turned her head slightly and her
wrathful eyes scanned the path. He was nowhere in sight. She turned
back again and seemed to gather herself up. Her shoulders rose and she
drew in her breath.

"What do you send me a message like that for?" she said in a low   177
fierce voice, barely above a whisper but with the force of a shout in its
concentrated fury. "How am I a hog and me both? How am I saved and
from hell too?" Her free fist was knotted and with the other she gripped
the hose, blindly pointing the stream of water in and out of the eye of the
old sow whose outraged squeal she did not hear.

The pig parlor commanded a view of the back pasture where their   178
twenty beef cows were gathered around the hay-bales Claud and the boy
had put out. The freshly cut pasture sloped down to the highway. Across
it was their cotton field. The sun was behind the wood, very red, looking
over the paling of trees like a farmer inspecting his own hogs.

"Why me?" she rumbled. "It's no trash around here, black or white,   179
that I haven't given to. And break my back to the bone every day working. And do for the church."

She appeared to be the right size woman to command the arena be-   180
fore her. "How am I a hog?" she demanded. "Exactly how am I like
them?" and she jabbed the stream of water at the shoats. "There was
plenty of trash there. It didn't have to be me."

"If you like trash better, go get yourself some trash then," she railed.   181
"You could have made me trash. Or a nigger. If trash is what you wanted
why didn't you make me trash?" She shook her fist with the hose in it
and a water snake appeared momentarily in the air. "I could quit working
and take it easy and be filthy," she growled. "Lounge about the sidewalks

all day drinking root beer. Dip snuff and spit in every puddle and have it all over my face. I could be nasty."

"Or you could have made me a nigger. It's too late for me to be a nig- 182 ger," she said with deep sarcasm, "but I could act like one. Lay down in the middle of the road and stop traffic. Roll on the ground."

In the deepening light everything was taking on a mysterious hue. 183 The pasture was growing a peculiar grassy green and the streak of highway had turned lavender. She braced herself for a final assault and this time her voice rolled out over the pasture. "Go on," she yelled, "call me a hog! Call me a hog again. From hell. Call me a wart hog from hell. Put that bottom rail on top. There'll still be a top and bottom!"

A garbled echo returned to her. 184

A final surge of fury shook her and she roared, "Who do you think 185 you are?"

The color of everything, field and crimson sky, burned for a moment 186 with a transparent intensity. The question carried over the pasture and across the highway and the cotton field and returned to her clearly like an answer from beyond the wood.

She opened her mouth but no sound came out of it. 187

A tiny truck, Claud's, appeared on the highway, heading rapidly out 188 of sight. Its gears scraped thinly. It looked like a child's toy. At any moment a bigger truck might smash into it and scatter Claud's and the niggers' brains all over the road.

Mrs. Turpin stood there, her gaze fixed on the highway, all her mus- 189 cles rigid, until in five or six minutes the truck reappeared, returning. She waited until it had had time to turn into their own road. Then like a monumental statue coming to life, she bent her head slowly and gazed, as if through the very heart of mystery, down into the pig parlor at the hogs. They had settled all in one corner around the old sow who was grunting softly. A red glow suffused them. They appeared to pant with a secret life.

Until the sun slipped finally behind the tree line, Mrs. Turpin re- 190 mained there with her gaze bent to them as if she were absorbing some abysmal life-giving knowledge. At last she lifted her head. There was only a purple streak in the sky, cutting through a field of crimson and leading, like an extension of the highway, into the descending dusk. She raised her hands from the side of the pen in a gesture hieratic and profound. A visionary light settled in her eyes. She saw the streak as a vast swinging bridge extending upward from the earth through a field of living fire. Upon it a vast horde of souls were rumbling toward heaven. There were whole companies of white-trash, clean for the first time in their lives, and bands of black niggers in white robes, and battalions of freaks and lunatics shouting and clapping and leaping like frogs. And bringing up the end of the procession was a tribe of people whom she recognized at once as those who, like herself and Claud, had always had a little of everything and the God-given wit to use it right. She leaned forward to observe them closer. They were marching behind the others with great dignity, accountable as they had always been for good order and common sense and respectable behavior. They alone were on key. Yet she could see by their shocked and altered faces that even their virtues were being burned away. She lowered her hands and gripped the rail of the hog pen, her eyes small but fixed unblinkingly on what lay ahead. In a moment the vision faded but she remained where she was, immobile.

At length she got down and turned off the faucet and made her slow way on the darkening path to the house. In the woods around her the invisible cricket choruses had struck up, but what she heard were the voices of the souls climbing upward into the starry field and shouting hallelujah.

191

• • •

THINKING ABOUT LITERATURE

1. What is Mrs. Turpin's revelation? What causes it? What, if anything, does it teach her about herself?

2. On what basis does Mrs. Turpin classify people? What categories does she identify? How do hogs fit into her system of classification?

3. How would you classify Mrs. Turpin, the "white-trash woman," and the "pleasant lady" in terms of their attitudes toward blacks? Whose attitudes do you find most—and least—offensive?

JOURNAL ENTRY

What dangers do you see in classification systems like Mrs. Turpin's? Who—or what—is most at risk? Why?

THEMATIC CONNECTIONS

- "What's in a Name?" (page 5)
- "Just Walk On By" (page 186)
- "On the Meaning of Plumbing and Poverty" (page 288)
- "The Untouchable" (page 448)

WRITING ASSIGNMENTS FOR CLASSIFICATION AND DIVISION

1. Choose a film you have seen recently and list all the elements that you consider significant—plot, direction, acting, special effects, and so on. Then further subdivide each category (for instance, listing each of the special effects). Using this list as an organizational guide, write a review of the film.

2. Write an essay in which you classify the teachers or bosses you have had into several distinct categories and make a judgment about the relative effectiveness of the individuals in each group. Give each category a name, and be sure your essay has a thesis statement.

3. What styles of dress do you observe on your college campus? Establish four or five distinct categories, and write an essay in which you classify students on the basis of how they dress. Give each group a descriptive title.

4. Do some research to help you identify the subclasses of a large class of animals or plants. Write an essay in which you enumerate and describe the subclasses in each class for an audience of elementary school students.

5. Violence in sports is considered by many to be a serious problem. Write an essay in which you express your views on this problem. Use a classification-and-division structure, categorizing information according to sources of violence (such as the players, the nature of the game, or the fans).

6. Classify television shows according to type (action, drama, and so forth), audience (preschoolers, school-age children, adults, and so forth), or any other logical principle. Write an essay based on your system of classification, making sure to include a thesis statement. For instance, you might assert that the relative popularity of one kind of program over others reveals something about television watchers, or that one kind of program shows signs of becoming obsolete.

7. Write a lighthearted essay discussing kinds of snack foods, cartoons, pets, status symbols, toys, shoppers, vacations, weight-loss diets, hairstyles, or drivers.

8. Write an essay in which you assess the relative merits of several different politicians, news broadcasts, or academic majors.

9. What kinds of survival skills does a student need to get through college successfully? Write a classification-and-division essay in which you identify and discuss several kinds of skills, indicating why each category is important. If you like, you may write your essay in the form of a letter to a beginning college student.

10. After attending a party, lecture, or concert, write an essay in which you divide the people you observe there into categories according to some logical principle. Include a thesis statement that indicates how different the various groups are.

COLLABORATIVE ACTIVITY FOR CLASSIFICATION AND DIVISION

Working in groups, devise a classification system that encompasses all the different kinds of popular music favored by the members of your group. You may begin with general categories like country, pop, and rhythm and blues, but you should also include more specific categories, such as heavy metal and rap, in your classification system. After you decide on categories and subcategories that represent the tastes of all members of your group, fill in examples for each category. Then devise several different options for arranging your categories into an essay.

9

DEFINITION

WHAT IS DEFINITION?

A **definition** tells what a term means and how it is different from other terms in its class. In the following paragraph from *Nothing to Declare*, Mary Morris defines *traveler*:

Topic sentence

How do you know if you are a traveler? What are the telltale signs? As with most compulsions, such as being a gambler, a kleptomaniac, or a writer, the obvious proof is that you can't stop. If you are hooked, you are hooked. One sure sign of travelers is their relationship to maps. I cannot say how much of my life I have spent looking at maps, but there is no map I won't stare at and study. I love to measure each detail with my thumb, to see how far I have come, how far I've yet to go. I love maps the way stamp collectors love stamps. Not for their usefulness, but rather for the sheer beauty of the object itself. I love to look at a map, even if it is a map of Mars, and figure out where I am going and how I am going to get there, what route I will take. I imagine what adventures might await me even though I know that the journey is never what we plan for; it's what happens between the lines.

Extended definition defines term by means of analogy, exemplification, and description

Whenever you take an exam, you are likely to encounter questions that require definitions. You might, for example, be asked to define *behaviorism*; tell what a *cell* is; explain the meaning of the literary term *naturalism*; include a comprehensive definition of *mitosis* in your answer; or define *authority*. Such exam questions cannot always be answered in one or two sentences. In fact, the definitions they call for often require several paragraphs.

Most people think of definition in terms of dictionaries, which give brief, succinct explanations of what words mean. But definition also includes explaining what something, or even someone, *is*—that is, its essential nature. Sometimes a definition requires a paragraph, an essay, or even a whole book. These longer, more complex definitions are called **extended definitions.**

Extended definitions are useful for many academic assignments besides exams. A thoughtful definition can clarify a precise term or a general concept. Definitions can explain abstractions like *freedom* or controversial terms like *right to life* or **slang** terms, informal expressions whose meanings may vary from locale to locale or change as time passes. In a particular writing situation, a definition may be essential because a term has more than one meaning, because you are using it in an unusual way, or because you believe the term is unfamiliar to your readers.

Many extended-definition essays include shorter **formal definitions** like those in dictionaries. Moreover, essays in which patterns of development are dominant often incorporate brief definitions to clarify points or explain basic information for the reader. Whether it appears in another kind of essay or acts as a focus for an extended definition, the brief formal definition (often called a *dictionary definition*) establishes the basic meaning of a term.

Formal Definitions

Look at any dictionary, and you will notice that all definitions have a standard three-part structure. First, they present the *term* to be defined, then the general *class* it is a part of, and finally the *qualities that differentiate it* from the other terms in the same class.

Term	Class	Differentiation
Behaviorism	is a theory	that regards the objective facts of a subject's actions as the only valid basis for psychological study.
A cell	is a unit of protoplasm	with a nucleus, cytoplasm, and an enclosing membrane.
Naturalism	is a literary movement	whose original adherents believed that writers should treat life with scientific objectivity.
Mitosis	is the process	of nuclear division of cells, consisting of prophase, metaphase, anaphase, and telophase.
Authority	is the power	to command and require obedience.

Supplying a dictionary definition of each term you use is seldom necessary or desirable. Readers will often know what a word means or be able to look it up. Sometimes, however, defining your terms is essential—for example, when a word has several meanings, each of which might fit your context, or when you want to use a word in a special way. In a long definition essay, a brief formal definition helps to introduce readers to the extended definition or to support the essay's thesis. Remember, formal definitions include the term, its class, and its distinguishing qualities—the three components that pinpoint what something is and what it is not.

Extended Definitions

An extended definition includes the three basic parts of a formal definition—the term, its class, and its distinguishing characteristics. Beyond these essentials, an extended definition does not follow a set pattern of development. Instead, it uses whatever strategies best suit the term being defined and the writing situation. In fact, any one (or more than one) of the essay patterns illustrated in this book can be used to structure a definition essay.

USING PATTERNS OF DEVELOPMENT.   As you plan your essay and jot down your ideas about the term or subject, you will see which patterns are most useful. The formal definitions of the five terms discussed previously, for example, could be expanded with five different patterns of development.

• *Exemplification* To explain *behaviorism,* you could give examples. Carefully chosen cases could show how this theory of psychology applies in different situations. These examples could help readers see exactly how behaviorism works and what it can and cannot account for. Often, examples are the clearest way to explain something unusual, especially when it is unfamiliar to your readers. Defining dreams as "the symbolic representation of mental states" might convey little to readers who do not know much about psychology. But a few examples would help you make your point. Many students have dreams about taking exams—perhaps dreaming that they are late for the test, that they remember nothing about the course, or that they are writing their answers in disappearing ink. You might explain the nature of dreams by interpreting these particular dreams, which may reflect anxiety about a course or about school in general.

• *Description* You can explain the nature of something by describing it. For example, the concept of a *cell* is difficult to grasp from just a formal definition, but your readers would understand the concept more clearly if you were to explain what a cell looks like, possibly with the aid of a diagram or two. Concentrating on the cell membrane, cytoplasm, and nucleus, you could detail each structure's appearance and function. These descriptions would enable readers to visualize the whole cell and understand its workings. Of course, description involves more than the visual: a definition of Italian cooking might describe the taste and smell, as well as the appearance, of ravioli, and a definition of Parkinson's disease might include a description of how its symptoms feel to a patient.

• *Comparison and contrast* An extended definition of *naturalism* could employ a comparison-and-contrast structure. Naturalism is one of several major movements in American literature, and its literary aims could be contrasted with those of other literary movements, such as romanticism or realism. Or you might compare and contrast the plots and characters of several naturalistic works with those of romantic or realistic works. If you needed to define something unfamiliar, you could compare it to something familiar to your readers. For example, your readers may never have heard of the Chinese dish called sweet-and-sour cabbage, but you can help them imagine it by saying it tastes something like cole slaw. You can also define a thing by contrasting it with something unlike it, especially if the two have some qualities in common. One way to explain the British sport of rugby is by contrasting it with American football, which is not as violent.

• *Process* An extended definition of *mitosis* should be organized as a process analysis because mitosis is a process. You could explain the stages of mitosis, pointing out the transitions from one phase to another. By tracing the process from stage to stage, you would be able to clearly define this type of cell division for your readers. Similarly, some objects must be defined in terms of what they do. For example, because a computer carries out certain processes, an extended definition of a computer would probably include a process analysis.

• *Classification and division* Finally, you could define *authority* by using classification and division. Basing your extended definition on the model developed by the German sociologist Max Weber, you could divide the class *authority* into the subclasses *traditional authority, charismatic authority,* and *legal-bureaucratic authority.* Then, by explaining each type of authority, you would clarify this very broad term for your readers. In both extended and formal definitions, classification and division can be very useful. By saying what class something belongs to, you are explaining what kind of thing it is. For instance, *monetarism* is an economic theory; *The Adventures of Huckleberry Finn* is a novel; *emphysema* is a disease. And by dividing that class into subclasses, you are defining something more specifically. Emphysema, for instance, is a disease of the lungs, which classifies it with tuberculosis but not with appendicitis.

USING OTHER STRATEGIES.   In addition to using various patterns of development, you can expand a definition by using other strategies:

• You can define a term by using **synonyms** (words with similar meanings).
• You can define a term by using *negation* (telling what it is *not*).
• You can define a term by using *enumeration* (listing its characteristics).
• You can define a term by using **analogies** (comparisons that identify similarities between the term and something dissimilar).
• You can define a term by discussing its *origin and development* (the word's derivation, original meaning, and usages).

Whatever form your definitions take, make certain that they are clear and that they actually define. Be sure to provide a true definition, not just a descriptive statement such as "Happiness is a four-day weekend." Likewise, repetition is not definition, so don't include the term you are defining in your definition. For instance, the statement "abstract art is a school of artists whose works are abstract" clarifies nothing for your readers. Finally, define as precisely as possible. Name the class of the term you are defining—for example, state "mitosis is *a process in which* a cell divides" rather than "mitosis is *when* a cell divides"—and define this class as narrowly and as accurately as you can. Be specific when you differentiate your term from other members of its class. Careful attention to the language and structure of your definition will help readers understand your meaning.

STRUCTURING A DEFINITION ESSAY

A definition essay should have an *introduction,* a *body,* and a *conclusion.* Although a formal definition strives for objectivity, an extended definition may not. Instead, it may define a term in a way that reflects your attitude toward the subject or your reason for defining it. For example, your extended-definition paper about literary *naturalism* might argue that the significance of this movement's major works has been underestimated by literary scholars. Or your definition of *authority* might criticize its abuses. In such cases the thesis statement provides a focus for a definition essay, telling readers *your* approach to the definition.

Suppose you are assigned a short paper in your introductory psychology course. You decide to examine *behaviorism.* First, you have to determine whether your topic is appropriate for a definition essay. If the topic suggests a response such as "The true nature of A is B" or "A means B," then it is a definition. Of course, you can define *behaviorism* as a *word* in one sentence, or possibly two. But to explain the *concept* of behaviorism and its position in the field of psychology, you must go beyond the dictionary.

Second, you have to decide what kinds of explanations are most suitable for your topic and for your intended audience. If you are trying to define *behaviorism* for readers who know very little about psychology, you might use comparisons that relate behaviorism to your readers' experiences, such as how they were raised or how they train their pets. You might also use examples, but the examples would relate not to psychological experiments or clinical treatment but to experiences in everyday life. If, however, you direct your paper to your psychology instructor, who obviously already knows what behaviorism is, your purpose is to show that you know, too. One way to do this is to compare behaviorism to other psychological theories. Another way is to give examples of how behaviorism works in practice. You could also briefly summarize the background and history of the theory. (In a term paper you might use all of these strategies.)

After considering your paper's scope and audience, you might decide that because behaviorism is somewhat controversial, your best strategy is to supplement a formal definition with examples showing how behaviorist assumptions and methods are applied in specific situations. These examples, drawn from your class notes and textbook, will support your thesis that behaviorism is a valid approach for treating certain psychological dysfunctions. Together, your examples will define *behaviorism* as it is understood today.

An informal outline for your essay might look like this:

Introduction	Thesis statement—Contrary to its critics' assertions, behaviorism is a valid approach for treating a wide variety of psychological dysfunctions.
Background:	Definition of behaviorism, including its origins and evolution
First example:	The use of behaviorism to help psychotics function in an institutional setting
Second example:	The use of behaviorism to treat neurotic behavior, such as chronic anxiety, a phobia, or a pattern of destructive acts
Third example:	The use of behaviorism to treat normal but antisocial or undesirable behavior, such as heavy smoking or overeating
Conclusion:	Restatement of thesis or review of key points

Notice how the three examples in this paper define behaviorism with the complexity, detail, and breadth that a formal definition could not duplicate. It is more like a textbook explanation—and, in fact, textbook explanations are often written as extended definitions.

▶ A STUDENT WRITER: DEFINITION

The following student essay, written by Ajoy Mahtab for a composition course, defines the untouchables, a caste whose members are shunned in India. In his essay Ajoy, who grew up in Calcutta, presents a thesis that is sharply critical of the practice of ostracizing untouchables.

```
                        The Untouchable
Introduction:            A word that is extremely common in India       1
background           yet uncommon to the point of incomprehension
                     in the West is the word untouchable. It is a
                     word that has had extremely sinister connota-
                     tions throughout India's history. A rigorously
                     worked-out caste system existed in traditional
                     Indian society. At the top of the social lad-
                     der sat the Brahmins, the clan of the priest-
                     hood. These people had renounced the material
                     world for a spiritual one. Below them came the
                     Kshatriyas, or the warrior caste. This caste
```

included the kings and all their nobles along
with their armies. Third on the social ladder
were the Vaishyas, who were the merchants of
the land. Trade was their only form of livelihood. Last came the Shudras--the menials.
Shudras were employed by the prosperous as
sweepers and laborers. Originally a person's
caste was determined only by his profession.
Thus, if the son of a merchant joined the
army, he automatically converted from a Vaishya
to a Kshatriya. However, the system soon became
hereditary and rigid. Whatever one's occupation, one's caste was determined from birth
according to the caste of one's father.

Outside of this structure were a group of   2
people, human beings treated worse than dogs
and shunned far more than lepers, people who
were not considered even human, people who
defiled with their very touch. These were the

Formal definition   Achhoots: the untouchables. The word <u>untouch-</u>
<u>able</u> is commonly defined as "that which cannot
or should not be touched." In India, however,
it was taken to a far greater extreme. The

Historical back-   untouchables of a village lived in a separate
ground   community downwind of the borders of the village. They had a separate water supply, for
they would make the village water impure if
they were to drink from it. When they walked
they were made to bang two sticks together
continuously so that passersby could avoid an
untouchable's shadow. Tied to their waists,
trailing behind them, was a broom that would
clean the ground they had walked on. The
penalty for not following these or any other
rules was death for the untouchable and, in
many instances, for the entire untouchable
community.

Present situation   One of the pioneers of the fight against   3
untouchability was Mahatma Gandhi. Thanks to
his efforts and those of many others, untoucha-

bility no longer presents anything like the horrific picture painted above. In India today, in fact, recognition of untouchability is punishable by law. Theoretically, there is no such thing as untouchability anymore. But old traditions linger on, and such a deep-rooted fear passed down from generation to generation cannot disappear overnight. Even today, caste is an important factor in most marriages. Most Indian surnames reveal a person's caste immediately, and so it is a difficult thing to hide. The shunning of the untouchable is more prevalent in South India, where the general public is much more devout, than in the North. Some people would rather starve than share food and water with an untouchable. This concept is very difficult to accept in the West, but it is true all the same.

Example

I remember an incident from my childhood. 4
I could not have been more than eight or nine at the time. I was on a holiday staying at my family's house on the river Ganges. There was a festival going on and, as is customary, we were giving the servants small presents. I was handing them out when an old lady, bent with age, slowly hobbled into the room. She stood in the far corner of the room all alone, and no one so much as looked at her. When the entire line ended, she stepped hesitantly forward and stood in front of me, looking down at the ground. She then held a cloth stretched out in front of her. I was a little confused about how I was supposed to hand her her present, since both her hands were holding the cloth. Then, with the help of prompting from someone behind me, I learned that I was supposed to drop the gift into the cloth without touching the cloth itself. It was only later that I found out that she was an untouchable.

This was the first time I had actually come
face to face with prejudice, and it felt like
a slap in the face. That incident was burned
into my memory, and I do not think I will ever
forget it.

**Conclusion
begins**

5

The word <u>untouchable</u> is not often used in
the West, and when it is, it is generally used
as a complimentary term. For example, an avid
fan might say of an athlete, "He was absolutely untouchable. Nobody could even begin to
compare with him." It seems rather ironic that
a word could be so favorable in one culture
and so derogatory in another. Why does a word
that gives happiness in one part of the world
cause pain in another? Why does the same word
have different meanings to different people
around the globe? Why do certain words cause
rifts and others forge bonds? I do not think
anyone can tell me the answer.

**Conclusion
continues**

6

No actual parallel can be found today that
compares to the horrors of untouchability. For
an untouchable, life itself was a crime. The
day was spent just trying to stay alive. From

Thesis statement

the misery of the untouchables, the world
should learn a lesson: isolating and punishing
any group of people is dehumanizing and
immoral.

Points for Special Attention

THESIS STATEMENT.   Ajoy Mahtab's assignment was to write an extended definition of a term he assumed would be unfamiliar to his audience. Because he had definite ideas about the unjust treatment of the
untouchables, Ajoy wanted his essay to have a strong thesis that communicated his disapproval. Still, because he knew his American classmates
would need a good deal of background information before they would
accept such a thesis, he decided not to present it in his introduction.
Instead, he decided to lead up to his thesis gradually and state it at the
end of his essay. When other students in the class reviewed his draft, this
subtlety was one of the points they reacted to most favorably.

STRUCTURE.   Ajoy's introduction establishes the direction of his essay by introducing the word he will define; he then places this word in context by explaining India's rigid caste system. In paragraph 2 he gives the formal definition of the word *untouchable* and goes on to sketch the term's historical background. Paragraph 3 explains the status of the un-touchables in present-day India, and paragraph 4 gives a vivid example of Ajoy's first encounter with an untouchable. As he begins his conclusion in paragraph 5, Ajoy brings his readers back to the word his essay de-fines. Here he uses two strategies to add interest: he contrasts one con-temporary American usage of *untouchable* with its derogatory meaning in India, and he asks a series of **rhetorical questions** (questions asked for ef-fect and not meant to be answered). In paragraph 6 Ajoy presents a sum-mary of his position to lead into his thesis statement.

PATTERNS OF DEVELOPMENT.   This essay uses a number of strategies commonly encountered in extended definitions: it includes a formal defi-nition, explains the term's origin, and explores some of the term's conno-tations. In addition, the essay incorporates several familiar patterns of development. For instance, paragraph 1 uses classification and division to explain India's caste system; paragraphs 2 and 3 use brief examples to illustrate the plight of the untouchable; and paragraph 4 presents a narra-tive. Each of these patterns enriches the definition.

Focus on Revision

Because the term Ajoy defined was so unfamiliar to his classmates, many of the peer editing worksheets asked for more information. One suggestion in particular—that he draw an **analogy** between the unfamil-iar term *untouchable* and a more familiar concept—appealed to Ajoy as he planned his revision. Another student suggested that Ajoy could compare untouchables to other groups who are shunned—for example, people with AIDS. Although Ajoy states in his conclusion that no parallel exists, an attempt to find common ground between untouchables and other groups could make his essay more meaningful to his readers—and bring home to them an idea that is distinctly foreign. Such a connection could also make his conclusion especially powerful.

The readings that follow use exemplification, description, narration, and other methods of developing extended definitions. As you can see, no one pattern is more appropriate than another for a definition paper. (In fact, combining several patterns is often the most effective way to define the significant aspects of a term.) Your choice of pattern or patterns should evolve naturally from your knowledge of the material, your pur-pose, and the needs of your audience.

JOHN KENNETH GALBRAITH

One of the twentieth century's most influential economists, John Kenneth Galbraith (1908–   ) was born in Iona Station, Ontario, Canada, the son of a farmer. He studied agriculture at the University of Toronto and received advanced degrees in economics at the University of California at Berkeley. He became a U.S. citizen in 1937. Galbraith has taught economics at Harvard and Princeton and has held a number of important government positions, most notably ambassador to India and economic advisor to Presidents Kennedy and Johnson. He is the author of more than thirty books, including *American Capitalism: The Concept of Countervailing Power* (1952), *The Affluent Society* (1958), *The New Industrial State* (1967), *The Age of Uncertainty* (1977), *Economics in Perspective: A Critical History* (1987), and *The Good Society* (1996). He has also written novels and travel journals. Galbraith often critiques those who advocate absolute free markets; he has always been concerned with the effects of economic policy on minorities and the poor. In the following essay, which originally appeared on the *New York Times* Op-Ed page in 1995, Galbraith considers the word *burden* as it is used by critics who refer to "the burden imposed by government on the citizen."

Our Forked Tongue

In these last years, and notably in these past months, we have heard much of the burden imposed by government on the citizen. Nothing has been more emphasized in speech and possibly also in thought. This comment is not meant to regret this concern, as some might suppose: rather, it is to clarify the way the word "burden" is now employed. It has a very special connotation, of which all who cherish good or anyhow accepted English usage should be aware.

As now used, "burden" applies only to a very specific range of government activities. Many are not a burden and are not to be so described. Defense expenditure is definitely not a burden; indeed, increases therein are now being proposed. That there is now no wholly plausible enemy does not affect the situation. Similarly, in recent years large sums, in a range upward from $50 billion, have been appropriated to bail out failed financial institutions, specifically the savings and loan associations. This was not a burden. A clear distinction must be made between a burden and an admittedly unfortunate and costly financial misadventure.

Social Security is not a burden; in no politically acceptable discourse is it so described. Nor are farm price and income supports, although recipients regularly command incomes of a hundred grand or more. Medicare is basically not a burden and is not to be so described. There are many lesser items of expenditure that are not a burden, including health care for members of the Congress.

453

On the other hand, some functions of government are a heavy bur-   4
den. Notable are welfare payments, especially those to unmarried mothers and their children. Likewise expenditures for food stamps and child
nutrition. While Medicare is not a burden, Medicaid is a real burden.*

Education is a somewhat special case. While private education is not   5
a burden, public education, especially in our cities, can be a very heavy
load. Here, as elsewhere, burden bears no necessary relation to cost.

And here one sees the rule by which students of contemporary   6
English usage should be guided. Whether a public function or service or
regulation is or is not a burden depends on the income of the individual
so helped or favored.

As with all linguistic rules there can be exceptions. The National   7
Endowment for the Arts, support to public broadcasting, a few other
items not specifically designed for the poor, are a burden. The exceptions,
as ever, make the rule.

It is the generally accepted purpose of language to convey meaning.   8
All who use or hear the word "burden" should know the precise and subtle meaning that it conveys. Basically something is a burden when it is not
for the rich, not for the merely affluent, but for the poor.

•   •   •

COMPREHENSION

1. How does Galbraith define *burden?* Where does he give his formal definition
   of the word? Why do you think he presents this definition where he does?

2. In paragraph 1, when Galbraith speaks of "all who cherish good or anyhow
   accepted English usage," what distinction do you think he means to make
   between *good* and *accepted* English? Why is this distinction important?

3. What distinction does Galbraith draw between a burden and "an admittedly unfortunate and costly financial misadventure" (2)?

4. What examples does Galbraith give of programs that are burdens? Of those
   that are not burdens? What do the programs in each group have in common?

5. Why, according to Galbraith, is education a "special case" (5)?

6. Why do the National Endowment for the Arts and public broadcasting
   qualify as burdens even though they are not designed for the poor? Does
   Galbraith state the reason or merely imply it? Why?

PURPOSE AND AUDIENCE

1. A person who speaks with a forked tongue is someone who is taking two
   different positions at the same time—in other words, a liar. What effect

---

*EDS. NOTE—Medicare is government-supported health insurance for retired peo-
ple; Medicaid is government-supported health-care benefits for the poor and disabled.

do you think Galbraith might reasonably expect the title "Our Forked Tongue" to have on his readers? Do you think this title is a good choice? Why or why not?

2. Is Galbraith's purpose in this essay to criticize social priorities or to criticize the use of language to justify those priorities? Do you think his primary target is government or individuals? Explain your reasoning.

STYLE AND STRUCTURE

1. Where does Galbraith define by enumeration? By negation? Why is negation a particularly effective strategy for this essay?

2. How could Galbraith use additional strategies to strengthen his definition? For example, could he discuss the origin and development of the word *burden?* Could he use **synonyms** or **analogies?** If so, where?

3. How would you characterize Galbraith's tone in this essay? Does he seem to be angry or bitter, or does he seem disheartened by what he observes?

4. Where does Galbraith use sarcasm? Do you think the sarcasm is appropriate? Necessary? Do you think Galbraith could reach more readers by adopting a more neutral tone? Explain your reasoning.

5. Do you think the essay would be more convincing if Galbraith had provided historical background for the social and political situation he describes—for example, discussions of other programs that were (or were not) perceived as burdens? Why or why not?

6. In paragraph 3 Galbraith sets down a rule: "Medicare is basically not a burden and is not to be so described." Where else does he use this kind of language? Who does he imply has established these rules? What is his attitude toward these rule makers?

VOCABULARY PROJECTS

1. Define each of the following words as it is used in this selection.
   therein (2)   plausible (2)   discourse (3)

2. Look up the word *burden* in a dictionary. How does the dictionary's primary definition differ from Galbraith's? How do you account for this difference?

JOURNAL ENTRY

What is your emotional response to Galbraith's essay? Do you agree with him? Do you share his political position?

WRITING WORKSHOP

1. Write an essay in which you define *burden* at a personal level, by giving examples of the kinds of things you consider burdens. You might want to

develop your definition essay with comparison and contrast, exploring the differences between a *burden* and a *responsibility*.

2. What state, local, or national government program do you consider to be the biggest burden on citizens? Why? Write a definition essay in which you support your thesis with a single extended example.

3. Sometimes a person can be a burden. Define *burden* by explaining in what sense you find a particular friend or family member to be a burden to you—or in what respects you believe you are or have been a burden to someone else.

COMBINING THE PATTERNS

What pattern does Galbraith use most often to develop his definition? Where does he use this pattern? Could he have used **narration** to support his thesis? Where? Do you think he *should* have expanded his essay with a paragraph or two of narrative? Why or why not?

THEMATIC CONNECTIONS

- "The Human Cost of an Illiterate Society" (page 192)
- "On the Meaning of Plumbing and Poverty" (page 288)
- "On Dumpster Diving" (page 609)
- "A Modest Proposal" (page 625)

JOSÉ ANTONIO BURCIAGA

José Antonio Burciaga was born in 1940 in El Chuco, Texas, and served in the U.S. Air Force from 1960 to 1964. He graduated from the University of Texas at El Paso in 1968 and attended the Corcoran School of Art and the San Francisco Art Institute. Burciaga has been a resident fellow in the Chicano residences at Stanford University since 1985. He is the founder of Disseños Literarios, a publishing company in California, and he contributes fiction, poetry, and articles to many anthologies as well as to journals and newspapers, including the *Texas Monthly*, the *Denver Quarterly*, the *Christian Science Monitor*, and the *Los Angeles Times*. Burciaga has published several books of poems, drawings, and essays, including the poetry collection *Undocumented Love* (1992) and the essay collections *Drink Cultura* (1993) and *Give 'Em an Inch and They'll Take the Whole Enchilada* (1994). "Tortillas," originally titled "I Remember Masa," was first published in *Weedee Peepo* (1988), a bilingual collection of essays in Spanish and English. In this essay Burciaga discusses the numerous uses and transformations of the tortilla.

Tortillas

My earliest memory of *tortillas* is my *Mamá* telling me not to play with them. I had bitten eyeholes in one and was wearing it as a mask at the dinner table.

As a child, I also used *tortillas* as hand warmers on cold days, and my family claims that I owe my career as an artist to my early experiments with *tortillas*. According to them, my clowning around helped me develop a strong artistic foundation. I'm not so sure, though. Sometimes I wore a *tortilla* on my head, like a *yarmulke*, and yet I never had any great urge to convert from Catholicism to Judaism. But who knows? They may be right.

For Mexicans over the centuries, the *tortilla* has served as the spoon and the fork, the plate and the napkin. *Tortillas* originated before the Mayan civilizations, perhaps predating Europe's wheat bread. According to Mayan mythology, the great god Quetzalcoatl, realizing that the red ants knew the secret of using maize as food, transformed himself into a black ant, infiltrated the colony of red ants, and absconded with a grain of corn. (Is it any wonder that to this day, black ants and red ants do not get along?) Quetzalcoatl then put maize on the lips of the first man and woman, Oxomoco and Cipactonal, so that they would become strong. Maize festivals are still celebrated by many Indian cultures of the Americas.

When I was growing up in El Paso, *tortillas* were part of my daily life. I used to visit a *tortilla* factory in an ancient adobe building near the open *mercado* in Ciudad Juárez. As I approached, I could hear the rhythmic slapping of the *masa* as the skilled vendors outside the factory formed it into balls and patted them into perfectly round corn cakes be-

457

tween the palms of their hands. The wonderful aroma and the speed with which the women counted so many dozens of *tortillas* out of warm wicker baskets still linger in my mind. Watching them at work convinced me that the most handsome and *deliciosas tortillas* are handmade. Although machines are faster, they can never adequately replace generation-to-generation experience. There's no place in the factory assembly line for the tender slaps that give each *tortilla* character. The best thing that can be said about mass-producing *tortillas* is that it makes possible for many people to enjoy them.

In the *mercado* where my mother shopped, we frequently bought   5
taquitos de nopalitos, small tacos filled with diced cactus, onions, tomatoes, and *jalapeños.* Our friend Don Toribio showed us how to make delicious, crunchy *taquitos* with dried, salted pumpkin seeds. When you had no money for the filling, a poor man's *taco* could be made by placing a warm *tortilla* on the left palm, applying a sprinkle of salt, then rolling the *tortilla* up quickly with the fingertips of the right hand. My own kids put peanut butter and jelly on *tortillas,* which I think is truly bicultural. And speaking of fast foods for kids, nothing beats a *quesadilla,* a *tortilla* grilled-cheese sandwich.

Depending on what you intend to use them for, *tortillas* may be made   6
in various ways. Even a run-of-the-mill *tortilla* is more than a flat corn cake. A skillfully cooked homemade *tortilla* has a bottom and a top; the top skin forms a pocket in which you put the filling that folds your *tortilla* into a taco. Paper-thin *tortillas* are used specifically for *flautas,* a type of taco that is filled, rolled, and then fried until crisp. The name *flauta* means *flute,* which probably refers to the Mayan bamboo flute; however, the only sound that comes from an edible *flauta* is a delicious crunch that is music to the palate. In México *flautas* are sometimes made as long as two feet and then cut into manageable segments. The opposite of *flautas* is *gorditas,* meaning *little fat ones.* These are very thick small *tortillas.*

The versatility of *tortillas* and corn does not end here. Besides being   7
tasty and nourishing, they have spiritual and artistic qualities as well. The Tarahumara Indians of Chihuahua, for example, concocted a corn-based beer called *tesgüino,* which their descendants still make today. And everyone has read about the woman in New Mexico who was cooking her husband a *tortilla* one morning when the image of Jesus Christ miraculously appeared on it. Before they knew what was happening, the man's breakfast had become a local shrine.

Then there is *tortilla* art. Various Chicano artists throughout the   8
Southwest have, when short of materials or just in a whimsical mood, used a dry *tortilla* as a small, round canvas. And a few years back, at the height of the Chicano movement, a priest in Arizona got into trouble with the Church after he was discovered celebrating mass using a *tortilla* as the host. All of which only goes to show that while the *tortilla* may be a lowly corn cake, when the necessity arises, it can reach unexpected distinction.

• • •

COMPREHENSION

1. What exactly is a tortilla?

2. List the functions—both practical and whimsical—tortillas serve.

3. In paragraph 7 Burciaga cites the "spiritual and artistic qualities" of tortillas. Do you think he is being serious? Explain your reasoning.

PURPOSE AND AUDIENCE

1. Burciaga states his thesis explicitly in his essay's final sentence. Paraphrase this thesis. Why do you think he does not state it sooner?

2. Do you think Burciaga expects most of his readers to be of Hispanic descent? To be familiar with tortillas? How can you tell?

3. Why do you think Burciaga uses humor in this essay? Is it consistent with his essay's purpose? Could the humor have a negative effect on his audience? Explain.

4. Why are tortillas so important to Burciaga? Is it just their versatility he admires, or do they represent something more to him?

STYLE AND STRUCTURE

1. Where does Burciaga provide a formal definition of *tortilla?* Why does he locate this formal definition at this point in his essay?

2. Burciaga uses many Spanish words, but he defines only some of them—for example, *taquitos de nopalitos* and *quesadilla* in paragraph 5 and *flautas* and *gorditas* in paragraph 6. Why do you think he defines some terms but not others?

3. Does Burciaga use **synonyms** or negation to define *tortilla?* Does he discuss the word's origin? If so, where? If not, do you think any of these strategies would improve his essay? Explain.

VOCABULARY PROJECTS

1. Define each of the following words as it is used in this selection.
   yarmulke (2)   absconded (3)   concocted (7)
   maize (3)   adobe (4)

2. Look up each of the following words in a Spanish-English dictionary and (if possible) supply its English equivalent.
   mercado (4)   *masa* (4)
   deliciosas (4)   *jalapeños* (5)

JOURNAL ENTRY

Explore some additional uses—practical or frivolous—for tortillas that Burciaga does not discuss.

WRITING WORKSHOP

1. Write an essay in which you define a food that is important to your family, ethnic group, or circle of friends. Use several patterns of development, as Burciaga does. Assume that your audience is not very familiar with the food you define.

2. Relying primarily on description and exemplification, define a food that is sure to be familiar to all your readers. Don't name the food until your essay's last sentence.

3. Write an essay defining a food—but include a thesis statement that paints a very favorable portrait of a much-maligned food (for example, Spam or brussels sprouts) or a very negative picture of a popular food (for example, chocolate or ice cream).

COMBINING THE PATTERNS

Burciaga uses several patterns of development in his extended definition. Where, for example, does he use **description, narration, process,** and **exemplification?** Does he use any other patterns? Explain.

THEMATIC CONNECTIONS

- "Once More to the Lake" (page 142)
- "Aria: A Memoir of a Bilingual Childhood" (page 357)
- "Let's Tell the Story of All America's Cultures" (page 552)
- "The Park" (page 604)

JUDY BRADY

Judy Brady was born in San Francisco in 1937 and earned a B.F.A. in painting from the University of Iowa in 1962. She has raised two daughters, worked as a secretary, and published articles on many social issues. Brady has been active in the women's movement since 1969, and this article appeared in the first issue of *Ms.* magazine in 1972. She has edited *Women and Cancer* (1990), an anthology of writings by women, and *One in Three: Women with Cancer Confront an Epidemic* (1991). In "I Want a Wife," Brady adopts an ironic tone to present a definition of what she believes society considers the ideal wife.

I Want a Wife

I belong to that classification of people known as wives. I am A Wife. And, not altogether incidentally, I am a mother.

Not too long ago a male friend of mine appeared on the scene fresh from a recent divorce. He had one child, who is, of course, with his ex-wife. He is looking for another wife. As I thought about him while I was ironing one evening, it suddenly occurred to me that I, too, would like to have a wife. Why do I want a wife?

I would like to go back to school so that I can become economically independent, support myself, and, if need be, support those dependent upon me. I want a wife who will work and send me to school. And while I am going to school I want a wife to take care of my children. I want a wife to keep track of the children's doctor and dentist appointments. And to keep track of mine, too. I want a wife to make sure my children eat properly and are kept clean. I want a wife who will wash the children's clothes and keep them mended. I want a wife who is a good nurturant attendant to my children, who arranges for their schooling, makes sure that they have an adequate social life with their peers, takes them to the park, the zoo, etc. I want a wife who takes care of the children when they are sick, a wife who arranges to be around when the children need special care, because, of course, I cannot miss classes at school. My wife must arrange to lose time at work and not lose the job. It may mean a small cut in my wife's income from time to time, but I guess I can tolerate that. Needless to say, my wife will arrange and pay for the care of the children while my wife is working.

I want a wife who will take care of *my* physical needs. I want a wife who will keep my house clean. A wife who will pick up after my children, a wife who will pick up after me. I want a wife who will keep my clothes clean, ironed, mended, replaced when need be, and who will see to it that my personal things are kept in their proper place so that I can find what I need the minute I need it. I want a wife who cooks the meals, a wife who is a *good* cook. I want a wife who will plan the menus, do the necessary grocery shopping, prepare the meals, serve them pleasantly, and then do the cleaning up while I do my studying. I want a wife who will care for me when I am sick and sympathize with my pain and loss of time from school. I want a wife to go along when our family takes a vacation so that someone can continue to care for me and my children when I need a rest and change of scene.

I want a wife who will not bother me with rambling complaints about   5
a wife's duties. But I want a wife who will listen to me when I feel the need to explain a rather difficult point I have come across in my course of studies. And I want a wife who will type my papers for me when I have written them.

I want a wife who will take care of the details of my social life. When   6
my wife and I are invited out by my friends, I want a wife who will take care of the babysitting arrangements. When I meet people at school that I like and want to entertain, I want a wife who will have the house clean, will prepare a special meal, serve it to me and my friends, and not inter-rupt when I talk about things that interest me and my friends. I want a wife who will have arranged that the children are fed and ready for bed before my guests arrive so that the children do not bother us. I want a wife who takes care of the needs of my guests so that they feel comfort-able, who makes sure that they have an ashtray, that they are passed the hors d'oeuvres, that they are offered a second helping of the food, that their wine glasses are replenished when necessary, that their coffee is served to them as they like it. And I want a wife who knows that some-times I need a night out by myself.

I want a wife who is sensitive to my sexual needs, a wife who makes   7
love passionately and eagerly when I feel like it, a wife who makes sure that I am satisfied. And, of course, I want a wife who will not demand sexual attention when I am not in the mood for it. I want a wife who as-sumes the complete responsibility for birth control, because I do not want more children. I want a wife who will remain sexually faithful to me so that I do not have to clutter up my intellectual life with jealousies. And I want a wife who understands that *my* sexual needs may entail more than strict adherence to monogamy. I must, after all, be able to relate to people as fully as possible.

If, by chance, I find another person more suitable as a wife than the   8
wife I already have, I want the liberty to replace my present wife with an-other one. Naturally, I will expect a fresh new life; my wife will take the children and be solely responsible for them so that I am left free.

When I am through with school and have a job, I want my wife to   9
quit working and remain at home so that my wife can more fully and completely take care of a wife's duties.

My God, who *wouldn't* want a wife?   10

• • •

COMPREHENSION

1. In one sentence, define what Brady means by *wife*. Does this ideal wife actually exist? Explain.

2. List some of the specific duties of the wife Brady describes. Into what five general categories does Brady arrange these duties?

3. What complaints does Brady apparently have about the life she actually leads? To what does she seem to attribute her problems?

4. Under what circumstances does Brady say she would consider leaving her wife? What would happen to the children if she left?

PURPOSE AND AUDIENCE

1. This essay was first published in *Ms.* magazine. In what sense is it appropriate for the audience of this feminist publication? Where else can you imagine it appearing?

2. Does this essay have an explicitly stated thesis? If so, where is it? If the thesis is implied, paraphrase it.

3. Do you think Brady *really* wants the kind of wife she describes? Explain.

STYLE AND STRUCTURE

1. Throughout the essay, Brady repeats the words "I want a wife." What is the effect of this repetition?

2. The first and last paragraphs of this essay are quite brief. Does this weaken the essay? Why or why not?

3. In enumerating a wife's duties, Brady frequently uses the verb *arrange*. What other verbs does she use repeatedly? How do these verbs help her make her point?

4. Brady never uses the personal pronouns *he* or *she* to refer to the wife she defines. Why not?

5. Comment on Brady's use of phrases like *of course* (2, 3, and 7), *needless to say* (3), *after all* (7), *by chance* (8), and *naturally* (8). What do these expressions contribute to the sentences in which they appear? To the essay as a whole?

VOCABULARY PROJECTS

1. Define each of the following words as it is used in this selection.
   nurturant (3)   replenished (6)   adherence (7)
   monogamy (7)

2. Going beyond the dictionary definitions, decide what Brady means to suggest by the following words. Is she using any of these words sarcastically? Explain.

proper (4)   necessary (6)   suitable (8)
pleasantly (4)   demand (7)   free (8)
bother (6)   clutter up (7)

JOURNAL ENTRY

Do you think Brady's 1972 characterization of a wife is still accurate today? Which of the characteristics she describes have remained the same? Which have changed? Why?

WRITING WORKSHOP

1. Write an essay in which you define your ideal spouse.

2. Write an essay entitled "I Want a Husband." Taking an **ironic** stance, use society's notions of the ideal husband to help you shape your definition.

3. Read "The Company Man" (page 465). Using ideas gleaned from that essay and "I Want a Wife," as well as your own ideas, write a definition essay called "The Ideal Couple." Your essay can be serious or humorous. Develop your definition with examples.

COMBINING THE PATTERNS

Like most **definition** essays, "I Want a Wife" uses several patterns of development. Which ones does it use? Which of these do you consider most important for supporting Brady's thesis? Why?

THEMATIC CONNECTIONS

- "My Mother Never Worked" (page 81)
- "Sex, Lies, and Conversation" (page 350)
- "The Men We Carry in Our Minds" (page 387)
- "The Company Man" (page 465)

ELLEN GOODMAN

Ellen Goodman was born in 1941 in Newton, Massachusetts, and graduated from Radcliffe College in 1963. After working for *Newsweek* and the *Detroit Free Press,* she began working for the *Boston Globe* in 1967. She is now a columnist and associate editor at the newspaper. Her regular column, "At Large," has been syndicated since 1976, and she has published several volumes of her columns, including *Close to Home* (1975) and, most recently, *Value Judgments* (1993). Goodman, who is a frequent commentator on television and radio, received a Pulitzer Prize for commentary in 1980. She is also the author of *Turning Points* (1979), an examination, based on interviews, of changes in men's and women's lives as a result of the feminist movement. "The Company Man," from *Close to Home,* defines what clinicians call a "workaholic." Goodman develops her definition with an extended example of a man who literally worked himself to death.

The Company Man

He worked himself to death, finally and precisely, at 3:00 A.M. Sunday morning. 1

The obituary didn't say that, of course. It said that he died of a coronary thrombosis—I think that was it—but everyone among his friends and acquaintances knew it instantly. He was a perfect Type A, a workaholic, a classic, they said to each other and shook their heads—and thought for five or ten minutes about the way they lived. 2

This man who worked himself to death finally and precisely at 3:00 A.M. Sunday morning—on his day off—was fifty-one years old and a vice-president. He was, however, one of six vice-presidents, and one of three who might conceivably—if the president died or retired soon enough—have moved to the top spot. Phil knew that. 3

He worked six days a week, five of them until eight or nine at night, during a time when his own company had begun the four-day week for everyone but the executives. He worked like the Important People. He had no outside "extracurricular interests," unless, of course, you think about a monthly golf game that way. To Phil, it was work. He always ate egg salad sandwiches at his desk. He was, of course, overweight, by 20 or 25 pounds. He thought it was okay, though, because he didn't smoke. 4

On Saturdays, Phil wore a sports jacket to the office instead of a suit, because it was the weekend. 5

He had a lot of people working for him, maybe sixty, and most of them liked him most of the time. Three of them will be seriously considered for his job. The obituary didn't mention that. 6

But it did list his "survivors" quite accurately. He is survived by his wife, Helen, forty-eight years old, a good woman of no particular marketable skills, who worked in an office before marrying and mothering. 7

465

She had, according to her daughter, given up trying to compete with his work years ago, when the children were small. A company friend said, "I know how much you will miss him." And she answered, "I already have."

"Missing him all these years," she must have given up part of herself which had cared too much for the man. She would be "well taken care of." 8

His "dearly beloved" eldest of the "dearly beloved" children is a hard-working executive in a manufacturing firm down South. In the day and a half before the funeral, he went around the neighborhood researching his father, asking the neighbors what he was like. They were embarrassed. 9

His second child is a girl, who is twenty-four and newly married. She lives near her mother and they are close, but whenever she was alone with her father, in a car driving somewhere, they had nothing to say to each other. 10

The youngest is twenty, a boy, a high-school graduate who has spent the last couple of years, like a lot of his friends, doing enough odd jobs to stay in grass and food. He was the one who tried to grab at his father, and tried to mean enough to him to keep the man at home. He was his father's favorite. Over the last two years, Phil stayed up nights worrying about the boy. 11

The boy once said, "My father and I only board here." 12

At the funeral, the sixty-year-old company president told the forty-eight-year-old widow that the fifty-one-year-old deceased had meant much to the company and would be missed and would be hard to replace. The widow didn't look him in the eye. She was afraid he would read her bitterness and, after, all, she would need him to straighten out the finances—the stock options and all that. 13

Phil was overweight and nervous and worked too hard. If he wasn't at the office, he was worried about it. Phil was a Type A, a heart-attack natural. You could have picked him out in a minute from a lineup. 14

So when he finally worked himself to death, at precisely 3:00 A.M. Sunday morning, no one was really surprised. 15

By 5:00 P.M. the afternoon of the funeral, the company president had begun, discreetly of course, with care and taste, to make inquiries about his replacement. One of three men. He asked around: "Who's been working the hardest?" 16

•   •   •

COMPREHENSION

1. In one sentence, define *the company man*. What does Goodman's extended definition convey that your one-sentence definition lacks?

2. When Phil's widow is told by a friend, "I know how much you will miss him," she answers, "I already have" (7). What does she mean?

3. Why does Phil's oldest son go around the neighborhood researching his father?

4. Why doesn't Phil's widow look the company president in the eye?

5. What kind of man will the company president seek for Phil's replacement?

PURPOSE AND AUDIENCE

1. What point is Goodman trying to make in this essay? Does she succeed? Explain.

2. What assumptions does Goodman make about her readers? What effect do you think she hopes the essay will have on her audience?

3. Why does Goodman imply her thesis and not state it?

STYLE AND STRUCTURE

1. Why does Goodman state the time of Phil's death at both the beginning and the end of her essay?

2. Is there a reason why Goodman waits until the end of paragraph 3 before she refers to the company man by name? Explain.

3. What is the effect of the bits of dialogue Goodman includes?

4. Goodman tells Phil's story in a flat, impersonal way. How does this tone help her achieve her purpose?

5. Why does Goodman put quotation marks around the phrases *extracurricular interests* (4), *survivors* (7), *missing him all these years, well taken care of* (8), and *dearly beloved* (9)?

VOCABULARY PROJECTS

1. Define each of the following words as it is used in this selection.

   coronary thrombosis (2)   classic (2)   stock options (13)
   workaholic (2)   conceivably (3)

2. This essay's style and vocabulary are quite informal. Substitute a more formal word or phrase for each of these expressions:

   top spot (3)   odd jobs (11)   all that (13)
   okay (4)   grab at (11)   a heart-attack natural (14)

   How does each substitution change the sentence in which it appears?

JOURNAL ENTRY

Do you know anyone like Phil? What do you think really motivates people like him? Do you believe such forces drive women as well as men?

WRITING WORKSHOP

1. Write an essay defining the workaholic student (or the procrastinating student). As Goodman does, use an extended example to support your thesis.

2. Write a definition essay in which you define the company man (or the company woman), but use comparison and contrast to organize your definition.

3. Write a brief obituary for Phil, one that might appear in his company's newsletter. Using the title "A Valued Employee," develop the obituary as a definition essay. Your aim is to show readers what traits such an employee must have—and to present those traits as desirable ones.

COMBINING THE PATTERNS

Goodman relies on **narration** to develop her definition. Is this a good choice? Why? What other patterns of development would be helpful?

THEMATIC CONNECTIONS

- "Midnight" (page 165)
- "The Peter Principle" (page 169)
- "Suicide Note" (page 305)
- "The Catbird Seat" (page 474)

BRUNO BETTELHEIM

Bruno Bettelheim (1903–1990) was born in Vienna, Austria, and studied psychology at the University of Vienna, receiving his doctorate in 1938. During the Nazi occupation of Austria, he was imprisoned in concentration camps at Dachau and Buchenwald. Released in 1939 through American intervention, Bettelheim made his way to the United States. A psychoanalyst by training, Bettelheim taught child psychology at the University of Chicago and for thirty years ran the Orthogenic School for children with emotional problems. He was particularly concerned with autistic children, seeing in their trauma something of the scars of the concentration camp. Among Bettelheim's better-known books are *Love Is Not Enough: The Treatment of Emotionally Disturbed Children* (1950), *The Informed Heart: Autonomy in a Mass Age* (1960), and *The Uses of Enchantment: The Meaning and Importance of Fairy Tales* (1976). In "The Holocaust," which appeared in the collection *Surviving and Other Essays* (1979), he criticizes the use of the word *holocaust* to refer to the Nazis' mass murder of Jews.

The Holocaust

To begin with, it was not the hapless victims of the Nazis who named their incomprehensible and totally unmasterable fate the "holocaust." It was the Americans who applied this artificial and highly technical term to the Nazi extermination of the European Jews. But while the event when named as mass murder most foul evokes the most immediate, most powerful revulsion, when it is designated by a rare technical term, we must first in our minds translate it back into emotionally meaningful language. Using technical or specially created terms instead of words from our common vocabulary is one of the best-known and most widely used distancing devices, separating the intellectual from the emotional experience. Talking about "the holocaust" permits us to manage it intellectually where the raw facts, when given their ordinary names, would overwhelm us emotionally—because it was catastrophe beyond comprehension, beyond the limits of our imagination, unless we force ourselves against our desire to extend it to encompass these terrible events.

This linguistic circumlocution began while it all was only in the planning stage. Even the Nazis—usually given to grossness in language and action—shied away from facing openly what they were up to and called this vile mass murder "the final solution of the Jewish problem." After all, solving a problem can be made to appear like an honorable enterprise, as long as we are not forced to recognize that the solution we are about to embark on consists of the completely unprovoked, vicious murder of millions of helpless men, women, and children. The Nuremberg* judges of

---

*EDS. NOTE—After World War II, Nuremberg was the seat of the international tribunal for war crimes.

these Nazi criminals followed their example of circumlocution by coining a neologism out of one Greek and one Latin root: genocide. These artificially created technical terms fail to connect with our strongest feelings. The horror of murder is part of our most common human heritage. From earliest infancy on, it arouses violent abhorrence in us. Therefore, in whatever form it appears we should give such an act its true designation and not hide it behind polite, erudite terms created out of classical words.

To call this vile mass murder "the holocaust" is not to give it a special name emphasizing its uniqueness which would permit, over time, the word becoming invested with feelings germane to the event it refers to. The correct definition of *holocaust* is "burnt offering." As such, it is part of the language of the psalmist, a meaningful word to all who have some acquaintance with the Bible, full of the richest emotional connotations. By using the term "holocaust," entirely false associations are established through conscious and unconscious connotations between the most vicious of mass murders and ancient rituals of a deeply religious nature.   3

Using a word with such strong unconscious religious connotations when speaking of the murder of millions of Jews robs the victims of this abominable mass murder of the only thing left to them: their uniqueness. Calling the most callous, most brutal, most horrid, most heinous mass murder a burnt offering is a sacrilege, a profanation of God and man.   4

Martyrdom is part of our religious heritage. A martyr, burned at the stake, is a burnt offering to his god. And it is true that after the Jews were asphyxiated, the victims' corpses were burned. But I believe we fool ourselves if we think we are honoring the victims of systematic murder by using this term, which has the highest moral connotations. By doing so, we connect for our own psychological reasons what happened in the extermination camps with historical events we deeply regret, but also greatly admire. We do so because this makes it easier for us to cope; only in doing so we cope with our distorted image of what happened, not with the events the way they did happen.   5

By calling the victims of the Nazis martyrs, we falsify their fate. The true meaning of *martyr* is: "One who voluntarily undergoes the penalty of death for refusing to renounce his faith" (*Oxford English Dictionary*). The Nazis made sure that nobody could mistakenly think that their victims were murdered for their religious beliefs. Renouncing their faith would have saved none of them. Those who had converted to Christianity were gassed, as were those who were atheists, and those who were deeply religious Jews. They did not die for any conviction, and certainly not out of choice.   6

Millions of Jews were systematically slaughtered, as were untold other "undesirables," not for any convictions of theirs, but only because they stood in the way of the realization of an illusion. They neither died for their convictions, nor were they slaughtered because of their convictions, but only in consequence of the Nazis' delusional belief about what was required to protect the purity of their assumed superior racial endowment, and what they thought necessary to guarantee them the living   7 space they believed they needed and were entitled to. Thus while these millions were slaughtered for an idea, they did not die for one.

Millions—men, women, and children—were processed after they had   8
been utterly brutalized, their humanity destroyed, their clothes torn from their bodies. Naked, they were sorted into those who were destined to be murdered immediately, and those others who had a short-term usefulness as slave labor. But after a brief interval they, too, were to be herded into the same gas chambers into which the others were immediately piled, there to be asphyxiated so that, in their last moments, they could not prevent themselves from fighting each other in vain for a last breath of air.

To call these most wretched victims of a murderous delusion, of de-   9
structive drives run rampant, martyrs or a burnt offering is a distortion invented for our comfort, small as it may be. It pretends that this most vicious of mass murders had some deeper meaning; that in some fashion the victims either offered themselves or at least became sacrifices to a higher cause. It robs them of the last recognition which could be theirs, denies them the last dignity we could accord them: to face and accept what their death was all about, not embellishing it for the small psychological relief this may give us.

We could feel so much better if the victims had acted out of choice.   10
For our emotional relief, therefore, we dwell on the tiny minority who did exercise some choice: the resistance fighters of the Warsaw ghetto, for example, and others like them. We are ready to overlook the fact that these people fought back only at a time when everything was lost, when the overwhelming majority of those who had been forced into the ghettos had already been exterminated without resisting. Certainly those few who finally fought for their survival and their convictions, risking and losing their lives in doing so, deserve our admiration; their deeds give us a moral lift. But the more we dwell on these few, the more unfair are we to the memory of the millions who were slaughtered—who gave in, did not fight back—because we deny them the only thing which up to the very end remained uniquely their own: their fate.

• • •

COMPREHENSION

1. To what does the term *holocaust* generally refer? Why does Bettelheim object to this use of the term?

2. What objection does Bettelheim have to the term *genocide?*

3. How, according to Bettelheim, are the victims of the Nazis different from religious martyrs? Specifically, what does he mean in paragraph 7 when he says that "while these millions were slaughtered for an idea, they did not die for one"?

4. What does Bettelheim mean in paragraph 10 when he says, "We could feel so much better if the victims had acted out of choice"? Do you agree with him? Why or why not?

PURPOSE AND AUDIENCE

1. What basic information does Bettelheim seem to expect his readers to know about the Holocaust? How can you tell?

2. Bettelheim seems to assume most people reading his essay will share his associations with the words *holocaust* and *martyr*. Do you think he is correct? Would his arguments work for readers who do not share what Bettelheim calls "our religious heritage" (5)?

3. What do you think Bettelheim meant to accomplish by writing this essay? Is he making a point about language or about the Holocaust?

STYLE AND STRUCTURE

1. Where does Bettelheim supply information on the origin of the term *holocaust?* Is this information necessary? Why or why not?

2. Throughout this essay Bettelheim uses first-person pronouns (such as *we* and *our*) instead of third-person pronouns. What, if anything, does he accomplish by using these pronouns?

3. Bettelheim, himself a Holocaust survivor, uses very strong language—for example, "this vile mass murder" (3)—to condemn the Nazis' actions. Find other examples of such language in the essay. Are these strongly negative words necessary, or could Bettelheim have made his point with more neutral language?

4. In paragraph 6 Bettelheim includes a definition from the *Oxford English Dictionary*. Why does he include this definition? Do you think he should have provided extended definitions of *holocaust?* Of *genocide?* Of any other term used in his essay? Why or why not?

5. What does Bettelheim achieve by using words like *processed* and *sorted* in paragraph 8?

6. Reread paragraph 9. Do you think Bettelheim is too emotional? Given his subject matter, could you argue that he is perhaps not emotional enough?

VOCABULARY PROJECTS

1. Define each of the following words as it is used in this selection.

hapless (1)	invested (3)	sacrilege (4)
circumlocution (2)	germane (3)	profanation (4)
neologism (2)	psalmist (3)	martyrdom (5)
abhorrence (2)	callous (4)	

2. What other term besides *holocaust* could be applied to what Bettelheim terms "the vile mass murder" committed by the Nazis?

JOURNAL ENTRY

Although *holocaust* once meant "burnt offering," its meaning, like those of many other words, has changed over time; now, the term is used most often to designate the Nazi extermination of Jews. Do you think Bettelheim is too rigid when he objects to the application of the term *holocaust* beyond what he calls its "correct definition" (3)? How would you respond to him?

WRITING WORKSHOP

1. Many people object to the use of the term *victim* to designate those the Nazis brutalized, yet Bettelheim seems to have no problem with this term. Look up the word *victim* in the dictionary. Then, write a letter to Bettelheim challenging the use of the term *victim* in the context in which he uses it. Develop your letter as a definition, and use negation to help you define *victim*.

2. Write an essay in which you use examples to develop an extended definition of the word **euphemism,** a polite term for an unpleasant concept.

3. Write an essay that defines the term *survivor* as it is commonly used in expressions like *cancer survivor, Holocaust survivor,* and *incest survivor.* Use narration and description to develop your definition.

COMBING THE PATTERNS

Where in this essay does Bettelheim use **cause and effect?** Where does he use **description? Exemplification?** Would a paragraph of **narration**—for example, a story told by a victim of the Nazi death camps—strengthen his case? Explain your reasoning.

THEMATIC CONNECTIONS

- "'What's in a Name?'" (page 5)
- "Thirty-Eight Who Saw Murder Didn't Call the Police" (page 86)
- "Shooting an Elephant" (page 91)
- "The Ways We Lie" (page 414)

JAMES THURBER

James Thurber (1894–1961) was born in Columbus, Ohio, and graduated from The Ohio State University in 1919. He joined the staff of the *New Yorker* in 1927, contributing his humorous and satirical stories, anecdotes, and sketches even after he resigned from the magazine in 1933. As his eyesight deteriorated, Thurber began to write more than he drew; he was almost totally blind for the last fifteen years of his life. His numerous books include *Is Sex Necessary?* (1929, with E. B. White); *My Life and Hard Times* (1933); *My World and Welcome to It* (1942), containing the well-known story "The Secret Life of Water Mitty"; *Men, Women, and Dogs* (1943); *The Thurber Carnival* (1945); and *The Thirteen Clocks* (1950), a fable for children. Thurber also wrote a comedy with Elliott Nugent called *The Male Animal* (1940), which was produced on Broadway and later made into a film. His last book was *The Years with Ross* (1959), a biography of *New Yorker* editor Harold Ross as well as a memoir of Thurber's years on the staff of the magazine. In "The Catbird Seat," the main character builds a case against an office rival and then plots her murder.

The Catbird Seat

Mr. Martin bought the pack of Camels on Monday night in the most   1
crowded cigar store on Broadway. It was theater time and seven or eight men were buying cigarettes. The clerk didn't even glance at Mr. Martin, who put the pack in his overcoat pocket and went out. If any of the staff at F & S had seen him buy the cigarettes, they would have been astonished, for it was generally known that Mr. Martin did not smoke, and never had. No one saw him.

It was just a week to the day since Mr. Martin had decided to rub out   2
Mrs. Ulgine Barrows. The term "rub out" pleased him because it suggested nothing more than the correction of an error—in this case an error of Mr. Fitweiler. Mr. Martin had spent each night of the past week working out his plan and examining it. As he walked home now he went over it again. For the hundredth time he resented the element of imprecision, the margin of guesswork that entered into the business. The project as he had worked it out was casual and bold, the risks were considerable. Something might go wrong anywhere along the line. And therein lay the cunning of his scheme. No one would ever see in it the cautious, painstaking hand of Erwin Martin, head of the filing department at F & S, of whom Mr. Fitweiler had once said, "Man is fallible but Martin isn't." No one would see his hand, that is, unless it were caught in the act.

Sitting in his apartment, drinking a glass of milk, Mr. Martin re-   3
viewed his case against Mrs. Ulgine Barrows, as he had every night for seven nights. He began at the beginning. Her quacking voice and braying laugh had first profaned the halls of F & S on March 7, 1941 (Mr. Martin had a head for dates). Old Roberts, the personnel chief, had introduced

her as the newly appointed special adviser to the president of the firm, Mr. Fitweiler. The woman had appalled Mr. Martin instantly, but he hadn't shown it. He had given her his dry hand, a look of studious concentration, and a faint smile. "Well," she had said looking at the papers on his desk, "are you lifting the oxcart out of the ditch?" As Mr. Martin recalled that moment, over his milk, he squirmed slightly. He must keep his mind on her crimes as a special adviser, not on her peccadillos as a personality. This he found difficult to do, in spite of entering an objection and sustaining it. The faults of the woman as a woman kept chattering on in his mind like an unruly witness. She had, for almost two years now, baited him. In the halls, in the elevator, even in his own office, into which she romped now and then like a circus horse, she was constantly shouting out these silly questions at him. "Are you lifting the oxcart out of the ditch? Are you tearing up the pea patch? Are you hollering down the rain barrel? Are you scraping around the bottom of the pickle barrel? Are you sitting in the catbird seat?"

It was Joey Hart, one of Mr. Martin's two assistants, who had explained what the gibberish meant. "She must be a Dodger fan," he had said. "Red Barber announces the Dodger games over the radio and he uses those expressions—picked 'em up down South." Joey had gone on to explain one or two. "Tearing up the pea patch" meant going on a rampage; "sitting in the catbird seat" meant sitting pretty, like a batter with three balls and no strikes on him. Mr. Martin dismissed all this with an effort. It had been annoying, it had driven him near to distraction, but he was too solid a man to be moved to murder by anything so childish. It was fortunate, he reflected as he passed on to the important charges against Mrs. Barrows, that he had stood up under it so well. He had maintained always an outward appearance of polite tolerance. "Why, I even believe you like the woman," Miss Paird, his other assistant, had once said to him. He had simply smiled.

A gavel rapped in Mr. Martin's mind and the case proper was resumed. Mrs. Ulgine Barrows stood charged with willful, blatant, and persistent attempts to destroy the efficiency and system of F & S. It was competent, material, and relevant to review her advent and rise to power. Mr. Martin had got the story from Miss Paird, who seemed always able to find things out. According to her, Mrs. Barrows had met Mr. Fitweiler at a party, where she had rescued him from the embraces of a powerfully built drunken man who had mistaken the president of F & S for a famous retired Middle Western football coach. She had led him to a sofa and somehow worked upon him a monstrous magic. The aging gentleman had jumped to the conclusion there and then that this was a woman of singular attainments, equipped to bring out the best in him and in the firm. A week later he had introduced her into F & S as his special adviser. On that day confusion got its foot in the door. After Miss Tyson, Mr. Brundage, and Mr. Bartlett had been fired and Mr. Munson had taken his hat and stalked out, mailing in his resignation later, old Roberts had been emboldened to speak to Mr. Fitweiler. He mentioned that Mr. Munson's department had been "a little disrupted" and hadn't they perhaps better resume the old system there? Mr. Fitweiler had said certainly not. He had the greatest faith in Mrs. Barrows' ideas. "They require a little seasoning, a little seasoning, is all," he had added. Mr. Roberts had given it up. Mr. Martin reviewed in detail all the changes wrought by Mrs. Barrows. She had begun chipping at the cornices of the firm's edifice and now she was swinging at the foundation stones with a pickaxe.

Mr. Martin came now, in his summing up, to the afternoon of   6
Monday, November 2, 1942—just one week ago. On that day, at 3 P.M., Mrs. Barrows had bounced into his office. "Boo!" she had yelled. "Are you scraping around the bottom of the pickle barrel?" Mr. Martin had looked at her from under his green eyeshade, saying nothing. She had begun to wander about the office, taking it in with her great, popping eyes. "Do you really need *all* these filing cabinets?" she had demanded suddenly. Mr. Martin's heart had jumped. "Each of these files," he had said, keeping his voice even, "plays an indispensable part in the system of F & S." She had brayed at him, "Well, don't tear up the pea patch!" and gone to the door. From there she had bawled, "But you sure have got a lot of fine scrap in here!" Mr. Martin could no longer doubt that the finger was on his beloved department. Her pickaxe was on the upswing, poised for the first blow. It had not come yet; he had received no blue memo from the enchanted Mr. Fitweiler bearing nonsensical instructions deriving from the obscene woman. But there was no doubt in Mr. Martin's mind that one would be forthcoming. He must act quickly. Already a precious week had gone by. Mr. Martin stood up in his living room, still holding his milk glass. "Gentlemen of the jury," he said to himself, "I demand the death penalty for this horrible person."

The next day Mr. Martin followed his routine, as usual. He polished   7
his glasses more often and once sharpened an already sharp pencil, but not even Miss Paird noticed. Only once did he catch sight of his victim; she swept past him in the hall with a patronizing "Hi!" At five-thirty he walked home, as usual, and had a glass of milk, as usual. He had never drunk anything stronger in his life—unless you could count ginger ale. The late Sam Schlosser, the S of F & S, had praised Mr. Martin at a staff meeting several years before for his temperate habits. "Our most efficient worker neither drinks nor smokes," he had said. "The results speak for themselves." Mr. Fitweiler had sat by, nodding approval.

Mr. Martin was still thinking about that red-letter day as he walked   8
over to the Schrafft's on Fifth Avenue near Forty-sixth Street. He got there, as he always did, at eight o'clock. He finished his dinner and the financial page of the *Sun* at a quarter to nine, as he always did. It was his custom after dinner to take a walk. This time he walked down Fifth Avenue at a casual pace. His gloved hands felt moist and warm, his forehead cold. He transferred the Camels from his overcoat to a jacket pocket. He wondered, as he did so, if they did not represent an unnecessary note

of strain. Mrs. Barrows smoked only Luckies. It was his idea to puff a few puffs on a Camel (after the rubbing-out), stub it out in the ashtray holding her lipstick-stained Luckies, and thus drag a small red herring* across the trail. Perhaps it was not a good idea. It would take time. He might even choke, too loudly.

Mr. Martin had never seen the house on West Twelfth Street where   9
Mrs. Barrows lived, but had a clear enough picture of it. Fortunately, she had bragged to everybody about her ducky first-floor apartment in the perfectly darling three-story redbrick. There would be no doorman or other attendants; just the tenants of the second and third floors. As he walked along, Mr. Martin realized that he would get there before nine-thirty. He had considered walking north on Fifth Avenue from Schrafft's to a point from which it would take him until ten o'clock to reach the house. At that hour people were less likely to be coming in or going out. But the procedure would have made an awkward loop in the straight thread of his casualness, and he had abandoned it. It was impossible to figure when people would be entering or leaving the house, anyway. There was a great risk at any hour. If he ran into anybody, we would sim-ply have to place the rubbing-out of Ulgine Barrows in the inactive file forever. The same thing would hold true if there were someone in her apartment. In that case he would just say that he had been passing by, rec-ognized her charming house, and thought to drop in.

It was eighteen minutes after nine when Mr. Martin turned into   10
Twelfth Street. A man passed him, and a man and a woman talking. There was no one within fifty paces when he came to the house, halfway down the block. He was up the steps and in the small vestibule in no time, pressing the bell under the card that said "Mrs. Ulgine Barrows." When the clicking in the lock started, he jumped forward against the door. He got inside fast, closing the door behind him. A bulb in a lantern hung from the hall ceiling on a chain seemed to give a monstrously bright light. There was nobody on the stair, which went up ahead of him along the left wall. A door opened down the hall in the wall on the right. He went to-ward it swiftly, on tiptoe.

"Well, for God's sake, look who's here!" bawled Mrs. Barrows, and   11
her braying laugh rang out like the report of shotgun. He rushed past her like a football tackle, bumping her. "Hey, quit shoving!" she said, closing the door behind them. They were in her living room, which seemed to Mr. Martin to be lighted by a hundred lamps. "What's after you?" she said. "You're as jumpy as a goat." He found he was unable to speak. His heart was wheezing in his throat. "I—yes," he finally brought out. She was jabbering and laughing as she started to help him off with his coat. "No, no," he said. "I'll put it there." He took it off and put it on a chair near the door. "Your hat and gloves, too," she said. "You're in a lady's

---

*EDS. NOTE—Something introduced to divert attention from the main issue.

house." He put his hat on top of the coat. Mrs. Barrows seemed larger than he had thought. He kept his gloves on. "I was passing by," he said. "I recognized—is there anyone here?" She laughed louder than ever. "No," she said, "we're all alone. You're as white as a sheet, you funny man. Whatever *has* come over you? I'll mix you a toddy." She started toward a door across the room. "Scotch-and-soda be all right? But say, you don't drink, do you?" She turned and gave him her amused look. Mr. Martin pulled himself together. "Scotch-and-soda will be all right," he heard himself say. He could hear her laughing in the kitchen.

Mr. Martin looked quickly around the living room for the weapon.   12
He had counted on finding one there. There were andirons and a poker and something in a corner that looked like an Indian club. None of them would do. It couldn't be that way. He began to pace around. He came to a desk. On it lay a metal paper knife with an ornate handle. Would it be sharp enough? He reached for it and knocked over a small brass jar. Stamps spilled out of it and it fell to the floor with a clatter. "Hey," Mrs. Barrows yelled from the kitchen, "are you tearing up the pea patch?" Mr. Martin gave a strange laugh. Picking up the knife, he tried its point against his left wrist. It was blunt. It wouldn't do.

When Mrs. Barrows reappeared, carrying two highballs, Mr. Martin,   13
standing there with his gloves on, became acutely conscious of the fantasy he had wrought. Cigarettes in his pocket, a drink prepared for him—it was all too grossly improbable. It was more than that; it was impossible. Somewhere in the back of his mind a vague idea stirred, sprouted. "For heaven's sake, take off those gloves," said Mrs. Barrows. "I always wear them in the house," said Mr. Martin. The idea began to bloom, strange and wonderful. She put the glasses on a coffee table in front of a sofa and sat on the sofa. "Come over here, you odd little man," she said. Mr. Martin went over and sat beside her. It was difficult getting a cigarette out of the pack of Camels, but he managed it. She held a match for him, laughing. "Well," she said, handing him his drink, "this is perfectly marvelous. You with a drink and a cigarette."

Mr. Martin puffed, not too awkwardly, and took a gulp of the high-   14
ball. "I drink and smoke all the time," he said. He clinked his glass against hers. "Here's nuts to that old windbag, Fitweiler," he said, and gulped again. The stuff tasted awful, but he made no grimace. "Really, Mr. Martin," she said, her voice and posture changing, "you are insulting our employer." Mrs. Barrows was now all special adviser to the president. "I am preparing a bomb," said Mr. Martin, "which will blow the old goat higher than hell." He had only had a little of the drink, which was not strong. It couldn't be that. "Do you take dope or something?" Mrs. Barrows asked coldly. "Heroin," said Mr. Martin. "I'll be coked to the gills when I bump that old buzzard off." "Mr. Martin!" she shouted, getting to her feet. "That will be all of that. You must go at once." Mr. Martin took another swallow of his drink. He tapped his cigarette out in the ashtray and put the pack of Camels on the coffee table. Then he got up. She stood

glaring at him. He walked over and put on his hat and coat. "Not a word about this," he said, and laid an index finger against his lips. All Mrs. Barrows could bring out was "Really!" Mr. Martin put his hand on the doorknob. "I'm sitting in the catbird seat," he said. He stuck his tongue out at her and left. Nobody saw him go.

Mr. Martin got to his apartment, walking, well before eleven. No one   15
saw him go in. He had two glasses of milk after brushing his teeth, and he felt elated. It wasn't tipsiness, because he hadn't been tipsy. Anyway, the walk had worn off all effects of the whisky. He got in bed and read a magazine for a while. He was asleep before midnight.

Mr. Martin got to the office at eight-thirty the next morning, as usual.   16
At a quarter to nine, Ulgine Barrows, who had never before arrived at work before ten, swept into his office. "I'm reporting to Mr. Fitweiler now!" she shouted. "If he turns you over to the police, it's no more than you deserve!" Mr. Martin gave her a look of shocked surprise. "I beg your pardon?" he said. Mrs. Barrows snorted and bounced out of the room, leaving Miss Paird and Joey Hart staring after her. "What's the matter with that old devil now?" asked Miss Paird. "I have no idea," said Mr. Martin, resuming his work. The other two looked at him and then at each other. Miss Paird got up and went out. She walked slowly past the closed door of Mr. Fitweiler's office. Mrs. Barrows was yelling inside, but she was not braying. Miss Paird could not hear what the woman was saying. She went back to her desk.

Forty-five minutes later, Mrs. Barrows left the president's office and   17
went into her own, shutting the door. It wasn't until half an hour later that Mr. Fitweiler sent for Mr. Martin. The head of the filing department, neat, quiet, attentive, stood in front of the old man's desk. Mr. Fitweiler was pale and nervous. He took his glasses off and twiddled them. He made a small, bruffing sound in his throat. "Martin," he said, "you have been with us more than twenty years." "Twenty-two, sir," said Mr. Martin. "In that time," pursued the president, "your work and your— uh—manner have been exemplary." "I trust so, sir," said Mr. Martin. "I have understood, Martin," said Mr. Fitweiler, "that you have never taken a drink or smoked." "That is correct, sir," said Mr. Martin. "Ah, yes." Mr. Fitweiler polished his glasses. "You may describe what you did after leaving the office yesterday, Martin," he said. Mr. Martin allowed less than a second for his bewildered pause. "Certainly, sir," he said. "I walked home. Then I went to Schrafft's for dinner. Afterward I walked home again. I went to bed early, sir, and read a magazine for a while. I was asleep before eleven." "Ah, yes," said Mr. Fitweiler again. He was silent for a moment, searching for the proper words to say to the head of the filing department. "Mrs. Barrows," he said finally, "Mrs. Barrows has worked hard, Martin, very hard. It grieves me to report that she has suffered a severe breakdown. It has taken the form of a persecution complex accompanied by distressing hallucinations." "I am very sorry, sir," said

Mr. Martin. "Mrs. Barrows is under the delusion," continued Mr. Fitweiler, "that you visited her last evening and behaved yourself in an—uh—unseemly manner." He raised his hand to silence Mr. Martin's little pained outcry. "It is the nature of these psychological diseases," Mr. Fitweiler said, "to fix upon the least likely and most innocent part as the—uh—source of persecution. These matters are not for the lay mind to grasp, Martin. I've just had my psychiatrist, Dr. Fitch, on the phone. He would not, of course, commit himself, but he made enough generalizations to substantiate my suspicions. I suggested to Mrs. Barrows when she had completed her—uh—story to me this morning, that she visit Dr. Fitch, for I suspected a condition at once. She flew, I regret to say, into a rage, and demanded—uh—requested that I call you on the carpet. You may not know, Martin, but Mrs. Barrows had planned a reorganization of your department—subject to my approval, of course, subject to my approval. This brought you, rather than anyone else, to her mind—but again that is a phenomenon for Dr. Fitch and not for us. So, Martin, I am afraid Mrs. Barrows' usefulness here is at an end." "I am dreadfully sorry, sir," said Mr. Martin.

It was at this point that the door to the office blew open with the suddenness of a gas-main explosion and Mrs. Barrows catapulted through it. "Is the little rat denying it?" she screamed. "He can't get away with that!" Mr. Martin got up and moved discreetly to a point beside Mr. Fitweiler's chair. "You drank and smoked at my apartment," she bawled at Mr. Martin, "and you know it! You called Mr. Fitweiler an old windbag and said you were going to blow him up when you got coked to the gills on your heroin!" She stopped yelling to catch her breath and a new glint came into her popping eyes. "If you weren't such a drab, ordinary little man," she said, "I'd think you'd planned it all. Sticking your tongue out, saying you were sitting in the catbird seat, because you thought no one would believe me when I told it! My God, it's really too perfect!" She brayed loudly and hysterically, and the fury was on her again. She glared at Mr. Fitweiler. "Can't you see how he has tricked us, you old fool? Can't you see his little game?" But Mr. Fitweiler had been surreptitiously pressing all the buttons under the top of his desk and employees of F & S began pouring into the room. "Stockton," said Mr. Fitweiler, "you and Fishbein will take Mrs. Barrows to her home. Mrs. Powell, you will go with them." Stockton, who had played a little football in high school, blocked Mrs. Barrows as she made for Mr. Martin. It took him and Fishbein together to force her out of the door into the hall, crowded with stenographers and office boys. She was still screaming imprecations at Mr. Martin, tangled and contradictory imprecations. The hubbub finally died out down the corridor.

"I regret that this has happened," said Mr. Fitweiler. "I shall ask you to dismiss it from your mind, Martin." "Yes, sir," said Mr. Martin, anticipating his chief's "That will be all" by moving to the door. "I will dismiss it." He went out and shut the door, and his step was light and quick in the

18

19

hall. When he entered his department he had slowed down to his customary gait, and he walked quietly across the room to the W20 file, wearing a look of studious concentration.

•   •   •

THINKING ABOUT LITERATURE

1. Define *catbird seat*. What is the term's origin?

2. What patterns of development does Thurber use to develop the definition of *catbird seat*?

3. If Mrs. Barrows had kept quiet about her encounter with Mr. Martin, *she* would have been in the catbird seat. Why, then, do you suppose she did not keep silent?

JOURNAL ENTRY

Could this story of office rivalry have been written about two men? About two women? Explain.

THEMATIC CONNECTIONS

- "The Open Window" (page 100)
- "The Peter Principle" (page 169)
- "The Spider and the Wasp" (page 223)
- "The Company Man" (page 465)

WRITING ASSIGNMENTS FOR DEFINITION

1. Choose a document or ritual that is a significant part of your religious or cultural heritage. Define it, using any pattern or combination of patterns you choose but making sure to include a formal definition somewhere in your essay. Assume your readers are not familiar with the term you are defining.

2. Write an essay defining *catbird seat,* using narration to explain a time when you were "sitting pretty."

3. The readings in this chapter define (among other things) a food, a family role, and an occupational role. Write an essay in which you define one of these topics—for instance, spaghetti (food), a stepmother (family role), or the modern baseball player (occupational role).

4. Do some research to learn the meaning of one of these medical conditions: angina, migraine, Hodgkin's disease, Down syndrome, osteoporosis, poliomyelitis, Alzheimer's disease. Then, write an extended definition essay explaining the condition to an audience of high school students.

5. Use an extended example to support a thesis in an essay that defines *racism, sexism,* or another type of bigoted behavior.

6. Choose a term that is central to one of your courses—for instance, *naturalism, behaviorism,* or *authority*—and write an essay in which you define the term. Assume that your audience is made up of students who have not yet taken the course. You may begin with an overview of the term's origin if you believe this is appropriate. Then, develop your essay with examples and **analogies** that will facilitate your audience's understanding of the term.

7. Assume your audience is from a culture that is not familiar with modern American pastimes. Write a definition essay for this audience in which you describe the form and function of a Frisbee, a Barbie doll, a G.I. Joe action figure, a skateboard, or baseball cards.

8. Review any one of the following narrative essays from Chapter 2, and use it to help you develop an extended definition of one of the following terms.
   "Only Daughter"—alienation
   "Finishing School"—prejudice
   "My Mother Never Worked"—work
   "Thirty-Eight Who Saw Murder Didn't Call the Police"—apathy
   "Shooting an Elephant"—power

9. What constitutes an education? Define the term *education* by identifying several different sources of knowledge, formal or informal, and explaining what each contributes. You might read—or reread—"Finishing School" (page 75), "Reading the River" (page 126), or "The Human Cost of an Illiterate Society" (page 192).

10. What qualifies someone to be a hero? Developing your essay with a single extended example or a series of examples, define the word *hero.*

Include a formal definition, and try to incorporate at least one paragraph in which you define the term by explaining and illustrating what a hero is *not*.

COLLABORATIVE ACTIVITY FOR DEFINITION

Working as a group, choose one of the following words to define: *pride, hope, sacrifice, courage, justice.* Then, define the term with a series of extended examples drawn from films that members of your group have seen, with each of you developing an illustrative paragraph based on a different film. (Before beginning, your group may decide to focus on one particular genre of film.) When each paragraph has been read by everyone in the group, work together to formulate a thesis that asserts the vital importance of the quality your examples have defined. Finally, write suitable opening and closing paragraphs for the essay, and arrange the body paragraphs in a logical order, adding transitions where necessary.

10
ARGUMENTATION

WHAT IS ARGUMENTATION?

Argumentation is a reasoned, logical way of asserting the soundness of a position, belief, or conclusion. Argumentation takes a stand—supported by evidence—and urges people to share the writer's perspective and insights. In the following paragraph from "Test-Tube Babies: Solution or Problem?" Ruth Hubbard argues that before we endorse further development of the technology that allows for the creation of test-tube babies, we should consider the consequences:

Issue identified	In vitro fertilization of human eggs and the implantation of early embryos into women's wombs are new biotechnologies that may enable some women to bear
Background presents both sides of issue	children who have hitherto been unable to do so. In that sense, it may solve their particular infertility problems. On the other hand, this technology poses unpredictable hazards since it intervenes in the process of fertilization, in the first cell divisions of the fertilized egg, and in the implantation of the embryo into the uterus. At present we have no way to assess in what ways and to what extent these interventions may affect the women or the babies they acquire by this procedure. Since the use of the
Topic sentence (takes a stand)	technology is only the beginning, the financial and technical investments it represents are still modest. It is therefore important that we, as a society, seriously consider the wisdom of implementing and developing it further.

Argumentation can have any of several purposes: to convince other people to accept—or at least acknowledge the validity of—your position; to defend your position, even if others cannot be convinced to agree; or to question or refute a position you believe to be misguided, untrue, dangerous, or evil, without necessarily offering an alternative.

Argumentation and Persuasion

Although the terms *persuasion* and *argumentation* are frequently used interchangeably, they do not mean the same thing. **Persuasion** is a general term that refers to the method by which a writer moves an audience to adopt a belief or follow a course of action. To persuade an audience, a writer relies on various appeals—to the emotions, to reason, or to ethics.

Argumentation is the appeal to reason. In an argument a writer connects a series of statements so that they lead logically to a conclusion. Argumentation is different from persuasion in that it does not try to move an audience to action; its primary purpose is simply to demonstrate that certain ideas are valid and others are not. Unlike persuasion, argumentation has a formal structure: an argument makes points, supplies evidence, establishes a logical chain of reasoning, refutes opposing arguments, and accommodates the views of an audience.

As the readings in this chapter demonstrate, however, most effective arguments combine several appeals: even though their primary appeal is to logic, they may also appeal to emotions. For example, you could use a combination of logical and emotional appeals to argue against lowering the drinking age in your state from twenty-one to eighteen. You could appeal to *reason* by constructing an argument leading to the conclusion that the state should not condone policies that have a high probability of injuring or killing citizens. You could support your conclusion by presenting statistics showing that alcohol-related traffic accidents kill more teenagers than disease does. You could also cite a study showing that when the drinking age was raised from 18 to 21, fatal accidents declined. In addition, you could include an appeal to the *emotions* by telling a particularly sad story about an eighteen-year-old alcoholic or by pointing out how an increased number of accidents involving drunk drivers would cost taxpayers more money and could even cost some of them their lives. These appeals to your audience's emotions could strengthen your argument by widening its appeal. Keep in mind, however, that in an effective argument emotion does not take the place of logic; it supports and reinforces it.

The appeals you choose and how you balance them depend in part on your purpose and your sense of your audience. As you consider what strategies to use, remember that some extremely effective appeals are unfair. Although most people would agree that lies, threats, and appeals to greed and prejudice are unacceptable ways of reaching an audience, such appeals are used in political campaigns, international diplomacy, and daily conversation. Nevertheless, in your college writing you should use only those appeals that most people would consider fair.

Choosing a Topic

In an argumentative essay, as in all writing, choosing the right topic is important. Ideally, your topic should be one in which you have an intellectual or emotional stake. Still, you should still be open-minded and willing to consider all sides of a question. If the evidence goes against your position, you should be willing to change your thesis. And you should be able, from the outset, to consider your topic from other people's viewpoints; this will help you determine how much they know about your topic, what their beliefs are, and how they are likely to react. You can then use this knowledge to build your case. If you cannot be open-minded, then you should choose another topic that you can deal with more objectively.

Other factors should also influence your selection of a topic. You should be well informed about your topic. In addition, you should choose an issue narrow enough to be treated effectively in the space available to you, or be willing to confine your discussion to one aspect of a broad issue. It is also important to consider your purpose—what you expect your argument to accomplish and how you wish your audience to respond. If your topic is so far-reaching that you cannot identify what you want to convince readers to think, or if your purpose is so idealistic that your expectations of their response are impossible or unreasonable, your essay will suffer.

Taking a Stand

After you have chosen your topic, you are ready to take your stand— to state the position you will argue in the form of a thesis. Consider the following thesis statement:

> Education is the best way to address the problem of increased drug use among teenagers.

This thesis says you believe that increased drug use is a problem among teenagers, that there is more than one possible solution to this problem, and that education is a better solution than any other. In your argument you will have to support each of these three points logically and persuasively.

After stating your thesis, you should examine it to make sure it is *debatable.* There is no point in arguing a statement of fact or a point that most people accept as self-evident. A good argumentative thesis contains a proposition that at least some people would object to. A good way to test the suitability of your thesis for an argumentative essay is to formulate an **antithesis,** a statement that asserts the opposite position. If you know that some people would support the antithesis, you can be certain that your thesis is indeed debatable.

Thesis:	Because immigrants have contributed much to the development of the United States, immigration quotas should be relaxed.
Antithesis:	Even though immigrants have contributed much to the development of the United States, immigration quotas should not be relaxed.

Analyzing Your Audience

Before writing any essay, you should analyze the characteristics, values, and interests of your audience. In argumentation it is especially important to consider what beliefs or opinions your readers are likely to have and whether your audience is likely to be friendly, neutral, or hostile to your thesis. It is probably best to assume that some, if not most, of your readers are at least skeptically neutral—that they are open to your ideas but need to be convinced. This assumption will keep you from making claims you cannot support. If your position is controversial, you should assume that an informed and determined opposition is looking for holes in your argument.

In an argumentative essay, you face a dual challenge. You must appeal to readers who are neutral or even hostile to your position, and you must influence those readers so that they are more receptive to your viewpoint. For example, it would be relatively easy to convince college students that tuition should be lowered or instructors that faculty salaries should be raised. You could be reasonably sure, in advance, that each group would be friendly and would agree with your position. But argument requires more than telling people what they already believe. It would be much harder to convince college students that tuition should be raised to pay for an increase in instructors' salaries or to persuade instructors to forgo raises so that tuition can remain the same. Remember, your audience will not just take your word for the claims you make. You must provide evidence that will support your thesis and reasoning that will lead logically to your conclusion.

Gathering and Documenting Evidence

All the points you make in your paper must be supported. If they are not, your audience will dismiss them as unfounded, irrelevant, or unclear. Sometimes you can support a statement with appeals to emotion, but most of the time you support the points of your argument by appealing to reason—by providing **evidence,** facts and opinions in support of your position.

As you gather evidence and assess its effectiveness, keep in mind that evidence in an argumentative essay never proves anything conclusively. If it did, there would be no debate and hence no point in arguing. The best evidence can do is convince your audience that an assertion is reasonable and worth considering.

KINDS OF EVIDENCE.   Evidence can be fact or opinion. *Facts* are statements that most people agree are true and that can be verified independently. Facts—including statistics—are the most commonly used type of evidence. It is a fact, for example, that fewer people per year were killed in automobile accidents in the 1980s than in the 1960s. Facts may be drawn from your own experience as well as from reading and observation. It may, for instance, be a fact that you yourself may have had a serious automobile accident. Quite often, facts are more convincing when they are supplemented by *opinions,* or interpretations of facts. To connect your facts about automobile accidents to the assertion that the installation of airbags on all cars and trucks could reduce deaths still further, you could cite the opinions of an expert—consumer advocate Ralph Nader, for example. His statements, along with the facts and statistics you have assembled and your own interpretations of those facts and statistics, could convince readers that your solution to the problem of highway deaths is reasonable.

Keep in mind that not all opinions are equally convincing. The opinions of experts are more convincing than are those of individuals who have less knowledge of an issue. Your personal opinions can be excellent evidence (provided you are knowledgeable about your subject), but they are usually less convincing to your audience than expert opinions or facts. In the final analysis, what is important is not just the quality of the evidence but also the credibility of the person offering it.

What kind of evidence might change readers' minds? That depends on the readers, the issue, and the facts at hand. Put yourself in the place of your readers, and ask what would make them receptive to your thesis. Why should a student agree to pay higher tuition? You might concede that tuition is high but point out that it has not been raised for three years, while the college's costs have kept going up. The cost of heating and maintaining the buildings has increased, and professors' salaries have not, with the result that several excellent teachers have recently left the college for higher-paying jobs. Furthermore, cuts in federal and state funding have already caused a reduction in the number of courses offered. Similarly, how could you convince a professor to agree to accept no raise at all, especially in light of the fact that faculty salaries have not keep up with inflation? You could say that because cuts in government funding have already reduced course offerings and because the government has also reduced funds for student loans, any further rise in tuition to pay faculty salaries will cause some students to drop out—and that in turn would cost some instructors their jobs. As you can see, the evidence and reasoning you use in an argument depend to a great extent on whom you want to persuade and what you know about them.

CRITERIA FOR EVIDENCE.   As you select and review material, choose your evidence with three criteria in mind:

Your evidence should be *relevant.* It should support your thesis and be pertinent to the argument you are making. As you present evidence, be careful not to concentrate so much on a specific example that you lose sight of the point you are supporting. Such digressions may confuse your readers. For example, in arguing for mandatory HIV testing for all health-care workers, one student made the point that AIDS is at epidemic proportions. To illustrate this point, he offered a discussion of the bubonic plague in fourteenth-century Europe. Although interesting, this example was not relevant. To show its relevance, the student would have to link his discussion to his assertions about AIDS, possibly by comparing the spread of the bubonic plague in the fourteenth century to the spread of AIDS today.

Your evidence should be *representative*. It should represent the *full range* of opinions about your subject, not just one side or another. For example, in an essay in which you argued against the use of animals in medical experimentation, you would not just use information provided by animal rights activists. You would also use information supplied by medical researchers, pharmaceutical companies, and possibly medical ethicists. In addition, the examples and expert opinions you include should be typical, not aberrant. Suppose you are writing an essay in support of building a trash-to-steam plant in your city. To support your thesis, you present the example of Baltimore, which has a successful trash-to-steam program. As you consider your evidence, ask yourself if Baltimore's experience with trash-to-steam is typical. Did other cities have less success? Take a close look at the opinions that disagree with the position you plan to take. If you understand your opposition, you will be able to refute it effectively when you write your paper.

Your evidence should be *sufficient*. Include enough evidence to support your claims. The amount of evidence you need depends on the length of your paper, your audience, and your thesis. It stands to reason that you would use fewer examples in a two-page paper than in a ten-page research assignment. Similarly, an audience that is favorably disposed to your thesis might need only one or two examples to be convinced, whereas a skeptical audience would need many more. As you develop your thesis, think about the amount of support you will need to write your paper. You may decide that a narrower, more limited thesis will be easier to support than one that is more inclusive.

DOCUMENTATION OF EVIDENCE.   As soon as you decide on a topic, you should begin to gather your evidence. Sometimes you will be able to use your own ideas and observations to support your claims. Most of the time, however, you will have to go to the library and search reference books, print indexes, and computer databases to locate the facts and expert opinions you need. Whenever you use such evidence in your paper, you have to *document* it by providing the source of the evidence. You can do this by following a format such as the one recommended by the Modern Language Association (MLA) and explained in the Appendix of this book. If you don't document your sources, your readers are likely to dismiss your evidence, thinking it is inaccurate, unreliable, or simply false. **Documentation** gives readers the ability to judge the sources you cite and to consult them if they wish. When you document sources, you are telling your readers that you are honest and have nothing to hide. Documentation also helps you avoid **plagiarism**—presenting the ideas or words of others as if they were your own. Certainly you don't have to document every idea you use in your paper. **Common knowledge**—information you could easily find in several reference sources—can be presented without documentation. You must, however, document any use of a direct quotation and any ideas that are the original conclusions of your source.

Dealing with the Opposition

When gathering evidence, keep in mind that you cannot ignore arguments against your position. In fact, you should specifically address the most obvious—and sometimes the not-so-obvious—objections to your case. Try to anticipate the objections that a reasonable person would have to your thesis. By directly addressing these objections in your essay, you will help convince readers that your arguments are sound. This part of an argument, called **refutation,** is essential to making the strongest case possible.

You can refute opposing arguments by showing that they are unsound, unfair, or weak. Frequently, you will present contrasting evidence to show the weakness of your opponent's points and to reinforce your own case. Careful use of definition and cause-and-effect analysis may also prove effective. In the following passage from the classic essay "Politics and the English Language," George Orwell refutes an opponent's argument:

> I said earlier that the decadence of our language is probably curable. Those who deny this would argue, if they produced an argument at all, that language merely reflects existing social conditions, and that we cannot influence its development by any direct tinkering with words and constructions. So far as the general tone or spirit of a language goes, this may be true, but it is not true in detail. Silly words and expressions have often disappeared, though not through any evolutionary process but owing to the conscious actions of a minority.

Orwell begins by stating the point he wants to make. He goes on to define the argument against his position, and then he identifies its weakness. Later in the essay Orwell bolsters his argument by presenting two examples that support his point.

When an opponent's argument is so compelling that it cannot be easily dismissed, you should concede its strength. By acknowledging that a point is well taken, you reinforce the impression that you are a fair-minded person. If possible, identify the limitations of the opposing position and then move your argument to more solid ground. Often an opponent's strong point addresses only *one* facet of a multifaceted problem.

When planning an argumentative essay, write down all possible arguments against your thesis that you can identify. Then, as you marshal your evidence, you can decide which points you will refute, keeping in mind that careful readers will expect you to refute the most compelling of your opponent's arguments. Take care, though, not to distort an opponent's argument by making it seem weaker than it actually is. This technique, called creating a *straw man,* can backfire and actually turn fair-minded readers against you.

Using Rogerian Argument

Psychologist Carl Rogers has written about how to argue without assuming an adversarial relationship. According to Rogers, traditional strategies of argument rely on confrontation—proving that an opponent's position is wrong. With this method of arguing, one person is "wrong" and one is "right." By attacking an opponent and repeatedly hammering home the message that his or her arguments are incorrect or misguided, a writer forces the opponent into a defensive position. The result is conflict, disagreement, and frequently ill will and hostility.

Rogers recommends that you think of the members of your audience as colleagues, not adversaries. With this approach, now known as **Rogerian argument,** you enter into a cooperative relationship with readers. Instead of refuting opposing arguments, you negotiate to determine points of agreement. The result is that you collaborate to find solutions that are mutually satisfying. By adopting a conciliatory attitude, you demonstrate your respect for opposing points of view and your willingness to compromise and work toward a position that both you and those who disagree with you will find acceptable. To use a Rogerian strategy in your writing, follow the guidelines below.

☑ GUIDELINES FOR USING ROGERIAN ARGUMENT

- Begin by summarizing opposing viewpoints.
- Carefully consider the position of those who disagree with you. What are their legitimate concerns? If you were in their place, how would you react?
- Present opposing points of view accurately and fairly. Demonstrate your respect for the ideas of those who disagree with you.
- Concede the strength of a compelling opposing argument.
- Think of the concerns that you and your opposition share.
- Demonstrate to readers how they will benefit from the position you are defining.

DEDUCTIVE AND INDUCTIVE ARGUMENTS

In an argument, you may move from evidence to conclusion in two basic ways. One method, called **deductive reasoning,** proceeds from a general premise or assumption to a specific conclusion. Deduction is what most people mean when they speak of logic. Using strict logical form, deduction holds that if all the statements in the argument are true, the conclusion must also be true. The other method of moving from evidence to conclusion is called **inductive reasoning.** Induction proceeds from individual observations to a more general conclusion and uses no strict form. It requires only that all the relevant evidence be stated and that the conclusion fit the evidence better than any other conclusion would. Most written arguments use a combination of deductive and inductive reasoning, but it is simpler to discuss and illustrate them separately.

Using Deductive Arguments

The basic form of a deductive argument is a **syllogism.** A syllogism consists of a *major premise,* which is a general statement; a *minor premise,* which is a related but more specific statement; and a *conclusion,* which has to be drawn from those premises. Consider the following example:

Major premise:	All Olympic runners are fast.
Minor premise:	Florence Griffith Joyner is an Olympic runner.
Conclusion:	Therefore, Florence Griffith Joyner is fast.

As you can see, if you grant each of the premises, then you must also grant the conclusion—and it is the only conclusion you can properly draw. You cannot conclude that Florence Griffith Joyner is slow because that conclusion contradicts the premises. Nor can you conclude (even if it is true) that Florence Griffith Joyner is tall because that conclusion goes beyond the premises.

Of course this argument seems obvious, and it is much simpler than an argumentative essay would be. But a deductive argument's premises can be fairly elaborate. The Declaration of Independence, which appears later in this chapter, has at its core a deductive argument that might be summarized in this way:

Major premise:	Tyrannical rulers deserve no loyalty.
Minor premise:	King George III is a tyrannical ruler.
Conclusion:	Therefore, King George III deserves no loyalty.

The major premise is a truth the Declaration claims is self-evident. Much of the Declaration consists of evidence to support the minor premise that King George is a tyrannical ruler. And the conclusion, because it is drawn from those premises, has the force of irrefutable logic:

the king deserves no loyalty from his American subjects, who are therefore entitled to revolt against him.

When a conclusion follows logically from the major and minor premises, then the argument is said to be *valid*. But if the syllogism is not logical, the argument is not valid and the conclusion is not sound. For example, the following syllogism is not logical:

Major premise:	All dogs are animals.
Minor premise:	All cats are animals.
Conclusion:	Therefore, all dogs are cats.

Of course the conclusion is absurd. But how did we wind up with such a ridiculous conclusion when both premises are obviously true? The answer is that although both cats and dogs are animals, cats are not included in the major premise of the syllogism, which deals only with dogs. Therefore, the form of the syllogism is defective, and the argument is invalid. Here is another example of an invalid argument:

Major premise:	All dogs are animals.
Minor premise:	Ralph is an animal.
Conclusion:	Therefore, Ralph is a dog.

This error in logic occurs when the minor premise refers to a term in the major premise that is *undistributed*—that is, it covers only some of the items in the class it denotes. In the major premise, *dogs* is the distributed term; it designates *all dogs*. The minor premise, however, refers not to *dogs* but to *animals*, which is undistributed because it refers only to animals that are dogs. As the minor premise establishes, Ralph is an animal, but it does not follow that he is also a dog. He could be a cat, a horse, or even a human being.

Even if a syllogism is valid—that is, correct in its form—its conclusion will not necessarily be *true*. The following syllogism draws a false conclusion:

Major premise:	All dogs are brown.
Minor premise:	My poodle Toby is a dog.
Conclusion:	Therefore, Toby is brown.

As it happens, Toby is black. The conclusion is false because the major premise is false: many dogs are *not* brown. If Toby were actually brown, the conclusion would be correct, but only by chance, not by logic. To be *sound*, a syllogism must be both logical and true.

The advantage of a deductive argument is that if you convince your audience to accept your major and minor premises, the force of logic should bring them to accept your conclusion. Therefore, you should try to select premises that you know your audience accepts or that are self-evident—that is, premises that most people believe to be true. Don't assume, however, that "most people" refers only to your friends and acquaintances. Consider, too, those who may hold different views. If you think that your premises are too controversial or difficult to establish firmly, you should use inductive reasoning.

Using Inductive Arguments

Inductive arguments move from specific examples or facts to a general conclusion. Unlike deduction, induction has no distinctive form, and its conclusions are less definitive than those of syllogisms whose forms are valid and whose premises are clearly true. Still, much inductive thinking (and writing based on that thinking) tends to follow a certain process. First, you usually decide on a question to be answered—or, especially in scientific work, you identify a tentative answer to such a question, called a *hypothesis*. Then, you gather all the evidence you can find that is relevant to the question and that may be important to finding the answer. Finally, you move from your evidence to your conclusion by making an *inference* that answers the question and takes the evidence into account. Here is a very simple example of the inductive process:

Question:	How did that living-room window get broken?
Evidence:	There is a baseball on the living-room floor.
	The baseball was not there this morning.
	Some children were playing baseball this afternoon.
	They were playing in the vacant lot across from the window.
	They stopped playing a little while ago.
	They aren't in the vacant lot now.
Conclusion:	One of the children hit or threw the ball through the window. Then they all ran away.

The conclusion, because it takes all of the evidence into account, seems obvious. But if it turned out that the children had been playing softball, not baseball, that one additional piece of evidence would make the conclusion doubtful—and the true answer could not be inferred. Even if the conclusion is believable, you cannot necessarily assume it is true: after all, the window could have been broken in some other way. For example, perhaps a bird flew against it, and perhaps the baseball in the living room had gone unnoticed all day, making the second piece of "evidence" on the list above not true.

Because inductive arguments tend to be more complicated than the preceding example, it is not always easy to move from the evidence you have collected to a sound conclusion. Of course, the more information you gather, the smaller the gap between your evidence and your conclusion. Still, the crucial step from evidence to conclusion can be a big one, sometimes requiring what is called an *inductive leap*. With induction, conclusions are never certain, only highly probable. Although induction does not point to any particular type of conclusion the way deduction does, making sure that your evidence is *relevant, representative,* and *sufficient* (see pages 489–490) can increase the probability that your conclusion will be sound.

Considering possible conclusions is a good way to avoid reaching an unjustified or false conclusion. In the preceding example, a hypothesis like this one might follow the question:

Hypothesis: One of those children playing baseball broke the living-room window.

Many people stop reasoning at this point, without considering the evidence. But when the gap between your evidence and your conclusion is too great, you may reach a hasty conclusion or one that is not borne out by the facts. This well-named error is called *jumping to a conclusion* because it amounts to a premature inductive leap. In induction, the hypothesis is merely the starting point. The rest of the inductive process continues as if the question were still to be answered—as in fact it is until all the evidence has been taken into account.

Using Toulmin Logic

Another method for structuring arguments has been advanced by philosopher Stephen Toulmin. Known as **Toulmin logic,** this method is an effort to describe argumentation as it actually occurs in everyday life. Toulmin puts forth a model that divides arguments into three parts: the *claim,* the *grounds,* and the *warrant.* The **claim** is the main point of the essay. Usually the claim is stated directly as the thesis, but in some arguments it may be implied. The **grounds**—the material a writer uses to support the claim—can be evidence (facts or expert opinion) or appeals to the emotions or values of the audience. The **warrant** is the inference that connects the claim to the grounds. It can be a belief that is taken for granted or an assumption that underlies the argument.

In its simplest form, an argument following Toulmin logic would look like this:

Claim: Carol should be elected class president.

Grounds: Carol is an honor student.

Warrant: A person who is an honor student would make a good class president.

When you formulate an argument using Toulmin logic, you can still use inductive and deductive reasoning. You derive your claim inductively from facts and examples, and you connect the grounds and warrant to your claim deductively. For example, the deductive argument in the Declaration of Independence that was summarized on page 493 can be represented this way:

Claim:	King George III deserves no loyalty.
Grounds:	King George III is a tyrannical ruler. (supported by facts and examples)
Warrant:	Tyrannical rulers deserve no loyalty.

As Toulmin points out, the clearer your warrant, the more likely readers will be to agree with it. Notice that in the two preceding examples, the warrants are very explicit.

Recognizing Fallacies

Fallacies are statements that may sound reasonable or true but are deceptive and dishonest. When your readers detect them, such statements can backfire and turn even a sympathetic audience against your position. Here are some of the more common fallacies that you should avoid:

BEGGING THE QUESTION.   Begging the question is a logical fallacy that assumes in the premise what the arguer should be trying to prove in the conclusion. This tactic asks readers to agree that certain points are self-evident when they are not.

> The unfair and shortsighted legislation that limits free trade is clearly a threat to the American economy.

Restrictions against free trade may or may not be unfair and shortsighted, but emotionally loaded language does not constitute proof. The statement begs the question because it assumes what it should be proving—that restrictive legislation is dangerous.

ARGUMENT FROM ANALOGY.   An **analogy** is a form of comparison that explains an unfamiliar element by comparing it to a more familiar one. Although analogies can explain abstract or unclear ideas, they do not constitute proof. An argument based on an analogy frequently ignores important dissimilarities between the two things being compared. When this occurs, the argument is fallacious.

> The overcrowded conditions in some parts of our city have forced people together like rats in a cage. Like rats, they will eventually turn on one another, fighting and killing until a balance is restored. It is therefore necessary that we vote to appropriate funds to build low-cost housing.

No evidence is offered that people behave like rats under these or any other conditions. Just because two things have some characteristics in common, you should not assume they are alike in other respects.

PERSONAL ATTACK (ARGUMENT *AD HOMINEM*).   This fallacy tries to divert attention from the facts of an argument by attacking the motives or character of the person making the argument.

> The public should not take seriously Dr. Mason's plan for upgrading county health services. He is a recovering alcoholic whose second wife recently divorced him.

This attack on Dr. Mason's character says nothing about the quality of his plan. Sometimes a connection exists between a person's private and public lives—for example, a case of conflict of interest. But no evidence of such a connection is presented here.

HASTY OR SWEEPING GENERALIZATION. Sometimes called *jumping to a conclusion,* this fallacy occurs when a conclusion is reached on the basis of too little evidence.

> Our son Marc really benefited socially from going to nursery school; I think every child should go.

Perhaps other children would benefit from nursery school, and perhaps not, but no conclusion about children in general can be reached on the basis of one child's experience.

FALSE DILEMMA (EITHER/OR FALLACY). This fallacy occurs when you suggest that only two alternatives exist even though there may be others.

> We must choose between life and death, between intervention and genocide. There can be no neutral position on this issue.

An argument like this oversimplifies issues and forces people to choose between extremes instead of exploring more moderate positions.

EQUIVOCATION. This fallacy occurs when the meaning of a key term changes at some point in an argument. Equivocation makes it seem as if a conclusion follows from premises when it actually does not.

> As a human endeavor, computers are a praiseworthy and even remarkable accomplishment. But how human can we hope to be if we rely on computers to make our decisions?

The use of *human* in the first sentence refers to the entire human race. In the second sentence *human* means "merciful" or "civilized." By subtly shifting this term to refer to qualities characteristic of people as opposed to machines, the writer makes the argument seem more sound than it is.

RED HERRING. This fallacy occurs when the focus of an argument is changed to divert the audience from the actual issue.

> The mayor has proposed building a new baseball-only sports stadium. How can he even consider allocating millions of dollars to this irresponsible scheme when so many professional baseball players have drug problems?

The focus of this argument should be the merits of the sports stadium. Instead, the writer shifts to the irrelevant issue of athletes' drug use.

You Also (*Tu Quoque*).   This fallacy asserts that an opponent's argument has no value because the opponent does not follow his or her own advice.

> How can that judge favor stronger penalties for convicted drug dealers? During his confirmation hearings, he admitted he had smoked marijuana as a student.

Appeal to Doubtful Authority.   Often people will attempt to bolster an argument with references to experts or famous people. These appeals are valid when the person quoted or referred to is an expert in the area being discussed. They are not valid, however, when the individuals cited have no expertise on the issue.

> According to Ted Koppel, interest rates will remain low during the next fiscal year.

Although Ted Koppel is a respected journalist, he is not an expert in business or finance. Therefore, his pronouncements about interest rates are no more than a personal opinion or, at best, an educated guess.

Misleading Statistics.   Although statistics are a powerful form of factual evidence, they can be misrepresented or distorted in an attempt to influence an audience.

> Women will never be competent firefighters; after all, 50 percent of the women in the city's training program failed the exam.

Here the writer has neglected to mention that there were only two women in the program. Because this statistic is not based on a large enough sample, it cannot be used as evidence to support the argument.

Post Hoc, Ergo Propter Hoc (After This, Therefore Because of This).   This fallacy, known as *post hoc reasoning,* assumes that because two events occur close together in time, the first must be the cause of the second.

> Every time a Republican is elected president a recession follows. If we want to avoid another recession, we should elect a Democrat.

Even if it were true that recessions always occur during the tenure of Republican presidents, no causal connection has been established. (See pages 261–62.)

Non Sequitur (It Does Not Follow).   This fallacy occurs when a statement does not logically follow from a previous statement.

> Disarmament weakened the United States after World War I. Disarmament also weakened the United States after the Vietnam War. For this reason, gun control will weaken the United States.

The historical effects of disarmament have nothing to do with current efforts to control the sale of guns. Therefore, the conclusion is a *non sequitur.*

STRUCTURING AN ARGUMENTATIVE ESSAY

An argumentative essay, like other kinds of essays, has an *introduction,* a *body,* and a *conclusion.* But an argumentative essay has its own special structure, one that ensures that ideas are presented logically and convincingly. The Declaration of Independence follows the classic design typical of many arguments:

Introduction:	Introduces the issue
	States the thesis
Body:	Induction—offers evidence to support the thesis
	Deduction—uses syllogisms to support the thesis
	States the arguments against the thesis and refutes them
Conclusion:	Sums up the argument if it is long and complex
	Restates the thesis in different words
	Makes a forceful closing statement

Jefferson begins the Declaration by presenting the issue that the document addresses: the obligation of the people of the American colonies to tell the world why they must separate from Great Britain. Next Jefferson states his thesis that because of the tyranny of the British king, the colonies must replace his rule with another form of government. In the body of the Declaration, he offers as evidence twenty-eight examples of injustice endured by the colonies. Following the evidence, Jefferson refutes counterarguments by explaining how time and time again the colonists have appealed to the British for redress, but without result. In his concluding paragraph, he restates the thesis and reinforces it one final time. He ends with a flourish: speaking for the representatives of the United States, he explicitly dissolves all political connections between England and America.

Not all arguments, however, follow this pattern. Your material, your thesis, your purpose, your audience, the type of argument you are writing, and the limitations of your assignment all help you determine the strategies you use. If your thesis is especially novel or controversial, for example, the refutation of opposing arguments may come first. In this instance, opposing positions might even be mentioned in the introduction—provided they are discussed more fully later in the argument.

Suppose your journalism instructor gives you the following assignment:

Select a controversial topic that interests you, and write a brief editorial about it. Direct your editorial to readers who do not share your views, and try to convince them that your position is reasonable. Be sure to ac-knowledge the view your audience holds and to refute possible criti-cisms of your argument.

You are well informed about one local issue because you have just read a series of articles on it. A citizen group is lobbying for a local ordinance that would authorize government funding for parochial schools in your community. Since you have also recently studied the constitutional doc-trine of separation of church and state in your American government class, you know you could argue fairly and strongly against the position taken by this group.

An informal outline of your essay might look like this:

Issue introduced:	Should public tax revenues be spent on aid to parochial schools?
Thesis statement:	Despite the pleas of citizen groups like Parochial School Parents United, using tax dollars to sup-port church-affiliated schools directly violates the U.S. Constitution.
Evidence (deduction):	Explain general principle of separation of church and state in the Constitution.
Evidence (induction):	Present recent examples of court cases interpret-ing and applying this principle.
Evidence (deduction):	Explain how the Constitution and the court cases apply to your community's situation.
Opposition refuted:	Identify and respond to arguments used by Parochial School Parents United. Concede the point that parochial schools educate many chil-dren who would otherwise have to be educated in public schools at taxpayers' expense.
Conclusion:	Sum up the argument, restate the thesis, and end with a strong closing statement.

▶ **A STUDENT WRITER: ARGUMENTATION**

The following editorial, written by Matt Daniels for his college newspa-per, illustrates a number of the techniques discussed earlier in the chapter.

                    An Argument against the Anna Todd Jennings
                                Scholarship
Introduction   Recently, a dispute has arisen over the   1
                    "Caucasian-restricted" Anna Todd Jennings

Summary of controversy

scholarship.* Anna Jennings died in 1955, and her will established a trust that granted a scholarship of up to $15,000 for a deserving student. Unfortunately, Jennings, who had certain racist views, limited her scholarship to "Caucasian students." After much debate with family and friends, I, a white, well-qualified, and definitely deserving student, have decided not to apply for the scholarship. It

Thesis statement

is my view that despite arguments to the contrary, applying for the Anna Todd Jennings scholarship furthers the racist ideas that were held by its founder.

Argument (deductive)

Most people would agree that racism in any form is an evil that should be opposed. The Anna Todd Jennings scholarship is a subtle but nonetheless dangerous expression of racism. It explicitly discriminates against African-Americans, Asians, Latinos, Native Americans, and others. By providing a scholarship for whites only, Anna Jennings frustrates the aspirations of groups who until recently had been virtually kept out of the educational mainstream. On this basis alone, students should refuse to apply and should actively work to encourage the school to challenge the racist provisions of Anna Todd Jennings's will. Such challenges have been upheld by the courts: the striking down of a similar clause in the will of the eighteenth-century financier Stephen Girard is just one example.

2

Argument (inductive)

The school itself must share some blame in this case. Students who applied for the Anna Todd Jennings scholarship were unaware of its restrictions. The director of the financial aid office has acknowledged that he knew

3

---

*EDS. NOTE—This essay discusses an actual situation, but the name of the scholarship has been changed here.

Evidence

about the racial restrictions of the scholarship but thought that students should have the
right to apply anyway. In addition, the materials distributed by the financial aid office
gave no indication that the award was limited
to Caucasians. Students were required to fill
out forms, submit financial statements, and
forward transcripts. In addition to this material, all students were told to attach a
recent photograph to their application. Little
did the applicants know that the sole purpose
of this innocuous little picture was to distinguish whites from nonwhites. By keeping
secret the restrictions of the scholarship,
the school has put students, most of whom are
not racists, in the position of unwittingly
endorsing Anna Jennings's racism. Thus, both
the school and the unsuspecting students have
been in collusion with the administrators of
the Anna Todd Jennings trust.

**Conclusion
(based on evi-
dence)**

**Refutation of
opposing argu-
ment**

The problem facing students is how best to   4
deal with the generosity of a racist. A recent
edition of the school paper contained several
letters saying that students should accept Anna
Jennings's scholarship money. One student said,
"If we do not take that money and use our education to topple the barriers of prejudice, we
are giving the money to those who will use the
money in the opposite fashion." This argument,
although attractive, is flawed. If an individual accepts a scholarship with racial restrictions, then he or she is actually endorsing the
principles behind it. If a student does not
want to appear to endorse racism, then he or
she should reject the scholarship, even if this
action causes hardship or gives adversaries a
momentary advantage. To do otherwise is to further the cause of the individual who set up
the scholarship. The best way to register a

protest is to work to change the requirement
for the scholarship and to encourage others not
to apply as long as the racial restrictions
exist.

**Refutation of
opposing argu-
ment**

Another student letter made the point that   5
a number of other restricted scholarships are
available at the school and no one seems to
question them. For example, one is for the
children of veterans, another is for women, and
yet another is earmarked for African-Americans.
Even though these scholarships have restrictions, to say that all restrictions are the
same is to make a hasty generalization. Women,
African-Americans, and the children of veterans
are groups who deserve special treatment. Both
women and African-Americans have been discriminated against for years, and many educational
opportunities have been denied them. Earmarking
scholarships for them is simply a means of
restoring some measure of equality. The children of veterans have been singled out because
their parents have rendered an extraordinary
service to their country. Whites, however, do
not fall into either of these categories.
Special treatment for them is based solely on
race and has nothing to do with any objective
standard of need or merit.

Conclusion

I hope that by refusing to apply for the   6
Anna Todd Jennings scholarship, I have encouraged other students to think about the issues
involved in their own decisions. All of us have

**Restatement of
thesis**

a responsibility to ourselves and to society.
If we truly believe that racism in all its
forms is evil, then we have to make a choice

**Concluding
statement**

between sacrifice and hypocrisy. Faced with
these options, our decision should be clear:
accept the loss of funds as an opportunity to
explore your values and fight for principles in
which you believe; if you do, this opportunity
is worth far more than any scholarship.

Points for Special Attention

GATHERING EVIDENCE.   Because of his involvement with his subject, Matt Daniels was able to provide examples from his own experience to support his points and did not have to do much research. Still, Matt did have to spend a lot of time thinking about ideas and selecting evidence. He had to review the requirements for the scholarship and decide on the arguments he would make. In addition, he reviewed an article that appeared in the school newspaper and the letters students wrote in response to the article. He then chose material that would create interest and add authority to his arguments.

Certainly statistics, studies, and expert testimony, if they exist, would strengthen Matt's argument. But even without such evidence, an argument such as this one, based on strong logic and personal experience, can be quite compelling.

REFUTING OPPOSING ARGUMENTS.   Matt devotes two paragraphs to presenting and refuting arguments made by those who believe qualified students should apply for the scholarship despite its racial restrictions. He begins this section by asking a **rhetorical question**—a question asked not to elicit an answer but to further the argument. He goes on to present what he considers the two best arguments against his thesis—that students should take the money and work to fight racism and that other scholarships at the school have restrictions. Matt counters these arguments by identifying a flaw in the logic of the first argument and by pointing to a fallacy, a hasty generalization, in the second.

AUDIENCE.   Because his essay was written as an editorial for his college newspaper, Matt assumed his audience would be familiar with the issue he was discussing. Letters to the editor of the paper convinced him that his position was unusual, and he decided that his readers, mostly students and instructors, would have to be persuaded that his points were valid. To achieve this end, he was careful to present himself as a reasonable person, to explain issues that he believes are central to his case, and to avoid *ad hominem* attacks. In addition, he made sure to avoid sweeping generalizations and name-calling and to include many details to support his assertions and convince readers that his points are worth considering.

ORGANIZATION.   Matt uses several strategies discussed earlier in the chapter. He begins his essay by introducing the issue he is going to discuss and then states his thesis: "Applying for the Anna Todd Jennings scholarship furthers the racist ideas that were held by its founder."

Because Matt had given a good deal of thought to his subject, he was able to construct two fairly strong arguments to support his position. His first argument is deductive. He begins by stating a premise that he believes is self-evident—that most people think racism should be opposed. The rest of this argument follows a straightforward deductive pattern:

Major premise:	Racism is an evil that should be opposed.
Minor premise:	The Anna Todd Jennings scholarship is racist.
Conclusion:	Therefore, the Anna Todd Jennings scholarship should be opposed.

Matt ends his first argument with a piece of factual evidence that reinforces his conclusion: the successful challenge to the will of financier Stephen Girard, which limited admittance to Girard College in Philadelphia to white male orphans.

Matt's second argument is inductive, asserting that the school has put students in the position of unknowingly supporting racism. The argument begins with Matt's hypothesis and presents the fact that even though the school is aware of the racist restrictions of the scholarship, it has done nothing to make students aware of them. According to Matt, the school's knowledge (and tacit approval) of the situation leads to the conclusion that the school is in collusion with those who manage the scholarship.

In his fourth and fifth paragraphs, Matt refutes two criticisms of his argument. Although his conclusion is rather brief, it does effectively reinforce and support his main idea. Matt ends his essay by recommending a course of action to his fellow students.

Focus on Revision

Matt constructed a solid argument that addresses the central issue very effectively. However, some students on the newspaper's editorial board thought he should add a section giving more information about Anna Todd Jennings and her bequest. These students believed that such information would help them understand the implications of accepting her money. As it now stands, the essay dismisses Anna Todd Jennings as a racist, but biographical material and excerpts from the will—both of which appeared in the school paper—would enable readers to grasp the extent of her prejudice. Matt decided to follow up on this advice and to strengthen his conclusion as well. He thought that including the exact words of Anna Todd Jennings's will would help him to reinforce his points forcefully and memorably.

The essays that follow represent a wide variety of topics. Each, however, presents an argument to support a controversial thesis. In three cases, essays that take opposing stands on the same issue are paired in debates. In an additional debate, four essays on a single topic are included to present a greater variety of viewpoints. As you read each essay, try to identify the strategies that each author uses to convince readers.

THOMAS JEFFERSON

Thomas Jefferson was born in 1743 at Shadwell, in what is now Albemarle County, Virginia. He attended the College of William and Mary and became a lawyer. Jefferson was elected to the House of Burgesses, Virginia's colonial legislature, in 1769 and began a distinguished political career. In 1774 he wrote a daring pamphlet titled *A Summary View of the Rights of British Americans,* in which he denied all British parliamentary authority over America. He was named a delegate to the Second Continental Congress in Philadelphia, and on June 11, 1776, he was elected to join Benjamin Franklin, John Adams, Roger Sherman, and Robert Livingston in drafting a declaration of independence. The draft was written entirely by Jefferson, with suggestions from the other commission members. (Congress amended it to remove a passage containing a strong statement against slavery.) Jefferson also served as governor of Virginia; minister to France; secretary of state in President George Washington's first cabinet; vice president under John Adams; and finally president—the first to be inaugurated in Washington—from 1801 to 1809. During his retirement, Jefferson founded the University of Virginia. He wrote only one book, *Notes on the State of Virginia,* but his published writings and correspondence fill sixty volumes. He died on July 4, 1826. The Declaration of Independence challenges a basic assumption of the age in which it was written—the divine right of kings. To accomplish his ends, Jefferson follows many of the principles of argumentative writing. The Declaration is a model of clarity and precision that attempts to establish and support its thesis by means of irrefutable logic and reason.

The Declaration of Independence

When in the course of human events, it becomes necessary for one people to dissolve the political bonds which have connected them with another, and to assume among the powers of the earth, the separate and equal station to which the Laws of Nature and of Nature's God entitle them, a decent respect to the opinions of mankind requires that they should declare the causes which impel them to the separation.   1

We hold these truths to be self-evident, that all men are created equal, that they are endowed by their Creator with certain unalienable rights, that among these are life, liberty and the pursuit of happiness. That to secure these rights, governments are instituted among men, deriving their just powers from the consent of the governed. That whenever any form of government becomes destructive to these ends, it is the right of the people to alter or to abolish it, and to institute new government, laying its foundation on such principles and organizing its powers in such form, as to them shall seem most likely to effect their safety and happiness. Prudence, indeed, will dictate that governments long established should not be changed for light and transient causes; and accordingly all experi-   2 ence hath shown, that mankind are more disposed to suffer, while evils are sufferable, than to right themselves by abolishing the forms to which they are accustomed. But when a long rain of abuses and usurpations, pursuing invariably the same object, evinces a design to reduce them under absolute despotism, it is their right, it is their duty, to throw off such government, and to provide new guards for their future security. Such has been the patient sufferance of these Colonies; and such is now the necessity which constrains them to alter their former systems of government. This history of the present king of Great Britain is a history of repeated injuries and usurpations, all having in direct object the establishment of an absolute tyranny over these States. To prove this, let facts be submitted to a candid world.

He has refused his assent to laws, the most wholesome and necessary 3 for the public good.

He has forbidden his Governors to pass laws of immediate and press- 4 ing importance, unless suspended in their operation till his assent should be obtained; and when so suspended, he has utterly neglected to attend to them.

He has refused to pass other laws for the accommodation of large dis- 5 tricts of people, unless those people would relinquish the right of representation in the legislature, a right inestimable to them and formidable to tyrants only.

He has called together legislative bodies at places unusual, uncom- 6 fortable, and distant from the depository of their public records, for the sole purpose of fatiguing them into compliance with his measure.

He has dissolved representative houses repeatedly, for opposing with 7 manly firmness his invasions on the rights of people.

He has refused for a long time, after such dissolutions, to cause others 8 to be elected; whereby the legislative powers, incapable of annihilation, have returned to the people at large for their exercise; the State remaining in the meantime exposed to all the dangers of invasion from without and convulsions within.

He has endeavoured to prevent the population of these states; for that 9 purpose obstructing the laws for naturalization of foreigners; refusing to pass others to encourage their migration hither, and raising the conditions of new appropriations of lands.

He has obstructed the administration of justice, by refusing his assent 10 to laws for establishing judiciary powers.

He has made judges dependent on his will alone, for the tenure of 11 their offices, and the amount and payment of their salaries.

He has erected a multitude of new offices, and sent hither swarms of 12 officers to harass our people, and eat out their substance.

He has kept among us, in times of peace, standing armies without the 13 consent of our legislatures.

He has affected to render the military independent of and superior to 14 the civil power.

He has combined with others to subject us to a jurisdiction foreign to   15
our constitution, and unacknowledged by our laws; giving his assent to
their acts of pretended legislation:

For quartering large bodies of troops among us: 16

For protecting them, by a mock trial, from punishment for any mur-   17
ders which they should commit on the inhabitants of these States:

For cutting off our trade with all parts of the world: 18

For imposing taxes on us without our consent: 19

For depriving us in many cases of the benefits of trial by jury: 20

For transporting us beyond seas to be tried for pretended offences: 21

For abolishing the free system of English laws in a neighbouring   22
Province, establishing therein an arbitrary government, and enlarging its
boundaries so as to render it at once an example and fit instrument for introducing the same absolute rule into these Colonies:

For taking away our Charters, abolishing our most valuable laws,   23
and altering fundamentally the forms of our governments:

For suspending our own legislatures, and declaring themselves in-   24
vested with power to legislate for us in all cases whatsoever.

He had abdicated government here, by declaring us out of his protec-   25
tion and waging war against us.

He has plundered our seas, ravaged our coasts, burnt our towns, and   26
destroyed the lives of our people.

He is at this time transporting large armies of foreign mercenaries to   27
complete the works of death, desolation and tyranny, already begun with
circumstances of cruelty and perfidy scarcely paralleled in the most bar-
barous ages, and totally unworthy the head of a civilized nation.

He has constrained our fellow citizens taken captive on the high seas   28
to bear arms against their country, to become the executioners of their
friends and brethren, or to fall themselves by their hands.

He has excited domestic insurrections amongst us, and has endeav-   29
oured to bring on the inhabitants of our frontiers, the merciless Indian
savages, whose known rule of warfare, is an undistinguished destruction
of all ages, sexes, and conditions.

In every stage of these oppressions we have petitioned for redress in   30
the most humble terms: our repeated petitions have been answered only
by repeated injury. A prince whose character is thus marked by every act
which may define a tyrant is unfit to be the ruler of a free people.

Nor have we been wanting in attention to our British brethren. We   31
have warned them from time to time of attempts by their legislature to
extend an unwarrantable jurisdiction over us. We have reminded them of
the circumstances of our emigration and settlement here. We have appealed to their native justice and magnanimity, and we have conjured
them by the ties of our common kindred to disavow these usurpations,
which would inevitably interrupt our connections and correspondence.
They too have been deaf to the voice of justice and of consanguinity. We
must, therefore, acquiesce in the necessity, which denounces our separa-

tion, and hold them, as we hold the rest of mankind, enemies in war, in peace friends.

We, therefore, the Representatives of the United States of America, in   32
General Congress assembled, appealing to the Supreme Judge of the world for the rectitude of our intentions, do, in the name, and by authority of the good people of these Colonies, solemnly publish and declare, That these United Colonies are, and of right ought to be, Free and Independent States; that they are absolved from all allegiance to the British Crown, and that all political connection between them and the state of Great Britain, is and ought to be totally dissolved; and that as Free and Independent States, they have full power to levy war, conclude peace, contract alliances, establish commerce, and to do all other acts and things which Independent States may of right do. And for the support of this declaration, with a firm reliance on the protection of Divine Providence, we mutually pledge to each other our lives, our fortunes, and our sacred honor.

•   •   •

COMPREHENSION

1. What "truths" does Jefferson assert are "self-evident"?

2. What does Jefferson say is the source from which governments derive their powers?

3. What reasons does Jefferson give to support his premise that the United States should break away from Great Britain?

4. What conclusions about the British crown does Jefferson draw from the evidence he presents?

PURPOSE AND AUDIENCE

1. What is the major premise of Jefferson's argument? Should Jefferson have done more to establish the truth of this premise?

2. The Declaration of Independence was written during a period now referred to as the Age of Reason. In what ways has Jefferson tried to make his document appear reasonable?

3. For what audience (or audiences) is the document intended? Which groups of readers would have been most likely to accept it? Explain.

4. How effectively does Jefferson anticipate and refute the opposition?

5. In paragraph 31, following the list of grievances, why does Jefferson address his "British brethren"?

6. At what point does Jefferson state his thesis? Why does he state it where he does?

STYLE AND STRUCTURE

1. Does the Declaration of Independence rely primarily on inductive or deductive reasoning? Identify examples of each.

2. What techniques does Jefferson use to create smooth and logical transitions from one paragraph to another?

3. Why does Jefferson list all of his twenty-eight grievances? Why doesn't he just summarize them or mention a few representative grievances?

4. Jefferson begins the last paragraph of the Declaration of Independence with "We, therefore." How effective is this conclusion? Explain.

VOCABULARY PROJECTS

1. Define each of the following words as it is used in this selection.

   station (1)   evinces (2)   tenure (11)
   impel (1)   despotism (2)   jurisdiction (15)
   self-evident (2)   sufferance (2)   arbitrary (22)
   endowed (2)   candid (2)   insurrections (29)
   deriving (2)   depository (6)   disavow (31)
   prudence (2)   dissolutions (8)   consanguinity (31)
   transient (2)   annihilation (8)   rectitude (32)
   usurpations (2)   appropriations (9)   levy (32)

2. Underline ten words that have negative connotations. How does Jefferson use these words to help him make his point? Do you think words with more neutral connotations would strengthen or weaken his case? Why?

3. What words does Jefferson use that are rarely used today? Would the Declaration of Independence be more meaningful to today's readers if it were updated, with more familiar words substituted? To help you formulate your response, try rewriting a paragraph or two, and assess your updated version.

JOURNAL ENTRY

Do you think Jefferson is being fair to the king? Do you think he should be?

WRITING WORKSHOP

1. Following Jefferson's example, write a declaration of independence from your school, job, family, or any other institution with which you are associated.

2. Write an essay in which you state a grievance you share with other members of some group, and then argue for the best way to eliminate the grievance.

3. In an argumentative essay written from the point of view of King George III, try to convince the colonists that they should not break away from Great Britain. If you can, refute some of the points Jefferson lists in the Declaration.

COMBINING THE PATTERNS

The middle section of the Declaration of Independence is developed by means of **exemplification;** it presents a series of examples to support Jefferson's assertion that the colonists have experienced "repeated injuries and usurpations" (2). Are these examples relevant? Representative? Sufficient? Effective? What other pattern of development could Jefferson have used to support his assertion?

THEMATIC CONNECTIONS

- "The 'Black Table' Is Still There" (page 284)
- "Grant and Lee: A Study in Contrasts" (page 330)
- "Letter from Birmingham Jail" (page 513)
- "What, Then, Is to Be Done?" (page 530)

MARTIN LUTHER KING JR.

Martin Luther King Jr. was born in 1929 in Atlanta, Georgia, and was assassinated in 1968 in Memphis, Tennessee. He graduated from Morehouse College in 1948 and received his B.D. from the Crozer Theological Seminary in 1951. After receiving his doctorate in systematic theology from Boston University in 1955, King became pastor of the Dexter Avenue Baptist Church in Montgomery, Alabama. He led a 382-day bus boycott in Montgomery that led to the 1956 Supreme Court decision declaring the Alabama law requiring racial segregation on buses unconstitutional. In 1957, King was elected president of the newly formed Southern Christian Leadership Conference. During this time he developed a philosophy of nonviolent protest that characterized his actions throughout the rest of his career. In 1963, King launched a campaign against segregation in Birmingham, Alabama, that met fierce opposition from police as well as from white moderates, who saw him as dangerous. He was also a leader of the March on Washington in August of 1963, where he delivered his famous "I Have a Dream" speech. King was awarded the Nobel Peace Prize in 1964, becoming the youngest person ever to win the prize. His books include *Stride Towards Freedom* (1958), *Why We Can't Wait* (1964), and *Where Do We Go From Here: Chaos or Community?* (1967). His shorter writings are collected in *A Testament of Hope* (1968), edited by James M. Washington, and *The Words of Martin Luther King* (1983), selected by Coretta Scott King. During the Birmingham demonstrations, King was arrested and jailed for eight days. He wrote his "Letter from Birmingham Jail" to white clergymen to explain his actions and answer those who urged him to call off the demonstrations. Having much in common with the Declaration of Independence, "Letter from Birmingham Jail" is a well-reasoned defense of demonstrations and civil disobedience.

Letter from Birmingham Jail

April 16, 1963

My Dear Fellow Clergymen:

While confined here in the Birmingham city jail, I came across your recent statement calling my present activities "unwise and untimely." Seldom do I pause to answer criticism of my work and ideas. If I sought to answer all the criticisms that cross my desk, my secretaries would have little time for anything other than such correspondence in the course of the day, and I would have no time for constructive work. But since I feel that you are men of genuine good will and that your criticisms are sincerely set forth, I want to try to answer your statement in what I hope will be patient and reasonable terms.

I think I should indicate why I am here in Birmingham, since you have been influenced by the view which argues against "outsiders coming in." I have the honor of serving as president of the Southern Christian Leadership Conference, an organization operating in every southern state, with headquarters in Atlanta, Georgia. We have some eighty-five affiliated organizations across the South, and one of them is the Alabama Christian Movement for Human Rights. Frequently we share staff, educational, and financial resources with our affiliates. Several months ago the affiliate here in Birmingham asked us to be on call to engage in a nonviolent direct-action program if such were deemed necessary. We readily consented, and when the hour came we lived up to our promise. So I, along with several members of my staff, am here because I was invited here. I am here because I have organizational ties here.

But more basically, I am in Birmingham because injustice is here. Just   3 as the prophets of the eighth century B.C. left their villages and carried their "thus saith the Lord" far beyond the boundaries of their home towns, and just as the Apostle Paul left his village of Tarsus and carried the gospel of Jesus Christ to the far corners of the Greco-Roman world, so am I compelled to carry the gospel of freedom beyond my own home town. Like Paul, I must constantly respond to the Macedonian call for aid.

Moreover, I am cognizant of the interrelatedness of all communities   4 and states. I cannot sit idly by in Atlanta and not be concerned about what happens in Birmingham. Injustice anywhere is a threat to justice everywhere. We are caught in an inescapable network of mutuality, tied in a single garment of destiny. Whatever affects one directly, affects all indirectly. Never again can we afford to live with the narrow, provincial, "outside agitator" idea. Anyone who lives inside the United States can never be considered an outsider anywhere within its bounds.

You deplore the demonstrations taking place in Birmingham. But   5 your statement, I am sorry to say, fails to express a similar concern for the conditions that brought about the demonstrations. I am sure that none of you would want to rest content with the superficial kind of social analysis that deals merely with effects and does not grapple with underlying causes. It is unfortunate that demonstrations are taking place in Birmingham, but it is even more unfortunate that the city's white power structure left the Negro community with no alternative.

In any nonviolent campaign there are four basic steps: collection of   6 the facts to determine whether injustices exist; negotiation; self-purification; and direct action. We have gone through all these steps in Birmingham. There can be no gainsaying the fact that racial injustice engulfs this community. Birmingham is probably the most thoroughly segregated city in the United States. Its ugly record of brutality is widely known. Negroes have experienced grossly unjust treatment in courts. There have been more unsolved bombings of Negro homes and churches in Birmingham than in any other city in the nation. These are the hard, brutal facts of the case. On the basis of these conditions, Negro leaders sought to negotiate with the city fathers. But the latter consistently refused to engage in good-faith negotiation.

Then, last September, came the opportunity to talk with leaders of   7
Birmingham's economic community. In the course of the negotiations,
certain promises were made by the merchants—for example, to remove
the stores' humiliating racial signs. On the basis of these promises, the
Reverend Fred Shuttlesworth and the leaders of the Alabama Christian
Movement for Human Rights agreed to a moratorium on all demonstrations. As the weeks and months went by, we realized that we were the
victims of a broken promise. A few signs, briefly removed, returned; the
others remained.

As in so many past experiences, our hopes had been blasted, and the   8
shadow of deep disappointment settled upon us. We had no alternative
except to prepare for direct action, whereby we would present our very
bodies as means of laying our case before the conscience of the local and
the national community. Mindful of the difficulties involved, we decided
to undertake a process of self-purification. We began a series of workshops
on nonviolence, and we repeatedly asked ourselves: "Are you able to accept blows without retaliating?" "Are you able to endure the ordeal of
jail?" We decided to schedule our direct-action program for the Easter season, realizing that except for Christmas, this is the main shopping period
of the year. Knowing that a strong economic-withdrawal program would
be the by-product of direct action, we felt that this would be the best time
to bring pressure to bear on the merchants for the needed change.

Then it occurred to us that Birmingham's mayoral election was com-   9
ing up in March, and we speedily decided to postpone action until after
election day. When we discovered that the Commissioner of Public Safety,
Eugene "Bull" Connor, had piled up enough votes to be in the run-off, we
decided again to postpone action until the day after the run-off so that the
demonstrations could not be used to cloud the issues. Like many others,
we waited to see Mr. Connor defeated, and to this end we endured postponement after postponement. Having aided in this community need, we
felt that our direct-action program could be delayed no longer.

You may well ask, "Why direct action? Why sit-ins, marches, and so   10
forth? Isn't negotiation a better path?" You are quite right in calling for
negotiation. Indeed, this is the very purpose of direct action. Nonviolent
direct action seeks to create such a crisis and foster such a tension that a
community which has constantly refused to negotiate is forced to confront the issue. It seeks so to dramatize the issue that it can no longer be
ignored. My citing the creation of tension as part of the work of the non-
violent-resistor may sound rather shocking. But I must confess that I am
not afraid of the word "tension." I have earnestly opposed violent tension, but there is a type of constructive, nonviolent tension which is necessary for growth. Just as Socrates felt that it was necessary to create a
tension in the mind so that individuals could rise from the bondage of
myths and half-truths to the unfettered realm of creative analysis and
objective appraisal, so must we see the need for nonviolent gadflies to
create the kind of tension in society that will help men rise from the dark

depths of prejudice and racism to the majestic heights of understanding and brotherhood.

The purpose of our direct-action program is to create a situation so   11
crisis-packed that it will inevitably open the door to negotiation. I therefore concur with you in your call for negotiation. Too long has our beloved Southland been bogged down in a tragic effort to live in monologue rather than dialogue.

One of the basic points in your statement is that the action that I and   12
my associates have taken in Birmingham is untimely. Some have asked: "Why didn't you give the new city administration time to act?" The only answer that I can give to this query is that the new Birmingham administration must be prodded about as much as the outgoing one, before it will act. We are sadly mistaken if we feel that the election of Albert Boutwell as mayor will bring the millennium to Birmingham. While Mr. Boutwell is a much more gentle person than Mr. Connor, they are both segregationists, dedicated to maintenance of the status quo. I have hoped that Mr. Boutwell will be reasonable enough to see the futility of massive resistance to desegregation. But he will not see this without pressure from devotees of civil rights. My friends, I must say to you that we have not made a single gain in civil rights without determined legal and nonviolent pressure. Lamentably, it is an historical fact that privileged groups seldom give up their privileges voluntarily. Individuals may see the moral light and voluntarily give up their unjust posture; but, as Reinhold Niebuhr* has reminded us, groups tend to be more immoral than individuals.

We know through painful experience that freedom is never voluntar-   13
ily given by the oppressor; it must be demanded by the oppressed. Frankly, I have yet to engage in a direct-action campaign that was "well timed" in the view of those who have not suffered unduly from the disease of segregation. For years now I have heard the word "Wait!" It rings in the ear of every Negro with piercing familiarity. This "Wait" has almost always meant "Never." We must come to see, with one of our distinguished jurists, that "justice too long delayed is justice denied."

We have waited for more than 340 years for our constitutional and   14
God-given rights. The nations of Asia and Africa are moving with jetlike speed toward gaining political independence, but we still creep at horse-and-buggy pace toward gaining a cup of coffee at a lunch counter. Perhaps it is easy for those who have never felt the stinging darts of segregation to say, "Wait." But when you have seen vicious mobs lynch your mothers and fathers at will and drown your sisters and brothers at whim; when you have seen hate-filled policemen curse, kick, and even kill your black brothers and sisters; when you see the vast majority of your twenty million Negro brothers smothering in an airtight cage of poverty in the midst of an affluent society; when you suddenly find your tongue twisted

---

*Eds. note—American religious and social thinker (1892–1971).

and your speech stammering as you seek to explain to your six-year-old daughter why she can't go to the public amusement park that has just been advertised on television, and see tears welling up in her eyes when she is told that Funtown is closed to colored children, and see ominous clouds of inferiority beginning to form in her little mental sky, and see her beginning to distort her personality by developing an unconscious bitterness toward white people; when you have to concoct an answer for a five-year-old son who is asking, "Daddy, why do white people treat colored people so mean?"; when you take a cross-country drive and find it necessary to sleep night after night in the uncomfortable corners of your automobile because no motel will accept you; when you are humiliated day in and day out by nagging signs reading "white" and "colored"' when your first name becomes "nigger," your middle name becomes "boy" (however old you are) and your last name becomes "John," and your wife and mother are never given the respected title "Mrs."; when you are harried by day and haunted at night by the fact that you are a Negro, living constantly at tiptoe stance, never quite knowing what to expect next, and are plagued with inner fears and outer resentments; when you are forever fighting a degenerating sense of "nobodiness"—then you will understand why we find it difficult to wait. There comes a time when the cup of endurance runs over, and men are no longer willing to be plunged into the abyss of despair. I hope, sirs, you can understand our legitimate and unavoidable impatience.

You express a great deal of anxiety over our willingness to break   15 laws. This is certainly a legitimate concern. Since we so diligently urge people to obey the Supreme Court's decision of 1954 outlawing segregation in the public schools, at first glance it may seem rather paradoxical for us consciously to break laws. One may well ask: "How can you advocate breaking some laws and obeying others?" The answer lies in the fact that there are two types of laws: just and unjust. I would be the first to advocate obeying just laws. One has not only a legal but a moral responsibility to obey just laws. Conversely, one has a moral responsibility to disobey unjust laws. I would agree with St. Augustine that "an unjust law is no law at all."

Now, what is the difference between the two? How does one deter-   16 mine whether a law is just or unjust? A just law is a man-made code that squares with the moral law or the law of God. An unjust law is a code that is out of harmony with the moral law. To put it in the terms of St. Thomas Aquinas:* An unjust law is a human law that is not rooted in eternal law and natural law. Any law that uplifts human personality is just. Any law that degrades human personality is unjust. All segregation statutes are unjust because segregation distorts the soul and damages the personality. It gives the segregator a false sense of superiority and the segregated a

---

*EDS. NOTE—Italian philosopher and theologian (1225–1274).

false sense of inferiority. Segregation, to use the terminology of the Jewish philosopher Martin Buber, substitutes an "I-it" relationship for an "I-thou" relationship and ends up relegating persons to the status of things. Hence segregation is not only politically, economically, and sociologically unsound, it is morally wrong and sinful. Paul Tillich* has said that sin is separation. Is not segregation an existential expression of man's tragic separation, his awful estrangement, his terrible sinfulness? Thus it is that I can urge men to obey the 1954 decision of the Supreme Court, for it is morally right; and I can urge them to disobey segregation ordinances, for they are morally wrong.

Let us consider a more concrete example of just and unjust laws. An 17
unjust law is a code that a numerical or power majority group compels a minority group to obey but does not make binding on itself. This is *difference* made legal. By the same token, a just law is a code that a majority compels a minority to follow and that it is willing to follow itself. This is *sameness* made legal.

Let me give another explanation. A law is unjust if it is inflicted on a 18
minority that, as a result of being denied the right to vote, had no part in enacting or devising the law. Who can say that the legislature of Alabama which set up that state's segregation laws was democratically elected? Throughout Alabama all sorts of devious methods are used to prevent Negroes from becoming registered voters, and there are some counties in which, even though Negroes constitute a majority of the population, not a single Negro is registered. Can any law enacted under such circumstances be considered democratically structured?

Sometimes a law is just on its face and unjust in its application. For 19
instance, I have been arrested on a charge of parading without a permit. Now, there is nothing wrong in having an ordinance which requires a permit for a parade. But such an ordinance becomes unjust when it is used to maintain segregation and to deny citizens the First-Amendment privilege of peaceful assembly and protest.

I hope you are able to see the distinction I am trying to point out. In 20
no sense do I advocate evading or defying the law, as would the rabid segregationist. That would lead to anarchy. One who breaks an unjust law must do so openly, lovingly, and with a willingness to accept the penalty. I submit that an individual who breaks a law that conscience tells him is unjust, and who willingly accepts the penalty of imprisonment in order to arouse the conscience of the community over its injustice, is in reality expressing the highest respect for law.

Of course, there is nothing new about this kind of civil disobedience. 21
It was evidenced sublimely in the refusal of Shadrach, Meshach, and Abednego to obey the laws of Nebuchadnezzar, on the ground that a higher moral law was at stake. It was practiced superbly by the early

---

*Eds. note—American philosopher and theologian (1886–1965).

Christians, who were willing to face hungry lions and the excruciating pain of chopping blocks rather than submit to certain unjust laws of the Roman Empire. To a degree, academic freedom is a reality today because Socrates practiced civil disobedience. In our own nation, the Boston Tea Party represented a massive act of civil disobedience.

We should never forget that everything Adolph Hitler did in   22
Germany was "legal" and everything the Hungarian freedom fighters did in Hungary was "illegal." It was "illegal" to aid and comfort a Jew in Hitler's Germany. Even so, I am sure that, had I lived in Germany at the time, I would have aided and comforted my Jewish brothers. If today I lived in a Communist country where certain principles dear to the Christian faith are suppressed, I would openly advocate disobeying that country's anti-religious laws.

I must make two honest confessions to you, my Christian and Jewish   23
brothers. First, I must confess that over the past few years I have been gravely disappointed with the white moderate. I have almost reached the regrettable conclusion that the Negro's great stumbling block in his stride toward freedom is not the White Citizens Counciler or the Ku Klux Klanner, but the white moderate, who is more devoted to "order" than to justice; who prefers a negative peace which is the absence of tension to a positive peace which is the presence of justice; who constantly says, "I agree with you in the goal you seek, but I cannot agree with your methods of direct action"; who paternalistically believes he can set the timetable for another man's freedom; who lives by a mythical concept of time and who constantly advised the Negro to wait for a "more convenient season." Shallow understanding from people of good will is more frustrating than absolute misunderstanding from people of ill will. Lukewarm acceptance is much more bewildering than outright rejection.

I had hoped that the white moderate would understand that law and   24
order exist for the purpose of establishing justice and that when they fail in this purpose they become the dangerously structured dams that block the flow of social progress. I had hoped that the white moderate would understand that the present tension in the South is a necessary phase of the transition from an obnoxious negative peace, in which the Negro passively accepted his unjust plight, to a substantive and positive peace, in which all men will respect the dignity and worth of human personality. Actually, we who engage in nonviolent direct action are not the creators of tension. We merely bring to the surface the hidden tension that is already alive. We bring it out in the open, where it can be seen and dealt with. Like a boil that can never be cured so long as it is covered up but must be opened with all its ugliness to the natural medicines of air and light, injustice must be exposed, with all the tension its exposure creates, to the light of human conscience and the air of national opinion, before it can be cured.

In your statement you assert that our actions, even though peaceful,   25
must be condemned because they precipitate violence. But is this a logical

assertion? Isn't this like condemning a robbed man because his posses-
sion of money precipitated the evil act of robbery? Isn't this like condemning Socrates because his unswerving commitment to truth and his
philosophical inquiries precipitated the act by the misguided populace in
which they made him drink hemlock? Isn't this like condemning Jesus
because his unique God-consciousness and never-ceasing devotion to
God's will precipitated the evil act of crucifixion? We must come to see
that, as the federal courts have consistently affirmed, it is wrong to urge
an individual to cease his efforts to gain his basic constitutional rights because the quest may precipitate violence. Society must protect the robbed
and punish the robber.

I had also hoped that the white moderate would reject the myth con-   26
cerning time in relation to the struggle for freedom. I have just received a
letter from a white brother in Texas. He writes: "All Christians know that
the colored people will receive equal rights eventually, but it is possible
that you are in too great a religious hurry. It has taken Christianity almost
two thousand years to accomplish what it has. The teachings of Christ
take time to come to earth." Such an attitude stems from a tragic misconception of time, from the strangely irrational notion that there is something in the very flow of time that will inevitably cure all ills. Actually,
time itself is neutral; it can be used either destructively or constructively.
More and more I feel that the people of ill will have used time much more
effectively than have the people of good will. We will have to repent in
this generation not merely for the hateful words and actions of the bad
people, but for the appalling silence of the good people. Human progress
never rolls in on wheels of inevitability; it comes through the tireless efforts of men willing to be co-workers with God, and without his hard
work, time itself becomes an ally of the forces of social stagnation. We
must use time creatively, in the knowledge that the time is always ripe to
do right. Now is the time to make real the promise of democracy and
transform our pending national elegy into a creative psalm of brotherhood. Now is the time to lift our national policy from the quicksand of
racial injustice to the solid rock of human dignity.

You speak of our activity in Birmingham as extreme. At first I was   27
rather disappointed that fellow clergymen would see my nonviolent efforts as those of an extremist. I began thinking about the fact that I stand
in the middle of two opposing forces in the Negro community. One is a
force of complacency, made up in part of Negroes who, as a result of long
years of oppression, are so drained of self-respect and a sense of "some-
bodiness" that they have adjusted to segregation; and in part of a few
middle-class Negroes who, because of a degree of academic and economic security and because in some ways they profit by segregation,
have become insensitive to the problems of the masses. The other force is
one of bitterness and hatred, and it comes perilously close to advocating
violence. It is expressed in the various black nationalist groups that are
springing up across the nation, the largest and best-known being Elijah

Muhammad's Muslim movement. Nourished by the Negro's frustration over the continued existence of racial discrimination, this movement is made up of people who have lost faith in America, who have absolutely repudiated Christianity, and who have concluded that the white man is an incorrigible "devil."

I have tried to stand between these two forces, saying that we need 28 emulate neither the "do-nothingism" of the complacent nor the hatred and despair of the black nationalist. For there is the more excellent way of love and nonviolent protest. I am grateful to God that, through the influence of the Negro church, the way of nonviolence became an integral part of our struggle.

If this philosophy had not emerged, by now many streets of the South 29 would, I am convinced, be flowing with blood. And I am further convinced that if our white brothers dismiss as "rabble-rousers" and "outside agitators" those of us who employ nonviolent direct action, and if they refuse to support our nonviolent efforts, millions of Negroes will, out of frustration and despair, seek solace and security in black-nationalist ideologies—a development that would inevitably lead to a frightening racial nightmare.

Oppressed people cannot remain oppressed forever. The yearning for 30 freedom eventually manifests itself, and that is what has happened to the American Negro. Something within has reminded him of his birthright of freedom, and something without has reminded him that it can be gained. Consciously or unconsciously, he has been caught up by the *Zeitgeist,* and with his black brothers of Africa and his brown and yellow brothers of Asia, South America, and the Caribbean, the Untied States Negro is moving with a sense of great urgency toward the promised land of racial justice. If one recognizes this vital urge that has engulfed the Negro community, one should readily understand why public demonstrations are taking place. The Negro has many pent-up resentments and latent frustrations, and he must release them. So let him march; let him make prayer pilgrimages to the city hall; let him go on freedom rides—and try to understand why he must do so. If his repressed emotions are not released in nonviolent ways, they will seek expression through violence; this is not a threat but a fact of history. So I have not said to my people, "Get rid of your discontent." Rather, I have tried to say that this normal and healthy discontent can be channeled into the creative outlet of nonviolent direct action. And now this approach is being termed extremist.

But though I was initially disappointed at being categorized as an ex- 31 tremist, as I continued to think about the matter I gradually gained a measure of satisfaction from the label. Was not Jesus an extremist for love: "Love your enemies, bless them that curse you, do good to them that hate you, and pray for them which despitefully use you, and persecute you." Was not Amos an extremist for justice: "let justice roll down like waters and righteousness like an everflowing stream." Was not Paul an extremist for the Christian gospel: "I bear in my body the marks of the Lord Jesus."

Was not Martin Luther an extremist: "Here I stand; I cannot do otherwise, so help me God." And John Bunyan: "I will stay in jail to the end of my days before I make a butchery of my conscience." And Abraham Lincoln: "This nation cannot survive half slave and half free." And Thomas Jefferson: "We hold these truths to be self-evident, that all men are created equal. . . . " So the question is not whether we will be extremists, but what kind of extremists we will be. Will we be extremists for hate or for love? Will we be extremists for the preservation of injustice or for the extension of justice? In that dramatic scene of Calvary's hill three men were crucified. We must never forget that all three were crucified for the same crime—the crime of extremism. Two were extremists for immorality, and thus fell below their environment. The other, Jesus Christ, was an extremist for love, truth, and goodness, and thereby rose above his environment. Perhaps the South, the nation, and the world are in dire need of creative extremists.

I hoped that the white moderate would see this need. Perhaps I was 32 too optimistic; perhaps I expected too much. I suppose I should have realized that few members of the oppressor race can understand the deep groans and passionate yearnings of the oppressed race, and still fewer have the vision to see that injustice must be rooted out by strong, persistent, and determined action. I am thankful, however, that some of our white brothers in the South have grasped the meaning of this social revolution and committed themselves to it. They are still all too few in quantity, but they are big in quality. Some—such as Ralph McGill, Lillian Smith, Harry Golden, James McBride Dabbs, Ann Braden, and Sarah Patton Boyle—have written about our struggle in eloquent and prophetic terms. Others have marched with us down nameless streets of the South. They have languished in filthy, roach-infested jails, suffering the abuse and brutality of policemen who view them as "dirty nigger-lovers." Unlike so many of their moderate brothers and sisters, they have recognized the urgency of the movement and sensed the need for powerful "action" antidotes to combat the disease of segregation.

Let me take note of my other major disappointment. I have been so 33 greatly disappointed with the white church and its leadership. Of course, there are some notable exceptions. I am not unmindful of the fact that each of you has taken some significant stands on this issue. I commend you, Reverend Stallings, for your Christian stand on this past Sunday, in welcoming Negroes to your worship service on a nonsegregated basis. I commend the Catholic leaders of this state for integrating Spring Hill College several years ago.

But despite these notable exceptions, I must honestly reiterate that I 34 have been disappointed with the church. I do not say this as one of those negative critics who can always find something wrong with the church. I say this as a minister of the gospel, who loves the church; who was nurtured in its bosom; who has been sustained by its spiritual blessings and who will remain true to it as long as the cord of life shall lengthen.

When I was suddenly catapulted into the leadership of the bus 35 protest in Montgomery, Alabama, a few years ago, I felt we would be supported by the white church. I felt that the white ministers, priests, and rabbis of the South would be among our strongest allies. Instead, some have been outright opponents, refusing to understand the freedom movement and misrepresenting its leaders; all too many others have been more cautious than courageous and have remained silent behind the anesthetizing security of stained-glass windows.

In spite of my shattered dreams, I came to Birmingham with the hope 36 that the white religious leadership of this community would see the justice of our cause and, with deep moral concern, would serve as the channel through which our just grievances could reach the power structure. I had hoped that each of you would understand. But again I have been disappointed.

There was a time when the church was very powerful—in the time 37 when the early Christians rejoiced at being deemed worthy to suffer for what they believed. In those days the church was not merely a thermometer that recorded the ideas and principles of popular opinion; it was a thermostat that transformed the mores of society. Whenever the early Christians entered a town, the people in power became disturbed and immediately sought to convict the Christians for being "disturbers of the peace" and "outside agitators." But the Christians pressed on, in the conviction that they were "a colony of heaven," called to obey God rather than man. Small in number, they were big in commitment. They were too God-intoxicated to be "astronomically intimidated." By their effort and example they brought an end to such ancient evils as infanticide and gladiatorial contests.

Things are different now. So often the contemporary church is a 38 weak, ineffectual voice with an uncertain sound. So often it is an archdefender of the status quo. Far from being disturbed by the presence of the church, the power structure of the average community is consoled by the church's silent—and often even vocal—sanction of things as they are.

But the judgment of God is upon the church as never before. If 39 today's church does not recapture the sacrificial spirit of the early church, it will lose its authenticity, forfeit the loyalty of millions, and be dismissed as an irrelevant social club with no meaning for the twentieth century. Every day I meet young people whose disappointment with the church has turned into outright disgust.

Perhaps I have once again been too optimistic. Is organized religion 40 too inextricably bound to the status quo to save our nation and the world? Perhaps I must turn my faith to the inner spiritual church, the church within the church, as the true *ekklesia** and the hope of the world. But again I am thankful to God that some noble souls from the ranks of

---

*Eds. note—Greek word for the early Christian church.

organized religion have broken loose from the paralyzing chains of conformity and joined us as active partners in the struggle for freedom. They have left their secure congregations and walked the streets of Albany, Georgia, with us. They have gone down the highways of the South on torturous rides for freedom. Yes, they have gone to jail with us. Some have been dismissed from their churches, have lost the support of their bishops and fellow ministers. But they have acted in the faith that right defeated is stronger than evil triumphant. Their witness has been the spiritual salt that has preserved the true meaning of the gospel in these troubled times. They have carved a tunnel of hope through the dark mountain of disappointment.

I hope the church as a whole will meet the challenge of this decisive 41 hour. But even if the church does not come to the aid of justice, I have no despair about the future. I have no fear about the outcome of our struggle in Birmingham, even if our motives are at present misunderstood. We will reach the goal of freedom in Birmingham and all over the nation, because the goal of America is freedom. Abused and scorned though we may be, our destiny is tied up with America's destiny. Before the pilgrims landed at Plymouth, we were here. Before the pen of Jefferson etched the majestic words of the Declaration of Independence across the pages of history, we were here. For more than two centuries our forebears labored in this country without wages; they made cotton king; they built the homes of their masters while suffering gross injustice and shameful humiliation—and yet out of a bottomless vitality they continued to thrive and develop. If the inexpressible cruelties of slavery could not stop us, the opposition we now face will surely fail. We will win our freedom because the sacred heritage of our nation and the eternal will of God are embodied in our echoing demands.

Before closing I feel impelled to mention one other point in your 42 statement that has troubled me profoundly. You warmly commended the Birmingham police for keeping "order" and "preventing violence." I doubt that you would have so warmly commended the police force if you had seen its dogs sinking their teeth into unarmed, nonviolent Negroes. I doubt that you would so quickly commend the policemen if you were to observe their ugly and inhumane treatment of Negroes here in the city jail; if you were to watch them push and curse old Negro women and young Negro girls; if you were to see them slap and kick old Negro men and young boys; if you were to observe them, as they did on two occasions, refuse to give us food because we wanted to sing our grace together. I cannot join you in your praise of the Birmingham police department.

It is true that the police have exercised a degree of discipline in han- 43 dling the demonstrators. In this sense they have conducted themselves rather "nonviolently" in public. But for what purpose? To preserve the vile system of segregation. Over the past few years I have consistently preached that nonviolence demands that the means we use must be as pure as the ends we seek. I have tried to make clear that it is wrong to use immoral means to attain moral ends. But now I must affirm that it is just as wrong, or perhaps even more so, to use moral means to preserve immoral ends. Perhaps Mr. Connor and his policemen have been rather nonviolent in public, as was Chief Pritchett in Albany, Georgia, but they have used the moral means of nonviolence to maintain the immoral end of racial injustice. As T. S. Eliot has said, "The last temptation is the greatest treason: To do the right deed for the wrong reason."

I wish you had commended the Negro sit-inners and demonstrators 44
of Birmingham for their sublime courage, their willingness to suffer, and their amazing discipline in the midst of great provocation. One day the South will recognize its real heroes. They will be the James Merediths,* with the noble sense of purpose that enables them to face jeering and hostile mobs, and with the agonizing loneliness that characterizes the life of the pioneer. They will be old, oppressed, battered Negro women, symbolized in a seventy-two-year old woman in Montgomery, Alabama, who rose up with a sense of dignity and with her people decided not to ride segregated buses, and who responded with ungrammatical profundity to one who inquired about her weariness: "My feets is tired, but my soul is at rest." They will be the young high school and college students, the young ministers of the gospel and a host of their elders, courageously and nonviolently sitting in at lunch counters and willingly going to jail for conscience' sake. One day the South will know that when these disinherited children of God sat down at lunch counters, they were in reality standing up for what is best in the American dream and for the most sacred values in our Judaeo-Christian heritage, thereby bringing our nation back to those great wells of democracy which were dug deeply by the founding fathers in their formulation of the Constitution and the Declaration of Independence.

Never before have I written so long a letter. I'm afraid it is much too 45
long to take your precious time. I can assure that it would have been much shorter if I had been writing from a comfortable desk, but what else can one do when he is alone in a narrow jail cell, other than write long letters, think long thoughts, and pray long prayers?

If I have said anything in this letter that overstates the truth and indi- 46
cates an unreasonable impatience, I beg you to forgive me. If I have said anything that understates the truth and indicates my having a patience that allows me to settle for anything less than brotherhood, I beg God to forgive me.

I hope this letter finds you strong in the faith. I also hope that circum- 47
stances will soon make it possible for me to meet each of you, not as an integrationist or a civil-rights leader but as a fellow clergyman and a Christian brother. Let us all hope that the dark clouds of racial prejudice

---

*EDS. NOTE—James Meredith was the first African-American to enroll at the University of Mississippi.

will soon pass away and the deep fog of misunderstanding will be lifted from our fear-drenched communities, and in some not too distant tomorrow the radiant stars of love and brotherhood will shine over our great nation with all their scintillating beauty.

Yours for the cause of Peace and Brotherhood,
Martin Luther King Jr.

•   •   •

COMPREHENSION

1. King says he seldom answers criticism. Why, then, does he decide to do so in this instance?

2. Why do the other clergymen consider King's activities to be "unwise and untimely" (1)?

3. What reasons does King give for the demonstrations? Why does he think it is too late for negotiations?

4. What does King say *wait* means to black people?

5. What are the two types of laws King defines? What is the difference between the two?

6. What does King find illogical about the claim that the actions of his followers precipitate violence?

7. Why is King disappointed in the white church?

PURPOSE AND AUDIENCE

1. Why, in the first paragraph, does King establish his setting (the Birmingham city jail) and define his intended audience?

2. Why does King begin his letter with a reference to his audience as "men of genuine good will" (1)? Is this phrase ironic in light of his later criticism of them? Explain.

3. What indication is there that King is writing his letter to an audience other than his fellow clergymen?

4. What is the thesis of this letter? Is it stated or implied?

STYLE AND STRUCTURE

1. Where does King seek to establish that he is a reasonable person?

2. Where does King address the objections of his audience?

3. As in the Declaration of Independence, transitions are important in King's letter. Identify the transitional words and phrases that connect the different parts of his argument.

4. Why does King cite Jewish, Catholic, and Protestant philosophers to support his position?

5. King relies heavily on appeals to authority (Augustine, Aquinas, Buber, Tillich, and so forth). Why do you think he uses this strategy?

6. King uses both induction and deduction in his letter. Find an example of each, and explain how they function in the argument.

7. Throughout the body of his letter, King criticizes his audience of white moderates. In his conclusion, however, he seeks to reestablish a harmonious relationship with them. How does he do this? Is he successful?

VOCABULARY PROJECTS

1. Define each of the following words as it is used in this selection.

affiliate (2)	devotee (12)	reiterate (34)
cognizant (4)	estrangement (16)	intimidate (37)
mutuality (4)	ordinances (16)	infanticide (37)
provincial (4)	anarchy (20)	inextricably (40)
gainsay (6)	elegy (26)	scintillating (47)
unfettered (10)	incorrigible (27)	
millennium (12)	emulate (28)	

2. Locate five **allusions** to the Bible in this essay. How do these allusions help King express his ideas?

3. In paragraph 14 King refers to his "cup of endurance." To what is this a reference? How is the original phrase worded?

JOURNAL ENTRY

Do you believe King's remarks go too far? Do you believe they do not go far enough? Explain.

WRITING WORKSHOP

1. Write an argumentative essay in which you support a deeply held belief of your own. Assume that your audience, like King's, is not openly hostile to your position.

2. Assume that you are a militant political leader writing a letter to Martin Luther King Jr. Argue that King's methods do not go far enough. Be sure to address potential objections to your position. You might want to go to the library and read some newspapers and magazines from the 1960s to help you prepare your argument. (Be sure to document all material you borrow from your sources. See the Appendix.)

3. Read your local newspaper for several days, collecting articles about a controversial subject that interests you. Using information from the articles, take a position on the issue, and write an essay supporting it. (Be sure to document all material you borrow from your sources. See the Appendix.)

COMBINING THE PATTERNS

In "Letter from Birmingham Jail," King includes several passages of **narration.** Find two of these passages, and discuss what use King makes of narration. Why do you think narration plays such an important part in King's argument?

THEMATIC CONNECTION

DEBATE:
Immigration

"Give me your tired, your poor, / Your huddled masses yearning to breathe free." These lines from Emma Lazarus's poem "The New Colossus" are engraved on the base of the Statue of Liberty. They affirm the fact that when the statue was dedicated, the United States welcomed immigrants from all lands and all stations in life. Certainly there were times when nativist sentiment boiled over into hostility and violence against "foreigners," but on the whole, the message was clear: the United States was the only country in the world that offered unrestricted immigration to the people of other countries. Indeed, immigration is a major part of our identity as a nation. We are, as the maxim goes, a nation of immigrants.

Not until the end of the nineteenth century did Congress raise the question of limiting access to this country. At that time, however, critics argued against open immigration on two grounds: first, that there was no longer any room for new immigrants, and second, that immigration was changing the demographics of the nation. These arguments eventually prevailed, and in 1924 Congress passed legislation that established strict quotas, bringing a century of open immigration to an end. Some of the same arguments raised at the beginning of the century are being made today by those who would limit, or in some cases entirely end, immigration. For example, today's critics of American immigration policy say that in an era of global competition the United States can no longer provide jobs to new immigrants. In addition, they point out that since 1965, when new, less restrictive immigration quotas were instituted, the United States has accepted so many immigrants from developing nations that the racial and ethnic character of the country is changing. For some, the current immigration situation signals the beginning of the end for the United States. For others, it underscores the hope and promise that has always been at the heart of the American dream.

The two essays that follow summarize the debate that is currently swirling around the issue of immigration. In "What, Then, Is to Be Done?" Peter Brimelow argues passionately for limiting immigration. According to Brimelow, the 1965 Immigration Act has created a situation that "will lead to conflict, repression and, perhaps, ultimately to a threat thought extinct in American politics for more than a hundred years: secession." In "Five Myths about Immigration," David Cole takes the opposite position, pointing out that many myths exist about the subject of immigration. According to Cole, these myths cloud the debate and ultimately cause politicians and their constituents to make scapegoats out of people who want nothing more than the opportunities traditionally offered to all immigrants to this country.

PETER BRIMELOW

Born in Warrington, England, Peter Brimelow (1947–   ) received his B.A. in history and economics at the University of Sussex in 1970; as a Fulbright scholar, he received an M.B.A. in 1972 from Stanford University in California. After working as a securities analyst for a Canadian firm, Brimelow joined the staff of Toronto's *Financial Post*. He moved to *Maclean's* magazine as business editor in 1976, wrote a column for the *Toronto Sun* syndicate from 1980 to 1982, and later served as a contributing editor to *Barron's* and as an associate editor at *Fortune*. Now a U.S. citizen, he is currently a senior editor at *Forbes* and *National Review* as well as a columnist for the *London Times*. His books include *The Wall Street Gurus: How You Can Profit from the Investment Letters* (1986) and *The Patriot Game* (1987). Brimelow's latest book, the controversial *Alien Nation: Common Sense about America's Immigration Disaster* (1995), predicts disaster unless the United States drastically changes its immigration policy. Brimelow is especially critical of the Immigration Act of 1965, which abolished preferences for immigrants from northern and western Europe and gave priority to family reunification over an immigrant's skills and ability to find a job. In this chapter from *Alien Nation*, Brimelow offers his blueprint for resolving what he considers a crisis.

What, Then, Is to Be Done?

. . . The tradition of British medical science is entirely opposed
to any emphasis on [treatment]. British medical specialists are
usually quite content to trace the symptoms and define the
cause. It is the French, by contrast, who begin by describing the
treatment and discuss the diagnosis later, if at all. We feel
bound to adhere in this to the British method, which may not
help the patient but which is unquestionably more scientific.
> —C. NORTHCOTE PARKINSON
> "Injelititis, or, Palsied Paralysis,"
> *Parkinson's Law* (1958)

Just over one hundred years ago, at a Chicago meeting of the 1
American Historical Society in 1893, a young historian called Frederick Jackson Turner read a paper on "The Significance of the Frontier in American History." The argument he set forth was to dominate Americans' thinking about themselves for more than a generation.

Turner began by noting that the Bureau of the Census had just announced that there was no longer a continuous line of free, unsettled land visible on the U.S. map. The American "frontier" had closed. 2

For the first time since the Puritans came down the gangplank with a 3 watchful eye cocked on the distant tree line, America was no longer bounded by a clear point beyond which civilization ceased. There was no longer a distinct region where Americans could always go to claim land of their own, to escape from authority, to begin their lives anew.

Closing along with the frontier, said Turner, was "the first period of   4
American history." He argued that the frontier had shaped the American
character—its informality, equality, self-reliance. And he worried about
what would happen without the social "safety valve" that the frontier
had represented.

A century later, the second period of American history may be closing   5
too. It may be time to face the fact that the United States can no longer be
an "immigrant country."

IMMIGRATION POLICY IN A DECOLONIZED AMERICA

For Americans even to think about their immigration policy, given   6
the political climate that has prevailed since the 1960s, involves a sort of
psychological liberation movement. In Eugene McCarthy's terms,
America would have to stop being a colony of the world. The implications are shocking, even frightening: that Americans, without feeling
guilty, can and should seize control of their country's destiny.

If they did, what would a decolonized American immigration policy   7
look like?

Remember that the United States has been on an immigration binge   8
since 1965. The hangover will be terrible; the temptation to take another
drink overwhelming. But the alternative is dissolution. To recover, the patient needs a relentless, driving will. And he must accept extreme measures, such as total abstinence, which have become tragically necessary
because of thirty years of irresponsible policy.

The first step is absolutely clear: 9

- **The 1965 Immigration Act, and its amplifications in 1986 and 1990,
  have been a disaster and must be repealed.**

And a future, American, immigration policy must be shaped by these   10
four principles:

- *The United States must regain control of its borders—over both illegal and legal
  immigration.*
- *Immigration must be treated as a luxury for the United States, not as a necessity.*
- *The costs of any immigration should fall on the immigrant, not on native-born
  Americans.*
- *Any immigration must meet a fundamental test: What does it mean for "The
  National Question"? Will it help or hurt the ability of the United States to sur-
  vive as a nation-state—the political expression of that interlacing of ethnicity
  and culture that now constitutes the American nation?*

Ideally, working out the details of a future, American immigration   11
policy deserves at least as much intellectual energy as immigration enthusiasts have poured into thinking up rationalizations for the current
chaos. But here are some quick suggestions:

ILLEGAL IMMIGRATION: END IT

First Line of Defense: The Border

The Border Patrol should be increased from its present four thou-   12
sand—under the circumstances, a Border Patrol the size of the Los
Angeles Police Department (about eight thousand) seems hardly unreasonable. The border, especially the crucial one hundred miles where 90
percent of apprehensions occur, should be sealed (at long last) with a
fence, a ditch, and whatever other contrivances that old Yankee ingenuity
finds appropriate. Consideration should be given to jailing repeat offend-
ers, perhaps in special prisons, for at least as long as is necessary to dis-
rupt the economic patterns that have currently developed around lax
border enforcement.

Second Line of Defense: Inside the United States

The Immigration and Naturalization Service's Investigations   13
Division, its main enforcement unit in the United States, should be increased as urgently as the Border Patrol. Presently, it has a mere 1,650 employees—and there are at least 4 million illegals here. A second Operation
Wetback, the much-reviled anti-illegals drive of 1954, will be necessary.
This will require coordinated effort by all levels of government, including
federal agencies like the Internal Revenue Service and the Department of
Housing and Urban Development, which currently decline to cooperate
with immigration-law enforcement. Americans may eventually have to
carry identification cards like many Europeans—and legal U.S. resident
aliens, whose official status is affirmed by the famous "green card," now
actually blue. (Perhaps the Clinton administration's proposed universal
health-care card could serve.) Libertarians will dislike this, but it is hardly
more an encroachment on personal freedom than the income tax. The economic basis of the illegal-immigrant presence in the United Sates must be
systematically attacked. This attack must go beyond tactics like employer
sanctions and the ending of direct and indirect subsidies from the
American taxpayer to reach strategic points, like the ability of illegals to
remit money to their countries of origin without proof of legal residence.
Blocking financial flows in this way proved useful in the drug war. Other
drug war expedients suggested by Huber Hanes, a former Border Patrol
officer who has been circulating a proposed Border Line and Boundary
bill: fining illegals, who typically carry large amounts of cash, and depu-
tizing local police to enforce federal immigration law, which—puzzling to
non-lawyers—they currently cannot do.

State and local governments that refuse to cooperate must be pun-   14
ished. (Just imagine what would happen if they were practicing segregation.) Deportation procedures, for both legal and illegal aliens, should be
streamlined, and criminal aliens automatically deported.

There must under no circumstances be another amnesty.*   15

Both on the border and inside the United States, the national effort   16
against illegal immigration must be constantly reinforced by legislation.
U.S. immigration law has already been significantly weakened by activist
judges. But there is nothing sacred about a wrongheaded judicial ruling.
The answer is to pass another law. When Americans do seize control of
their immigration policy again, it will inevitably take the form of an epic
clash between the legislative and judicial branches.

And the moral pressure will be intense.   17

A common argument will be that employed in mid-1993 by   18
Representative José Serrano (D.–New York), the Puerto Rican–born chairman of the Congressional Hispanic Caucus, while denouncing an anti-
illegal-immigrant amendment to the Clinton administration's national
service plan: *"I resent having to prove I'm a citizen. . . . "*

To this, the American answer must be: *tough.* Life is unfair, as another   19
Democrat—President John F. Kennedy—once memorably noted.
Representative Serrano has, presumably, ample means to prove his identity. I will be happy to do the same (I don't mind now, actually) when
there are 2 to 3 million illegal Englishmen crossing the border every year.

Could any American politician be so callous?   20

Well, do they want to keep their country?   21

LEGAL IMMIGRATION: CUT IT BACK—OR CUT IT OFF?

Quality

Current policy should be reversed: skilled immigration must be fa-   22
vored before family reunification. To put it another way, the United States
could do without that portion of the current influx that is below the average American's educational achievement.

The immigrant influx could be further reharmonized with U.S. labor-   23
market conditions by requiring more potential immigrants to have offers
of employment. Since an immigrant's country of origin turns out to be an
excellent predictor of likely success or failure in the United States, the admissions policy might take account of this reality. (Isn't honesty the best
policy? To end abuse of their asylum process, in 1987 the British frankly
banned a whole list of specified "troublesome" nationalities from approaching immigration officials while in transit—including Somalis,
Iranians, and Libyans.) A further possibility: Ben Wattenberg's idea of an
English-language requirement for immigrants.

No immigration should be permitted from countries that do not   24
allow reciprocal emigration from the United States.

---

*EDS. NOTE—The 1986 Immigration Reform Act allowed many illegal immigrants
to apply for legal resident alien status without fear of deportation.

Quantity

America needs another time-out from immigration. It needs another pause for digestion, to match the Great Lulls of 1790–1840 and 1925–65. [25]

This means a *drastic cutback of legal immigration.* From the current 1 million a year to perhaps 400,000, the target suggested by the Rockefeller Commission on Population Growth and the American Future in 1972. Or 350,000, as proposed by Reverend Theodore Hesburgh's Select Commission on Immigration and Refugee Policy in 1981. Or 300,000, as proposed by FAIR* in 1992—which the organization describes as a "moratorium" because it would mean zero net immigration, since up to some 300,000 people are estimated to leave the United States each year. [26]

Or, maybe, even less. There is a case for an *immediate temporary cutoff of all immigration*—say three to five years. Thereafter it might be advisable to adopt the more flexible Australian and Canadian approach. These countries have no specific immigrant total written into law, and can vary the total accepted yearly according to their labor-market conditions (and to public opinion—ultimately the only legitimate arbiter). Returning the INS** to the Labor Department from the Justice Department, as proposed by Vernon M. Briggs, Jr., in his *Mass Immigration and the National Interest,* might reduce the current legalistic–civil rights bias. When you have a hammer, as Justice Department lawyers do, everything looks like a nail. [27]

Whatever the total, however, cutting back immigration certainly means *radical reform of the "family-reunification" policy.* Currently, the United States is the only industrialized country that allows the automatic immigration of "non-nuclear" extended-family members. Had immigration been restricted just to the "nuclear" family members of American citizens—parents, spouses, and dependent children—only about 250,000 immigrants would have entered in 1992. (And even this flow would diminish in time, because many of these sponsoring American citizens are actually themselves recent immigrants.) [28]

But an automatic quarter million immigrants a year, before any skilled immigration at all, is still a lot. In the end, the fact must be faced: *even close family reunification is not sacred.* The restrictionist legislation in the 1920s, for example, made no provision for it. (And, of course, families can be reunited in two ways—the immigrant can always leave.) [29]

This is a distressing prospect. I know. Maggy and I benefited personally from the generous American policy on family reunification. She is a Canadian, and I was a resident alien in the United States when I married her. Then, because of our marriage, she herself was admitted as a legal resident alien. [30]

---

*EDS. NOTE—The Federation for American Immigration Reform.
**EDS. NOTE—The U.S. Immigration and Naturalization Service.

But this was a legal right—hardly a moral right. It was a privilege   31
granted by American policy. And the truth is that our lives would not have
been destroyed if Maggy had not been permitted to immigrate. I would
probably be writing a book on Canadian immigration policy right now.

Cutting back on immigration also means *cutting back on "refugees,"*   32
"asylees," and the various other special categories that have been slipped
through Congress by interest-group lobbying. Probably all these categories should be abolished entirely. Any individual member of one of
them, of course, could apply to immigrate in the usual way.

COSTS MUST FALL ON THE IMMIGRANTS

Anything that artificially distorts the demand for immigrants, no-   33
tably financial transfers by the government, must be reviewed critically.
Payments to illegal immigrants must be eliminated. This includes the transfer
implicit in free public education, which means another clash with the
judges: the Supreme Court's split-decision *Plyler v. Doe* ruling (1982) forc-
ing school systems to accept the children of illegals. And it means a prin-
cipled stand against all forms of government-imposed "bilingualism."

No immigrant should count as a member of a "protected class" for   34
the purposes of U.S. affirmative action programs. Instead, Americans
should be asking themselves: *if the "protected classes" are so oppressed in the
United States that they must be rescued by this unprecedented government intervention, how can it be right to allow more of these protected classes to immigrate into this oppression?*

IMMIGRATION AND THE NATIONAL QUESTION

[Earlier] I raised what I described as *The National Question:*   35

- **Is America still that interlacing of ethnicity and culture that we call a
  nation? Can the United States survive as a nation-state, the political expression of that nation?**

To begin at the most sensitive point: 36

The American nation of 1965, nearly 90 percent white, was explicitly   37
promised that the new immigration policy would not shift the country's
racial balance. But it did.

Race is destiny in American politics. Its importance has only been in-   38
tensified by the supposedly color-blind civil rights legislation of the
1960s—which paradoxically has turned out to mean elaborate race-con-
scious affirmative action programs. Any change in the racial balance must
obviously be fraught with consequences for the survival and success of
the American nation.

It is simply common sense that Americans have a legitimate interest   39
in their country's racial balance. It is common sense that they have a right
to insist that their government stop shifting it. Indeed, it seems to me that
they have a right to insist that it be shifted back.

This does not necessarily mean an absolute ban on any group.   40
"Numbers are of the essence," in the words of Enoch Powell, the prophetic
critic of Britain's disastrous postimperial immigration policy. In small
numbers, all kinds of immigrants can arrive in America and be assimi-
lated. Culture is a substitute for ethnicity. But numbers so high that they
shift the American demographic balance make this impossible.

One right that Americans certainly have is the right to insist that im-   41
migrants, whatever their race, become Americans. The full force of public
policy should be placed behind another "Americanization" campaign,
modeled on that during the last Great Wave of Immigration. All diversion
of public funds to promote "diversity," "multiculturalism," and foreign-
language retention must be struck down as subversive of this American
ideal. Hyphenated identities must remain a private matter, as throughout
most of American history. An English-language requirement for potential
immigrants would make Americanization easier. The English-language
requirement for citizenship should be enforced and the various recent exceptions, such as for spouses and the elderly, abolished—they were symbolic gestures anyway, and now the symbols are needed elsewhere. There
must be a concerted legislative attack on bilingual manifestations, beginning with the U.S. Department of Education's promotion of "bilingual"
education. (The Quebec government's defense of French through restrictions on English should be studied with care.) A Constitutional amendment making English the official language of the United States could be a
decisive step.

The Census Bureau's category of "Hispanic" should be abolished. It   42
should be replaced with a national-origin or racial classification where
appropriate.

Judging immigration in the context of the National Question sounds   43
grim. But actually it could relax the tension. For example, it focuses attention on the demographic impact of immigration. Admitting elderly parents (leaving aside the issue of whether they are likely to become a public
charge) would obviously not have a long-term demographic impact.

In the context of the National Question, the ultimate issue is not   44
whether foreigners show up in the United States but when they are admitted to the national community and obtain full political rights and
privileges. In an era of mass movement, the fact that the children of
even illegal immigrants are automatically U.S. citizens is plainly out-
dated. It must be ended, by amending the Constitution if necessary. It
may also be time to consider lengthening the five-year waiting period
before immigrants can naturalize—perhaps to ten years, as in Italy and
Germany, or even to fourteen years, as it was in the United States from
1798 to 1801.

"Nationalize, then naturalize" was one of the Know Nothings'* slogans. 45
But today American citizenship is being acquired in much the same spirit as
a driver's license. This is why you regularly read of "American citizens"
being involved in peculiar political intrigues in foreign countries—of which
becoming prime minister of Greece (Andreas Papandreou) and running for
the presidency of Serbia (Milan Panic) are among the most respectable.

And, in turn, this makes immigration control difficult. Public policy 46
is currently unable to discriminate between a new immigrant citizen's
arranged marriage back in the old country and a tenth-generation
American's foreign spouse. It probably should.

Again, discouraging foreign residents' access to the political commu- 47
nity may seem rather grim. But actually it could relax the tension. Many
foreign residents in the United States are perfectly happy with their half-
and-half status. (For example, the British. They are notoriously laggardly
about naturalizing, largely because they don't feel foreign in the first
place.) Recently, there have been cases of famous foreign-born wives only
reluctantly agreeing to naturalize because estate-tax law has been changed
to discriminate savagely, and foolishly, against resident noncitizens.

It may be time for the United States to consider moving to a concep- 48
tion of itself more like that of Switzerland: tolerating a fairly large foreign
presence that comes and goes, but rarely if ever naturalizes. It may be
time to consider reviving a version of the *bracero* program, the agricultural guest-workers program that operated from the 1940s to the 1960s,
allowing foreign workers to move in and out of the country in a controlled way, without permanently altering its demography and politics.
(Many immigration critics dislike "guest-worker" programs because the
"guests" tend to become permanent and deepen the "channels" followed
by illegal immigrants. But it is hard to see how this could be worse than
the current massive combination of illegal immigration and "citizen children." And it may be a transitional solution, allowing the U.S. immigration era to close without unnecessary hardship.)

This new conception may be a shock to American sensibilities. Many 49
Americans, like my students at the University of Cincinnati Law School,
are under the charming impression that foreigners don't really exist. But
they also tend to think that, if foreigners really do exist, they ought to become Americans as quickly as possible.

However, the fact is that we—foreigners—are, in some sense, all 50
Americans now, just as Jefferson said everyone had two countries, his
own and France, in the eighteenth century. That is why we are here, just
as the entire world flocked to Imperial Rome. The trick the Americans
face now is to be an empire in fact, while remaining a democratic republic
in spirit. Avoiding the Romans' mistake of diluting their citizenship into
insignificance may be the key.

---

*EDS. NOTE—A nineteenth-century political movement opposed to allowing fur-
ther immigration to the United States.

SHIPWRECK AND SALVAGE

What do I really think will happen?   51

In politics as elsewhere, if you ask a stupid question, you get a stupid   52
answer—or at any rate a terse answer. And asking people if they want
their communities to be overwhelmed by weird aliens with dubious
habits is a stupid question. The answer is inevitable.

Until now in America, chance circumstances and shifts in public pol-   53
icy have always combined to change this question before that inevitable
answer became too embarrassing. But the greater the number of immigrants, and the greater their difference from the American mainstream,
the louder and ruder the answer will be.

The political elite may choose not to hear. Others, however, will.   54

I think... *that immigration restriction is inevitable in America.* It will be   55
resisted hysterically. It will be sabotaged in every possible way. It will
probably require repeated legislation. But that will only intensify the ultimate nationalist eruption.

And no political issue, once it reaches the surface, has more elemental   56
power than immigration. It could quite easily destroy the present politi-
cal-party system, as it helped to do in the years before the Civil War.

Precisely because of the bitterness of the battle, and because of the   57
need to find any sheltering compromise, the ultimate restriction will probably be as crude as anything seen in the 1920s. To avoid the embarrassing
question *"Who?"* politicians may find it simpler to answer the question
"How Many?" with *"None."* Immigration could be ended entirely.

This would be tragic for the United States. But it would not be, in the   58
full sense, a tragedy. Immigration is a luxury, not a necessity.

But I also suspect that the immigration cutoff will be too late.   59
Diversity, the buzzword of the 1990s, will prove *divisive*—the now-forgot-
ten buzzword of the 1970s. The contradictions of a society as deeply divided as the United States must now inexorably become, as a result of the
post-1965 influx, will lead to conflict, repression, and, perhaps, ultimately
to a threat thought extinct in American politics for more than a hundred
years: secession.

Deep into the twenty-first century, throughout the lifetime of my little   60
son, American patriots will be fighting to salvage as much as possible
from the shipwreck of their great republic. It will be a big wreck, and
there will be a lot to salvage. But the struggle must be contrasted sadly
with the task of completing the "Great Society"* upon which Americans
were encouraged to think they were embarking in 1965.

And the politicians and pundits who allowed this to happen truly de-   61
serve, and will certainly receive... the curses of those who come after.

---

*EDS. NOTE—A term used by President Lyndon Johnson to encompass his "war"
on poverty and racism, which he believed would create universal prosperity.

• • •

COMPREHENSION

1. What two periods in American history does Brimelow define? What do they have to do with immigration?

2. What does Brimelow mean when he says, "America would have to stop being a colony of the world" (6)?

3. What are Brimelow's specific suggestions for changing America's current immigration policy?

4. How has immigration affected the racial balance of the country? According to Brimelow, what are the effects of this shift? What does Brimelow think the country's response to this shift should be?

5. According to Brimelow, what will happen if the current immigration policy is maintained?

PURPOSE AND AUDIENCE

1. What attitudes about immigration does Brimelow have? Does he expect his readers to share these assumptions? How do you know?

2. At what point does Brimelow state his thesis? What would he have gained or lost by stating it later?

3. Brimelow concedes little to his opposition. Should he have conceded more? Does he seem reasonable? Angry? Strident? Friendly? Something else? Explain.

STYLE AND STRUCTURE

1. In his introduction, Brimelow refers to Frederick Jackson Turner's famous paper, "The Significance of the Frontier in American History." Is this an effective introduction? Why or why not?

2. Is Brimelow's argument mainly inductive or deductive? In addition to appealing to logic, does Brimelow appeal to the emotions? If so, where?

3. How well does Brimelow support his assertions? Which assertions does he support adequately? Which ones need more support?

4. Where does Brimelow refute arguments against his position? How well does he refute these arguments?

5. What are the advantages of the headings that appear in the essay? Do they have any disadvantages?

6. How well does Brimelow sum up his argument in his conclusion? Could he have been more forceful? Explain.

VOCABULARY PROJECTS

1. Define each of the following words as it is used in this selection.

colony (6)
interlacing (10)
ethnicity (10)
encroachment (13)
sanctions (13)
subsidies (13)
remit (13)
expedients (13)
reunification (22)
asylum (23)

reciprocal (24)
moratorium (26)
bilingualism (33)
unprecedented (34)
fraught (38)
postimperial (40)
diversity (41)
naturalizing (47)
sabotaged (55)
secession (59)

2. Brimelow makes frequent use of italics. What words does he put in italics? What is the point of this strategy? Does the use of italics add to or detract from Brimelow's argument? Explain.

JOURNAL ENTRY

Identify two or three logical fallacies in Brimelow's essay, and bracket the parts of the essay that contain these fallacies. Then, write a paragraph about how these fallacies affect your response to the essay.

WRITING WORKSHOP

1. Write an essay in which you refute three or four of Brimelow's arguments, showing how the arguments are illogical or false. Be sure to include an introduction in which you state your thesis and a conclusion that reinforces your main ideas.

2. Assume that you are a recent immigrant to the United States. Write a letter to Brimelow in which you respond to his assertion, "it may be time to face the fact that the United States can no longer be an 'immigrant country'" (5).

3. Write an argumentative essay in which you present your own set of immigration laws. What criteria would you use to deny someone admission to this country? What criteria would you use to grant someone citizenship?

COMBINING THE PATTERNS

Paragraphs 1 through 5 rely on **comparison and contrast.** What two things are being compared? Why does one part of the comparison get more emphasis than the other? What do you think Brimelow is trying to establish with this comparison?

THEMATIC CONNECTIONS

- "Two Ways to Belong in America" (page 340)
- "Aria: A Memoir of a Bilingual Childhood" (page 357)
- "Let's Tell the Story of All America's Cultures" (page 552)

DAVID COLE

David Cole (1958–   ) was born in Princeton, New Jersey, and is a graduate of Yale University and the Yale Law School. Currently a professor of constitutional law at the Georgetown University Law Center, he volunteers as a staff attorney with the Center for Constitutional Rights in Chevy Chase, Maryland. Cole has published articles in numerous law journals, including the *Yale Law Journal* and the *Stanford Law Review,* and has contributed Op-Ed pieces to the *New York Times,* the *Washington Post,* the *Wall Street Journal,* and other newspapers. He also writes a monthly column for *Legal Times,* a publication for the Washington legal community. The following essay originally appeared in the *Nation,* a weekly publication with a strong liberal viewpoint. In it Cole attempts to counter the argument that the United States has a serious immigration problem. He also tries to dispel the idea that legal, noncitizen residents should not have the same rights as citizens.

Five Myths about Immigration

For a brief period in the mid-nineteenth century, a new political movement captured the passions of the American public. Fittingly labeled the "Know-Nothings," their unifying theme was nativism. They liked to call themselves "Native Americans," although they had no sympathy for people we call Native Americans today. And they pinned every problem in American society on immigrants. As one Know-Nothing wrote in 1856: "Four-fifths of the beggary and three-fifths of the crime spring from our foreign population; more than half the public charities, more than half the prisons and almshouses, more than half the police and the cost of administering criminal justice are for foreigners."

At the time, the greatest influx of immigrants was from Ireland, where the potato famine had struck, and Germany, which was in political and economic turmoil. Anti-alien and anti-Catholic sentiments were the order of the day, especially in New York and Massachusetts, which received the brunt of the wave of immigrants, many of whom were dirt-poor and uneducated. Politicians were quick to exploit the sentiment: There's nothing like a scapegoat to forge an alliance.

I am especially sensitive to this history: My forebears were among those dirt-poor Irish Catholics who arrived in the 1860s. Fortunately for them, and me, the Know-Nothing movement fizzled within fifteen years. But its pilot light kept burning, and is turned up whenever the American public begins to feel vulnerable and in need of an enemy.

Although they go by different names today, the Know-Nothings have returned. As in the 1850s, the movement is strongest where immigrants are most concentrated: California and Florida. The objects of prejudice are of course no longer Irish Catholics and Germans; 140 years later, "they" have become "us." The new "they"—because it seems "we" must always have a "they"—are Latin Americans (most recently, Cubans), Haitians, and Arab-Americans, among others.

But just as in the 1850s, passion, misinformation, and short-sighted fear often substitute for reason, fairness, and human dignity in today's immigration debates. In the interest of advancing beyond know-nothingism, let's look at five current myths that distort public debate and government policy relating to immigrants.   5

§ *America is being overrun with immigrants.* In one sense, of course, this is true, but in that sense it has been true since Christopher Columbus arrived. Except for the real Native Americans, we are a nation of immigrants.   6

It is not true, however, that the first-generation immigrants' share of our population is growing. As of 1990, foreign-born people made up only 8 percent of the population, as compared with a figure of about 15 percent from 1870 to 1920. Between 70 and 80 percent of those who immigrate every year are refugees or immediate relatives of U.S. citizens.   7

Much of the anti-immigrant fervor is directed against the undocumented, but they make up only 13 percent of all immigrants residing in the United States, and only 1 percent of the American population. Contrary to popular belief, many such aliens do not cross the border illegally but enter legally and remain after their student or visitor visa expires. Thus, building a wall at the border, no matter how high, will not solve the problem.   8

§ *Immigrants take jobs from U.S. citizens.* There is virtually no evidence to support this view, probably the most wide-spread misunderstanding about immigrants. As documented by a 1994 A.C.L.U.* Immigrants' Rights Project report, numerous studies have found that immigrants actually create more jobs than they fill. The jobs immigrants take are of course easier to see, but immigrants are often highly productive, run their own businesses, and employ both immigrants and citizens. One study found that Mexican immigration to Los Angeles County between 1970 and 1980 was responsible for 78,000 new jobs. Governor Mario Cuomo reports that immigrants own more than 40,000 companies in New York, which provide thousands of jobs and $3.5 billion to the state's economy every year.   9

§ *Immigrants are a drain on society's resources.* This claim fuels many of the recent efforts to cut off government benefits to immigrants. However, most studies have found that immigrants are a net benefit to the economy because, as a 1994 Urban Institute report concludes, "immigrants generate significantly more in taxes paid than they cost in services received." The Council of Economic Advisers similarly found in 1986 that "immigrants have a favorable effect on the overall standard of living."   10

Anti-immigrant advocates often cite studies purportedly showing the contrary, but these generally focus only on taxes and services at the local or state level. What they fail to explain is that because most taxes go to the   11

---

*EDS. NOTE—The American Civil Liberties Union.

federal government, such studies would also show a net loss when applied to U.S. citizens. At most, such figures suggest that some redistribution of federal and state monies may be appropriate; they show nothing unique about the costs of immigrants.

Some subgroups of immigrants plainly impose a net cost in the short   12
run, principally those who have most recently arrived and have not yet "made it." California, for example, bears substantial costs for its disproportionately large undocumented population, largely because it has on average the poorest and least educated immigrants. But that has been true of every wave of immigrants that has ever reached our shores; it was as true of the Irish in the 1850s, for example, as it is of Salvadorans today. From a long-term perspective the economic advantages of immigration are undeniable.

Some have suggested that we might save money and diminish incen-   13
tives to immigrate illegally if we denied undocumented aliens public services. In fact, undocumented immigrants are already ineligible for most social programs, with the exception of education for schoolchildren, which is constitutionally required, and benefits directly related to health and safety, such as emergency medical care and nutritional assistance to poor women, infants, and children. To deny such basic care to people in need, apart from being inhumanly callous, would probably cost us more in the long run by exacerbating health problems that we would eventually have to address.

§ *Aliens refuse to assimilate, and are depriving us of our cultural and politi-*   14
cal unity. This claim has been made about every new group of immigrants to arrive on U.S. shores. Supreme Court Justice Stephen Field wrote in 1884 that the Chinese "have remained among us a separate people, retaining their original peculiarities of dress, manners, habits, and modes of living, which are as marked as their complexion and language." Five years later, he upheld the racially based exclusion of Chinese immigrants. Similar claims have been made over different periods of our history about Catholics, Jews, Italians, Eastern Europeans, and Latin Americans.

In most instances, such claims are simply not true; "American cul-   15
ture" has been created, defined, and revised by persons who for the most part are descended from immigrants once seen as anti-assimilationist. Descendants of the Irish Catholics, for example, a group once decried as separatist and alien, have become Presidents, senators, and representatives (and all of these in one family, in the case of the Kennedys). Our society exerts tremendous pressure to conform, and cultural separatism rarely survives a generation. But more important even if this claim were true, is this a legitimate rationale for limiting immigration in a society built on the values of pluralism and tolerance?

§ *Noncitizen immigrants are not entitled to constitutional rights.* Our gov-   16
ernment has long declined to treat immigrants as full human beings, and nowhere is that more clear than in the realm of constitutional rights. Although the Constitution literally extends the fundamental protections

in the Bill of Rights to all people, limiting to citizens only the right to vote and run for federal office, the federal government acts as if this were not the case.

In 1893 the executive branch successfully defended a statute that re-   17
quired Chinese laborers to establish their prior residence here by the testi-mony of "at least one credible white witness." The Supreme Court ruled that this law was constitutional because it was reasonable for Congress to presume that nonwhite witnesses could not be trusted.

The federal government is not much more enlightened today. In a   18
pending case I'm handling in the Court of Appeals for the Ninth Circuit, the Clinton Administration has argued that permanent resident aliens lawfully living here should be extended no more First Amendment rights than aliens applying for first-time admission from abroad—that is, none. Under this view, students at a public university who are citizens may express themselves freely, but students who are not citizens can be deported for saying exactly what their classmates are constitutionally entitled to say.

Growing up, I was always taught that we will be judged by how we   19
treat others. If we are collectively judged by how we have treated immi-grants—those who appear today to be "other" but will in a generation be "us"—we are not in very good shape.

. . .

COMPREHENSION

1. Who were the "Know-Nothings"? What was their attitude toward immigrants?
2. According to Cole, why will "building a wall at the border" (8) not stop the majority of illegal immigrants?
3. Why does Cole believe it is a mistake to think that immigrants take jobs from U.S. citizens?
4. Why, according to Cole, is it a mistake to deny undocumented immigrants public services?
5. How does Cole respond to the charge that many immigrants simply refuse to assimilate? Why, according to him, is this statement not true?

PURPOSE AND AUDIENCE

1. Does Cole expect his readers to share the myths that he says "distort pub-lic debate and government policy relating to immigrants" (5)? How do you know?
2. What is Cole's thesis? Where does he state it?
3. Do you think Cole respects his readers' intelligence, or does he seem to talk down to them?

STYLE AND STRUCTURE

1. Why does Cole begin his essay by referring to the Know-Nothings? How was their movement similar to current anti-immigration movements?

2. Where does Cole attempt to refute the major arguments against his position? How successful is he?

3. In paragraph 6 Cole concedes a point to his opposition. How successful is this strategy? What other strategy might have worked here? Explain.

4. How effectively does Cole support the points he makes? What kinds of support does he use? For example, does he use personal opinion? Expert opinion? Statistics? Case studies? Do you think he offers enough support, or should he have offered more?

5. In his conclusion, Cole says that the federal government is no more enlightened today than it was in 1893, when Congress required Chinese laborers to establish residence by having the testimony of a white witness. Do you think Cole risks alienating some of his readers with this statement? Why or why not?

VOCABULARY PROJECTS

1. Define each of the following words as it is used in this selection.

   nativism (1)   undocumented (8)
   almshouses (1)   callous (13)
   turmoil (2)   rationale (15)
   scapegoat (2)   pluralism (15)

2. In paragraph 1 Cole quotes the Know-Nothings, who refer to immigrants as the *foreign population* and *foreigners*. Throughout his essay, however, Cole himself uses the terms *immigrants* and *permanent resident aliens*. What does each set of terms suggest? How are their connotations different?

JOURNAL ENTRY

Do you think the United States benefits from a policy that ensures a constant influx of immigrants? What are the advantages and disadvantages of this policy?

WRITING WORKSHOP

1. Write an essay in which you argue against Cole's position. Be sure to refute each of his major arguments.

2. How do you think Cole would respond to Brimelow's essay? Choose a section of Brimelow's essay, and refute it by using any of Cole's points that are relevant to Brimelow's argument.

3. Consider Cole's assertion that immigrants are *not* a drain on society's re-sources. Although he makes an effective argument, his position is not without critics—Brimelow, for example. Write an essay in which you consider whether or not immigrants are a financial benefit to American society. To support your thesis, supplement your own observations and experience with both "Five Myths about Immigration" and "What, Then, Is to Be Done?" as well as another source you find at the library or on the Internet. (Make sure you document all material you borrow from your sources. See the Appendix for information on documentation.)

COMBINING THE PATTERNS

In paragraph 14 Cole uses **narration.** Why does he include this paragraph? What point does he hope to make? Is he successful? Why or why not?

THEMATIC CONNECTIONS

DEBATE:
Multicultural Education

There once was a time when most American educators and scholars could agree on what constituted a good education. The list of authors and works that all educated people were supposed to have read was referred to as the *canon*. In recent years, however, some critics have charged that the canon, as it has traditionally been established, is like an exclusive club, with otherwise qualified members kept out for reasons of class, gender, and race. Indeed, when one examines the traditional canon, it is clear that with few exceptions the viewpoints represented are male, middle class, and white. For this reason, some educators have proposed a more inclusive, multicultural curriculum that exposes students to more works by women, people of color, and writers from different cultural backgrounds. The result has been that literature, history, and other courses at many high schools and colleges are now more culturally diverse than they were several years ago.

A fierce debate rages, however, around the issue of multicultural education. Critics charge that some teachers care less about the intellectual quality of the works on their reading lists than they do about the racial and ethnic backgrounds of the authors represented. Others contend that multicultural courses are more concerned with making students feel good about themselves than with fostering critical thinking. Still others say the curriculum is being broadened at the expense of the great works of Western thought that reinforce our society's basic values.

The two essays that follow reflect the ongoing debate about multicultural education. In "Multiculturalism Is Misguided," Trudy Rubin argues that multicultural education is hostile to the study of Western civilization and "wrongfully misguided." In "Let's Tell the Story of All America's Cultures," Ji-Yeon Mary Yuhfill takes the opposite position, asserting that children should understand that the history of the United States is the story of people from many different cultures struggling to make a better life for themselves.

![decorative border]

TRUDY RUBIN

Trudy Rubin graduated from Smith College in 1965 and received her master's degree from the London School of Economics in 1966. Before joining the *Philadelphia Inquirer*, where she is a foreign affairs columnist and a member of the newspaper's editorial board, she worked for the British magazine *Economist* as a staff writer on American politics and for the *Christian Science Monitor* as a national correspondent and then as a Middle East correspondent. Rubin has lived in Prague (where, as a radio correspondent, she reported on Czechoslovakia's short-lived effort to throw off Soviet domination in 1968) as well as in London, Jerusalem, Cairo, and Beirut, and she travels frequently in the Middle East, Russia, Europe, and Asia. She has published articles in several newspapers and magazines, including the *Atlantic Monthly*, the *New Republic*, and the *Nation*. "Multiculturalism Is Misguided" argues that while American universities are preoccupied with the virtues of multiculturalism and the faults of Western civilization, the rest of the world is trying to learn from the history and political theory of Western democracies.

Multiculturalism Is Misguided

1   This week I traveled to my alma mater, Smith College, to take part in an informal dialogue among alumnae, faculty, and students on the goals of a women's liberal arts college in uncertain times.

2   Smith, a small, elite women's college, is smack in the middle of the raging national debate over multiculturalism. Smith's president, Mary Maples Dunn, has made "diversity" the college's premier issue, including a major campaign to recruit minority students, faculty, and staff and to introduce more "multicultural" material on race and ethnicity into courses.

3   Many colleges and universities, such as Dartmouth, Wisconsin, and Mount Holyoke, now require students to take Third World or ethnic studies courses but not courses in Western civilization. Smith has no course requirements at all. But that may not continue to be the case.

4   The Smith administration believes that a stronger multicultural slant is necessary to enable students to cope with a more interdependent world, in which nonwhite minorities will make up a bigger share of the U.S. population.

5   As someone who makes a living by traveling around the world, observing its staggering changes, I feel the hopes invested in "multiculturalism" are woefully misguided, especially since they are so often driven by a hostility toward the study of Western civilization. Many of the academic backers of multiculturalism seem to believe that Western liberal thought has spawned only imperialism, racism, and sexism. They ignore the fact that much of the rest of the world is looking West for something very different.

6   All over the globe, in China, Africa, Southeast Asia, Soviet Asia, the Soviet Union, Eastern Europe, Latin America, elites and the public at

large are struggling to find political formulas that give ordinary people a say in how they are governed and instill tolerance for different political views. In many of these places the most urgent need is to find a way for different ethnic groups to coexist without killing each other. In most of these struggles, women still play a painfully subordinate role.

From Korea to the Middle East, from Ukraine to Moscow to the Baltics, supporters of democracy are looking to the experience, history, literature, and political theory of Western democracies for clues as to how to establish the tolerant systems that they seek. 7

In Moscow, politicians walk around carrying copies of the U.S. Constitution and James Madison's Federalist Papers, trying to grasp the idea of opposition politics and to learn how the American states managed to stay together with only one civil war. Little in their history or religion has prepared them for the give-and-take of democratic politics. And so they look West. 8

In the Middle East, young intellectuals have told me that democracy may not be possible because of Islamic beliefs that link mosque and state and because of the widespread belief in one Arab nation, which undermines respect for state democratic institutions. As for the rights of women, in Iran young women are beaten for letting bits of hair stick out of a head scarf, and in Saudi Arabia women can't even drive. In that region, the idea that the state must respect an individual's God-given human rights gets short shrift. 9

In Burma, China, and elsewhere in Asia, leaders claim that the concept of inalienable human rights is antithetical to Asian culture. In Africa, I have seen the remnants of tribal slavery and the most brutal racism. In no Third World culture have I seen anything close to the respect—however imperfect—that women are accorded in Western societies. Some of my most horrible discussions have been with African women discussing the commonly accepted practice of clitoridectomy. 10

It is European culture, primarily the Anglo-Saxon tradition, that has given the world the concepts of the rule of law, individual rights, cultural freedom, and pluralistic democracy. All over the world I have had the American Declaration of Independence quoted to me. No one was interested in Thomas Jefferson's history as a white male slave owner. What they were concerned about was the argument that individuals were entitled to "life, liberty and the pursuit of happiness." 11

And so I find it bewildering to return home to the debate on multiculturalism, many of whose adherents seem to believe that a dilettantish dip into Third World studies will help American students deal with America's and the world's ills. This is a deception, which taken to extremes can polarize minority students, rather than making them aware of the unique cultural heritage that they are entitled to share. 12

With all the immense mistakes made by the West, including the overweening sin of slavery, it is still Western history and culture that has given men and women the greatest possibility to fight for change. 13

In today's world, one can't assume that students arrive at college   14
versed in European and American history or political theory. It is these
lessons that American students most need to study, to prevent America
from going the way of Yugoslavia or Lebanon.

It's fine to offer students the chance to study other cultures, so long as   15
those classes are taught without false illusions, laying out the flaws of
Third World cultures as well as their beauties. But if required, those studies should be in conjunction with the study of Western civilization. That
tradition, white Anglo-Saxon though it may be, belongs to all of us.
Without it, the very idea of diversity would be a joke.

● ● ●

COMPREHENSION

1. Why does the Smith College administration believe more multicultural
   education is necessary?

2. Why do you think Rubin makes a point of saying that she is someone
   who makes her living traveling around the world?

3. According to Rubin, what misconception do the academic backers of
   multiculturalism have?

4. What does Rubin say that people from all over the world look for from
   the West?

5. According to Rubin, why should American students study Western civilization?

PURPOSE AND AUDIENCE

1. What attitudes does Rubin assume her readers have about her subject?
   Explain your conclusion.

2. At what point does Rubin state her thesis? What would she have gained
   or lost by stating it later?

3. What opposing point does Rubin concede? What do you think she hopes
   to gain by doing so?

STYLE AND STRUCTURE

1. Rubin supports her thesis by presenting examples from all the major re-
   gions of the world. Why do you think she does this? Could she have
   eliminated some examples?

2. Do Rubin's anecdotes adequately support her thesis? What other kinds
   of evidence could she have used?

3. Where does Rubin refute arguments against her position?

4. Is Rubin's argument primarily inductive or deductive? Explain.

5. How well does Rubin sum up her argument in her last paragraph? Would a stronger closing statement improve her essay? If so, how?

VOCABULARY PROJECTS

1. Define each of the following words as it is used in this selection.

ethnicity (2)	mosque (9)	adherents (12)
imperialism (5)	clitoridectomy (10)	polarize (12)
subordinate (6)	Anglo-Saxon (11)	overweening (13)

2. In paragraph 12 Rubin clearly reveals her bias in the phrase *dilettantish dip*. What other words and phrases show Rubin's attitude toward her subject? What would be the effect of substituting words that have more neutral connotations?

JOURNAL ENTRY

Do you think Rubin overstates her case? If so, do you think her overstatements are intentional? How do they affect you?

WRITING WORKSHOP

1. Write an argumentative essay in which you support Rubin's position that the white Anglo-Saxon tradition "belongs to all of us" (15). Use examples from your own experience to support your thesis.

2. Write an essay in which you refute Rubin's argument. The body of your essay should point out the weaknesses of Rubin's points, not make your own argument in favor of multicultural education.

3. Write an essay in which you argue that your college or university courses would (or would not) be strengthened by the addition of more multicultural material.

COMBINING THE PATTERNS

Paragraphs 6 through 10 rely on **classification and division.** What is being divided? Into what categories are the elements being sorted? How does Rubin strengthen her argument with this pattern of development?

THEMATIC CONNECTIONS

- "Only Daughter" (page 70)
- "Shooting an Elephant" (page 91)
- "Mother Tongue" (page 393)
- "The Untouchable" (page 448)

⟨⟨⟨⟨⟨⟨⟨⟨⟨⟨⟨⟨⟨⟨⟨⟨⟨⟨⟨

JI-YEON MARY YUHFILL

Ji-Yeon Mary Yuhfill was born in Seoul, South Korea, in 1965 and moved to the United States with her family in 1970. She received a master's degree in cognitive science from Stanford University in 1987 and has completed graduate work at the University of Pennsylvania. Yuhfill has worked as an agricultural reporter for the *Omaha World-Herald* and as a general assignment reporter for *New York Newsday*. In "Let's Tell the Story of All America's Cultures" Yuhfill argues for a multicultural curriculum that would give students a more inclusive view of history.

Let's Tell the Story of All America's Cultures

I grew up hearing, seeing, and almost believing that America was white—albeit with a little black tinged here and there—and that white was best. 1

The white people were everywhere in my 1970s Chicago childhood: Founding Fathers, Lewis and Clark, Lincoln, Daniel Boone, Carnegie,* presidents, explorers, and industrialists galore. The only black people were slaves. The only Indians were scalpers. 2

I never heard one word about how Benjamin Franklin was so impressed by the Iroquois federation of nations that he adapted that model into our system of state and federal government. Or that the Indian tribes were systematically betrayed and massacred by a greedy young nation that stole their land and called it the United States. 3

I never heard one word about how Asian immigrants were among the first to turn California's desert into fields of plenty. Or about Chinese immigrant Ah Bing, who bred the cherry now on sale in groceries across the nation. Or that plantation owners in Hawaii imported labor from China, Japan, Korea, and the Philippines to work the sugar cane fields. I never learned that Asian immigrants were the only immigrants denied U.S. citizenship, even though they served honorably in World War I. All the immigrants in my textbook were white. 4

I never learned about Frederick Douglass, the runaway slave who became a leading abolitionist and statesman, or about black scholar W. E. B. Du Bois. I never learned that black people rose up in arms against slavery. Nat Turner** wasn't one of the heroes in my childhood history class. 5

---

*EDS. NOTE—Andrew Carnegie (1935–1919), American industrialist and philanthropist.
**EDS. NOTE—Leader of a slave rebellion in Virginia in 1831.

I never learned that the American Southwest and California were already settled by Mexicans when they were annexed after the Mexican-American War. I never learned that Mexico once had a problem keeping land-hungry white men on the U.S. side of the border.   6

So when other children called me a slant-eyed chink and told me to go back where I came from, I was ready to believe that I wasn't really an American because I wasn't white.   7

America's bittersweet legacy of struggling and failing and getting another step closer to democratic ideals of liberty and equality and justice for all wasn't for the likes of me, an immigrant child from Korea. The history books said so.   8

Well, the history books were wrong.   9

Educators around the country are finally realizing what I realized as a teenager in the library, looking up the history I wasn't getting in school. America is a multicultural nation, composed of many people with varying histories and varying traditions who have little in common except their humanity, a belief in democracy, and a desire for freedom.   10

America changed them, but they changed America too.   11

A committee of scholars and teachers gathered by the New York State Department of Education recognizes this in their recent report, "One Nation, Many Peoples: A Declaration of Cultural Interdependence."   12

They recommend that public schools provide a "multicultural education, anchored to the shared principles of a liberal democracy."   13

What that means, according to the report, is recognizing that America was shaped and continues to be shaped by people of diverse backgrounds. It calls for students to be taught by people of diverse backgrounds. It calls for students to be taught that history is an ongoing process of discovery and interpretation of the past, and that there is more than one way of viewing the world.   14

Thus, the westward migration of white Americans is not just a heroic settling of an untamed wild, but also the conquest of indigenous peoples. Immigrants were not just white, but Asian as well. Blacks were not merely passive slaves freed by northern whites, but active fighters for their own liberation.   15

In particular, according to the report, the curriculum should help children "to access critically the reasons for the inconsistencies between the ideals of the U.S. and social realities. It should provide information and intellectual tools that can permit them to contribute to bringing reality closer to the ideals."   16

In other words, show children the good with the bad, and give them the skills to help improve their country. What could be more patriotic?   17

Several dissenting members of the New York committee publicly worry that America will splinter into ethnic fragments if this multicultural curriculum is adopted. They argue that the committee's report puts the focus on ethnicity at the expense of national unity.   18

But downplaying ethnicity will not bolster national unity. The history   19
of America is the story of how and why people from all over the world
came to the United States, and how in struggling to make a better life for
themselves, they changed each other, they changed the country, and they
all came to call themselves Americans.

E pluribus unum. Out of many, one.   20

This is why I, with my Korean background, and my childhood tor-   21
mentors, with their lost-in-the-mist-of-time-European backgrounds, are
all Americans.

It is the unique beauty of this country. It is high time we let all our   22
children gaze upon it.

• • •

COMPREHENSION

1. What did Yuhfill believe while she was growing up?

2. What was Yuhfill never taught as a child? What is the result of her ignorance?

3. According to Yuhfill, what are educators all around the country finally
   realizing? What is the result of their change in thinking?

4. What does the committee formed by the New York State Department of
   Education mean when it says public schools should give students "a
   multicultural education, anchored to the shared principles of a liberal
   democracy"? (13)

5. According to Yuhfill, "downplaying ethnicity will not bolster national
   unity" (19). Why not?

PURPOSE AND AUDIENCE

1. What credentials does Yuhfill present to establish her expertise? Are they
   sufficient? Why or why not?

2. Where does Yuhfill state her thesis? Would the beginning of her essay be
   a better place for her thesis statement? Explain your reasoning.

3. Does Yuhfill assume her audience is friendly, hostile, or neutral? How
   can you tell?

4. Do you think Yuhfill's essay is too personal and subjective? Would a less
   emotional, more objective tone be more effective? Explain.

STYLE AND STRUCTURE

1. In the first part of her essay (3–6), Yuhfill repeats the words "I never
   heard" and "I never learned." What is the effect of this repetition? How
   does it help her make her point?

2. Yuhfill refers extensively to a New York State Department of Education report. Do these references adequately support her argument? Do you think she relies too much on a single source? Explain.

3. In paragraph 18 Yuhfill mentions the dissenting members of the committee that wrote the report. How effectively does she refute their objections? What else could she have said?

4. Yuhfill's essay was originally published as a newspaper column and therefore contains a number of one- and two-sentence paragraphs. How effective are these short paragraphs? Should they be combined with other paragraphs? Explain.

5. Yuhfill ends her essay with a one-sentence conclusion. How well does this conclusion reinforce her points? What other concluding strategy could she have used?

VOCABULARY PROJECTS

1. Define each of the following words as it is used in this selection.

albeit (1)	annexed (6)	inconsistencies (16)
federation (3)	legacy (8)	ethnicity (18)
abolitionist (5)	indigenous (15)	

2. Yuhfill uses many terms that have built-in value judgments. Identify several of these terms (*land-hungry* white men [6], for example), and substitute terms with more neutral connotations.

JOURNAL ENTRY

Paragraph 21 presents a conclusion ("This is why I . . . "). Do you think Yuhfill includes enough information in the essay to justify this conclusion? Why or why not?

WRITING WORKSHOP

1. Yuhfill gives a number of reasons why schools should adopt a multicultural curriculum. Write an essay in which you discuss the possible drawbacks of such a curriculum.

2. In the early 1990s, when the New York City Board of Education tried to mandate a multicultural curriculum, it met a good deal of resistance. Some people complained that the board was trying to impose its way of thinking on children. Others said the curriculum idealized many aspects of minority culture. Still others objected to some of the books students were required to read. Write a letter to the editor of the *New York Times* in which you outline the type of multicultural curriculum you would like to see in a public elementary school. What kinds of material would you accept? What kinds would you reject?

3. Write an essay in which you discuss whether or not it is the responsibility of the public schools to tell the story of each ethnic group's contributions to the United States.

COMBINING THE PATTERNS

Paragraphs 3 through 6 rely on **exemplification.** What does Yuhfill hope to accomplish with this series of short examples? Is she successful? Would fewer examples discussed in more depth be more effective? Explain your reasoning.

THEMATIC CONNECTIONS

- "Grant and Lee: A Study in Contrasts" (page 330)
- "Aria: A Memoir of a Bilingual Childhood" (page 357)
- "An Argument against the Anna Todd Jennings Scholarship" (page 501)

DEBATE:
Date Rape

The phenomenon known as date rape has existed for a long time, but in recent years it has become an important issue on many college campuses. The rise of feminism has called attention to the problem and has led to campus programs to help both male and female students avoid situations that could lead to date rape. Some colleges have even published behavior codes in an attempt to sensitize students to this issue. (Antioch College, for example, has instituted a widely publicized code requiring students to ask a partner's permission at each stage of intimacy.)

Given the lack of controversy about the seriousness of rape, one might ask, "What is there to debate about date rape? Isn't rape always rape?" But for many people the issue is not this simple. Some argue that many incidents characterized as date rape are not rape at all. What actually occurs in these situations, they say, is a miscommunication that results in sex, which the woman may not really want or may later regret but which cannot be fairly characterized as rape. Others say drugs and alcohol frequently play a part in what are labeled *date rapes.* How can a woman cry "rape," they ask, when she has contributed to the situation? Finally, some say that by applying the term *rape* to situations like these, date-rape activists diminish the seriousness of "real" rape resulting from physical force or threats of violence. In response to these arguments, activists say such excuses continue a long tradition of women's subjugation. The vast majority of men, they argue, bestow their affections only on willing recipients, and the charge that large numbers of them are being falsely accused of rape by fickle or vindictive women not only ignores the facts but itself trivializes the severity of the crime.

The two writers in this section express opposite opinions about date rape. In "It's a Jungle Out There," Camille Paglia asserts that the only way to eliminate date rape is for women to take responsibility for their own actions. In "Common Decency," Susan Jacoby argues that there should be no distinction between rape and date rape because men should be expected to understand when "no" means "no."

CAMILLE PAGLIA

Camille Paglia was born in 1947 in Endicott, New York, graduated from the State University of New York at Binghamton in 1968, and received her doctorate from Yale University in 1974. She has taught at Bennington College, Wesleyan University, Yale, the University of New Haven, and, since 1984, at the University of the Arts in Philadelphia. Paglia has published three books: *Sexual Personae: Art and Decadence from Nefertiti to Emily Dickinson* (1990), a best-selling scholarly work that examines pornographic elements in art and literature beginning in ancient Egypt and Greece; *Sex, Art, and American Culture* (1992), a collection of provocative articles, interviews, book reviews, and lectures on popular culture, in which the following piece appears; and the essay collection *Vamps and Tramps* (1994). In "It's a Jungle Out There," which first appeared in *New York Newsday* in 1991, Paglia argues that feminism misleads women by offering them a fantasy of sexual empowerment instead of warning them of the inevitability of male sexual aggression.

It's a Jungle Out There

Rape is an outrage that cannot be tolerated in civilized society. Yet feminism, which has waged a crusade for rape to be taken more seriously, has put young women in danger by hiding the truth about sex from them.

In dramatizing the pervasiveness of rape, feminists have told young women that before they have sex with a man, they must give consent as explicit as a legal contract's. In this way, young women have been convinced that they have been the victims of rape. On elite campuses in the Northeast and on the West Coast, they have held consciousness-raising sessions, petitioned administrations, demanded inquests. At Brown University, outraged, panicky "victims" have scrawled the names of alleged attackers on the walls of women's rest rooms. What marital rape was to the '70s, "date rape" is to the '90s.

The incidence and seriousness of rape do not require this kind of exaggeration. Real acquaintance rape is nothing new. It has been a horrible problem for women for all of recorded history. Once fathers and brothers protected women from rape. Once the penalty for rape was death. I come from a fierce Italian tradition where, not so long ago in the motherland, a rapist would end up knifed, castrated, and hung out to dry.

But the old clans and small rural communities have broken down. In our cities, on our campuses far from home, young women are vulnerable and defenseless. Feminism has not prepared them for this. Feminism keeps saying the sexes are the same. It keeps telling women they can do anything, go anywhere, say anything, wear anything. No, they can't. Women will always be in sexual danger.

One of my male students recently slept overnight with a friend in a passageway of the Great Pyramid in Egypt. He described the moon and sand, the ancient silence and eerie echoes. I will never experience that. I am a woman. I am not stupid enough to believe I could ever be safe there. There is a world of solitary adventure I will never have. Women have always known these somber truths. But feminism, with its pie-in-the-sky fantasies about the perfect world, keeps young women from seeing life as it is.

We must remedy social injustice whenever we can. But there are some 6 things we cannot change. There are sexual differences that are based in biology. Academic feminism is lost in a fog of social constructionism. It believes we are totally the product of our environment. This idea was invented by Rousseau.* He was wrong. Emboldened by dumb French language theory, academic feminists repeat the same hollow slogans over and over to each other. Their view of sex is naive and prudish. Leaving sex to the feminists is like letting your dog vacation at the taxidermist's.

The sexes are at war. Men must struggle for identity against the over- 7 whelming power of their mothers. Women have menstruation to tell them they are women. Men must do or risk something to be men. Men become masculine only when other men say they are. Having sex with a woman is one way a boy becomes a man.

College men are at their hormonal peak. They have just left their moth- 8 ers and are questing for their male identity. In groups, they are dangerous. A woman going to a fraternity party is walking into Testosterone Flats, full of prickly cacti and blazing guns. If she goes, she should be armed with resolute alertness. She should arrive with girlfriends and leave with them. A girl who lets herself get dead drunk at a fraternity party is a fool. A girl who goes upstairs alone with a brother at a fraternity party is an idiot. Feminists call this "blaming the victim." I call it common sense.

For a decade, feminists have drilled their disciples to say, "Rape is a 9 crime of violence but not of sex." This sugar-coated Shirley Temple nonsense has exposed young women to disaster. Misled by feminism, they do not expect rape from the nice boys from good homes who sit next to them in class.

Aggression and eroticism are deeply intertwined. Hunt, pursuit, and 10 capture are biologically programmed into male sexuality. Generation after generation, men must be educated, refined, and ethically persuaded away from their tendency toward anarchy and brutishness. Society is not the enemy, as feminism ignorantly claims. Society is woman's protection against rape. Feminism, with its solemn Carry Nation** repressiveness, does not see what is for men the eroticism or fun element in rape, especially the wild, infectious delirium of gang rape. Women who do not understand rape cannot defend themselves against it.

----

*EDS. NOTE—Jean-Jacques Rousseau (1712–1778), a French philosopher and political theorist.

**EDS. NOTE—An American temperance leader and advocate of women's suffrage (1846–1911), who became legendary for her use of a hatchet to destroy liquor and other contents of saloons.

The date-rape controversy shows feminism hitting the wall of its own   11
broken promises. The women of my '60s generation were the first respectable girls in history to swear like sailors, get drunk, stay out all
night—in short, to act like men. We sought total sexual freedom and
equality. But as time passed, we woke up to cold reality. The old double
standard protected women. When anything goes, it's women who lose.

Today's young women don't know what they want. They see that   12
feminism has not brought sexual happiness. The theatrics of public rage
over date rape are their way of restoring the old sexual rules that were
shattered by my generation. Because nothing about the sexes has really
changed. The comic film *Where the Boys Are* (1960), the ultimate expression of '50s man-chasing, still speaks directly to our time. It shows smart,
lively women skillfully anticipating and fending off the dozens of strategies with which horny men try to get them into bed. The agonizing date-
rape subplot and climax are brilliantly done. The victim, Yvette Mimieux,
makes mistake after mistake, obvious to the other girls. She allows herself
to be lured away from her girlfriends and into isolation with boys whose
character and intentions she misreads. *Where the Boys Are* tells the truth. It
shows courtship as a dangerous game in which the signals are not verbal
but subliminal.

Neither militant feminism, which is obsessed with politically correct   13
language, nor academic feminism, which believes that knowledge and
experience are "constituted by" language, can understand pre-verbal or
non-verbal communication. Feminism, focusing on sexual politics, cannot
see that sex exists in and through the body. Sexual desire and arousal cannot be fully translated into verbal terms. This is why men and women
misunderstand each other.

Trying to remake the future, feminism cut itself off from sexual his-   14
tory. It discarded and suppressed the sexual myths of literature, art, and
religion. Those myths show us the turbulence, the mysteries and passions
of sex. In mythology we see men's sexual anxiety, their fear of women's
dominance. Much sexual violence is rooted in men's sense of psychological weakness toward women. It takes many men to deal with one woman.
Woman's voracity is a persistent motif. Clara Bow,* it was rumored, took
on the USC football team on weekends. Marilyn Monroe, singing
"Diamonds Are a Girl's Best Friend," rules a conga line of men in tuxes.
Half-clad Cher, in the video for "If I Could Turn Back Time," deranges a
battleship of screaming sailors and straddles a pink-lit cannon. Feminism,
coveting social power, is blind to woman's cosmic sexual power.

To understand rape, you must study the past. There never was and   15
never will be sexual harmony. Every woman must take personal responsibility for her sexuality, which is nature's red flame. She must be prudent
and cautious about where she goes and with whom. When she makes a

---

*EDS. NOTE—An American actress in silent movies (1905–1965).

mistake, she must accept the consequences and, through self-criticism, re-solve never to make that mistake again. Running to Mommy and Daddy or the campus grievance committee is unworthy of strong women. Posting lists of guilty men in the toilet is cowardly, infantile stuff.

The Italian philosophy of life espouses high-energy confrontation. A   16
male student makes a vulgar remark about your breasts? Don't slink off to whimper and simper with the campus shrinking violets. Deal with it. On the spot. Say, "Shut up, you jerk! And crawl back to the barnyard where you belong!" In general, women who project this take-charge attitude to-ward life get harassed less often. I see too many dopey, immature, self-pity-ing women walking around like melting sticks of butter. It's the Yvette Mimieux syndrome: Make me happy. And listen to me weep when I'm not.

The date-rape debate is already smothering in propaganda churned   17
out by the expensive Northeastern colleges and universities, with their overconcentration of boring, uptight academic feminists and spoiled, af-fluent students. Beware of the deep manipulativeness of rich students who were neglected by their parents. They love to turn the campus into hysterical psychodramas of sexual transgression, followed by assertions of parental authority and concern. And don't look for sexual enlighten-ment from academe, which spews out mountains of books but never looks at life directly.

As a fan of football and rock music, I see in the simple, swaggering   18
masculinity of the jock and in the noisy posturing of the heavy-metal gui-tarist certain fundamental, unchanging truths about sex. Masculinity is aggressive, unstable, combustible. It is also the most creative cultural force in history. Women must reorient themselves toward the elemental powers of sex, which can strengthen or destroy.

The only solution to date rape is female self-awareness and self-control.   19
A woman's number one line of defense is herself. When a real rape occurs, she should report it to the police. Complaining to college committees be-cause the courts "take too long" is ridiculous. College administrations are not a branch of the judiciary. They are not equipped or trained for legal in-quiry. Colleges must alert incoming students to the problems and dangers of adulthood. Then colleges must stand back and get out of the sex game.

• • •

COMPREHENSION

1. According to Paglia, how does feminism mislead women?

2. How does Paglia explain the prevalence of date rape in our society?

3. According to Paglia, "Women who do not understand rape cannot defend themselves against it" (10). What does she say women must understand?

4. Why, according to Paglia, do men and women misunderstand each other?

5. What is Paglia's solution to the problem of rape?

PURPOSE AND AUDIENCE

1. Does Paglia assume her readers are hostile, friendly, or neutral? How can you tell?

2. Is Paglia primarily addressing men, women, or both? How do you know?

3. Is Paglia's purpose to change people's ideas or to change their behavior? Explain.

STYLE AND STRUCTURE

1. Paglia makes no effort to hide her feelings toward those who disagree with her ideas. Underline the words that show her opinion of her opposition. How would you describe her tone? Reasonable? Angry? Sarcastic? Frustrated? Impatient?

2. Throughout her essay Paglia makes personal attacks against what she calls "academic feminists" and "militant feminists." Do you think these attacks strengthen or undercut her argument? Explain your reasoning.

3. Is Paglia's argument primarily inductive or deductive? Explain.

4. How effectively does Paglia refute the arguments against her position?

5. What strategy does Paglia use to conclude her essay? Is this a wise choice?

VOCABULARY PROJECTS

1. Define each of the following words as it is used in this selection.

pervasiveness (2)	eroticism (10)	motif (14)
incidence (3)	delirium (10)	conga line (14)
solitary (5)	subliminal (12)	transgression (17)
taxidermist (6)	turbulence (14)	spews (17)
testosterone (8)	voracity (14)	combustible (18)

2. Find several examples of **colloquialisms** Paglia uses in her essay. Do they help her make her point more clearly, or do they undermine her credibility?

JOURNAL ENTRY

Some of Paglia's critics have charged that she is more interested in shining the spotlight on herself than in addressing issues. After reading her essay, do you think this criticism is justified?

WRITING WORKSHOP

1. What do you think should be done to prevent date rape? Do you, like Paglia, think the solution is up to women? Or do you think the responsibility lies elsewhere?

2. Write an essay in which you take two of Paglia's points and refute them either by questioning their accuracy or by identifying flaws in their logic.

3. Find out what your college's policy is concerning date rape. Write an editorial for your school newspaper or a memo to the dean of students in which you argue that the policy is sound—or that it should be modified.

COMBINING THE PATTERNS

Paragraph 12 is developed by means of **exemplification**. What point is Paglia making? How does her example help her make it? Should she have used a series of brief examples instead of a single extended example? Why or why not?

THEMATIC CONNECTIONS

- "Just Walk On By" (page 186)
- "Sexism in English: A 1990s Update" (page 401)
- "I Want a Wife" (page 461)

SUSAN JACOBY

Susan Jacoby is a freelance writer. Fluent in Russian, she lived in the Soviet Union from 1969 to 1971 and wrote two books on her experiences and research there, *Moscow Conversations* (1972) and *Inside Soviet Schools* (1974). Jacoby also collaborated with Yelena Khanga on a biography of Khanga's family, *Soul to Soul: The Story of a Black Russian American Family 1865–1992* (1992). Jacoby has worked as an education reporter for the *Washington Post* and is a regular contributor to *Cosmopolitan, Glamour, McCall's* and *Good Housekeeping*. She is the author of *Wild Justice: The Evolution of Revenge* (1983) and *The Possible She* (1979), a collection of essays from her research and magazine writings. In "Common Decency," published in 1991, Jacoby argues that excusing date rape on the grounds of "mixed signals" demeans men as well as women.

Common Decency

She was deeply in love with a man who was treating her badly. To assuage her wounded ego (and to prove to herself that she could get along nicely without him), she invited another man, an old boyfriend, to a dinner *à deux** in her apartment. They were on their way to the bedroom when, having realized that she wanted only the man who wasn't there, she changed her mind. Her ex-boyfriend was understandably angry. He left her apartment with a not-so-politely phrased request that she leave him out of any future plans. 1

And that is the end of the story—except for the fact that he was eventually kind enough to accept her apology for what was surely a classic case of "mixed signals." 2

I often recall this incident, in which I was the embarrassed female participant, as the controversy over "date rape" . . . heats up across the nation. What seems clear to me is that those who place acquaintance rape in a different category from "stranger rape"—those who excuse friendly social rapists on grounds that they are too dumb to understand when "no" means no—are being even more insulting to men than to women. 3

These apologists for date rape—and some of them are women—are really saying that the average man cannot be trusted to exercise any impulse control. Men are nasty and men are brutes—and a woman must be constantly on her guard to avoid giving a man any excuse to give way to his baser instincts. 4

If this view were accurate, few women would manage to get through life without being raped, and few men would fail to commit rape. For the reality is that all of us, men as well as women, send and receive innumer- 5

---

*EDS. NOTE—French expression meaning "between two people" or "private."

able mixed signals in the course of our sexual lives—and that is as true in marital beds at age 50 as in the back seats of cars at age 15.

Most men somehow manage to decode these signals without using superior physical strength to force themselves on their partners. And most women manage to handle conflicting male signals without, say, picking up carving knives to demonstrate their displeasure at sexual rejection. This is called civilization.   6

Civilized is exactly what my old boyfriend was being when he didn't use my muddleheaded emotional distress as an excuse to rape me. But I don't owe him excessive gratitude for his decent behavior—any more than he would have owed me special thanks for not stabbing him through the heart if our situations had been reversed. Most date rapes do not happen because a man honestly mistakes a woman's "no" for a "yes" or a "maybe." They occur because a minority of men—an ugly minority, to be sure—can't stand to take "no" for an answer.   7

This minority behavior—and a culture that excuses it on grounds that boys will be boys—is the target of the movement against date rape that has surfaced on many campuses during the past year.   8

It's not surprising that date rape is an issue of particular importance to college-age women. The campus concentration of large numbers of young people, in a unsupervised environment that encourages drinking and partying, tends to promote sexual aggression and discourage inhibition. Drunken young men who rape a woman at a party can always claim they didn't know what they were doing—and a great many people will blame the victim for having been there in the first place.   9

That is the line adopted by antifeminists like Camille Paglia, author of the controversial *Sexual Personae: Art and Decadence from Nefertiti to Emily Dickinson.* Paglia, whose views strongly resemble those expounded 20 years ago by Norman Mailer in *The Prisoner of Sex,* argues that feminists have deluded women by telling them they can go anywhere and do anything without fear of rape. Feminism, in this view, is both naïve and antisexual because it ignores the power of women to incite uncontrollable male passions.   10

Just to make sure there is no doubt about a woman's place, Paglia also links the male sexual aggression that leads to rape with the creative energy of art. "There is no female Mozart," she has declared, "because there is no female Jack the Ripper." According to this "logic," one might expect to discover the next generation of composers in fraternity houses and dorms that have been singled out as sites of brutal gang rapes.   11

This type of unsubtle analysis makes no distinction between sex as an expression of the will to power and sex as a source of pleasure. When domination is seen as an inevitable component of sex, the act of rape is defined not by a man's actions but by a woman's signals.   12

It is true, of course, that some women (especially the young) initially resist sex not out of real conviction but as part of the elaborate persuasion and seduction rituals accompanying what was once called courtship.   13

And it is true that many men (again, especially the young) take pride in the ability to coax a woman a step further than she intended to go.

But these mating rituals do not justify or even explain date rape. Even the most callow youth is capable of understanding the difference between resistance and genuine fear; between a halfhearted "no, we shouldn't" and tears or screams; between a woman who is physically free to leave a room and one who is being physically restrained. 14

The immorality and absurdity of using mixed signals as an excuse for rape is cast in high relief when the assault involves one woman and a group of men. In cases of gang rape in a social setting (usually during or after a party), the defendants and their lawyers frequently claim that group sex took place but no force was involved. These upright young men, so the defense invariably contends, were confused because the girl had voluntarily gone to a party with them. Why, she may have even displayed sexual interest in *one* of them. How could they have been expected to understand that she didn't wish to have sex with the whole group? 15

The very existence of the term "date rape" attests to a slow change in women's consciousness that began with the feminist movement of the late 1960's. Implicit in this consciousness is the conviction that a woman has the right to say no at any point in the process leading to sexual intercourse—and that a man who fails to respect her wishes should incur serious legal and social consequences. 16

The other, equally important half of the equation is respect for men. If mixed signals are the real cause of sexual assault, it behooves every woman to regard every man as a potential rapist. 17

In such a benighted universe, it would be impossible for a woman (and, let us not forget, for a man) to engage in the tentative emotional and physical exploration that eventually produces a mature erotic life. She would have to make up her mind right from the start in order to prevent a rampaging male from misreading her intentions. 18

Fortunately for everyone, neither the character of men nor the general quality of relations between the sexes is that crude. By censuring the minority of men who use ordinary socializing as an excuse for rape, feminists insist on sex as a source of pure pleasure rather than as a means of social control. Real men want an eager sexual partner—not a woman who is quaking with fear or even one who is ambivalent. Real men don't rape. 19

• • •

COMPREHENSION

1. Why does Jacoby believe those who excuse "friendly social rapists" (3) are being more insulting to men than to women?

2. According to Jacoby, why do most date rapes occur?

3. Why is date rape a particularly important issue for college-age women?

4. According to Jacoby, why does using mixed signals as an excuse for rape show a lack of respect for men?

5. What does Jacoby mean in paragraph 16 when she says, "the very existence of the term *date rape* attests to a slow change in women's consciousness that began with the feminist movement of the late 1960's"?

PURPOSE AND AUDIENCE

1. Does Jacoby seem to be addressing her remarks primarily to men, to women, or to both? Explain.

2. How does Jacoby establish her credentials in the area of date rape? Should she have done more in this regard?

3. What preconceptions does she seem to think her readers have about her subject? Explain.

STYLE AND STRUCTURE

1. Jacoby begins her essay with a personal anecdote. How effective is this strategy? Would another strategy have been more effective?

2. How accurate is Jacoby's summary of Camille Paglia's position? How effectively does she refute Paglia's points?

3. What other arguments does Jacoby refute? How effective are these refutations?

4. What evidence does Jacoby use to support her points? Would other kinds of evidence strengthen her argument? Explain.

5. How well does Jacoby summarize her argument in her final paragraph? What new point does she introduce? Is this a wise strategy? Explain.

VOCABULARY PROJECTS

1. Define each of the following words as it is used in this selection.

assuage (1)	elaborate (13)	rampaging (18)
innumerable (5)	rituals (13)	ambivalent (19)

2. What does Jacoby mean by the phrase *common decency?* What connotations does it have?

3. *Date rape* is also referred to as *acquaintance rape.* What does each term suggest? How do the connotations of these terms differ? Which do you believe is more accurate?

JOURNAL ENTRY

Do you agree with Jacoby when she says apologists for date rape are even more insulting to men than they are to women?

WRITING WORKSHOP

1. Who makes a better argument, Paglia or Jacoby? Write an essay in which you summarize the positions of both writers and then support one or the other. Include the reasons why you prefer one argument over the other, and use material from both essays to support your points.

2. What do you think Camille Paglia would say about Jacoby's argument? Assuming you are Paglia, write a letter to Jacoby responding to the specific points she makes in her essay.

3. Write an essay in which you support Jacoby's point that "mating rituals do not justify or even explain date rape" (14). Use examples from personal experience (your own or someone else's) to support your thesis.

COMBINING THE PATTERNS

Paragraph 14 relies on **comparison and contrast.** What two things are being contrasted? Should Jacoby have developed her series of contrasts in more depth? For instance, should she have used narrative examples? What would be the advantages and disadvantages of such a strategy?

THEMATIC CONNECTIONS

- "Thirty-Eight Who Saw Murder Didn't Call the Police" (page 86)
- "The Lottery" (page 247)
- "Sex, Lies, and Conversation" (page 350)

DEBATE CASEBOOK:
Media Violence

Violence is a disturbing and sometimes frightening undercurrent of life in the United States. In any given year, more murders occur in any one of our major cities than in all of the British Isles combined. This fact has not been lost on lawmakers, especially those running for reelection. Violent behavior (and how to curb it) has been a frequent issue in elections. Although the causes of violent crime are complex, some people look for a single cause that will point to a quick fix for the problem. In the 1950s, for example, parents and educators blamed graphically violent comic books for an increase in juvenile crime. In the 1970s, pressure from Congress caused Hollywood to institute a rating system so that parents could judge the suitability of movies. More recently, lawmakers mandated that a V-chip, enabling parents to block violent or sexually explicit programs, be built into all new television sets.

The debate about the connection between media violence and violent behavior heats up whenever a particularly horrible crime is linked to a movie. In one case, for example, two teenagers went on a murder spree and blamed their actions on Oliver Stone's movie *Natural Born Killers.* In another case, five young men seemingly imitated a scene from the movie *The Money Train* and killed a New York City subway toll clerk by setting him on fire. Movies, however, are not the only culprits. In 1996, Paladin Press, publisher of the how-to manual *The Hit Man,* was unsuccessfully sued by the family of a woman whose killer apparently followed a set of detailed instructions outlined in the book. In another apparent case of life imitating art, a woman who had seen the made-for-television movie *The Burning Bed* set her abusive husband on fire.

The four essays in this casebook examine the issue of media violence. In "Unnatural Killers," lawyer and best-selling author John Grisham argues that filmmaker Oliver Stone should be held legally accountable for the aftereffects of his movie *Natural Born Killers.* A guilty verdict against Stone, says Grisham, will show Hollywood that it will have to rein itself in and take responsibility for its own actions. In "Memo to John Grisham" Stone replies, accusing Grisham of leading a witch hunt. According to Stone, Grisham has singled out his film for blame, ignoring the more direct causes of the crimes committed by those who saw his movie. In "Violent Films Cry 'Fire' in Crowded Theaters," attorney Michael Zimecki argues that legal precedents exist for finding filmmakers negligent when they make movies that glorify violence. Finally, in "Frankenstein Must Be Destroyed: Chasing the Monster of TV Violence," Brian Siano argues that the link between TV violence and violent behavior has never been conclusively established. In addition, says Siano, many TV shows that include violence not only are entertaining but also teach children the value of fair play and courage.

JOHN GRISHAM

One of the country's best-selling writers, John Grisham (1955–) almost failed English composition in high school. Born in Jonesboro, Arkansas, he played high school football, graduated from Mississippi State University, and received his law degree from the University of Mississippi. A practicing lawyer from 1981 to 1990, he also served as a member of the Mississippi House of Representatives from 1984 to 1990. His first novel, *A Time to Kill* (1989), was written in fits and starts while he was practicing law. It was not an immediate success. For his second book, Grisham consciously studied the characterization and plotting of best-selling novels; the result was *The Firm* (1991), which remained on the *New York Times* best-seller list for almost a year. Other blockbusters followed in quick succession: *The Pelican Brief* (1992), *The Client* (1993), *The Chamber* (1994), *The Rainmaker* (1995), *The Runaway Jury* (1996), and *The Partner* (1997). Many of his books have been made into successful films. In 1995 (as Grisham relates in the following essay, which originally appeared in the *Oxford American*) a friend of his was killed by a pair of teenagers; the two were allegedly influenced by Oliver Stone's film *Natural Born Killers*. Grisham, who has brought a wrongful-death lawsuit against Stone and others involved in the film, argues here that Hollywood has a responsibility to stop glamorizing and glorifying murder and mayhem.

Unnatural Killers

The town of Hernando, Mississippi has five thousand people, more 1 or less, and is the seat of government for DeSoto County. It is peaceful and quiet, with an old courthouse in the center of the square. Memphis is only fifteen minutes away, to the north, straight up Interstate 55. To the west is Tunica County, now booming with casino fever and drawing thousands of tourists.

For ten years I was a lawyer in Southaven, a suburb to the north, and 2 the Hernando courthouse was my hangout. I tried many cases in the main courtroom. I drank coffee with the courthouse regulars, ate in the small cafes around the square, visited my clients in the nearby jail.

It was in the courthouse that I first met Mr. Bill Savage. I didn't know 3 much about him back then, just that he was soft-spoken, exceedingly polite, always ready with a smile and a warm greeting. In 1983, when I first announced my intentions to seek an office in the state legislature, Mr. Savage stopped me in the second-floor rotunda of the courthouse and offered me his encouragement and good wishes.

A few months later, on election night as the votes were tallied and the 4 results announced to a rowdy throng camped on the courthouse lawn, it became apparent that *I* would win my race. Mr. Savage found me and expressed his congratulations. "The people have trusted you," he said. "Don't let them down."

He was active in local affairs, a devout Christian and solid citizen   5
who believed in public service and was always ready to volunteer. For
thirty years, he worked as the manager of a cotton gin two miles outside
Hernando on a highway that is heavily used by gamblers anxious to get
to the casinos in Tunica.

Around five P.M., on March 7, 1995, someone entered Bill Savage's office   6
next to the gin, shot him twice in the head at point-blank range, and took his
wallet, which contained a few credit cards and two hundred dollars.

There were no witnesses. No one heard gunshots. His body was dis-   7
covered later by an insurance salesman making a routine call.

The crime scene yielded few clues. There were no signs of a struggle.   8
Other than the bullets found in the body, there was little physical evidence. And since Bill Savage was not the kind of person to create ill will
or maintain enemies, investigators had nowhere to start. They formed the
opinion that he was murdered by outsiders who'd stopped by for a fast
score, then hit the road again, probably toward the casinos.

It had to be a simple robbery. Why else would anybody want to mur-   9
der Bill Savage?

The townspeople of Hernando were stunned. Life in the shadows of   10
Memphis had numbed many of them to the idea of random violence, but
here was one of their own, a man known to all, a man who, as he went
about his daily affairs, minding his own business, was killed in his office
just two miles from the courthouse.

The next day, in Poncharoula, Louisiana, three hundred miles   11
south, and again just off Interstate 55, Patsy Byers was working the late
shift at a convenience store. She was thirty-five years old, a happily
married mother of three, including an eighteen-year-old who was
about to graduate from high school. Patsy had never worked outside
the home, but had taken the job to earn a few extra dollars to help with
the bills.

Around midnight, a young woman entered the convenience store   12
and walked to a rack where she grabbed three chocolate bars. As she approached the checkout counter, Patsy Byers noticed the candy, but she
didn't notice the .38. The young woman thrust it forward, pulled the trigger, and shot Patsy in the throat.

The bullet instantly severed Patsy's spinal cord, and she fell to the   13
floor bleeding. The young woman screamed and fled the store, leaving
Patsy paralyzed under the cash register.

The girl returned. She'd forgotten the part about the robbery. When   14
she saw Patsy she said, "Oh, you're not dead yet."

Patsy began to plead. "Don't kill me," she kept saying to the girl who   15
stepped over her and tried in vain to open the cash register. She asked
Patsy how to open it. Patsy explained it as best she could. The girl fled
with $105 in cash, leaving Patsy, once again, to die.

But Patsy did not die, though she will be a quadriplegic for the rest of 16
her life.

The shooting and robbery was captured on the store's surveillance 17
camera, and the video was soon broadcast on the local news. Several full
facial shots of the girl were shown.

The girl, however, vanished. Weeks, and then months, passed with- 18
out the slightest hint to her identity making itself known.

Authorities in Louisiana had no knowledge of the murder of Bill 19
Savage, and authorities in Mississippi had no knowledge of the shooting
of Patsy Byers, and neither state had reason to suspect the two shootings
were committed by the same people.

The crimes, it was clear, were not committed by sophisticated crimi- 20
nals. Soon two youths began bragging about their exploits. And then an
anonymous informant whispered to officials in Louisiana that a certain
young woman in Oklahoma was involved in the shooting of Patsy Byers.

The young woman was Sarah Edmondson, age nineteen, the daugh- 21
ter of a state court judge in Muskogee, Oklahoma. Her uncle is the
Attorney General of Oklahoma. Her grandfather once served as
Congressman, and her great uncle was Governor and then later a U.S.
Senator. Sarah Edmondson was arrested on June 2, 1995, at her parents'
home, and suddenly the pieces fell into place.

Sarah and her boyfriend, Benjamin Darras, age eighteen, had drifted 22
south in early March. The reason for the journey has not been made clear.
One version has them headed for Florida so that Ben could finally see the
ocean. Another has them aiming at New Orleans and Mardi Gras. And a
third is that they wanted to see the Grateful Dead concert in Memphis,
but, not surprisingly, got the dates mixed-up.

At any rate, they stumbled through Hernando on March 7, and 23
stayed just long enough, Sarah says, to kill and rob Bill Savage. Then they
raced deeper south until they ran out of money. They decided to pull another heist. This is when Patsy Byers met them.

Though Sarah and Ben have different socioeconomic backgrounds, 24
they made a suitable match. Sarah, a member of one of Oklahoma's most
prominent political families, began using drugs and alcohol at the age of
thirteen. At fourteen she was locked up for psychiatric treatment. She has
admitted to a history of serious drug abuse. She managed to finish high
school, with honors, but then dropped out of college.

Ben's family is far less prominent. His father was an alcoholic who di- 25
vorced Ben's mother twice, then later committed suicide. Ben too has a
history of drug abuse and psychiatric treatment. He dropped out of high
school. Somewhere along the way he met Sarah, and for awhile they lived
that great American romance—the young, troubled, mindless drifters
surviving on love.

Once they were arrested, lawyers got involved, and the love affair 26
came to a rapid end. Sarah blames Ben for the killing of Bill Savage. Ben

blames Sarah for the shooting of Patsy Byers, Sarah has better lawyers, and it appears she will also attempt to blame Ben for somehow controlling her in such a manner that she had no choice but to rob the store and shoot Patsy Byers. Ben, evidently, will have none of this. It looks as if he will claim his beloved Sarah went into the store only to rob it, that he had no idea whatsoever that she planned to shoot anyone, that, as he waited outside in the getaway car, he was horrified when he heard a gunshot. And so on.

It should be noted here that neither Ben nor Sarah have yet been tried   27 for any of these crimes. They have not been found guilty of anything, yet. But as the judicial wheels begin to turn, deals are being negotiated and cut. Pacts are being made.

Sarah's lawyers managed to reach an immunity agreement with the   28 State of Mississippi in the Savage case. Evidently, she will testify against Ben, and in return will not be prosecuted. Her troubles will be confined to Louisiana, and if convicted for the attempted murder of Patsy Byers and the robbing of the store, Sarah could face life in prison. If Ben is found guilty of murdering and robbing Bill Savage, he will most likely face death by lethal injection at the state penitentiary in Parchman, Mississippi. Juries in Hernando are notorious for quick death verdicts.

On January 24, 1996, during a preliminary hearing in Louisiana,   29 Sarah testified, under oath, about the events leading up to both crimes. It is from this reported testimony that the public first heard the appalling details of both crimes.

According to Sarah, she and Ben decided to travel to Memphis to see   30 the Grateful Dead. They packed canned food and blankets, and left the morning of March 6. Sarah also packed her father's .38, just in case Ben happened to attack her for some reason. Shortly before leaving Oklahoma, they watched the Oliver Stone movie *Natural Born Killers.*

For those fortunate enough to have missed *Natural Born Killers,* it is   31 the repulsive story of two mindless young lovers, Mickey (Woody Harrelson) and Mallory (Juliette Lewis), who blaze their way across the Southwest, killing everything in their path while becoming famous. According to the script, they indiscriminately kill fifty-two people before they are caught. It seems like many more. Then they manage to kill at least fifty more as they escape from prison. They free themselves, have children, and are last seen happily rambling down the highway in a Winnebego.

Ben loved *Natural Born Killers,* and as they drove to Memphis he   32 spoke openly of killing people, randomly, just like Mickey spoke to Mallory. He mentioned the idea of seizing upon a remote farmhouse, murdering all its occupants, then moving on to the next slaughter. Just like Mickey and Mallory.

We do not know, as of yet, what role Sarah played in these discus-   33 sions. It is, of course, her testimony we're forced to rely upon, and she claims to have been opposed to Ben's hallucinations.

They left Memphis after learning the concert was still a few days 34
away, and headed south. Between Memphis and Hernando, Ben again
talked of finding an isolated farmhouse and killing a bunch of people.
Sarah said it sounded like he was fantasizing from the movie. They left
Interstate 55, drove through Hernando and onto the highway leading to
the cotton gin where Bill Savage was working in his office.

Ben was quite anxious to kill someone, she says. 35

He professed a sudden hatred for farmers. This was the place where 36
they would kill, he said, and told Sarah to stop the car a short distance
away so he could test-fire the gun. It worked. They then drove to the gin,
parked next to Bill Savage's small office. Ben told her to act "angelic," and
then they went inside.

Ben asked Bill Savage for directions to Interstate 55. Sarah says that 37
Mr. Savage knew they were up to something. As he gave directions, he
walked around the desk toward Ben, at which point Ben removed the
.38 and shot Mr. Savage in the head. "He threw up his hands and made
a horrible sound," she testified. There was a brief struggle between the
two men, a struggle that ended when Ben shot Mr. Savage for the second time.

Sarah claims to have been so shocked by Ben's actions that she 38
started to run outside, then, after a quick second thought, decided to
stand by her man. Together they rummaged through Mr. Savage's pockets and took his wallet.

Back in the car, Ben removed the credit cards from the wallet, threw 39
the driver's license out the window, and found two one-hundred-dollar
bills. According to Sarah, "Ben mocked the noise the man made when Ben
shot him. Ben was laughing about what happened and said the feeling of
killing was powerful."

You see, the Mickey character in *Natural Born Killers* felt much the 40
same way. He sneered and laughed a lot when he killed people, and then
he sneered and laughed some more after he killed them. He felt powerful.
Murder for Mickey was the ultimate thrill. It was glorious. Murder was a
mystical experience, nothing to be ashamed of and certainly nothing to be
remorseful about. In fact, remorse was a sign of weakness. Mickey was,
after all, a self-described "natural born killer." And Mickey encouraged
Mallory to kill.

Ben encouraged Sarah. 41

After the murder of Mr. Savage, he and Sarah drove to New Orleans, 42
where they roamed the streets of the French Quarter. Ben repeatedly assured Sarah that he felt no aftershocks from committing the murder. He
felt fine. Just like Mickey. He pressed her repeatedly to kill someone herself. "It's your turn," he kept saying. And, "We're partners."

Sarah, as might be expected, claims she was completely repulsed by 43
Ben's demands that she slay the next person. She claims that she considered killing herself as an alternative to surrendering to Ben's demands
that she shed blood.

But Sarah did not kill herself. Instead, she and Ben drove to   44
Ponchatoula for their ill-fated meeting with Patsy Byers.

According to Sarah, she did not want to rob the store, and she cer-   45
tainly didn't wish to shoot anyone. But they were out of money, and, just
like Mickey and Mallory, robbery was the most convenient way to survive. Ben selected the store, and, through some yet-to-be-determined variety of coercion, forced her out of the car and into the store, with the gun.
It was, after all, her turn to kill.

In *Natural Born Killers,* we are expected to believe that Mickey and Mallory   46
are tormented by demons, and that they are forced to commit many of their
heinous murders, not because they are brainless young idiots, but because evil
forces propel them. They both suffered through horrible, dysfunctional childhoods, their parents were abusive, etc. Demons have them in their clutches,
and haunt them, and stalk them, and make them slaughter fifty-two people.

This demonic theme, so as not to be missed by even the simplest   47
viewer, recurs, it seems, every five minutes in the movie.

Guess what Sarah Edmondson saw when she approached the check-   48
out stand and looked at Patsy Byers? She didn't see a thirty-five-year-old
woman next to the cash register. No.

She saw a "demon." And so she shot it.   49

Then she ran from the store. Ben, waiting in the car, asked where the   50
money was. Sarah said she forgot to take the money. Ben insisted she return to the store and rob the cash register.

We can trust the judicial systems of both Mississippi and Louisiana to   51
effectively deal with the aftermath of the Sarah and Ben romance. Absent
a fluke, Sarah will spend the rest of her life behind bars in a miserable
prison and Ben will be sent to death row at Parchman, where he'll endure
an indescribable hell before facing execution. Their families will never be
the same. And their families deserve compassion.

The wife and children and countless friends of Bill Savage have al-   52
ready begun the healing process, though the loss is beyond measure.

Patsy Byers is a quadriplegic for life, confined to a wheelchair, faced   53
with enormous medical bills, unable to hug her children or do any one of
a million things she did before she met Sarah Edmondson. She's already
filed a civil suit against the Edmondson family, but her prospects of a
meaningful physical recovery are dim.

A question remains: Are there other players in this tragic episode?   54
Can fault be shared?

I think so.   55

Troubled as they were, Ben and Sarah had no history of violence.   56
Their crime spree was totally out of character. They were confused, disturbed, shiftless, mindless—the adjectives can be heaped on with shov-
els—but they had never hurt anyone before.

Before, that is, they saw a movie. A horrific movie that glamorized   57
casual mayhem and bloodlust. A movie made with the intent of glorifying random murder.

Oliver Stone has said that *Natural Born Killers* was meant to be a 58 satire on our culture's appetite for violence and the media's craving for it. But Oliver Stone always takes the high ground in defending his dreadful movies. A satire is supposed to make fun of whatever it is attacking. But there is no humor in *Natural Born Killers*. It is a relentlessly bloody story designed to shock us and to further numb us to the senselessness of reckless murder. The film wasn't made with the intent of stimulating morally depraved young people to commit similar crimes, but such a result can hardly be a surprise.

Oliver Stone is saying that murder is cool and fun, murder is a high, a 59 rush, murder is a drug to be used at will. The more you kill, the cooler you are. You can be famous and become a media darling with your face on magazine covers. You can get by with it. You will not be punished.

It is inconceivable to expect either Stone or the studio executives to 60 take responsibility for the aftereffects of their movie. Hollywood has never done so; instead, it hides behind its standard pious First Amendment arguments, and it pontificates about the necessities of artistic freedom of expression. Its apologists can go on, ad nauseam, about how meaningful even the most pathetic film is to social reform.

It's no surprise that *Natural Born Killers* has inspired several young 61 people to commit murder. Sadly, Ben and Sarah aren't the only kids now locked away and charged with murder in copycat crimes. Since the release of the movie, at least several cases have been reported in which random killings were executed by troubled young people who claim they were all under the influence, to some degree, of Mickey and Mallory.

Any word from Oliver Stone? 62

Of course not. 63

I'm sure he would disclaim all responsibility. And he'd preach a bit 64 about how important the film is as a commentary on the media's insatiable appetite for violence. If pressed, he'd probably say that there are a lot of crazies out there, and he can't be held responsible for what they might do. He's an *artist* and he can't be bothered with the effects of what he produces.

I can think of only two ways to curb the excessive violence of a film 65 like *Natural Born Killers*. Both involve large sums of money—the only medium understood by Hollywood.

The first way would be a general boycott of similar films. If people re- 66 fused to purchase tickets to watch such an orgy of violence as *Natural Born Killers*, then similar movies wouldn't be made. Hollywood is pious, but only to a point. It will defend its crassest movies on the grounds that they are necessary for social introspection, or that they need to test the limits of artistic expression, or that they can ignore the bounds of decency as long as these movies label themselves as satire. This all works fine if the box office is busy. But let the red ink flow and Hollywood suddenly has a keen interest in rediscovering what's mainstream.

Unfortunately, boycotts don't seem to work. The viewing public is a   67
large, eclectic body, and there are usually enough curious filmgoers to
sustain a controversial work.

So, forget boycotts.   68

The second and last hope of imposing some sense of responsibility on   69
Hollywood, will come through another great American tradition, the lawsuit. Think of a movie as a product, something created and brought to
market, not too dissimilar from breast implants, Honda three-wheelers,
and Ford Pintos. Though the law has yet to declare movies to be products, it is only one small step away. If something goes wrong with the
product, whether by design or defect, and injury ensues, then its makers
are held responsible.

A case can be made that there exists a direct causal link between the   70
movie *Natural Born Killers* and the death of Bill Savage. Viewed another
way, the question should be: Would Ben have shot innocent people *but for*
the movie? Nothing in his troubled past indicates violent propensities.
But once he saw the movie, he fantasized about killing, and his fantasies
finally drove them to their crimes.

The notion of holding filmmakers and studios legally responsible for   71
their products has always been met with guffaws from the industry.

But the laughing will soon stop. It will take only one large verdict   72
against the likes of Oliver Stone, and his production company, and perhaps the screenwriter, and the studio itself, and then the party will be
over. The verdict will come from the heartland, far away from Southern
California, in some small courtroom with no cameras. A jury will finally
say enough is enough; that the demons placed in Sarah Edmondson's
mind were not solely of her making.

Once a precedent is set, the litigation will become contagious, and the   73
money will become enormous. Hollywood will suddenly discover a desire to rein itself in.

The landscape of American jurisprudence is littered with the remains of   74
large, powerful corporations which once thought themselves bulletproof and
immune from responsibility for their actions. Sadly, Hollywood will have to
be forced to shed some of its own blood before it learns to police itself.

Even sadder, the families of Bill Savage and Patsy Byers can only   75
mourn and try to pick up the pieces, and wonder why such a wretched
film was allowed to be made.

• • •

COMPREHENSION

1. What do Sarah Edmondson and Benjamin Darras have in common? How
   do they claim the movie *Natural Born Killers* influenced them?

2. Who does Grisham believe should share the responsibility for the two
   murders Ben and Sarah committed?

3. According to Grisham, how does Oliver Stone defend the violent content of *Natural Born Killers?* How does Grisham respond to Stone's arguments?

4. In paragraph 60 Grisham says, "It is inconceivable to expect either Stone or the studio executives to take responsibility for the aftereffects of their movie." Why is it inconceivable?

5. What does Grisham think should be done to eliminate excessive violence from movies like *Natural Born Killers?*

PURPOSE AND AUDIENCE

1. What is the thesis of this essay? At what point does Grisham state it? Why does he wait as long as he does?

2. What do you think Grisham hopes to accomplish with his essay? Does he want to change attitudes? Call people to action? Accomplish something else? Explain.

3. This essay appeared in a magazine that Grisham publishes, the *Oxford American: A Magazine of the South.* Does Grisham seem to assume that his readers share his ideas about movie violence? Do you think he considers his readers hostile, friendly, or neutral? What makes you think so?

STYLE AND STRUCTURE

1. Is Grisham appealing mainly to logic or to his readers' emotions? On what do you base your conclusions?

2. What specific arguments does Grisham put forward to support his thesis? How effective do you think these arguments are?

3. At what point does Grisham refute the arguments against his thesis? Are there other arguments he should have addressed? If so, what are they?

4. What is Grisham's attitude toward Stone? Do Grisham's criticisms ever take the form of an *ad hominem* attack? Explain.

5. Grisham ends his essay with a one-sentence conclusion. How effective is this conclusion? Does it reinforce the main point of the essay? What other strategy could Grisham have used to conclude his essay?

VOCABULARY PROJECTS

1. Define each of the following words as it is used in this selection.

tallied (4)	depraved (58)
quadriplegic (16)	apologists (60)
socioeconomic (24)	guffaws (71)
heinous (46)	

2. Throughout this essay, Grisham uses words that contain built-in judgments. For example, in paragraph 23 Grisham says Sarah and Ben "*stum-*

bled through Hernando." Underline as many of these words as you can. How do they affect your response to this essay? Should Grisham have avoided using such words? Why or why not?

JOURNAL ENTRY

Does Grisham ever establish a strong link between *Natural Born Killers* and the crimes committed by Sarah Edmondson and Benjamin Darras? What other factors could have influenced their actions?

WRITING WORKSHOP

1. Write a letter from Grisham to Stone in which you argue why he should-n't make films that glorify violence. Use material from Grisham's essay as well as from the next selection, Stone's "Memo to John Grisham: What's Next—'A Movie Made Me Do It'?" to support your argument.

2. Assume you are a member of the jury in Benjamin Darras's trial. Would you accept or reject the defense's contention that *Natural Born Killers* compelled Darras to commit murder? Write an essay in which you explain your decision. Use facts from Grisham's essay to support your verdict.

3. Rent a copy of *Natural Born Killers* from a video store and view it. Then, write an editorial for your local paper in which you discuss the movie's violent content. Do you think the movie is, as Stone says, a satire of today's violent society? Or do you think, as Grisham says, that the movie glorifies senseless violence? Make sure your thesis statement clearly presents your assessment of the film.

COMBINING THE PATTERNS

This essay begins with a long **narrative** account of the crimes committed by Sarah Edmondson and Benjamin Darras. Why do you think Grisham begins his essay this way? Could he have made his point as effectively with **description?** Why or why not?

THEMATIC CONNECTIONS

- "Just Walk On By" (page 186)
- "Samuel" (page 202)
- "It's Just Too Late" (page 294)
- "It's a Jungle Out There" (page 558)

OLIVER STONE

Controversial filmmaker Oliver Stone (1946–   ) was born in New York City and educated at Yale. He served in Vietnam during the war, returning home a highly decorated infantry specialist. He then studied film at New York University and in the following years wrote screenplays for violent but well-received films like *Midnight Express* (1978) and *Scarface* (1983). His directorial debut came with *Salvador* (1986), about the revolution then taking place in El Salvador; it was followed that same year by *Platoon,* a drama set during the Vietnam War, which won the Academy Award for best picture and earned Stone the award for best director. Next came the highly successful *Wall Street* (1987) and *Born on the Fourth of July* (1989), for which Stone received another best-director Oscar. His films *JFK* (1991) and *Nixon* (1995) sparked considerable debate about the fictionalization of film biography. *Natural Born Killers* (1995) created almost as much controversy because of its apparent glorification of casual murder; while not a box-office hit, the film found a cult audience after it was released on videotape. In the following essay, commissioned by *LA Weekly* as a response to John Grisham's essay "Unnatural Killers," Stone argues that his film had no influence on the couple who killed Grisham's friend and that Grisham's advocacy of "silencing artists" is only a small step from taking away freedom of speech altogether.

Memo to John Grisham: What's Next—"A Movie Made Me Do It"?

The hunt for witches to explain society's ills is ancient in our blood, but unholy for that nonetheless. The difference is that now we do not blame the village hag and her black cat, but the writer and the photographer and the filmmaker. Increasingly indicted by art and fearful of technology, our society scours them for scapegoats, in the process ignoring Shakespeare, who reminds us that artists do not invent nature but merely hold up to it a mirror. That the mirror now is electronic or widescreen or cyberspace is all the more intimidating to the unschooled, and the more tempting to the lawyers.

John Grisham predictably draws upon the superstition about the magical power of pictures to conjure up the undead specter of censorship. Too sophisticated to clamor for government intervention, he calls instead for civil action. Victims of crimes should, he declares, rise up against the purveyors of culture high and low and demand retribution, thereby "sending a message" about the mood of the popular mind. And so we arrive at yet another, more modern, more typically American superstition: that the lawsuit is the answer to everything. Fall victim to a crime acted out in the movies and all you have to do is haul the director into court. Has your father been brutalized? Sue Oedipus and call Hamlet as a wit-

ness. Do you hate your mother? Blame Medea and Joan Crawford.* And
has your lawyer-husband been unfaithful? Why, then slap a summons on
John Grisham, since, after all, he wrote *The Firm.*

Grisham is at pains to insist that before seeing my film *Natural Born*   3
Killers, accused murderers Ben Darras (18) and Sarah Edmondson (19)
had "never hurt anyone." But, even by his own admission, Ben and Sarah
are deeply disturbed youths with histories of drug and/or alcohol abuse
and psychiatric treatment. Ben's alcoholic father divorced his mother
twice, then committed suicide. Grisham mentions as if it is insignificant
that Sarah carried a gun because she feared that Ben would attack her. Far
from never having hurt anyone, it seems Ben and Sarah had for years
been hurting themselves and their families, and it was only a matter of
time until they externalized their anger.

It is likely that, whether they had seen *Natural Born Killers* or *The Green*   4
Berets or a *Tom and Jerry* cartoon the night before their first crime, Ben and
Sarah would have behaved in exactly the way they did. And it is equally
clear that the specific identity of the victim was entirely irrelevant. "Ben
was quite anxious to kill someone," Grisham states, and Sarah was ready
to help. And at the crucial moment when the carefully twisted springs of
their psyches finally uncoiled, as they were bound to do, not I nor Newt
Gingrich nor Father Sullivan of Boys Town could or did influence them.

Did *Natural Born Killers* have an impact on members of its audience?   5
Undoubtedly. Did it move some to a heightened sensitivity toward violence? It did, some. Does it reveal a truth about the media's obsession
with the senseless sensational? Ask O.J. Simpson. But did it drive Ben and
Sarah to commit two murders? No. If they are guilty, perhaps a negligent
or abusive upbringing, combined with defects in their psyches, *did.*
Parents, school, and peers shape children from their earliest days, not
films. And, once grown and gone horribly wrong, those children must answer for their actions—not Hollywood directors. An elementary principle
of our civilization is that people are responsible for their own actions. If
Dan White, the killer of San Francisco Supervisor Harvey Milk and
Mayor George Moscone, could claim that "Twinkies made me do it,"
what's next—"A movie made me do it"?

A recent study showed that the average teenager spends 15,000 hours   6
a year watching television, compared with 11,000 hours a year in school.
According to the study, most programs contain violence, and fully half
of these violent acts do not depict the victim's injuries or pain.
Astonishingly, only 16 percent of all programs show the long-term effects
of violence, while three-quarters of the time, perpetrators of violence on
television go unpunished. Is it just possible that these 15,000 hours of

---

*EDS. NOTE—Oedipus, Hamlet, and Medea are tragic figures of classical drama.
Former Hollywood star Joan Crawford was accused of child abuse by her adopted
daughter in a best-selling memoir.

mostly violent TV programming might have had slightly more effect on these two youngsters than two hours of *Natural Born Killers?*

Grisham points to "at least several" anonymous youths who claim to   7
have committed crimes under the influence "to some degree" of my film. Leaving aside the self-serving vagueness of this statement, we might ask: How many thousands of murders have been committed under the influence of alcohol? Yet Grisham does not call for the breweries and distilleries to be shut down by lawsuits. How many homicidal lunatics have purchased guns? Yet he mounts no campaign to close the weapons factories. Even if we admit, for the sake of argument, that Ben and Sarah were influenced by a film, only a lawyer in search of a client could see in this an indictment of the entertainment industry and not of the teenage killers and those who reared them.

Grisham disparages the First Amendment (which also protects the   8
films that have sprung from Grisham's own brainless works of fiction) and those who believe in it. He has nothing to say, however, about the Second Amendment, which permits gun-toting crazies to litter the American landscape with bodies. To my mind, his priorities are severely distorted. But then, the First Amendment protects even the views of those who don't believe in it. In America, we call that freedom of speech.

It gives me a shiver of fear when an influential lawyer and writer ar-   9
gues, as Grisham does, that a particular work of art *should never have been allowed to be made.* Strangle art in its infancy, he suggests, and society will be a better place. One might more persuasively argue that cold-blooded murderers should be strangled in their infancy. Yet as with human infants, we can never know the outcome of nascent art, and so both must be protected and nurtured, precisely for society's sake. For it is only a small step from silencing art to silencing artists, and then to silencing those who support them, and so on, until, while we may one day live in a lawyer's paradise, we will surely find ourselves in a human hell.

• • •

COMPREHENSION

1. In paragraph 1 Stone says that the function of an artist is to hold a mirror up to nature. What does he mean? How does this statement help explain why he made a movie as violent as *Natural Born Killers?*

2. In paragraphs 1 and 2, Stone calls Grisham's attack against *Natural Born Killers* a witch hunt. What does he mean? Do you agree?

3. In criticizing Grisham's article, Stone implies that Grisham is engaging in *post hoc* reasoning. At what point in his essay does Stone suggest this? Do you agree that Grisham's article is flawed by *post hoc* reasoning? Why or why not?

4. According to Stone, what impact does *Natural Born Killers* have on audiences? What impact does he say television has on viewers?

5. In paragraphs 7 and 8, Stone says that Grisham targets his movie while ignoring other possible causes of violence. What other causes can you identify? How persuasive is Stone's line of reasoning?

PURPOSE AND AUDIENCE

1. What preconceptions does Stone have about movie violence? Does he expect his readers to share his ideas? How do you know?

2. Do you think Stone respects his readers' intelligence, or does he talk down to his audience? Explain.

3. Why do you think Stone wrote this essay? What is his purpose?

4. Is Stone's argument likely to appeal to those who already think television and movies are too violent? Does he make any attempt to appeal to readers who are hostile to his position? If so, where?

STYLE AND STRUCTURE

1. Stone begins his essay by comparing Grisham's attack against *Natural Born Killers* to a witch hunt. Is this a good strategy? Is it likely to alienate some of his readers? Why or why not?

2. Where does Stone attempt to refute Grisham's major points? How successful is he in doing so?

3. In paragraph 5 Stone concedes some points to his opposition. Is this a good strategy, or should he have denied any connection between movie violence and societal violence?

4. In paragraph 8 Stone asks why those who want to censor him don't consider the implications of the Second Amendment, "which permits gun-toting crazies to litter the American landscape with bodies." What effect does the phrase *gun-toting crazies* have on you? Does Stone seem to overstate his case? Why or why not?

5. How effective is Stone's conclusion? Does it adequately restate his position? Is his point about lawyers valid or is it an *ad hominem* attack? Explain.

VOCABULARY PROJECTS

1. Define each of the following words as it is used in this selection.

   scapegoats (1)   retribution (2)
   cyberspace (1)   perpetrators (6)
   specter (2)   nascent (9)

2. At times, Stone's feelings come through. Underline words and phrases in the essay that show his attitude toward Grisham. How would you describe his tone?

JOURNAL ENTRY

Do you believe there is a link between movie violence and societal violence? Do you think that seeing a movie such as *Natural Born Killers* can cause someone to do something he or she would not normally do?

WRITING WORKSHOP

1. Do you believe, as Stone does, that filmmakers should not be legally responsible for the consequences of their films? Or do you agree with Grisham when he says that filmmakers, like car manufacturers, are involved in a commercial enterprise and should be liable for damages caused by their products? Write an essay in which you argue for one side or the other.

2. Stone says that people like Grisham are creating a society in which people no longer have to take responsibility for their actions. Do you agree with Stone? Write an essay in which you argue for or against this position. Use your own experiences as well as examples from the news to support your points.

3. Assume you are either Ben Darras or Sarah Edmondson. Write a letter to Stone in which you argue that he is responsible for the crime you committed. Use the facts of the case as presented in Grisham's and Stone's essays to bolster your argument.

COMBINING THE PATTERNS

Stone includes several paragraphs organized according to a **cause-and-effect** pattern. Find two of these paragraphs, and determine how they help Stone support his thesis.

THEMATIC CONNECTIONS

- "Thirty-Eight Who Saw Murder Didn't Call the Police" (page 86)
- "Who Killed Benny Paret?" (page 270)
- "The Holocaust" (page 469)

MICHAEL ZIMECKI

Michael Zimecki (1950–) was born in Detroit, Michigan, and received his
B.A. from the University of Pittsburgh and an M.A. from Carnegie Mellon.
For many years he was a medical writer affiliated with the University of
Pittsburgh Medical School. After receiving a law degree from Duquesne
University, Zimecki established a private practice in Pittsburgh. He contributed the following essay to the *National Law Journal* in 1996. Several
months earlier, in New York City, a group of young men had set on fire a subway clerk in a token booth, apparently influenced by a similar incident depicted in the film *Money Train,* which had been recently released. Noting
other such copycat incidents, Zimecki argues that "movies are a significant
cause of the violence that has become so prevalent in our society."

Violent Films Cry "Fire" in Crowded Theaters

The late Richard Weaver, professor of rhetoric at the University of   1
Chicago, was fond of reminding his students that "ideas have consequences."

Bad ideas can have abominable consequences. Nevertheless, U.S.   2
courts have permitted moviemakers, magazine publishers, and other members of the mass media to represent some of the most odious and repulsive
scenes imaginable, "on the confidence," as Circuit Judge Alvin B. Run once
said, "that the benefits society reaps from the free flow and exchange of
ideas outweigh the costs society endures by receiving reprehensible or dangerous ideas." *Herceg v. Hustler Magazine Inc.,* 814 F.2d 1017 (1987).

In 1995, a few days after Thanksgiving, a group of five young men   3
torched a subway token booth in Brooklyn, N.Y., trapping the toll clerk
inside. He died of his burns within the week. The act that caused his
death bore an eerie resemblance to two scenes from the recently released
Columbia Pictures movie *Money Train.* In the movie, a pyromaniac sets
token booths on fire by squirting a flammable liquid through the token
slots and throwing in a lighted match.

Senate Majority Leader Bob Dole, the *Wall Street Journal,* the head of   4
the New York Transit Authority and New York's police commissioners
were quick to blame the movie for sparking a copycat crime. As it turned
out, the movie may not have been responsible. Shortly after his arrest, the
youth accused of squirting the flammable liquid denied that the movie
had any connection to the incident. In a letter to the *New York Times,* Jack
Valenti, President and CEO of the Motion Picture Association of America,
could scarcely contain his glee.

For its part, Columbia Pictures steadfastly maintained that it was   5
merely holding a mirror up to life, noting that its film was based on a series of attacks in New York subway stations in 1988.

It may be premature to conclude that *Money Train* did or did not play   6
a part in the 1995 Thanksgiving incident: As of this writing, police have
declined to say whether any of the men in custody saw the movie.
Moreover, two suspects remain at large, and the match-thrower, who
could face a capital murder charge, has not been identified.

One thing is certain: Life and art exert a strong tug on each other.   7

Money Train was not the only such example. In 1993, a Pennsylvania   8
youth died after he attempted to duplicate a scene from *The Program*. In a
peculiar display of male bravado, he lay down on the center line of a
highway and was run over by a car.

In an earlier era, the perpetrators of the 1974 Hi-Fi Murders in Ogden,   9
Utah, forced their victims to drink liquid Drano after watching a similar
scene in the Clint Eastwood picture *Magnum Force*.

That same year, a 9-year-old girl was raped with a bottle by a group   10
of juveniles at a San Francisco beach—just days after the nationwide tele-
cast of the film *Born Innocent*, which showed a young girl being sexually
assaulted with a plunger. The parents of the San Francisco girl subsequently sued NBC for her physical and emotional injuries, alleging that
they were attributable to the broadcaster's negligence and recklessness in
airing the film. *Olivia N. v. National Broadcasting Co. Inc.*, 178 Cal. Rptr.
888, 126 Cal. App.3d 488 (1982). Although the suit proved to be unsuc-
cessful, it was nonetheless a signal attempt to expand tort liability for
speech outside the area of defamation.

COURTS SUPPORT FILMMAKERS

U.S. courts have routinely rejected attempts to hold filmmakers liable   11
in tort for the harm they cause. Plaintiffs' attorneys seeking recovery on a
theory of strict products liability have encountered some of the same difficulties that have impeded anti-gun and anti-tobacco litigation: Movies
are meant to be seen, just as guns are meant to be fired and cigarettes to
be smoked, and there is nothing defective about a product that accom-
plishes its purpose all too well. In fact, brutally violent films are especially popular box-office fare.

The biggest obstacle to plaintiff's attorneys, however, isn't the courts'   12
rejection of claims based on negligence, nuisance or products liability. It's
the courts' narrow interpretation of "incitement."

Speech that advocates violence but that does not incite imminent   13
harm is protected by the First Amendment under the U.S. Supreme
Court's holding in *Brandenburg v. Ohio*, 396 U.S. 444, 23 L.Ed.2d 430, 89
S.Ct. 1827 (1969).

In *Brandenburg*, the high court overturned the conviction of a   14
Klansman under Ohio's criminal syndicalism statute for saying that
"there might have to be some revengence [sic] taken", if "our President,
our Congress, our Supreme Court continues to suppress the white,

Caucasian race." The finding of the court was that the mere advocacy of violence is not enough.

As Justice William O. Douglas wrote in his concurring opinion, the line between what is permissible and what is not is "the line between ideas and overt acts." The Klansman was on the constitutionally protected side of the line because he was not advocating violent deeds now, in the temporal present; his message had an abstract, rather than an urgent, quality. By contrast, someone who falsely shouts "fire" in a crowded theater has impermissibly crossed the line because his speech is "brigaded with action."   15

But what about a film that shouts "fire" in that same, proverbially crowded theater? Film industry executives maintain that movies portray violence but do not advocate it; to the contrary, industry spokespeople claim, the perpetrators of movie violence typically get their comeuppance by film's end.   16

Unfortunately, filmmakers say one thing while showing another. As social psychologist Albert Bandura observed more than 20 years ago, the message of most violent films is not that "crime does not pay," but rather that the wages of violent sin are pretty good except for an occasional mishap.   17

Indifferent to the anti-social repercussions of their cinematic special effects, violent movies such as *Money Train* advocate violence implicitly, if not explicitly. Violence is as much a product of external reinforcement as internal pathology. By modeling, legitimizing, and sanctioning violence, movies do not just loosen restraints on those who are already predisposed to violence. Violent movies actively promote aggressive behavior as a social norm.   18

LEGALLY FLAWED DEFINITION

By any definition other than the legal one, this would constitute "incitement." The rub, of course, is that harm delayed is no harm at all under the *Brandenburg* standard, which distinguishes violence that takes to the streets from violence that erupts in the theater. While fine in theory, the *Brandenburg* concept of "speech brigaded with action" gets reduced in practice to "Take it outside, boys!"—which is poor advice to a schoolchild and hardly more sagacious as a constitutional principle.   19

The difference between a risk of eventual harm and immediate bodily injury has been minimized of late in the toxic torts arena, where medical monitoring awards embrace the principle that a polluter should not be allowed to escape responsibility for his actions simply because environmentally induced cancers are late-developing. Violence, too, can fester for years.   20

Unfortunately, constitutional law has been slow to appreciate the toxic power of words, slow to recognize that exposure to cruel and degrading images is like exposure to a carcinogen, slower still to understand that speech and act occupy a continuum of cause and effect.   21

The premier of *Money Train* may not have been a substantial factor in bringing about the death of subway token clerk Harry Kaufman. But   22 movies are a significant cause of the violence that has become so prevalent in our society. Film-inspired violence may not be "imminent" in the constitutional sense, but the constitutional difference between "I will kill you now" and "I will kill you later" is cold comfort to the victims of movie-modeled murder.

The problem is that we, as a society, are becoming increasingly deadened and desensitized to violence through repeated exposure to its display. Under *Brandenburg,* the onslaught continues. But film industry executives should take heed: Violence is now so imminent in our society that a wrong look can get you shot on many street corners. The hour has come at last, and the rough beast that the poet William Butler Yeats warned about is already born. As we continue to split hairs, failing to address the need for legislation, we can take comfort in the cliché, "Enjoy yourself. It's later than you think." 23

• • •

COMPREHENSION

1. According to Zimecki, why have courts in the United States allowed moviemakers and magazine publishers "to represent some of the most odious and repulsive scenes imaginable" (2)?

2. In paragraph 7 Zimecki says, "Life and art exert a strong tug on each other." What does he mean? What examples does he offer to support this statement?

3. Why have courts routinely rejected attempts to hold filmmakers liable on the theory of product liability? How has the narrow interpretation of *incitement* created an obstacle for plaintiffs?

4. According to Zimecki, in what way do certain types of films shout "fire" in a crowded theater?

5. What does Zimecki mean when he says, "Unfortunately, constitutional law has been slow to appreciate the toxic power of words" (21)?

PURPOSE AND AUDIENCE

1. At what point does Zimecki state his thesis? Why does he wait as long as he does?

2. Is this essay aimed at an audience of lawyers or at a more general audience? How do you know?

3. What is Zimecki's purpose in writing this essay? Is it to change attitudes? To bring about legislation? To change policy? Explain.

STYLE AND STRUCTURE

1. Zimecki begins his essay with a quotation by Richard Weaver. Why do you think he chose this quotation? What other strategies could he have used to introduce his essay?

2. This essay appeared in the *National Law Journal*. If Zimecki were to rewrite the essay for *People* magazine, what kinds of changes would he need to make? What additional support would he need? Explain.

3. Do you think Zimecki undercuts his case by conceding the point that "*Money Train* may not have been a substantial factor in bringing about the death of subway token clerk Harry Kaufman" (22)? Why or why not?

4. What evidence does Zimecki use to support his assertions? Why do you think he chose this type of support?

5. Zimecki concludes his essay with a quotation that he admits is a cliché. How effective is this strategy? Would another quotation be more effective? Explain your reasoning.

VOCABULARY PROJECTS

1. Define each of the following words as it is used in this selection.

repulsive (2)	liability (11)
reaps (2)	incitement (12)
endures (2)	advocacy (14)
reprehensible (2)	impermissibly (15)
pyromaniac (3)	brigaded (15)
capital (6)	repercussions (18)
attributable (10)	pathology (18)
negligence (10)	norm (18)
defamation (10)	sagacious (19)
tort (11)	carcinogen (21)

2. What is the dictionary definition of *incitement?* What additional meanings does Zimecki say the word has acquired?

JOURNAL ENTRY

Do you believe the courts should hold filmmakers responsible for the effects of their movies? What would be the possible effects on movies of such a change in policy?

WRITING WORKSHOP

1. Write an essay in which you argue that moviemakers should not be held responsible for the consequences of their films. Consider the effect on free expression of holding moviemakers liable years after their movies are released. Make sure you refute Zimecki's arguments against your position.

2. Using as evidence several violent movies you have seen, write an essay in which you argue that by glorifying violence, certain films encourage violent behavior.

3. How do you think Zimecki would respond to Stone's essay? Choose a section of Stone's essay, and refute it using any of Zimecki's points that are relevant to the issue.

COMBINING THE PATTERNS

In paragraph 15 Zimecki uses **comparison and contrast** to make his point. What point is he making? Would a paragraph of cause and effect be just as effective here? Why or why not?

THEMATIC CONNECTIONS

- "Thirty-Eight Who Saw Murder Didn't Call the Police" (page 86)
- "It's Just Too Late" (page 294)
- "How the Lawyers Stole Winter" (page 345)

BRIAN SIANO

Brian Siano was born in Cherry Hill, New Jersey, in 1963. He graduated from Temple University and now works as a freelance writer based in Philadelphia. Formerly a senior editor and columnist at the *Humanist,* a journal that promotes secular humanist values, Siano continues to be a regular contributor. He has also written for the *Skeptic,* the *Philadelphia Inquirer,* and *In the Life.* In "Frankenstein Must Be Destroyed," which originally appeared in the *Humanist* in 1994, Siano argues that although there is a correlation between the excessive viewing of TV violence and the acting out of aggressive impulses, no causal connection between the two has been established.

Frankenstein Must Be Destroyed: Chasing the Monster of TV Violence

Here's the scene: Bugs Bunny, Daffy Duck, and a well-armed Elmer   1
Fudd are having a stand-off in the forest. Daffy the rat-fink has just exposed Bugs' latest disguise, so Bugs takes off the costume and says, "That's right, Doc, I'm a wabbit. Would you like to shoot me now or wait until we get home?"

"Shoot him now! Shoot him now!" Daffy screams.   2

"You keep out of this," Bugs says. "He does not have to shoot you now."   3

"He does *so* have to shoot me now!" says Daffy. Full of wrath, he storms   4
up to Elmer Fudd and shrieks, "And I *demand* that you shoot me now!"

Now, if you *aren't* smiling to yourself over the prospect of Daffy's   5
beak whirling around his head like a roulette wheel, stop reading right now. This one's for a very select group: those evil degenerates (like me) who want to corrupt the unsullied youth of America by showing them violence on television.

Wolves' heads being conked with mallets in Tex Avery's *Swing Shift*   6
Cinderella. Dozens of dead bodies falling from a closet in *Who Killed Who?* A sweet little kitten seemingly baked into cookies in Chuck Jones' *Feed the Kitty.* And best of all, Wile E. Coyote's unending odyssey of pain in *Fast and Furious* and *Hook, Line, and Stinker.* God, I love it. The more explosions, crashes, gunshots, and defective ACME catapults there are, the better it is for the little tykes.

Shocked? Hey, I haven't even gotten to *The Three Stooges* yet.   7

The villagers are out hunting another monster—the Frankenstein of   8
TV violence. Senator Paul Simon's hearings in early August 1993 provoked a fresh round of arguments in a debate that's been going on ever since the first round of violent kids' shows—*Sky King, Captain Midnight,* and *Hopalong Cassidy*—were on the air. More recently, Attorney General Janet Reno has taken a hard line on TV violence. "We're fed up with ex-

cuses," she told the Senate, arguing that "the regulation of violence is constitutionally permissible" and that, if the networks don't do it, "government should respond." Reno herself presents a fine example, given her rotisserielike tactics with the Branch Davidian sect in Waco, or her medieval record on prosecuting "satanic ritual abuse" cases in Florida. (At least she wasn't as baffled as Senator Ernest Hollings, who kept referring to *Beavis and Butt-head* as *Buffcoat and Beaver*.)

Simon claims to have become concerned with this issue because, three years ago, he turned on the TV in his hotel room and was treated to the sight of a man being hacked apart with a chainsaw. (From his description, it sounds like the notorious scene in Brian de Palma's *Scarface*—itself censored to avoid an X-rating—but Simon never said what network, cable, or pay-per-view channel he saw it on.) This experience prompted him to sponsor a three-year antitrust exemption for the networks, which was his way of encouraging them to voluntarily "clean house." But at the end of that period, the rates of TV violence hadn't changed enough to satisfy him, so Simon convened open hearings on the subject in 1993.

If Simon was truly concerned with the content of television programming, the first question that comes to mind is why he gave the networks an antitrust exemption in the first place. Thanks to Reagan-era deregulation, ownership of the mass media has become steadily more concentrated in the hands of fewer and fewer corporations. . . .

There's a reason we should be concerned about this issue of media ownership: television influences people. That's its job. Advertisers don't spend all that money on TV commercials because they have no impact. Corporations don't dump money into PBS shows like *The McLaughlin Group* or *Firing Line* unless they are getting their point across. *Somebody* is buying stuff from the Home Shopping Network and keeping Rush Limbaugh's ratings up. Then, too, we all applaud such public-service initiatives as "Don't Drink and Drive" ads, and I think most of us would be appalled if Donatello of the *Teenage Mutant Ninja Turtles* lit up a Marlboro or chugged a fifth of Cutty Sark. So it's not unreasonable to wonder whether violent television might be encouraging violent behavior.

The debate becomes even more impassioned when we ask how children might be affected. The innocent, trusting little tykes are spending hours bathed in TV's unreal colors, and their fantasy lives are inhabited by such weirdos as Wolverine and Eek the Cat. Parents usually want their kids to grow up sharing their ideals and values, or at least to be well-behaved and obedient. Tell parents that their kids are watching *Beavis and Butt-head* in their formative years and you set off some major alarms.

There are also elitist, even snobbish, attitudes toward pop culture that help to rationalize censorship. One is that the corporate mass-market culture of TV isn't important enough or "art" enough to deserve the same free-speech protection as James Joyce's *Ulysses* or William Burrough's

*Naked Lunch.** The second is that rational, civilized human beings are supposed to be into Shakespeare and Scarlatti, not Pearl Jam and *Beavis and Butt-head.* Seen in this "enlightened" way, the efforts of Paul Simon are actually for *our own good.* And so we define anything even remotely energetic as "violent," wail about how innocent freckle-faced children are being defiled by such fare as *NYPD Blue,* and call for a Council of Certified Nice People who will decide what the rest of us get to see. A recent *Mother Jones* article by Carl Cannon (July/August 1993) took just this hysterical tone, citing as proof "some three thousand research studies of this issue."

Actually, there aren't 3,000 studies. In 1984, the *Psychological Bulletin*   14 published an overview by Jonathan Freedman of research on the subject. Referring to the "2,500 studies" figure bandied about at the time (it's a safe bet that 10 years would inflate this figure to 3,000), Freedman writes:

> The reality is more modest. The large number refers to the complete bibliography on television. References to television and aggression are far fewer, perhaps around 500. . . . The actual literature on the relation between television violence and aggression consists of fewer than 100 independent studies, and the majority of these are laboratory experiments. Although this is still a substantial body of work, it is not vast, and there are only a small number of studies dealing specifically with the effects of television violence outside the laboratory.

The bulk of the evidence for a causal relationship between television   15 violence and violent behavior comes from the research of Leonard Eron of the University of Illinois and Rowell Huesmann of the University of Michigan. Beginning in 1960, Eron and his associates began a large-scale appraisal of how aggression develops in children and whether or not it persists into adulthood. (The question of television violence was, originally, a side issue to the long-term study.) Unfortunately, when the popular press writes about Eron's work, it tends to represent his methodology in the simplest of terms: *Mother Jones* erroneously stated that his study "followed the viewing habits of a group of children for twenty-two years." It's this sort of sloppiness, and overzealousness to prove a point, that keeps people from understanding the issues or raising substantial criticisms. Therefore, we must discuss Eron's work in some detail. . . .

Eron's team selected the entire third-grade population of Columbia   16 County, New York, testing 870 children and interviewing about 75 to 80 percent of their parents. Several trends became clear almost immediately. Children with less nurturing parents were more aggressive. Children who more closely identified with either parent were less aggressive. And children with low parental identification who were punished tended to be *more* aggressive (an observation which required revision of the behavioral model).

---

*EDS. NOTE—Serious works of fiction that were banned because they were considered "obscene."

Ten years later, Eron and company tracked down and reinterviewed   17
about half of the original sample. (They followed up on the subjects in
1981 as well.) Many of the subjects—now high-school seniors—demonstrated a persistence in aggression over time. Not only were the "peer-
nominated" ratings roughly consistent with the third-grade ratings, but
the more aggressive kids were three times as likely to have a police record
by adulthood.

Eron's team also checked for the influences on aggression which they   18
had previously noted when the subjects were eight. The persistent influences were parental identification and socioeconomic variables. Some
previously important influences (lack of nurturance, punishment for aggression) didn't seem to affect the subjects' behavior as much in young
adulthood. Eron writes of these factors:

> Their effect is short-lived and other variables are more important in pre-
> dicting later aggression. Likewise, contingencies and environmental
> conditions can change drastically over 10 years, and thus the earlier con-
> tingent response becomes irrelevant.

It's at this stage that Eron mentions television as a factor:

> One of the best predictors of how aggressive a young man would be at
> age 19 was the violence of the television programs he preferred when he
> was 8 years old. Now, because we had longitudinal data, we could say
> with more certainty, on the basis of regression analysis, partial correla-
> tion, path analysis, and so forth, that there indeed was a cause-and-effect
> relation. *Continued research, however, has indicated that the causal effect is
> probably bidirectional: Aggressive children prefer violent television, and the vio-
> lence on television causes them to be more aggressive.*   [italics added]

. . . Eron's data reveals that aggressive kids who turn into aggressive   19
adults like aggressive television. But this is a correlation; it is not proof of a
causal influence. If aggressive kids like eating strawberry ice cream more
often than the class wusses did, that too would be a predictor, and one
might speculate on some anger-inducing chemical in strawberries.

Of course, the relation between representational violence and its in-   20
fluence on real life isn't as farfetched as that. The problem lies in determining precisely the nature of that relation, as we see when we look at the
laboratory studies conducted by other researchers. Usually, the protocol
for these experiments involves providing groups of individuals with entertainment calibrated for violent content, and studying some aspect of
behavior after exposure—response to a behavioral test, which toys the
children choose to play with, and so forth. But the results of these tests
have been somewhat mixed. Sometimes the results are at variance with
other studies, and many have methodological problems. For example,
which "violent" entertainment is chosen? Bugs Bunny and the *Teenage
Mutant Ninja Turtles* present action in very different contexts, and in one
study, the Adam West *Batman* series was deemed nonviolent, despite
those *Pow! Bam! Sock!* fistfights that ended every episode.

Many of the studies report that children do demonstrate higher levels   21
of interpersonal aggression shortly after watching violent, energetic entertainment. But a 1971 study by Feshbach and Singer had boys from
seven schools watch preassigned violent and nonviolent shows for six
weeks. The results were not constant from school to school—and the boys
watching the *nonviolent* shows tended to be more aggressive. Another
protocol, carried out in Belgium as well as the United States, separated
children into cottages at an institutional school and exposed certain
groups to violent films. Higher aggression was noted in *all* groups after
the films were viewed, but it returned to a near-baseline level after a week
or so. (The children also rated the less violent films as less exciting, more
boring, and sillier than the violent films—indicating that maybe kids *like*
a little rush now and then.) Given the criticisms of the short-term-effects
studies, and the alternate interpretations of the longitudinal studies, is
this matter really settled?

Eron certainly thinks so. Testifying before Simon's committee in   22
August [1993], he declared that "the scientific debate is over" and called
upon the Senate to reduce TV violence. His statement did not include any
reference to such significant factors as parental identification—which, as
his own research indicates, can change the way children interpret physical punishment. And even though Rowell Huesmann concurred with
Eron in similar testimony before a House subcommittee, Huesmann's
1984 study of 1,500 youths in the United States, Finland, Poland, and
Australia argued that, assuming a causal influence, television might be
responsible for 5 percent of the violence in society. At *most*.

This is where I feel one has to part company with Leonard Eron. He is   23
one of the most respected researchers in his field, and his work points to
an imperative for parents in shaping and sharing their children's lives.
But he has lent his considerable authority to such diversionary efforts as
Paul Simon's and urged us to address, by questionable means, what only
might be causing a tiny portion of real-live violence.

Some of Eron's suggestions for improving television are problematic   24
as well. In his Senate testimony, Eron proposed restrictions on televised
violence from 6:00 AM to 10:00 PM—which would exclude pro football,
documentaries about World War II, and even concerned lawperson Janet
Reno's proudest moments. Or take Eron's suggestion that, in televised
drama, "perpetrators of violence should not be rewarded for violent
acts." I don't know what shows Eron's been watching, but all of the cop
shows I remember usually ended with the bad guys getting caught or
killed. And when Eron suggests that "gratuitous violence that is not necessary to the plot should be reduced or abandoned," one has to ask just
who decides that it's "not necessary"? Perhaps most troubling is Eron's
closing statement:

For many years now Western European countries have had monitoring
of TV and films for violence by government agencies and have *not* per-

mitted the showing of excess violence, especially during child viewing hours. And I've never heard complaints by citizens of those democratic countries that their rights have been violated. If something doesn't give, we may have to institute some such monitoring by government agencies here in the U.S.A. If the industry does not police itself, then there is left only the prospect of official censorship, distasteful as this may be to many of us. . . .

[In addition], there's the anecdotal evidence—loudly trumpeted as such by Carl Cannon in *Mother Jones*—where isolated examples of entertainment-inspired violence are cited as proof of its pernicious influence. Several such examples have turned up recently. A sequence was edited out of the film *The Good Son* in which McCaulay Culkin drops stuff onto a highway from an overhead bridge. (As we all know, nobody ever did this before the movie came out.) The film *The Program* was re-edited when some kids were killed imitating the film's characters, who "proved their courage" by lying down on a highway's dividing line. Perhaps most notoriously, in October 1993 a four-year-old Ohio boy set his family's trailer on fire, killing his younger sister; the child's mother promptly blamed MTV's *Beavis and Butt-head* for setting a bad example. But a neighbor interviewed on CNN reported that the family didn't even have cable television and that the kid had a local rep as a pyromaniac months before. This particular account was not followed up by the national media, which, if there were no enticing *Beavis and Butt-head* angle, would never have mentioned this fire at a low-income trailer park to begin with.   25

Numerous articles about media-inspired violence have cited similar stories—killers claiming to be Freddy Kreuger, kids imitating crimes they'd seen on a cop show a few days before, and so forth. In many of these cases, it is undeniably true that the person involved took his or her inspiration to act from a dramatic presentation in the media—the obvious example being John Hinckley's fixation on the film *Taxi Driver.** (Needless to say, Bible-inspired crimes just don't attract the ire of Congress.) But stories of media-inspired violence are striking mainly because they're so *atypical* of the norm; the vast majority of people don't take a movie or a TV show as a license to kill. Ironically, it is the *abnormality* of these stories that ensures they'll get widespread dissemination and be remembered long after the more mundane crimes are forgotten.   26

Of course, there are a few crazies out there who will be unfavorably influenced by what they see on TV. But even assuming that somehow the TV show (or movie or record) shares some of the blame, how does one predict what future crazies will take for inspiration? What guidelines would ensure that people write, act, or produce something that *will not upset a psychotic?* Not only is this a ridiculous demand, it's insulting to the   27

---

*EDS. NOTE—Hinckley attempted to assassinate President Ronald Reagan after stalking actress Jodie Foster, who appeared in *Taxi Driver.*

public as well. We would all be treated as potential murderers in order to gain a hypothetical 5 percent reduction in violence.

In crusades like this—where the villagers pick up their torches and go   28
hunting after Frankenstein—people often lose sight of what they're defending. I've read reams of statements from people who claim to know what television does to kids; but what do *kids* do with television? Almost none of what I've read gives kids any credit for thinking. None of these people seems to remember what being a kid is like.

When *Jurassic Park* was released, there was a huge debate over   29
whether or not children should be allowed to see it. Kids like to see dinosaurs, people argued, but this movie might scare them into catatonia. There was even the suspicion that Steven Spielberg and company were being sneaky and underhanded by making a film about dinosaurs that was terrifying. These objections were actually taken seriously. But kids like dinosaurs because they're big, look really weird, and scare the hell out of everything around them. Dinosaurs *kick ass.* What parent would tell his or her child that dinosaurs were *cute?* (And how long have these "concerned parents" been *lying* to their kids about the most fearsome beasts ever to shake the earth?)

Along the same lines, what kid hasn't tried to gross out everyone at   30
the dinner table by showing them his or her chewed-up food? Or tried using a magnifying glass on an ant-hill on a hot day? Or clinically inspected the first dead animal he or she ever came across? Sixty years ago, adults were terrified of *Frankenstein* and fainted at the premiere of *King Kong.* But today, *Kong* is regarded as a fantasy story, *Godzilla* can be shown without the objections of child psychologists, and there are breakfast cereals called Count Chocula and Frankenberry. Sadly, there are few adults who seem to remember how they identified more with the monsters. Who wanted to be one of those stupid villagers waving torches at Frankenstein? That's what our *parents* were like.

But it's not just an issue of kids liking violence, grossness, or comic-   31
book adventure. About 90 percent of the cartoon shows I watched as a child were the mass-produced sludge of the Hanna-Barbera Studios—like *Wacky Races, The Jetsons,* and *Scooby Doo, Where Are You?* I can't remember a single memorable moment from any of them. But that Bugs Bunny sequence at the beginning of this article (from *Rabbit Seasoning,* 1952, directed by Chuck Jones) was done from memory, and I have no doubt that it's almost verbatim.

I know that, even at the age of eight or nine, I had some rudimentary   32
aesthetic sense about it all. There was something hip and complex about the Warner Bros. cartoons, and some trite, insulting *sameness* to the Hanna-Barbera trash, although I couldn't quite understand it then. Bugs Bunny clearly wasn't made for kids according to some study on social-interaction development. Bugs Bunny was meant to make adults laugh as much as children. Kids can also enjoy entertainment ostensibly created

for adults—in fact, that's often the most rewarding kind. I had no trouble digesting *Jaws,* James Bond, and Clint Eastwood "spaghetti westerns" in my preteen years. And I'd have no problems with showing a 10-year-old *Jurassic Park,* because I know how much he or she would love it.

Another example: Ralph Bakshi's brilliant *Mighty Mouse* series was 33 canceled after the Reverend Donald Wildmon claimed it showed the mouse snorting coke. Kids don't organize mass write-in campaigns, and I hate to see them lose something wonderful just because some officious crackpot decides it was corrupting their morals. Perhaps aspartame-drenched shows like *Barney and Friends* or *Widget* (a purple, spermy little alien who can do magic) encourage children to be good citizens, but they also encourage kids to be docile and unimaginative—just the sort of "good citizens" easily manipulated by the likes of Wildmon.

I don't enjoy bad television with lots of violence, but I'd rather not 34 lose *decent* shows that use violence for good reason. Shows like *Star Trek, X-Men,* or the spectacular *Batman: The Animated Series* can give kids a sense of adventure while teaching them about such qualities as courage, bravery, and heroism. Even better, a healthy and robust spirit of irrever-ence can be found in Bugs Bunny, *Ren and Stimpy,* and *Tiny Toons.* Some of these entertainments—like adventure stories and comic books of the past—can teach kids how to be really *alive.*

Finally, if we must have a defense against the pernicious influence of 35 the mass media, it cannot be from the Senate's legislation or the pro-nouncements of social scientists. It must begin with precisely the qualities I described above—especially irreverence. One good start is Comedy Central's *Mystery Science Theater 3000,* where the main characters, forced to watch horrendous movies, fight back by heckling them. Not surpris-ingly, children love the show, even though most of the jokes go right over their curious little heads. They recognize a kindred spirit in *MST 3000.* Kids want to stick up for themselves, maybe like Batman, maybe like Bugs Bunny, or even like Beavis and Butt-head—but always against a world made by adults.

You know, *adults*—those doofuses with the torches, trying to burn up 36 Frankenstein in the old mill.

•   •   •

COMPREHENSION

1. Why, according to Siano, should we be concerned about who owns the media?

2. From what research does the bulk of evidence for a relationship between television violence and violent behavior come? According to Siano, what is the problem with the way the popular press reports on this research?

3. What does Eron conclude about the relationship between television vio-lence and violent behavior? Is he able to say there is a causal influence? On what issue does Siano say he disagrees with Eron?

4. According to Siano, what is the problem with anecdotal evidence about television violence and violent behavior?

5. What reasons does Siano give for not wanting to eliminate violence from children's television shows?

PURPOSE AND AUDIENCE

1. What is the thesis of this article? Is it explicitly stated? If so, where?

2. What strategies does Siano use to appeal to his audience? Is he trying to appeal to their reason? Their emotions? Do you think he succeeds in winning their trust? Explain.

3. How would you describe Siano's tone? Is he serious? Sarcastic? Funny? How can you tell?

STYLE AND STRUCTURE

1. Siano begins his essay by discussing some cartoons. What is the purpose of this introduction? Is it consistent in tone and content with the discussion that follows? Would the essay be more convincing without this introduction? Why or why not?

2. In paragraph 8 Siano says, "The villagers are out hunting another monster—the Frankenstein of TV violence." Why does Siano compare TV violence to Frankenstein?

3. Siano spends a good bit of time refuting those who say there is a causal relationship between TV violence and violent behavior. How effectively does Siano refute the claims made by Eron? By those who present anecdotal evidence?

4. Siano presents his own arguments in the last section of his essay. Are the points he makes in this section convincing? What other points could he have made?

5. Siano ends his essay with a one-sentence conclusion. How memorable is this conclusion? What are its advantages and disadvantages?

VOCABULARY PROJECTS

1. Define each of the following words as it is used in this selection.

permissible (8)	interpersonal (21)
antitrust (9)	diversionary (23)
exemption (9)	pernicious (25)
deregulation (10)	fixation (26)
methodology (15)	atypical (26)
erroneously (15)	norm (26)
contingent (18)	catatonia (29)
correlation (19)	sludge (31)
representational (20)	irreverence (34)

2. When he summarizes Eron's research, Siano uses technical words such as *sample, variable,* and *baseline.* Do you think less technical language would improve the essay? What tentative conclusions can you draw about the use of **jargon** in essays aimed at a wide general audience? (This essay first appeared in the *Humanist.*)

JOURNAL ENTRY

Do you agree or disagree with Siano's contention that TV (or, for that matter, movies and song lyrics) shouldn't be censored just because there are "a few crazies out there who will be influenced by what they see on TV" (27)?

WRITING WORKSHOP

1. Do you think there is a relationship between TV violence and violent behavior in children? Write an argumentative essay in which you take a position on this issue. Use your own personal experience as well as information from the essay to support your ideas.

2. Watch and take notes on five or six different cartoons on television. Then, write an essay in which you agree or disagree with Siano's ideas about cartoon violence. For example, do the best cartoons, as Siano says, encourage children to have a healthy spirit of irreverence for the adult world? Or does Siano ignore some of the more pernicious aspects of cartoon violence?

3. Write a letter to Eron in which you argue for or against his statement, "If the industry does not police itself, then there is left only the prospect of official censorship, distasteful as this may be to many of us" (24).

COMBINING THE PATTERNS

Siano structures paragraphs 25 and 26 as **exemplification** paragraphs. What point is he trying to make? Does he provide enough examples? Should he have provided more? Should he have discussed the examples he mentions in more depth?

THEMATIC CONNECTIONS

- "Who Killed Benny Paret?" (page 270)
- "Television: The Plug-In Drug" (page 274)

WRITING ASSIGNMENTS FOR ARGUMENTATION

1. Write an essay in which you discuss a teacher's right to strike. Address the major arguments against your position, and maintain an objective stance.

2. Assume that a library in your town has decided that certain books are objectionable and has removed them from the shelves. Write a letter to the local paper in which you argue for or against the library's actions. Make a list of the major arguments that you could refute, and address some of them in your essay. Remember to respect the views of your audience and to address them in a respectful manner.

3. Write an essay in which you argue for or against the right of a woman to keep the baby after she has agreed to be a surrogate mother for another woman.

4. Write an essay in which you discuss under what circumstances, if any, animals should be used for scientific experimentation.

5. Write an essay in which you argue for or against the proposition that women soldiers should be able to serve in combat situations.

6. Research some criminal cases that resulted in the death penalty. Write an essay in which you use these accounts to support your arguments either for or against the death penalty. Don't forget to give credit to your sources. See the Appendix for information about documentation.

7. Write an argumentative essay in which you discuss whether there are any situations in which a nation has an obligation to go or not to go to war.

8. Write an essay in which you discuss whether health-care workers—doctors, nurses, and dentists, for example—should be required to be tested for the AIDS virus.

9. In the Declaration of Independence, Jefferson says that all individuals are entitled to "life, liberty, and the pursuit of happiness." Write an essay in which you argue that these rights are not absolute.

10. Write an argumentative essay on one of these topics: Should high school students be required to take sex-education courses? Should fraternities/sororities be abolished? Should teachers be required to pass periodic competency tests? Should the legal drinking age be raised (or lowered)? Should any workers be required to submit to random drug testing?

COLLABORATIVE ACTIVITY FOR ARGUMENTATION

Working with three other students, select a controversial topic—one not covered in any of the debates in this chapter—that interests all of you. (You can review the Writing Assignments for Argumentation listed above to get ideas.) State your topic the way a topic is stated in a formal debate:

Resolved: The United States should suspend all immigration quotas.

Then, divide into two two-member teams, and decide which team will take the pro position and which will take the con. Each team should list the arguments on its side of the issue and then write two or three paragraphs summarizing its position. Finally, each group should stage a ten-minute debate—five minutes for each side—in front of the class. (The pro side presents its argument first.) At the end of each debate, the class should discuss which side has presented the stronger arguments.

11

COMBINING THE PATTERNS

Few essays are pure process essays or exemplification essays or models of any other single pattern of development; in fact, nearly every essay, including those in this text, combines a variety of patterns. Even though an essay may be organized primarily as, say, a comparison and contrast, it is still likely to include sentences, paragraphs, and even groups of paragraphs shaped by other patterns of development. In fact, combining various patterns in a single essay gives writers the flexibility to express their ideas most effectively. (For this reason, every essay in Chapters 2 through 10 of this text is followed by Combining the Patterns questions that focus on how the essay uses other patterns of development along with its dominant pattern.)

In this chapter we include essays that are somewhat more challenging than most others in the text. These essays illustrate how different patterns of development work together in a single piece of writing. We have annotated the first two essays—"The Park" by Michael Huu Truong, a student, and "On Dumpster Diving" by Lars Eighner—to identify the various patterns these writers use. Truong's essay relies primarily on narration, description, and exemplification to express his memories of childhood. Eighner's combines sections of definition, exemplification, classification and division, cause and effect, comparison and contrast, and process; at the same time, he tells the story (narration) and provides vivid details (description) of his life as a homeless person. Following these annotated essays are two additional selections that combine patterns: Jonathan Swift's classic satire "A Modest Proposal" and Alice Walker's contemporary essay "In Search of Our Mothers' Gardens." Each of the essays in this chapter is followed by the same types of questions that accompany the other reading selections in the text.

▶ **A STUDENT WRITER: COMBINING THE PATTERNS**

This essay was written for a first-year composition course in response to the assignment "Write an essay about the person and/or place that defined your childhood."

The Park

Background

    My childhood did not really begin until thirteen years ago, when I first came to this country from the rural jungle of Vietnam. I can't really remember much from this period, and the things I do remember are vague images that I have no desire or intention to discuss. However, my childhood in the States was a lot different, especially after I met my friend **Thesis statement** James. While it lasted, it was paradise. 1

Narrative begins

    It was a cold wintry day in February after a big snowstorm--the first I'd ever seen. My **Description: effects of cold** lips were chapped, my hands were frozen stiff, and my cheeks were burning from the biting wind, and yet I loved it. I especially loved **Comparison and contrast: U.S. vs. Vietnam** the snow. I had come from a country where the closest things to snow were white paint and cotton balls. But now, I was in America. On that frosty afternoon, I was determined to build a snowman. I had seen them in books, and I had heard they could talk. I knew they could come alive, and I couldn't wait. 2

    "Eyryui roeow ierog," said a voice that **Description: James** came out of nowhere. I turned around, and right in my face was a short, red-faced (probably from the cold wind) Korean kid with a dirty, runny nose. I responded, "Wtefkjkr ruyjft gsdfr" in my own tongue. We understood each other perfectly, and we expressed our understanding with a smile. **Narration: the first day** Together, we built our first snowman. We were disappointed that evening when the snowman just stood there; however, I was happy because I had made my first friend. 3

Analogies

    Ever since then we've been a team like Abbott and Costello (or, when my cousin joined 4

us, The Three Stooges). The two of us were
inseparable. We could've made the greatest
Krazy Glue commercial ever.

Narration: what they did that summer

The summer that followed the big snow-   5
storm, from what I can recall, was awesome. We
were free like comets in the heavens, and we
did whatever our hearts wanted. For the most
part, our desires were fulfilled in a little
park across the street. This park was ours; it
was like our own planet guarded by our own
robot army (disguised as trees). Together we
fought against the bigger people who always
tried to invade and take over our world. The
enemy could never conquer our fortress because
they would have to destroy our robots, penetrate our force field, and then defeat us;
this last feat would be impossible.

Narrative continues

This park was our fantasy land where   6
everything we wished for came true and
everything we hated was banished forever. We

Examples: what they banished

banished vegetables, cheese, bigger people,
and--of course--girls. The land was enchanted,
and we could be whatever we felt like. We were
super ninjas one day and millionaires the
next; we became the heroes we idolized and
lived the lives we dreamed about. I had the

Examples: super-hero fantasies

strength of Bruce Lee and Superman; James possessed the power of Clint Eastwood and the
Bionic Man. My weapons were the skills of
Bruce and a cape. James, however, needed a
real weapon for Clint, and the weapon he made
was awesome. The Death Ray could destroy a
building with one blast, and it even had a
shield so James was always protected. Even
with all his mighty weapons and gadgets,
though, he was still no match for Superman and
Bruce Lee. Every day, we fought until death
(or until our parents called us for dinner).

Narrative continues

When we became bored with our super pow-   7
ers, the park became a giant spaceship. We

Examples: new worlds and planets

traveled all over the Universe, conquering and exploring strange new worlds and mysterious planets. Our ship was a top secret, indestructible space warship called the X-007. We went to Mars, Venus, Pluto, and other alien planets, destroying all the monsters we could find. When necessary, our spacecraft was transformed into a submarine for deep-sea adventures. We found lost cities, unearthed treasures, and saved Earth by destroying all the sea monsters that were plotting against us. We became heroes--just like Superman, Bruce Lee, the Bionic Man, and Clint Eastwood.

Cause and effect: prospect of school leads to problems

James and I had the time of our lives in the park that summer. It was great--until we heard about the horror of starting school. Shocked and terrified, we ran to our fortress to escape. For some reason, though, our magic kingdom had lost its powers. We fought hard that evening, trying to keep the bigger people out of our planet, but the battle was soon lost. Bruce Lee, Superman, the Bionic Man, and Clint Eastwood had all lost their special powers.   8

Narrative continues

School wasn't as bad as we'd thought it would be. The first day, James and I sat there with our hands folded. We didn't talk or move, and we didn't dare look at each other (we would've cracked up because we always made these goofy faces). Even though we had pens that could be transformed into weapons, we were still scared.   9

Description: school

Everyone was darker or lighter than we were, and the teacher was speaking a strange language (English). James and I giggled as she talked. We giggled softly when everyone else talked, and they laughed out loud when it was our turn to speak.   10

Narrative continues

The day dragged on, and all we wanted to do was go home and rebuild our fortress. Finally, after an eternity, it was almost   11 three o'clock. James and I sat at the edge of our seats as we counted under our breath: "10, 9, 8, 7, 6, 5, 4, 3, 2, 1." At last the bell sounded. We dashed for the door and raced home and across the street--and then we stopped. We stood still in the middle of the street with our hearts pounding like the beats of a drum. The cool September wind began to pick up, and everything became silent. We stood there and

Description: the fence

watched the metal of the fence reflect the beautiful colors of the sun. It was beautiful, and yet we hated everything about it. The new metal fence separated us from our fortress, our planet, our spaceship, our submarine--and, most important of all, our heroes and our dreams.

We stood there for a long time. As the sun slowly turned red and sank beneath the ground, so did our dreams, heroes, and hearts. Darkness soon devoured the park, and after a while we walked home with only the memories of the summer that came after the big snowstorm.

12

Points for Special Attention

WRITING A PERSONAL EXPERIENCE ESSAY.   Michael's assignment specified that he was to write an essay about an experience that would help his readers—other students—understand what his childhood was like. Because it was a personal experience essay, Michael was free to use the first-person pronouns *I* and *we* as well as contractions, neither of which would be acceptable in a more formal essay.

THESIS STATEMENT.   Because Michael's primary purpose in this essay was to communicate personal feelings and impressions, an argumentative thesis statement (such as "If every television in the United States disappeared, more people would have childhoods like mine") would have been inappropriate. Still, Michael states his thesis explicitly in order to unify his essay around the dominant impression he wants to convey: "While it lasted, it was paradise."

COMBINING THE PATTERNS.   Michael also had more specific purposes, and these determined the patterns that shape his essay. His essay's dominant pattern is *narration,* but to help students visualize the person (James) and the place (the park) he discusses, he includes sections that *describe* and give concrete, specific *examples* as well as summarize his daily routine. These patterns work together to create an essay that *defines* the nature of his childhood.

TRANSITIONS.   The transitions between the individual sentences and paragraphs of Michael's essay—"now," "Ever since," "The summer that followed the big snowstorm"—serve primarily to move readers through time. This is appropriate because *narration* is the dominant pattern governing his essay's overall structure.

DETAIL.   Michael's essay is full of specific detail—for example, quoted bits of dialogue in paragraph 3 and names of his heroes and of particular games (and related equipment and weapons) elsewhere. The descriptive details that recreate the physical scenes—in particular, the snow, cold, frost, and wind of winter and the sun reflected in the fence—are vivid enough to help readers visualize the places Michael writes about.

FIGURATIVE LANGUAGE.   Michael's essay describes a time when his imagination wandered without the restraints of adulthood. Appropriately, he uses rich figurative language—"We were free like comets in the heavens"; "The park became a giant spaceship"; "We found lost cities, unearthed treasures, and saved Earth"; "darkness soon devoured the park"—to evoke the time and place he describes.

Focus on Revision

Michael's assignment asked him to write about his childhood, and he chose to focus on his early years in the United States. When his peer editing group discussed his essay, however, a number of students were curious about his life in Vietnam. Some of them thought he should add a paragraph summarizing the "vague images" he remembered of his earlier childhood, perhaps contrasting it with his life in the United States, as he does in passing in paragraph 2. An alternate suggestion, made by one classmate, was that Michael consider deleting the sentence that states he has "no desire or intention" to discuss this part of his life, since it raises issues his essay doesn't address. After thinking about these ideas, Michael decided to revise his essay by adding a brief paragraph about his life in Vietnam, contrasting the park and his friendship with James to some of his earlier memories.

Each of the following essays combines several patterns, blending strategies to achieve the writer's purpose.

LARS EIGHNER

Lars Eighner was born in 1948 and grew up in Houston, Texas. He attended the University of Texas at Austin for three years before dropping out and going to work in a state mental hospital. After leaving this job over a policy dispute in 1988 and falling behind in his rent payments, Eighner became homeless. He traveled for three years with his dog, Lizbeth, between Austin and Los Angeles, earning some money writing stories for magazines. Some of his fiction had already been collected in *Bayou Boy and Other Stories* (1985). Eighner now lives in Austin. His most recent publications are *Whispered in the Dark* (1995) and the novel *Pawn to Queen Four* (1995). Eighner's memoir of his homelessness, *Travels with Lizbeth* (1993), was written on a personal computer found in a Dumpster, and portions of the book were published serially in the *Utne Reader*, *Harper's* magazine, *The Pushcart Prizes XVII*, and the *Threepenny Review*, where this chapter first appeared in 1991. "On Dumpster Diving" details the practical dangers as well as the many possibilities of scavenging from Dumpsters.

On Dumpster Diving

This chapter was composed while the author was homeless. The present tense has been preserved.

Definition: Dumpster

Long before I began Dumpster diving I was impressed with Dumpsters, enough so that I wrote the Merriam-Webster research service to discover what I could about the word *Dumpster*. I learned from them that it is a proprietary word belonging to the Dempsey Dumpster company. Since then I have dutifully capitalized the word, although it was lowercased in almost all the citations Merriam-Webster photocopied for me. Dempsey's word is too apt. I have never heard these things called anything but Dumpsters. I do not know anyone who knows the generic name for these objects. From time to time I have heard a wino or hobo give some corrupted credit to the original and call them Dipsy Dumpsters.

Narration: Eighner's story begins

I began Dumpster diving about a year before I became homeless.

Definition: *diving*

I prefer the word *scavenging* and use the word *scrounging* when I mean to be obscure. I have heard people, evidently meaning to be polite, use the word *foraging*, but I prefer to reserve that word for gathering nuts and berries and such, which I do also according to the season and the opportunity. *Dumpster diving*

1

2

3

seems to me to be a little too cute and, in my case, inaccurate because I lack the athletic ability to lower myself into the Dumpsters as the true divers do, much to their increased profit.

I like the frankness of the word *scavenging,* which I 4 can hardly think of without picturing a big black snail on an aquarium wall. I live from the refuse of others. I am a scavenger. I think it a sound and honorable niche, although if I could I would naturally prefer to live the comfortable consumer life, perhaps—and only perhaps—as a slightly less wasteful consumer, owing to what I have learned as a scavenger.

Narration: story continues

While Lizbeth and I were still living in the shack 5 on Avenue B as my savings ran out, I put almost all my sporadic income into rent. The necessities of daily life I began to extract from Dumpsters. Yes, we ate from them. Except for jeans, all my clothes came from

Exemplification: things found in Dumpsters

Dumpsters. Boom boxes, candles, bedding, toilet paper, a virgin male love doll, medicine, books, a typewriter, dishes, furnishings, and change, sometimes amounting to many dollars—I acquired many things from Dumpsters.

Thesis statement

I have learned much as a scavenger. I mean to put 6 some of what I have learned down here, beginning with the practical art of Dumpster diving and proceeding to the abstract.

What is safe to eat? 7

After all, the finding of objects is becoming something of an urban art. Even respectable employed people will sometimes find something tempting sticking out of a Dumpster or standing beside one. Quite a number of people, not all of them of the bohemian type, are willing to brag that they found this or that piece of trash. But eating from Dumpsters is what separates the dilettanti from the professionals. Eating safely from the Dumpsters involves three principles: using the senses and common sense to evaluate the condition of the found materials, knowing the Dumpsters of a given area and checking them regularly, and seeking always to answer the question "Why was this discarded?"

Comparison and contrast: Dumpster divers vs. others

Perhaps everyone who has a kitchen and a regular 9 supply of groceries has, at one time or another, made a sandwich and eaten half of it before discovering mold on the bread or got a mouthful of milk before realizing the milk had turned. Nothing of the sort is likely to happen to a Dumpster diver because he is constantly reminded that most food is discarded for a reason. Yet a lot of perfectly good food can be found in Dumpsters.

Classification and division: different kinds of food found in Dumpsters and their relative safety

Canned goods, for example, turn up fairly often in the Dumpsters I frequent. All except the most phobic people will be willing to eat from a can, even if it came from a Dumpster. Canned goods are among the safest foods to be found in Dumpsters but are not utterly foolproof.   10

Although very rare with modern canning methods, botulism is a possibility. Most other forms of food poisoning seldom do lasting harm to a healthy person, but botulism is almost certainly fatal and often the first symptom is death. Except for carbonated beverages, all canned goods should contain a slight vacuum and suck air when first punctured. Bulging, rusty, and dented cans and cans that spew when punctured should be avoided, especially when the contents are not very acidic or syrupy.   11

Heat can break down the botulin, but this requires much more cooking than most people do to canned goods. To the extent that botulism occurs at all, of course, it can occur in cans on pantry shelves as well as in cans from Dumpsters. Need I say that home-canned goods are simply too risky to be recommended.   12

From time to time one of my companions, aware of the source of my provisions, will ask, "Do you think these crackers are really safe to eat?" For some reason it is most often the crackers they ask about.   13

This question has always made me angry. Of course I would not offer my companion anything I had doubts about. But more than that, I wonder why he cannot evaluate the condition of the crackers for himself. I have no special knowledge and I have been wrong before. Since he knows where the food comes from, it seems to me he ought to assume some of the responsibility for deciding what he will put in his mouth. For myself I have few qualms about dry foods such as crackers, cookies, cereal, chips, and pasta if they are free of visible contaminates and still dry and crisp. Most often such things are found in the original packaging, which is not so much a positive sign as it is the absence of a negative one.   14

Raw fruits and vegetables with intact skins seem perfectly safe to me, excluding of course the obviously   15 rotten. Many are discarded for minor imperfections that can be pared away. Leafy vegetables, grapes, cauliflower, broccoli, and similar things may be contaminated by liquids and may be impractical to wash.

Candy, especially hard candy, is usually safe if it   16
has not drawn ants. Chocolate is often discarded only because it has become discolored as the cocoa butter de-emulsified. Candying, after all, is one method of food preservation because pathogens do not like very sugary substances.

All of these foods might be found in any Dumpster   17
and can be evaluated with some confidence largely on the basis of appearance. Beyond these are foods that cannot be correctly evaluated without additional information.

I began scavenging by pulling pizzas out of the   18
Dumpster behind a pizza delivery shop. In general, prepared food requires caution, but in this case I knew when the shop closed and went to the Dumpster as soon as the last of the help left.

Such shops often get prank orders; both the orders   19
and the products made to fill them are called *bogus*. Because help seldom stays long at these places, pizzas are often made with the wrong topping, refused on delivery for being cold, or baked incorrectly. The products to be discarded are boxed up because inventory is kept by counting boxes: A boxed pizza can be written off; an unboxed pizza does not exist.

I never placed a bogus order to increase the sup-   20
ply of pizzas and I believe no one else was scavenging in this Dumpster. But the people in the shop became suspicious and began to retain their garbage in the shop overnight. While it lasted I had a steady supply of fresh, sometimes warm pizza. Because I knew the Dumpster I knew the source of the pizza, and because I visited the Dumpster regularly I knew what was fresh and what was yesterday's.

Cause and effect: why Eighner visits certain Dumpsters; why students throw out food

The area I frequent is inhabited by many affluent   21
college students. I am not here by chance; the Dumpsters in this area are very rich. Students throw out many good things, including food. In particular they tend to throw everything out when they move at the end of a semester, before and after breaks, and around midterm, when many of them despair of college. So I find it advantageous to keep an eye on the academic calendar.

Students throw food away around breaks because 22
they do not know whether it has spoiled or will spoil
before they return. A typical discard is a half jar of
peanut butter. In fact, nonorganic peanut butter does
not require refrigeration and is unlikely to spoil in any
reasonable time. The student does not know that, and
since it is Daddy's money, the student decides not to
take a chance. Opened containers require caution and
some attention to the question "Why was this discarded?" But in the case of discards from student apartments, the answer may be that the item was thrown out
through carelessness, ignorance, or wastefulness. This
can sometimes be deduced when the item is found with
many others, including some that are obviously perfectly good.

Some students, and others, approach defrosting a 23
freezer by chucking out the whole lot. Not only do the
circumstances of such a find tell the story, but also the
mass of frozen goods stays cold for a long time and
items may be found still frozen or freshly thawed.

Yogurt, cheese, and sour cream are items that are 24
often thrown out while they are still good. Occasionally
I find cheese with a spot of mold, which of course I just
pare off, and because it is obvious why such a cheese
was discarded, I treat it with less suspicion than an apparently perfect cheese found in similar circumstances.
Yogurt is often discarded, still sealed, only because the
expiration date on the carton had passed. This is one of
my favorite finds because yogurt will keep for several
days, even in warm weather.

Students throw out canned goods and staples at the 25
end of semesters and when they give up college at
midterm. Drugs, pornography, spirits, and the like are
often discarded when parents are expected—Dad's Day,
for example. And spirits also turn up after big party
weekends, presumably discarded by the newly re-
formed. Wine and spirits, of course, keep perfectly well
even once opened, but the same cannot be said of beer.

My test for carbonated soft drinks is whether they 26
still fizz vigorously. Many juices or other beverages
are too acidic or too syrupy to cause much concern,
provided they are not visibly contaminated. I have
discovered nasty molds in the vegetable juices, even
when the product was found under its original seal; I
recommend that such products be decanted slowly
into a clear glass. Liquids always require some care.

Example: a liquid that requires care

One hot day I found a large jug of Pat O'Brien's Hurricane mix. The jug had been opened but was still ice cold. I drank three large glasses before it became apparent to me that someone had added the rum to the mix, and not a little rum. I never tasted the rum, and by the time I began to feel the effects I had already ingested a very large quantity of the beverage. Some divers would have considered this a boon, but being suddenly intoxicated in a public place in the early afternoon is not my idea of a good time.

I have heard of people maliciously contaminating 27 discarded food and even handouts, but mostly I have heard of this from people with vivid imaginations who have had no experience with Dumpsters themselves. Just before the pizza shop stopped discarding its garbage at night, jalapeños began showing up on most of the thrown-out pizzas. If indeed this was meant to discourage me, it was a wasted effort because I am a native Texan.

For myself, I avoid game, poultry, pork, and egg- 28 based foods, whether I find them raw or cooked. I seldom have the means to cook what I find, but when I do I avail myself of plentiful supplies of beef, which is often in very good condition. I suppose fish becomes disagreeable before it becomes dangerous. Lizbeth is happy to have any such thing that is past its prime and, in fact, does not recognize fish as food until it is quite strong.

Home leftovers, as opposed to surpluses from 29 restaurants, are very often bad. Evidently, especially among students, there is a common type of personality that carefully wraps up even the smallest leftover and shoves it into the back of the refrigerator for six months or so before discarding it. Characteristic of this type are the reused jars and margarine tubs to which the remains are committed. I avoid ethnic foods I am unfamiliar with. If I do not know what it is supposed to look like when it is good, I cannot be certain I will be able to tell if it is bad.

No matter how careful I am I still get dysentery at 30 least once a month, oftener in warmer weather. I do not want to paint too romantic a picture. Dumpster diving has serious drawbacks as a way of life.

Process: how to scavenge

I learned to scavenge gradually, on my own. Since 31 then I have initiated several companions into the trade. I have learned that there is a predictable series of stages a person goes through in learning to scavenge.

At first the new scavenger is filled with disgust   32
and self-loathing. He is ashamed of being seen and
may lurk around, trying to duck behind things, or he
may try to dive at night. (In fact, most people instinctively look away from a scavenger. By skulking
around, the novice calls attention to himself and
arouses suspicion. Diving at night is ineffective and
needlessly messy.)

Every grain of rice seems to be a maggot.   33
Everything seems to stink. He can wipe the egg yolk
off the found can, but he cannot erase from his mind
the stigma of eating garbage.

That stage passes with experience. The scavenger   34
finds a pair of running shoes that fit and look and
smell brand-new. He finds a pocket calculator in perfect working order. He finds pristine ice cream, still
frozen, more than he can eat or keep. He begins to understand: People throw away perfectly good stuff, a
lot of perfectly good stuff.

At this stage, Dumpster shyness begins to dissi-   35
pate. The diver, after all, has the last laugh. He is finding all manner of good things that are his for the
taking. Those who disparage his profession are the
fools, not he.

He may begin to hang on to some perfectly good   36
things for which he has neither a use nor a market.
Then he begins to take note of the things that are not
perfectly good but are nearly so. He mates a Walkman
with broken earphones and one that is missing a bat-
tery cover. He picks up things that he can repair.

At this stage he may become lost and never re-   37
cover. Dumpsters are full of things of some potential
value to someone and also of things that never have
much intrinsic value but are interesting. All the
Dumpster divers I have known come to the point of
trying to acquire everything they touch. Why not take
it, they reason, since it is all free? This is, of course,
hopeless. Most divers come to realize that they must
restrict themselves to items of relatively immediate
utility. But in some cases the diver simply cannot control himself. I have met several of these pack-rat types.
Their ideas of the values of various pieces of junk
verge on the psychotic. Every bit of glass may be a diamond, they think, and all that glisters,* gold.

---

*EDS. NOTE—Glitters.

Cause and effect: why Eighner gains weight when he scavenges

I tend to gain weight when I am scavenging. 38 Partly this is because I always find far more pizza and doughnuts than water-packed tuna, nonfat yogurt, and fresh vegetables. Also I have not developed much faith in the reliability of Dumpsters as a food source, although it has been proven to me many times. I tend to eat as if I have no idea where my next meal is coming from. But mostly I just hate to see food go to waste and so I eat much more than I should. Something like this drives the obsession to collect junk.

Cause and effect: why Eighner collects junk

As for collecting objects, I usually restrict myself 39 to collecting one kind of small object at a time, such as pocket calculators, sunglasses, or campaign buttons. To live on the street I must anticipate my needs to a certain extent: I must pick up and save warm bedding I find in August because it will not be found in Dumpsters in November. As I have no access to health care, I often hoard essential drugs, such as antibiotics and antihistamines. (This course can be recommended only to those with some grounding in pharmacology. Antibiotics, for example, even when indicated are worse than useless if taken in insufficient amounts.) But even if I had a home with extensive storage space, I could not save everything that might be valuable in some contingency.

I have proprietary feelings about my Dumpsters. 40 As I have mentioned, it is no accident that I scavenge from ones where good finds are common. But my limited experience with Dumpsters in other areas suggests to me that even in poorer areas, Dumpsters, if attended with sufficient diligence, can be made to yield a livelihood. The rich students discard perfectly good kiwi fruit; poorer people discard perfectly good apples. Slacks and Polo shirts are found in one place; jeans and T-shirts in the other. The population of competitors rather than the affluence of the dumpers most affects the feasibility of survival by scavenging. The large number of competitors is what puts me off the idea of trying to scavenge in places like Los Angeles.

Comparison and contrast: Dumpsters in rich and poorer areas

Curiously, I do not mind my direct competition, 41 other scavengers, so much as I hate the can scroungers.

Cause and effect: why people scrounge cans

People scrounge cans because they have to have a 42 little cash. I have tried scrounging cans with an able-bodied companion. Afoot a can scrounger simply cannot make more than a few dollars in a day. One can extract the necessities of life from the Dumpsters directly with far less effort than would be required to accumulate the equivalent value in cans. (These observations may not hold in places with container redemption laws.)

Can scroungers, then, are people who must have small amounts of cash. These are drug addicts and winos, mostly the latter because the amounts of cash are so small. Spirits and drugs do, like all other commodities, turn up in Dumpsters and the scavenger will from time to time have a half bottle of a rather good wine with his dinner. But the wino cannot survive on these occasional finds; he must have his daily dose to stave off the DTs. All the cans he can carry will buy about three bottles of Wild Irish Rose.   43

I do not begrudge them the cans, but can scroungers tend to tear up the Dumpsters, mixing the contents and littering the area. They become so specialized that they can see only cans. They earn my contempt by passing up change, canned goods, and readily hockable items.   44

Comparison and contrast: can scroungers vs. true scavengers

There are precious few courtesies among scavengers. But it is common practice to set aside surplus items: pairs of shoes, clothing, canned goods, and such. A true scavenger hates to see good stuff go to waste, and what he cannot use he leaves in good condition in plain sight.   45

Can scroungers lay waste to everything in their path and will stir one of a pair of good shoes to the bottom of a Dumpster, to be lost or ruined in the muck. Can scroungers will even go through individual garbage cans, something I have never seen a scavenger do.   46

Cause and effect: why scavengers do not go through individual garbage cans

Individual garbage cans are set out on the public easement only on garbage days. On the other days going through them requires trespassing close to a dwelling. Going through individual garbage cans without scattering litter is almost impossible. Litter is likely to reduce the public's tolerance of scavenging. Individual cans are simply not as productive as Dumpsters; people in houses and duplexes do not move so often and for some reason do not tend to discard as much useful material. Moreover, the time required to go through one garbage can that serves one household is not much less than the time required to go through a Dumpster that contains the refuse of twenty apartments.   47

But my strongest reservation about going through   48
individual garbage cans is that this seems to me a very
personal kind of invasion to which I would object
if I were a householder. Although many things in
Dumpsters are obviously meant never to come to
light, a Dumpster is somehow less personal.

I avoid trying to draw conclusions about the peo-   49
ple who dump in the Dumpsters I frequent. I think it
would be unethical to do so, although I know many
people will find the idea of scavenger ethics too funny
for words.

Examples: things found in Dumpsters

Dumpsters contain bank statements, correspon-   50
dence, and other documents, just as anyone might expect. But there are also less obvious sources of
information. Pill bottles, for example. The labels bear
the name of the patient, the name of the doctor, and
the name of the drug. AIDS drugs and antipsychotic
medicines, to name but two groups, are specific and
are seldom prescribed for any other disorders. The
plastic compacts for birth-control pills usually have
complete label information.

Despite all of this sensitive information, I have   51
had only one apartment resident object to my going
through the Dumpster. In that case it turned out the
resident was a university athlete who was taking bets
and who was afraid I would turn up his wager slips.

Occasionally a find tells a story. I once found a small   52
paper bag containing some unused condoms, several
partial tubes of flavored sexual lubricants, a partially
used compact of birth-control pills, and the torn pieces
of a picture of a young man. Clearly she was through
with him and planning to give up sex altogether.

Dumpster things are often sad—abandoned teddy   53
bears, shredded wedding books, despaired-of sales
kits. I find many pets lying in state in Dumpsters.
Although I hope to get off the streets so that Lizbeth
can have a long and comfortable old age, I know this
hope is not very realistic. So I suppose when her time
comes she too will go into a Dumpster. I will have no
better place for her. And after all, it is fitting, since for
most of her life her livelihood has come from the
Dumpster. When she finds something I think is safe
that has been spilled from a Dumpster, I let her have it.
She already knows the route around the best ones. I
like to think that if she survives me she will have a

chance of evading the dog catcher and of finding her sustenance on the route.

Silly vanities also come to rest in the Dumpsters. I am a rather accomplished needleworker. I get a lot of material from the Dumpsters. Evidently sorority girls, hoping to impress someone, perhaps themselves, with their mastery of a womanly art, buy a lot of embroider-by-number kits, work a few stitches horribly, and eventually discard the whole mess. I pull out their stitches turn the canvas over, and work an original design. Do not think I refrain from chuckling as I make gifts from these kits. 54

I find diaries and journals. I have often thought of compiling a book of literary found objects. And perhaps I will one day. But what I find is hopelessly commonplace and bad without being, even unconsciously, camp. College students also discard their papers. I am horrified to discover the kind of paper that now merits an A in an undergraduate course. I am grateful, however, for the number of good books and magazines the students throw out. 55

In the area I know best I have never discovered vermin in the Dumpster, but there are two kinds of kitty surprise. One is alley cats whom I meet as they leap, claws first, out of Dumpsters. This is especially thrilling when I have Lizbeth in tow. The other kind of kitty surprise is a plastic garbage bag filled with some ponderous, amorphous mass. This always proves to be used cat litter. 56

City bees harvest doughnut glaze and this makes the Dumpster at the doughnut shop more interesting. My faith in the instinctive wisdom of animals is always shaken whenever I see Lizbeth attempt to catch a bee in her mouth, which she does whenever bees are present. Evidently some birds find Dumpsters profitable, for birdie surprise is almost as common as kitty surprise of the first kind. In hunting season all kinds of small game turn up in Dumpster, some of it, sadly, not entirely dead. Curiously, summer and winter, maggots are uncommon. 57

The worst of the living and near-living hazards of the Dumpsters are the fire ants. The food they claim is not much of a loss, but they are vicious and aggressive. It is very easy to brush against some surface of the Dumpster and pick up half a dozen or more fire ants, usually in some sensitive area such as the under- 58 arm. One advantage of bringing Lizbeth along as I make Dumpster round is that, for obvious reasons, she is very alert to ground-based fire ants. When Lizbeth recognizes a fire-ant infestation around our feet, she does the Dance of the Zillion Fire Ants. I have learned not to ignore this warning from Lizbeth, whether I perceive the tiny ants or not, but to remove ourselves at Lizbeth's first *pas de bourée.** All the more so because the ants are the worst in the summer months when I wear flip-flops if I have them. (Perhaps someone will misunderstand this. Lizbeth does the Dance of the Zillion Fire Ants when she recognizes more fire ants than she cares to eat, not when she is being bitten. Since I have learned to react promptly, she does not get bitten at all. It is the isolated patrol of fire ants that falls in Lizbeth's range that deserves pity. She finds them quite tasty.)

Process: how to go through a Dumpster

By far the best way to go through a Dumpster is to lower yourself into it. Most of the good stuff tends to settle at the bottom because it is usually weightier than the rubbish. My more athletic companions have often demonstrated to me that they can extract much good material from a Dumpster I have already been over. 59

To those psychologically or physically unprepared to enter a Dumpster, I recommend a stout stick, preferably with some barb or hook at one end. The hook can be used to grab plastic garbage bags. When I find canned goods or other objects loose at the bottom of a Dumpster, I lower a bag into it, roll the desired object into the bag, and then hoist the bag out—a procedure more easily described than executed. Much Dumpster diving is a matter of experience for which nothing will do except practice. 60

Dumpster diving is outdoor work, often surprisingly pleasant. It is not entirely predictable; things of interest turn up every day and some days there are finds of great value. I am always very pleased when I can turn up exactly the thing I most wanted to find. Yet in spite of the element of chance, scavenging more than most other pursuits tends to yield returns in some proportion to the effort and intelligence brought to bear. It is very sweet to turn up a few dollars in change from a Dumpster that has just been gone over by a wino. 61

*EDS. NOTE—A ballet step.

The land is now covered with cities. The cities are   62
full of Dumpsters. If a member of the canine race is
ever able to know what it is doing, then Lizbeth knows
that when we go around to the Dumpsters, we are
hunting. I think of scavenging as a modern form of
self-reliance. In any event, after having survived nearly
ten years of government service, where everything is
geared to the lowest common denominator, I find it re-
freshing to have work that rewards initiative and effort. Certainly I would be happy to have a sinecure
again, but I am no longer heartbroken that I left one.

I find from the experience of scavenging two rather   63
deep lessons. The first is to take what you can use and
let the rest go by. I have come to think that there is no
value in the abstract. A thing I cannot use or make useful, perhaps by trading, has no value however rare or
fine it may be. I mean useful in some broad sense—
some art I would find useful and some otherwise.

**Cause and effect:
results of
Eighner's
experiences as a
scavenger**

I was shocked to realize that some things are not   64
worth acquiring, but now I think it is so. Some material
things are white elephants that eat up the possessor's
substance. The second lesson is the transience of material being. This has not quite converted me to a dualist,*
but it has made some headway in that direction. I do
not suppose that ideas are immortal, but certainly mental things are longer lived than other material things.

Once I was the sort of person who invests objects   65
with sentimental value. Now I no longer have those
objects, but I have the sentiments yet.

Many times in our travels I have lost everything   66
but the clothes I was wearing and Lizbeth. The things I
find in Dumpsters, the love letters and rag dolls of so
many lives, remind me of this lesson. Now I hardly pick
up a thing without envisioning the time I will cast it
aside. This I think is a healthy state of mind. Almost
everything I have now has already been cast out at least
once, proving that what I own is valueless to someone.

Anyway, I find my desire to grab for the gaudy   67
bauble has been largely sated. I think this is an attitude I
share with the very wealthy—we both know there is
plenty more where what we have came from. Between
us are the rat-race millions who nightly scavenge the
cable channels looking for they know not what.

I am sorry for them.   68

---

*EDS. NOTE—Someone who believes the world consists of two opposing forces,
such as mind and matter.

• • •

COMPREHENSION

1. In your own words, give a formal definition of *Dumpster diving.*

2. List some of Eighner's answers to the question "Why was this discarded?" (8). What additional reasons can you think of?

3. What foods does Eighner take particular care to avoid? Why?

4. In paragraph 30 Eighner comments, "Dumpster diving has serious drawbacks as a way of life." What drawbacks does he cite in his essay? What additional drawbacks are implied?

5. Summarize the stages in the process of learning to scavenge.

6. In addition to food, what else does Eighner scavenge for? Into what general categories do these items fall?

7. Why does Eighner hate can scroungers?

8. What lessons has Eighner learned as a Dumpster diver?

PURPOSE AND AUDIENCE

1. In paragraph 6 Eighner states his purpose: to record what he has learned as a Dumpster diver. What additional purposes do you think he had in setting his ideas down on paper?

2. Do you think most readers are apt to respond to Eighner's essay with sympathy? Pity? Impatience? Contempt? Disgust? How do you react? Why?

3. Why do you think Eighner chose not to provide any background about his life—his upbringing, education, or work history—before he became homeless? Do you think this decision was a wise one? How might such information (for example, any of the details in the headnote that precedes the essay) have changed readers' reactions to his discussion?

4. In paragraph 8 Eighner presents three principles one must follow to eat safely from a Dumpster; in paragraphs 59–60 he explains how to go through a Dumpster; and throughout the essay he includes many cautions and warnings. Clearly, he does not expect his audience to take up Dumpster diving. What, then, is his purpose in including such detailed explanations?

5. When Eighner begins paragraph 9 with "Perhaps everyone who has a kitchen, . . ." he encourages readers to identify with him. In what other ways does he help readers imagine themselves in his place? Are these efforts successful? Explain.

6. What effect do you think the essay's last line is calculated to have on readers? What effect does it have on you?

STYLE AND STRUCTURE

1. Eighner opens his essay with a very conventional strategy: an extended definition of *Dumpster diving.* What techniques does he use in paragraphs

1 through 3 to develop his definition? Is beginning with a definition the best strategy for this essay? Why or why not?

2. This long essay contains four one-sentence paragraphs. Why do you think Eighner isolates these sentences? Do you think any of them should be combined with an adjacent paragraph? Explain your reasoning.

3. As the introductory comment notes, Eighner retained the present tense even though he was no longer homeless when the essay was published. Why do you think he preserved the present tense? Was this a good decision?

4. Eighner's essay includes a number of lists that catalog items with which he came in contact (for example, in paragraphs 5 and 50). Identify as many of these lists as you can. Why do you think Eighner includes such extensive lists?

VOCABULARY PROJECTS

1. Define each of the following words as it is used in this selection.

proprietary (1)	decanted (26)	contingency (39)
niche (4)	ingested (26)	feasibility (40)
sporadic (5)	avail (28)	stave (43)
bohemian (8)	skulking (32)	commonplace (55)
dilettanti (8)	stigma (33)	vermin (56)
phobic (10)	pristine (34)	sinecure (62)
pared (15)	dissipate (35)	transience (64)
de-emulsified (16)	disparage (35)	gaudy(67)
pathogens (16)	intrinsic (37)	bauble (67)
staples (25)		

2. In paragraph 2 Eighner suggests several alternative words for *diving* as he uses it in his essay. Consult a dictionary to determine the connotations of each of his alternatives. What are the pros and cons of substituting one of these words for *diving* in Eighner's title and throughout the essay?

JOURNAL ENTRY

In paragraphs 21–25 Eighner discusses the discarding of food by college students. Does your own experience support his observations? Do you think he is being too hard on students, or does his characterization seem accurate?

WRITING WORKSHOP

1. Write an essay about a homeless person you have seen in your community. Use any patterns you like to structure your paper. When you have finished, annotate your essay to identify the patterns you have used.

2. Write a memo to your school's dean of students recommending steps that can be taken on your campus to redirect discarded (but edible) food to the homeless. Use process and exemplification to structure your memo.

3. Taking Eighner's point of view and using information from his essay, write an argumentative essay with a thesis statement that takes a strong position against homelessness and recommends government and/or private measures to end it. If you like, you may write your essay in the form of a statement by Eighner to a congressional committee.

COMBINING THE PATTERNS

Review the annotations that identify each pattern of development used in this essay. Which patterns seem to be most effective in helping you understand and empathize with the life of a homeless person? Why?

THEMATIC CONNECTIONS

- "The Human Cost of an Illiterate Society" (page 192)
- "On the Meaning of Plumbing and Poverty" (page 288)
- "The Untouchable" (page 448)

▶▶▶▶▶▶▶▶▶▶▶▶▶▶▶▶▶

JONATHAN SWIFT

Born in Dublin, Ireland, to English parents, Jonathan Swift (1667–1745) received his degree from Dublin's Trinity College. He spent much of his life journeying between England, where he wished to be part of the literary establishment, and Ireland, where he was ordained an Anglican priest and had a modest income. Strongly involved in English and Irish literary and political debates, Swift wrote a number of satires, including *The Battle of the Books* and *Tale of a Tub,* and numerous political pamphlets. Today he is best remembered for *Gulliver's Travels* (1726), a tale of fantastic voyages to lands of tiny people, giants, and talking horses; the story was considered sharply satirical at the time but is now read as a fable of human foibles. A fierce advocate of the Irish people in their struggle under sometimes harsh British rule, Swift also published several works supporting the Irish cause. The following sharply ironic essay was written during the height of a terrible famine, a time when the British were proposing a devastating tax on an impoverished Irish citizenry. It was meant as an indictment of British callousness and greed. Note that Swift does not write in his own voice here but adopts the persona of one who does not recognize the barbarity of his "solution."

A Modest Proposal

It is a melancholy object those who walk through this great town* or travel in the country, where they see the streets, the roads, and cabin doors, crowded with beggars of the female sex, followed by three, four, or six children, all in rags and importuning every passenger for an alms. These mothers, instead of being able to work for their honest livelihood, are forced to employ all their time in strolling to beg sustenance for their helpless infants, who, as they grow up, either turn thieves for want of work, or leave their dear native country to fight for the Pretender in Spain, or sell themselves to the Barbadoes.** 1

I think it is agreed by all parties that this prodigious number of children in the arms, or on the backs, or at the heels of their mothers, and frequently of their fathers, is in the present deplorable state of the kingdom a very great additional grievance; and therefore whoever could find out a fair, cheap, and easy method of making these children sound, useful members of the commonwealth would deserve so well of the public as to have his statue set up for a preserver of the nation. 2

But my intention is very far from being confined to provide only for the children of professed beggars; it is of a much greater extent, and shall take in the whole number of infants at a certain age who are born of par- 3

---

*EDS. NOTE—Dublin.

**EDS. NOTE—Many young Irishmen left their country to fight as mercenaries in Spain's civil war or to work as indentured servants in the West Indies.

ents in effect as little able to support them as those who demand our charity in the streets.

As to my own part, having turned my thoughts for many years upon this important subject, and maturely weighed the several schemes of the other projectors, I have always found them grossly mistaken in their computation. It is true, a child just dropped from its dam may be supported by her milk for a solar year, with little other nourishment; at most not above the value of two shillings, which the mother may certainly get, or the value in scraps, by her lawful occupation of begging; and it is exactly at one year old that I propose to provide for them in such a manner as instead of being a charge upon their parents or the parish, or wanting food and raiment for the rest of their lives, they shall on the contrary contribute to the feeding, and partly to the clothing, of many thousands.   4

There is likewise another great advantage in my scheme, that it will prevent those involuntary abortions, and that horrid practice of women murdering their bastard children, alas, too frequent among us, sacrificing the poor innocent babies, I doubt, more to avoid the expense than the shame, which would move tears and pity in the most savage and inhuman breast.   5

The number of souls in this kingdom being usually reckoned one million and a half, of these I calculate there may be about two hundred thousand couples whose wives are breeders, from which number I subtract thirty thousand couples who are able to maintain their own children, although I apprehend there cannot be so many under the present distress of the kingdom; but this being granted, there will remain an hundred and seventy thousand breeders. I again subtract fifty thousand for those women who miscarry, or whose children die by accident or disease within the year. There only remain an hundred and twenty thousand children of poor parents annually born. The question therefore is, how this number shall be reared and provided for, which, as I have already said, under the present situation of affairs, is utterly impossible by all the methods hitherto proposed. For we can neither employ them in handicraft nor agriculture; we neither build houses (I mean in the country) nor cultivate land. They can very seldom pick up livelihood by stealing till they arrive at six years old, except where they are of towardly parts,* although I confess they learn the rudiments much earlier, during which time they can however be looked upon only as probationer, as I have been informed by a principal gentleman in the country of Cavan, who protested to me that he never knew above one or two instances under the age of six, even in a part of the kingdom so renowned for the quickest proficiency in that art.   6

I am assured by our merchants that a boy or a girl before twelve years old is no salable commodity; and even when they come to this age, they   7

---

*EDS. NOTE—Precocious.

will not yield above three pounds, or three pounds and half a crown at most on the Exchange; which cannot turn to account either to the parents or the kingdom, the charge of nutriment and rags having been at least four times that value.

I shall now therefore humbly propose my own thoughts, which I hope will not be liable to the least objection. 8

I have been assured by a very knowing American of my acquaintance in London, that a young healthy child well nursed is at a year old a most delicious, nourishing, and wholesome food, whether stewed, roasted, baked, or boiled; and I make no doubt that it will equally serve in fricasee or a ragout. 9

I do therefore humbly offer it to public consideration that of the hundred and twenty thousand children, already computed, twenty thousand may be reserved for breed, whereof only one fourth part to be males, which is more than we allow to sheep, black cattle, or swine; and my reason is that these children are seldom the fruits of marriage, a circumstance not much regarded by our savages, therefore one male will be sufficient to serve four females. That the remaining hundred thousand may at a year old be offered in sale to the persons of quality and fortune through the kingdom, always advising the mother to let them suck plentifully in the last month, so as to render them plump and fat for a good table. A child will make two dishes at an entertainment for friends; and when the family dines alone, the fore or hind quarter will make a reasonable dish, and seasoned with a little pepper or salt, will be very good boiled on the fourth day, especially in winter. 10

I have reckoned upon a medium that a child just born will weigh twelve pounds, and in a solar year if tolerably nursed increaseth to twenty-eight pounds. 11

I grant this food will be somewhat dear, and therefore very proper for landlords, who, as they have already devoured most of the parents, seem to have the best title to the children. 12

Infant's flesh will be in season throughout the year, but more plentiful in March, and a little before and after. For we are told by a grave author, an eminent French physician,* that fish being a prolific diet, there are more children born in Roman Catholic countries about nine months after Lent, than at any other season; therefore, reckoning year after Lent, the markets will be more glutted than usual, because the number of popish infants is at least three to one in this kingdom; and therefore it will have on other collateral advantage, by lessening the number of Papists** among us. 13

I have already computed the charge of nursing a beggar's child (in which list I reckon all cottages, laborers, and four fifths of the farmers) to be about two shillings per annum, rags included; and I believe no gentleman would repine to give ten shillings for the carcass of a good fat child, 14

---

*EDS. NOTE—Francois Rabelais, a sixteenth-century satirical writer.
**EDS. NOTE—Roman Catholics.

which, as I have said, will make four dishes of excellent nutritive meat, when he hath only some particular friend or his own family to dine with him. Thus the squire will learn to be a good landlord, and grow popular among the tenants; the mother will have eight shillings net profit, and be fit for work till she produces another child.

Those who are more thrifty (as I must confess the times require) may [15] flay the carcass; the skin of which artificially* dressed will make admirable gloves for ladies, and summer boots for fine gentlemen.

As to our city of Dublin, shambles** may be appointed for this purpose in the most convenient parts of it, and butchers we may be assured [16] will not be wanting; although I rather recommend buying the children alive, and dressing them hot from the knife as we do roasting pigs.

A very worthy person, a true lover of his country, and whose virtues I [17] highly esteem, was lately pleased in discoursing on this matter to offer a refinement upon my scheme. He said that many gentlemen of his kingdom, having of late destroyed their deer, he conceived that the want of venison might be well supplied by the bodies of young lads and maidens, not exceeding fourteen years of age nor under twelve, so great a number of both sexes in every county being now ready to starve for want of work and service; and these to be disposed of by their parents, if alive, or otherwise by their nearest relations. But with due deference to so excellent a friend and so deserving a patriot I cannot be altogether in his sentiments; for as to the males, my American acquaintance assured me from frequent experience that their flesh was generally tough and lean, like that of our schoolboys, by continual exercise, and their taste disagreeable; and to fatten them would not answer the charge. Then as to the females, it would, I think with humble submission, be a loss to the public, because they soon would become breeders themselves; and besides, it is not improbable that some scrupulous people might be apt to censure such a practice (although indeed very unjustly) as a little bordering upon cruelty; which, I confess, hath always been with me the strongest objection against any project, how well soever intended.

But in order to justify my friend, he confessed that this expedient was [18] put into his head by the famous Psalmanazar,*** a native of the island Formosa, who came from thence to London above twenty years ago, and in conversation told my friend that in his country when any young person happened to be put to death, the executioner sold the carcass to the persons of quality as a prime dainty; and that in his time the body of a plump girl of fifteen, who was crucified for an attempt to poison the emperor, was sold to the Imperial Majesty's prime minister of state, and other great mandarins of the court, in joints from the gibbet, at four hun-

---

*EDS. NOTE—Skillfully.
**EDS. NOTE—A slaughterhouse or meat market.
***EDS. NOTE—Frenchman who passed himself off as a native of Formosa.

dred crowns. Neither indeed can I deny that if the same use were made of several plump young girls in this town, who without one single groat to their fortunes cannot stir abroad without a chair,* and appear at the playhouse and assemblies in foreign fineries which they never will pay for, the kingdom would not be the worse.

Some persons of a desponding spirit are in great concern about the vast number of poor people who are aged, diseased, or maimed, and I have been desired to employ my thoughts what course may be taken to ease the nation of so grievous an encumbrance. But I am not in the least pain upon that matter, because it is very well known that they are every day dying and rotting by cold and famine, and filth and vermin, as fast as can be reasonably expected. And as to the younger laborers, they are now in almost as hopeful a condition. They cannot get work, and consequently pine away for want of nourishment to a degree that if any time they are accidentally hired to common labor, they have not strength to perform it; and thus the country and themselves are happily delivered from the evils to come. 19

I have too long digressed, and therefore shall return to my subject. I think the advantages by the proposal which I have made are obvious and many, as well as of the highest importance. 20

For first, as I have already observed, it would greatly lessen the number of Papists, with whom we are yearly overrun, being the principal breeders of the nation as well as our most dangerous enemies; and who stay at home on purpose to deliver the kingdom to the Pretender, hoping to take their advantage by the absence of so many good Protestants, who have chosen rather to leave their country than to stay at home and pay tithes against their conscience to an Episcopal curate. 21

Secondly, the poorer tenants will have something valuable of their own, which by law may be made liable to distress,** and help to pay their landlord's rent, their corn and cattle being already seized and money a thing unknown. 22

Thirdly, whereas the maintenance of an hundred thousand children, from two years old and upwards, cannot be computed at less than ten shillings a piece per annum, the nation's stock will be thereby increased fifty thousand pounds per annum, besides the profit of a new dish introduced to the tables of all gentlemen of fortune in the kingdom who have any refinement in taste. And the money will circulate among ourselves, the goods being entirely of our own growth and manufacture. 23

Fourthly, the constant breeders, besides the gain of eight shillings sterling per annum by the sale of their children, will be rid of the charge for maintaining them after the first year. 24

Fifthly, this food would likewise bring great custom to taverns, where the vintners will certainly be so prudent as to procure the best receipts*** 25

---

*Eds. note—A sedan chair; that is, a portable, covered chair designed to seat one person and then to be carried by two men.

**Eds. note—Property could be seized by creditors.

***Eds. note—Recipes.

for dressing it to perfection, and consequently have their houses frequented by all the fine gentlemen, who justly value themselves upon their knowledge in good eating; and a skillful cook, who understands how to oblige his guests, will contrive to make it as expensive as they please.

Sixthly, this would be a great inducement to marriage, after which all   26
wise nations have either encouraged by rewards or enforced by laws and penalties. It would increase the care and tenderness of mothers toward their children, when they were sure of a settlement for life to the poor babes, provided in some sort by the public, to their annual profit instead of expense. We should see an honest emulation among the married women, which of them could bring the fattest child to the market. Men would become as fond of their wives during the time of pregnancy as they are now of their mares in foal, their cows in calf, or sows when they are ready to farrow; nor offer to beat or kick them (as is too frequent a practice) for fear of miscarriage.

Many other advantages might be enumerated. For instance, the addi-   27
tion of some thousand carcasses in our exportation of barreled beef, the propagation of swine's flesh, and improvements in the art of making good bacon, so much wanted among us by the great destruction of pigs, too frequent at our tables, which are no way comparable in taste or magnificence to a well-grown, fat, yearling child, which roasted whole will make a considerable figure at a lord mayor's feast or other public entertainment. But this and many others I omit, being studious of brevity.

Supposing that one thousand families in this city would be constant   28
customers for infants' flesh, besides others who might have it at merry meetings, particularly weddings and christenings, I compute that Dublin would take off annually about twenty thousand carcasses, and the rest of the kingdom (where probably they will be sold somewhat cheaper) the remaining eighty thousand.

I can think of no one objection that will possibly be raised against this   29
proposal, unless it should be urged that the number of people will be thereby much lessened in the kingdom. This I freely own, and it was indeed one principal design in offering it to the world. I desire the reader will observe; that I calculate my remedy for this one individual kingdom of Ireland and for no other than ever was, is, or I think ever can be upon earth. Therefore, let no man talk to me of other expedients: of taxing our absentees at five shillings a pound: of using neither clothes nor household furniture except what is of our own growth and manufacture: of utterly rejecting the materials and instruments that promote foreign luxury: of curing the expensiveness of pride, vanity, idleness, and gaming in our women: of introducing a vein of parsimony, prudence, and temperance: of learning to love our country, in the want of which we differ even from Lowlanders and the inhabitants of Topinamboo:* of quitting our animosi-

---

*EDS. NOTE—A place in the Brazilian jungle.

ties and factions, nor acting any longer like the Jews,* who were murdering one another at the very moment their city was taken: of being a little cautious not to sell our country and conscience for nothing: of teaching landlords to have at least one degree of mercy toward their tenants: lastly, of putting a spirit of honesty, industry, and skill into our shopkeepers; who, if a resolution could now be taken to buy only our native goods, would immediately unite to cheat and exact upon us in the price, the measure, and the goodness, nor could ever yet be brought to make one fair proposal of just dealing, though often and earnestly invited to it.

Therefore, I repeat, let no man talk to me of these and the like expedients, till he hath at least some glimpse of hope that there will ever be some hearty and sincere attempt to put them in practice.**   30

But as to myself, having been wearied out for many years with offering vain, idle, visionary thoughts, and the length utterly despairing of success, I fortunately fell upon this proposal, which, as it is wholly new, so it hath something solid and real, of no expense and little trouble, full in our own power, and whereby we can incur no danger in disobliging England. For this kind of commodity will not bear exploration, the flesh being of too tender a consistence to admit a long continuance in salt, although perhaps I could name a country which would be glad to eat up our whole nation without it.   31

After all, I am not so violently bent upon my own opinion as to reject any offer proposed by wise men, which shall be found equally innocent, cheap, easy, and effectual. But before something of that kind shall be advanced in contradiction to my scheme, and offering a better, I desire the author or authors will be pleased maturely to consider two points. First, as things now stand, how they will be able to find food and raiment for an hundred thousand useless mouths and backs. And secondly, there being a round million of creatures in human figure throughout this kingdom, whose sole subsistence put into a common stock would leave them in debt two million of pounds sterling, adding those who are beggars by profession to the bulk of farmers, cottagers, and laborers, with their wives and children who are beggars in effect; I desire those politicians who dislike my overture, and may perhaps be so bold to attempt an answer, that they will first ask the parents of these mortals whether they would not at this day think it a great happiness to have been sold for food at a year old in this manner I prescribe, and thereby have avoided such a perpetual scene of misfortunes as they have since gone through by the oppression of landlords, the impossibility of paying rent without money or trade, the want of common sustenance, with neither house nor clothes to cover them from the inclemencies of the weather, and the most inevitable prospect of entailing the like or greater miseries upon their breed forever.   32

---

*Eds. note—In the first century B.C., the Roman general Pompey was able to conquer Jerusalem in part because the citizenry was divided among rival factions.

**Eds. note—Note that these measures represent Swift's true proposal.

I profess, in the sincerity of my heart, that I have not the least per- 33
sonal interest in endeavoring to promote this necessary work, having no
other motive than the public good of my country, by advancing our trade,
providing for infants, relieving the poor, and giving some pleasure to the
rich. I have no children by which I can propose to get a single penny; the
youngest being nine years old, and my wife past childbearing.

• • •

COMPREHENSION

1. What problem does Swift identify? What general solution does he recommend?

2. What advantages does Swift see in his plan?

3. What does he see as the alternative to his plan?

4. What clues indicate that Swift is not serious about his proposal?

5. In paragraph 29 Swift lists and rejects a number of "other expedients."
   What are they? Why do you think he presents and rejects these ideas?

PURPOSE AND AUDIENCE

1. Swift's target here is the British government, in particular its poor treatment of the Irish. How would you expect British government officials to
   respond to his proposal? How would you expect Irish readers to react?

2. What do you think Swift hoped to accomplish in this essay? Do you
   think his purpose was simply to amuse and shock, or do you think he
   wanted to change people's minds—or even inspire them to take some
   kind of action? Explain.

3. In paragraphs 6, 14, 23, and elsewhere, Swift presents a series of mathe-
   matical calculations. What effect do you think he expected these compu-
   tations to have on his readers?

4. Explain why each of the following groups might have been offended by
   this essay: women, Catholics, butchers, poor people.

5. How do you think Swift expected the appeal in his conclusion to affect
   his audience?

STYLE AND STRUCTURE

1. In paragraph 6 Swift uses the word *breeders* to refer to fertile women.
   What connotations does this word have? Why does he use it rather than a
   more neutral alternative?

2. What purpose does paragraph 8 serve in the essay? Do the other short
   paragraphs have the same function? Explain.

3. Swift's remarks are presented as an argument. Where, if anywhere, does
   he anticipate and refute his readers' objections?

4. Swift applies to infants many words usually applied to animals who are slaughtered to be eaten—for example, *fore or hind quarter* (10) and *carcass* (15). List as many examples of this usage as you can. Why do you think Swift uses such words?

5. Throughout his essay Swift cites the comments of others—"our merchants" (7), "a very knowing American of my acquaintance" (9), and "an eminent French physician" (13), for example. Cite additional examples. What, if anything, does he accomplish by referring to these people?

6. A **satire** is a piece of writing that uses wit, **irony,** and ridicule to attack foolishness, incompetence, or evil. How does "A Modest Proposal" fit this definition of satire?

7. Evaluate the strategy Swift uses to introduce each advantage he cites in paragraphs 21 through 26.

8. Swift uses a number of parenthetical comments in his essay—for example, in paragraphs 14, 17, and 26. Identify all of his parenthetical comments, and consider what they contribute to the essay.

9. Swift begins paragraph 20 with "I have too long digressed, and therefore shall return to my subject." Has he in fact been digressing? Explain.

VOCABULARY PROJECTS

1. Define each of the following words as it is used in this selection.

importuning (1)	rudiments (6)	encumbrance (19)
alms (1)	nutriment (7)	tithes (21)
prodigious (2)	repine (14)	vintners (25)
professed (3)	flay (15)	expedients (29)
dam (4)	scrupulous (17)	parsimony (29)
reckoned (6)	censure (17)	temperance (29)
apprehend (6)	desponding (19)	raiment (32)

2. The title states that Swift's proposal is a "modest" one; elsewhere he says that he proposes his ideas "humbly" (8). Why do you think he chooses these words? Does he really mean to present himself as modest and humble?

JOURNAL ENTRY

What is your emotional reaction to this essay? Do you find it amusing or offensive? Why?

WRITING WORKSHOP

1. Write a "modest proposal," either straightforward or satirical, for solving a problem in your school or community.

2. Write a "modest proposal" for achieving one of these national goals:

• Eliminating welfare dependency

• Making health care more affordable

- Improving public education
- Eliminating teenage pregnancy
- Reducing the use of illegal drugs

3. Write a letter to an executive of the tobacco industry, a television network, or an industry that threatens the environment. In your letter, set forth a "modest proposal" for making the industry more responsible.

COMBINING THE PATTERNS

What patterns of development does Swift use in his argument? Annotate the essay to identify each pattern. Use the annotations accompanying the preceding essay, "On Dumspter Diving," as a guide.

THEMATIC CONNECTIONS

- "The Embalming of Mr. Jones" (page 240)
- "The Irish Famine, 1845–1849" (page 265)
- "I Want a Wife" (page 461)
- The Declaration of Independence (page 507)
- "What, Then, Is to Be Done?" (page 530)

▶▶▶▶▶▶▶▶▶▶▶▶▶▶▶▶▶▶▶

ALICE WALKER

Born in Eatontown, Georgia, one of eight children in a family of sharecrop-pers, Alice Walker (1944–) today often explores feminist and antiracist themes in her writing. After attending Spelman College in Atlanta, Walker received her B.A. from Sarah Lawrence College in New York in 1965. In 1968 she published *Once*, a volume of poems (some of which grew out of her active participation in the civil rights movement). Her following two novels, *The Third Life of Grange Copeland* (1970) and *Meridian* (1976), and her short story collections, *In Love & Trouble* (1973) and *You Can't Keep A Good Woman Down* (1981), established her as a major literary voice. It was the publication of *The Color Purple* in 1982, however, that brought her wide public attention; this best-selling novel won the Pulitzer Prize for fiction and served as the basis for a popular film directed by Steven Spielberg. More recent novels include *The Temple of My Familiar* (1989) and *Possessing the Secret of Joy* (1992). Walker has also published several more poetry collections; two highly influential collections of essays, *In Search of Our Mothers' Gardens: Womanist Prose* (1983) and *Living by the Word* (1988); and a memoir about the filming of *The Color Purple, The Same River Twice* (1996). In the following essay, she considers the roots of black female literature and, in particular, the creative contributions of poor countrywomen, the "mothers" of the title.

In Search of Our Mothers' Gardens

I described her own nature and temperament. Told how they
needed a larger life for their expression. . . . I pointed out that
in lieu of proper channels, her emotions had overflowed into
paths that dissipated them. I talked, beautifully I thought,
about an art that would be born, an art that would open the
way for women the likes of her. I asked her to hope, and build
up an inner life against the coming of that day. . . . I sang, with a
strange quiver in my voice, a promise song.

–JEAN TOOMER,
"Avey," Cane

The poet speaking to a prostitute who falls asleep while he's talking—   1

When the poet Jean Toomer walked through the South in the early   2
twenties, he discovered a curious thing: black women whose spirituality was so intense, so deep, so *unconscious*, that they were themselves unaware of the richness they held. They stumbled blindly through their lives: creatures so abused and mutilated in body, so dimmed and confused by pain, that they considered themselves unworthy even of hope. In the selfless abstractions their bodies became to the men who used them, they became more than "sexual objects," even more than mere women: they became "Saints." Instead of being perceived as whole persons, their bodies became shrines, what was thought to be their minds became temples suitable for worship. These crazy Saints stared out at the

world, wildly, like lunatics—or quietly, like suicides; and the "God" that was in their gaze was as mute as a great stone.

Who were these Saints? These crazy, loony, pitiful women? 3

Some of them, without a doubt, were our mothers and grandmothers. 4

In the still heat of the post-Reconstruction South, this is how they 5 seemed to Jean Toomer: exquisite butterflies trapped in an evil honey, toiling away their lives in an era, a century, that did not acknowledge them, except as "the *mule* of the world." They dreamed dreams that no one knew—not even themselves, in any coherent fashion—and saw visions no one could understand. They wandered or sat about the countryside crooning lullabies to ghosts, and drawing the mother of Christ in charcoal on courthouse walls.

They forced their minds to desert their bodies and their striving spirits 6 sought to rise, like frail whirlwinds from the hard red clay. And when those frail whirlwinds fell, in scattered particles, upon the ground, no one mourned. Instead, men lit candles to celebrate the emptiness that remained, as people do who enter a beautiful but vacant space to resurrect a God.

Our mothers and grandmothers, some of them: moving to music not 7 yet written. And they waited.

They waited for a day when the unknown thing that was in them 8 would be made known; but guessed, somehow in their darkness, that on the day of their revelation they would be long dead. Therefore to Toomer they walked, and even ran, in slow motion. For they were going nowhere immediate, and the future was not yet within their grasp. And men took our mothers and grandmothers, "but got no pleasure from it." So complex was their passion and their calm.

To Toomer, they lay vacant and fallow as autumn fields, with harvest 9 time never in sight: and he saw them enter loveless marriages, without joy; and become prostitutes, without resistance, and become mothers of children, without fulfillment.

For these grandmothers and mothers of ours were not Saints, but 10 Artists; driven to a numb and bleeding madness by the springs of creativity in them for which there was no release. They were Creators, who lived lives of spiritual waste, because they were so rich in spirituality—which is the basis of Art—that the strain of enduring their unused and unwanted talent drove them insane. Throwing away this spirituality was their pathetic attempt to lighten the soul to a weight their work-worn, sexually abused bodies could bear.

What did it mean for a black woman to be an artist in our grandmoth- 11 ers' time? In our great-grandmothers' day? It is a question with an answer cruel enough to stop the blood.

Did you have a genius of a great-great-grandmother who died under 12 some ignorant and depraved white overseer's lash? Or was she required to bake biscuits for a lazy backwater tramp, when she cried out in her soul to paint watercolors of sunsets, or the rain falling on the green and peaceful pasturelands? Or was her body broken and forced to bear children (who were more often than not sold away from her)—eight, ten, fifteen, twenty children—when her one joy was the thought of modeling heroic figures of rebellion, in stone or clay?

How was the creativity of the black woman kept alive, year after   13
year and century after century, when for most of the years black people have been in America, it was a punishable crime for a black person to read or write? And the freedom to paint, to sculpt, to expand the mind with an action did not exist. Consider, if you can bear to imagine it, what might have been the result if singing, too, had been forbidden by law. Listen to the voices of Bessie Smith, Billie Holiday, Nina Simone, Roberta Flack, and Aretha Franklin, among others, and imagine those voices muzzled for life. Then you may begin to comprehend the lives of our "crazy," "Sainted" mothers and grandmothers. The agony of the lives of women who might have been Poets, Novelists, Essayists, and Short-Story Writers (over a period of centuries), who died with their real gifts stifled within them.

And, if this were the end of the story, we would have cause to cry out   14
in my paraphrase of Okot p'Bitek's great poem:

O, my clanswomen
Let us all cry together!
Come,
Let us mourn the death of our mother,
The death of a Queen
The ash that was produced
By a great fire!
O, this homestead is utterly dead
Close the gates
With *lacari* thorns,
For our mother
The creator of the Stool is lost!
And all the young women
Have perished in the wilderness!

But this is not the end of the story, for all the young women—our   15
mothers and grandmothers, *ourselves*—have not perished in the wilderness. And if we ask ourselves why, and search for and find the answer, we will know beyond all efforts to erase it from our minds, just exactly who, and of what, we black American women are.

One example, perhaps the most pathetic, most misunderstood one,   16
can provide a backdrop for our mothers' work: Phillis Wheatley,* a slave in the 1700s.

---

*Eds. note—Eventually achieving her freedom, Wheatley (1753?–1784) published several volumes of poetry and is considered the first important African-American writer in the United States.

Virginia Woolf,* in her book *A Room of One's Own,* wrote that in order   17
for a woman to write fiction she must have two things, certainly: a room of
her own (the key and lock) and enough money to support herself.

What then are we to make of Phillis Wheatley, a slave, who owned   18
not even herself? This sickly, frail black girl who required a servant of her
own at times—her health was so precarious—and who, had she been
white, would have been easily considered the intellectual superior of all
women and most of the men in the society of her day.

Virginia Woolf wrote further, speaking of course not of our Phillis,   19
that "any woman born with a great gift in the sixteenth century [insert
"eighteenth century," insert "black woman," insert "born or made a
slave"] would certainly have gone crazed, shot herself, or ended her days
in some lonely cottage outside the village, half witch, half wizard [insert
"Saint"], feared and mocked at. For it needs little skill and psychology to
be sure that a highly gifted girl who had tried to use her gift for poetry
would have been so thwarted and hindered by contrary instincts [add
"chains, guns, the lash, the ownership of one's body by someone else,
submission to an alien religion"], that she must have lost her health and
sanity to a certainty."

The key words, as they relate to Phillis, are "contrary instincts." For   20
when we read the poetry of Phillis Wheatley—and when we read the
novels of Nella Larsen or the oddly false-sounding autobiography of that
freest of all black women writers, Zora Hurston**—evidence of "contrary
instincts" is everywhere. Her loyalties were completely divided, as was,
without question, her mind.

But how could this be otherwise? Captured at seven, a slave of   21
wealthy, doting whites who instilled in her the "savagery" of the Africa
they "rescued" her from...one wonders if she was even able to remember
her homeland as she had known it, or as it really was.

Yet, because she did not try to use her gift for poetry in a world that   22
made her a slave, she was "so thwarted and hindered by...contrary instincts, that she...lost her health...." In the last years of brief life, burdened not only with the need to express her gift but also with a penniless,
friendless "freedom" and several small children for whom she was forced
to do strenuous work to feed, she lost her health, certainly. Suffering from
malnutrition and neglect and who knows what mental agonies, Phillis
Wheatley died.

So torn by "contrary instincts" was black, kidnapped, enslaved   23
Phillis that her description of "the Goddess"—as she poetically called the
Liberty she did not have—is ironically, cruelly humorous. And, in fact,

---

*EDS. NOTE—Early-twentieth-century English essayist and novelist.
**EDS. NOTE—Larsen (1891–1964) wrote realistic novels about black and white re-
lations; Hurston (1903–1960) is noted for her folklore research and novels and stories
that reproduce southern black dialect.

has held Phillis up to ridicule for more than a century. It is usually read prior to hanging Phillis's memory as that of a fool. She wrote:

> The Goddess comes, she moves divinely fair,
> Olive and laurel binds her *golden* hair.
> Wherever shines this native of the skies,
> Unnumber'd charms and recent graces rise. [My italics]

It is obvious that Phillis, the slave, combed the "Goddess's" hair   24
every morning; prior, perhaps, to bringing in the milk, or fixing her mistress's lunch. She took her imagery from the one thing she saw elevated above all others.

With the benefit of hindsight we ask, "How could she?"   25

But at last, Phillis, we understand. No more snickering when your   26
stiff, struggling, ambivalent lines are forced on us. We know now that you were not an idiot or a traitor; only a sickly little black girl, snatched from your home and country and made a slave; a woman who still struggled to sing the song that was your gift, although in a land of barbarians who praised you for your bewildered tongue. It is not so much what you sang, as that you kept alive, in so many of our ancestors, *the notion of song.*

Black women are called, in the folklore that so aptly identifies one's   27
status in society, "the *mule* of the world," because we have been handed the burdens that everyone else—*everyone* else—refused to carry. We have also been called "Matriarchs," "Superwomen," and "Mean and Evil Bitches." Not to mention "Castraters" and "Sapphire's Mama." When we have pleaded for understanding, our character has been distorted; when we have asked for simple caring, we have been handed empty inspirational appellations, then stuck in the farthest corner. When we have asked for love, we have been given children. In short, even our plainer gifts, our labors of fidelity and love, have been knocked down our throats. To be an artist and a black woman, even today, lowers our status in many respects, rather than raises it: and yet, artists we will be.

Therefore we must fearlessly pull out of ourselves and look at and   28
identify with our lives the living creativity some of our great-grandmothers were not allowed to know. I stress *some* of them because it is well known that the majority of our great-grandmothers knew, even without "knowing" it, the reality of their spirituality, even if they didn't recognize it beyond what happened in the singing at church—and they never had any intention of giving it up.

How they did it—those millions of black women who were not   29
Phillis Wheatley, or Lucy Terry or Frances Harper or Zora Hurston or Nella Larsen or Bessie Smith; or Elizabeth Catlett, or Katherine Dunham,*

---

*EDS. NOTE—Successful black female artists; the first five were writers, Smith was a singer and songwriter, Catlett a sculptor, and Dunham a dancer and choreographer.

either—brings me to the title of this essay, "In Search of Our Mothers' Gardens," which is a personal account that is yet shared, in its theme and its meaning, by all of us. I found, while thinking about the far-reaching world of the creative black woman, that often the truest answer to a question that really matters can be found very close.

In the late 1920s my mother ran away from home to marry my father. Marriage, if not running away, was expected of seventeen-year-old girls. By the time she was twenty, she had two children and was pregnant with a third. Five children later, I was born. And this is how I came to know my mother: she seemed a large, soft, loving-eyed woman who was rarely impatient in our home. Her quick, violent temper was on view only a few times a year, she battled with the white landlord who had the misfortune to suggest to her that her children did not need to go to school. 30

She made all the clothes we wore, even my brothers' overalls. She made all the towels and sheets we used. She spent the summers canning vegetables and fruits. She spent the winter evenings making quilts enough to cover all our beds. 31

During the "working" day, she labored beside—not behind—my father in the fields. Her day began before sunup, and did not end until late at night. There was never a moment for her to sit down, undisturbed, to unravel her own private thoughts; never a time free from interruption—by work or the noisy inquiries of her many children. And yet, it is to my mother—and all our mothers who were not famous—that I went in search of the secret of what has fed that muzzled and often mutilated, but vibrant, creative spirit that the black woman has inherited, and that pops out in wild and unlikely places to this day. 32

But when, you will ask, did my overworked mother have time to know or care about feeding the creative spirit? 33

The answer is so simple that many of us have spent years discovering it. We have constantly looked high, when we should have looked high—and low. 34

For example: in the Smithsonian Institution in Washington, D.C., there hangs a quilt unlike any other in the world. In fanciful, inspired, and yet simple and identifiable figures, it portrays the story of the Crucifixion. It is considered rare, beyond price. Though it follows no known pattern of quilt-making, and though it is made of bits and pieces of worthless rags, it is obviously the work of a person of powerful imagination and deep spiritual feeling. Below this quilt I saw a note that says it was made by "an anonymous Black woman in Alabama, a hundred years ago." 35

If we could locate this "anonymous" black woman from Alabama, she would turn out to be one of our grandmothers—an artist who left her mark in the only materials she could afford, and in the only medium her position in society allowed her to use. 36

As Virginia Woolf wrote further, in *A Room of One's Own:* 37

Yet genius of a sort must have existed among women as it must have existed among the working class. [Change this to "slaves" and "the wives of the daughters of sharecroppers."] Now and again an Emily Brontë or a Robert Burns [change this to "a Zora Hurston or a Richard Wright"] blazes out and proves its presence. But certainly it never got itself on to paper. When, however, one reads of a witch being ducked, of a woman possessed by devils [or "Sainthood"], of a wise woman selling herbs [our root workers], or even a very remarkable man who had a mother, then I think we are on the track of a lost novelist, a suppressed poet, of some mute and inglorious Jane Austen.... Indeed, I would venture to guess that Anon, who wrote so many poems without signing them, was often a woman....

And so our mothers and grandmothers have, more often than not   38
anonymously, handed on the creative spark, the seed of the flower they themselves never hoped to see: or like a sealed letter they could not plainly read.

And so it is, certainly, with my own mother. Unlike "Ma" Rainey's*   39
songs, which retained their creator's name even while blasting forth from Bessie Smith's mouth, no song or poem will bear my mother's name. Yet so many of the stories that I write, that we all write, are my mother's stories. Only recently did I fully realize this: that through years of listening to my mother's stories of her life, I have absorbed not only the stories themselves, but something of the manner in which she spoke, something of the urgency that involves the knowledge that her stories—like her life—must be recorded. It is probably for this reason that so much of what I have written is about characters whose counterparts in real life are so much older than I am.

But the telling of these stories, which came from my mother's lips as   40
naturally as breathing, was not the only way my mother showed herself as an artist. For stories, too, were subject to being distracted, to dying without conclusion. Dinners must be started, and cotton must be gathered before the big rains. The artist that was and is my mother showed itself to me only after many years. This is what I finally noticed:

Like Mem, a character in *The Third Life of Grange Copeland,* my mother   41
adorned with flowers whatever shabby house we were forced to live in. And not just your typical straggly country stand of zinnias, either. She planted ambitious gardens—and still does—with over fifty different varieties of plants that bloom profusely from early March until late November. Before she left home for the fields, she watered her flowers, chopped up the grass, and laid out new beds. When she returned from the fields she might divide clumps of bulbs, dig a cold pit, uproot and replant rose, or prune branches from her taller bushes or trees—until night came and it was too dark to see.

---

*EDS. NOTE—Famous blues singer and songwriter of the early twentieth century.

Whatever she planted grew as if by magic, and her fame as a grower   42
of flowers spread over three counties. Because of her creativity with her
flowers, even my memories of poverty are seen through a screen of
blooms—sunflowers, petunias, roses, dahlias, forsythia, spirea, delphini-
ums, verbena . . . and on and on.

And I remember people coming to my mother's yard to be given cut-   43
tings from her flowers; I hear again the praise showered on her because
whatever rocky soil she landed on, she turned into a garden. A garden so
brilliant with colors, so original in its design, so magnificent with life and
creativity, that to this day people drive by our house in Georgia—perfect
strangers and imperfect strangers—and ask to stand or walk in my
mother's art.

I notice that it is not only when my mother is working in her flowers   44
that she is radiant, almost to the point of being invisible—except as
Creator: hand and eye. She is involved in work her soul must have.
Ordering the universe in the image of her personal conception of Beauty.

Her face, as she prepares the Art that is her gift, is a legacy of respect   45
she leaves to me, for all that illuminates and cherishes life. She has
handed down respect for the possibilities—and the will to grasp them.

For her, so hindered and intruded upon in so many ways, being an   46
artist has still been a daily part of her life. This ability to hold on, even in
very simple ways, is work black women have done for a very long time.

This poem is not enough, but it is something, for the woman who lit-   47
erally covered the holes in our walls with sunflowers:

> They were women then
> My mama's generation
> Husky of voice—Stout of
> Step
> With fists as well as
> Hands
> How they battered down
> Doors
> And ironed
> Starched white
> Shirts
> How they led
> Armies
> Headragged Generals
> Across mined
> Fields
> Booby-trapped
> Kitchens
> To discovery books
> Desks
> A place for us

How they knew what we
Must know
Without knowing a page
Of it
Themselves.

Guided by my heritage of a love of beauty and a respect for   48
strength—in search of my mother's garden, I found my own.

And perhaps in Africa over two hundred years ago, there was just   49
such a mother; perhaps she painted vivid and daring decorations in oranges and yellows and greens on the walls of her hut; perhaps she sang—in a voice like Roberta Flack's—*sweetly* over the compounds of her village; perhaps she wove the most stunning mats or told the most ingenious stories of all the village storytellers. Perhaps she was herself a poet—though only her daughter's name is signed to the poems that we know.

Perhaps Phillis Wheatley's mother was also an artist.   50

Perhaps in more than Phillis Wheatley's biological life is her mother's   51
signature made clear.

• • •

COMPREHENSION

1. Why does Walker describe southern black women in the 1920s as "crazy, loony, pitiful women" (3)? What strengths did these women have?

2. In paragraph 5 Walker describes southern black women as "exquisite butterflies trapped in an evil honey." What is this "evil honey"? What does Walker believe poet Jean Toomer means when he characterizes these women as "the mule of the world"?

3. What is the "music not yet written" (7) to which Walker says these women moved? What, according to Walker, were they waiting for?

4. Walker sees the women not as saints but as something else. How does she characterize them? Why?

5. In paragraph 11 Walker asks, "What did it mean for a black woman to be an artist in our grandmothers' time?" In paragraph 13 she asks how their creativity was kept alive. Paraphrase her answers to these questions.

6. Why, according to Walker, is what she describes in paragraphs 1 through 14 "not the end of the story"? What is the rest of this story?

7. Paraphrase the story of Phillis Wheatley's life. What does her story contribute to Walker's essay?

8. What, specifically, does Walker believe black women should do? In what sense should they see their mothers and grandmothers as positive examples? As negative examples? Why does she call this essay "In Search of Our Mothers' Gardens"?

9. How does Walker link herself with her mother and grandmother? What legacy have they left her?

PURPOSE AND AUDIENCE

1. This essay was first published in *Ms.*, a feminist magazine. Do you think it is a feminist essay? Explain.

2. In this essay, Walker addresses African-American women. What does she advise her readers? Do you think her recommendations are relevant to women of other races? To men? Why or why not?

3. What is Walker's thesis? Do you think she expects her audience to be sympathetic to this position? Explain your reasoning.

STYLE AND STRUCTURE

1. The essay opens with a quotation from noted African-American novelist and poet Jean Toomer. Is this an effective opening strategy? Why do you think Walker begins her essay this way?

2. Throughout her essay Walker (sometimes quoting Toomer) uses elaborate figurative language to describe the women she is writing about. Give examples of some of the metaphors she uses, and evaluate their effectiveness. Do you think she uses enough figurative language? Too much? Explain.

3. In paragraphs 14, 23, and 37, Walker quotes three women writers; in paragraph 47, she presents a poem of her own. What do these excerpts have in common? Do you think they are distracting digressions or vital components of the essay? Explain.

4. Is Walker's tone sorrowful? Bitter? Regretful? Strident? On what do you base your conclusion?

5. Why does Walker summarize her own mother's life in paragraphs 30 through 32? What is the connection between the life of Walker's mother and the life of Phillis Wheatley? Do you think the biographical information Walker provides about these two women is necessary? Why or why not?

6. Walker introduces some of her key ideas with questions. For example, in paragraph 3 she asks, "Who were these Saints?" Where else does she ask questions? Does she answer them? Why do you suppose she uses this strategy instead of making direct statements?

VOCABULARY PROJECTS

1. Define each of the following words as it is used in this selection.

overseer (12)	barbarians (26)	counterparts (39)
lash (12)	matriarchs (27)	

2. What images are usually associated with the word *garden*? Is *garden* simply a metaphor for art in this essay, or does it have other meanings as well?

JOURNAL ENTRY

In paragraph 27 Walker says "To be an artist and a black woman, even today, lowers our status in many respects, rather than raises it." Do you agree with Walker's statement? Do you think it is true for all women? For any artist?

WRITING WORKSHOP

1. In what sense might you see yourself as an artist? What kinds of creative expression do you believe constitute your own garden? Using a series of examples, develop an essay about these ideas.

2. Interview your mother or grandmother (or another female relative) on the subject of the creative outlets available to women of her generation—and the obstacles to those outlets. Use narration, exemplification, and cause and effect to shape an essay about their experiences and those of their peers.

3. Think about the various kinds of art Walker discusses in this essay—everything from poetry to quilting to singing to gardening. Do you consider all her examples legitimate kinds of art, or do you have different standards? Write a definition of *art* using classification and division as well as exemplification to develop your definition.

COMBINING THE PATTERNS

What patterns of development does Walker use in her essay? Annotate the essay to identify each pattern. Use the annotations accompanying "On Dumpster Diving" (which appears earlier in this chapter) as a guide.

THEMATIC CONNECTIONS

- "My Mother Never Worked" (page 81)
- "The Way to Rainy Mountain" (page 136)
- "The Men We Carry in Our Minds" (page 387)
- "Mother Tongue" (page 393)

WRITING ASSIGNMENTS FOR COMBINING THE PATTERNS

1. Reread Michael Huu Truong's essay at the beginning of this chapter. Responding to the same assignment he was given ("Write an essay about the person and/or place that defined your childhood"), use several different patterns to communicate to readers what your childhood was like.

2. Write an essay about the political, social, or economic events that you believe have dominated and defined your life, or a stage in your life. Use **cause and effect** and any other patterns you think are appropriate to explain and illustrate why these events were important to you and how they affected you.

3. Develop a thesis statement that draws a general conclusion about the nature, quality, or effectiveness of advertising in print media (in newspapers or magazines or on billboards). Write an essay that supports this thesis statement with a series of very specific paragraphs. Use the patterns of development that best help you to characterize particular advertisements.

4. Exactly what do you think it means to be an American? Write a **definition** essay that answers this question, developing your definition with whatever patterns best serve your purpose.

5. Many of the essays in this text recount the writers' personal experiences. Identify one essay in which a writer describes experiences that are either similar to your own or in sharp contrast to your own. Then, write a **comparison-and-contrast** essay in which you *either* compare *or* contrast your experiences with those of the writer. Use several different patterns to develop your essay.

COLLABORATIVE ACTIVITY FOR COMBINING THE PATTERNS

Working in pairs, choose two essays from Chapters 2 through 10 of this text. Then, working individually, identify the various patterns of development used in each essay. When you have finished, exchange ideas with the other student in your group. Have both of you identified the same patterns in each essay? If not, try to reach a consensus. Then, working together, choose one of the two essays, and write a paragraph summarizing why each pattern is used and explaining how the various patterns work together.

APPENDIX: USING AND DOCUMENTING SOURCES

When you write about the essays in this book, they become *sources* for your writing. In any college class you may use material from many other sources as well—books, journals, newspapers, magazines, and the Internet. Every time you use material that is not yours, you need to acknowledge it in your writing. You do this with **documentation,** a formal way of giving credit to the sources from which you borrow words or ideas.

This appendix gives an overview of how to use sources. It also discusses the documentation style recommended by the Modern Language Association (MLA), which is used by teachers of the humanities (including composition).* Other academic disciplines use different methods of documentation. For example, if you were writing a paper for a psychology course, you would use the format recommended by the American Psychological Association (APA). If you have questions about what documentation style to use, ask your instructor for guidance and then consult the appropriate manual or handbook.

PARAPHRASING, SUMMARIZING, AND USING QUOTATIONS

When you use information from sources in your writing, you do not always quote the exact words of your sources. Instead, you frequently use *paraphrase* and *summary.*

When you **paraphrase,** you present the ideas of a passage in your own words, following the order and emphasis of the original. Here is a passage from David Cole's "Five Myths about Immigration" (see p. 543) followed by a paraphrase:

ORIGINAL: Some have suggested that we might save money and diminish incentives to immigrate illegally if we denied undocumented aliens public services. In fact, undocumented immigrants are already

---

*For further information see the *MLA Handbook for Writers of Research Papers,* 4th ed. (New York: MLA, 1995) and guidelines for documenting Internet sources at <http://www.mla.org>.

ineligible for most social programs, with the exception of education for schoolchildren, which is constitutionally required, and benefits directly related to health and safety, such as emergency medical care and nutritional assistance to poor women, infants, and children. To deny such basic care to people in need, apart from being inhumanly callous, would probably cost us more in the long run by exacerbating health problems that we would eventually have to address.

PARAPHRASE: According to David Cole, one popular belief is that denying access to public services would reduce the number of illegal immigrants. The truth, however, is that most benefits, except for those for some basic health and education services, are already unavailable to undocumented aliens. To eliminate these services would not only increase suffering but would also cost taxpayers more later on (543).

Notice that the lead-in to the paraphrase ("According to David Cole") is a **running acknowledgment,** a phrase that identifies the author of a source. The paraphrase itself is followed by parenthetical documentation. None of the distinctive phrasing of the original appears in the paraphrase; if it did, it would be enclosed in quotation marks.

When you write a **summary,** you also put the ideas of a source in your own words. But unlike a paraphrase, a summary conveys only the basic meaning of a passage, without following the order and emphasis of the original. For this reason, a summary is always shorter than the original. Notice how the following summary presents the basic idea of the Cole passage:

SUMMARY: David Cole observes that denying benefits will not solve the problem of undocumented aliens (543).

Like a paraphrase, a summary identifies the author and the page number of the source, and does not use the phrasing of the original. (Keep in mind, when you write paraphrases and summaries, that they present just the ideas of the original, not your opinions.)

When you **quote,** you present the exact words of a source, enclosed in quotation marks. Quotations give your readers the flavor of an original source, and they can lend the authority of an expert to your essay. Whenever possible, however, you should put information from your sources in your own words. Because quotations tend to break the flow of an essay, they distract readers. For this reason, use a quotation only when it is so memorable that putting it in your own words would seriously weaken its effect, or when it is so complex that any attempt to paraphrase it would change its meaning.

When you do use a quotation, integrate it smoothly into your essay so that readers will understand why you are using it and how it relates to your discussion. In the following passage, the writer uses a quotation without showing how it relates to the rest of her discussion:

AWKWARD: Multicultural education does have its place in the current college curriculum. "But if required, those studies should be in conjunction with the study of Western civilization" (Rubin 548).

To clarify her purpose and integrate the quotation smoothly into her essay, the writer should use a running acknowledgement.

INTEGRATED: Multicultural education does have its place in the current college curriculum. But, *as Trudy Rubin points out,* studies of other cultures "should be in conjunction with the study of Western civilization" (548).

For the sake of clarity and variety, you can place a running acknowledgment at various points in a sentence. You can also use different words to introduce the quoted remarks—for example, *points out, observes, comments, notes, remarks,* and *concludes.*

> *As Trudy Rubin observes,* "studies of other cultures should be in conjunction with the study of Western civilization" (548).

> "In today's world," *Rubin notes,* "one can't assume that students arrive at college versed in European or American history or political theory" (550).

> Studies of other cultures "should be in conjunction with the study of Western civilization," *comments Trudy Rubin* in her essay "Multiculturalism Is Misguided" (548).

If you have to omit a word or phrase from a quotation, show the omission by substituting an ellipsis—three spaced periods—for the deleted words.

> According to Rubin, "With all the immense mistakes made by the West, . . . it is still Western history and culture that has given men and women the greatest possibility to fight for change" (549).

Notice that in the preceding sentence the deleted words directly follow internal punctuation (a comma), so the punctuation in the original quotation is retained.

AVOIDING PLAGIARISM

As a rule, you must document any words or ideas from an outside source that are not **common knowledge**—factual information widely available in reference works. To present information from another source as if it were your own (whether intentionally or unintentionally) is to commit **plagiarism**—and, make no mistake about it, *plagiarism is theft.* You can avoid committing plagiarism by understanding what you must document and what you do not have to document.

☑ **GUIDELINES FOR AVOIDING PLAGIARISM**

YOU SHOULD DOCUMENT

- Word-for-word quotations from a source
- Ideas from a source that you put in your own words
- Tables, charts, graphs, or statistics from a source

YOU DO NOT NEED TO DOCUMENT

- Your own ideas
- Common knowledge
- Familiar quotations

Whenever you consult a source to get ideas for your writing, be careful to avoid the errors that commonly lead to plagiarism. The following paragraph from Brian Siano's "Frankenstein Must Be Destroyed: Chasing the Monster of TV Violence" (see Chapter 10) and the four scenarios that follow it will help you understand these common errors.

> **ORIGINAL:**   Of course, there are a few crazies out there who will be unfavorably influenced by what they see on TV. But even assuming that somehow the TV show (or movie or record) shares some of the blame, how does one predict what future crazies will take for inspiration? What guidelines would ensure that people write, act, or produce something that *will not upset a psychotic?* Not only is this a ridiculous demand, it's insulting to the public as well. We would all be treated as potential murderers in order to gain a hypothetical 5 percent reduction in violence.

DOCUMENT YOUR SOURCES

> **PLAGIARISM:**   Even if we were to control the programs that are shown on television, we would decrease violence in society by perhaps 5 percent.

Even though the writer does not quote Siano directly, she still must identify him as the source of the borrowed material.

> **CORRECT:**   According to Brian Siano, even if we were to control the programs that are shown on television, we would decrease violence in society by perhaps 5 percent (Siano 596-97).

PLACE BORROWED WORDS IN QUOTATION MARKS

> **PLAGIARISM:**   According to Brian Siano, there will always be a few crazies out there who will be unfavorably influenced by what they see on TV (596).

Although the writer cites Siano as his source, his passage incorrectly uses Siano's exact words without quoting them.

CORRECT (BORROWED WORDS IN QUOTATION MARKS): According to Brian Siano, there will always be "a few crazies out there who will be unfavorably influenced by what they see on TV" (596).

CORRECT (BORROWED WORDS PUT INTO WRITER'S OWN WORDS): According to Brian Siano, some unstable people will commit crimes because of the violence they see in the media (596).

USE YOUR OWN WORDING

PLAGIARISM: Naturally, there will always be people who are affected by what they view on television. But even if we agree that television programs can influence people, how can we really know what will make people commit crimes? How can we be absolutely sure that a show will not disturb someone who is insane? The answer is that we can't. To pretend that we can is insulting to law-abiding citizens. We can't treat everyone as if they were criminals just to reduce violence by a small number of people (Siano 596-97).

Even though the writer acknowledges Siano as her source, and even though she does not use Siano's exact words, her passage closely follows the order, emphasis, and syntax and phrasing of the original. Notice in the following passage how the writer lets her own voice guide the discussion and uses a single distinctive quotation from the original.

CORRECT: According to Brian Siano, we should not censor a television program just because "a few crazies" may be incited to violence (596). Not only would such censorship deprive the majority of people of the right to watch what they want, but it will not significantly lessen the violence in society (596-97).

DISTINGUISH YOUR IDEAS FROM THE SOURCE'S IDEAS

PLAGIARISM: Any attempt to control television violence will quickly reach the point of diminishing returns. There is no way to make absolutely certain that a particular television program will not cause a disturbed person to commit a crime. It seems silly, then, to treat the majority of people as "potential murderers" just to control the behavior of a few (Siano 597).

In the preceding passage it appears that only the quotation in the last sentence is borrowed from Siano's article. In fact, so are the ideas in the second sentence. The writer should use a running acknowledgment (such as "According to Siano") to acknowledge the borrowed material in this sentence and to indicate where it begins.

> **CORRECT:** Any attempt to control television violence will quickly reach the point of diminishing returns. According to Brian Siano, there is no way to make absolutely certain that a particular television program will not cause a disturbed person to commit a crime (596). It seems silly, then, to treat the majority of people as "potential murderers" just to control the behavior of a few (597).

(Note that a quotation requires separate parenthetical documentation.)

USING MLA STYLE TO CITE AND DOCUMENT SOURCES

MLA documentation format consists of *parenthetical references* within a paper that refer to a *Works Cited* list at the end of the paper.

Parenthetical References in the Text

A parenthetical reference should include just enough information to guide readers to a specific entry in your Works Cited list. A typical parenthetical reference consists of the author's last name and the page number: (Grisham 724). If you use more than one work by the same author, include a shortened form of the title in the parenthetical reference: (Grisham, Pelican 47). Notice that there is no *p.* before the page number and that no punctuation precedes the page number.

Whenever possible, identify the author of a source in a running acknowledgment. If you do this, include only the page number in parentheses. (Note that with summaries and paraphrases, end punctuation comes after the parenthetical reference.) For information on placement of punctuation with parenthetical references and quotations, see "Guidelines for Formatting Quotations" on page 653.

▶ As John Grisham observes in "Unnatural Killers," Oliver
   Stone celebrates gratuitous violence (576).

Place documentation so that it doesn't interrupt the flow of your ideas, preferably at the end of a sentence. Notice how the preceding example differentiates the writer's ideas from the ideas of the source by beginning with a running acknowledgment ("As John Grisham observes") and by ending with a parenthetical reference.

The format for parenthetical references departs from these guidelines in three special situations:

WHEN YOU ARE CITING A WORK BY TWO AUTHORS

▶ Film violence has been increasing during the past ten years
   (Williams and Yorst 34).

> ☑ **GUIDELINES FOR FORMATTING QUOTATIONS**
>
> - **Short quotations** Quotations of no more than four typed lines are run in with text. End punctuation follows the parenthetical reference (which follows the quotation marks).
>
>   ```
>   According to Grisham, there are "only two ways to
>   curb the excessive violence of films like Natural
>   Born Killers" (576).
>   ```
>
> - **Long quotations** Quotations of more than four lines are set off from the text. Indent long quotations ten spaces, or one inch, from the left-hand margin, and do not enclose the passage in quotation marks. The first line of a long quotation does not have a paragraph indent. If a quoted passage has more than one paragraph, indent the first line of each subsequent paragraph three additional spaces (or one-quarter inch). Introduce a long quotation with a colon, and place the parenthetical reference one space *after* the end punctuation.
>
>   ```
>   Grisham believes that eventually the courts will act to
>   force studio executives to accept responsibility for the
>   effects of their products:
>        But the laughing will soon stop. It will take only
>        one large verdict against the likes of Oliver Stone,
>        and his production company, and perhaps the screen-
>        writer, and the studio itself, and then the party
>        will be over. The verdict will come from the heart-
>        land, far away from Southern California, in some
>        small courtroom with no cameras. (577)
>   ```

WHEN YOU ARE CITING A WORK WITHOUT A LISTED AUTHOR

▶
```
Ever since cable television came on the scene, shows with
graphically violent content have become common ("Cable
Wars" 76).
```

WHEN YOU ARE CITING AN INDIRECT SOURCE

If you use a statement by one author that is quoted in the work of another author, show this by including the abbreviation *qtd. in* ("quoted in").

▶
```
When speaking of television drama, Leonard Eron, of the
University of Illinois, says "perpetrators of violence should
not be rewarded for violent acts" (qtd. in Siano 595).
```

The Works Cited List

The Works Cited list includes all the works you cite. Use the following guidelines to help you prepare your list.

☑ **GUIDELINES FOR PREPARING THE WORKS CITED LIST**
- Begin the Works Cited list on a new page after the last page of text.
- Number the Works Cited page as the next page of the paper.
- Center the heading *Works Cited* one inch from the top of the page; don't underline the heading or put it in quotation marks.
- Double-space the list.
- List entries alphabetically according to the author's last name.
- Alphabetize unsigned articles according to the first major word of the title.
- Begin each entry flush with the left-hand margin.
- Indent second and subsequent lines five spaces (or one-half inch).
- Separate each division of the entry—author, title, and publication information—by a period and one space.

The following sample entries cover the situations you will encounter most often. Make certain that you follow the formats exactly as they appear below.

Books

BOOK BY ONE AUTHOR

List the author, last name first. Underline the title. Include the city of publication and a shortened form of the publisher's name—for example, *Prentice* for *Prentice Hall* or *Harcourt* for *Harcourt Brace College Publishers.* Use the abbreviation *UP* for *University Press,* as in *Princeton UP* and *U of Chicago P.* End with the date of publication.

▶ Brown, Charles T. The Rock and Roll Story. Englewood
       Cliffs: Prentice, 1983.

BOOK BY TWO OR THREE AUTHORS

List second and subsequent authors, first name first, in the order in which they are listed on the title page.

▶ Coe, Sophie D., and Michael D. Coe. The True History of
       Chocolate. New York: Thames, 1996.

BOOK BY MORE THAN THREE AUTHORS

List only the first author, followed by the abbreviation *et al.* ("and others").

▶ Sklar, Robert E., et al. Movie-Made America: A Cultural
       History of American Movies. New York: Random, 1994.

TWO OR MORE BOOKS BY THE SAME AUTHOR

List two or more books by the same author in alphabetical order according to title. After the first entry, type three unspaced hyphens followed by a period. This takes the place of the author's name.

▶ Angelou, Maya. Getting Together in My Name. New York:
     Bantam, 1980.

   ---. I Know Why the Caged Bird Sings. New York: Bantam,
     1985.

EDITED BOOK

▶ Dickinson, Emily. The Complete Poems of Emily Dickinson.
     Ed. Thomas H. Johnson. New York: Little, 1990.

TRANSLATION

▶ García Márquez, Gabriel. Love in the Time of Cholera.
     Trans. Edith Grossman. New York: Knopf, 1988.

REVISED EDITION

▶ Gans, Herbert J. The Urban Villagers. 2nd ed. New York:
     Free, 1982.

ANTHOLOGY

▶ Kirszner, Laurie G., and Stephen R. Mandell, eds. Patterns
     for College Writing. 7th ed. New York: St. Martin's,
     1998.

ESSAY IN AN ANTHOLOGY

▶ Grisham, John. "Unnatural Killers." Patterns for College
     Writing. 7th ed. Ed. Laurie G. Kirszner and Stephen R.
     Mandell. New York: St. Martin's, 1998. 570-77.

MORE THAN ONE ESSAY IN THE SAME ANTHOLOGY

List each essay separately with a cross-reference to the entire anthology.

▶ Grisham, John. "Unnatural Killers." Kirszner and Mandell
     570-77.

  Kirszner, Laurie G., and Stephen R. Mandell, eds. Patterns
     for College Writing. 7th ed. New York: St. Martin's,
     1998.

  Stone, Oliver. "Memo to John Grisham: What's Next--'A Movie
     Made Me Do It'?" Kirszner and Mandell 580-82.

SECTION OR CHAPTER OF A BOOK

▶   Gordimer, Nadine. "Once upon a Time." <u>Jump and Other</u>
        <u>Stories</u>. New York: Farrar, 1991.

Periodicals

ARTICLE IN A JOURNAL WITH CONTINUOUS PAGINATION
THROUGHOUT AN ANNUAL VOLUME

Some scholarly journals have continuous pagination; that is, one issue
might end on page 234 and the next begins with page 235. In this case, the
volume number is followed by the date of publication in parentheses.

▶   Allen, Dennis W. "Horror and Perverse Delight: Faulkner's
        'A Rose for Emily.'" <u>Modern Fiction Studies</u> 30 (1984):
        685-96.

ARTICLE IN A JOURNAL WITH SEPARATE PAGINATION IN EACH ISSUE

For a journal in which each issue begins with page 1, the volume
number is followed by a period and the issue number and then by the
date. Leave no space after the period.

▶   Lindemann, Erika. "Teaching as a Rhetorical Art." <u>CEA Forum</u>
        15.2 (1985): 9-12.

ARTICLE IN A MONTHLY MAGAZINE

If an article doesn't appear on consecutive pages—for example, if it
begins on page 43, skips to page 47, and continues on page 49—include
only the first page followed by a plus sign.

▶   O'Brien, Conor Cruise. "Thomas Jefferson: Radical and
        Racist." <u>Atlantic Monthly</u> Oct. 1996: 43+.

ARTICLE IN A WEEKLY OR BIWEEKLY MAGAZINE (SIGNED OR UNSIGNED)

▶   Miller, Arthur. "Why I wrote <u>The Crucible</u>." <u>New Yorker</u> 21
        Oct. 1996: 158-63.

    "The Dead Don't Tell Lies." <u>Time</u> 28 Oct. 1996: 37.

ARTICLE IN A NEWSPAPER

▶   Haberman, Clyde. "Is Graffiti 'Art'?" <u>New York Times</u> 22
        Oct. 1996, late ed.: B1.

EDITORIAL OR LETTER TO THE EDITOR

▶   "High Taxes Kill Cities." Editorial. <u>Philadelphia Inquirer</u>
        8 Aug. 1995, late ed., sec. 1: 17.

Internet Sources

When citing Internet sources appearing on the World Wide Web, include both the date of electronic publication (or latest update, or posting) and the date you accessed the source. Some of the following examples include only the date of access, meaning that the date of publication was not available.

SCHOLARLY PROJECT

▶ New Brunswick History Department: Oral History Archives of
    WW-II. Ed. G. Kurt Piehler. 16 Oct. 1997. Rutgers U. 11
    Nov. 1997 <http://history.rutgers.edu/oralhistory/
    orlinf.htm>.

PROFESSIONAL SITE

▶ The American Dialect Society. Brigham Young U. 20 Aug.
    1997. 11 Nov. 1997 <http://www.et.byu.edu/~lilliek/
    ads/index.htm>.

PERSONAL SITE

▶ Lynch, Jack. Home page. 11 Nov. 1997 <http://
    dept.english.upenn.edu/~jlynch>.

BOOK

If information about print publication is given, include it in your entry.

▶ Maugham, W. Somerset. Of Human Bondage. Garden City, NY:
    Doubleday, Doran, 1915. The English Server Fiction
    Collection. Ed. Martha Cheng and Geoff Sauer. 12 May
    1994. Carnegie Mellon U. 11 Nov. 1997 <http://
    eserver.org/fiction/of-human.bondage.txt>.

POEM

▶ Poe, Edgar Allan. "The Raven." The CMU Poetry Index of
    Canonical Verse. 12 June 1993. 11 Nov. 1997 <http://
    eserver.org/poetry/the-raven.txt>.

ARTICLE IN A REFERENCE DATABASE

▶ "Estonia." The 1996 World Factbook. 12 Mar. 1997. Central
    Intelligence Agency. 11 Nov. 1997 <http://www.odci.gov/
    cia/publications/nsolo/factbook/en.htm>.

ARTICLE IN A JOURNAL

▶ Becker, Trudy Harrigton. "Ambiguity and the Female Warrior:
    Vergil's Camilla." Electronic Antiquity 4.1 (1997). 11

Nov. 1997 <gopher://babel.its.utas.edu.au:70/00/
Publications/
Electronic%20Antiquity%20%3A%20Communicating%20The%Classics/
4%2C1-August1997/%2802%29Articles/Becker-Vergil>.

ARTICLE IN A MAGAZINE

▶ Webb, Michael. "Playing at Work." Metropolis Online. Nov.
       1997. 11 Nov. 1997 <http://www.metropolismag.com/nov97/
       eames/eames.html>.

POSTING TO A DISCUSSION LIST

Be sure to include the phrase "Online posting."

▶ Thune, W. Scott. "Emotion and Rationality in Argument."
       23 Mar. 1997. Online posting. CCCC/97 Online. 11 Nov.
       1997 <http://www.missouri.edu/HyperNews/get/cccc98/
       proplink/12.html>.

Other Nonprint Sources

TELEVISION OR RADIO PROGRAM

▶ "Prime Suspect 3." Writ. Lynda La Plante. With Helen
       Mirren. Mystery! WNET, New York. 28 Apr. 1994.

VIDEOTAPE, MOVIE, RECORD, OR SLIDE PROGRAM

▶ Murray, Donald. Interview with John Updike. Dir. Bruce
       Schwartz. Videocassette. Harcourt, 1997.

PERSONAL INTERVIEW

▶ Garcetti, Gilbert. Personal interview. 7 May 1994.

LECTURE

▶ Rosenberg, Vivian. "Family Relationships in American
       Literature." Humanities 108. Drexel University,
       Philadelphia. 24 Oct. 1996.

MATERIAL ACCESSED THROUGH A COMPUTER SERVICE

When citing information from a commercial computer service such as
BRS, CompuServe, America Online, Lexis/Nexis, or Prodigy, include the
name of the medium (Online), the computer service (America Online),
and the date you accessed the material.

▶ Glicken, Natalie. "Brady Defends Gun Law in Court." Con-
    gressional Quarterly. Online. America Online. 10 Oct.
    1996.

If the material you are citing has appeared in print, include the print publication information before the electronic information. Use the abbreviation *n. pag.* ("no pagination") if no pages are given.

▶ "Downsizing Means New Jobs." New York Times 13 Apr. 1995,
    late ed.: C2. New York Times Online. Online. Nexis. 17
    Sept. 1996.

MATERIAL ACCESSED ON A CD-ROM

In addition to the publication information, include the medium (CD-
ROM), the vendor (UMI-Proquest), and the date you accessed the information.

▶ "Downsizing Means New Jobs." New York Times 13 Apr. 1995,
    late ed.: C2. New York Times Ondisc. CD-ROM. UMI-
    Proquest. 17 Sept. 1996.

COMPUTER PROGRAM

Include the name of the author (if given), the medium (CD-ROM or
Diskette), the city of publication, the name of the publisher, and the year
of publication.

▶ Interactive Sign Language: Fingerspelling and Numbers. CD-
    ROM. Seattle: Palatine, 1996.

Cahan, Benjamin, et al. Three by Five. Diskette. Santa
    Monica: MacToolkit, 1994.

The following paper, written for a composition class, follows the conventions of MLA documentation style. The paper uses three sources from
this text, one additional print source, and one source accessed from the
Internet.

Note: When you use quotations from one or two sources that the entire
class has read, your instructor may allow you to use *informal documentation.*
Because both the instructor and the class know the sources you are using,
you may be permitted to omit a Works Cited list and simply supply the authors' last names and the page numbers in parentheses.

Rogers 1

Allison Rogers
English 122-83
Essay 3
8 May 1997

Violence in the Media

Mickey and Mallory, two characters in Oliver Stone's film Natural Born Killers, travel across the Southwest killing a total of fifty-two people. After watching this movie, two teenagers went on a crime spree of their own and killed one person and wounded another, paralyzing her for the rest of her life. At their trial, their defense was that watching Natural Born Killers had made them commit their crimes and that Hollywood, along with the director of the movie, Oliver Stone, was to blame. As creative as this defense is, it somehow misses the mark. The power of the media to shape lives may be great, but **Thesis statement** no amount of violence on the screen can eliminate a person's responsibility for his or her actions, especially when it comes to committing serious crimes like murder.

Running acknowledgment cites author, so parenthetical reference includes only page number. Why are teens drawn to movies such as Natural Born Killers? Lewis H. Lapham believes that movies have become more violent because stress and anxiety makes the public's demand for violence stronger (13). True, if we are living in violent times, then movies simply reflect the world around us. Even so, is there a link between violent movies and television shows and violent behavior?

Paragraph combines quotation and paraphrase from Grisham article with student's own observations.

According to John Grisham, Oliver Stone's Natural Born Killers "inspired" two teenagers "to commit murder" (576). Grisham goes on to say that since the movie was released, several murders have been committed by troubled young people who claimed "they were under the influence...of Mickey and Mallory" (576). This scapegoat defense keeps reappearing as the violence in our everyday lives escalates: "I am not to blame," says the perpetrator. "That movie (or television show) made me do it."

Paragraph combines clearly documented paraphrases of Stone and Siano articles with student's own conclusions

The idea that violence in the media causes violent behavior is not supported by the facts. When one looks at Ben and Sarah, the two teenagers who supposedly imitated Mickey and Mallory, it is clear that factors other than Natural Born Killers influenced their decision to murder. Both young adults were deeply disturbed and had long histories of drug and alcohol abuse as well as psychiatric treatment (Stone 581). In addition, no clear experimental link between the violent shows and aggressive behavior has been discovered. Many studies have shown that after watching violent television shows, children tend to act aggressively, but after about a week they return to their normal pattern of behavior (Siano 595). The most that can be concluded from these studies is that the link between media violence and violent behavior is not clear.

What, then, are we supposed to make of the "copycat crimes" that are clearly inspired by the media? As Siano points out, there is a body of anecdotal evidence that supports the link between these "copycat crimes" and media violence (596). At one time or another, all of

us have read reports of a person imitating a
crime that he or she saw in a movie. Two
problems exist with this type of "evidence,"
however. The first problem is that in most
cases, the movie is never definitely linked to
the crime. For example, after the movie The
Money Train was released, a clerk in a New
York City subway token booth was set on fire
in much the same way a subway token clerk was
in the movie. Naturally, it is tempting to say
that the movie inspired the crime. But at the
time of the crime, several newspapers reported
that the act depicted in the movie was not
unusual and had in fact occurred at least
twice in the year before the movie's release.
So the question remains: did the movie cause
the violence, or did it simply reflect a kind
of violent behavior that was already present
in society? The truth is that we cannot answer
this question conclusively.

The second problem with anecdotal evidence is that it is not representative. The
crimes that are inspired by the media--killers
imitating Freddy Krueger, for example--are
unusual. As Siano says, most people who watch
a violent movie do not go out and commit
crimes. It is the "few crazies...who will be
unfavorably influenced by what they see"
(596). In other words, only a few people will
have extreme reactions, and because they are
mentally unbalanced, we cannot predict what
will set them off. It could be a movie like
Natural Born Killers, but it could also be a
Bugs Bunny cartoon or a Three Stooges movie.
The point is that society should not limit the
right of the majority to watch the movies and
television shows they want to see just because

No documentation necessary for factual information that appears in several sources.

Ellipsis indicates material deleted from quotation

Rogers 4

a few unbalanced individuals may go out and
commit crimes after seeing these presentations.

Certainly the media have some effect,
particularly on very young children who are
easily influenced by the violence they see.
For this reason, some might say that movie
violence should be prohibited. Children do not
understand the seriousness of violence, so
they naturally want to act it out. We have
all heard a child's brain being compared to a
sponge. With this in mind, parents need to
accept and understand their responsibility for
supervising what their children watch on "the
tube." The monitoring of what children see
needs to begin at home, where it is the parents' job to give their children a strong
sense of what is real and what is false.
Lapham states, for example, that each of his
children understood, well before the age of
nine, that violence in the video games Die
Hard and Lethal Weapon 2 was simulated (13).
One way parents can help supervise their children's viewing habits is to take the time to
view shows along with them, discussing after
the show is over what they have viewed. If
parents cannot watch television with their
children, they can buy devices that deny access
to objectionable programs. In fact, as of 1998,
all television sets are required by law to be
equipped with a V-chip that viewers can program
to automatically block out shows that are not
suitable for children (National).

The media have already taken steps to
improve the situation. For example, rating
systems now in place can help. These give the
audience the opportunity to judge the suitability of a movie before they go to see it

Parenthetical reference to online source includes only title because no author was listed.

or of a television program before they turn it on. Clearly, however, more needs to be done to enforce these rating systems. If a movie is being shown at a theater, the rating must be strictly enforced by the management. This could be done by having the attendant ask for some form of identification, such as a driver's license. (As you read this, you might be thinking, "But they already do this!" True, but how many R-rated movies did you get into when you were underage?) In addition, any movie or television show containing violence should not be shown on stations whose audience is primarily children, such as Nickelodeon or the Disney Channel, even at night. The time of day should not matter. When you think of Nickelodeon or Disney, The Brady Bunch and Mickey Mouse should come to mind, not Dirty Harry.

Last two paragraphs need no documentation because they represent student's own ideas.

Conclusion

There is no doubt that violence is learned and that violent media images encourage violent behavior. It is not clear, however, that violent movies and television shows will actually cause a person to commit a crime. For this reason, it is not fair or right to hold the media responsible for the possible effects of their productions. Placing the blame on the media is just an easy way to sidestep the hard questions of what is causing so much violence in our society and what we can do about it. If we prohibit violent programs, we will only deprive many people of their right to view the programs of their choice, and we will prevent creative artists from expressing themselves freely. In the process, these restrictions will also deprive society of a good deal of worthwhile entertainment.

Rogers 6

Works Cited

Grisham, John. "Unnatural Killers." Kirszner and
    Mandell 570-77.

Kirszner, Laurie G., and Stephen R. Mandell, eds.
    Patterns for College Writing. 7th ed. New
    York: St. Martin's, 1998.

Lapham, Lewis H. "Notebook." Harper's Apr. 1994:
    11-15.

National Crime Prevention Council. "Self, Home, and
    Family: Protecting Yourself: Turning Off Media
    Violence." 26 Nov. 1996 <http://www.ncpc.org/
    1safe6dc.html>.

Siano, Brian. "Frankenstein Must Be Destroyed:
    Chasing the Monster of TV Violence." Kirszner
    and Mandell 591-98.

Stone, Oliver. "Memo to John Grisham: What's Next--
    'A Movie Made Me Do It'?" Kirszner and Mandell
    580-82.

GLOSSARY

Abstract/Concrete language Abstract language names concepts or qualities that cannot be directly seen or touched: *love, emotion, evil, anguish.* Concrete language denotes objects or qualities that can be perceived by the senses: *fountain pen, leaky, shouting, rancid.* Abstract words are sometimes needed to express ideas, but they are very vague unless used with concrete supporting detail. The abstract phrase "The speaker was overcome with emotion" could mean almost anything, but the addition of concrete language clarifies the meaning: "He clenched his fist and shook it at the crowd" (anger).

Allusion A brief reference to literature, history, the Bible, mythology, popular culture, and so on that readers are expected to recognize. An allusion evokes a vivid impression in very few words. "The gardener opened the gate, and suddenly we found ourselves in Eden" suggests in one word (*Eden*) the stunning beauty of the garden the writer visited.

Analogy A form of comparison that explains an unfamiliar element by comparing it to another that is more familiar. Analogies also enable writers to put abstract or technical information in simpler, more concrete terms: "The effect of pollution on the environment is like that of cancer on the body."

Annotating The technique of recording one's responses to a reading selection by writing notes in the margins of the text. Annotating a text might involve asking questions, suggesting possible parallels with other selections or with the reader's own experience, arguing with the writer's points, commenting on the writer's style, or defining unfamiliar terms or concepts.

Antithesis A viewpoint opposite to one expressed in a *thesis.* In an argumentative essay, the thesis must be debatable. If no antithesis exists, the writer's thesis is not debatable. (See also **Thesis.**)

Antonym A word opposite in meaning to another word. *Beautiful* is the antonym of *ugly. Synonym* is the antonym of *antonym.*

Argumentation The form of writing that takes a stand on an issue and attempts to convince readers by presenting a logical sequence of points supported by evidence. Unlike *persuasion,* which uses a number of different appeals, argumentation is primarily an appeal to reason. (See Chapter 10.)

Audience The people "listening" to a writer's words. Writers who are sensitive to their audience will carefully choose a tone, examples, and allusions that their readers will understand and respond to. For instance, an effective article attempting to persuade high school students not to drink alcohol would use examples and allusions pertinent to a teenager's life. Different examples would be chosen if the writer were addressing middle-aged members of Alcoholics Anonymous.

Basis of comparison A fundamental similarity between two or more things that enables a writer to compare them. In a comparison of how two towns react to immigrants, the basis of comparison might be that both towns have a rapidly expanding immigrant population. (If one of the towns did not have any immigrants, this comparison would be illogical.)

Body paragraphs The paragraphs that develop and support an essay's thesis.

Brainstorming An invention technique that can be done individually or in a group. When writers brainstorm on their own, they jot down every fact or idea that relates to a particular topic. When they brainstorm in a group, they discuss a topic with others and write down the useful ideas that come up.

Causal chain A sequence of events in which one event causes another event, which in turn causes yet another event.

Cause and effect The pattern of development that discusses either the reasons for an occurrence or the observed or predicted consequence of an occurrence. Often both causes and effects are discussed in the same essay. (See Chapter 6.)

Causes The reasons for an event, situation, or phenomenon. An *immediate cause* is an obvious one; a *remote cause* is less easily perceived. The *main cause* is the most important cause, whether it is immediate or remote. Other, less important causes that nevertheless encourage the effect in some way (for instance, by speeding it up or providing favorable circumstances for it) are called *contributory causes.*

Chronological order The time sequence in which events occur. Chronological order is often used to organize a narrative; it is also used to structure a process essay.

Claim In Toulmin logic, the thesis or main point of an essay. Usually the claim is stated directly, but sometimes it is implied. (See also **Toulmin logic.**)

Classification and division The pattern of development that uses these two related methods of organizing information. *Classification* involves searching for common characteristics among various items and grouping them accordingly, thereby imposing orderly or randomly organized information. *Division* breaks up an entity into smaller groups or elements. Classification generalizes; division specifies. (See Chapter 8.)

Cliché An overused expression, such as *beauty is in the eye of the beholder, the good die young,* or *a picture is worth a thousand words.*

Clustering A method of invention whereby a writer groups ideas visually by listing the main topic in the center of a page, circling it, and surrounding it with words or phrases that identify the major points to be addressed. The writer then circles these words or phrases, creating new clusters or ideas for each of them.

Coherence The tight relationship between all the parts of an effective piece of writing. Such a relationship ensures that the writing will make sense to readers. For a piece of writing to be coherent, it must be logical and orderly, with effective *transitions* making the movement between sentences and paragraphs clear. Within and between paragraphs, coherence may also be enhanced by the repetition of key words and ideas, by the use of pronouns to refer to nouns mentioned previously, and by the use of parallel sentence structure.

Colloquialisms Expressions that are generally appropriate for conversation and informal writing but not usually acceptable for the writing you do in college, business, or professional settings. Examples of colloquial language include contractions; clipped forms (*dorm* for *dormitory, exam* for *examination*); vague expressions like *kind of* and *sort of*; conversation fillers like *you know*; and other informal words and expressions, such as *get across* for *communicate* and *kids* for *children.*

Common knowledge Factual information that is widely available in reference sources. Writers do not need to document common knowledge.

Comparison and contrast The pattern of development that focuses on similarities and/or differences between two or more subjects. In a general sense, *comparison* shows how two or more subjects are alike; *contrast* shows how they are different. (See Chapter 7.) (See also **Point-by-point comparison; Subject-by-subject comparison.**)

Conclusion The group of sentences or paragraphs that brings an essay to a close. To *conclude* means not only "to end" but also "to resolve." Although a conclusion does not resolve all the issues in an essay, the conclusion is the place to show that they *have* been resolved. An effective conclusion indicates that the writer is committed to what has been expressed, and it is the writer's last chance to leave an impression of confidence with readers.

Concrete language See **Abstract/Concrete language.**

Connotation The associations, meanings, or feelings a word suggests beyond its literal meaning. Literally, the word *home* means one's place of residence, but *home* also connotes warmth and a sense of belonging. (See also **Denotation.**)

Contributory cause See **Causes.**

Deductive reasoning The method of reasoning that moves from a general premise to a specific conclusion. Deductive reasoning is the opposite of *inductive reasoning.* (See also **Syllogism.**)

Definition An explanation of a word's meaning; the pattern of development in which a writer explains what something or someone is. See Chapter 9. (See also **Extended definition; Formal definition.**)

Denotation The literal meaning of a word. The denotation of *home* is "one's place of residence." (See also **Connotation.**)

Description The pattern of development that presents a word picture of a thing, a person, a situation, or a series of events. (See Chapter 3.) (See also **Objective description; Subjective description.**)

Digression A remark or series of remarks that wanders from the main point of a discussion. In a personal narrative, a digression may be entertaining because of its very irrelevance, but in other kinds of writing it is likely to distract and confuse readers.

Division See **Classification and division.**

Documentation The formal way of giving credit to the sources from which a writer borrows words or ideas. Documentation allows readers to evaluate a writer's sources and to consult them if they wish. Papers written for classes in English and related disciplines use the documentation style recommended by the Modern Language Association (MLA).(See Appendix.)

Dominant impression The mood or quality that is central to a piece of writing.

Essay A short work of nonfiction writing on a single topic that usually expresses the author's impressions or opinions. An essay may be organized around one of the patterns of development presented in Chapters 2 through 10 of this book, or it may combine several of these patterns.

Euphemism A polite term for an unpleasant concept (*passed on* is a euphemism for *died*).

Evidence Facts and opinions used to support a statement, position, or idea. *Facts,* which may include statistics, may be drawn from research or personal experience; *opinions* may represent the conclusions of experts or the writer's own ideas.

Example A concrete, specific illustration of a general point.

Exemplification The pattern of development that uses a single extended *example* or a series of shorter examples to support a thesis. (See Chapter 4.)

Extended definition A paragraph-, essay-, or book-length definition developed by means of one or more of the rhetorical strategies discussed in this book.

Fallacy A statement that resembles a logical argument but is not. Logical fallacies are often persuasive, but they unfairly manipulate readers to win agreement. Fallacies include begging the question; argument from analogy; personal (*ad hominem*) attacks; hasty or sweeping generalizations; false dilemmas (the either/or fallacy); equivocation; red herrings, you also (*tu quoque*); appeals to doubtful authority; distorting statistics; *post hoc* reasoning; and *non sequiturs*.

Figures of speech (also known as *figurative language*) Imaginative language used to suggest a special meaning or create a special effect. Three of the most common figures of speech are *similes, metaphors,* and *personification.*

Formal definition A brief explanation of a word's meaning as it appears in the dictionary.

Freewriting A method of invention that involves writing without stopping for a fixed period—perhaps five or ten minutes—without paying attention to spelling, grammar, or punctuation. The goal of freewriting is to let ideas flow and get them down on paper.

Grounds In Toulmin logic, the material that a writer uses to support a claim. Grounds may be evidence (facts or expert opinions) or appeals to the emotions or values of an audience. (See also **Toulmin logic.**)

Highlighting A technique used by a reader to record responses to a reading selection by marking the text with symbols. Highlighting a text might involve underlining important ideas, boxing key terms, numbering a series of related points, circling unfamiliar words (or placing question marks next to them), drawing vertical lines alongside an interesting or important passage, drawing arrows to connect related points, or placing asterisks next to discussions of the selection's central issues or themes.

Hyperbole Deliberate exaggeration for emphasis or humorous effect: "I froze to death out in the storm"; "She has hundreds of boyfriends"; "Senior year passed by in a second." The opposite of a hyperbole is *understatement.*

Imagery A set of verbal pictures of sensory experiences. These pictures, conveyed through concrete details, make a description vivid and immediate to the reader. Some images are literal ("The cows were so white they almost glowed in the dark"); others are more figurative ("The black and white cows looked like maps, with the continents in black and the seas in white"). A pattern of imagery (repeated images of, for example, shadows, forests, or fire) may run through a piece of writing.

Immediate cause See **Causes.**

Inductive reasoning The method of reasoning that moves from specific evidence to a general conclusion based on this evidence. Inductive reasoning is the opposite of *deductive reasoning.*

Instructions A kind of process essay whose purpose is to enable readers to *perform* a process. Instructions use the present tense and speak directly to readers: "Walk at a moderate pace for twenty minutes."

Introduction An essay's opening. Depending on the length of an essay, the introduction may be one paragraph, several paragraphs, or even a few pages long. In an introduction, a writer tries to encourage the audience to read the essay that follows. Therefore, the writer must choose tone and diction carefully, indicate what the paper is about, and suggest to readers what direction it will take.

Invention (also known as *prewriting*) The stage of writing in which a writer explores the writing assignment, focuses ideas, and ultimately decides on a thesis for an essay. A writer might begin by thinking through the requirements of the assignment—the essay's purpose, length, and audience. Then, using one or more methods of invention—such as *freewriting, looping, questions for probing, brainstorming, clustering,* and *journal writing*—the writer can proceed to formulate a tentative thesis and begin to write the essay.

Irony Language that points to a discrepancy between two different levels of meaning. *Verbal irony* is characterized by a gap between what is actually stated and what is really meant, which often has the opposite meaning—for instance, "his humble abode" (referring to a millionaire's estate). *Situational irony* points to a discrepancy between what actually happens and what readers expect will happen. This kind of irony is present, for instance, when a character, trying to frighten a rival, ends up being frightened himself. *Dramatic irony* occurs when the reader understands more about what is happening in a story than the character who is telling the story does. For example, a narrator might tell an anecdote that he intends to illustrate how clever he is, while it is obvious to the reader from the story's events that the narrator has made a fool of himself because of his gullibility. (See also **Sarcasm.**)

Jargon The specialized vocabulary of a profession or academic field. Although the jargon of a particular profession is an efficient means of communication within that field, it may not be clear or meaningful to readers outside that profession.

Journal writing A method of invention that involves recording ideas that emerge from reading or other experiences and then exploring them in writing.

Looping A method of invention that involves isolating one idea from a piece of freewriting and using this idea as a focus for a new piece of freewriting.

Main cause See **Causes.**

Metaphor A comparison of two dissimilar things that does not use the words *like* or *as* ("Not yet would they veer southward to the caldron of the land that lay below"—N. Scott Momaday).

Narration The pattern of development that tells a story. (See Chapter 2.)

Objective description A detached, factual picture presented in as plain and direct a manner as possible. Although pure objectivity is difficult if not impossible to achieve, writers of science papers, technical reports, and news articles, among others, strive for precise language that is free of value judgments.

Paragraph The basic unit of an essay. A paragraph is composed of related sentences that together express a single idea. This main idea is often stated in a single *topic sentence.* Paragraphs are also graphic symbols on the page, mapping the progress of the ideas in the essay and providing visual breaks for readers.

Parallelism The use of similar grammatical elements within a sentence or sentences. "I like hiking, skiing, and to cook" is not parallel because *hiking* and *skiing* are gerund forms (*-ing*) while *to cook* is an infinitive form. Revised for parallelism, the sentence could read either "I like hiking, skiing, and cooking" or "I like to hike, to ski, and to cook." As a stylistic technique, parallelism can provide emphasis through repetition—for example, "Walk groundly, talk profoundly, drink roundly, sleep soundly" (William Hazlitt). Parallelism is also a powerful oratorical technique: "Until justice is blind to color, until education is unaware of race, until opportunity is unconcerned with the color of men's skins, emancipation will be a proclamation but not a fact" (Lyndon B. Johnson). Finally, parallelism can increase *coherence* within a paragraph or an essay.

Paraphrase The restatement of another person's words in one's own words, following the order and emphasis of the original. Paraphrase is frequently used in source-based papers, where the purpose is to use information gathered during research to support the ideas in the paper. For example, Jonathan Kozol's "Illiterates cannot travel freely. When they attempt to do so, they encounter risks that few of us can dream of" (page 196) might be paraphrased like this: "According to Jonathan Kozol, people who cannot read find travel extremely risky."

Personification Describing concepts or objects as if they were human ("the chair slouched"; "the wind sighed outside the window").

Persuasion The method by which a writer moves an audience to adopt a belief or follow a course of action. To persuade an audience, a writer relies on the various appeals—to the emotions, to reason, or to ethics. Persuasion is different from *argumentation,* which appeals primarily to reason.

Plagiarism Presenting the words or ideas of someone else as if they were one's own (whether intentionally or unintentionally). Plagiarism should always be avoided.

Point-by-point comparison A comparison in which the writer first makes a point about one subject and then follows it with a comparable point about the other subject. (See also **Subject-by-subject comparison.**)

Post hoc reasoning A logical fallacy that involves looking back at two events that occurred in chronological sequence and wrongly assuming that the first event caused the second. For example, just because a tree falls after a thunderstorm, one cannot automatically assume that the storm caused the tree to fall.

Prewriting See **Invention.**

Principle of classification In a classification-and-division essay, the quality the items have in common. For example, if a writer were classifying automobiles, one principle of classification might be "repair records."

Process The pattern of development that presents a series of steps in a procedure in chronological order and shows how this sequence of steps leads to a particular result. (See Chapter 5.)

Process explanation A kind of process essay whose purpose is to enable readers to understand a process rather than perform it.

Purpose A writer's reason for writing. A writer's purpose may, for example, be to entertain readers with an amusing story, to inform them about a dangerous disease, to move them to action by enraging them with an example of injustice, or to change their perspective by revealing a hidden dimension of a person or situation.

Quotation The exact words of a source, enclosed in quotation marks. A quotation should be used only for particularly memorable statements, or when a paraphrase would change the meaning of the original.

Refutation The attempt to counter an opposing argument by revealing its weaknesses. Three of the most common weaknesses are logical flaws in the argument, inadequate evidence, and irrelevance. Refutation greatly strengthens an argument by showing that the writer is aware of the complexity of the issue and has considered opposing viewpoints.

Remote cause See **Causes.**

Rhetorical question A question asked for effect and not meant to be answered.

Rogerian argument A strategy put forth by psychologist Carl Rogers that rejects the adversarial approach that characterizes many arguments. Rather than attacking the opposition, Rogers suggests acknowledging the validity of opposing positions. By finding areas of agreement, a Rogerian argument reduces conflict and increases the chance that the final position will satisfy all parties.

Running acknowledgment The phrase that identifies the author of a paraphrase, summary, or quotation. "According to Judy Brady" and "As Amy Tan notes" are examples of running acknowledgments.

Sarcasm Deliberately insincere and biting irony—for example, "That's okay—I love it when you borrow things and don't return them."

Satire Writing that uses wit, irony, and ridicule to attack foolishness, incompetence, or evil in a person or idea. Satire has a different purpose from comedy, which usually intends simply to entertain. For a classic example of satire, see Jonathan Swift's "A Modest Proposal," page 625.

Sexist language Language that stereotypes people according to gender. Writers often use plural constructions to avoid sexist language. For example, *the doctors . . . they* can be used instead of *the doctor . . . he.* Words such as *police officer* and *firefighter* can be used instead of *policeman* and *fireman.*

Simile A comparison of two dissimilar things using the words *like* or *as* ("Hills Like White Elephants"—Ernest Hemingway).

Slang Informal words whose meanings vary from locale to locale or change as time passes. Slang is frequently associated with a particular group of people—for example, bikers, musicians, or urban youth. Slang is inappropriate in college writing.

Subject-by-subject comparison A comparison organized by subject rather than by the points on which the subjects are being compared. (See also **Point-by-point comparison.**)

Subjective description A description that contains value judgments (*a saintly woman,* for example). Whereas objective language is distanced from an event or object, *subjective language* is involved. A subjective description focuses on the author's reaction to the event, conveying not just a factual record of details but also their significance. Subjective language may include poetic or colorful words that impart a judgment or an emotional response (*stride, limp, meander, hobble, stroll, plod,* or *shuffle* instead of *walk*). Subjective descriptions often include *figures of speech.*

Summary The ideas of a source as presented in one's own words. Unlike a paraphrase, a summary conveys only a general sense of a passage, without following the order and emphasis of the original.

Syllogism A basic form of deductive reasoning. Every syllogism includes three parts: a major premise that makes a general statement ("Confinement is physically and psychological damaging"); a minor premise that makes a related but more specific statement ("Zoos confine animals"); and a conclusion drawn from these two premises ("Therefore, zoos are physically and psychologically damaging to animals").

Symbol A person, event, or object that represents something more than its literal meaning.

Synonym A word with the same basic meaning as another word. A synonym for *loud* is *noisy.* Most words in the English language have several synonyms, but each word has unique nuances or *connotations.*

Thesis An essay's main idea; the idea that all the points in the body of the essay support. A thesis may be implied, but it is usually stated explicitly in the form of a *thesis statement.* In addition to conveying the essay's main idea, the thesis statement may indicate the writer's approach to the subject and the writer's purpose. It may also indicate the pattern of development that will structure the essay.

Topic sentence A sentence stating the main idea of a paragraph. Often, but not always, the topic sentence opens the paragraph.

Toulmin logic A method of structuring an argument according to the way arguments occur in everyday life. Developed by philosopher Stephen Toulmin, Toulmin logic divides an argument into three parts: the *claim,* the *grounds,* and the *warrant.*

Transitions Words or expressions that link ideas in a piece of writing. Long essays frequently contain *transitional paragraphs* that connect one part of the essay to another. Writers use a variety of transitional expressions, such as *afterward, because, consequently, for instance, furthermore, however,* and *likewise.* See the list of transitions on page 41.

Understatement Deliberate de-emphasis for effect: "The people who live near the Mississippi River are not exactly looking forward to more flooding"; "Emily was a little upset about flunking out of school." The opposite of understatement is *hyperbole.*

Unity The desirable attribute of a paragraph in which every sentence relates directly to the paragraph's main idea. This main idea is often stated in a *topic sentence.*

Warrant In Toulmin logic, the inference that connects the claim to the grounds. The warrant can be a belief that it is taken for granted or an assumption that underlies the argument. (See also **Toulmin logic.**)

Writing process The sequence of tasks a writer undertakes when writing an essay. During *invention,* or *prewriting,* the writer gathers information and ideas and develops a thesis. During the *arrangement* stage, the writer organizes material into a logical sequence. During *drafting and revision,* the essay is actually written and then rewritten. Finally, during *editing,* the writer puts the finishing touches on the essay by correcting misspellings, checking punctuation, searching for grammatical inaccuracies, and so on. These stages occur in no fixed order; many effective writers move back and forth among them. (See Chapter 1.)

(Acknowledgments continued from p. iv)

Bruce Catton, "Grant and Lee: A Study in Contrasts." From *The American Story,* edited by Earl Schenck Miers. Copyright © U.S. Capitol Historical Society. All rights reserved. Reprinted by permission of the United States Capitol Historical Society.

Sandra Cisneros, "Only Daughter." First published in *Glamour,* November 1990. Copyright © 1990 by Sandra Cisneros. Reprinted by permission of Susan Bergholz Literary Services, New York. All rights reserved.

Leah Hager Cohen, "Words Left Unspoken." From *Train Go Sorry.* Copyright © 1994 by Leah Hager Cohen. Reprinted with permission of Houghton Mifflin Co. All rights reserved.

David Cole, "Five Myths about Immigration." From *The Nation,* October 17, 1994. Copyright © 1994 *The Nation.* Reprinted by permission of the publisher.

Norman Cousins, "Who Killed Benny Paret?" From *Present Tense,* a collection of editorials by Norman Cousins. Published by McGraw Hill. Copyright © 1967 by Norman Cousins. Reprinted with the permission of Eleanor Cousins.

Christopher Daly, "How the Lawyers Stole Winter." From *The Atlantic Monthly,* March 1995. Copyright © 1995 Christopher Daly. Reprinted by permission of the author.

Annie Dillard, "In the Jungle." From *Teaching a Stone to Talk* by Annie Dillard. Copyright © 1982 by Annie Dillard. Reprinted by permission of HarperCollins Publishers, Inc.

Lars Eighner, "On Dumpster Diving." From *Travels with Lizbeth: Three Years on the Road and on the Streets* by Lars Eighner. Copyright © 1993 by Lars Eighner. Reprinted with the permission of St. Martin's Press Incorporated.

Stephanie Ericsson, "The Way We Lie." From *Companion into the Dawn* by Stephanie Ericsson (New York: HarperCollins, 1995). Copyright © 1992 by Stephanie Ericsson. Originally published in *Utne Reader.* Permission granted by Rhoda Weyer Agency, NY.

John Kenneth Galbraith, "Our Forked Tongue." From *The New York Times* Op-Ed page, February 6, 1995. Copyright © 1995 by The New York Times, Co. Reprinted by permission.

Martin Gansberg, "38 Who Saw Murder Didn't Call the Police." From *The New York Times,* March 27, 1964. Copyright © 1964 by The New York Times Co. Reprinted by permission.

Henry Louis Gates, Jr., "What's in a Name?" Originally printed in *Dissent,* Fall 1989. Copyright © 1989 Henry Louis Gates, Jr. Reprinted with permission of author.

Ellen Goodman, "The Company Man." From *Close to Home* by Ellen Goodman. Copyright © 1979 by The Washington Post Company. Reprinted with the permission of Simon & Schuster.

Lawrence Otis Graham, "The 'Black Table' Is Still There." From *The New York Times* Op-Ed page, February 3, 1991. Copyright © 1991 by The New York Times Co. Reprinted by permission.

John Grisham, "Unnatural Killers." From *The Oxford American,* Spring 1996, pp. 2–5. Reprinted by permission.

Shirley Jackson, "The Lottery." From *The Lottery* by Shirley Jackson. Copyright © 1948, 1949 by Shirley Jackson. Renewed © 1976, 1977 by Laurence Hyman, Barry Hyman, Mrs. Sarah Webster, and Mrs. Joanne Schnurer. Reprinted by permission of Farrar, Straus & Giroux, Inc.

Susan Jacoby, "Common Decency." From *The New York Times Magazine,* May 9, 1991. Copyright © 1991 by Susan Jacoby. Reprinted by permission of Georges Borchardt, Inc. for the author.

Martin Luther King, Jr., "Letter from Birmingham Jail." Reprinted by arrangement with The Heirs to the Estate of Martin Luther King, Jr., c/o Writers House, Inc. as agent for the proprietor. Copyright © 1963 by Martin Luther King, Jr., copyright renewed 1991 by Coretta Scott King.

Jonathan Kozol, "The Human Cost of an Illiterate Society." From *Illiterate America* by Jonathan Kozol. © 1985 by Jonathan Kozol. Used by permission of Doubleday, a division of Bantam Doubleday Dell Publishing Group, Inc.

Richard Lederer, "English Is a Crazy Language." From *Crazy English* by Richard Lederer. Copyright © 1989 by Richard Lederer. Reprinted with the permission of Pocket Books, a Division of Simon & Schuster.

Robert M. Lilienfeld and William L. Rathje, "Six Enviro-Myths." *The New York Times* Op-Ed page, January 21, 1996. Copyright © 1996 by The New York Times Co. Reprinted by permission

Edward Mendelson, "The Word and the Web." *The New York Times,* June 2, 1996 (Book Review section). Copyright © 1996 by The New York Times Co. Reprinted by permission.

Janice Mirikitani, "Suicide Note." From *Shedding Silence* by Janice Mirikitani. Copyright © 1987 by Janice Mirikitani. Reprinted by permission of the publisher, Ten Speed Press/Celestial Arts.

Jessica Mitford, "The Embalming of Mr. Jones." From *The American Way of Death* by Jessica Mitford. Copyright © 1963, 1978 by Jessica Mitford. All rights reserved. Reprinted by permission of the Estate of Jessica Mitford.

N. Scott Momaday, "The Way to Rainy Mountain." From *The Reporter,* January 26, 1997. Copyright © 1967 by The University of New Mexico Press. Reprinted by permission.

Bharati Mukherjee, "Two Ways to Belong in America." *The New York Times* Op-Ed page, September 22, 1996. Copyright © 1991 by The New York Times Co. Reprinted by permission.

Alleen Pace Nielsen, "Sexism in English: A 1990's Update." From "Sexism in English: A Feminist View" from Female Studies VI: Closer to the Ground: Womans Classes, Criticism, Programs—1972, edited by Nancy Hoffman, Cynthia Secor, Adrian Tinsley, Copyright © 1972 by Nancy Hoffman, Cynthia Secor, Adrian Tinsley. Updated by Alleen Pace Nielsen, English Department, Arizona State University, Tempe, AZ 85287-0302. Reprinted with her permission.

Flannery O'Connor, "Revelation." From *Everything That Rises Must Converge* by Flannery O'Connor. Copyright © 1964, 1965 by The Estate of Flannery O'Connor. Reprinted with the permission of Farrar, Straus & Giroux, Inc.

George Orwell, "Shooting an Elephant." From *Shooting an Elephant and Other Essays* by George Orwell. Copyright © 1950 by Sonia Brownell Orwell and renewed 1978 by Sonia Pitt-Rivers. Reprinted by permission of Harcourt Brace & Company. Copyright © Mark Hamilton as literary executor of the estate of the late Sonia Brownell Orwell and Martin Secker and Warburg Ltd.

Camille Paglia, "It's a Jungle Out There." From *Sex, Art and American Culture.* Copyright © 1992 by Camille Paglia. Reprinted with the permission of Vintage Books, a Division of Random House, Inc.

Grace Paley, "Samuel." From *Enormous Changes at the Last Minute* by Grace Paley. Copyright © 1968, 1974 by Grace Paley. Reprinted with permission of Farrar, Straus & Giroux, Inc.

Laurence J. Peter and Raymond Hull, Excerpt from *The Peter Principle.* Copyright © 1969 by William Morrow & Company, Inc. Reprinted by permission of William Morrow & Company, Inc.

Alexander Petrunkevitch, "The Spider and the Wasp." From *Scientific American,* August 1952. Copyright © 1952 and renewed © 1980 by Scientific American, Inc. Reprinted with the permission of Scientific American.

Katherine Anne Porter, "The Grave." From *The Leaning Tower and Other Stories.* Copyright © 1944 and renewed 1972 by Katherine Anne Porter. Reprinted by permission of Harcourt Brace & Company.

Richard Rodriguez, "Aria." Copyright © 1980 by Richard Rodriguez. Originally appeared in *American Scholar.* Reprinted by permission of Georges Borchardt, Inc., for the author.

Trudy Rubin, "Multiculturalism Is Misguided." From *The Philadelphia Inquirer,* October 25, 1991. Reprinted with the permission of The Philadelphia Inquirer.

Scott Russell Sanders, "The Men We Carry in Our Minds." From *The Paradise of Bombs* (Athens, GA: The University of Georgia Press, 1984). Originally in *Milkweed*

Chronicle. Copyright © 1984 by Scott Russell Sanders. Reprinted with the permission of the author and Virginia Kidd, Literary Agent.

Melanie Scheller, "On the Meaning of Plumbing and Poverty." Copyright © 1990 by Melanie Scheller. Originally published in and reprinted with permission of the The *Independent Weekly,* 1990 (Durham, NC).

Brian Siano, "Frankenstein Must Be Destroyed." From *The Humanist,* Jan/Feb 1994. Reprinted by permission of the author.

Brent Staples, "Just Walk On By: A Black Man Ponders His Power to Alter Public Space." From *Harper's,* December 1986. Reprinted with permission of the author. Brent Staples writes editorials on politics and culture for *The New York Times.* He is the author of a memoir, *Parallel Time: Growing Up in Black and White.*

Oliver Stone, "Memo to John Grisham: What's Next—'A Movie Made Me Do It'?" *LA Weekly,* March 29-April 4, 1996, p. 39. Reprinted by permission of the author.

Amy Tan, "Mother Tongue." Copyright © 1990 by Amy Tan. First appeared in *Threepenny Review.* Reprinted by permission of Amy Tan and Sandra Dijkstra Literary Agency.

Deborah Tannen, "Sex, Lies and Conversation." From *You Just Don't Understand* by Deborah Tannen, Ph.D. Copyright © 1990 by Deborah Tannen, Ph.D. Reprinted by permission of William Morrow & Company, Inc.

James Thurber, "The Catbird Seat." From *The Thurber Carnival* (New York: Harper, 1945.) Copyright © 1945 by James Thurber. Copyright © 1973 by Helen Thereby and Rosemary A. Thurber. Reprinted by arrangement with Rosemary A. Thurber c/o The Barbara Hogenson Agency.

Calvin Trillin, "It's Just Too Late." Copyright © 1984 by Calvin Trillin. Originally appeared in *The New Yorker.* Reprinted with the permission of Lescher & Lescher, Ltd.

Garry Trudeau, "Anatomy of a Joke." *The New York Times,* August 1, 1993. Copyright © 1993 by The New York Times Co. Reprinted with permission of The New York Times and Universal Press Syndicate. All rights reserved.

Mark Twain, "Reading the River." Reprinted by permission of Oxford University Press.

John Updike, "Ex–Basketball Player." From *The Carpenter Hen and Other Tame Creatures* by John Updike. Copyright © 1957, 1982 by John Updike. Reprinted by permission of Alfred A. Knopf, Inc.

Alice Walker, "In Search of Our Mothers' Gardens." From *In Search of Our Mothers' Gardens: Womanist Prose.* Copyright © 1974 by Alice Walker. Reprinted by permission of Harcourt Brace & Company.

E. B. White, "Once More to the Lake." From *One Man's Meat* by E. B. White. Copyright © 1941 by E. B. White. Reprinted by permission of HarperCollins Publishers, Inc.

Marie Winn, "Television: The Plug-In Drug." Originally titled "Family Life" from *The Plug-In Drug,* revised edition by Marie Winn Miller. Copyright © 1977, 1985 by Marie Winn Miller. Used by permission of Viking Penguin, a division of Penguin Books USA, Inc.

Malcolm X, "My First Conk." From *The Autobiography of Malcolm X* by Malcolm X, with the assistance of Alex Haley. Copyright © 1964 by Alex Haley and Malcolm X and copyright © 1965 by Alex Haley and Betty Shabazz. Reprinted by permission of Random House, Inc.

Ji-Yeon Mary Yuhfill, "Let's Tell the Story of All America's Cultures." From *The Philadelphia Inquirer,* December 12, 1993. Reprinted by permission.

Michael Zimecki, "Violent Films Cry 'Fire' in Crowded Theaters." From *The National Law Journal,* February 19, 1996. Michael Zimecki is an attorney in Pittsburgh, PA. Reprinted by permission of the author.

William Zinsser, "College Pressures." Copyright © 1979 by William K. Zinsser. Published in Blair & Ketchum's *Country Journal,* Vol. VI, No. 4, April 1979. Reprinted by permission of the author.

INDEX
OF TERMS,
AUTHORS,
AND TITLES